GEONEXUS

CANADIAN AND WORLD ISSUES

GEONEXUS

CANADIAN AND WORLD ISSUES

Author Team

Graham Draper

Patricia Healy

THOMSON

NELSON

Australia   Canada   Mexico   Singapore   Spain   United Kingdom   United States

THOMSON

NELSON

Geonexus: Canadian and World Issues

by Graham Draper and Patricia Healy

Director of Publishing
David Steele

Publisher
Carol Stokes

Executive Managing Editor, Development
Cheryl Turner

Program Manager
Kevin Linder

Project Editor
Debbie Davies-Wright

Developmental Editor
Shirley Tessier

Editorial Assistant
Kim Toffan

Executive Managing Editor, Production
Nicola Balfour

Copy Editor
Evan Turner

Production Coordinator
Sharon Latta Paterson

Creative Director
VISU*TronX* Services

Interior Design
VISU*TronX* Services

Cover Design
VISU*TronX* Services

Composition
VISU*TronX* Services

Photo Research and Permissions
Robyn Craig
Elaine Freedman

Printer
Transcontinental Printing Inc.

Reviewers
The authors and publisher gratefully acknowledge the contributions of the following educators:
Linda Barrett, Niagara DSB, ON
Skid Crease, ECONEXUS Ltd., ON
Peggy Karas, Toronto DSB, ON
Marion Kupper, Dufferin/Peel DSB, ON
Carole Locke, York Region DSB, ON
Andrew Lovatt, Ottawa-Carleton DSB, ON
Gale May, York Region DSB, ON
Paul Melim, Windsor-Essex CDSB, ON
Elaine Rubinoff, York University
Fraser Scott, York Region DSB, ON
Kim Wallace, Halton DSB, ON

National Library of Canada Cataloguing in Publication Data

Draper, Graham A.
Geonexus: Canadian and world issues

Includes index.
ISBN 0-7725-2933-7

1. Geography. I. Healy, Patricia II. Title.

G128.D73 2002   910
C2002-900510-8

To my parents, Frances and Paul, for instilling the belief that I can be and do anything I choose to.

Trisha Healy

Table of Contents

Preface

Objectives

Geonexus: Canadian and World Issues was developed to provide comprehensive, meaningful information about global events and to help students arrive at a deeper understanding of how the serious issues facing Canadians are interconnected; how our actions have an impact on people and ecosystems around the world; and how the issues have an impact on our communities at the local, regional, national, and global level.

We live in a world where the proliferation of technology has created more than instant access to information—it has created a borderless global village where economic, environmental, political, and social events in one country can and often do have an impact on a global scale. Events such as the collapse of the Soviet Union, the bombing of the World Trade Center, the loss of biodiversity, or the AIDS pandemic on the African continent are more than isolated incidents—they are interwoven with an array of complex issues, which left unchecked may lead to catastrophic consequences around the world. It is critical, therefore, that we educate ourselves about these issues as a first step to finding solutions.

Researchers and scientists have already begun to look at global issues, analysing their economic, political, environmental, and social aspects. But analysts are beginning to realize that breaking issues into smaller, isolated topics will not lead to solutions. To understand the pieces is not to understand the whole. What is needed is an approach that explores the relationships and connections among all aspects of the issues. These *interrelationships* create a **nexus**—a set of complex connections we are just beginning to understand.

Geographic education with its broad perspective and skills of synthesis and spatial analysis is a good way to promote this understanding and to encourage students to engage in lifelong learning—to become the critical thinkers and creative problem solvers of the future.

Organization

Geonexus: Canadian and World Issues is presented in thematic sections beginning with an introduction to and overview of world issues, differing worldviews, how the media reports and distorts, and how we receive and process this information. Students are then asked to apply this understanding to a geographic inquiry of various environmental, social, and political issues. The text concludes by encouraging students to find solutions for a better future.

The material has a number of key themes threaded throughout, including methodologies used by scientists/geographers to achieve solutions, balanced points of view to illustrate the need for co-operative action by stakeholders, and a focus on the communities in which people around the world live, with suggestions as to how students can apply what they have learned and how they can contribute to the development of a sustainable healthy future for their local community.

Features

A variety of features interspersed throughout the text can be used to:
- provide context and clarity;
- encourage critical thinking about the issues;

- promote discussion;
- apply knowledge and skills;
- assess student achievement and understanding of concepts and skills outlined in the curriculum expectations;
- conduct research beyond the scope of the text.

Fact Files offer relevant, intriguing information related to issues under discussion.

66 The power of population is infinitely greater than the power in the earth to produce subsistence for man. *99*

Thomas Robert Malthus, economist (1766–1834)

Quotations offer thought-provoking perspectives and intriguing ideas related to topics under discussion.

Case Studies explore, study, and analyse specific instances of broader ideas and issues and their implications in the real world, providing context and clarity.

Commentaries encourage critical analysis of articles or excerpts that reflect on significant aspects of issues.

News Clips highlight a variety of perspectives on issues.

Geographic Methods provide details about geotechnologies and other methodologies used by geographers in the real world to investigate and analyse issues.

Profiles provide details about people and organizations working to find and implement solutions to issues.

Make a Difference features identify ways that individuals can get involved in environmental, economic, and social aspects of issues to change conditions for the better.

Web Links provide valuable Internet sites that can be used to begin additional research and inquiry.

Related Issues suggest current, relevant topics suitable for independent or class study.

In-text Links direct students to additional coverage or similar topics covered elsewhere in the text.

Canadian Connections highlight Canadian connections, perspectives, and roles in global issues.

Counterpoints highlight opposing viewpoints from a variety of worldviews, ideologies, and perspectives on topics.

Interact questions and activities related to the issues under study appear throughout the text to assess understanding of concepts and skills outlined in the curriculum expectations.

INTERACT

Analyse, Apply, and Interact questions and activities appear at the end of each chapter to challenge students to think critically about the issues, apply their knowledge and skills, and conduct research beyond the scope of the text.

ANALYSE, APPLY, AND INTERACT

Geotechnical applications offer opportunities for geotechnical analysis, are noted at chapter end, and are collected in an appendix in the Teacher's Resource.

GIS

Data Appendix is a useful tool for comparison, research, and statistical analysis as students investigate world issues.

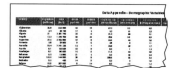

It is our hope that, through their exploration of the connections and linkages of the critical issues that affect this planet, students will view the future with a positive and thoughtful attitude.

Graham Draper
Patricia Healy

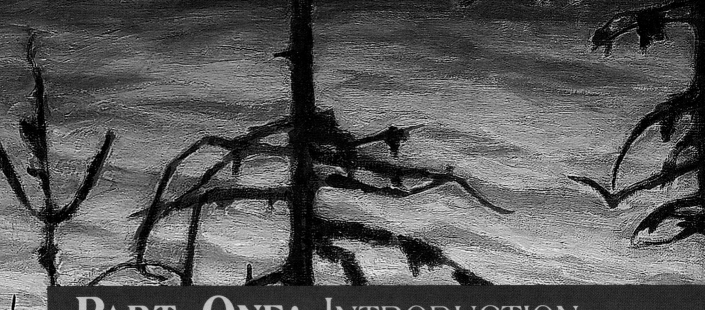

HARRIS, Lawren S. Canadian 1885-1970. BEAVER SWAMP, Algoma 1920. Oil on Canvas, 120.7 x 141.0 cm. ART GALLERY OF ONTARIO, Toronto. Gift of Ruth Massey Tovell, in memory of Harold Murchison Tovell, 1953.

PART ONE: INTRODUCTION

Chapter 1: Ways of Seeing— World Issues, Worldviews

By the end of this chapter, you will:

- demonstrate an understanding of the interdependence of ecology and economics;

- explain why places and regions are important to the identities of selected human groups;

- explain how points of view and paradigms influence an individual's perception of a place;

- analyse geographic issues that arise from the impact of human activities on the environment in different regions of the world;

- evaluate approaches, policies, and principles relating to the protection and sustainability of the planet's life support systems;

- explain how people perceive resources and sustainable development differently at different times and in different places;

- identify awareness levels and viewpoints relating to a geographic issue by conducting a survey in the school or local community;

- evaluate and communicate the perspectives and arguments of various stakeholders involved in a geographic issue;

- select and apply geographic skills, methods, and technologies to gather, analyse, and synthesize ideas and information;

- describe biases that may inform different viewpoints and perspectives on geographic issues;

- demonstrate an understanding of the possibility of a number of alternative solutions to any geographic problem or issue;

- evaluate and effectively use information from a variety of primary and secondary sources (including mainstream and alternative print, broadcasting, and electronic sources) when conducting geographic inquiries, and apply relevant data when making decisions and solving problems;

- analyse how the media influence public opinion on geographic issues;

- draw conclusions or make judgements or predictions on the basis of reasoned analysis;

- use written, oral, and visual communication skills to present the results of geographic inquiry and analysis effectively.

A GLOBAL PERSPECTIVE

Until the 1960s no one had ever seen Earth in its entirety. Every astronaut who has ventured into the black void of space, from the first explorers to current inhabitants of space stations, has turned to look back at Earth and has been amazed at the sight of the whole, round, beautiful, blue-and-green planet that we call home. Astronauts can clearly see how thin the layer of atmosphere is that we all depend on for air, and how closely connected it is to the land and water. This relatively new perspective has caused a radical shift in the way we view life on Earth. From such a perspective, conflicts caused by differences in religion, access to resources, and political **ideologies** seem unwise.

Some of the advantages of the billions of dollars that have been spent on space exploration programs include:

- a new and different view of our world from space;
- a rise in awareness and public concern for the planet we live on;
- a turn toward investigating environmental problems by many scientists;
- some new laws and regulations enacted by governments to protect the natural environment;
- a rise in non-governmental organizations (NGOs) acting to protect peoples and the natural environment;
- new products developed by business and industry for pollution control, waste management, and renewable energy.

The Global Village

Advances in technology, especially in transportation and communications, have brought people around the world so close together that they can communicate and visit with one another almost as easily as if they lived in the same village. When Marshall McLuhan, a Canadian communications theorist, first used the term "global village" in 1967, the Internet did not exist. Now, the World Wide Web has brought the image of a global village even closer to reality. People from diverse cultures and distant parts of the world can communicate almost instantaneously. This media form has become just like a village square where people can meet to exchange ideas and views. The global village has its own institutions such as the United Nations (UN), World Bank, and International Court. While all people are part of the global society, many individuals do not have equal opportunities to share in the world's resources and to take part in their communities in a meaningful way. Human activities play a significant role in shaping the economic, social, political, and environmental conditions in which we live. The effects of human activity on Earth have become global as well as local in scale and no one can accurately predict the consequences.

> 66 The real voyage of discovery lies not in seeking new lands but in seeing with new eyes. 99
>
> *Marcel Proust, writer, France (1871–1922)*

> **FACT FILE**
>
> The global village does not extend everywhere. For example, there are thousands of villages in India that are not connected by roads.

We Are All in This Together

As our lives become faster-paced and more complicated, we must deal with a greater number of issues, increasingly difficult decisions, and the resulting shift in the way we perceive ourselves and the world around us. As the pace of change in the world accelerates, as a staggering amount of information becomes available, as technology advances, and as international connections increase, people need knowledge and skills in order to solve the fundamental issues they face. The first step toward real solutions and change is better understanding.

> 66 The entire history of automobiles, airplanes, antibiotics, oral contraceptives, nuclear energy, computers, plastics, satellites and xerography is encompassed by the span of a single human life. 99
>
> *David Suzuki, scientist, journalist*

Knowledge Is Power

This chapter provides an overview of the issues facing Canadians as part of the global community. It offers a number of strategies to help deal with these issues. Throughout the text, you will find a feature called Make a Difference. There are many people reaching out in kind and simple ways to help bridge cultural and economic gaps and to help protect the environment. Make a Difference outlines the accomplishments of people and organizations around the world in their efforts to find solutions to the issues. It provides ideas and opportunities for young people to demonstrate initiative and to take action.

The more we know about an issue, the better we understand how its implications affect us and our communities on a local, national, and global scale, and the better prepared we are to take appropriate action. When we understand the issues, we can act, not out of guilt, but from the perspective of knowledge and justice.

Facts and figures are not as useful in helping us deal with the issues as firsthand experience and connecting with people who see and think about the world differently from us. When we listen to and get to know someone a little better, we still may not agree with his or her viewpoint, but we tend to gain a more sophisticated understanding. Hearing from a young child from Zimbabwe who is coping with HIV/AIDS, or a refugee from Afghanistan, we realize that all people have the same basic needs and that problems and issues throughout the world tend to share similar root causes. We gain a more intelligent and discerning view of the world and are better able to negotiate and compromise to find solutions. There are no perfect answers and no single individual or institution can solve an issue. But by working together, a variety of alternatives can be tried, and each participant can contribute to a solution.

Young people need to understand the economic, political, social, and environmental implications of global issues. They need a vision of how their actions and choices affect others and how they can contribute to the world around them. Young people have more at stake in the outcome of issues, as they will spend a large part of their lives as parents, workers, voters, and leaders in a future that will be very different from the world of today. Most people want to live in a more humane, just, civilized, and healthy international community. Almost everyone agrees that we need to be more environmentally responsible, but approaches to achieving these desirable goals and determining the extent of our responsibility vary considerably.

> " ...the advent of billions more people on the planet, each consuming more energy and materials and each with more technological power to produce, invent, communicate, travel and destroy, has sharply increased the density, intensity, and pace of human interactions; it has helped shift power from states and governments to individuals and sub-groups; and it has generated a multitude of environmental and **epidemiological** stresses, some of them global in scope. "
>
> *Thomas Homer-Dixon, professor, University of Toronto; director, Peace and Conflict Studies Program*

THINK GLOBALLY, ACT LOCALLY

This phrase is commonly heard in discussions about world issues. It refers to the need to develop an understanding of the global context within which our actions toward the environment and other people take place. Problems and issues at a local, community level are often connected to wider issues at national and global levels. Global issues that can affect the local community include terrorism, migration of refugees, changing global trading patterns, ozone layer depletion, and global climate change. Within the local community, situations such as habitat destruction, invasive species, acid rain, depletion of fisheries, or unemployment are symptomatic of wider issues. People are often encouraged to act locally because actions that benefit the community can also contribute to a global effect. Examples of this effect include conserving energy, reducing our use of pesticides and chlorofluorocarbons (CFCs), buying responsibly, and supporting NGOs that contribute to humanitarian aid or environmental protection strategies in other parts of the world.

Globalization

We hear a lot of talk about globalization but what does it mean and why is it significant? Economic globalization is based on a free-market economy, free trade, and free movement of capital within an essentially borderless world. Most people in developed countries now rely on farmers and manufacturers in faraway places to provide many of their basic necessities and consumer wants. Economies are no longer tied to a place or society. Interaction among national economies and the rapid flow of private money, ideas, technology, goods, and services around the world are increasing. This reality is supported by international organizations including the International Monetary Fund (IMF), the World Bank, many national governments, and most conventional economists who believe that globalization is good for all. In addition, huge transnational corporations (TNCs) invest wherever costs are lowest and profits are greatest. They control the market as well as the mainstream media in an attempt to achieve economic efficiency and to maximize profits.

 See Chapter 2 for more information about media control.

Economic interaction is only one aspect of globalization. There are also important technological, cultural, political, social, and environmental components. Technological aspects of globalization are related to new communications technologies and the information revolution, which has spread around the world. Cultural aspects involve the spread of cultural characteristics, such as the consumption of western television programs, advertising and products, and a fear among smaller groups of an erosion of cultural identity. Political aspects are related to the lessening of the power that nation states have to control their economies and social programs. No national government can withstand the economic control of the capital market on the flow of money. Social aspects involve the spread of a way of life based on the importance of the individual as a consumer, and the erosion of social controls to protect workers from layoffs and poor working conditions, to provide education and health care, and to protect the environment. Environmental aspects of globalization involve the spread of environmental degradation, including pollution, climate change, and loss of biodiversity. Environmental issues tend to ignore national boundaries. An increased awareness of environmental issues related to globalization has coincided with the development of a free market and growth-based economy. One reason for this is the power of the World Trade Organization (WTO) to challenge a country's environmental laws.

Statistical evidence shows that, despite claims of the benefits of continued globalization and economic growth, these benefits do not always trickle down to all segments of society as predicted. For example, poverty rates in parts of Asia have declined significantly but there is a concentration of economic power in the hands of a small group of elite decision makers and a growing gap between rich and poor. Some economists predict continued evolution of the international monetary system will result in a single world currency.

> **FACT FILE**
>
> UN data clearly show the trend of an increasing income gap between the 20% of the world's population living in wealthier developed countries, who benefit from receiving 86% of total Gross Domestic Product (GDP), and the 20% living in the poorest countries, who receive only 1% of GDP. That same wealthiest 20% controls 82% of world export markets and almost 70% of direct foreign investment.

> **FACT FILE**
>
> Poverty is a key issue that affects all countries, including Canada. In 1989, the Canadian government claimed that child poverty would be gone by 2000. In 2001, there were almost 200 000 more children living in poverty.

> "A growing number of free trade agreements, more or less secret multilateral negotiations, and the inclusion, in all economic discussions, of sensitive areas such as culture, the environment, social support networks, and management of the health care system should leave no one indifferent."
>
> *Jocelyn Coulon, director, Lester B. Pearson Canadian International Peacekeeping Training Centre*

A number of issues related to globalization are of concern to a large and increasingly vocal group of people in our society who, although they encompass a wide range of interests, have come to be known as the anti-globalization movement. These people hope to bring about some kind of change, based on a more inclusive democracy, a more equal sharing of wealth and power, and a better quality of life for all. Globalization is seen by philosopher Christopher Lund as a human ⟨rather than a natural creation that lies within the realm of human choice. We can support it or resist it; approve it or condemn it.

Globalization Has Its Benefits

While globalization is often seen to be a threat to individual rights, freedoms, and quality of life, there can be a positive side to globalization. Global health and safety standards have improved conditions in many parts of the world. Few people question the benefit to poorer countries of improved basic health care needs such as vaccinations. International negotiations have resulted in worldwide protection of natural and cultural heritage sites, declarations of human and children's rights, and treaties such as the UN Chemicals Treaty, formally known as the Stockholm Convention

on Persistent Organic Pollutants. Signed by 122 countries in May 2001, the UN Chemicals Treaty aims to stop manufacturing some of the most dangerous, toxic chemicals ever created, and includes US$150 million in funding to help developing countries change to safer alternatives.

> ❝ The globalization of the music market and the technology of multiple-channel recording has made it possible to create fresh sounds for the world market with exotica from all over the world. Everything from *zouk, rhi,* and *jit* from Africa and *salsa* from the Caribbean islands to the chants of India known as *bhangra* are mixed with a variety of American pop genres to produce a blend that is promoted around the world as "world beat." "Lambada," promoted by French entrepreneurs as the dance craze of Brazil, is Bolivian in origin. A recorded version of this music performed by mostly Senegalese musicians became a global hit. ❞
>
> Richard J. Barnett and John Cavanaugh, authors, Global Dreams, Imperial Corporations and the New World Order, *1994*

The globalization of music is another noticeable effect. Eighty percent of the world trade in music is controlled by just four transnational recording companies: Vivendi Universal (France), Sony (Japan), AOL Time-Warner (U.S.), and Bertelsmann BMG (Germany). Music from all over the world is now mixed or adapted to create musical styles that will appeal to a huge world market. The increasing dominance of Anglo-American pop music may continue to see more influence of regional music styles such as tropical rhythms or native drums to appeal to an increasing market. The marketing of popular music through the Internet and music download sites may lead to a homogenization of popular music at the expense of regional sounds. On the other hand, greater accessibility to different cultural musical sounds for the consumer may promote more internationally successful musicians from countries outside Europe and America.

FACT FILE

Global Village is a CBC radio show that has broadcast reports featuring the music and musical life of 84 different countries.

FIGURE 1.1 Music from Lima Highlands, Peru; Soweto, South Africa; and Tuva on the Siberian/Mongolian border.

A parable

Once upon a time there was a class
and the students expressed disapproval of
    their teacher.
Why should they be concerned with
global interdependency, global problems
and what others of the world were thinking,
    feeling, and doing?
And the teacher said she had a dream in which
    she
saw one of her students fifty years from today.
The student was angry and said,
'Why did I learn so much detail about the past
and the administration of my country
and so little about the world?'
He was angry because no one told him
that as an adult he would be faced
almost daily with problems of a
global interdependent nature, be they
problems of peace, security, quality
of life, food, inflation, or scarcity
of natural resources.

The angry student found he was the
victim as well as the beneficiary.
'Why was I not warned? Why was
I not better educated? Why
did my teachers not tell me about
the problems and help me understand
I was a member of an interdependent human
    race?'
With even greater anger the student shouted,
'You helped me extend my hands with
    incredible machines,
my eyes with telescopes and microscopes,
my ears with telephones, radios, and sonar,
my brain with computers,
but you did not help me extend
my heart, love, concern
to the entire human family.
You, teacher, gave me half a loaf.

Jon Rye Kinghorn

INTERACT

1. With other members of your class, brainstorm:
   a) a list of ways that the world can be seen as a global village;
   b) a list of specific local actions that people in your community can take to help solve global problems, and the impact these actions are likely to have.
2. Create a concept web with the term "globalization" in the centre connected to surrounding terms that represent the various components of globalization. Below each term, write two or three key words to describe that component and draw lines to illustrate connections between the components.
3. How do you see globalization? Create a chart that identifies positive and negative impacts. Conduct some additional research to add ideas to your chart. Write a paragraph explaining why you feel either the positive or negative side outweighs the other.
4. What are the main goals of the anti-globalization movement? Which groups make up this segment of society?
5. Why is it said that globalization results in a "borderless world"?
6. In the quote on page 3, what does Thomas Homer-Dixon mean by:
   a) "a shift in power"?
   b) epidemiological stresses?
7. What are the advantages and disadvantages of the globalization of music?

What Is an Issue?

We hear the word "issue" a lot but what does it really mean? What is the difference between a problem and an issue? A problem is usually smaller than an issue, requires a solution, but does not necessarily involve different viewpoints or a disagreement on how to solve it. An issue is a complex problem also requiring a solution. It has many different sides, involves some dispute, and has become a matter of concern to many people. For example, one's pet running away from home is a problem. The way some people mistreat animals is an issue.

Issues arise because of disagreements about people's aspirations for a desirable future. How people see the future usually depends on their cultural and experiential background as well as their **worldview**. Issues can generate a range of feelings, including surprise, shock, concern, anger, or anxiety. People certainly seem to have opinions about current controversial issues, but what do they really know about the wider aspects of the issue? Are their opinions informed?

a)

b)

c)

d)

g)

h)

f)

e)

FIGURE 1.2 Identify the issues portrayed in these photographs.

FIGURE 1.3 When faced with so many issues, it is difficult to know which ones to focus on. Which issues are important in your life?

Because issues have complex causes and effects, it is important to know how to investigate and understand issues and to look for a way to be part of the solution. Considering all of the information can help to clarify and define an issue. For example, before we can determine how much of our forests we can cut down to supply us with wood and paper without jeopardizing the ability of people in the future to use those forests, we need accurate information about the rate and conditions under which forests can regenerate, as well as about the impact of logging on other species, soil, water, and air. The best we can do is to collect this information from scientific research and from the observations of people, often indigenous people, who have watched the forest ecosystem over many years, and ensure that important facts are not left out. Since nature involves ever-changing, self-organizing processes that we do not fully understand, collecting complete and accurate information can be a difficult task.

When identifying the causes and effects of issues, we must consider the complex interrelationships that exist among people, living things, and other components of the biosphere including air, water, and land. By studying issues, we gain a context within which to build our lives. We can better understand our connections and relationships with our own community and with the rest of the world.

> " Nature is not only more complex than we think, it is more complex than we *can* think. "
>
> *David Suzuki, scientist, environmentalist*

What Are the Issues?

Life in the global village is disorderly. Human activities are the source of many issues, including those that affect the environment, social justice, peace and war, and geopolitics.

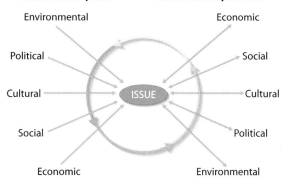

Causes and Aspects

Environmental
Political
Cultural
Social
Economic

ISSUE

Effects and Implications

Economic
Social
Cultural
Political
Environmental

FIGURE 1.4 While some issues have a particular focus, most are more complex and have aspects of all these components.

INTERACT

1. For each of the issues illustrated in the photos in Figure 1.2, identify an economic, political, social, cultural, and environmental aspect or connection.
2. With other members of your class, brainstorm a list of issues that you feel are important to your lives now and in the future. Classify them into various headings that you design, such as Local versus Global. Diamond rank them according to their significance and need for solutions. This is a way of ranking the importance of items without having to agree on an exact order. It works best when there are seven or nine items to be ranked. Try to reach a consensus to rank the issues according to the following diamond patterns:

   For seven issues:

   1
   2   2
   3   3
   2   2
   3   3
   2

For nine issues:

1
2   2
3   3
4   4
5
3

3. Work in small groups to map out on chart paper a dependency word web that shows the ways people in your community are dependent on one another.
4. Choose one global issue that interests you. Conduct research to identify some of the causes and effects of the issue for people and their environment. Complete a cause and effect chart using your findings.
5. Identify several reasons why it is beneficial for young people to gain an understanding of global issues and their implications.

INVESTIGATING AND ANALYSING ISSUES

The Science of Inquiry

When investigating the world around us, scientists use a systematic process to develop new knowledge, insight, and understanding. Science deals with measurement, experimentation, observation and interpretation of data, and development of hypotheses that can be tested and then accepted or rejected. Until very recently, science usually provided important information about isolated parts of the world without a focus on how these parts are interconnected. It ignored the idea that the whole is greater than the sum of its parts. This approach is called **reductionism**. Reductive fallacy is drawing a conclusion that is too simplistic or exclusive because it ignores any complexity that does not fit with a particular viewpoint.

Geographic Inquiry: A Detailed Process for Investigating and Analysing Issues

The following chart provides a framework to illustrate what goes on throughout the process of geographic inquiry. However, the process is dynamic and approaches can vary. Some of the steps may occur simultaneously. The suggested questions and strategies may not be appropriate or necessary for all inquiries. The inquiry may take a broad, general approach to the issue rather than studying part of it in detail. In this case, the focus questions would be used to guide the research.

Steps in the Process	How to Do It	Questions You May Ask	Suggested Strategies
1. Identify and clarify the issue.	Ask speculative questions to help define and focus the issue. Relate the issue to an appropriate context.	What do I think this issue is all about? What part of the issue will be studied in detail? Over what time period does the issue have an effect? What are the local/global connections? How might people in my community be affected?	Key focus questions may be reworded into a hypothesis or theory. This step may require some brief initial research—starting a KWL (Know/Want to Know/Learned) chart may be helpful.
2. Conduct research to acquire information.	Read and interpret maps, statistics, **mainstream** and **alternative media**, including documentaries, Web sites, books, and periodicals. Collect data from primary sources using surveys, interviews with experts or stakeholders, and fieldwork. Synthesize additional material into your organizer (Step 3) from videos, class discussion, and other sources as you continue through the process.	What type of information is needed? What sources need to be tapped? Who is involved and why? Why is the issue controversial? What are the economic, political, social, cultural, and environmental aspects of the issue?	For primary research techniques such as surveys and interviews to be effective, questions should be prepared carefully in advance to elicit the information you seek. Surveys identify opinions and attitudes of stakeholders or assess awareness of the general public. Interviews may be held with local government members, environmental agencies, NGOs, and other stakeholders.
3. Organize the information collected.	Design a recording sheet that allows new information to be added easily (synthesis).		A graphic organizer or chart with subheadings can be a useful way to organize material.
4. Analyse and evaluate the information.	Apply critical thinking skills and select the most accurate, relevant, and reliable material. Ensure that multiple viewpoints are represented.	(See Geographic Methods: Steps to Critical Analysis on page 15.) What has been the role of media in bringing this issue to prominence?	Draw concept webs to show how various aspects of the issue are connected.

Steps in the Process	How to Do It	Questions You May Ask	Suggested Strategies
4. Analyse and evaluate the information. *(continued)*	Explain your observations and geographical relationships. Classify values and perspectives. Does the information have a particular bias?	What trends and patterns are evident? What predictions can be made for future change based on trends? What are the most significant relationships and impacts?	Create an impact chart to indicate how likely various impacts are to occur. Analyse statistics and explain patterns and relationships.
5. Draw conclusions.	Answer the focus questions based on the information that has been gathered. Make inferences and draw conclusions from your findings.	Do I have enough information to make a decision? What more information is needed? Has the hypothesis been proven or have the focus questions been answered?	
6. Make recommendations for solutions.	Prioritize aspects of the issue according to a need for solution. Recommend alternative actions. Decide on the most appropriate action.	What are the possible positive and negative outcomes of each action? What was your initial viewpoint on this issue? What information supported your views?	Try to collect ideas for solutions from other similar situations or from people with experience. Consider factors such as resources available, time, costs and benefits of various solutions, sustainability, and stakeholder views.
7. Communicate results of the inquiry.	Communication can take a variety of forms, including oral presentation, written report, letter, or newsletter. Design a campaign, pamphlet, or display.	Does my report answer the questions posed throughout the process? Is any further action necessary?	Support the findings of your report with visuals, including maps, diagrams, statistics, and charts.
8. Reflect and take action.	Assess your own inquiry process. Take some action to make a difference.	What sources of information do you disagree with? Have you modified your viewpoint? How does the issue affect you personally and how does it affect other members of your community? What are the options for actions you can take based on your conclusions?	Develop an action plan.

Despite impressive advances in science and technology, and significant improvements in quality of life for many around the world, issues related to poverty, hunger, resources, violence, and environmental degradation are still prevalent. Issues are often dealt with in the realm of politics, as this is usually the area where power is wielded and decisions are made. Resolving issues can be difficult because people with opposing views may be reluctant to examine alternative outlooks or implement plans they disagree with.

Geographers are often called social scientists but in reality geography is different from other social sciences like history or anthropology. In order to make sense of complex issues, geographers often use a step-by-step process of research, analysis, and decision making called the geographic inquiry method. There is no one correct way of conducting research and, even within different disciplines, there are many variations. All methods, however, strive to draw valid, relevant conclusions and to apply them in an effort to find solutions to problems and issues.

Geographic Perspectives

Geographers look at how space on Earth is organized and the patterns that result from human and natural processes. We use geographic skills and concepts to make decisions on a daily basis about things such as how to get to a place to meet friends, where to shop, go to school, take a vacation, or where to live. The need for geographic knowledge is increasing. Geography helps us to think systematically about issues. To cope with them effectively, tomorrow's citizens need to be geographically literate. This requires gathering, organizing, and analysing information to answer questions and make reasoned judgements about:

- where things, people, and other species are;
- why they are there;
- why and how they move from place to place;
- how they interact with other people, species, and places;
- how they interact with resources, technologies, and environmental constraints, and the resulting impacts;
- how processes cause observable patterns on Earth's surface;
- what is significant about the effects and implications of these patterns;
- what alternatives exist for solutions to related problems and issues.

> " Our main dilemma is not a lack of information or technological capability. Rather our problem is inherent in the way we perceive our relationship with the rest of Nature and our role in the grand scheme of things. "
>
> *Paul Ehrlich, ecologist, Stanford University, U.S.A.*

Two Methods of Research

Scientific Method	Geographic Inquiry Method
1. Decide on the problem.	1. Clarify and focus the problem/issue.
2. Write a hypothesis.	2. Conduct research from varied sources.
3. Design and conduct an experiment.	3. Organize and record collected data.
4. Observe relationships.	4. Evaluate the data.
5. Formulate conclusions.	5. Draw conclusions.
6. Apply results.	6. Select alternative solutions.
7. Present information.	7. Communicate results of the inquiry.
	8. Take action.

adapted from Information Studies, Ontario School Library Association, 1998

FIGURE 1.5 Not all research fits into such a neat package, nor are these methods bias and value free. The power of creative and imaginative thinking and intuition to solve problems and issues can also be significant.

Seeing the world from a geographic perspective requires the interpretation of many tools such as fieldwork, media, maps, photographs, satellite images, and geographic information systems (GIS). This distinctive approach is essential for the analysis, synthesis, and evaluation needed to help people make sense of a complicated world and improve their capacity to find solutions to problems. People who are geographically literate understand how the many components of natural and human systems are interconnected. They are able to make informed decisions and to work toward improving their local, national, and global communities.

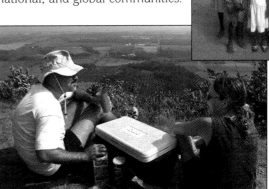

PROFILE

Baron Alexander von Humboldt

FIGURE 1.6

Although he lived to be 90, Baron Alexander von Humboldt was not around on September 15, 1869, when Americans celebrated his one-hundredth birthday. Headlines in the *New York Times* recorded the event. Humboldt was a geographer. He was also a philosopher, explorer, naturalist, and writer. Charles Darwin was one of his followers. Humboldt became famous for his exploration of the Andes mountains, Orinoco River, and surrounding jungles of Venezuela, and for enthralling the public with his knowledge of previously unheard of plants, animals, and peoples of the exotic natural world. Before the advent of specialization and reductionism, in the nineteenth century—when many began to see nature as an object unrelated to humans and broken down into its smallest components—Humboldt understood the "chain of connection" among all elements of life, including humans. He spoke out strongly against the assumption of superior and inferior peoples and slavery. Humboldt first used the word "cosmos" (from the Greek *kosmos*) to describe the nature of the world's interconnections.

FIGURE 1.7 A quick look at the photographs reveals a Haitian family and some pleasant scenery. People tend to judge what they see from the characteristics and standards of their own society, often considering their way of life normal and even superior. This is called **ethnocentrism**. A geographic way of seeing can involve a closer, more objective, **holistic** look. The family shown (upper right) has far fewer material goods than most Canadians, but appears to have all the basic necessities and seems to be happy. What environmental issue can be seen with a closer look at the scenic photo ?

INTERACT

1. Identify a local issue currently being discussed in your community. What aspects of the issue are connected to the wider global community?
2. Identify a global issue and explain how it may affect your own community.
3. Conduct research on an issue of your choice. Complete a KWL chart, and then create an impact chart to identify several potential impacts that different aspects of the issue could have on people and the natural environment. In the final column of your impact chart, indicate whether you feel that each impact is likely or not very likely to occur.
4. Using an atlas, identify and record as many places in the world as you can that are named after Humboldt.

GETTING THE WHOLE STORY

People in developed countries like Canada are often passive observers of misery in far-off places through their exposure to the presentation of issues by the electronic or print media. They can be lulled into complacency with the use of euphemistic language—for instance, civilians killed in military operations being referred to as "collateral damage." They may not even be aware that people in all places are influenced by events and activities in other parts of the world.

We are continually bombarded with media messages. Yet the information we receive often has little context or history. Issues are presented in simple, "black and white" terms rather than in the much more complex shades of grey that exist in reality. Mainstream media provides so-called "in-depth" reports on issues that last two or three minutes, but which provide little information on how you are personally connected or what you can do about the issue.

Media has great power when it comes to increasing awareness of an issue and can play a role in shaping public opinion. With all the rather simplistic **rhetoric** we hear in the media and so-called factual claims about different viewpoints on current issues, how do we know what to believe? Many people just accept what others tell them or what they hear and see in the media. They form opinions based on limited or biased information. In order to make a positive contribution as citizens of the global world we now live in, we need to challenge our own views as well as those of others before we can put our skills to effective use.

 See Chapter 2 for more information about the role of media in analysing issues.

Critical Thinking

Critical thinking is a process of using cognitive skills that are useful in our everyday lives. It can help us:

- separate fact from opinion;
- gain full information about a topic;
- consider what information is missing before drawing conclusions;
- challenge commonly held assumptions;
- consider different points of view;
- take a stand on an issue and support it with reliable information;
- learn how to compromise and negotiate;
- make informed choices and decisions;
- realize that anyone can be wrong, including the "experts";
- explore possibilities and see new ways of behaving in the world;
- "put ourselves in the shoes of another";
- understand the cultural, social, political, economic, and environmental contexts that shape people's views and behaviour.

Make a Difference

As we study issues affecting Canadians and other peoples in the world and become more aware of the realities of life on our planet, we are faced with moral and ethical choices. If we are concerned enough to investigate and analyse the issues, we should be able to identify what we think are better ways of thinking, seeing, and acting. If we oppose an action taken by government, industry, or some other group, we should propose alternative solutions or our protest is merely empty rhetoric.

We may become politically active, or make decisions about how to change our consumption habits. As we realize that our actions do have an effect on other people and places, we should refuse to be passive observers. You can make a difference.

FIGURE 1.8 You can make a difference.

Steps to Critical Analysis

Critical analysis is a way to use critical-thinking skills to evaluate information. As you gather details from different media sources, it is important to use a discerning eye to analyse and evaluate their validity. This process can be adapted to a wide range of media, including cartoons, advertising, and television documentaries. Ask yourself the following questions:

1. What is the main message (e.g., of the article, cartoon, brochure)?
2. What is the purpose (e.g., to inform, influence, persuade, entertain) of the information given?
3. What data (e.g., facts, statistics, opinions) does the author use to support the main message?
4. Who is the author or creator?
5. What bias can you identify? (Look for any main points of view or facts that may be missing, "loaded" words used to persuade, or irrelevant facts.)
6. What is your own bias?
7. How does this sample of media make you feel?
8. What can you conclude about the main message? (Do you have enough information yet to make a conclusion?)

 See Chapter 20 for more information about finding solutions and taking action.

> **"** There's a big world out there where people have much bigger problems than I do. I saw the health care field as a way to address these broader issues. It's your right to find out the truth of what's happening in the world and what you can do to change it. It's important to *think outside the box*; break the mold and have a richer quality of life by making life better for others. These are people with hearts, goals, beautiful stories, sad stories, tragedies. Nevertheless they're just people and they deserve the same human rights. Why are they any less significant than me? Do whatever you can to raise awareness, make a donation, participate in a concert. *The important thing is to care.* **"**
>
> *Dr. Samantha Knott, War Child Canada*

WAYS OF SEEING THE WORLD

There are clearly different ways of looking at things. What is happiness? What is success? Some people use material wealth and the accumulation of the products of technology and industry as criteria. However, if attaining this kind of happiness and success destroys the long-term supply of natural resources and has a detrimental effect on health, our actions are self-defeating in the long term. There is growing evidence that our consumptive lifestyle is unsustainable.

What influences how we see an issue? One of the assumptions of current western thinking is that there is an important link between our worldview and our behaviour. Different worldviews inspire different patterns of behaviour. Worldviews are often evaluated based on the way of life each tends to foster. A recurring theme is that, in order to create a sustainable human society living in a healthy natural environment, simple acts such as recycling or using public transportation, instead of driving, will not be enough. We need to change our way of thinking about how people relate to nature. This assumption supports the need to change our worldview from an **anthropocentric** view, the belief that humans should dominate nature, to an **ecocentric** view, or a new ecological **paradigm**, which values all parts of ecosystems and recognizes that people are one part of the interrelated whole that is nature.

A Sense of Place

What place is home to you? Do you have more than one place you call home? How connected do you feel to that place? Do you miss it when you are away?

Understanding the basic geographic concept of place can serve as a personal framework for our understanding and feelings about a place. Understanding how people can form connections to a place can help us appreciate the perspectives of others and foster the co-operation and communication required for solving problems. Understanding the natural and human characteristics of one's home, and how the two interact, is critical to our understanding of the integral role that humans play within an ecosystem. This understanding helps people make informed decisions about where to live, travel, work, locate various human activities, and find opportunities and solutions. The way people think and feel about their home depends on characteristics such as cultural background, gender, age, occupation, values, and various personal experiences. A bond with a particular landscape can inspire a sense of identity and connection between oneself and the natural world.

> **❝** We need a new system of values, which recognizes the organic unity between humankind and nature and promotes the ethic of global responsibility. **❞**
>
> *Mikhail Gorbachev, former president of the Soviet Union, founder of Green Cross International*

a)

b)

f)

c)

e)

g)

d)

FIGURE 1.9 Perceptions of a particular place vary significantly, depending on your point of view. How might each of the individuals portrayed perceive these places?

excerpt from
"From swamp-ugly to wetland harmony"
by Rick Boychuk
Canadian Geographic magazine
May/June 2000

"Ever come across a landscape that could only be described as plug-ugly? Okay, some strip malls and maybe those wastelands on the edge of every city where junkyards and used-oil outfits and slaughterhouses tend to locate. But I mean an out-of-the-municipal-limits sort of landscape that appeared grotesque or hideous?

HARRIS, Lawren S. Canadian 1885-1970. BEAVER SWAMP, Algoma 1920. Oil on Canvas, 120.7 x 141.0 cm. ART GALLERY OF ONTARIO, Toronto. Gift of Ruth Massey Tovell, in memory of Harold Murchison Tovell, 1953.

FIGURE 1.10 "Beaver Swamp" by Lawren Harris.

Nature may be inconvenient and occasionally bug-ridden, tangled, windswept or desolate, but the environmental ethic of our age has taught us to appreciate the beauty of its harmonious complexity. Every flutter of a butterfly's wings matters. The disappearance of the homely little Oregon spotted frog…means the loss of a "unique and irreplaceable genetic lineage." Saving the frog means preserving its habitat, wetlands that were once considered worthless. Every hectare of barren, soggy ground we drain for bright new subdivisions robs a frog species of its home. It also steals a sustaining element from one of the water systems we take so much for granted in this country….

The painting in Figure 1.10 is by Lawren Harris of Group of Seven fame. Entitled *Beaver Swamp, Algoma*, it was exhibited in Toronto in 1921 and provoked a comment from *Saturday Night* magazine critic Hector Charlesworth. The painting of the swamp, he wrote, is a "repulsive, forbidding thing. One felt like taking a dose of quinine every time one looked at it. If ugliness is real beauty, they have yet to prove it to a very large mass of the assembled public."

Done. Proved. Clayton Rubec, an Environment Canada scientist who has devoted himself to preserving Canada's wetlands, says Charlesworth's comments "reflect the mood of a bygone era. They are echoes of a time when swamps and marshes and sloughs were home to the bogeyman, mosquito-plagued mudholes that any Canadian of real virtue would quickly drain and put to the plough…. Today, we see in them what Charlesworth didn't—diversity, harmony, and beauty plainly evident to a large mass of the assembled public."

Critical Analysis
1. How have the public's general views of wetlands changed?
2. What factors do you think are responsible for the change?
3. Conduct research using an Internet search engine to discover what is meant by the phrases "every flutter of a butterfly's wings matters," and "one felt like taking a dose of quinine."
4. Conduct research to:
   a) discover the percentage of Ontario's and/or Canada's original wetlands that remain intact;
   b) create a list of "services" that wetlands provide for humans and other species.

How people feel about a place can give rise to hopes and struggles for improved living conditions, freedom from oppression, and sovereignty.

 See Chapter 17 for more information about nationalism.

Making Sense of the World

Scientific and geographic inquiry provide two ways of viewing and making sense of the world, but there are many other ways as well. **Epistemology** is what philosophers call our approach to understanding how complex natural systems work. There are two main epistemologies. One involves collection of data and careful analysis, experiments, and testing of theories—a narrow **mechanistic** approach. The other, a more holistic ecological approach, looks at a whole system. The view that natural systems tend to be stable and balanced is part of the mechanistic view that most governments, corporations, and western policies tend to follow as they attempt to extract **maximum sustained yields** from natural resources. In other words, take as much of a renewable resource such as forests or fish as possible without seriously depleting the supply for future generations. In many cases, the amount of resources taken far exceeds this maximum sustained yield. Some ecologists believe that nature is resilient. This view tends to make a careful limiting of the amount of resources we take seem unnecessary. Our impacts on nature are very great and growing, making it difficult to predict how long the resources will last.

A clear example can be found in the collapsed cod fishery off the Atlantic coast of Canada. The federal Department of the Environment in its 1976 *Policy for Canada's Commercial Fisheries* stated that management of the resource should be guided by economic and social issues, rather than biological realities. This was because, in the past, management had been in the interests of the people rather than the fish. The 1976 management plan ignored the interconnections of the real world and failed to predict the complete collapse of the fishery 16 years later, clearly not in the interest of the people or the fish. Despite the moratorium placed on cod fishing in 1992, by 2002 stocks were even lower.

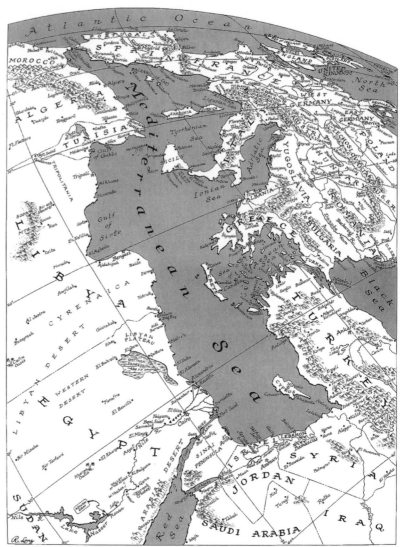

World Eagle © 2001 Russel H. Lenz

FIGURE 1.11 A map of North Africa and Europe as seen from the Middle East.

> 66 Science is a tool that can be used to provide the ecological insights needed to save the Earth and its natural values. Instead, billions of dollars are spent each year on applied research in biotechnology, chemistry, the military, industrial agriculture, and the like. This human-centred research increases short-term profits and competitiveness and improves industrial output, defense capability, health, comforts and food production. But what is the cost to our planet and the security of our future? 99
>
> *Ted Mosquin, from "Anthro-pocentric Science Fiddles while the Earth Burns" in* Borealis magazine, 1992

Perceptions of Places on Maps

What do you see when you look at a map of the world? It depends on your perspective. Why do we usually place our globes with the North Pole side up? When seen from space, there is no real up or down with respect to Earth's position. Our view of the world can be shaped by the maps we use. Consider what is at the centre of most of the world maps you see. The Atlantic Ocean and western countries form the focal point. Children in Japan use maps that place Japan at the centre and have a different outlook on the relative significance of Japan's location with respect to other parts of the world.

See Chapter 2 for more information about maps and their implications.

A Sampling of Values, Ethics, and Worldviews

Throughout your study of Canadian and world issues, you will learn about and analyse a number of local and global issues. All of them will involve different stakeholders with different opinions. It helps to understand where people's opinions come from, why certain decisions are made about the issues, and why people choose to act in different ways. Opinions often evolve from different values, ethics, and worldviews. As global issues increase and intensify, interest in ethics and worldviews, including those related to the environment, business, health care, animal welfare, media, government, and computer technology, is growing.

Values, ethics, and worldviews are shaped by culture and experience. People with different worldviews can logically investigate and analyse the same information about an issue in a similar way but come to very different conclusions. Decisions made to resolve issues should consider the ethics and worldviews held by the stakeholders involved.

The word "value" comes from an ancient Latin word meaning strong and heroic. Values are beliefs about the worth of an idea, person, thing, or behaviour. They indicate what we consider to be important. An ethic is a system of moral standards that depends on our values and guides us on what we think is right and wrong and what we consider appropriate behaviour when interacting with other people and with the environment. Worldviews are larger, commonly shared philosophies about important life questions, the nature of reality, and the role of humans within it that are based on our values and ethics. Theorists divide worldviews into various groupings. One group divides people according to whether they are optimistic or pessimistic about the future. Another group considers anthropocentric and ecocentric worldviews.

In the anthropocentric worldview, humans are seen as conquerors of nature and are disconnected from it. They have greater value than other species and individual rights are valued. Science and technology are of prime importance and are used to control and manage nature for human use. People make use of natural resources to satisfy their needs and accumulate wealth. Technology solves most problems and issues. This worldview, which is dominant in western society, is sometimes described as expansionist, mechanistic, or technocratic. Conventional—sometimes called neoclassical—economics is part of this worldview.

In the ecocentric worldview, nature is seen as a kaleidoscope of patterns and processes that constantly change over time and space. All life forms are related and all species have equal intrinsic value. Humans are unique but decisions made must consider not only all other species, but abiotic (non-living) components of ecosystems as well (see Figure 1.13).

Conflicting Views of Economy

Economists with a more ecocentric worldview are often called green or ecological economists. They see ecology and economy as working together to create ways of production and distribution of goods and services that respect the complex nature of Earth's natural systems. Green economists are concerned with social and environmental relationships. They have developed ways to measure the economic activity of a country that take into account the long-term costs of using up valuable resources and creating pollution. People with this worldview believe that economic measures such as Gross National Product (GNP) and GDP are misleading as they overstate progress, ignoring environmental degradation and depletion of the resources that form the natural capital that supports the system. Green economists include in their accounting the "free" services that nature provides, which form the foundation that supports all societies and economies.

Conventional economists tend to take nature's services for granted. Nature's free services include:

■ natural water flows for agricultural, industrial, and household uses;
■ the formation of soil;
■ erosion control;
■ air-cleaning services by trees;

- pollination for plant reproduction, including agricultural crops;
- biological control of pests and diseases.

The oil spill from the *Exxon Valdez*, which dumped nearly 50 million L of oil off the coast of Alaska in 1989, actually boosted the GNP. That is because billions of dollars were spent to treat the mess, jobs were created, and resources were consumed. The more people who get divorced, have car accidents, or get serious diseases like cancer, the better the economy appears to be doing. That is because money is spent on lawyers, repairs, doctors, medicines, and so on. One alternative way to measure how well the economy is doing is to replace the GDP with the green economists' Index of Sustainable Economic Welfare (ISEW) or Genuine Progress Indicator (GPI). These indicators show a different picture of the economy as they recognize factors such as loss of wetlands or forests and rising health care costs, which result from pollution or tobacco use. Alternative measures of economic progress such as these have been found commonly at universities, in various magazines, and at NGO Web sites, but until very recently have been ignored by mainstream media and the political realm. Because of this monopoly on ideas, a great deal of useful discussion did not reach the public in Canada, until the federal finance minister, Paul Martin, expressed interest in new ways of measuring economic progress such as GPI, in 2001.

> " The economy is dependent on the ecosphere; the bottom line of the economy, so to speak. "
>
> *Dr. Dianne Draper,*
> *University of Calgary,*
> *Canada*

COUNTERPOINT Challenging the concept of economic growth seems pointless. Most westerners want the bigger house, the more expensive car. The global economy needs to grow. Economic growth leads to a much better quality of life. It is the best way to bring the poor, disadvantaged, and marginalized groups into the mainstream of an economy. Economic growth leads to increased food security, better health care, and reduced poverty. Developed countries like Canada and the U.S. benefit as the economies of developing nations expand, becoming more open and market-oriented. This expansion also helps to reduce poverty, which contributes to political instability and exacerbates global issues such as rapid population growth, the spread of infectious diseases, and environmental degradation. Free markets are good for the environment because they generate growth that attacks the root cause of environmental degradation, and result in environmental policies and technological innovations that help the environment. Technology means progress and new developing technologies will solve most of our problems.

Within these two main worldviews—anthropocentric and ecocentric—there are several subgroups. Two of these subgroups are traditional ecological knowledge (TEK) and stewardship. Stewardship is based on the idea that God created nature so that it has inherent value and, while we may make use of it, it must be protected. Humans have a special place in nature and should be caretakers of Earth and its peoples. It puts part of the blame for problems on one of the early assump-

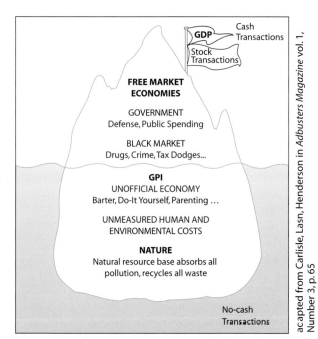

acapted from Carlisle, Lasn, Henderson in *Adbusters Magazine* vol. 1, Number 3, p. 65

FIGURE 1.12 Conventional economists deal mostly with the top of the iceberg.

FACT FILE

The words "ecology" and "economy" both come from the Greek root word "*oikos*", meaning "the house."

A Spectrum of Ethics

	Ecocentric (Species centred: ecosystem processes of prime importance)	Biocentric (Species centred: humans have equal value to other species)	Anthropocentric (People centred)	Econocentric/Technocentric (Growth/industry centred)
Values:	• nature has intrinsic value • deep attachment to place • nature is delicately balanced • integration of facts/values/thoughts/feelings	• people are an important part of nature • human activities must work within nature's limits	• nature is manageable • nature has resource value • economic growth with concern for social justice and environment • take what we need plus profit	• nature is ours for the taking • nature is abundant, hostile, controllable • people are above nature • separation of facts/values/thoughts/feelings
Knowledge:	• holistic, interconnections • science has limits • wisdom of elders **• long-term focus on issues—consider several generations into the future** • small scale community solutions • flexible • purists • "green" economics	• soft technology (e.g., renewable energy) • TEK (traditional ecological knowledge) • ecology and economy are interconnected—need a common goal and collaboration to solve problems	• appropriate technology **• short-term focus on problem solving** • pragmatic approach	• reductionist scientific paradigm • confidence in science and technology • ignores wisdom of elders and native peoples **• short-term focus on problem solving** • large-scale corporate solutions
Society:	• redistribution of wealth • spiritualism, sharing • social democracy with strong social safety net	• governments cannot do it all • local communities control their own destinies	• public/private sectors have joint responsibilities • technology extends human ability (e.g., submarines take us into oceans)	• conventional economics • mindless consumerism (value material goods) • industrial paradigm • rich–poor gap inevitable • privatization • progress is the modern religion • militarism
	Ecoterrorism	**Activism** **Gaia hypothesis** **Ecofeminism**		**Economic terrorism**

FIGURE 1.13 Our ethics have a lot to do with the worldviews we hold. What are the effects of decisions made by people with particular worldviews on the sustainability of human and natural systems? This spectrum could be seen as ethnocentric as it applies most widely to western societies in developed countries. Many poor people in developing countries are preoccupied with survival and unable to take care of their environment. For example, recycling and reusing may be a way of life out of sheer necessity.

tions of Christianity, the idea that nature was given to humans to dominate.

TEK is the accumulated knowledge, based on a set of values and beliefs that have been passed down from generation to generation of Aboriginal peoples, about the relationship of all living beings—including humans—with each other and with their environment. It is an understanding of how natural systems and processes operate and a belief that all things are interconnected. Nature is strongly valued as it plays a vital role in the social, economic, and cultural life of various groups of Aboriginal peoples. In the past, western scientists rejected TEK as anecdotal and unscientific. Today, TEK is being much more widely used in many parts of the world, including Canada, as governments and scientists are realizing the tremendous value it has, and that it actually is a form of science. There are many cases of studies on resources and wildlife that have been conducted in Canada's Arctic, where TEK either disputed or confirmed the results of the studies, with far more accurate results than did western scientific methods. Both science and TEK have validity and can complement one another.

Religion and Worldviews

Religion is a major component of culture that can shape worldviews. Most major religions and spiritual beliefs express similar values and ethics such as various interpretations of the "golden rule" (i.e., Do unto others as you would have them do unto you). Most major religions express a reverence for nature and a belief in the idea that people should act as stewards or caretakers of nature. However, there are many people within each religion who find it difficult to comply with these values or who simply pay lip service to them. Religious differences are attributes that can keep people from uniting together. In many ways, religion can be the most divisive force in the world and there are many religious conflicts around the globe. Some conflicts are rooted in religious fundamentalism, while others are more economically based.

> " Traditional knowledge is science, and the sooner…scientists make use of that traditional knowledge, the better it will be for their research. Aboriginal people wish to be involved in science and they will be involved in research whether through legislation, the permit process, or voluntary action. Partnerships are a vital part of the strategy we must adopt in together seeking imaginative, innovative and perhaps unexpected, solutions. "
>
> *George Hobson, director, Polar Continental Shelf Project, winner of Northern Science Award for outstanding contribution to Arctic research*

> " If everyone could see the image of God in his/her neighbour, do you think we should still need tanks and generals? "
>
> *Mother Teresa, Catholic nun, missionary*

 See Chapter 3 for more information about the political spectrum.

INTERACT

1. For each of the following statements, suggest the values, ethics, or worldviews that the speaker has.
   a) Those tree huggers just want to protect things like spotted owls and they don't really care if people lose their jobs.
   b) Progress is best measured by the flow of money.
   c) Humans are only one species among millions where even the smallest bacterium is as important as any other species for the well-being of the whole organism, the biosphere.
   d) The world cannot be left as it is, it has to be improved. Progress is bringing roads, bridges, and airports to help develop the economy.
   e) "Until he extends the circle of compassion to all living things, man will not himself find peace." *Dr. Albert Schweitzer*

f) Using animals to test whether cosmetics are safe or for military experiments to test the effects of new weapons is necessary to keep humans safe.

g) Modern industrial society has embarked on a suicidal course. We're destroying all our life-support systems and we must change our ways or we will eliminate life on the planet.

2. What do you value the most? How does your most significant value compare with those of other members of your class? With other members of your class, create a list of values and attitudes that young people today will need to acquire to become responsible citizens in the twenty-first century.

A Sustainable Future

A fundamental concept underlying many of the local and global issues that you will study is sustainability. Defining sustainable development is difficult but achieving it may be much more so. The current challenge facing humans revolves around the question of how we can satisfy the needs of a growing population without destroying our life-supporting natural systems and ruining the chances for future generations to do the same.

Many people have adopted sustainable development as a desirable goal for human activity. However, groups with different worldviews hold completely different interpretations and make different decisions on how to achieve sustainability. Someone with an ecocentric worldview would say that economic growth, which is a continued increase in the quantity of resources, technology, and wealth, cannot be sustained forever on a planet with finite resources. Sustainable economic development implies a better quality of life without necessarily consuming more resources. Economic development based on conserving, reducing our high consumption rates, and sharing resources more equally is much more likely to be sustainable. Whether our economy can continue to keep on growing is an ongoing debate that has widespread implications for the future health of people and the planet.

 See Chapters 4 and 20 for more information about sustainable development.

Web Links

- Ethical dimensions of Earth and its natural ecosystems and ecocentrism: <www.ecospherics.net>
- Green Cross International: <www.globalgreen.org>
- Links to world issues ethics sites: <http://carbon.cudenver.edu/~jjuhasz/ethiclinks.html>

Related Issues

- The ethics of animal rights
- The role of technology in solving problems

GIS **Measuring Quality of Life Using the HDI, GDI, and Gini**

ANALYSE, APPLY, AND INTERACT

1. Use critical thinking skills as outlined on page 15 to analyse a magazine ad or television commercial.

2. What is your place—a favourite location where you like to be and feel most comfortable? It can be in a natural setting, a vacation destination, or a place as simple as a spot within your home.
   a) Write a 150–200-word detailed description of your place, why it is important to you, and the factors that have determined your perception of your place.
   b) What role has your worldview played in determining the kinds of places that are important or valuable to you?

3. Collect newspaper clippings that show direct and indirect connections between the community and the wider world. Classify them under different headings of your choice.

4. Create a definition for the terms "paradigm," "ideology," "ethnocentrism," "holistic," "context," "norms," and "think outside the box." How do these terms relate to "worldview"?

5. Conduct research on Christianity, Islam, Judaism, Hinduism, Buddhism, Jain, and any other religions or spiritual beliefs of your choice, to compare their worldviews relating to
   a) the "golden rule" (i.e., Do unto others as you would have them do unto you.) and b) the relationship of humans with nature. What are the implications of your findings for solving global issues?

6. Brainstorm a list of well-known people in the world who have spoken out to take a stand on a particular issue or event. Place them in an appropriate spot on Figure 1.13, **A Spectrum of Ethics**. Where do you and your peers fit in the ethical spectrum? Are you and your peers generally optimistic or pessimistic about the future? Explain your answer.

7. Conduct research and write a one-page description of some of the ways Canadians view themselves. Include a section on how some others view Canadians.

8. Collect two letters to the editor of a regional or national newspaper. Critically analyse the viewpoints expressed in the letters. Have the authors used critical-thinking skills in expressing their views? Explain why or why not.

9. Humans are said to have intellectual, emotional, spiritual, and physical needs. Rank the order in which these needs are met by a typical secondary school education. Would you say that your education is reductionist or holistic? Explain your answer.

10. What do you value? To many people, a swamp is just a wasteland to be filled in and developed. Development such as a shopping mall provides jobs, activities, and services for people. Conduct some research on the role that swamps and marshes play in an ecosystem as well as the benefits they provide for humans. Write a one-page explanation, outlining your position on the question of whether or not to drain a hypothetical swamp in your community to build a shopping mall. Which do you value more? Debate the issue with someone in your class who has taken the opposite view.

11. Design a survey that you can use to collect information about the attitudes of friends, family, and community members about a few global issues. Create questions that will reveal what they consider to be the "hot" issues, how they feel about them, key questions related to the issues that they would like to resolve, and their ideas for resolving them. Identify the most common worldview of the people in your survey.

12. Write a 250–300-word explanation, using specific examples, of how religion can promote both tolerance and intolerance.

13. Use the step-by-step process outlined in Geographic Inquiry: A Detailed Process for Investigating and Analysing Issues, on pages 10–11, to analyse a geographic issue of your choice.

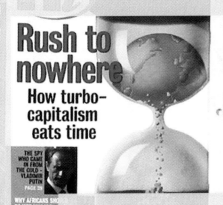

Managing and Monitoring:
Tools for Sustainable Development

Chapter 2: The Media and Global Issues

By the end of this chapter, you will

- explain how points of view and paradigms influence an individual's perceptions of a place;

- analyse selected global trends and evaluate their effects on people and environments at the local, national, and global levels;

- explain how people perceive resources and sustainable development differently at different times and in different places;

- demonstrate an understanding of how economies and environments in some places may be affected by decisions made in other places;

- evaluate the performance of a selected transnational corporation with respect to the promotion of environmental sustainability and human rights;

- evaluate the cultural, economic, and environmental impact of changing technology;

- identify awareness levels and viewpoints relating to a geographic issue by conducting a survey in the school or local community;

- describe biases that may inform different viewpoints and perspectives on geographic issues;

- demonstrate an ability to distinguish between fact and opinion in information sources;

- evaluate and effectively use information from a variety of primary and secondary sources when conducting geographic inquiries, and apply relevant data when making decisions and solving problems;

- analyse how the media influence public opinion on geographic issues;

- draw conclusions or make judgements or predictions on the basis of reasoned analysis;

- use different types of maps and images to analyse the consequences of human activities or environmental phenomena;

- use maps to analyse change over time in a place.

THE GLOBAL MEDIA

As you will learn throughout this text, globalization is a powerful force, shaping the world. As we have transformed from an industrial to an information society, globalization of the media has kept pace. Communications technology has made it possible for information to move across borders and around the world instantaneously. Each successive development in communications technology has brought a corresponding increase in the number of ideas we must process. Satellite coverage provides real-time information about national and international concerns from the Olympics to civil wars and about global issues such as famine, deforestation, and climate change. One remarkable aspect of globalization has been the emergence of the ever-expanding Internet network, which can send a vast array of information anywhere on Earth, contributing to the spread of democracy, changing the way business and government conduct daily activities, and generating wealth.

> **Everyone has the right to freedom of opinion and expression; this right includes freedom to hold opinions without interference and to seek, receive and impart information and ideas through any media and regardless of frontiers.**
>
> *UN Universal Declaration of Human Rights, Article 19*

Almost all information about the world beyond our immediate experience comes to us through media, mainly in electronic and print forms. While all forms of media contain messages about values and beliefs, about 95% of the media the average citizen is exposed to is considered **mainstream media**. Diverse views are not commonly expressed in mainstream media and are, therefore, not readily available to most people. The messages received from these dominant media play a role in shaping public opinion on most issues from foreign policy to fast food.

Exposure to media has become a major factor in shaping the economic, political, social, cultural, and environmental make-up of the world. Not everyone has equal access to media, and an information gap exists between rich and poor, and between the more powerful groups in society and those who are marginalized. Individuals cannot address serious issues if they are unaware of their underlying causes and interconnections. Accurate and complete information is needed to enhance awareness of issues and to build skills of critical thinking, **analysis**, and **synthesis**. A related issue is that decisions are often made by those in power without consulting the people most affected by the decisions. Due to a lack of political will or funding, accurate and complete information and ideas on which to base policies, such as those intended to reduce poverty, are not sought out.

The United Nations (UN) considers this need a priority. World leaders, representatives of non-governmental organizations (NGOs), and the private sector have planned to meet at UN World Summits on the Information Society in Geneva, Switzerland, in 2003 and Tunis, Tunisia, in 2005 to address issues concerning media. They intend to develop goals and action plans to make sure that the world community, as a whole, benefits from the "information society."

Getting the Information

In a democratic society, information should be designed to help people become well informed and better able to protect themselves. As we are exposed to the hectic pace of modern life and receive e-mail, faxes, telephone messages, and many other stimuli from work, school, family, and friends, it is easy to become overwhelmed. There are so many opposing claims and ideas in all types of information—political, commercial, and environmental—that it is hard to tell **rhetoric** from reality. For example, most of what is shown on television about global trade meetings is confrontation and violence, instead of the peaceful demonstrations and the tireless work of politicians and officials that are much more common.

> **We need to communicate that knowledge and wisdom [to] people we know, love, respect and spend time with. We need to live richer lives as a result of that information—not just amass it and bombard ourselves with it.**
>
> *David Shenk, computer and media analyst, author,* Data Smog

The glut of contradictory information can lead to a feeling of powerlessness as busy people have less time for reflection and tend to

FIGURE 2.1 Media includes all of the industries and products that communicate information.

become less critical but more sceptical of what they hear.

Accurate, well-balanced information allows individuals to form opinions and to make informed decisions on whether and how to take action. But what is the quality of the information received? Who decides what information to convey? Access to a great deal more information does not necessarily mean people are better informed. Information itself is a resource. To be used effectively, it has to be turned into knowledge and understanding. A wide variety of views about issues, including our own, must be studied and challenged before analysis of the issues can be effective.

Information for Survival

In ancient times, humans sought information about the world that they needed for survival. Their information came from all the senses: sight, sound, smell, taste, and touch. After the Industrial Revolution, technological advances such as the telegraph and the television began to inundate people with different kinds of infor-

mation. Rather than getting information actively from the senses, many people now passively observe and may even become indifferent to much of the information they receive.

The rise of large newspaper chains in the nineteenth century and their desire to increase sales led to an increase in sensational or scandalous stories of crimes, celebrity events, wars, and disasters. This change in how information was presented and in what information was selected could actually trigger events and turn events into crises. The early wealthy press barons like William Randolph Hearst in the United States manipulated the news and were influential in creating the Spanish-American and Boer Wars. Elite groups continue to influence society today.

> "Show half a dozen people a story about an earthquake and ask for their reactions. A filmmaker sees it one way, an insurance broker another, an engineer, a firefighter, a travel agent, a child—all making use of the story in different ways. All of them doing their own analysis. All of them helpless without the basic facts."
>
> *Paul Knox, journalist*

News networks still welcome dramatic, sensational events and claim that the public demands them. Technology is so advanced that media can be completely created or manufactured—a fabrication rather than the whole truth. Analysis may be conducted, conclusions drawn, and opinions formed without accurate, impartial information.

> "We can watch a murder on television, or something just as lurid and awful, and continue to eat our chicken sandwich. We don't even get upset by it…this may have created the sense of impotence that people feel. "
>
> *Neil Postman,*
> *media analyst, author,*
> *Amusing Ourselves to Death*

People still use their eyes and ears to absorb information and still need that information to make important and informed decisions about their communities and their survival. They must know if the water is safe to drink. They should know the root causes of a conflict before going off to war. They should understand the changing nature of today's information as it shapes attitudes, beliefs, views, and behaviour.

Constructing Reality

People interested in the natural environment may lack the time and means to explore wild places, so they tend to do this through film, television, and other media. A documentary showing beautiful views of wildlife in a pristine environment does not show reality. The collage of images portrayed focuses on the fascinating or thrilling aspects of a natural environment, missing the integral activity that goes on at night or up in the highest canopy layer. Real time is sped up so that "digestible bites" of carefully selected and filtered information fit within the framework of a television show, contributing to our lack of real understanding of the long, slow-paced time frame of nature. Life in the modern world

> "Sometimes the media ignore history, sometimes they manufacture it. Sometimes they deliver messages, sometimes they make up messages and deliver them, sometimes they don't deliver the messages that were sent. They are complicit, like many other social forces, far more so than they can evade by claiming messenger status. "
>
> *Rick Salutin, columnist*

FIGURE 2.2 For many people, the only experience of a wild natural environment comes from imagined participation through media.

encourages speed. Media images change several times a minute. Our view of reality becomes distorted. Many people feel they are exempt from this effect and wise enough to sort it out, but the distortion is so pervasive that it becomes a form of reality.

INTERACT

1. Brainstorm a list of information that you need to **a)** function comfortably in your community and **b)** survive.
2. What primary sources of information about other people and places do you have access to other than mainstream media?
3. Keep a journal for a week to calculate the percentage of your total waking time that is spent exposed to various kinds of media.
4. Who are the powerful elite in our society? Suggest ways in which they could influence the outcome of important issues.
5. Investigate to find two or three techniques that can be used by media to manufacture or "construct" reality.
6. Using specific media samples such as a news broadcast or article, photograph, or advertisement, explain how media can **a)** distort our view of reality and **b)** influence public opinion.

WHO OWNS THE MEDIA AND DOES IT MATTER?

In the first half of the twentieth century, governments used institutions such as the Canadian Broadcasting Corporation (CBC) to distribute information in order to protect freedom of speech, cultural identity, and diversity and to avoid commercialization. The general public owns public broadcasting, which has been seen as the forum for voices that might not otherwise be heard and where unbiased debate can and should take place. Publicly owned media provide information and analysis that allows the public to act effectively in the interest of their communities. However, the publicly owned media are receiving decreasing government support amid increased pressure to avoid controversy and debate of sensitive issues. In Ontario, TVO has been under threat of privatization.

As regulations under negotiation at the World Trade Organization (WTO) reduce the ability of governments to provide subsidies or incentives to support public broadcasting, regular funding cuts, the necessity for increased use of advertising, and campaigns for public and private donations have become common. As a solution to

FIGURE 2.3 The Internet is seen as a way to deliver consumers to advertisers. America on Line (AOL)'s favourite links steer more than 22 million subscribers in many corporate-friendly directions, including toward offerings by its own company, Time Warner.

inadequate funding, some people have suggested taxes on the use of public airwaves or on mass advertising.

Global Media Giants

Huge transnational corporations (TNCs) control public airwaves in a vast, horizontally and **vertically integrated** system of media, including books, music, movies, radio, television, and the Internet. They use the public airwaves at no cost and face few regulations or public interest obligations. They have a vested interest in what is reported and how. The global media industry is dominated by just a few companies. None of these existed before 1990 as the media conglomerates of today. Many of these companies own stock in each other's companies and jointly operate ventures around the world. Some have common shareholders and board of director members, including representatives of government and other large TNCs. The following companies represent the media elite of the world:

- **Disney**—ABC television, radio networks, ESPN (including ESPN Sports Zone Web site), A&E, History channel, Disney Channel, several major film and video production companies (including Disney, Buena Vista, and Miramax), magazine and newspaper publishing through subsidiaries Fairchild and Chilton Publications, Hyperion Books, several music labels, theme parks and resorts, a cruise line, a chain of high-tech arcade game stores, and interest in hockey and baseball teams
- **General Electric**—NBC, CNBC, and, along with Microsoft, MSNBC
- **AOL Time Warner**—CNN
- **SONY**—music (Columbia, CBS, and Epic records), movies (Columbia, Tristar, and Loew's theatres)
- **News Corporation** (owned by Rupert Murdoch)—Fox TV, 20th Century Fox, *TV Guide* magazine, 175 newspapers worldwide (including *London Times* and *New York Post*), and book publishing (HarperCollins)
- **Viacom**—CBS, Blockbuster, Showtime, MTV, Paramount Pictures, Famous Players, Simon and Schuster
- **Vivendi**—MCA records, MP3.com, the world's third largest book publisher (including Houghton Mifflin, the world's second

largest educational publisher), Universal Studios, Home Shopping Network, Ticketmaster, Flipside on-line games

- **Bertelsmann**—the world's third largest conglomerate: book publishing (including Random House, Knopf, Doubleday, Ballantine publishers), magazines, newspapers, television, and radio and film production companies in 53 countries

The U.S. federal government passed laws that prevented any one company from owning both television stations and cable television franchises in the same market and restricted the maximum access of one company's television stations to 35% of households. In a lawsuit filed against these rules by four of the media giants Fox, AOL Time Warner, NBC, and Viacom—the U.S. Federal Court ruled in February 2002 that the ownership restrictions were arbitrary and not in the public interest, striking a further blow to diversity of ownership. Companies like Microsoft, AOL, Disney, and Vivendi (and Quebecor, CanWest, and Bell Globemedia in Canada) have invested heavily in the Internet, the next step of concentration of global communications.

> ## FACT FILE
>
> Athens, Greece, has 15 daily newspapers while 98% of the cities in North America have only one daily.

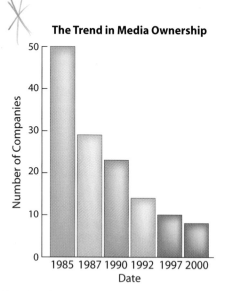

The Trend in Media Ownership

FIGURE 2.4 News sources in the U.S. are owned by fewer and fewer companies.

> " The multi-channel TV universe [will] be our salvation: There is no interest too small to be ignored as the big networks erode and minority tastes find critical mass through technology to satisfy every interest and need. "
>
> *William Thorsell, CEO, Royal Ontario Museum,*
> *former editor,* The Globe and Mail

Corporate control of media is being challenged by the nature of the system itself and by youth. Technology is beginning to fragment the markets of the large television networks as more and more specialty channels become available. More **pop culture** is being consumed, some of which is driven by youth with a more anti-corporate agenda.

Media Ownership in Canada

Although the Canadian Radio–Television Telecommunications Commission (CRTC) regulates media to ensure fair competition and diversity of ownership, media ownership is concentrated in Canada and just a few companies dominate the market:

- **Bell Globemedia**— *The Globe and Mail*, CTV, Sympatico–Lycos, TSN
- **CanWest Global**— *The National Post* and 14 daily metropolitan newspapers, Global TV, CHTV, Hamilton, Canada.com (news)
- **Shaw Communications** (Canada's second largest cable television company) —14 radio stations, specialty television networks (YTV, CMT)
- **Hollinger Inc.** (owned by Conrad Black)— about two dozen community newspapers in Canada and many in the U.S. as well as international newspapers (including *The Jerusalem Post*, *Chicago Sun-Times*, and *London Daily Telegraph*)

> ## FACT FILE
>
> In 2000, the CRTC issued new radio licences to Milestone Radio Inc.'s Flow Urban Music FM station, reflecting the musical traditions of Black musicians and Black-influenced music (including rhythm and blues, hip-hop, reggae, and calypso) and to Aboriginal Voices Radio with diverse cultural, spiritual, and news programming.

- **Quebecor**—16 *Sun* newspapers, including the *Ottawa Sun*, and *London Free Press*, Canoe.ca, Videotron cable in Quebec, and TVA (Quebec's largest private television network)
- **Rogers Communications** (Canada's largest cable television company)—Shopping Channel, CFMT, majority share of Sportsnet (Fox is the other shareholder), 65 magazines (including *Maclean's*, *Flare*), 29 radio stations, and the Toronto Blue Jays
- **Torstar**—*The Toronto Star*, *Hamilton Spectator*, *Kitchener–Waterloo Record*, *Guelph Mercury*, and 75 community newspapers, Harlequin Enterprises Publisher, Toronto Star Television, and about 40 Web sites

Much of the news has become entertainment and is driven by ratings and profit. The media owners tell us that people are not interested in serious issues. Intelligent, balanced commentary on issues of concern is not the responsibility of the media conglomerates. Their responsibility is not so much geared to the public interest, as it is in making profit for owners and shareholders.

> ❝ A free press is no longer free when competing voices disappear, yet the federal government has recently permitted two large corporations, CanWest and BCE Inc., to secure a stranglehold on Canada's major, privately-operated television and newspaper outlets. ❞
>
> *55 journalists from the Montreal Gazette*

INTERACT

1. Compare the roles played by public and private media in informing the public.
2. Explain your views on current media ownership patterns in North America. Identify the inherent bias that underlies your viewpoint.
3. Identify the forces that are threatening the survival of public media.
4. Brainstorm a list of ideas for encouraging the survival and growth of public media.

MANUFACTURING CONSENT

Perceptions about what is known are not always accurate. This idea has been exploited by media industries as they shape public opinion. The information presented in the news is often misleading and biased, missing a crucial point of view. It is filtered through a number of lenses before it reaches the public. We often get no information at all about important issues. Some **alternative media** sources provide annual reports on the important issues that did not make the news or that provide a view of world issues from a developing world perspective.

Noam Chomsky, an activist and well-known Massachusetts Institute of Technology (MIT) professor of linguistics, points out in his books, such as *Manufacturing Consent* that, while an authoritarian government can easily control the information received by the public, control cannot be imposed by force in a democracy. Limits are placed on democracy by subtle means used to control independent or dissident views, which might translate into political, social, or environmental action and be seen as a threat. The manufacturing of public consent is accomplished by setting the news agenda using various techniques. These techniques include selecting the topics and issues that will be reported, filtering information through different viewpoints such as editors, time constraints, limiting debate, and using a screening effect whereby one major event is used as a focus to distract from other significant events.

FACT FILE

A study conducted by Chomsky in the 1970s found that coverage in the *New York Times* of attempted genocide by the Pol Pot communist government in Cambodia received 1175 column inches of newspaper coverage while, at the same time, attempted genocide of people in East Timor by the Indonesian government, friendly to U.S. interests, received only 70 inches of coverage.

See Chapter 17 for more information about East Timor's struggle for independence.

FIGURE 2.5 Alternative media organizations report on news stories that do not make the mainstream media such as this celebration in Cochabamba, Bolivia, where farmers and students succeeded in stopping a World Bank–Bechtel Corporation plan to privatize their water supply.

Setting the Agenda

Chomsky sees society as consisting of a political class of about 20% of the population who are well-educated and play a role in decision making. They are not easily fooled by oversimplification and illusion, but, as the collective actions of mainstream media determines, selects, shapes, controls, and restricts what gets reported, public perceptions of the world can be made to satisfy the needs of the dominant elite. The consent of this group to government and corporate policy is crucial. The role of the remaining 80% of the population is to follow the rules, not to be challenged with critical perspectives or controversial ideas, and to be entertained.

Mass diversions such as national sports or shopping channels tend to pull these people away from things that matter more and reduce their interest in thinking critically about serious issues. Films about sports and the military often glorify unthinking obedience to those in positions of authority and portray stereotypical views of various groups, such as a negative view of Arab people in the 2001 film *Black Hawk Down*. The normal process of socialization in society and its institutions help to tell us what ideas, attitudes, and behaviours are acceptable.

Common Propaganda Strategies in Times of War

- Restrict free movement of journalists in conflict zones.

- Provide prepared information to journalists.

- Demonize the enemy and its leaders, using loaded language such as "evil empire" and stories of atrocities, fabricated or real, as justification for actions.

- Simplify the conflict to two sides when more are involved, ignoring the role played by groups such as TNCs or foreign governments.

- Use a double standard to judge atrocities and events of opposing sides.

- Narrow the focus of commentary; for example, use only retired military personnel.

- Treat government sources as fact instead of just one perspective.

- Omit historical and geopolitical context.

- Ignore critical perspectives or alternatives to violence and conflict.

FIGURE 2.6

Propaganda

The term "**propaganda**" is used to describe persuasive messages and the widespread promotion of particular ideas. There are many techniques used in communicating propaganda. A critical appreciation for the role of language is necessary for detecting propaganda. The language chosen to describe people and events can contribute to the "manufacturing" of public consent for policies that favour the dominant elite. This is particularly true in situations of military conflict. Few people want their country and youth to go to war. Even if a war is seen as right and legitimate by some, government and military leaders must often use "loaded words" to sell a war to persuade the public and win financial support from elected politicians.

Every war must be perceived to be a just cause that is a defence against or liberation from some menacing, murderous aggressor and his "cronies" and "henchmen," so that the world will become a better place. Stories of atrocities involving dead children are often used to help create this image. Leaders refer to the "theatre" of war and often use sports analogies and acronyms as a form of euphemism to soften the real horrors of war. Films of the time continue the message. The opposing side is cowardly, weak, and evil while "our" side is strong and good, with loyal heroes.

When **jargon** is used to manipulate or mislead, it becomes **doublespeak**. A commonly used example is the term **collateral damage**, a term referring to unintended civilian deaths.

Suppressing Dissent

After the September 11, 2001, terrorist attacks on the U.S., many journalists and broadcasters discussed a perceived silencing of dissent in mainstream media ostensibly because the American public was in no mood for criticism. Government officials said that people would have to be careful of what they said and that the best way they could deal with the tragedy was to get out and shop. In North America, a continent that prides itself on freedom of speech, dissent against the mainstream view was regarded as unpatriotic in the U.S. and, in Canada, unsupportive of our U.S. neighbours.

There are many "media truisms" or ideological beliefs that are presented in mainstream news media as true and that are rarely questioned. This acts as a subtle form of propaganda. Included is the view that there is no real alternative to the status quo and the competitive corporate culture. Despite these so-called truisms, there are always alternatives.

> **FACT FILE**
>
> In the 2000 film, *The Art of War*, a one-sided view of free trade is presented as the solution to economic problems in the world. Characters in the film who disagree are portrayed as criminals and extremists.

The Role of Journalists

Journalists make useful information accessible to citizens so that they get a sense of the wider world around them. Most journalists try to be

FIGURE 2.7 University of British Columbia professor Sunera Thobani was attacked through the media for expressing her views at a conference against the way the 2001 war in Afghanistan was run.

> 66 Political and media bile dumped this week on feminist academic Sunera Thobani are a startling lesson on how risky it is in Canada to publicly oppose mainstream thinking when the mainstream is on edge. Risky for whoever speaks out. Risky for whoever is in the same room as the person who speaks out— because Thobani's audience and two politicians unfortunate enough to be on the same podium with her have been subjected to much the same criticism. 99
>
> *Michael Valpy, journalist,* The Globe and Mail

fair, balanced, and responsible and to maintain ethical standards in reporting the news. Investigative journalists play an important role in forcing governments and companies to reveal negative information that is in the public interest. Good journalism is a source of information needed to achieve accountability and acts as a check on media control. However, some journalists are under pressure to write or air their reports before they have full information, simply to reach the public before

> **FACT FILE**
>
> In 1954, a Harvard sociologist found that 66% of Americans said that a Communist should not be permitted to speak and 60% said that an atheist should not be permitted to speak.

their competitors. The system, with its centralized control of editorial opinion about significant issues, is more likely to hire journalists that follow the values and truisms of mainstream media and who are interested in keeping their jobs. Editors tend to approve or alter stories to meet the expectations of corporate owners, acting as a filter for information. This can result in a kind of "group think" compliance with the attitudes and expectations of the corporate culture. Journalists who report in regions of war and conflict are not as able to report directly as in past conflicts. Since the conflicts of the 1960s through the early 1980s, when information was revealed by journalists to the world about the involvement and actions of western governments, primarily the U.S., their movement within war zones has been restricted and military and government sources provide them with much of their information.

> " As a journalist, I expect only one thing and that is to be lied to—by omission, distorted context, partial information if not directly— lied to by corporations, government and the military. "
>
> *Stephen Hume, senior writer, the* Vancouver Sun

> " [People] want entertainment and celebrities and sports and spectacles … crime and happy talk and sports and weather and very little else. …There's a great tendency to blame the people; why aren't they interested in things that affect their lives? But at the same time we aren't doing anything about encouraging that interest, stimulating that interest, providing what is necessary to make sure they get well informed. "
>
> *Lawrence Grossman, former president, NBC News and PBS*

Journalism can be a dangerous field. Journalists in many developing countries face censorship or even death threats for reporting views on issues that are not in the interests of the powerful groups in society. Many journalists working in conflict zones have been killed, either inadvertently, as an act of terrorism, or because they have been directly targeted as knowing too much about what is going on in a particular situation.

Media Think Truisms

- Private enterprise, while sometimes given to excess, is the core of our society and is beyond questioning.

- It's all very well to talk about alternative energy, organic agriculture, and preserving endangered species, but when there is a payroll to meet and stock prices to keep high, there is really no alternative.

- People who are wealthy got there because of ability and usually deserve our respect and admiration.

- People who are poor got there because of their own inability. Still, they deserve some form of charity as in food banks.

- Government debts are mostly due to lavish social programs, which we can no longer afford.

- Occasionally a tyrant in some part of the world threatens democracy and has to be put in his place, for the good of the world community and those in that country.

- Environmental problems are largely invented by irrational members of radical groups such as Greenpeace.

- Immigration laws in Canada are too lax. We let people in from minority cultures and they take advantage of our social programs and jobs.

- Unions have outlived their usefulness. Employers no longer try to abuse workers and government regulations protect workers.

- The news media are independent, socially responsible watchdogs who look out for the public interest.

FIGURE 2.8

adapted from excerpt from *Democracy's Oxygen, How Corporations Control the News* by James Winter, Professor of Communications, University of Windsor in *Mediacy*, Volume 19, Number 1, Winter 1997, p. 15

excerpt from

"CanWest censorship shameful"

by Haroon Siddiqui
The Toronto Star
March 10, 2002

Creeping censorship

The National Post appeared as an unapologetic right-wing paper. It was a welcome foil to the liberal *Toronto Star* in a city with four dailies. But in other cities, views different than [Conrad] Black's had trouble being heard, beyond letters to the editors.

With the advent of CanWest, the situation has worsened. The Aspers decreed in December that editorials written in their head office—on property rights, triple E Senate, military spending, the Israeli–Palestinian conflict, etc. must be run in all their major papers.

Among those who did not like it was Stephen Kimber, a columnist for their *Halifax Daily News* and director of journalism at King's College. His column was killed. He quit in protest. When Stephanie Domet criticized it in her column, it was canned. She quit too.

When Peter Worthington, of the Sun chain, wrote against all this, his syndicated column got canned from the Asper-owned *Windsor Star*. "They are trying to eliminate another point of view in other papers," he said.

Among those protesting were the Canadian Association of Journalists, Quebec Federation of Professional Journalists, Canadian University Press, PEN Canada and the National Conference of editorial Writers of North America, as well as 55 writers at the Asper's *Montreal Gazette* who withheld their bylines.

Another Halifax columnist, Peter Match, a professor at St. Mary's University, got canned after writing for the *Daily News* for 10 years, he said because he had been critical of Israel.

Doug Cuthand, a columnist for the *Leader-Post* in Regina and the *Star-Phoenix* in Saskatoon, compared the plight of Palestinians to that of aboriginals here. His column was killed, the first to meet such a fate in 10 years.

All this is chilling.

The *Montreal Gazette's* veteran reporter Bill Marsden was quoted as saying of his bosses: "They do not want any criticism of Israel. We do not run in our newspaper op-ed pieces that express criticism of Israel and what it's doing."

There is an irony here. CanWest media are often critical, and rightly so, of undemocratic Arabs who practise censorship against democratic Israel. Yet here we are in Canada witnessing creeping censorship of other views. …

I want to move on to some other shortcomings of the media. Despite the declarative demands of the Broadcast Act and CRTC guidelines, that the regulated media reflect our multicultural reality, neither private broadcasters nor the CBC reflect our growing diversity. They and our newspapers do not reflect our demography. This is bad journalism.

The point is best made in the Prairies, the cradle of immigration and multiculturalism. Canada today is more immigrant than the United States. Yet you would not know that from our media. An anti-immigrant narrative continues to dominate their content.

There are about 4.5 million visible minorities in Canada. That's larger than the population of Atlantic Canada. Yet these visible minorities are largely invisible in our media.

Even the original inhabitants of our land do not make it to mainstream media, except when they fit the stereotype and conservative commentators can heap some more abuse on them.

The aboriginal population of Saskatchewan is 10 per cent, about half of whom live in urban areas. Yet when I looked at a whole week's worth of the Leader-Post recently, the only photograph of an aboriginal was that of Grand Chief Ted Moses of the Cree in Quebec. No Saskatchewan aboriginal person had been allowed into the domain of the *Leader-Post*.

This is shameful.

There's no other way to say it.

Critical Analysis

1. What is CanWest?
2. Compare the viewpoints of the journalists and their employer, CanWest, in this conflict.
3. Explain what the author means by bad journalism and why he feels the situation is chilling.
4. How is public opinion in Canada shaped, according to the commentary?
5. Write a critical analysis of an editorial in a CanWest paper such as *The National Post* or one of their other local papers. Identify any underlying bias that is evident.
6. a) Check your local newspaper or regional section of a major newspaper for a week.
   b) Compare the coverage of stories with the multicultural make-up of your community.

1. Identify three filters that are used to manipulate information to construct reality.
2. For each of the points in Figure 2.8, **Media Think Truisms**, suggest an alternative viewpoint.
3. How might the use of state propaganda in developing countries affect economic and social development?
4. How might the use of propaganda in countries such as Canada and the U.S. affect geopolitical patterns?
5. Explain what is meant by **a)** setting the agenda and **b)** manufacturing consent and evaluate the ability of mainstream media to accomplish these.
6. What evidence does Noam Chomsky have that democracy is compromised in our society? What influence could this have on the outcome of critical issues?
7. Select two articles and two news programs from different sources on a current geopolitical conflict. Identify the program, time, date, type of story, and author. Evaluate the use of propaganda techniques as identified in Figure 2.6, **Common Propaganda Strategies in Times of War**.
8. Conduct Internet research to find various accounts of the number of people who were killed during the Khmer Rouge regime of Pol Pot during the 1970s. Write a 300-word conclusion about factual accuracy in geopolitical situations of violent conflict.
9. **a)** Along with other members of a group, study several articles on national or global issues in the front section of a major daily newspaper.
   b) Analyse the articles to find evidence of media think truisms and/or alternatives to those views.
   c) Identify examples of techniques used in the articles to influence public opinion.

PUBLIC RELATIONS— PERCEPTION OR REALITY?

Since the 1992 UN Conference on the Environment and Development known as the Earth Summit, the number of companies using the term "sustainable development" has increased significantly. Advertising that uses wilderness views or wildlife to sell products or that makes claims about sustainable practices and products that are environmentally responsible has also increased. This could be considered good news to those interested in sustaining a healthy environment because business and industry play such a huge role in whether or not sustainable development happens.

> **FACT FILE**
>
> While Starbucks advertised its policy of buying "fair trade" coffee in 2002, the amount spent on it was less than 1% of the total amount [the company] spent on coffee.

Many companies have denied the negative impacts of their activities on human and ecosystem health and actively lobby governments against taxes on pollution or carbon emissions and against regulations and laws that follow principles such as the **precautionary** and **polluter pays principles**.

 See Chapter 16 for more information about the precautionary and polluter pays principles.

It is difficult to sort through the claims made by different companies in their advertising, especially where false claims are suspected or where partial information is misleading. Some claims may be quite genuine and there are many companies that have made significant improvements in the way they do business. However, people become sceptical when they see the campaigns designed by transnational public relations companies such as Burson-Marsteller or Hill and Knowlton for clients such as big oil and tobacco companies, influencing people to believe that the products are good for them or that the practices are environmentally responsible.

Green or Greenwash? (four-point CARE system)

One way to find better information for analysing issues is to approach all claims, from different sides of the issue, with a degree of scepticism until substantial investigation can be undertaken. Many people do not have the time to do this for all but the most serious issues they may be concerned about. One way to deal with this problem is to maintain a precautionary approach. To help with the difficult task of analysing greenwash to separate it from legitimate claims, and to encourage public debate on the issue, Greenpeace has developed a four-point CARE system. A corporation that fails on any of the four points is probably in the greenwash business.

1. **Core Business** If a company's main business is based primarily on an activity that significantly contributes to environmental degradation, there is a strong presumption that its claims are greenwash. These companies would include forestry companies that clearcut old growth forests, making it impossible to implement the commitments made by 165 countries to protect species in the international Convention on Biological Diversity, and oil and coal companies whose products have been determined by UN scientists to be large sources of greenhouse gases.

2. **Advertising Practice** Any corporations that use the media for expensive campaigns that make environmental claims about at least one of their products while continuing to conduct "business as usual" practices with other products that involve the release of toxic chemicals or are energy intensive or inefficient are using greenwash.

3. **Research and Development (R&D)** Most corporations set aside funds to develop new products and processes. These funds could be used to develop cleaner technologies. If a significant percentage of the R & D budget is spent on developing cleaner, more sustainable practices, then the company has genuinely made a commitment towards a more sustainable future.

4. **Environmental Lobbying Record** Some corporations engage in doublespeak when they say one thing and do another, doing the entire business sector an injustice. A company that claims to be in favour of a cleaner environment loses all credibility if it lobbies government, either directly or through a coalition or institute which acts as a front group, against increased taxes or controls on polluting activities. If it threatens to close plants and move to another place with lower environmental standards, the corporation gets the greenwash tag. By contrast, many responsible corporations will use their name and experience to lobby in favour of policies and practices that reduce pollution.

adapted from <www.greenpeace.org/~comms/97/summit/greenwash.html>

FIGURE 2.9

Public relations is a multibillion dollar industry devoted to selling messages to the public. It has been called the "propaganda for hire" business and is increasingly involved in promoting special interests and in influencing public opinion. It must be recognized that all groups, including NGOs that are in favour of fair and sustainable solutions to environmental and social justice issues, may use public relations techniques to promote a point of view.

"**Greenwashing**" is a term used to describe the practices of companies or groups attempting to promote a positive environmental or social image to undermine and minimize the damage done to their **brand** or reputation by public criticism. This is done through political lobbying, financial contributions to political parties, and the use of public relations campaigns. At least ten TNCs have annual advertising budgets of more than US$1 billion each, more than most governments and corporations spend on environmental improvement. Public relations companies use a variety of techniques to create an image and shape public perceptions. These techniques include polling, focus groups, and watching young people's actions and language through one-way glass to track public opinion; using news releases, videos, and media campaigns to create fear or promote legends and myths; calling opposing claims **junk science**; and "hyping" their clients' environmental, social, and philanthropic commitment. Public relations companies will even conduct extensive letter writing and phone-in campaigns to government, purporting to represent the "**grass roots**."

Another technique companies may use is to lobby to make competing products more expensive through tariffs or even to make the competing product illegal. For example, until the middle of the twentieth century, industrial hemp played a huge role in the production of textiles, paper, canvas, rope, and thousands of other products. Because versatile hemp represented a serious commercial threat to their industries, large chemical and paper corporations used media and government connections and misinformation to manufacture hostility toward the hemp plant. Despite the fact that hemp is legally grown and used for many products in many countries around the world, including Canada, and despite the fact that it can be grown in an environmentally sustainable way on poorer soils without pesticides, it was made illegal in the U.S.

Detractors and critics of a product or company can be subjected to public relations campaigns designed to attack their credibility and to portray them as extremists or even as threats to national security. Techniques such as creating false connections, logical fallacies, and name-calling are used. For example, in some campaigns, environmentalists who believe in only non-violent action to encourage environmentally responsible practices have been portrayed as "ecoterrorists."

FACT FILE

The Global Climate Coalition, a creation of public relations company Burson-Marsteller for its client, the American Petroleum Industry, works actively in Australia and other countries to oppose the Kyoto Treaty on Carbon Emissions.

FACT FILE

A lawsuit was filed in California in 2001 against Nike for its corporate greenwashing campaign in which it claims it is a leader in the fight against Asian sweatshops.

Advertising

Advertising serves a useful purpose, providing information about products and services as well as financial support for many forms of media. There is nothing wrong with using mass communications to inform people about products. However, some advertising has become more than just promoting sales of consumer goods and services and expanding the market share.

Some social scientists are analysing the impact of **commercial pollution** as people are increasingly exposed to advertising. The message of advertising is not just conveyed in the usual way, on radio and television, but through telemarketing, junk mail, Web sites, corporate logos on clothing, in sports arenas, parks, along highways, bumper stickers, and in ads on buses and trains. Even schools and libraries that often lack adequate funding sell space for ads. This shapes and promotes a rampant consumerism by creating an image of necessity.

> " Shut up and shop is now the message that makes sense to advertiser dominated media... "
>
> *Danny Schechter, author, "Dung on all their houses" in* Toward Freedom *magazine, December/January 2000*

> " 'The Nature of Things' was to carry a special look at Canada's forestry practices. Before the program had even been completed or pre-screened, the forest industry took out newspaper ads condemning it and calling for public support … the CBC found itself under enormous pressure to have the program cut or watered down. The Canadian Imperial Bank of Commerce announced that it would not advertise on 'The Nature of Things' because of the episode. It was crude hardball, but to the CBC's credit, the program was not modified and was broadcast to wide public acclaim. "
>
> *David Suzuki, scientist, broadcaster, from Sez Who? From Naked Ape to Superspecies: A Personal Perspective on Humanity and the Global Eco-Crisis, Stoddart, p.95*

Consumers fit into a particular demographic group that can be targeted according to their tastes and ability to afford certain products. Some companies hire psychologists and anthropologists to find ways to appeal to different

zine article is not as important as the person watching or reading, who is being delivered to the advertiser by the program. People may feel they are not easily manipulated by advertising, but the average North American is exposed to 3000 advertisements a day and the images portrayed are pervasive.

Some stories that appear to be news stories are actually subtly disguised advertisements called **advertorials** or infomercials. One story reported on Ontario television news channels, about cleaning the roof of the Skydome in Toronto, was actually an ad for a soap company. Most people see no problem with advertorials as long as viewers know they are watching an advertisement that may encourage unnecessary consumption.

Companies use their economic power to persuade media not to air opposing views. Advertisers may threaten to pull their ads from a publication or program if some of the material to be presented does not fit within their own range of views. De Beers diamonds demands that their ads be placed far from any editorial with a negative "spin" on love or romance.

FACT FILE

Global spending on advertising was US$435 billion in 1998.

INTERACT

1. Considering what you have learned about media ownership, describe your chances of reading about or hearing a serious discussion about the dangers of corporate media control in **a)** mainstream media and **b)** alternative media.
2. How is your ability to analyse effectively geographic issues affected by current patterns of media ownership and by at least two of the techniques used to influence public opinion?

MCWORLD—A GLOBAL MONOCULTURE

Global media expansion has occurred not because of growth in providing public service but as a profit-making venture, delivering audiences to advertisers. Because companies are free to operate in every market and prefer to locate in places where there are lower wages, cheaper resources, and weaker labour or environmental laws, they continue to move into new countries to sell their products and commercialize aspects of local cultures.

As globalization accelerates, the media, accompanied by advertising and consumerism, are playing a role in making cultures more uniform. When attitudes and consumption habits are similar over a wide audience, it is possible to sell more of a product. There is a growing sense of how culture is becoming homogenized through the global marketplace as western commercial products flood the markets. The spread of western culture, sometimes referred to as McWorld, because of the proliferation of McDonald's fast-food restaurants in many countries, has become a controversial issue, and one that is not going to go away.

Cultural geographers study the positive and negative impacts of **cultural diffusion**. Cultural diffusion can bridge cultural divides to foster greater understanding among peoples exposed to foreign lifestyles, provide a richer, more stimulating mix of worldviews, ideas, music, and art. Some see the spread of not just one big culture, but many different cultures in all directions and recognize the resilience and adaptability of people to maintain important aspects of their unique cultures.

FIGURE 2.10 The art of decoration with henna paste to create mehndi designs has spread from Africa, South Asia, and the Middle East to countries all over the world.

 See Chapter 3 for more information about patterns of global power.

On the other hand, corporate attempts to commercialize many aspects of culture and spread the consumer lifestyle have reduced diversity. This can have a destabilizing effect as traditional craftspeople and artisans lose their livelihoods to competition from western products and as information becomes distorted through western media filters. Some see these influences as an assault on other unique cultures, even endangering indigenous languages and cultures. Or they see others rapidly adopting some of the worst aspects of American culture, including excessive consumerism, environmentally unsustainable practices, and products such as cigarettes and sports utility vehicles (SUVs). People tend to feel overwhelmed by the vast spending power of American media and

> 66 I want the culture of all lands to be blown about my house as freely as possible. But I refuse to be blown off my feet by any. 99
>
> *Mahatma Gandhi*

FACT FILE

In Mexico, more than 8 million people, or 10% of the population, have livelihoods related to traditional crafts.

corporations. Many feel increased pressure to acquire some of the vast array of things they see advertised. This can promote dissatisfaction as economic disparities are highlighted.

 See Chapter 5 for more information about global patterns of cultural diversity.

Large media conglomerates are the main drivers of a global monoculture as North American lifestyles and consumer products transform into a widespread culture industry. Another driver of the merging global culture is the large group of more than 800 million young people that have money to spend and time to spend it. A new industry of consultants called "cool hunters" has sprung up to discover and forecast trends in this most sought after demographic group—the 18- to 34-year-old consumer. They search out examples of what they see as "cutting edge" lifestyle for their corporate clients.

> 66 Fusion is going to be the term that everybody's going to use. There's going to be more blending, like Spanish music and punk—things that are so unrelated. 99
>
> *Amanda Freeman, cool hunter, Youth Intelligence*

FIGURE 2.11 In 2000, there were more than 500 million cars in the world, six times more than there were in 1950.

What Is Wrong with Consumerism?

We all want to have our basic needs met and maintain a comfortable standard of living. But in our society we have learned to consume much more than we really need to satisfy these aspirations. Some analysts view consumerism as a modern religion with the shopping mall as the church and advertisers as the priests. Some of the things we buy do make our lives more comfortable but we have more of them than we really need. Canadians use more energy per capita and produce more waste per capita than people in any other country. Many people buy out of habit, or to find happiness, as if they have lost other ways to give them joy such as experiencing the beauty of nature or helping others. Every product we buy comes from Earth. Buying more than we need increases pressure on Earth's resources and the size of our ecological footprint, and contributes to environmental degradation.

FIGURE 2.12 Most people in the world, even in the slums of Asian cities such as Jhuggi in New Delhi, have access at low cost to hundreds of television channels and networks imported from the U.S. India, in turn, exports many of its own television channels around the world. Where advertising has little impact, as in some remote villages, companies send out vans loaded with free samples of products such as Colgate toothpaste or Palmolive soap to capture a share of the vast Asian market.

> **FACT FILE**
>
> The world's biggest consumers include the 1.1 billion people, mainly in North America, Europe, and Australasia, with an annual income of more than US$10 000.

> **FACT FILE**
>
> In 1999, Sony created 4000 hours of television programs in languages other than English, including more than 30 hours a week in Hindi, broadcast all over the world, more than twice its output of English language shows.

FIGURE 2.13 Most of the incredible number of products we see on store shelves are unnecessary. Many highly processed or high in fat and sugars are unhealthy, and few will even exist in two or three years as new products replace them.

FACT FILE

In the 1990s, Canada became the Hollywood of the North where many U.S. films were made because of tax incentives provided by provincial and federal governments.

Pop Culture

Popular culture is a dynamic heterogeneous culture that allows a great deal of individualism, innovation, and change. Film studios, television networks, book publishers, and recording companies shape the popular culture of a society. Pop culture is reflected in every aspect of life, including clothing, food, music, and sports. Pop culture is associated with youth and western youth culture has spread quickly around the world. Hip-hop has been called the richest pop culture on Earth, both culturally and economically. It is complex, versatile, continually evolving, and expresses a wide range of political and social views in its main components: music, dance forms, and DJ-ing. Hip-hop culture has spread from its grass-roots origins in the inner cities of North America and exposed critical political and social issues affecting Black and Latino urban youth, including violence, racism, police brutality, and lack of living-wage job opportunities.

Global Culture and Consumerism

"Critics of western culture blast Coke and Hollywood but not organ transplants and computers."
Erla Zwingle, National Geographic Magazine, *August, 1999*

"There is fierce competition to sell to consumers worldwide, with increasingly aggressive advertising. On the social side local and national boundaries are breaking down in the setting of social standards and aspirations in consumption. Market research identifies 'global elites' and 'global middle classes' who follow the same consumption styles showing preferences for 'global brands'. There are 'global teens'—some 270 million 15 to 18 year olds in 40 countries—inhabiting a 'global space', a single pop culture world, soaking up the same videos and music and providing a huge market for designer running shoes, t-shirts and jeans."
Human Development Report 1998 Overview, *United Nations Development Programme (UNDP)*

"Often corporations are on the receiving end of the blame for the proliferation of vapid and worthless products. …We consumers are just as much responsible for contributing to this endemic exploration of frivolity."
Scott Hampton, creative resistance winner, Adbusters *magazine, Mar/April 2001*

"There is an alternative to corporate control. Corporations depend on us as consumers of their products. It would be easy to suck out the soft underbelly of a corporation that is not socially and environmentally responsible. We just don't have to buy what is offered."
Maude Barlow, chairperson, Council of Canadians

"The airwaves are incredibly valuable and commercial enterprises pay nothing for them. Some of their huge profits, a thin slice, should be taken off the top to provide a public freeway that serves people, connects to every home, every hospital, every school, every prison … [to] provide the kinds of material that society values and needs for its survival, and that democracy in particular requires, but that the marketplace, understandably and for very good reasons, is not providing."
Lawrence Grossman, former president, NBC News and PBS

FIGURE 2.14 Urban culture refers to the daily lives of youth living in the inner cities of North America.

Mainstream media may distort the public's understanding of what Black urban culture is. Media can reinforce negative stereotypes if it focuses only on the drugs, violence, and sexism of "gangsta rap." The majority of rap music though, with its rhythmic beats and complex rhyming language, centres on positive, community-minded, political, social, or "feel good" messages. A form of **alternative media**, rap not only spreads messages that help to empower Black youth, it celebrates the strength, pride, intelligence, style, creativity, and religion of Black cultures. Some aspects of the hip-hop lifestyle, mainly music and clothing, have a huge audience and represent a form of cross-cultural communication. Corporations and the media have stepped in to exploit this multibillion dollar market and sell Black urban culture to a much wider audience. Participate in the Lives of Youth (P.L.A.Y.) is the philanthropic wing of Nike. It sponsors inner-city sports programs and resurfaces basketball courts in exchange for high swoosh (Nike's logo) visibility. In wealthier neighbourhoods, this would be considered advertising and would be more expensive than charity.

Some popular music, as a form of alternative media, plays a strong role as a **paradigm shifter** in society. In the 1960s, many songs of

> ❝ The corporations can't own urban culture because no one can own someone's spirit and way of life. ❞
>
> *Rahsaan Harris,*
> *associate director,* Harlem Live

This so-called rational
international
language of money
is louder than the screams of the impoverished masses
as the free market passes
those from which the benefits were extracted.

They said prosperity was like water
that's going to trickle down,
well it must have evaporated before it hit the ground.
Take a walk down south
and visit a shanty town
nothing but poverty and neglect to be found.

The exception is for the global rulers
controlling the fields, the factories, the slaves, the consumers.
They were high on power like they were drug abusers.
It's a two-class system that's winners and losers.

In the new class war that's justified and endorsed
from their textbooks and their business reports
cause there's only one way and this is the course.
It's their vision of the world
and it's an endless resource.
This is the mission they can never abort.
It's exploitation called progress perpetuated by force.
Morals and money went through a divorce.
The only union here is the marriage of wealth and force.

> *Eric McIntyre, Rhyme for Reason*

FIGURE 2.15 What messages are conveyed by these rap lyrics?

> ❝ Just as the history of cool in America is really (as many have argued) a history of African–American culture—from jazz and blues to rock and roll to rap—for many of the superbrands, cool hunting simply means black-culture hunting. Which is why the cool hunters' first stop was the basketball courts of America's poorest neighbourhoods. ❞
>
> *Naomi Klein, columnist, author,* No Logo

rock and folk music focused on social and environmental themes. Since that time there have been hundreds of "ecorock" and protest songs, musicians and concerts that have communicated messages about concerns, revealed contradictions and illusions in society, and offered ways to change things.

Jihad vs McWorld
by Benjamin Barber
Ballantine Books
New York, 1996

McWorld is an entertainment shopping experience that brings together malls, multiplex movie theatres, theme parks, spectator sports arenas, fast-food chains (with their endless movie tie-ins), and television (with its burgeoning shopping networks) into a single vast enterprise that, on the way to maximizing its profits, transforms human beings.

Many people, the great majority in developed countries, a minority climbing toward the majority in developing countries, spend far too much of their time each day in one of the commercial habitations of the new world being "imagineered" (as the Disney people like to say) in Hollywood and its satellites—in front of a TV screen or at a mall or in a movie theatre or chewing on fast food while contemplating a promotion for a tie-in movie or buying some licensed piece of bric a brac; much more time than they spend in school, church, the library, a community service center, a political backroom, a volunteer house, or a playing field. Yet only these latter environments elicit active and engaged public behaviour and ask us to define ourselves as autonomous members of civic communities marked by culture or religion or other public values. ...

McWorld calls on us to see ourselves as private and solitary, interacting primarily via commercial transactions where 'me' displaces 'we'; and it permits private corporations whose only interest is their revenue stream to define by default the public goods of the individuals and communities they serve. NAFTA—McWorld's global strategy in its North American guise—serves American business as well as world markets and is unquestionably a policy geared to the future: but it does not and cannot serve American or global public interests such as full employment, the dignity of work, the creative civic use of forced leisure, environmental protection, social safety nets, and pension protection.

McWorld's advocates will argue that the 'market' does 'serve' individuals by empowering them to 'choose' but the choice is always about which items to buy and consume, never about whether to buy and consume anything at all; or about the right to earn an income that makes consumption possible; or about how to regulate and contain consumption so that it does not swallow up other larger public goods that cannot be advanced in the absence of democratic public institutions. In McWorld's global market, empowerment lies in the choice of toppings on a baked potato. The rest is passive consumption. When profit becomes the sole criterion by which we measure every good, every activity, every attitude, every cultural product, there is soon nothing but profit. In the empire of the market, the money hooligans are princes and largesse is king. ...

Go into a Protestant church in a Swiss village, a mosque in Damascus, the cathedral at Reims, a Buddhist temple in Bangkok, and though in every case you are visiting a place of worship with a common aura of piety, you know from one pious site to the next you are in a distinctive culture. Then sit in a multiplex movie box—or much the same thing, visit a spectator sports arena or a mall or a modern hotel or fast-food establishment in any city around the world—and try to figure out where you are. You are nowhere. You are everywhere. Inhabiting an abstraction. Lost in cyberspace. You are chasing pixels on a Nintendo: the world surrounding you vanishes. You are in front of or in or on MTV: universal images assault the eyes and global dissonance assaults the ears in a heart-pounding tumult that tells you everything except which country you are in. Where are you? You are in McWorld.

Critical Analysis
1. a) Compare activities that elicit active as opposed to passive behaviour.
   b) What are the implications of each kind of behaviour for addressing global issues?
2. Of which groups in society is the commentary critical?
3. How does exposure to McWorld transform people?
4. How does the author of this commentary feel about the move to a global monoculture?
5. Identify one idea from the commentary with which you most agree and one with which you most disagree. Explain your choices.
6. Write a paragraph that describes how you feel about the spread of McWorld.

1. List several factors that motivate TNCs to operate in other parts of the world.
2. Identify two current "cool" trends in consumer society and evaluate their lasting impact on people and the environment.
3. Explain the meaning of the term "paradigm shifter." Identify two paradigm shifters in our society and explain changes they have helped to bring about.
4. Select music lyrics that have a particular message on an issue of your choice and critically analyse the message.
5. Do you believe that cultures of the world are becoming more similar? Support your view with evidence and reasoned argument.
6. Conduct research to find a specific example of one positive and one negative aspect of cultural diffusion. Evaluate the positive and negative implications of a global monoculture.
7. Using the four-point CARE system outlined in Figure 2.9, **Green or Greenwash?**, conduct a CARE analysis on the corporation or group of your choice.
8. Using an advertising flyer or catalogue from a large retail store, analyse the message about the consumption ethic that is portrayed. What are the values represented? How is consumerism encouraged? What are the environmental and social implications or hidden costs of the values encouraged?

GETTING WISE TO THE MEDIA

A democracy is healthier when many voices are heard and when ideas compete in public discussion. The ability to access and analyse information is critically important if citizens hope to become part of the solution to world issues. Much of the media is controlled by large corporations that may not want the public to be "media literate." **Media literacy** is the ability to decode or deconstruct the "constructed" information that is received in order to find out the truth about the world and become better

> **"**I am not a seeker of truth ... just evidence. I will draw my own conclusions. **"**
>
> *Bernard Robertson-Dunn,*
> *Australian philosopher*

informed. With the proliferation of advertising, media literacy helps people to evaluate their role as consumers of information and of Earth's resources.

Media literacy gives consumers the tools to:
- access alternative viewpoints;
- look critically at powerful images, many of which are targeted at youth;
- get a "big picture" and more accurate view of the world, as media tends to fragment it;
- be aware of the techniques used to create propaganda, "spin," and how reality and public consent may be constructed;
- communicate effectively to get their own messages across;
- make wiser choices and better-informed decisions to become more effective global citizens.

Using Media to Analyse Geographic Issues

Analysing geographic issues requires an informed and critical understanding of the nature of media, the techniques used, and their impacts. Understanding where the media fits into the structure of society and how it relates to other systems of power and authority is essential. Conflict or war in the Middle East or Africa or debates about globalization or global climate change are condensed, simplified, and reduced to a few pictures and quick "sound bites," leaving out the real analysis and interconnections.

Geographers need to understand what places are really like, the nature and complexity of Earth's cultural mosaic, environmental patterns and issues, patterns and networks of economic interdependence, and the forces of global co-operation and conflict that shape divisions on Earth. It is difficult to make accurate and useful predictions about the future with only partial or misleading information. Information is not the same as knowledge or understanding or analysis. Explaining the facts is not the same as providing them.

> " Where is the wisdom we have lost in knowledge? Where is the knowledge we have lost in information? "
>
> *T.S. Eliot, poet*

Geographers have strong skills of synthesis in their ability to take data from a wide variety of sources and viewpoints, then organize and evaluate the data before drawing conclusions and making decisions. This is done much more effectively with media literacy.

 See Chapter 1 for more information about critical analysis.

Just the Facts

We need to be able to distinguish between facts and opinions, which are often intertwined; and between factual and editorial reporting. Facts are objective, unbiased bits of information about reality that are inarguable. Opinions are judgements or views about reality. Facts are not better than opinions, they are just different. Each fact is only a small part of the total reality. Facts can be used to support completely opposing opinions. Given the fact that the infant mortality rate in the U.S. decreased from 20 deaths per thousand live births to seven deaths per thousand over the twentieth century, your impression of U.S. health care might be favourable. Given the fact that infant mortality rates in the U.S. in 2000 were higher than all the other G7 countries, your impression would be less favourable.

FIGURE 2.16 A selection of alternative media sources.

What Is the Alternative?

Geographic analysis seeks alternative sources of information before views and opinions can be effectively formed. Alternative information must be synthesized with that which is more readily available from mainstream media. Alternative media provide an outlet for views that are not commonly expressed and that may be dismissed or vilified in mainstream media. Another purpose of alternative media is to report on issues in ways that introduce new ideas and raise different questions about how we should live with each other and with the natural environment. This challenges basic assumptions and helps people change the way they think about the world.

There are many sources of alternative media. They include public and alternative broadcasting, magazines, Web sites, publications by NGOs, "think tanks," and the arts. Alternative media can come from a wide political spectrum and, therefore, represent some extreme views. However, they can also originate from well-respected sources and institutions, including universities and international agencies. Much of the alternative media used by social scientists offers a broader perspective than mainstream media. Public broadcasting, for example, tends to be less biased, containing more than just the mainstream message of the day.

Alternative media challenges corporate control of public airwaves and the silencing of dissent. It promotes a democratic system that informs and empowers all members of society. The messages presented are often in favour of social and racial justice, ecological sustainability, co-operative citizen participation, diversification of control, government support for public broadcasting, and public disclosure of important information that people need to understand their world. Some sources, such as *New Internationalist* magazine, attempt to redress the imbalance of mainstream news dominated by events and preoccupations of the developed world by providing a view of each year's events from a developing world perspective.

Alternative media have exposed many of society's ills and enabled political pressure from intelligent and concerned citizens that has resulted in resolving issues. For example, books criticizing the food system led to the first food safety regulations in North America.

PROFILE

The Media Foundation— Using the Media to Change the Message

FIGURE 2.17 Media Foundation's ongoing High on the Hog campaign draws viewer attention to the fact that people in developed countries consume too much.

The Media Foundation is a Vancouver-based organization that uses different forms of media such as *Adbusters* magazine and television commercials, known as "uncommercials," to promote awareness of environmental and anti-consumerist messages and to provide an alternative view of our consumer society. The main issues covered include misleading corporate advertising, society's addiction to television and shopping, overconsumption of Earth's resources, and critiques of conventional economics.

Adbusters uncommercials are parodies that ridicule or deglamorize products that receive high amounts of advertising in mainstream media. One campaign includes changing consumer perceptions of McDonald's advertising by using an accurate formula to substitute the millions of gallons of grease served instead of the billions of hamburgers served around the world. The Media Foundation's social marketing branch, Powershift, produces an annual (November 23) *Buy Nothing Day* uncommercial, which challenges people to rethink their spending habits and their impact on Earth. As these are not the views corporations want the public to see, the Media Foundation has difficulty getting its ads broadcast, despite continued attempts to buy airtime on major networks. However, CNN Headline News did air the Buy Nothing day message in 2001.

FIGURE 2.18 What is the main message of this cartoon?

Political Cartoons

Some cartoons are designed not just to humour or entertain but also to express serious analysis about important local or global issues. Cartoons use graphic and visual art to express opinions and attitudes. Some media analysts believe that, because more people will read a cartoon than an editorial column, they have a wider impact on shaping public opinion about world issues.

INTERACT

1. Brainstorm a list of people and ideas that would be expressed more frequently in alternative rather than mainstream media.

2. Find a program schedule for a public or special interest broadcasting station in Ontario such as TVO or Vision TV. Study the programs listed and compare the coverage of world issues you consider important with that of a mainstream station.

3. Identify two ways to limit media control by a powerful elite and evaluate their effectiveness.

4. Select two articles on a geographic issue of your choice—one from a mainstream media source and one from an alternative media source. Underline the facts and opinions in each of the articles in two different colours. Attempt to rewrite the message of each article using only the facts. Evaluating the author's choice of facts and support given for opinions, write a conclusion about how informative each article is on the issue.

CASE STUDY

Canada's Forests

A visit to the Web site of the Forest Products Association of Canada (FPAC), <www.fpac.ca>, formerly the Canadian Pulp and Paper Association, reveals that the industry organization has made huge strides in improving forest management techniques and reducing the environmental impact of the forest products industry. Many of these claims may well be true. Critics have suggested, however, that the claims made on television and in newspaper ads, while perhaps not wrong, could be misleading.

The ads appear to be designed to make people feel that Canadian forests are in an enviable position in the world and that we should not worry about forests as they are well-managed and actually increasing. Do we accept the claims that almost all of Canada's original forest area still exists, and that forests have actually grown since 1970, or do we need to take a more in-depth look? An investigation reveals the following information:

- Statistical data from the UN shows that Canada's forest cover has not changed significantly in the 1990s, that U.S. forest cover has expanded by 1.7%, and that Mexico has lost 11% of its forest cover.
- Most of Canada's original forest was harvested long ago. Only a few remaining stands of old growth forest exist.
- Some forests have expanded naturally on marginal agricultural land that was abandoned.
- There are more forest plantations and reforested areas but these tree farms are not the same as original forests. They are often located

> " Our forest composition has suffered and important ecosystems such as the Acadian, Carolinian and Garry Oak forests are almost gone. We can have forest cover where we harvest twigs to make forest products or we can have complex forest ecosystem habitats. "
>
> Elizabeth May, former assistant to federal Minister of the Environment and current President of the Sierra Club of Canada

Canadian Forest Facts

- Canada has 10% of the world's forests by area and 30% of its boreal forest.

- Canada' logging of its old-growth and primary forests has made it the world's biggest timber exporter.

- In 1998, forest products accounted for $32 billion in trade and 830 000 jobs in Canada.

- Two-thirds of Canada's 140 000 species of plants, animals, and micro-organisms (excluding viruses) occur in the forests.

- Canada harvests 0.4% of its productive forest area annually, and fire and insect outbreaks affect 0.5%.

- Ninety-four percent of our forests are publicly owned, but 52% are under logging tenures.

- Roads, mines, and other activities fragment 95% of all major forested watersheds.

in logged areas, are more uniform in age and species, are higher in productivity because they grow faster, and are commercially more valuable. They are also more vulnerable to disease, insect infestation, fire, and severe weather such as windstorms and drought, and they support fewer wildlife species than natural forests do.

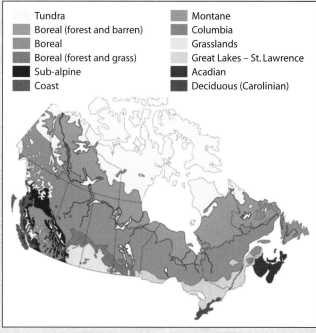

Legend:
- Tundra
- Boreal (forest and barren)
- Boreal
- Boreal (forest and grass)
- Sub-alpine
- Coast
- Montane
- Columbia
- Grasslands
- Great Lakes – St. Lawrence
- Acadian
- Deciduous (Carolinian)

FIGURE 2.19

- Many activities are going on in Canada's forests besides logging for pulp, paper, and wood products. These activities include:
  - oil and gas development;
  - hydroelectric projects that flood forest areas;
  - mining developments;
  - roads that accompany each development.
- The federal government reports that 24 million ha of Canadian forest lands have been converted to other uses, mainly agriculture, since Canada was settled by Europeans. However, of the forested area at settlement, 94.6% is still under some form of forest cover.
- According to the FPAC, their claim was based on forest *volume* rather than *area*. The Canadian Forest Service reports that collection of volume information reported from the provinces is inconsistent over time and from province to province.

FACT FILE

In Alberta's forests, there are 88 000 oil and gas wells, each with its own access road.

FIGURE 2.20 Seventy-five percent of major rainforest valleys on Vancouver Island have been logged, mainly using clear-cut methods.

Vancouver Island Forests, 1954 and 1999

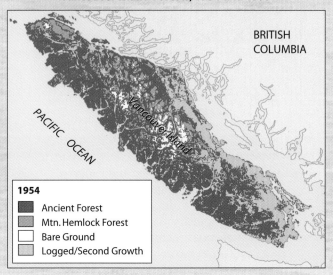

1954
- Ancient Forest
- Mtn. Hemlock Forest
- Bare Ground
- Logged/Second Growth

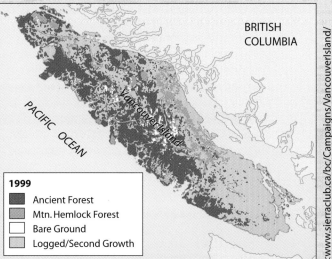

1999
- Ancient Forest
- Mtn. Hemlock Forest
- Bare Ground
- Logged/Second Growth

<www.sierraclub.ca/bc/Campaigns/VancouverIsland/ final_vi_webmaps/vi_small/vi_date>

FIGURE 2.21 By 1999, the ancient forests of British Columbia were 71% logged.

> "There is a sense of urgency, a sense that, at least in some parts of the boreal forest, time is running out for saving some of the vital functions that the forest provides such as wildlife habitat, watershed protection and carbon sinks."
>
> Nicholas Taylor, Canadian senator, chair, Senate Subcommittee on the Boreal Forest, 1999

> "Canada has overestimated timber growth by about 40% in some provinces leading to the desperate situation of harvesting rates approaching twice the replanting rate."
>
> S. Nillson, forest analyst, author, How Sustainable Are North America's Wood Supplies?

1. Select a cartoon with a political or environmental message. Write an explanation of the message and how it is portrayed.
2. Why is media literacy essential in effectively analysing geographic issues?
3. Conduct research to find and compare views on sustainable development as expressed in one mainstream media source and one alternative media source.
4. Using the steps to critical analysis outlined in Chapter 1 on page 15, write a critical analysis of a documentary or investigative news program. Do you feel adequately informed about the issue after watching the program? What other information is needed?
5. Analyse the trends and patterns shown in the photo in Figure 2.20 and the maps in Figure 2.21, **Vancouver Island Forests 1954 and 1999**, and Figure 7.22, **The Current Forest Cover Compared to Original Forests**, on pages 50 and 186, respectively. Write a 500-word conclusion on the state of Canada's forests.

GEOGRAPHIC METHODS

Maps and Worldviews

Maps, a commonly used geographic tool, are a form of media that show Earth's human and natural features as spatial data. While people are often sceptical about what they read or hear in media, people rarely question maps. Do maps really reflect reality or might they have a hidden agenda? People in different places and at different times have different perspectives from which to view the world. These views are based on language, cultural traditions and values, and varied natural environments. Even within a society, the kind of maps used and the way features are displayed can vary widely.

 See Chapter 1 for more information about ways of seeing and using maps.

Maps must generalize, symbolize, and simplify complex information. They show both qualitative data such as boundaries, rivers, and roads and quantitative data such as statistical indicators, altitude, or amount of precipitation. Quantitative data are often generalized or grouped as round numbers, statistical mean, or standard deviation values. Data from a specific point location may be shown, using shading or symbols, as part of a geographic region. These techniques provide information about general patterns that may vary from a map designed in another fashion.

Maps have been called a blend of science and art. As useful as they are for describing spatial relationships and for serving many other analytical purposes, maps are human creations and can have errors and bias that misrepresent reality, either intentionally or accidentally. As students of geography, you have produced your own maps. In doing so, you have made conscious design decisions about how to portray information, what to include, and what to leave out.

Maps are usually oriented so that the north is at the top. There is no scientific basis for this because Earth, spinning in space, does not have an "up" or a "down." It is just as realistic to display globes and maps "upside down." Ancient maps of Europe during the Middle Ages put the east on top, while early Arabic maps placed south at the top, possibly from the cultural perspective of looking toward Mecca. Dominant empires in the northern hemisphere during the time of exploration and colonialism began putting north on top in the early seventeenth century.

PROJECTING BIAS WITH MAP PROJECTIONS

How do you see the world? Because of the impossibility of accurately showing a round, three-dimensional object on a flat surface, world maps are unavoidably distorted and, therefore, biased. A world map that shows accurate shapes of land and sea features cannot show accurate sizes.

The Mercator projection, designed in the sixteenth century for navigation, is still used today by ship and airplane pilots and in many school atlases and texts.

The Gall-Peters projection dramatically improves the accuracy of land mass size but distorts its shape. The area that is considered the North or developed countries of the world covers 48.9 million km² while the South covers 90 million km². Yet both appear to be similar in area on most projections commonly used in North America and Europe. One's preference for a projection depends upon one's purpose in using a map. Foreign aid agencies and countries in the developing world tend to use the Gall-Peters projection.

> 66 Maps are subject to distortions arising from ignorance, greed, ideological blindness or motive. 99
>
> *Mark Monmonier, geographer, author,* How To Lie With Maps

> 66 ...the environmental map is also a racial map. The most polluting factories and the most dangerous dumps are located in the pockets of poverty where blacks, Indians, and Latinos live. 99
>
> *Eduardo Galeano, Latin American historian, author,* Upside Down: A Primer for the Looking-Glass World

> 66 Indigenous Americans communicated information about space and places through folk tales, gestures, ephemeral drawings, but theirs was not the cartography of commerce, navigation and warfare ... For the West, mapping has been all about assertions of economic and political dominance. Borders indicate agreed on limits to political power. Survey maps mark the limits of property owners' economic power... 99
>
> *Mark Monmonier,* Drawing the Line: Tales of Maps and Cartocontroversy

Map Projections

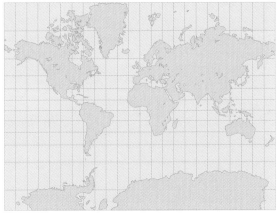

Mercator projection

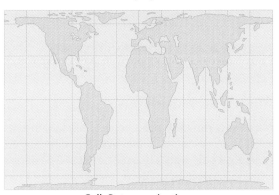

Gall–Peters projection

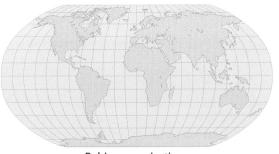

Robinson projection

FIGURE 2.22 Cartographers use many different map projections when transferring the surface of the globe onto paper. **Conformal projections** such as the **Mercator projection** show the true shape of continents but distort their size. **Equal-area projections** such as the **Gall–Peters projection** distort the shape but not the size. There are hundreds of **compromise projections** such as the **Robinson projection**.

Areas of Selected Land Masses (millions of km²)	
Asia	44.5
Africa	30.3
North America	19.6
South America	17.8
Antarctica	14.0
Europe	9.9
Greenland	2.2
China	9.3

FIGURE 2.23 Compare the actual size of land masses such as North America and Africa with how they appear in Figure 2.22, **Map Projections**.

"A knowledgeable map reader, recognizing that a map is both a simplification and a distortion of reality, will look for clues to the cartographer's purposes and biases."

Working With Maps,
U.S. Geological Survey

INTERACT

1. Examine Figure 2.22, **Map Projections**. Where on the maps do distortions appear to be the greatest? Expain why most maps used in Canada show the northern hemisphere at the top of the page.
2. Suggest a scenario in which a map could be used to influence public opinion.
3. How can maps and photographs be biased?

WEB LINKS

- The Atlas of Cyberspaces: <www.cybergeography.org/atlas>
- Corporate control in Canada's media industry: <www.cbc.ca/news/indepth/background/mediaownership.html>
- Media and democracy: <www.thirdworldtraveler.com/Media_control_propaganda/Media_Control.html>
- The Media Foundation: <www.adbusters.org>
- Independent news: <www.mediachannel.org>

RELATED ISSUES

- Media and gender issues
- Media and stereotyping cultures

GIS **Communication and Economic Development**

ANALYSE, APPLY, AND INTERACT

1. Prepare and conduct a demographic survey that analyses the reading habits of your friends, family, and other community members.
2. Working in a group, create a list of 10 media realities (statements that reflect characteristics of media).
3. Produce a poster, brochure, television commercial, or Web site that outlines the best way to use mass media wisely.
4. How does one's worldview influence one's perceptions of a place such as the inner city or a pristine forested valley? What role does the media play in influencing your perceptions of a place?
5. Analyse the impact of current patterns of media ownership on cultural diffusion.
6. **a)** Conduct research to create a list of as many of the holdings as possible of one of the global media giants, listed on pages 29–30.

b) Locate and label the holdings on an outline map of the world.

c) Write a 500-word analysis about the global reach of the company and its implications.

7. Debate the question: "Do the media create or reflect public opinion on global issues?"

8. Select an ad that uses some aspect of the natural environment to promote an unrelated product. Critically analyse the message and techniques used in the ad.

9. Choose one commonly used consumer product such as a can of cola, computer, cotton clothing, coffee, or a daily newspaper. Conduct research to find information on the following: the components of the product and its packaging, the interconnections involved in collecting and transporting the resources, growing or manufacturing the product and getting it to the consumer; the impact on people and the environment of these processes; action that can be taken to reduce the impact on people and the environment.

10. How has changing communications technology affected **a)** cultural geography and **b)** the media and its role in society?

11. Create a political cartoon or musical lyrics that portray a message about a global issue of your choice. Identify the techniques you have used to get your message across.

Chapter 3: Geopolitics—Patterns of Global Power

By the end of this chapter, you will

- analyse the causes and effects of economic disparities around the world;

- identify different methods of grouping countries and evaluate the implications of categorizing countries in these ways;

- identify ways in which countries and regions of the world are becoming increasingly interdependent;

- analyse the changing spatial distribution of political systems around the world;

- demonstrate an understanding of the interdependence of countries in the global economy;

- analyse instances of international coopera-tion and conflict and identify factors that contribute to each;

- describe the structure, membership, and activities of an international economic alliance in Africa or Asia;

- demonstrate an understanding of how economies and environments in some places may be affected by decisions made in other places;

- analyse geopolitical relationships between selected countries and regions;

- analyse the evolving geopolitical role of a selected region or country;

- demonstrate an understanding of how quality of life and employment prospects are related to the global economy;

- evaluate the performance of a selected transnational corporation with respect to the promotion of environmental sustainability and human rights;

- demonstrate an understanding of how the work of the United Nations and other organizations on poverty, disease, and the environment is directly related to your own life;

- demonstrate an understanding of the need to consider social differences when analysing global problems and issues.

THE NATURE OF GEOPOLITICS

Geopolitics is about which groups and places have power and how power is used to control territorial space and the activities within it. Geopolitical analysis examines interactions and conflicts within and among regions as well as between developed and developing coun-

> ❝ Globalization must be governed by the rule of law. Because the present structure of authority is territorially based, while most challenges are transboundary, we must explore new forms of a true, rules-based world system. ❞
>
> *Kimon Valaskakis, Canada's ambassador to the Organization for Economic Cooperation and Development (OECD), 1995–1999, president, the Club of Athens*

tries, states that are well integrated into the global economy, and those that are not. Geopolitics looks at how geographic concepts such as place, region, spatial interaction, environment, and the movement of people and goods create patterns of power and international interaction.

Strategic resource exploitation, nationalism and ethnicity, **hegemony**, imperialism, **economic colonialism**, trade, and foreign aid all play a role in shaping geopolitics.

Globalization is having a profound impact on geopolitical patterns around the world and the new century has already been called the "global" century. For the first time in history, everyone in the world is bound together in a global economic system that is no longer contained within national boundaries. Global changes are bringing new groups into the global power structure, including transnational corporations, international institutions, and economic and political alliances. The emerging imbalance between the **private** and **public sectors** has resulted in a loss of any real form of national control over many areas, including global finance, climate change, disease epidemics, and criminal activities. There is an increase in the cross-border flows of goods, services, investment and business transactions worth trillions of dollars, workers, refugees, technology, information, ideas, culture, and weapons. Some of these changes are happening faster than governments can effectively deal with them. This is giving rise to a number of issues related to **global governance**.

> ❝ Globalization could be the answer to many of the world's seemingly intractable problems. But this requires strong democratic foundations based on a political will to ensure justice and equality. ❞
>
> *Sharan Burrow, president, Australian Council of Trade Unions*

The continued integration of global markets provides the potential for greater material wealth while increasing the gap between "haves" and "have nots" and, consequently, the potential for political turmoil. As you analyse issues throughout this text, it is important to recognize the interconnections among political,

FIGURE 3.1 Rules of international trade law are used to export western culture through the sale of tobacco or fast foods as a way for people in developing countries to sample the lifestyle of the rich.

cultural, environmental, and economic factors. The components of **globalization** do not separate trade from politics or from the environment. For example, conflict and war may seem to be political issues but they usually have economic or cultural origins and can do great harm to **ecosystems**. The globalization of international trade encourages the spread of western culture in global markets as is evident in the spread of western brands such as McDonald's to most countries in the world.

FIGURE 3.2 Oil wells set on fire during the 1991 Gulf War damaged the Persian Gulf ecosystem, destroyed coral reefs and animals, and had a serious impact on human health.

FIGURE 3.3 In the past, political boundaries have acted as barriers to the spread of ideas and knowledge. With globalization and the advance of technology, especially airplanes and communications, national boundaries are superseded by international flows of people, ideas, culture, and capital.

ORGANIZING A COMPLEX WORLD

Geographers and international organizations tend to divide countries of the world into a variety of different groupings. One method of categorizing countries that was widely used in the past was to divide all the countries into "worlds"—the First World, the Second World, and the Third World. This scheme came about after World War II when geopolitical power was split between the capitalist western states (United States, France, Canada, etc.) and communist countries (Soviet Union, Poland, China, etc.). There were roughly 20 wealthy, industrialized, and democratic countries that called themselves the First World. The label "Second World" was used for communist countries, again numbering roughly 20 countries. This group was very diverse as it included industrialized countries like Poland and (at the time) poorly developed countries such as China. There remained about 20 other independent countries in the world that did not fit the first two categories. These places, including Mexico, Argentina, Liberia, and Thailand became known as the Third World. There were few commonalities among these countries except for the fact that they were less economically developed than First World countries. Thus, the label "Third World" quickly came to mean poor or undeveloped countries.

> **FACT FILE**
>
> High income economies are the countries in the world with a per capita GNP of more than US$10 000.

Global economic and political changes have made this scheme obsolete. The collapse of communism from 1989 to 1992 reduced Second World membership to just four or five communist countries. After World War II, the former colonies of the huge European empires became independent countries, inflating the membership of the Third World to over 150 countries. This category now included oil-rich (but non-industrialized) countries like Saudi Arabia and the poorest countries in sub-Saharan Africa. As a method for organizing countries, this scheme now has little value.

There are several other methods commonly used to categorize countries. The terms "South" and "North" are geopolitical terms that reflect the polarization of the world based on latitudinal and economic patterns. Since most rich countries are in the northern hemisphere, this method is not strongly supported by Australia and New Zealand—developed countries in the southern hemisphere. New regional trade alliances and the integration of **emerging economies** into the global marketplace are changing this view of a bipolar world into a more complex reality. Other schemes use terms like "Two-Thirds World" or "Majority World" to refer to the approximately three-quarters of the world's population that are relatively poor and non-industrialized. And, there are a host of labels that use the word "develop," including "less developed," "least developed," "developing," and the like. The differences among these terms are subtle and the use of different terms and labels can complicate discussion of the issues.

> **The traditional North–South nomenclature is of decreasing validity… as intraregional trade is becoming increasingly important in emerging economies. These developments make sense economically and geographically, but they don't fit easily with some North–South paradigms and the ideological baggage sometimes associated with them. To maintain a simple bipolar view of the world is, for the purposes of analysis, inappropriate and potentially misleading.**
>
> *Erik Nilsson, senior economist, Bank of Nova Scotia*

As Figure 3.4, **Regions of the World**, and Figure 3.5, **World Bank Classification of Countries**, show, there are many other ways to organize and divide the world into regions. Of course, any categorization scheme has fundamental flaws and subtle implications: each assumes that all the members of a category share the same characteristics. Categorical generalizations simply do not reflect reality. For example, all rich countries have poor people and all poor countries have rich people. Dividing the world into "haves" and "have nots" risks a "we" and "they" worldview and may foster **ethnocentrism** and arrogance. Nonetheless, a categorization scheme helps to simplify the complexities of the real world. Throughout most of this book, we will use the terms "developed" and "developing" to categorize countries. The label "developed countries" will refer to nations that have:

- high per capita incomes;
- economies that are diversified, including industries and services;
- forms of democratic governments;
- high qualities of life, including protection of human rights.

The label "developing countries" will refer to nations that have:

- relatively low per capita incomes;
- economies that are weak and not fully diversified;
- a variety of forms of government, some unstable and repressive, some democratic;
- relatively low qualities of life based on demographic, social, and economic indicators.

While this scheme does not account for emerging economies such as Korea, Thailand, and Chile experiencing rapid economic growth and movement toward democracy, it is often used by the United Nations (UN) and its definitions are widely accepted around the world. By using this scheme as a starting point, we can begin to identify patterns, explore relationships, and analyse real differences among countries.

> **One rich man plus six poor people, equals seven poor people.**
>
> *Hassan A. Sunmonu, secretary-general, Organization of African Trade Union Unity (OATUU)*

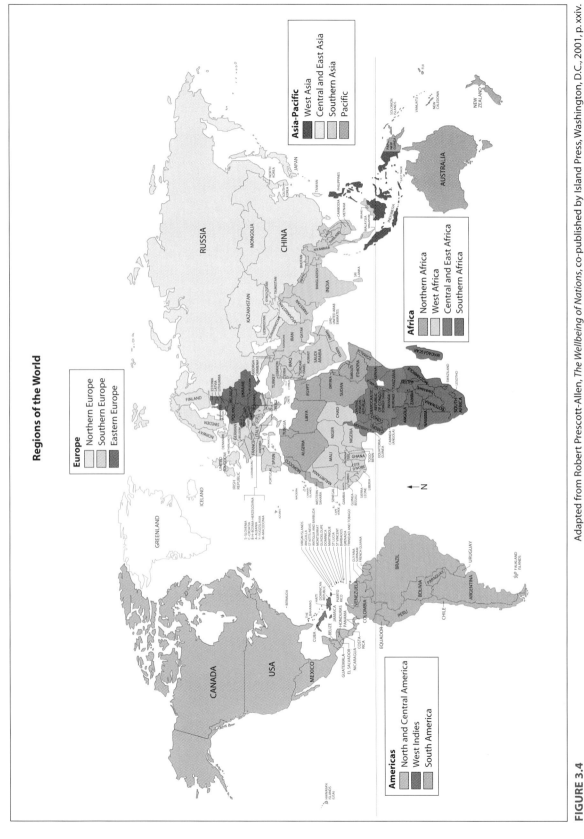

Regions of the World

Europe
- Northern Europe
- Southern Europe
- Eastern Europe

Americas
- North and Central America
- West Indies
- South America

Africa
- Northern Africa
- West Africa
- Central and East Africa
- Southern Africa

Asia-Pacific
- West Asia
- Central and East Asia
- Southern Asia
- Pacific

Adapted from Robert Prescott-Allen, *The Wellbeing of Nations*, co-published by Island Press, Washington, D.C., 2001, p. xxiv.

FIGURE 3.4

World Bank Classification of Countries

Segment	Approximate Population
Low-Income Economies	3 billion
Lower Middle-Income Economies	1.5 billion
Upper Middle-Income Economies	1 billion
High-Income Economies	820 million

FIGURE 3.5 The World Bank classifies countries into categories based on per capita **Gross National Product** (GNP). The categories are dynamic as economies grow or stagnate. For example, in 2001, Turkey moved from the upper-middle income to the lower-middle income segment and Honduras moved from low income to lower-middle income.

Canadian Family Income (average pretax income), 1989–1998

Income Segment	1989	1998	% change
Poorest 20%	10 388	8 627	−17
Lower-Middle 20%	31 427	27 486	−13
Middle 20%	48 776	46 835	−4
Upper-Middle 20%	67 790	68 505	+1
Richest 20%	114 178	124 681	+9

FIGURE 3.6 Economic divisions within a country are commonly used as organizers.

Maclean's magazine, August 28, 2000, p. 43

THE GEOPOLITICAL LANDSCAPE

The most noticeable geopolitical pattern is found when examining the arbitrary boundaries that divide Earth's surface into the mosaic of political and cultural regions that form some 192 countries.

A country or state is an independent political unit. It is concerned with secure borders, control of resources, and regional or international influence, along with administrative matters. The concept of a nation may coincide with a country or state but it has more of a cultural meaning. A **nation** is a group of people with a collective sense of belonging based on a common language and cultural background. **Nationalism** is a powerful political force and there are a number of nationalist movements of people with aspirations for political and economic self-determination and sovereignty. For example, the mountainous homeland of people known as the Kurds is divided between the countries of Turkey, Syria, Iraq, Iran, and Armenia. Twenty-five million Kurds have lived in the region, struggling for independence for centuries.

See Chapter 17 for more information about the Kurds' struggle for independence.

Some parts of the world are fragmented into many small countries while other countries cover vast amounts of territorial space. The 46 countries of Europe would fit easily within the boundaries of Canada. After World War II, when the colonial empires of countries such as Britain, France, Belgium, and the Netherlands collapsed, many new countries were created. When the former Soviet Union fell apart in 1991, 15 different countries in Northern and

Eastern Europe and Central Asia were recreated. Recently, a number of countries such as Yugoslavia, Czechoslovakia, and Ethiopia have fragmented into several smaller ones as a result of nationalistic aspirations based on ethnic and religious differences and conflict. Africa has 54 independent countries, most of which were created in the twentieth century.

Most of their boundaries make little practical sense as they do not follow the traditional tribal and ethnic boundaries, which has given rise to a number of violent conflicts and border disputes such as the continued chaos and ethnic conflict in the Democratic Republic of the Congo (despite a peace agreement signed by opposing forces).

FIGURE 3.7 Analysis of geopolitical landscapes can reveal remarkable patterns. This view of the political boundary between Haiti and the Dominican Republic illustrates how political differences such as resource protection regulations and economic differences such as the exploitation of wood supplies due to extreme poverty result in completely different human imprints on land.

 See Chapter 17 for more information about nationalism and Africa's boundaries.

INTERACT

1. Create your own definition for "geopolitics."
2. Make a list of six criteria that a country must meet in order for it to be defined as a country. How is the term "nation" different from the terms "country" or "state"?
3. Identify groups within Canada that consider themselves a nation.
4. **a)** Identify one main factor related to globalization that is causing countries to lose control over areas such as global finance, climate change, disease, and crime.
   b) In your opinion, should changes in the global power structure be considered positive, negative, or both? Explain your answer.
5. **a)** As a group, using Gross National Income in Purchasing Power Parity (GNI PPP) per capita statistics from the Data Appendix, write a definition for high and low income countries. Draw a line on a world map to estimate the approximate delineation of North and South. Share your map with other groups and discuss the reasons for any differences.
   b) Evaluate the use of general indicators of the standard of living of a country such as GNI PPP, GNP, and GDP.
6. Refer to Figure 3.5, **World Bank Classification of Countries**, and explain
   a) how these categories could be useful in analysing and addressing issues
   b) the fundamental flaws inherent in categorizing countries of the world.
7. Conduct research to find current events related to conflicts and disputes within the African continent. Produce an annotated map of Africa entitled Current Trouble Spots and explain the nature of each situation.

THE POLITICAL SPECTRUM

Politics is basically about power and wealth—who holds it and how it is used. Politics, whether at the international, national, community, or even personal level, influences almost all issues and aspects of our lives. Politics is sometimes thought of as pertaining to government, but this is a simplistic view. In reality, there have been and continue to be many different groups and even individuals who hold and exercise power over others. International institutions, regional organizations, large transnational corporations (TNCs), some non-governmental organizations (NGOs), criminal networks, and citizens are acting to gradually cause a shift in the power patterns of the past. Other groups that have been marginalized or exploited are struggling to gain power over their own lives.

> " While good politics fosters economic development and social cohesion and reduces corruption, bad politics breeds corruption, retards socio-economic development and may lead to civil conflicts and wars. "
>
> *African Development Bank,*
> *African Development*
> *Report, 2001*

When analysing geopolitical issues, it is important to understand the meaning of different political ideologies. An **ideology** is a set of values and beliefs about how people and groups in society should relate to one another and how power should be exercised. Ideology determines the ideals, goals, and form of government of a society and shapes its economic structure, policies, and laws. It can help us to understand the different types of political and economic systems that govern countries, as well as the political and economic **blocs** that contend for power. While the roots of many global conflicts are based in economic disparity and cultural clashes, differences in political ideology have also played a role.

Countries with governments at the extreme ends of the spectrum—dictatorships and totalitarian communist states—are places of human rights abuses and corruption. Political leaders in these countries do not follow the rule of law, nor do they allow public participation in the political process, provide information for their citizens, or honour their role as public trustees.

Political systems are continually evolving. For example, China is a communist country, but in 2002, capitalists were allowed to join the Communist Party for the first time. China also appears to be bowing to public pressure on human rights violations. China's politics change as its leaders become more interested in continued economic development, expanding participation in world trade, and promoting world peace. China's policy still supports nuclear proliferation and what it calls national reunification by bringing the unwilling citizens of Taiwan back under its control, but it appears to be interested in improving relations with the U.S. and other World Trade

FIGURE 3.8 Beijing, China, will host the 2008 Olympics and China will integrate its economy with the Association of South East Asian Nations (ASEAN) by 2010.

The Political Spectrum

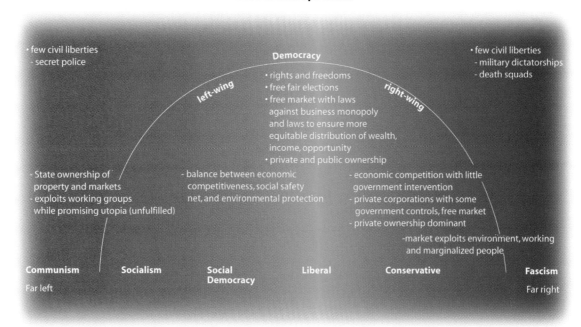

FIGURE 3.9 Different political–economic systems in the spectrum are represented as a linear continuum for simplicity. However, most people agree that because living conditions experienced at either end of the spectrum are similar and, in effect, closer together, the spectrum should be examined in a more cyclical (circular) way. Such diagrams are not perfect, but provide a general overview of the many variables and characteristics of a system.

How Leaders Left Office in Africa

	1970–1979	1980–1989	1990–1999	Total	Mean Time in Office (years)
Overthrown in coup, war, or invasion	30	22	22	74	5.7
Died of natural or accidental causes	3	4	3	10	11.7
Assassinated (not part of a coup)	0	1	3	4	7.8
Retired	2	5	9	16	11.7
Lost election	0	1	12	13	14.8

adapted from African Development Report 2001

FIGURE 3.10

Organization (WTO) members. Before joining the WTO in 2002, China had to agree to amend more than 500 of its domestic laws.

Democracy

Democracy originated in Greece in ancient times. It was a direct form of democracy wherein every man had the opportunity to vote on every law that was to be passed. Because women were not allowed to vote, we would not consider this a democracy today. According to Donald E. Whistler, author of *Conclusion: Devising Democracy*, democracy is defined as "a method for creating binding collective decisions

> ❝Fanaticism feeds on grievance. … The basic root cause [of terrorism] is neither religion nor poverty but lack of democracy, freedom and liberty. Democracy legitimates the struggle for power and provides safety valves for group anger; its denial drives dissent underground. Sometimes the mosque has been the only alternative rallying point in autocratic regimes kept in power by military might and harsh intelligence. … It is hard to imagine the Palestinian territories, Pakistan and Afghanistan as terrorist training bases … if they were well-off, middle class countries. ❞
>
> *Ramesh Thakur, vice-rector, United Nations University, Tokyo*

that are responsive to the wishes and values of a political society." Beliefs about the nature and spirit of democracy and how to achieve it vary widely. Democracy is often equated with capitalism but real democracy requires more than a free and open market; it must take social justice and a healthy environment into account. Holding elections does not always equal democracy. Elections in some countries are not free and fair but marred with intimidation tactics and corruption. Some new democracies in former military dictatorships particularly in Latin American countries such as Venezuela are fragile.

Democratic governments are expected to provide security for their citizens and to act to improve their quality of life. Laws are supposed to be designed to protect basic human rights and liberties as well as private property and collective national security. Governments have a difficult job balancing these tasks with policies that encourage economic growth. In the first decade of the twenty-first century, a large share of the world's population still do not have a voice in the decision-making process and are powerless in their struggle for equal opportunity. This is particularly the case for women in many countries. To be a real democ-

racy, a society must constantly strive to improve its political, economic, legal, and social systems for all members.

Politics and socio-economic policies vary considerably from one democracy to another. A democratic government may be right- or left-wing, but all real democracies fit somewhere near the middle of the political spectrum. Views from across the political spectrum have far-reaching implications for economic, cultural, and environmental policy making. India has had a democratically elected government for more than half a century, yet many of its citizens are not educated and human rights abuses and religious violence are common. Sweden and the U.S. are both considered democracies but life is quite different in the two countries. Social democracies such as that in Sweden are based on the belief that everyone in society, including workers and the disadvantaged, has the right to share in the wealth of the nation. Government

FIGURE 3.11 Sweden, with its strong social programs, such as this free daycare in Stockholm, as well as extensive health care, the right to a university education, parental leaves, and retirement benefits, is a social democracy.

FACT FILE

Between 1974 and 2000, the proportion of countries with a form of democratic government rose from 28% to over 60%. The United Nations Development Program (UNDP) reported that, in 1999 alone, 90 countries conducted local elections.

FIGURE 3.12 Aung San Suu Kyi and the National League for Democracy Party was elected by an overwhelming majority in Burma (Myanmar) in 1988. A brutally repressive military dictatorship took over, placing her under house arrest from 1989 until May 2002 when she was freed as a result of international public and economic pressure. This former "rice bowl" of Asia and its prosperous, educated population has been allowed by the military regime to deteriorate into a bankrupt land of poverty and fear. Suu Kyi was awarded the Nobel Peace Prize in 1991 and continues her struggle to bring the rightful democratic government to power in Myanmar.

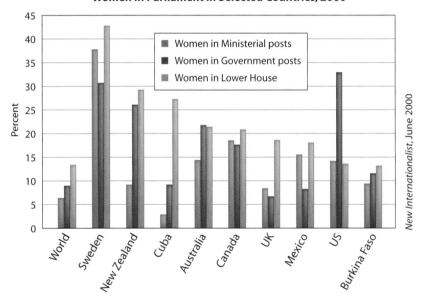

Women in Parliament in Selected Countries, 2000

New Internationalist, June 2000

FIGURE 3.13

policies may use regulations to interfere with free markets in order to provide a strong social safety net.

There has been a recent trend around the world toward the **multilateral** pursuit of common objectives such as the promotion of democracy and human rights, sustainable development, global peace, and most recently anti-terrorism. Currently, democracy is considered by the vast majority of people to be the best alternative for governance. Of 192 countries in the world, 120 are now considered to have some form of democratic government and the number of people living in a democracy has increased significantly since the end of World War II.

INTERACT

1. Explain what is meant by a strong social safety net. Evaluate the protection provided to all citizens by the social safety net of Ontario.

2. How is quality of life similar at opposite ends of the political spectrum? What factors differentiate opposite ends of the spectrum?

3. Analyse Figure 3.10, **How Leaders Left Office in Africa**. How does the table show political conditions in Africa? Why might these statistics not provide a valid picture of democratic change in Africa?

4. Compare the average length of time leaders are in office in European countries and African countries. Evaluate the significance of this difference for positive change.

5. Describe the changing geopolitical role of China and identify some factors responsible for the changes.

6. a) Suggest reasons for the lack of women in political positions as shown in Figure 3.13, **Women in Parliament in Selected Countries, 2000**.

   b) Predict how social, economic, and environmental policy might be different in a democracy where women hold one-half of the political positions.

7. In a group, discuss the meaning of the term "terrorism" and reach a consensus on a definition for the term.

8. How might democracy in a country reduce the risk of terrorism from groups within the country?

9. Conduct a case study of the evolving geopolitical situation in Myanmar that analyses the roles played by Aung San Suu Kyi and the military regime in the country's socio-economic development.

DISENCHANTED WITH DEMOCRACY

The amount of free and open political participation can be a measure of the strength of a democracy. As the forces of globalization take some of the power of states away, some analysts have noted the emergence of a widespread malaise about politics, including the belief that governments are losing their ability to govern effectively, that there may be little real difference in the outcomes of electing one political party over another, and that political leaders are unable to deal effectively with problems and issues. Many people, disenchanted with political parties, do not vote in elections.

According to the UN's *Human Development Report*, 90% of the people in the world do not participate in the decisions that affect their lives. With the way some electoral systems are designed, even in a democracy, a majority of the voting public may end up with a government that they did not choose. Some politicians may appear dishonest and the whole political process may seem corrupt. Many politicians have the interests of their constituents in mind when they run for office, but once elected, may find it difficult to manage the diverse demands of competing interests in a complex national and global system.

Another noticeable trend is the push by some groups within government and police forces for greater secrecy and less transparency. While most people would agree that some secrecy is necessary in times of war, the trend is noticeable in more familiar acts such as surveillance cameras on city streets, police forces using violent means to remove peaceful protesters at demonstrations, and organizations drafting international agreements behind closed doors. The World Trade Organization (WTO), for example, has been criticized as a closed, non-transparent decision-making body that offers no opportunity for citizen input. Defenders of the WTO say that the politicians who draft the agreements are acting as elected representatives of the people and should be left to do their job. While Canadians can make use of laws that provide access to public information, some governments do what they can to make the process difficult and expensive.

> " The streets are not the best place to discuss these highly complex issues. Some of the protestors are no more interested in open debate than officials at the IMF [International Monetary Fund] are. "
>
> *Joseph Stieglitz, Nobel prize-winning economist, former chief economist at the World Bank*

The cynicism about and alienation from the democratic process comes not just from the public but the private sector as well. Large corporations are spending millions of dollars to gain strategic advantage in the marketplace by sponsoring meetings of trade organizations like the WTO and in government by financially supporting political candidates. They are, in effect, circumventing the democratic process.

Some corporations have used a legal tactic known as **Strategic Lawsuits Against Public Participation (SLAPPs)** in an attempt to render their critics powerless to disrupt a company's industrial or resource development pursuits. A SLAPP is an intimidating attack on citizens who are exercising their democratic rights by merely voicing opposition to corporate policy through speaking out at a public meeting, signing a petition, writing articles or letters to a newspaper editor, and so on. While a SLAPP has little or no merit or hope of success, it can deter activists who are usually unable to afford the large amount of time and expensive legal cost to defend themselves. Canada's longest lasting

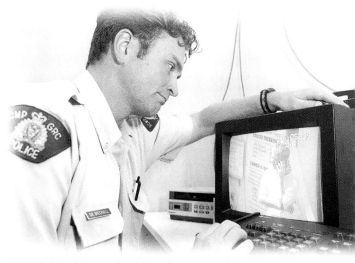

FIGURE 3.14 In 2002, Canada's privacy commissioner asked the Royal Canadian Mounted Police (RCMP) to remove the surveillance cameras from downtown Kelowna, B.C., considered an invasion of privacy and in violation of the UN declaration of Human Rights. Studies show that crime is not reduced by street cameras, although it may move to other parts of the city. The RCMP, citing the widespread support of the local community, has maintained the cameras.

and most notorious SLAPP was a multimillion dollar lawsuit, used in 1995, by Daishowa Inc., a Japanese pulp and paper transnational. Daishowa refused a moratorium on logging land that was part of a land claim dispute between the Lubicon Cree First Nation of northern Alberta and the Canadian government, until the claim was settled. The company obtained an injunction to stop the NGO Friends of the Lubicon from mounting a boycott campaign against the company's paper products. Daishowa even tried to prevent a Canadian law professor from publishing articles describing the case. In April 1998, a judge threw out Daishowa's attempt to silence the protestors, affirming their freedom of

> " It now seems clear to many social, environmental and poverty activists that state governments, international trading arrangements and large corporations are not a reliable set of institutions with which to run a small planet if any claim to justice or sustainability matters. "
>
> *Simon Dalby, chair of international governance, International Studies Association, Netherlands*

FIGURE 3.15 Smoke from tear gas and fires billows at an anti-globalization demonstration during the G8 summit in Genoa, Italy, in July 2001.

speech, but Daishowa continued to pursue an appeal that would overturn an Ontario court ruling permitting organized consumer boycotts.

> 66 Politics, whether by governments of the left or right, puts business at its center. It wants to encourage business to invest, to nurture it with low taxes.... It competes with other countries for its presence and vies with other political leaders for the acquaintanceship of the business superstars, led by Bill Gates. 99
>
> *John Lloyd, Moscow bureau chief and London-based journalist,*
> *Financial Times*

The Sierra Legal Defence Fund, an NGO, provided free legal services to the citizens group throughout the lengthy 12-year case. While there are fewer cases in Canada, thousands of SLAPPs are filed each year in the U.S., prompting about 20 states so far to pass anti-SLAPP legislation. The New Democratic Party (NDP) government of British Columbia passed Bill 10, the Protection of Public Participation Act in 2000 but the law was repealed in 2001 when the Liberal government was elected.

These societal changes are in part responsible for a complex decision-making process that is constantly evolving and responding to changing circumstances. People from all sectors and groups and from all points of view within society are starting to consider the implications of this dynamic political process for solving world issues.

Democratization and Civil Society

Many people are finding new ways to engage in democratic processes. There has been strong growth in people's concern for democracy, human rights, satisfying basic needs, protecting the environment, and promoting peace. Efforts to find solutions for issues with political, economic, environmental, and social justice components are fostering an interest in global governance and international law, expanding the reach of organizations such as the UN and the International Labour Organization (ILO). The same process is also having an opposing effect, encouraging people to concentrate on addressing issues within their own small communities.

 See Chapters 12 and 20 for more information about sustainable communities.

Trade unions were the first modern NGOs and while they are still quite powerful at national and international levels, their impact has levelled off with changes in global employment patterns and the trend toward free-market ideology. As business ideas are now the dominant way of thinking, less attention is paid to labour and there are downward pressures on wages and labour standards.

Many new organizations that advocate economic, social, cultural, and environmental goals and aspirations are emerging to challenge the corporate, technocratic approach to addressing global issues. A study of 42 countries, undertaken at the Center for Civil Society at Johns Hopkins University in Baltimore, U.S.A., revealed that the non-profit or **third sector** of society has grown so quickly (at four times the rate of the economy) that it will appear as significant in history as the creation of nation-states at the end of the nineteenth century. The collective

> 66 The World Bank recognizes that civil society organizations play an especially critical role in helping to amplify the voices of the poorest people in the decisions that affect their lives, and improve development effectiveness and sustainability. 99
>
> *The World Bank and*
> *Civil Society Report*

capacity of all these groups, generally referred to as **civil society**, is becoming increasingly influential. Some NGOs now act as advisors to national governments. For example, teams of lawyers with environmental law organizations have helped developing countries draft their own environmental protection laws.

Civil society plays an important role in identifying ways to improve conditions for people and ecosystems and to act as agents of change. The sustained pressure it places on governments and institutions has been credited for significant success in addressing world issues. It uses strategies such as boycotts, legal challenges, media campaigns, and promotion of corporate social responsibility. A growing trend is the use of lawsuits to force governments and businesses to follow a country's own laws or to stop projects without adequate environmental protection assessments.

In India, despite its poverty, public pressure has resulted in the courts closing hundreds of small businesses that were not complying with local laws. NGOs are credited with pushing many countries of the world into limiting the production and use of land mines and reducing the illegal trade in endangered species. Some NGOs tend to focus on narrow issues and block out the views of opposing stakeholders, while others are more skilled at conflict resolution and finding solutions. It is a challenge for governments at all levels to find ways for so many different voices and organizations to participate in a positive way.

The remarkable expansion in information technology and media has provided opportunity for increased interaction and democracy and a greater awareness of what is going on in the world but the reach of communication is not evenly spread. With satellite television and video equipment, governments cannot as easily isolate their citizens and censor information, although some authoritarian governments still try to do so. People everywhere are coming to understand how others around the world live. On the other hand, unequal access to the Internet has divided the world into those who are "connected" and those who are not. NGOs in developing countries experience more difficulty gathering information and financial resources. Access to the Internet for information and networking with other groups is not widespread in developing countries.

> " Leadership in the new millennium is not likely to come from the old familiar places like politics, mainstream media and business. It will come from ordinary people, health care workers, environmental and anti-poverty activists, new Canadians, First Nations people and most particularly, youth, who more than any other generation in our history will decide the values, ideology and lifestyle choices that will define Canadian culture for the 21st century. "
>
> *Maude Barlow, chairperson,*
> *Council for Canadians*

World Social Forum

Thousands of groups and NGOs, organized around a wide variety of issues from women's rights to protection of endangered species, have been networking via the Internet and meeting at the fringes of international conferences such as the UN Conferences on Population and Racism, the 2002 Earth Summit in Johannesburg, and at their own People's Forums. The World Social Forum has been created to bring these groups together as an alternative to the World Economic Forum where financial leaders of the G20 meet each year. Porto Allegre, Brazil, a city run by the worker's party with one of the most efficient public transportation systems in the world, was an appropriate location to meet in 2001. More than 60 000 people from 150 countries participated in the social forum, including almost 20 000 youth. The social forum represents a shift away from demonstrations against free trade and the ills of corporate globalization to a deeper analysis of how to make globalization a fairer and more equitable process.

Citizen Action

"In the packed corridors [at Porto Allegre], you were as likely to run into one of the international superstars of the struggle such as anti-war activist Noam Chomsky, Indian feminist Vandana Shiva or Nobel Peace Prize winner Rigoberta Menchu, as a poor campesino from Brazil's enormous Landless Peasant's Movement or Argentinean women with their pots and pans, fresh off the streets of Buenos Aires. There was a common critique of corporate globalization as a vicious greedy system that is creating more and more misery for people of the world and more and more devastation for the environment."

Judy Rebick, journalist, activist

"We are fighting for a world of compassion and caring against a world of greed and theft."

Vandana Shiva, biologist, author, activist, India

"The landless grow food on the lands they occupy when the World Bank commands the countries of the South not to grow their own food but rather to be a submissive beggar on the world market."

Edward Galeano, author

"The collective power of people to shape the future is greater now than ever before, and the need to exercise it is more compelling. Mobilizing that power to make life in the twenty-first century more democratic, more secure, and more sustainable is the foremost challenge of this generation."

"Our Global Neighbourhood," report of the Commission on Global Governance

"… The Canadian system has found ways of keeping governments in check other than by replacing them. The media are among the best educated and most critical in the world. Interest groups proliferate, dissidents abound. I have never seen a government successfully impose a major policy contrary to the popular will without being defeated in the next election. The system works."

John Ibbitson, political columnist

INTERACT

1. Make a list of the five most influential groups or institutions that affect geopolitical relationships. Explain your views to a classmate and discuss differences in your lists.
2. Brainstorm a list of factors that have the potential to bring about political change. Identify those factors that have been important in Canada's political evolution.
3. Discuss the advantages of democracy for African nations.
4. Democratic participation is usually expressed through voter turnout rates at elections. In your opinion, what factors in Canada result in low turnout rates? Suggest some of the consequences of low turnout rates. Identify additional ways that citizens may become involved in the democratic process.
5. Explain how SLAPPs undermine the democratic process.
6. What might be effective ways to support "civil societies" in developing countries? Give reasons for your ideas.
7. Do you agree or disagree with the prediction by Maude Barlow about Canadian leadership in the quote on page 69? In your opinion, how effective could this style of leadership be in addressing issues in Canada?

THE POWER SHIFT

Countries are becoming more interdependent and losing their individual dominance in a rapidly integrating global economy. This integration has coincided with the emergence of international alliances formed to enhance economic power, trade, and security. Today, these alliances, along with treaties and agreements, are a main form of interrelationships among countries.

The Role of the UN

The UN acts as an umbrella supranational organization whose many agencies set international policies to promote environmental and social well-being and security, including peacekeeping. One of its main goals is to encourage widespread acceptance of the universal values that are outlined in various UN declarations such as the Declaration of Human Rights and conventions such as the Law of the Sea Convention. It is the main forum where governments of the world can come together to try to solve the world's most challenging issues. The right to intervene in a country is seen as the responsibility of the UN in order to protect vulnerable populations at risk from civil wars, revolutions, state repression, and collapse. Some developing countries are opposed to this. However, military intervention is seen by the UN as a last resort after diplomatic efforts have failed.

When the UN Charter was written, the organization was seen as the world's police, charged with stopping aggression around the world. The UN has been successful at resolving conflicts in some places such as Cyprus and El Salvador while many other conflicts are ongoing or have ended in disaster. The countries with the most power at the UN are the permanent Security Council members—China, France, Russia, U.S., and UK. The big powers can and often do veto UN initiatives such as the veto of humanitarian aid to Kosovo by Russia during the conflict there in 1999.

 See Chapter 19 for more information about conflicts in various parts of the world.

Facts about the UN

- The UN was formed June 26, 1945, with 51 members.

- In 2002, there were 190 member countries.

- In 2001, 11 of the 190 delegations were headed by women.

- In 2001, the UN employed 64 700 people around the world with a budget of US$10.5 billion.

- Along with the powerful inner circle formed by the five permanent members of the Security Council, there are 10 additional countries on the council with two-year terms.

- The Secretariat is the UN's main administrative body.

- Switzerland was not a member because of its desire for neutrality and independence until it voted to join in a referendum in March 2002. It is home to the headquarters of more than 20 UN agencies.

- The U.S. owes the UN the most in unpaid fees. In 2001, it owed US$2.3 billion—more than 60% of the outstanding dues. It pays just enough to maintain its voting rights under Article 19 of the UN Charter.

- Between 1948 and 2001, the UN provided many international peacekeeping missions, the majority of them in the 1990s. Canada participated in 65 peace support missions between 1989 and 2001.

- Canada was elected as a non-permanent member of the Security Council for 1999 and 2000. During that time, as President of the Council, Canada advocated strongly for humanitarian concerns.

FIGURE 3.16

Kofi Annan

As secretary-general of the UN since1996, Kofi Annan has been a strong leader who has succeeded in bringing significant change to the UN. He has been under a great deal of pressure to show that the UN really can make a difference. He has focused on actions related to human rights and humanitarian law and has reached out to NGOs, private-sector philanthropists, and corporate leaders to work together against the root causes of conflict and to help civilians suffering under repressive governments, poverty, and ill health.

In 2000, Annan started a program known as the Global Compact to persuade transnational companies to be more responsible corporate citizens. By 2002, about 300 companies had pledged support, but only 30, mostly from Europe, had good enough conduct to allow them into the compact.

Annan has criticized countries such as Russia for human rights violations in subduing the uprising in Chechnya and the U.S. for its insistence on economic sanctions in Iraq that have had a negative impact on citizens—especially the elderly and children who are both vulnerable—with little effect on Saddam Hussein, the declared enemy of the U.S.

FIGURE 3.17

Annan's message to leaders of countries embroiled in conflicts has been to take their responsibilities more seriously and to negotiate with their opponents rather than expect the UN to solve conflicts for them.

During serious criticism of the UN for its failure to stop genocide in Rwanda or to save 7000 Bosnian Muslims from being killed by Serbs at Srebenica, Annan accepted full responsibility and took steps toward reform. He ensured that the UN dealt swiftly with scandals involving the local aid workers of NGOs and peacekeepers using food and aid as a form of sexual exploitation of children in refugee camps in West Africa. An urgent plan of action for protecting children and female refugees from sexual abuse, supervising aid workers, hiring more women as aid workers, and prosecuting violators was put into place by the UN High Commission for Refugees (UNHCR).

The world has changed significantly since the UN was created in 1945 and there has been criticism of its outdated structures and many calls for reform. Suggested reforms include changing the structure and membership of the Security Council to make it more representative, creating an Economic Council with enough control over the powers and processes in the world economy to make it more democratic, focusing more on conflict prevention, and dealing with the roots of problems. Despite the need for reform, the UN and its many agencies have made significant contributions to addressing these issues and to making the world a better place.

International Criminal Court

The UN has been trying for years with little success to deter war crimes and attempted genocide in places such as Cambodia, Rwanda, the Balkans, East Timor, Argentina, El Salvador, Guatemala, and Chile. The International Court of Justice was set up in 1945 as the judicial arm of the UN to enforce statutes and conventions, rule against the actions of a particular country, and resolve disputes between countries such as that over oil drilling rights on the continental shelf. It handles cases between states, not individuals. International Criminal Tribunals have been set up by the UN to prosecute leaders and

FIGURE 3.18 Canada has been a strong advocate at the UN for the protection of civilians and human security as well as state security. Canada is known around the world for its peacekeeping and conflict resolution skills.

others for crimes against humanity such as the 2002 trial of the former president of the former Yugoslavia, Slobodan Milosevic. However, these attempts at global justice have been accused of "selective justice," as not all crimes have been prosecuted and it has often taken a long time to set up ad hoc tribunals, allowing crucial evidence to be destroyed, the accused to disappear, or witnesses to be intimidated.

The International Criminal Court, which came into effect in July 2002, makes individuals, not just states, personally liable for the most serious crimes, including widespread murder of civilians, torture, and mass rape. Judges and prosecutors are to be elected by member states and the court is to be independent of the UN Security Council. Most of the 160 countries that met in Rome to create the court in 1998 endorsed the treaty, which required 60 countries to ratify it.

While Canada ratified the treaty, the U.S. government has not, because of objections from groups such as the U.S. military and a conservative Congress. The U.S. has a number of concerns about the credibility and effectiveness of an International Court. First, the U.S. government believes that its national judicial system is superior to an international one. Second, it fears that it would be a political rather than a judicial body. Third, it fears the possibility that U.S. personnel might be brought to the court accused of war crimes as a political ploy by hostile states.

> 66 The grown-ups who are here, the ministers, haven't seen a quarter of what I've seen. … I don't want to hear any more speeches. I want to know how they're going to take action. 99
>
> *Ewar Barzanji, 17-year-old Kurdish girl who fled northern Iraq*

FIGURE 3.19 UN headquarters in Manhattan, New York City.

MAKE A DIFFERENCE

Is it possible for one person to make a difference? As an individual, you cannot stop the genocide in Rwanda or make peace in a region of violent conflict. However, it is possible to participate actively in democracy and to shake up the status quo with enthusiasm, your own unique gifts, and what you have learned to make a difference in your own community or elsewhere in the world.

Canadian youth can get involved in the UN by participating in the Youth International Internship Program of the Department of Foreign Affairs and International Trade and the United Nations Association in Canada (UNAC). Several youth each year work in culturally diverse environments to gain a clearer understanding of the issues and challenges facing the world. Another way to get involved with the UN process is to take part in the Model UN in New York. Each year, more than 200 Canadian students from colleges and universities join thousands of students from other countries to attend Security Council sessions and defend their country's foreign policy in a model UN Assembly.

The Canadian Centre for Policy Development organizes events such as the National Forum for Youth on War-Affected Children held in major Canadian cities in 2000. Young people experiencing conflict attended and demanded that the problems and needs of war-affected children around the world be addressed in the following ways:

- Take a critical approach to sanctions on nations that target children rather than government leaders.
- Divert funding from war to education.
- Arrest and punish all war criminals.
- Provide aid for community organizations in war zones.
- Control gun sales and the arms trade to cut off small arms to war makers.

The demands were considered for international action at the UN General Assembly in September 2001. Subsequently, two new protocols were added to the Convention on the Rights of the Child at the UN Millennium Summit and signed by 50 countries to prevent children under the age of 18 from participating in armed conflict and eliminate trafficking in children, child prostitution, and child pornography.

Global Economic Institutions

The International Monetary Fund (IMF), based in Washington, maintains currency stability and exchange rates in a multilateral system through which money flows from one country to another. All 182 member-countries must peg their exchange rates to either gold or the U.S. dollar. Each country pays a membership fee, which is used to support members with temporary financial problems. The IMF generally supports the **neo-liberal economic model**—the free flow of money, goods, and services around the world.

The role of the WTO is to regulate world trade and to supervise the enforcement of national trade policies that generally work in favour of international banks and TNCs. In 1995, the WTO replaced the General Agreement on Tariffs and Trade (GATT). While the GATT agreement had no power to enforce tariffs and other agreements, the WTO can now legally impose trade sanctions on any country. No democratically elected body has the authority to intervene in the operations of the WTO. The

> **FACT FILE**
>
> The global economy (GDP for all countries) in 2001 totalled more than US$40 trillion.

WTO also has the power to invalidate regional trade agreements if they contain discriminatory rules against foreign trade, as was the case in 2001 when the Canada–U.S. auto pact was struck down. Main features of the WTO include the following:

- The General Agreement on Trade in Services (GATS) sets rules on services such as transportation, telecommunications, and banking for all WTO members.
- Trade-related intellectual property rights (TRIPS) deal with the protection of products that result from ideas, innovation, research, and design such as books, inventions, brand names, logos, and genetically modified plants.
- Trade-related investment measures (TRIMS) protect private and public investments and private property, even within another country's borders.

The Group of Twenty

The Group of Twenty (G20) is a forum of finance ministers and central bank governors from 20 countries. It was created to promote discussion and study issues related to the global economy and financial stability among industrialized and emerging economies. It includes the G7 countries (Canada, France, Germany, Italy, Japan, U.S., UK, and since 1997, Russia, making the G8) and eleven others (Argentina, Australia, Brazil, China, India, Indonesia, Mexico, Saudi Arabia, South Africa, South Korea, and Turkey), along with the European Union (EU), World Bank, and IMF. The leaders represent two-thirds of the world's population and almost 90% of its economic production. Canada's finance minister, Paul Martin, was the first chair of the G20 until 2001. Canada's objective was to provide a forum for the emerging economies to advance and reach consensus on issues of concern in an informal way that

" All I've heard about FTAA is either adamantly against globalization or blindly celebratory of it. The question is not whether to agree or disagree with it, but to criticize the intricate processes that lead to oppression and domination in specific locales, while continuing to make room for discussion and alternate solutions. "

Su Lin Lewis, in a letter to editor of The Globe and Mail, *Halifax*

the IMF and WTO have not allowed. Some geopolitical analysts believe that the G20 should shift its focus from making the emerging economies less vulnerable to financial crises toward a more equitable sharing of the world's prosperity.

Regional Alliances

Economic and political alliances have become a regular feature of the geopolitical landscape. The EU is the most economically powerful regional organization. The 15 member-countries have a common currency known as the euro, free movement across borders, and have given up some of their individual sovereign power for collective economic and security advantages. The EU and the North Atlantic Treaty Organization (NATO) have created a social democratic political entity in Europe that has a great deal of influence at the UN.

Political and economic cartels, organizations, and trade agreements such as the Organization of Petroleum Exporting Countries (OPEC), the Association of South East Asian Nations (ASEAN), Mercado Comun del Sur or the Common Market of the South (MERCOSUR), and the North American Free Trade Agreement (NAFTA) allow member nations to control resources such as oil or to enhance regional trade. NAFTA has had controversial and mixed results for groups within its three member countries (Canada, U.S., and Mexico). Along with the Free Trade of the Americas Agreement (FTAA), which comes into effect in 2005, NAFTA is part of an ambitious international plan to allow Mexico and other countries of the Americas access to the markets of Canada and the U.S., as well as to continue the process of modernization and democratization.

FACT FILE

NAFTA came into effect January 1, 1994. Seven years later, in 2001, 75% of Mexicans live in poverty, real wages are lower than in 1994, and unemployment is rising. On the other hand, democracy in Mexico is growing stronger.

FACT FILE

La Francophonie is a grouping of 52 countries and governments sharing the French language.

Key World Organizations

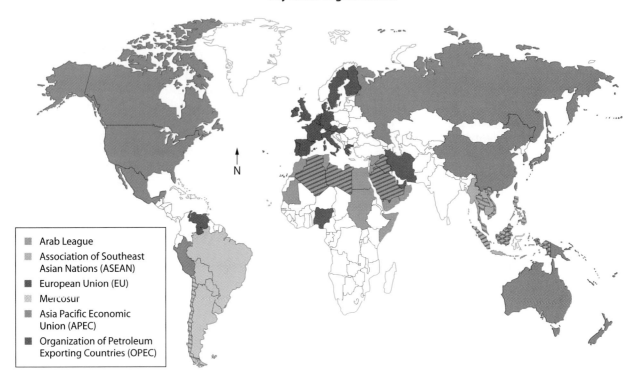

Arab League

Association of Southeast
Asian Nations (ASEAN)

European Union (EU)

Mercosur

Asia Pacific Economic
Union (APEC)

Organization of Petroleum
Exporting Countries (OPEC)

N

FIGURE 3.20

INTERACT

1. Explain what is meant when the WTO is described as "closed, and non-transparent." Conduct research to evaluate the WTO's role as a democratic institution.

2. Evaluate the potential of the ideas demanded by youth at the Canadian National Forum for Youth on War-Affected Children to effect positive change.

3. Create a diagram, showing the shift in power from national governments to TNCs, international bodies, and other groups.

4. While the UN has had some successes, there is much criticism of its performance. Investigate to find out what changes are needed to make the organization more effective. Explain your ideas.

5. Conduct research on the International Criminal Court. In your opinion, should there be an international justice system? Produce a one-page opinion statement on the topic. Some questions that you might consider are:
   - What values and ideologies would underlie the laws and procedures?
   - Who would enforce the laws?
   - How would the system be funded?

6. As members of economic alliances such as the EU, member states must give up some of their rights—in effect, give up some of their autonomy. Explain why rich and powerful countries like the UK choose to do this.

HOW TO BE A SUPERPOWER

By 1990, when the Cold War ended, the U.S. had evolved as the sole superpower. The U.S. is the only country with the political, military, and technological strength to match its economic hegemony. Other political entities such as the EU are powerful economically but less so politically. With its vast wealth and power, U.S. policies and actions have an effect on other parts of the world. It ranks highly in all the significant sources of power, including population size, literacy, natural resources, industrial and technological development, political stability, social cohesion, military strength, and diplomatic alliances.

U.S. foreign policy over the years has varied from **isolationist** to **interventionist**. The U.S. has been called on to perform many crisis interventions, peacekeeping, and humanitarian missions. While the U.S. government often builds coalitions and rallies its allies, it may take **unilateral** action and maintain the right of armed intervention without the authority of the UN Security Council.

An important geopolitical issue today centres on the rights and responsibilities of a superpower. Throughout the last century, the U.S. has become involved when its "national security interests" were affected. It has used whatever means it considers necessary to achieve its goals. For example, when the UN Security Council supported the position of the World Court at the Hague, Netherlands, which found the U.S. guilty of terror in its campaign against Nicaragua in the 1970s and 1980s, the U.S. simply vetoed the judgement. Some geopolitical analysts suggest that U.S. goals appear to be economic but the superpower also claims that the spread of democracy, rule of law, free markets, and the elimination of weapons of mass destruction are a top priority. The U.S. is perceived by many to control international institutions. Because it has used direct intervention for a variety of purposes such as in Grenada in 1983, Panama in 1989, Somalia in 1992, and Haiti in 1994 or covert action and subterfuge such as supporting a military coup in Chile in 1973, some anti-American feelings are held around the world, particularly in some developing countries. In the 1980s, US$3 billion worth of arms was provided to train a generation of people in guerilla warfare, hostage-taking, and the like to the "freedom fighting" Mujahadin in Afghanistan against the invading Soviet Union. Some factions of this group more recently turned to the next enemy—the U.S. itself—and became a prime U.S. target in the twenty-first century fight against terrorism. Some analysts argue that these policies are the best way to spread democracy and human rights to other places and that past U.S. policy has been appropriate, considering the strategic situation of the times. With its unrivalled power, the U.S. faces the challenge of creating a new and more stable world order, which many believe can only be achieved with the expanded participation of all countries.

As the U.S. has evolved into the world's only superpower, it serves as the main driver of economic growth. The U.S. considers the whole world and even outer space to be in its sphere of interest and has military bases and training forces in place around the world. The U.S. is often the only developed country that has refused to sign or ratify important international treaties such as the UN Conventions on Biological Diversity, Banning Land Mines, and Eliminating

> **FACT FILE**
>
> The U.S. is the world's biggest arms exporter, supplying about 40% of the developing world's weapons.

> **FACT FILE**
>
> In 2002, the U.S. sent military advisors to many countries, including the Philippines, to train local forces in their struggle against guerillas and terrorism.

> " Economic policy is today perhaps the most important part of U.S. interaction with the rest of the world. And yet, the culture of international economic policy in the world's most powerful democracy is not democratic. "
>
> *Joseph Stieglitz, Nobel prize winning economist and former chief economist at the World Bank (He was fired for criticizing the impact of World Bank policies.)*

Discrimination Against Women and has opted out of the 1972 Anti-Ballistic Missile Treaty. In not ratifying a treaty such as the Convention on the Rights of the Child (the U.S. and Somalia are the only two countries in the world who have not done so), it does not mean that the U.S. wants to violate children's rights. Rather, it prefers not to be accountable to anyone outside its own borders and sometimes initiates policies of its own to address the issues.

The U.S. is noted for its position against repressive dictatorships in Iraq, North Korea, and Cuba, but it has ignored serious violations of human rights in other places, such as Indonesia and Saudi Arabia, where its economic interests, particularly related to oil supply, are of more strategic importance. The U.S. media report far more on human rights abuses in Iran and Iraq than in Saudi Arabia.

> 66 As we help our friends increase their own security capability we are helping them in the global war on terrorism. 99
> *General Peter Pace, vice-chair, U.S. Joint Chiefs of Staff, February 2002*

 See Chapter 2 for more information about media influence on public opinion and Chapter 17 for more information about nationalism.

The U.S. promotes many alliances such as the Asia Pacific Economic Cooperation (APEC) forum around the world. APEC is an international organization for promoting open trade and economic integration and growth among its 21 member-countries around the Pacific Rim. This region represents a vitally important market for U.S. exports (US$500 billion in 2000).

The U.S. actively protects its allies. Canada benefits from the security provided by the much more powerful military forces and the radar, communication, and spy satellites used for military operations by the U.S. Canada co-operates closely with the U.S. military and the joint North American Aerospace Defence Command (NORAD) is run and staffed by both countries. NORAD is expected to tie in with the controversial plans for a ballistic missile defence shield and the "weaponizing" of space.

Sharing the Power

Other parts of the world, including China, the EU, and countries in Africa, are interested in playing a more active role on the world stage. China's power could increase significantly as it slowly integrates into the global economy and becomes a leader in an Asian free-trade zone. Its military power is expected to keep pace with economic growth.

The EU is emerging as a contender for a kind of collective superpower status, challenging U.S. dominance. Differences with the U.S. over trade matters and foreign policy initiatives have arisen as a result of differing worldviews on the role of institutions and regulations. Some U.S. policies in the Middle East have aroused protest among European leaders. The U.S. plan to extend the military war on terrorism in the first part of the twenty-first century to countries beyond Afghanistan met with little support. Europe's preferred strategy was to provide economic and political support through diplomacy and economic strategies in an effort to support the development of democracy.

> 66 There is no alternative to working together and using collective power to create a better world. 99
> *"Our Global Neighbourhood," report of the Commission on Global Governance*

Black Gold—The Strategic Resource

The world is dependent on oil. In 2001, Europe imported 60% of its oil, half of that from the Middle East. More than 80% of Japan's oil comes from the Middle East. The U.S. depends on Saudi Arabia for 25% of its oil supply, an important motive for helping to keep the Saudi royal family in power and for maintaining a strong military presence in Saudi Arabia.

The demand for oil and natural gas is increasing, especially in developing countries. At least 50% of the projected annual increase in global demand is expected to come from the emerging economies in the Pacific Rim and China. Economic growth in China is expected to increase demand for private cars and trucking, which has serious implications for pollution and global climate change.

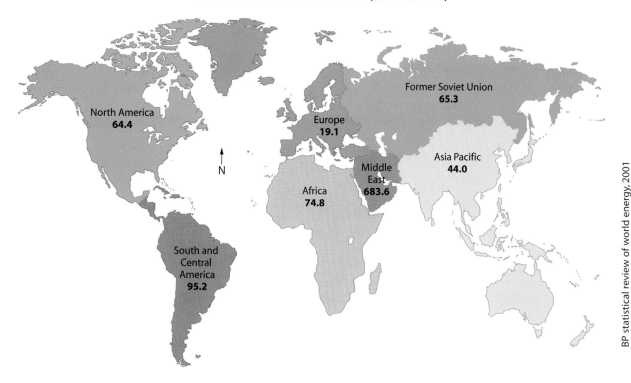

Proved Oil Reserves at End of 2000 (billion barrels)

North America
64.4

Former Soviet Union
65.3

Europe
19.1

Asia Pacific
44.0

Middle East
683.6

Africa
74.8

South and Central America
95.2

N

BP statistical review of world energy, 2001

FIGURE 3.21

The developed or industrialized countries consume more oil than developing countries. In North America, oil consumption is expected to increase by more than 8 million barrels a day between 2000 and 2020—an average annual growth rate of 1.5%. The control of a large part of the world's oil resources by countries in the Middle East and the suspicion that global terrorism is funded partly through oil has prompted the U.S. to rethink its energy supply situation. This will cause long-term and widespread change in geopolitical and economic patterns, particularly in the Middle East, and an impact on the natural environment as the developed world moves away from oil consumption to increased energy efficiency and cleaner, renewable supplies. Globalization and

FACT FILE

As of 2001, the U.S. produced about 40% of the oil it needs and imports the rest—1.2 million barrels a day from Saudi Arabia alone.

increased competition from non-OPEC oil-producing countries such as Norway, Russia, and Mexico will ensure less dependence on Middle East oil in the future. As the demand for Middle East oil goes down, governments in the region, with few other resources to export, will have to find alternative ways to generate revenue.

Energy Alternatives

Any move in the past away from oil dependency has met with opposition and threats of decreased political financing from two huge special interest groups—the transnational automobile and oil industries. There are signs that energy resource use patterns are beginning to change. The U.S. government is interested in freeing the economy from its reliance on Middle East

FACT FILE

If the fuel efficiency of cars improved by 2 km/L, 1.5 million barrels of oil a day would be saved.

> " Freedom from having to secure or defend oil supplies around the world [would mean] the United States could base its foreign policies even more purely on promoting democracy, freedom and open markets rather than on supporting regimes with whom we share few common values or interests beyond economics. "
>
> *Bill Richardson, former U.S. ambassador to the UN and former secretary of energy*

oil resources. Possible but controversial ways to accomplish this include:

- increasing reliance on non-OPEC oil producers, including Norway, Venezuela, Mexico, and Canada (including offshore and tar sands);
- accessing the vast oil resources of the Caspian Sea region via proposed pipeline routes to get the oil to market;
- drilling for oil in the environmentally sensitive Arctic Wildlife Refuge of Alaska (rejected by the U.S. senate in April 2002);
- exploiting small oil and gas supplies on the shores of the Great Lakes;
- implementing a comprehensive plan to increase energy efficiency in industry, heating and cooling, appliances, and transportation, including highly efficient jet engines and fuel cells;

FIGURE 3.22 The Toyota Prius is the world's first mass-produced car with a gas/electric hybrid engine. Cleaner technologies such as the Ballard fuel cell and electric vehicles are now available to the public but at a higher cost, although the health and environmental costs of not using cleaner energy are not included in the equation.

- investing in non-fossil fuel sources and alternative renewable energy sources such as solar, biomass, and wind and acceleration of the hydrogen age of energy;
- renewing interest in nuclear energy.

 See Chapter 19 for more information about the strategic role of oil in U.S. and Middle East geopolitics and Chapter 7 for more information about energy alternatives.

> " Fossil fuels are a one-time gift that lifted us up from subsistence agriculture and eventually should lead us to a future based on renewable resources… [but] no Caspian Sea exploration, no drilling in the South China Sea, no SUV [sport utility vehicle] replacements, no renewable energy projects can be brought on at a sufficient rate to avoid a bidding war for the remaining oil. "
>
> *Kenneth S. Deffeyes, Hubberts Peak: The Impending Oil Shortage, Princeton University Press, 2001*

The global supply of oil is declining by 5% a year. The discovery of additional reserves of oil in the future is unlikely as petroleum geologists have explored most of the globe. As oil and gas are depleted, shortages are likely to result in higher prices and disruptions in all sectors of the economy, especially transportation, energy, industry, and agriculture. Manufacturing industries that depend on petroleum products include agricultural fertilizers, pesticides, plastics, medicines, and cosmetics. Some analysts predict civil disturbances and harsher government policies as they struggle to provide adequate resources.

> " Everything is for sale in the new world order, even those areas we once considered sacred like water, health, education, and culture. Increasingly, these services and resources are controlled by a handful of transnational corporations operating outside of any national or international law. The top 200 global corporations are now so big, their combined sales surpass the combined economies of 182 countries and they have almost twice the economic clout of the poorest four-fifths of humanity. …Wal-Mart is bigger than 161 countries. Ford is bigger than South Africa. The merged Time Warner–America Online colossus has a market value greater than the economy of Australia. "
>
> *Maude Barlow, chairperson, Council for Canadians*

The Growth of Transnational Corporations

The first corporations began in the sixteenth century in the colonial empires of Europe. They were merchant companies that were granted a corporate charter that allowed them to conduct business with the financial risk limited to the amount that was invested. This privilege was not granted to individuals, placing the rights of corporations above them. The charters allowed the corporations to become very powerful and the states that issued them to expand their imperial interests to the colonies and help with war efforts with other empires. Even Adam Smith, the eighteenth-century capitalist, in his book *Wealth of Nations*, was concerned about the power of corporations to evade taxes and market laws, interfere with prices, and control trade.

> 66 You can have democracy or you can have corporate rule. You cannot have them both.
> *Ralph Nader, author, activist* 99

Much alarm has been expressed about the increasing power of transnational corporations (TNCs) and their exploitative practices. They control 80% of the world's trade and 80% of world food production. Many corporations do not pay any taxes although the profits of the top 200 corporations grew 362% between 1983 and 1999. As corporations get larger, they have more resources than the economies of many countries. There are about 63 000 TNCs with more than 690 000 subsidiaries around the world. The foreign subsidiaries of the top 100 transnationals have assets of more than US$2 trillion. A recent trend toward corporate merging has created larger and larger conglomerates with little government intervention (except in a few publicized cases such as Microsoft in 2001), despite the risk of monopolistic effects on the economy.

Corporations often talk publicly about their role in providing jobs. However, the reality is that the top 200 corporations employ less than 0.1% of the world's labour force. In the name of efficiency and increasing technology, downsizing and layoffs are the corporate norm. In 2001 alone, two million corporate jobs were lost worldwide.

Corporations have been able to use the rules of the WTO to force governments to weaken environmental legislation, labour standards, food safety, human rights, and cultural protection policies. One ruling struck down U.S. restrictions on the import of shrimp harvested by methods that trapped and killed turtles. This ruling led to the turtle costumes that were worn by some environmental activists in protests against the WTO in Seattle in December 1999.

Civil society has led campaigns against the actions of many TNCs, including Nestle, Nike, General Electric, Disney, and Shell, for their negative practices, including poor working conditions, profiteering, political interference, environmental damage, or cultural imperialism. Recently, however, some corporations have shown leadership and played positive roles in addressing issues of concern. Some corporations have integrated environmental or worker protection policies into their operations. Some have made significant

FACT FILE

In February 2002, Ford Motor Company laid off 35 000 workers, 22 000 in North America.

FACT FILE

The remarkable growth of some corporations is demonstrated by the case of Starbucks coffee bars. In 1989, the company had 50 coffee bars in North America. By 2002, it had more than 4700 coffee bars in cities around the world.

FACT FILE

A GenerAsians survey asked 5700 young people living in Asian countries to name their favourite food and drink. The results: young people in Australia, China, Hong Kong, Indonesia, Japan, Singapore, and Taiwan all picked McDonald's and Coca-Cola. Those from Malaysia picked Kentucky Fried Chicken and Coca-Cola, and those from Thailand picked Kentucky Fried Chicken and Pepsi.

FACT FILE

The 1999 film, *The Insider*, was based on the true story of a corporate "whistleblower" who revealed to the world how the transnational tobacco company he worked for lied to government and the public about the health hazards of smoking.

philanthropic donations to UN agencies and charitable causes. Many of the world's largest corporations belong to the World Business Council for Sustainable Development. Their definition of the key concept of sustainable development may not coincide exactly with those of other groups, but the concept is at least on the table for discussion. Energy efficiency, wise use of resources, and environmental protection are becoming more common as the long-term lower costs and benefits of such policies are realized. The desire to appear to be a good, socially responsible corporate citizen is a growing trend, as consumers and special interest groups increase their pressure. The Forest Stewardship Council certifies forest products produced using sustainable harvesting techniques. Home Depot is an example of a company that has chosen to sell the certified products.

FACT FILE

In 2002, the Canadian Democracy and Corporate Accountability Commission made 24 recommendations to guide business, government, and other regulatory bodies toward corporate social and environmental responsibility.

Comparing Wealth of Selected Corporations to Countries, 2000

Country or Corporation	GDP or Total Sales (US$ billions)	Country or Corporation	GDP or Total Sales (US$ billions)
Canada	677	Royal Dutch/Shell	190
Netherlands	375	IBM (International Business machines)	179
General Electric	372	Saudi Arabia	173
Australia	369	GlaxoSmithKline Pharmaceuticals	145
Microsoft	326	Indonesia	145
Exxon Mobil	300	Coca-Cola	130
Wal-Mart Stores	273	Venezuela	124
Argentina	269	Novartis Pharmaceuticals	114
Sweden	210	Thailand	114
BP (British Petroleum)	201	Philip Morris	113

World Development Indicators, World Bank, August 2002 and The world's largest companies, May 2002, Global 500, *Financial Times*, May 2002

FIGURE 3.23

INTERACT

1. Make a list of criteria that could be used as indicators of global power.
   a) In your opinion, what are the characteristics that define a superpower?
   b) In what ways does the U.S. meet these criteria?
2. a) What would the multiplier effect of massive layoffs in the automobile industry be?
   b) What additional industries and services would be affected by the layoffs?
3. Collect current events articles dealing with the role of the U.S. as a superpower. Write a 1000-word position paper that describes the interdependence of countries in the global economy and evaluates the geopolitical role played by the U.S.

4. Explain, using specific examples, how oil can be said to fuel geopolitical events and relationships in the world.
5. Investigate some of the international treaties and conventions that the U.S. has signed. For what reasons might the U.S. not sign treaties banning land mines, protecting children's rights, or eliminating discrimination against women?
6. Do corporations have a responsibility to society beyond profits and jobs?
   a) Investigate some specific examples of corporate responsibility.
   b) What are some additional actions that corporations could take to help improve social conditions?

THE SOUTH–NORTH GAP

The effect of global economic policies on developing countries gives rise to complex and controversial issues and widespread debate about who benefits.

66 In recent decades in the global economy, nearly one-fifth of the population has regressed—arguably one of the greatest economic failures of the twentieth century. 99

International Monetary Fund (IMF)

Of 142 member-countries of the WTO, 100 are developing countries. An additional 30 developing countries that have applied to join the organization are required to make economic and social changes to their national policies. In past meetings, wealthy countries have ignored the issues of concern to developing countries and have resisted their demands in areas such as reducing subsidies on agricultural exports and textiles and modifying the patent protection of pharmaceutical drugs. Despite claims of support for free trade, some developed countries subsidize agricultural production, which results in the dumping of food on global markets, keeping prices low. This ignores the crucial role of agriculture in the social and economic fabric of developing countries. Under

FACT FILE

The foreign debt of all developing countries in 2000 was US$2 trillion.

66 Poverty is the worst form of violence. 99

Mahatma Ghandi

Primary Commodity Prices		
Commodity Grouping	**% Change 1997–1998**	**% Change 1998–1999**
oil	−32.1	27.7
food (coffee, rice, sugar, fruits)	−12.7	−12.4
metals (copper, zinc, aluminum)	−16.3	−8.7

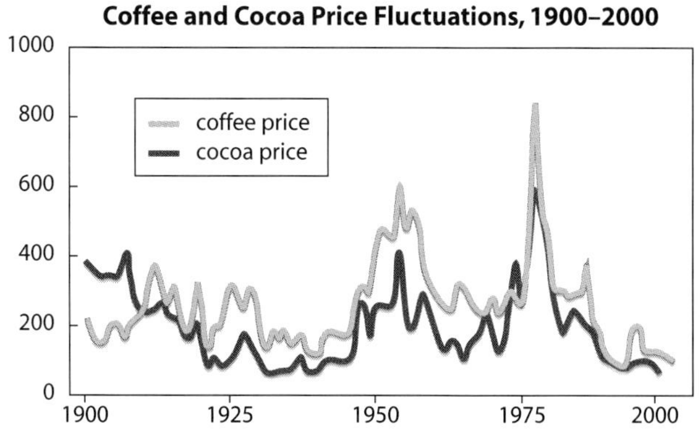

Coffee and Cocoa Price Fluctuations, 1900–2000

coffee price
cocoa price

adapted from Angus Deaton, *Commodity Prices and Growth in Africa*, vol. 13, no. 3, Summer 1999

FIGURE 3.24 Most developing countries are dependent on commodity exports for income. Real prices cannot rise as long as there is an unlimited supply of labour at subsistence wages. Savings resulting from technological advances on plantations and at refineries benefit consumers in industrialized countries.

WTO rules, countries are not allowed trade barriers to protect domestic agriculture and poor farmers.

 See Chapter 9 for more information about the world's food supply.

FIGURE 3.25 Free-trade zones in developing countries, such as the Jelepang free zone in Malaysia, employ mostly young women who make a fraction of the wages of western workers, assembling a wide range of products from IBM computers to GAP clothing.

❝ You don't need a doctorate in economics to know that when you have got 60 or more countries in the South all trying to export the same thing, prices in turn are going to plummet. ❞
South Movement, an NGO begun at La Trobe University, Australia

FACT FILE

Countries of the Middle East and Africa have 15% of the world's population but receive less than 4% of the total investment flow to developing countries.

Protesting the Status Quo

Trade and financial issues have become an international battle in the arena of public opinion. The wealthy elite and wealthy countries tend to see globalization in a more positive light. Proponents of economic growth and current trade rules claim that free trade and global market mechanisms work to the advantage of poor countries; that their problems are exacerbated by conditions in their own governments, societies, and economies, and that trade is better than aid. Others claim that it is not globalization itself that is the problem, but the effects on people and ecosystems of the inequities built into the global economic system; that trade, even free trade, is fine as long as it is fair trade. According to the NGO Oxfam, economic growth has the potential to reduce poverty if it results in more equal income distribution. East Asia is the only part of the world that is expected to meet UN and World Bank goals for reducing poverty by 2015 as policies there related to literacy, health, and access to productive resources result in a more equitable distribution of wealth. On the other hand, economic growth in Latin America and most of Africa has not been transformed into poverty reduction. Oxfam encourages governments to create the conditions in which poor people can work their way out of poverty, contributing to the wealth of their community and country along the way.

FACT FILE

The developing countries' share of world trade increased from 2.5% in 1970 to 3% in 2000, when the 48 poorest countries in the world accounted for 0.04% of world trade.

UK Department for International Development

FACT FILE

The UN's *Human Development Report, 1999* reported that the assets of the top three billionaires in the world are greater than the combined GDP of the least developed countries with a population of more than 600 million.

 See Chapter 14 for more information about solving the problems of poverty.

The amount of private and corporate money flowing to developing countries in the form of investments and loans grew from US$44 billion in 1990 to US$256 billion in 1997. Most of the trade and investments, however, occur among wealthy industrialized countries. Sudden reversals of private capital can create chain reactions that leave another region in financial crisis such as the Asian crisis where the economies of countries such as Indonesia, Thailand, Korea, Malaysia, and the Philippines collapsed in 1997.

Speculation on currency markets results in capital flows around the world that on a daily basis reach values twice as high as those for world trade. Investors and global banks gamble as they play bond and currency markets, making profits as currencies and interest rates fluctuate minute by minute. Most of the exchange of money is based on nothing real—there is no actual exchange of goods or services. In 1980, about 80% of the exchange of money around the world was based on the real exchange of goods and services, while 20% was speculative. By 2000, only 2% of the transactions were real and 98% speculative, and untouchable by any government. Some people and even governments, including that of Canada, have suggested a tax of less than 0.5% on speculative foreign exchange activity as a way of collecting funds for basic environmental and human needs. This is known as the **Tobin tax**, named after James Tobin, the Nobel-laureate economist from Yale University who developed the concept.

There is growing resistance to domination by these global economic institutions. For example, Guyana and several other countries have rejected structural adjustment programs that the IMF tried to impose that would result in less money for education and health care, rapid resource extraction, the exploitation of poorly paid non-union workers, and the growth of more cash crops for export to wealthy nations. They have developed alternative programs that focus on local and national solutions that reflect the needs of the majority of the population more than those of the elite groups in society and that balance their debt repayment with social needs such as food security.

Recently, developing countries, led by large economies such as South Africa, Brazil, and India have begun to exert more of the power of their sheer numbers at the WTO and in the formation of alliances. They

FACT FILE

In the decade of the 1990s, Latin American exports to Europe grew 29% while European exports to Latin America grew 164%.

FACT FILE

Senegal opened its markets by cutting industrial tariffs by almost 50% as required by the WTO rules, resulting in a loss of more than 30% of all manufacturing jobs in the country.

" When we talk about trade, we often focus on who is getting richer and who is getting poorer. But there is another divide at play: which countries are presented as diverse, complicated political landscapes where citizens have a range of divergent views and which countries seem to speak on the world stage in an ideological monotone. "

Naomi Klein, journalist, author, No Logo

FIGURE 3.26 Protests against the effects of globalization and for fairer trade are not found just in developed countries. Hundreds of thousands of Indian farmers joined a demonstration in New Delhi against the potential loss of their livelihoods due to current WTO rules that would encourage opening India's agricultural markets to free trade with developed countries.

have won some concessions, including clarifying WTO agreements on protection of intellectual property, the suspension of drug patents in case of a public health emergency, and postponement of discussion on issues relating to international investment and competition.

India threatened to walk out of the WTO talks in Doha, Qatar, in November 2001 when the EU insisted on including new and complex issues of concern. Many developing countries have argued that there are a number of clauses from previous WTO agreements that would benefit them that have never been implemented. Adding new issues would overload the agenda and ignore unfinished business.

The Group of 77

The Group of 77 is an alliance of developing countries that has begun to meet and work together to form a common front with greater collective power to negotiate more meaningful and effective trade policies at the WTO. While they support the idea of a global multilateral trading system as essential for both economic development and the eradication of poverty, they are beginning to make more effective demands for a more equitable share in global prosperity. The following statements are excerpts from declarations made by the Group of 77 and China to the WTO in meetings held in November 2001 and February 2002:

- We note that the developing countries have identified 104 implementation issues like trade and debt, and trade and transfer of technology, which emanate from the inadequate or faulty implementation of agreements. The establishment of mechanisms to meaningfully address these issues, which are of utmost concern to developing countries, should be urgently considered.
- We note with deep concern the substantial lag in the participation of developing countries in the trade in services.
- We reaffirm that the International Labour Organization (ILO) is the competent body to set and deal with all issues relating to labour standards. We, therefore, firmly oppose any linkage between trade and labour standards. We are also against the use of environmental standards as a new form of protectionism. We believe that issues relating to such standards should be dealt with by the competent international organizations and not the WTO.
- Developing countries cannot allow development agendas to be determined by interested parties in the North.

INTERACT

1. Identify several trends related to changes in the global economic power structure.
2. a) Identify at least six international trade concerns of developing countries.
   b) Make a prediction of how effectively these concerns will be met in the coming years.
3. Explain why commodity prices remain low and evaluate the effects of this trend on developing countries.

CASE STUDY

The Pan-African Movement

Pan-Africanism has been a movement since the end of the nineteenth century but, as African leaders realize that their states are not sustainable under the current poverty and conflict, the movement is growing. The Organization of African Unity (OAU) was formed in 1963 to help bring about the end of colonialism in Africa and to encourage unity among African nations. In March 2001 African heads of state, led by the leaders of South Africa, Egypt, Congo, and Ethiopia, replaced the OAU with the African Union, a Pan-African organization of united African states. The organization will have a continental parliament, court, and central bank to promote its principles. African leaders have pledged to use regional and co-operative mechanisms to act individually and collectively to:

- eradicate poverty and promote sustainable growth and development;
- foster active participation in the global economy;
- work with the international community to create better conditions for foreign investment and economic growth;
- develop infrastructure, education, health, agriculture, and information and communications technology;
- commit to good governance, democracy, and human rights, including gender equality;
- use intervention to resolve situations of conflict and political instability;
- use African private sector financing to foster development.

The most pressing concerns for 2002 were HIV/AIDS, transborder water issues, immigration within the African Union, and the impact on human rights of guerrilla-based liberation fronts in several countries. For the union to work effectively, power will need to be transferred down to local communities, enhancing real participatory democracy as well as upward to the continental administration. The rise of a large, well-organized civil society in Africa will help with these challenging goals and connect ordinary Africans with continent-wide policies. Full democracy and economic viability are still a long way off.

> " Unity will not make us rich, but it can make it difficult for Africa and the African peoples to be disregarded and humiliated. It will increase the effectiveness of the decisions we make and try to implement for our development. "
>
> *Julius Nyerere, former president of Tanzania and long-term leader of Pan-Africanism*

FIGURE 3.27 Casablanca, Morocco, reflects modern development and relative prosperity on the African continent.

excerpt from

"Impact of Angels"

by Tajudeen Abdul-Raheem, General Secretary of the
Pan-African Movement
in *New Internationalist*
August 2000, pp. 20–21

"In the last few years, international non-governmental organizations (NGOs) have become part of the landscape of Africa … with their Land Cruisers, Land Rovers, Pajeros, and other assorted four-wheel drives equipped with radio phones and advertising their endless projects.

So pervasive is their presence that there is virtually not a single district in most parts of Africa that does not have some form of contact with them. They come as private organizations, development agencies, religious groups, and so on. What unites them is that they are controlled, financed, and executively staffed by Europeans and North Americans. Wealth and direct or indirect backing from their governments put them above local community groups and NGOs in their host countries. …

No doubt many are involved in the charity business out of moral and political commitment. But it is also true that there are many who are doing it only for career purposes. Our misery is their job. If you are a disaster manager, what will you do if there are no more disasters? …

A typical case was that of post-genocide Rwandese refugees in former Zaire, Tanzania, and Burundi. The Ngara refugee settlement became the second biggest city in Tanzania after Dar-es-Salaam. Yet it was not under the control of the Government. It was controlled by NGOs. A trip there would have shocked any liberal conscience. Flags of different NGOs were hoisted in different compartments with the obvious suggestion to rival organizations: 'Keep off my refugees and I'll keep off yours.' Many of these NGOs did not wish the camps to be closed because their jobs and influence would go too. The pressure to make the camps habitable was turning them into permanent cities with amenities that the refugees were never going to get if they went back to their hills in Rwanda. …

The external brain drain from Africa is a dismal phenomenon that has been exacerbated by the economic crisis. … Thousands of Africans with university degrees or professional qualifications end up in dreary jobs in Europe or America, from cleaning the streets to working anti-social hours that would be refused by the natives. Meanwhile NGO employees almost all of them white, head back in the opposite direction. One might ask, if the NGOs genuinely wished to help, why could they not send African skills back to Africa with the same fantastic salaries and perks as the European experts?

But the internal brain drain is a less recognized problem. The few skilled people left behind in Africa are tempted away from public institutions by the NGOs who can afford to pay ten times what governments can afford. … Go to any university in Africa and you will find that the professors who are doing well are those with access to the foreign NGO community as consultants and researchers. …

The economic power of NGOs is precipitating a cultural crisis that is now very acute. It is not just that the colonial mentality is back in the shape of white expatriates treated as 'bosses' (and many of them are literally bosses to numerous domestic servants). But for African countries that already suffer from the debilitating effect of inferiority complexes brought about by slavery and colonialism, these new relations cannot do much for our collective morale, esteem and confidence. …

The African Unity agenda remains the only basis upon which Africans can reclaim their dignity and become equal partners with the rest of humanity. It is not that Africa does not need the help but at the moment it is too weak to determine where this help should be and how it should be used."

Critical Analysis

1. Outline the negative impacts of NGOs that the author describes.
2. a) Why is this view of NGOs not commonly heard in Canada?
   b) Explain the more typical Canadian view of the role of NGOs in Africa and other developing parts of the world.
3. Create a plan that the executive of a Canadian NGO could implement to avoid negative impact on African people and communities.
4. What is the author's idea for the best solution to the serious issues facing Africa?

Web Links

- World development indicators: <www.world-bank.org/data/wdi2000/index.htm>
- Third World Network: <www.twnside.org>
- Basel Action Network (a report card on which countries have ratified selected UN treaties): <www.ban.org>
- The Group of 77 developing countries: <www.G77.org>
- The Canadian Democracy and Corporate Accountability Commission: <www.corporate-accountability.ca>
- The Commission on Global Governance and Reforming the UN: <www.cgg.ch/welcome.html>
- International institutions and their policy decisions: <www.globalpolicy.org>
- South American alliance (links to many other alliances and trading blocs): <www.mercosur.org>
- Inter Parliamentary Union, Geneva, Switzerland: <www.ipu.org>

Related Issues

- Biopiracy and intellectual property rights
- Militarization of Space
- Impact of UN and U.S. economic sanctions in Iraq
- Geopolitics of water in the Middle East
- Who should control Antarctica?
- NAFTA and Chapter 11
- Canada–U.S. trade disputes
- The Global Trade Union Social Movement
- Child labour
- Environmental problems as a threat to national security

Analyse, Apply, and Interact

1. In your opinion, which is the best way to group countries to study world issues? Compare your "best" way to one other method of grouping countries.

2. What advantages does democracy as a form of government have for countries seeking to improve their level of development?

3. Explain how organizations such as an international court and regional alliances contribute to interdependence among the countries of the world.

4. From the perspective of developing countries, the rich, developed countries and TNCs hold tremendous geopolitical power. Identify three strategies that developing countries could use to counter the power held by others.

5. The first years of the twenty-first century have seen an enthusiasm to create a hemispheric free trade zone (FTAA) in the Americas. Based on your understanding of geopolitical relationships, what arguments might be made to support such a trading bloc and what arguments might be made to discourage it?

6. Using Internet sites that provide quotations, make a collection of quotations that express ideas about geopolitical power. Make up one statement to add to your collection that expresses your view of geopolitical power.

7. Conduct research to describe the structure, membership, and activities of an international economic alliance in Africa or Asia, such as the Organization of African Unity (OAU) or APEC.

8. Conduct research on a TNC to identify how it does and/or does not practise corporate social and environmental responsibility in the parts of the world in which it does business. In your report on the corporation, suggest changes that it might make in its practices and policies.

9. Suppose you wanted to take action to support the development of democracy in African countries such as Zimbabwe or Libya. Identify three organizations that you might contact to get information and ideas. Identify one action that you could take in your local area to support the development of democracy in Africa.

10. Prepare a case study of the geopolitical situation of a country of your choice. Describe the regional and global connections of that country and identify the groups that hold power in that country. Describe problems of a geopolitical nature that the country is struggling with. Make a prediction for the future that outlines your view of the geopolitical situation over the next five years.

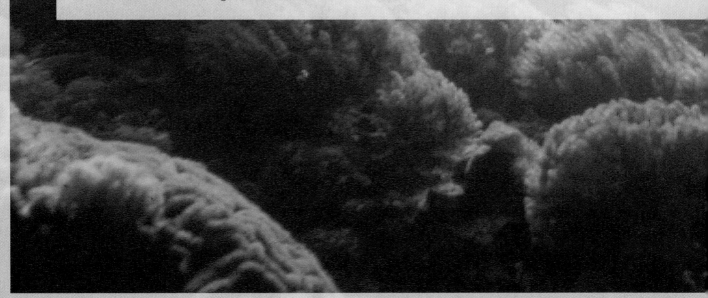

Chapter 4: Planetary Systems—Global Connections

By the end of this chapter, you will:

- explain the complex nature of the earth's natural and human systems;

- identify ways in which countries and regions of the world are becoming increasingly interdependent;

- analyse the distribution of the world's major biomes and determine the reasons for the observed patterns;

- compare the productivity and biodiversity of selected ecosystems;

- analyse selected global trends and evaluate their effects on people and environments at the local, national, and global level;

- explain the interactive nature of selected natural and human systems;

- identify current global sustainability issues and environmental threats;

- demonstrate an understanding of the technologies used in the analysis and synthesis of geographic data;

- describe biases that may inform different viewpoints and perspectives on geographic issues;

- explain why it is difficult to make accurate predictions relating to human use of the earth and its resources, and why some predictions are more (or less) accurate than others.

ALL IS NOT AS IT SEEMS

The world you live in is an astoundingly complex place. Although Earth may seem stable underfoot, you are spinning on an oblate spheroid object at 30 km a second. You are one of more than six billion passengers on this "spaceship Earth" on its journey around the sun. You are an individual, but you are also a community of countless organisms containing trillions of cells and quadrillions of bacteria and parasitic organisms, which see you as a "living pantry." You are just one member of one of the millions of species that makes up the thin layer of life known as the global biosphere. The biosphere is the largest **ecosystem**, encompassing the whole planet. It consists of biodiversity (all forms of life) and the ecological processes that cause complicated interactions among life forms (species) and between species and their environments.

FIGURE 4.1 Earth can be viewed as a spaceship hurtling through space with a crew of six billion and growing. It carries all the oxygen, food, and resources we need to survive, but there is no home base to return to for additional provisions, repairs, or for disposal of our wastes. Who is at the controls of spaceship Earth?

A WORLD OF CONNECTIONS

Global interdependence consists of a network of links, interactions, and relationships that encircle our world like an intricate spider's web. What do children in Mexico have to do with farmers in Great Britain and the nuclear accident in Chernobyl in 1986? What does the Gobi Desert in Mongolia have to do with you in the spring allergy season?

A catastrophic explosion at a nuclear power plant in Chernobyl, Ukraine, in April 1986 resulted in the release of large amounts of toxic radioactive material into the air, killing many people, affecting soil, vegetation, water, and buildings, and causing many cases of cancer. The effects of this accident will be felt for many years to come. Furthermore, the impact was not restricted to Europe. The radioactive material spread throughout Europe via wind currents, settling on farmers' fields in Great Britain. Dairy cattle feeding on affected grass produced milk contaminated with radioactive cesium. The milk, considered unfit for human consumption, was supposed to be destroyed, but unscrupulous business interests sold some of it as powdered milk. More than 2000 t of the contaminated milk was transported across the Atlantic Ocean to Mexico, where it was distributed to children, making them ill.

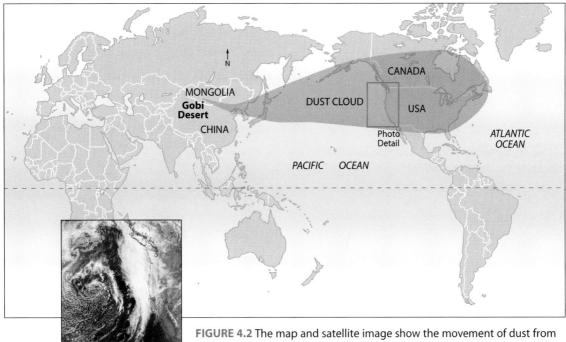

FIGURE 4.2 The map and satellite image show the movement of dust from Mongolia to eastern North America where it acts as an irritant. Dust storms can also serve a beneficial purpose as they carry nutrients like iron to plants and animals living in the oceans and rain forests.

Perhaps you know someone who is affected by spring allergies. In April 2001, a large sand and dust storm in the Gobi Desert was tracked by satellite as it moved east across China, then the Atlantic Ocean and North America. The dust cloud was clearly visible on satellite images and added to the springtime irritation of people far away. There are countless incidents involving interactions similar to these that illustrate the amazing web of global interconnections among human and natural **systems**.

The Complex Nature of Ecosystems

Ecosystems are communities of interacting organisms (**biotic** or living things) and the natural environment (**abiotic** or non-living) in which they live. They can be as small as a single leaf or as large as the whole planet. Large-scale physical processes on Earth's surface (e.g., **jet streams** in the atmosphere, the ring of earthquake and volcanic activity around the Pacific Ocean known as the Ring of Fire) as well as smaller local processes (e.g., riverbank flooding) combine to form diverse landscapes. These landscapes are important abiotic components

of ecosystems that provide a fascinating spatial distribution of different environments or habitats for people and other species (see Figures 4.7 and 4.8).

Ecosystems are constantly changing, dynamic systems powered by solar energy. Their components are intricately woven together in a complex set of relationships, including energy flow and nutrient cycles. Ecosystems help to recycle chemicals needed by living things to survive, recycle waste products, control pests within the system, and offer a pool of resources for all species to use.

Species within ecosystems also exert an influence on their natural environment. Some species, called **keystone species**, such as the prairie dogs of the Prairie grasslands, seem to play a more significant role in maintaining a balance. Other **indicator species**, such as the disappearing frogs of southern Ontario, appear to indicate trouble.

One crucial component of ecosystems is insects and micro-organisms. Insects are the most numerous, diverse, and successful species. Their **biomass** (total weight) outweighs that of all other species, including people, forests, and whales. Insects are vital to the health of our ecosystems and, although most insects are of great benefit to people, we have developed thousands of chemical **pesticides** to kill off those insects we consider detrimental to our activities. In the process, we disrupt food chains and harm other species, including birds, mammals, and fish.

 See Chapters 9 and 16 for more information about chemical pesticides.

FIGURE 4.3

Earth Components	
Basic Spheres	**Some Results of Human Impact**
Atmosphere	ozone depletion air pollution climate change
Biosphere	biodiversity loss deforestation desertification
Lithosphere	soil degradation weathering by polluted water or air toxic waste on land
Hydrosphere	biodiversity loss ocean and fresh water pollution wetland loss

FIGURE 4.4 The various "spheres" that form Earth's life-support systems are necessary for life. Most species use them as sources of raw materials and places to dispose of wastes. Only humans produce wastes that are not recycled through natural processes.

Ecosystems vary in how resilient they are to the effects of natural environmental changes such as fires or volcanic eruptions and to the subtle yet more dramatic effects of human impact. A greater diversity of species within an ecosystem usually indicates increased interconnections and more stability. Changes to one part of an ecosystem will affect other parts or may even affect the whole ecosystem. Changes in one ecosystem may affect other ecosystems.

FACT FILE

Scientists, unsure if their findings were typical of all Prairie ecosystems, discovered more than 2.5 billion viruses in one sample of water in a Saskatchewan dugout (a large excavation used to hold water collected from the spring thaw and from rainfall).

INTERACT

1. Compile a list of products derived from natural resources that you would use in a typical day. Select three and trace each one back to its original place within an ecosystem.
2. On an outline map of the world, label the places affected by the incident after the April 1986 Chernobyl nuclear explosion. Add flow arrows and appropriate labels, indicating the sequence of events. Choose an appropriate title for your map.
3. With a partner or in a small group, identify a few events or situations involving global interactions similar to the ones outlined so far. Add one of the situations of your choice to your world map from Question 2.
4. Refer to a map of wind patterns in an atlas and identify countries that would cause transboundary pollution in Canada.
5. Conduct research and refer to an atlas to identify some distant sources of pollution that potentially affect your own community.
6. Investigate to find out why amphibians such as frogs are considered indicator species.

DIVIDING THE LANDSCAPE

Biomes

People create regions to help them interpret Earth's complexities. **Biomes** are regions encompassing groups of interrelated ecosystems on a global scale. They cover large areas of Earth's terrestrial or marine surface. The location on Earth of particular biomes is largely determined by the climate of a region, but other factors also come into play (e.g., altitude, global atmospheric and oceanic circulation patterns, landforms, geology, proximity to bodies of water, availability of sunlight, salinity of soil or water). Combinations of climate and geology produce **biogeoclimatic** zones of distinctive types of vegetation, which in turn interact with the soil, providing habitat for plants and animals. **Biogeography** is the study of the geographic distribution of organisms.

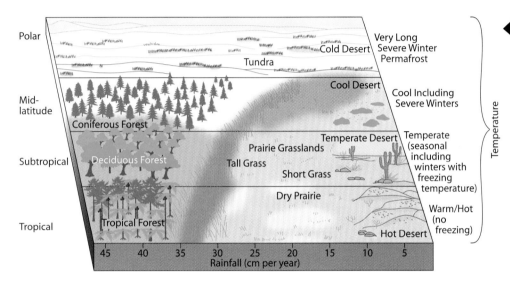

FIGURE 4.5 Combinations of precipitation and temperature determine the type of terrestrial biome or major ecosystem found in a region.

adapted from Bernard J. Nebel, *Environmental Science: The Way the World Works*, third edition, Prentice-Hall, Inc., 1990, p. 38

66 Thinking, planning and acting in the context of ecosystems is essential for today's environmental management and sustainability issues. 99
Environment Canada

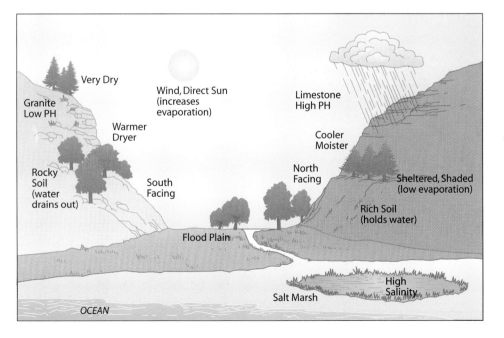

FIGURE 4.6 Local factors like wind patterns, slope gradient, bedrock type, and salinity create different microclimates and environments.

adapted from Bernard J. Nebel, *Environmental Science: The Way the World Works*, third edition, Prentice-Hall, Inc., 1990, p. 39

Map of Global Biomes

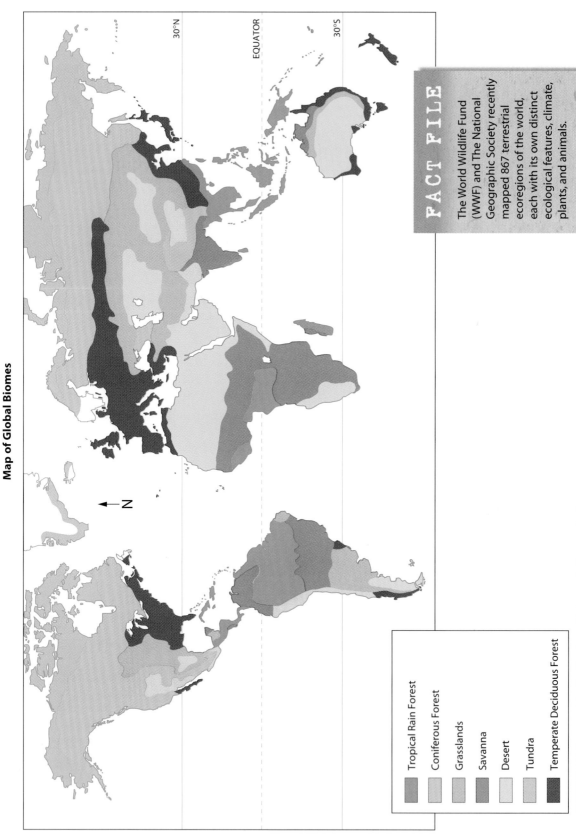

FACT FILE

The World Wildlife Fund (WWF) and The National Geographic Society recently mapped 867 terrestrial ecoregions of the world, each with its own distinct ecological features, climate, plants, and animals.

30°N

EQUATOR

30°S

N

Tropical Rain Forest
Coniferous Forest
Grasslands
Savanna
Desert
Tundra
Temperate Deciduous Forest

FIGURE 4.7 Geographic distribution of biomes follows a similar pattern to that of latitude, which affects climate.

Ecozones

"Ecozones" is the name given by geographers to ecosystems in Canada. They are similar to biomes although they cover smaller geographic areas. Because the unique combination of climate, soils, vegetation, wildlife, and geology, as well as modifications by humans, varies so significantly from place to place within them, the 15 terrestrial and 5 marine ecozones have been divided into 194 ecoregions and further subdivided into 1020 ecodistricts.

Bioregions

Another, more local, community-based framework for studying ecosystems, natural processes, and natural–human interactions is the **bioregion**. This is a geographic region of land and water whose boundaries are defined by either part or all of an ecosystem as well as the human community involved in using and managing the ecosystem in which it is situated. A bioregion is large enough to support important ecological processes like nutrient and waste recycling and to provide habitat for biological communities and keystone species. It is small enough for people who live there to consider it their home and worth looking after. It usually has a unique cultural identity and members of the community, local government, and business interests share responsibility for conservation, restoration, and planning and implementing sustainable management of its natural resources. A bioregion is often a small river **watershed**.

Canada's Terrestrial Ecozones

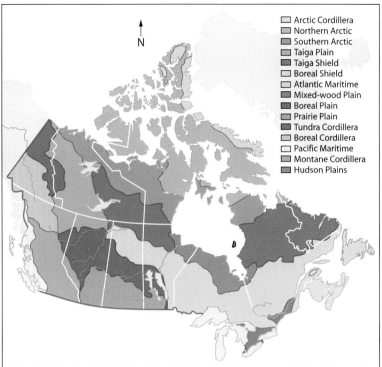

- ☐ Arctic Cordillera
- ☐ Northern Arctic
- ☐ Southern Arctic
- ☐ Taiga Plain
- ☐ Taiga Shield
- ☐ Boreal Shield
- ☐ Atlantic Maritime
- ☐ Mixed-wood Plain
- ☐ Boreal Plain
- ☐ Prairie Plain
- ☐ Tundra Cordillera
- ☐ Boreal Cordillera
- ☐ Pacific Maritime
- ☐ Montane Cordillera
- ☐ Hudson Plains

FIGURE 4.8

INTERACT

1. Explain why geographers divide Earth up into so many different regions when studying natural systems.
2. Draw a sketch map of the river watershed in which you live. Locate and label on the map major human and natural features, including arrows to show direction of water flow.
3. Create an interconnections chart or graphic organizer to illustrate how abiotic factors have helped to determine the characteristics of the ecozone in which you live.

HOW PRODUCTIVE ARE ECOSYSTEMS?

Biomes have different rates of productivity driven by **photosynthesis**. All plants need sunlight, carbon dioxide, water, and soil nutrients for photosynthesis, which is dependent on temperature, moisture, and nutrient availability. It is measured as the rate of formation of new biological material or the amount of energy produced per unit of Earth's surface over a period of time such as a year.

FIGURE 4.9 On a satellite image of global primary productivity, rain forests and other more productive biomes appear as dark green while deserts are yellow. Concentration of phytoplankton, an indicator of marine productivity, shows up as dark blue for high productivity and lighter blue for low. Patterns of diversity generally show a latitudinal gradient, with increasing diversity moving from the poles to the equator where warm climates, a greater supply of solar energy, and longer periods of time without disturbance from glaciation allow more biomass to be produced.

Most recent estimates of global **primary productivity** for terrestrial ecosystems are 90 to 120 × 1 000 000 000 tonnes of dry weight per year and 50 to 60 × 1 000 000 000 tonnes per year in the oceans. The more productive an ecosystem is, the more life it can support per unit area.

Because this primary biological production sustains all life on Earth, maintaining this productivity is the key to sustainability. **Sustainability** means that an ecosystem is able to maintain vital ecological processes and functions, biodiversity, and productivity indefinitely into the future. The world's human population is currently consuming about 40% of the primary production of Earth's ecosystems. If the world's population were to double, as some estimates predict, by 2050, people would use up all the biological material produced each year. Because the biological processes of Earth cannot sustain this level of consumption, the health of the environment and the quality of life for people are at risk.

 See Chapter 6 for more information about the carbon cycle and global climate change.

FIGURE 4.10 Local patterns are often superimposed on global patterns of productivity. The ocean around Antarctica is, uniquely, a very productive marine ecosystem. The Antarctic circumpolar current brings nutrient-rich water to the surface, which supports phytoplankton, the major food source for krill, a shrimplike organism that is food for many species of fish, birds, seals, and whales.

FIGURE 4.11 Tropical rain forests have the greatest diversity of species and are the most productive terrestrial ecosystem.

FIGURE 4.12 Oceans, which are not very productive, cover two-thirds of Earth's surface yet account for only one-third of Earth's total productivity. Coral reefs appear to be the most productive ecosystems in the marine world and are comprised of over 1000 species of reef-building corals, over 5000 species of fish, and many more species of invertebrates. In marine ecosystems, productivity is affected by sunlight, which penetrates only a few metres into the water, and by the amount and availability of nutrients like nitrogen.

FIGURE 4.13 Species diversity does not always indicate biological productivity or ecosystem resilience. For example, spartina is the only main plant species in coastal salt marshes that is responsible for the ecosystem's primary productivity. Yet, there is no evidence that salt marshes are in danger of extinction.

❝The dynamics of terrestrial ecosystems depend on the interactions between a variety of **biogeochemical cycles**, particularly the carbon cycle, the nutrient cycles, and the circulation of water—all of which may be modified indirectly by climate change and by direct human actions. ❞
Intergovernmental Panel on Climate Change, UNEP report 2000

INTERACT

1. In a sentence or two, explain how ecosystem productivity, resilience, and sustainability are connected.
2. Evaluate the significance to humans of the wide range in productivity from one biome to another.
3. Compare the patterns that appear on the world maps in Figure 4.7, **Map of Global Biomes**, and Figure 4.9, **Satellite Map of Global Primary Productivity**. What factors might account for similarities and differences in the patterns?

WHAT IS A SYSTEM?

Thinking about systems is at the heart of contemporary geography. It helps us understand how planet Earth actually works. It is useful to think in terms of systems because we are surrounded by them. We use the word "system" to describe something that is made up of different kinds of parts that join together to form an interconnected whole. With a system, the whole is more than the sum of its parts (synergy). A car is a system. Individually, the parts such as the steering wheel, brakes, cylinders, windshield wipers, and battery will not get you very far. However, joined together as parts of an interconnected whole, the car takes you places. It has characteristics that are qualitatively different from the characteristics of each part. No part of the car goes 20 km per litre of gasoline or can take you up a steep hill. Only the car as a functioning whole system can do these things.

Natural Systems

Natural systems include river or drainage systems, atmospheric and ocean circulation, energy and nutrient cycles, and the mosaic of countless ecosystems on Earth's surface.

FIGURE 4.14 Natural systems provide us with everything we need but can be hazardous. The devastating earthquake in January 2001 in the Gujarat region of India, the second deadliest in that country's recorded history, left 19 727 people dead and 600 000 people homeless. It took three months for communications, power, and transportation to return to near normal.

Characteristics of Natural Systems

Natural systems:

- support life;
- are driven by a constant flow of solar energy;
- are interconnected in a vast network of dynamic relationships;
- display synergy;
- operate in the atmosphere, hydrosphere, lithosphere, and biosphere;
- achieve stability through their linkages and can be quite resilient despite human intervention;
- contain organisms, including humans that feed on flows of energy and resources;
- recycle wastes through co-operation—a closed loop of cyclic changes;
- are somewhat self-regulating and seek balance and equilibrium;
- have boundaries and limits that may be difficult to identify;
- can be affected by external events and influences;
- operate on time lines of thousands or millions of years;
- are not well-understood by humans.

FIGURE 4.15

Human Systems

Human systems include human settlements, transportation and communication systems, patterns and networks of economic interdependence such as trade, and social interactions. They each have a profound influence on the natural systems they interact with and on each other. As population increases and technology changes, the number and speed of interactions increases. There are more and more people, organizations, and machines all linked in some way to one another. Human systems are becoming increasingly complex with many interdependent links to one another.

Because of **synergy**, the combined effect of changes in some parts of a system may be greater than the sum of their individual effects. This can make accurate predictions very difficult. Fisheries scientists were unable to predict that in the early 1990s the Atlantic cod fishery would collapse due to several interacting factors that are still not clearly understood. One factor was overfishing—which left 30 000 fishers dependent on government welfare and severely affected the economy of 700 communities in Newfoundland alone.

Examining and learning more about the incredible ways in which systems interact may help us manage an increasingly complex world and solve some of the problems and issues facing us.

Because humans interact differently with ecosystems in various regions of the world, the effects on natural systems may be felt differently by people living in different places. Usually, the poor suffer the most when ecosystems are damaged because they depend on them more for survival and may lack the capacity to deal with resulting problems. For example, the effect of drought in the Sahara Desert region may have a different impact on people living there, than on those experiencing drought in the southern United States.

c) forestry

d) agriculture

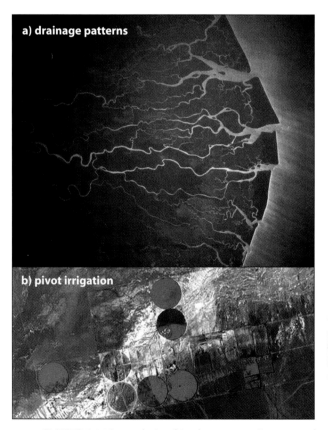

a) drainage patterns

b) pivot irrigation

INTERACT

1. Study the photographs in Figure 4.16 and identify the relationships you see among various systems.
2. Construct a diagram that traces the water you drink from precipitation to your tap. Shade natural systems and human systems in two different colours.

FIGURE 4.16 Interrelationships between various natural systems and between natural systems and human systems shape many patterns that we can see on Earth's surface. In remote sensing analysis, many satellite images do not show natural colour. In image b), the crops grown in the irrigated circles are shown in red, as the infrared part of the electromagnetic spectrum is very responsive to the type, health, and density of vegetation. Healthy plants have a high reflectivity of infrared light.

HUMAN IMPRINTS

If you fly from one end of Canada to the other on a clear day, you will see below you a continuous stretch of the human "footprint" on the land. In the past century especially, we have changed natural ecosystems so significantly that environments such as croplands, pastures, forest plantations, and cities are now considered to be anthropogenic or managed ecosystems. Biodiversity is lower in these systems, which support fewer **indigenous species**. Other species such as rats, mice, squirrels, raccoons, and domestic dogs and cats that thrive in cities may be more numerous.

Are Life-Support Systems at Risk?

People as well as all other living species depend on the natural systems within the biosphere's thin layer of life for survival. We must satisfy our need for air, water, food, shelter, clothing, energy, and materials to make goods. These things are intricately linked and we cannot do without them. For example, we cannot have food without water. In meeting our needs, humans use knowledge, ingenuity, and technology, and often, in ignorance or carelessness, modify natural systems and spaces. Farming,

FIGURE 4.18 Boardwalks are used at this wilderness resort in Alaska because footprints made in the fragile tundra soil and vegetation take hundreds of years to disappear.

FIGURE 4.19 An **anthropogenic ecosystem.** If a forest ecosystem is diminished by logging or replaced with reforestation using a single, harvestable tree species, ecosystem processes like water and nutrient recycling are adversely affected. More water is lost as run-off during heavy precipitation, or water flow may be reduced in a dry season. Soil erosion, landslides, and significant loss of species diversity result. A tree farm is not the same as a natural forest.

FIGURE 4.17 Agricultural patterns on the land in Big Beaver, Saskatchewan.

Global Trends and Pressures	Facts and Predictions for the Future
Rapidly expanding global economy	The global economy grew seven times between 1950 and 2000.
Population growth	Global population grew to six billion people from 1980 to 2000, an increase of 30%, and is predicted to reach between 9 and 14 billion by 2050.
Increasing energy consumption	Energy use per person has risen from about 70 kcal. per day in 1900 to over 300 kcal. per day in 2000.
Increasing demand for grain crops like wheat, rice, and maize	The demand is predicted to grow by 40% by 2020.
Increasing demand for water for industrial, agricultural, and daily domestic use	We use over 50% of Earth's freshwater run-off, depleting aquatic ecosystems. By 2025, two-thirds of the world's population will not have enough fresh water.
Increasing demand for wood for fuel and manufactured products	The demand is likely to double by 2020.
Increasing impact on the biosphere	From 1900 to 2050, human impact on the environment will have increased over 40 times, most of it occurring in the twenty-first century.

FIGURE 4.20

building homes and cities, creating jobs, acquiring resources such as minerals and forests, and disposing of our wastes have direct and indirect impacts on natural systems. Huge amounts of energy are used to change natural ecosystems into farmland and to manage farmland or timber plantations, to process and package food and goods, and to move goods from place to place. Ultimately, all economic development depends on Earth's natural resource base.

Based on objective interpretations of trends in environmental quality, many scientists believe that Earth's life-support systems are at risk, given current levels of resource exploitation, consumption, and population growth. Global pressures on ecosystems have caused people to overexploit them. Economic and political factors that influence what people, especially in the developed world, consume and from where in the world it comes encourage us to look for short-term gain rather than long-term stewardship.

Other social, economic, and political factors put human pressure on ecosystems. Each of these factors gives rise to serious circumstances:
- Increasing consumption habits as demand for goods and services continues to rise
- More widespread use of technology
- Dependence on oil, gas, and other fossil fuels

FACT FILE

Humans are the only species to grow continually in number and the only species to contaminate knowingly their source of life—air, water, and soil.

"Worldwide, governments spend about US$700 billion a year subsidizing environmentally unsound practices in the use of water, agriculture, energy, and transport...."

World Resources Institute, 2000

- Increasing emissions of CO_2 from cars and industries "hooked" on fossil fuels and the continuation of climate change
- Increasing emissions of nitrogen from agricultural practices and the burning of fossil fuels, affecting the balance of nutrients in many ecosystems
- The price paid for natural resources such as water or wood do not reflect the true cost to the environment of harvesting them, creating a tendency to overuse
- Armed conflict
- Government corruption
- Poverty forces some people to imperil the ecosystems on which they depend
- Loss of land tenure, particularly for rural poor in developing countries
- Greed, enterprise, ignorance, and inattention cause disregard for the natural limits that sustain ecosystems
- Lack of awareness and information about how natural and human systems interact
- Failure at all levels (from farmers to government decision makers) to make good use of available knowledge

FACT FILE

Between 1950 and 1990, the world volume of air transport increased over 100 times.

All of Earth's biomes have been affected to some degree by people, and there is no true "wilderness" left on the planet that is completely untouched by human activity. Transboundary pollution of heavy metals and **organochlorine chemicals** such as dioxins and chlordane, found in pesticides or industrial wastes, are a serious threat to Arctic peoples and other species. These chemicals, which

" The United Nations Development Programme, the United Nations Environment Programme, the World Bank, and the World Resources Institute reconfirm their commitment to making the viability of the world's ecosystems a critical development priority for the 21st century. "

World Resources Institute, 2000

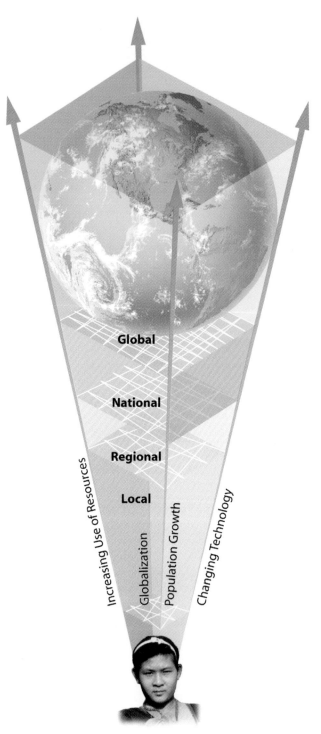

FIGURE 4.21 As one moves from the local to the global scale, the increasing links between human and natural systems create an incomprehensibly intricate web of interconnections.

make their way north through atmospheric and marine circulation patterns, bioaccumulate and become concentrated as they move up the Arctic food chain into the bodies of people and other top carnivore species such as polar bears. Scientists have even found trash in the most remote frontiers of the planet, such as empty cans of Coca-Cola under the Arctic ice.

FACT FILE

In the last 40 years of the twentieth century, global population doubled from three to six billion people while the number of kilometres travelled by people in all modes of motorized transport increased fivefold.

FIGURE 4.22 Because of high elevations, high snowfall, and cold temperatures, the Rockies, always thought to be pristine environments, have high levels of **persistent organic pollutants (POPs)** such as pesticides and industrial chemicals. The higher up the mountain scientists took their samples, the greater the level of pollutants that was found.

FIGURE 4.23 Garbage on Mount Everest (above) and empty fuel drums from World War II left in Iqaluit, Nunavut (right).

INTERACT

1. How do natural systems contribute to Canada's wealth?
2. Explain the statement, "A tree farm is not the same as a forest."
3. Do you agree that there is no wilderness left on planet Earth? Explain your answer.
4. Create an illustration that identifies changes in your local community resulting from human intervention and their causes.
5. List five arguments to support the view that Earth's life-support systems are at risk.

HAVE WE LOST OUR CONNECTIONS TO NATURE?

Despite our intimate dependence on Earth's natural systems, we are becoming more and more disconnected from them. How we interact with our environment gives rise to significant economic and political issues. Loss of **biodiversity**, global climate change, and conflict over unevenly distributed water resources affect people in developed and developing countries everywhere in the world. These issues provide us with the challenges of looking after our natural environment and using the resources it provides sustainably.

FIGURE 4. 24 Is there any better way to connect with nature? This tour, called "A Walk in the Clouds," takes nature buffs along a suspended walkway 20 m up in the treetops through 124 000 ha of mixed forest at Haliburton Forest near Algonquin Provincial Park.

excerpt from
The Ingenuity Gap
by Thomas Homer-Dixon
Knopf Canada, 2000

There is weirdness and wonder at both ends of nature's spatial spectrum, from the sky overhead to the soil below our feet. But in our modern cities we obscure the sky behind haze and light, and we pave over the soil. A wall of technology and its products now cuts us off from much of the universe around us. At the same time that we are altering our natural world one increment at a time, we are separating ourselves from this world. As a result, it seems less and less real, and we are less able to pick up the signals from our environment that could warn us of trouble; oblivious, we become yet more arrogant and sure of our powers. Arrogance distorts our ability to see which challenges around us really need our attention; and that, in turn, distorts the amount and kinds of ingenuity we supply.

Some skeptics might respond that it is simply not true that our ties to external reality are increasingly attenuated. Modern science and technology provide us with innumerable devices that allow us to probe and understand that external reality as never before and to communicate the results to specialists and the public. The Hubble space telescope extends our vision far into the universe, and electron microscopes allow us to investigate the biochemistry of soils. The Internet permits faster and more intensive dialogue among scientists about emerging ecological problems—like the disappearance of frogs. And the World Wide Web makes all this information far more accessible to the interested layman. In fact, these sceptics might conclude, humankind is more connected with non-human reality than ever before.

In many respects, these arguments are correct. But while our knowledge about the external world is undeniably greater and more widely available than ever before, it is still not reaching very many of us. Most of it is known only to particular interest groups and communities of specialists. And when it dribbles out of these communities, it usually goes no further than the intellectual elites of the wealthiest countries in the world, or is lost in the torrent of factoids distributed by popular media.… The everyday experience of a person living in industrialized countries or, more generally in the planet's megacities, barely touches on the natural world. On a day-to-day basis, most of us in rich countries are increasingly sealed within the hermetic and sometimes illusory world of the human-made, the human-scaled, and the human-imagined.

We are losing a sense of our place in the scheme of things; a sense of how strange the world is, and of the limits, ultimately, of our knowledge and control. We are losing the awe, the respect, and the recognition of mystery that remind us to be prudent.

Critical Analysis

1. Define the following terms used in the reading: "external reality," "attenuated," "factoids," "hermetic," "illusory," "prudent."
2. What credentials does the author have and what might his bias be?
3. What evidence does Thomas Homer-Dixon provide to assert that we are losing touch with the natural world?
4. How does he reply to sceptics who disagree with him?
5. What role has technology played in his argument?
6. Identify a point of view about technology that is missing.
7. Identify several global issues referred to in this reading.
8. Do you agree with Dr. Homer-Dixon that people are becoming increasingly disconnected from nature? Explain your answer.

PROFILE

Thomas Homer-Dixon

Thomas Homer-Dixon is an author and associate professor in the Department of Political Science at the University of Toronto. He is the director of the Peace and Conflict Studies Program. He is the author of many journal articles as well as books such as *Ecoviolence: Links among Environment, Population and Security* (Rowman and Littlefield, 1998); *Environment, Scarcity and Violence* (Princeton University Press, 1999); and *The*

Ingenuity Gap (Knopf Canada, 2000). He has travelled widely and is frequently asked to speak at universities such as Harvard and Princeton and to other diverse groups. In the late 1990s, Dr. Homer-Dixon was hired as a consultant on international relations and global environmental issues by senior officials in the Canadian and U.S. governments.

FIGURE 4.25

What Does This Have to Do with Me?

The dynamic links between natural and human systems have an impact on you. You should know ecosystems well. They are the forests where you hike, the lakes where you swim or get water, the beaches where you play, and the fields where you get your food. They are crucial to your survival. Consider the "rule of fours." You can survive about four minutes without oxygen, four hours without heat if your body is unprotected, four days without water, and four weeks without food.

Changes in the environment, such as the loss of global forests or shortages of fresh water, may seem far away, but the consequences can appear suddenly and be felt everywhere. As animal habitat shrinks, you may notice more wild animals, such as geese, coyotes, deer, or even bears, prowling in your backyard. If the environment in another part of the world becomes degraded, you will notice more reports of environmental refugees risking appalling conditions and putting their lives in jeopardy to try to reach the shores of asylum nations.

Severe storms such as tornadoes and the ice storm in Quebec in January 1998 can cause property damage. Your job prospects for the future may depend on the well-being of the global economy or continued supplies of natural resources. You and your family will likely pay more for clean, safe drinking water in the future. Are you planning to buy a sports utility vehicle (SUV)? Your choice of what and how much to buy has some reciprocal impact on another person, plant, animal, or place somewhere on the planet.

> **FACT FILE**
>
> Canadian consumers will have a choice of 77 different SUV models by 2006. Sales of the gas-guzzling vehicles were expected to rise 18% between 2001 and 2002.

On a Clear Day

Every time you drive a car you are adding to **smog** on a local scale and climate change on a global scale. A temperature inversion in the atmosphere can contribute to smog in the air you breathe. Smog is increasing and spreading across whole continents, forming a global haze. In parts of China, the brown air is so thick that it is difficult to see the smokestacks of the power plants and factories that produce the carbon dioxide, sulphur dioxide, nitric oxide, nitrogen dioxide, volatile organic compounds, **ozone**, and particles of soot that make up smog. Even what we consider wilderness has been affected. In recent summers, rural and "cottage country" regions of Ontario have experienced higher levels of ozone-laced smog than ever—as high as that in many cities.

> **FACT FILE**
>
> It takes 8500 kg of "stuff" from nature to make a 2-kg laptop computer.

 See Chapter 16 for more information about the environment and human health.

MAKE A DIFFERENCE

It All Adds Up

As a person in an industrialized country such as Canada, you use 80 tonnes of natural resources a year to produce what you use in goods and services. Each time you reduce, reuse, and recycle goods, or save water or energy, you will have a positive effect on patterns of environmental use. As an individual, your role may seem immeasurably small, but each act of consumption or conservation, when added to those of all others, has a cumulative and escalating effect. You are likely to experience the effects of ecosystem decline, whether water shortages or contamination or increased risks of some diseases like asthma and cancer due to environmental pollutants. At the same time, many people in their communities and in organizations are working to protect species, reduce damage to ecosystems or to manage them more sustainably, and to find solutions to problems and issues.

INTERACT

1. Explain the limitation of studying just one species within an ecosystem.
2. Use the World Wide Web to find the current "ecological footprint" of a typical Canadian. Compare this footprint to that of the average citizen in a developing country. Suggest factors to account for the significant difference between the two.

THE INFORMATION GAP

Scientists, geographers, and researchers know remarkably little about their home planet and its skeletal framework of ecosystems. We often study individual species instead of seeing ecosystems as part of a functioning whole, ignoring important interconnections. We lack the knowledge to accurately determine ecosystem capacities and interactions even within our local bioregions, let alone on a global scale. For example, we do not know how many plant and animal species there are in the world, nor do we know how increasing gasses such as carbon dioxide in the atmosphere will affect them. Some may adapt while others will surely disappear.

❝ In many respects, we really don't have a clue what we're doing. ❞

Thomas Homer-Dixon, director of peace and conflict studies, University of Toronto, Canada

 See Chapter 5 for more information about biodiversity loss.

Scientists around the world are seeking accurate information about how humans are changing Earth in ways that will affect quality of life for us and for future generations. Better understanding is essential if we are going to make decisions about living and working in ways that are economically and environmentally sustainable. We have some of the tools needed to continue to generate and analyse new information. A bigger question is whether we have the appropriate institutions in place and the will to act on what we know and what we learn.

COUNTERPOINT "Before there was science there was common sense—what a person acquires by paying attention. Aristotle had it. Shakespeare had it. Your grandmother probably had it. Common sense tells us that if we continue to dump millions of tonnes of poisons into our water and air, our environment will suffer. How much more do we need to know?" *Donald Hall, from a letter to the Editor,* The Globe and Mail, *July 2, 2001*

FACT FILE

We are constantly learning. We understand that deserts have low productivity, but a recent study conducted in a small canyon in California by the Nature Conservancy revealed some surprising results. Nine different habitat types were found. Within these types were over 3000 plant communities, each supporting many different species of animals including migratory species that also depend on the canyon, each species worth preserving.

❝ Satellites are too big, too expensive and organized too much around NASA [National Aeronautics and Space Administration] rather than around local and regional users of the information. There's too much emphasis on fancy science and too little on regional issues crucial for human habitation. ❞

Bruce Murray, geologist, California Institute of Technology

Monitoring Earth's Life-Support Systems

excerpts from

The Earth Observing System Project Science Office news releases
<http://eospso.gsfc.nasa.gov/eos_homepage>
May 30, 2001

Space-based maps are starting to replace more expensive and time-consuming traditional aerial photography. A major advance has been made in mapping Earth's surface by NASA's Earth Observing System Terra spacecraft, combined with new mapping methods developed by the Department of Geography at the University of Maryland [UM]. Estimates of deforestation, significantly better than those currently used by the United Nations, have been developed.

FIGURE 4.26 Settlement and deforestation surrounding the Brazilian town of Rio Branco (upper left) are see here in the striking "herringbone" deforestation patterns that cut through the rain forest. Rio Branco is the capital of the Brazilian state of Acre and is situated near the border with northeastern Bolivia. The town is a centre for the distribution of goods, including rubber, metals, medicinal plants, Brazil nuts, and timber. Colonization projects in the region are supported by farming, logging activities, and extensive cattle ranching. Much of the surrounding terrain is of a poorly-draining clay hardpan soil, and heavy rainfall periodically converts parts of the forested region to swamp.

"It is essential that we know accurately how much forest cover there is on our planet to help us conserve what is left and to make the best use of forest resources," said John Townshend, a professor in the Department of Geography and the Institute for Advanced Computer Studies at UM.

"The FAO (UN Food and Agriculture Organization) has recently made an enormous effort to derive statistics for forest cover for the world based on reports from the countries themselves. But these figures are simply not comparable from country to country and it is abundantly clear that for many countries the estimates are highly inaccurate."

Different definitions of what constitutes forest cover was one problem. In some cases areas from which trees had already been cut were still counted because that was the land's "intended" use.

"Our work and that of many other scientists show that the way forward to more useful estimates of forest cover lies with remote-imaging data. Remote sensing offers a globally repeatable and verifiable methodology, which doesn't have the problems of bias that are inherent when forest estimates are provided by various agencies within each country," said Ruth De Fries, an associate professor of geography.

An innovative global air pollution monitor called Measurements of Pollution in the Troposphere, or MOPITT, contributed to the Terra mission, was developed at the University of Toronto and built by COM DEV in Cambridge, Ontario, by the Canadian Space Agency.

For the first time, policy makers and scientists have a way to identify and track major sources of air pollution anywhere on Earth. This has given us the most complete view ever assembled of the world's air pollution churning through the atmosphere, crossing continents and oceans. MOPITT is making the first long-term global observations of the air pollutant carbon monoxide as Terra circles Earth from pole to pole, 16 times a day. "With these new observations you clearly see that air pollution is much more than a local problem. It's a global issue," said John Gille, MOPITT principal investigator at the U.S. National Center for Atmospheric Research in Boulder, Colorado. "The MOPITT observations represent a powerful new tool for identifying and quantifying pollution sources and for observing the transport of pollution in international and global scales," said atmospheric specialist Daniel J. Jacob of Harvard University, Cambridge, MA. "Such information will help us improve our understanding of the linkages between air pollution and global environmental change, and it will likely play a pivotal role in the development of international environmental policy."

NASA research has also recently provided more accurate and detailed maps of cities, which provide urban planners with a better understanding of city growth, and how rainfall runoff over paved surfaces impacts regional water quality.

Critical Analysis
1. What is the main purpose of the information provided in the reading?
2. Considering the source and purpose of the information, identify a possible bias.
3. Explain why scientists feel that information discovered using the new technology is important.
4. Evaluate the impact that new technologies such as this could have in solving global issues. Support your answer using specific examples.
5. Study the quote and the Counterpoint argument on page 109, and explain why the viewpoint expressed is not as enthusiastic about the use of satellite technology.

WEB LINKS

- Environment Canada:
  <www.ccea.org/ecozones>
- Natural and human systems within ecozones:
  <www.canadianbiodiversity.mcgill.ca/english/ecozones/ecozones.htm>
- World Resources Institute: <www.wri.org>
- Bioregions: <www.wri.org/wri/biodiv/bioregio.html>
- Maps: <www.nhq.nrcs.usda.gov/WSR/mapindx/maps.htm>
- Satellite images:
  <http://earthobservatory.nasa.gov>

RELATED ISSUES

- Global climate change
- Biodiversity loss
- International interdependence
- Wasteful consumption of resources
- Globalization

GIS **Regional Atlas of Socio-Economic Indicators**

ANALYSE, APPLY, AND INTERACT

1. Discuss the implications for people living in your region of the following statement: "Everywhere is downwind or downstream of somewhere else."

2. Draw a diagram that explains the natural processes affecting the unique productivity in the oceans surrounding the Antarctic continent.

3. Explain why it is difficult to make accurate predictions about future events.

4. Provide evidence that countries are becoming increasingly interdependent.

5. Suggest some opportunities within your region that could be exploited to help people "get in touch" with the natural environment.

6. **a)** Use information in the chapter to compile a list of five global trends that you consider to be environmental threats.
   b) Draw a graphic organizer, using arrows to show interconnections among as many of the threats and trends as you can.

7. Evaluate the effects of climate, including temperature range, precipitation amounts and seasonality, growing season, and hours of sunshine on types of housing, transportation, agriculture, fuel consumption, and recreational activities in your local bioregion.

8. Construct a mobile that represents the structure of a particular ecosystem or some other system. Present your mobile to a group in your class to show that, if one part of the mobile is tugged, reverberations are felt throughout the system.

9. Create an annotated photographic essay of your local bioregion to illustrate some interconnections among human and natural systems.

10. Discuss how likely you think it is that human knowledge, ingenuity, and technology will be able to solve significant global issues.

11. **a)** Describe remote sensing and its advantages.
    b) Research the education and qualifications required for a career as a geography professor working on a NASA project with remote-sensed data.

PART TWO: SUSTAINING PLANETARY SYSTEMS

Chapter 5: Biodiversity—Endangered Spaces, Endangered Species

By the end of this chapter, you will

- identify similarities and differences in the economic and political aspirations of selected regional or cultural groups within different countries;

- demonstrate an understanding of the need to respect the cultural and religious traditions of others;

- compare the productivity and biodiversity of selected ecosystems;

- analyse the impact of past and current trends in agriculture on natural and human systems;

- evaluate some of the ways of promoting sustainable development and assess their effectiveness in selected places and regions of the world;

- assess the contribution of selected government policies to sustainable resource development in Canada;

- identify current global sustainability issues and environmental threats;

- evaluate the role played by non-governmental organizations and local community initiatives in different parts of the world in promoting sustainable development and resource management;

- evaluate the effectiveness of an international strategy and agreement that has been designed to protect the global commons or address global issues;

- explain why it is difficult to make accurate predictions relating to human use of the earth and its resources, and why some predictions are more (or less) accurate than others.

WATCHING WHALES

For three months in the summer and fall of 2001, marine scientists watched the slow painful death of a right whale as it struggled off the Atlantic coast, entangled in 120 m of leaded fishing line. Some risked their lives trying to tranquilize and disentangle the whale, but their attempts failed. The fishing gear that was entangled in the mouth and fluke cut through blubber on the whale's back almost to its body cavity. The whale died from infection of the wounds.

Although protected from whaling since 1935, the population of right whales has not recovered and they have been declared an endangered species. Despite the birth of 200 calves in the 1980s and 1990s, there are currently only about 300 right whales left. Scientists believe the whales are suffering from reduced food sources and pollutants that harm their immune and reproductive systems, but another danger is more direct. More than 60% of the whales show scars from entanglement in fishing gear. With the efforts of scientists at marine biology institutes, some progress is being made in understanding whale habitat and physiology. New methods for disentangling whales and less damaging fishing gear are being studied. In spring 2002, the Canadian government changed the location of shipping lanes in the Bay of Fundy to reduce collisions between whales and ships.

FIGURE 5.1 Recent studies on the St. Lawrence River's beluga whale population have confirmed that they are sterile and on the verge of extinction. Some observers believe beluga carcasses are toxic from massive amounts of toxic run-off from agriculture and industries.

IS THE HUMAN SPECIES WAKING UP?

Humans have always been fascinated with the vast diversity of living things. We have also known for some time that the world's **ecosystems** and species are in danger. The World Conservation Union (IUCN), founded in 1948, was established to conserve biological resources. More recently, a great deal of concern has been expressed over the increasing impact of human activity on **biodiversity**. The headlines deal with the collapse of fisheries, contamination of water, effects of climate change, the extinction of species, or the dramatic increase in environmental refugees fleeing ravaged ecosystems. Yet few people understand the complexity, extent, and implications of the issues.

An Environics International survey found that the number of Canadians who are "very concerned about the state of wildlife and their habitat" rose from 48% to 54% between 1998 and 1999. Another Environics survey asked people to evaluate environmental protection laws and regulations as they are now applied in their country. In 28 out of 30 developed and developing countries, 61% to 91% of more than 35 000 respondents said that the laws do not go far enough.

We know surprisingly little about species and ecosystems and how human survival is dependent on them. No one knows how many species of plants and animals there are on Earth. Estimates vary widely, ranging from 10 to

> ## FACT FILE
>
> Since 1600, 484 animal and 654 plant species that we know of have become extinct because of human activity.

FIGURE 5.2 A frog sits in a pot of water that starts out comfortably warm. The water gradually heats up and so does the frog, so it does not notice the change until the water boils, killing the frog. This analogy has been used to describe how humans are changing the biosphere, without realizing the gravity of it, until it is too late.

FIGURE 5.3 We know of 270 000 plants, 3000 of which are used for food and between 25 000 and 50 000 of which are used for traditional medicines.

80 million. The Global Biodiversity Assessment of the United Nations Environment Program (UNEP) uses a working estimate of 13.6 million. We have discovered and named fewer than 2 million of them. More than half of these are insects, while **vertebrates**, including mammals, fish, birds, reptiles, and amphibians, make up only 2.5% of the total number of known species. **Invertebrates**, which play a critical role in ecological processes, are experiencing the greatest losses as their habitats are being destroyed at alarming rates.

Biological and social scientists have been progressing slowly with the monumental task of learning about plants and animals, how they interact within ecosystems, and how to preserve them. They are often hampered by lack of funding. In the meantime, species and ecosystems are disappearing before we even know they exist, let alone understand them.

There has been an unprecedented loss of biodiversity due to human activity in the last century. Although the rate of loss is accelerating, species extinction usually occurs gradually and is often not apparent until it is too late. Many improvements to the negative impact of human activity and many positive scientific advances have been made, yet the loss of species continues. We appear to be losing as

many as 20 000 species a year (although some scientists estimate the number to be higher at about 36 500 species a year). Projections of continued loss also vary widely from 2%–25% of all species by 2025. Even the low end of this estimate is 1000 times higher than the rate of natural extinction through Earth's ecological processes.

What Is Biodiversity?

Biodiversity refers to the great variety of unique species of plants, animals, and micro-organisms, as well as to the ecosystems of which they are a part. Biodiversity is a systems concept. While the soils, water, air, and living species are complex systems in themselves, they all interact in a larger, dynamic system. The various life forms that make up biodiversity form a hierarchy of three levels of organization:

- Genetic diversity—the genetic material in all the species within a region
- Species diversity—the different species of plants, animals, and micro-organisms
- Ecosystem diversity—the habitats, biological communities (groups of organisms that interact within a habitat), and natural processes (including **abiotic** components)

A Natural Event

Species extinction is a natural part of the evolutionary process, and the loss of some species will not necessarily affect the ability of an ecosystem to function. As many as 90% of the total species that have inhabited Earth are thought to have become extinct millions of years ago, during the five mass extinctions of geological history. Analysis of fossils tells us that the average lifetime of a species is between five and ten million years. There has been much speculation about why dinosaurs became extinct. Researchers now believe that they declined gradually from 35 different species 80 million years ago to just six species 65 million years ago. Many scientists support the theory that the Chicxulub comet, a giant asteroid, landed in the Yucatan Peninsula of Mexico, causing a global environmental collapse that wiped out the rest.

> 66 **The main reason we should fear the Sixth Extinction is that we ourselves stand a good chance of becoming one of its victims.** 99
>
> *Niles Eldridge, paleontologist*

INTERACT

1. Identify three issues related to the sustainability of the right whale population.
2. Conduct research to identify and define five mass extinctions of the past.
3. Account for the wide range in estimates of species totals and biodiversity loss.
4. Create a diagram, perhaps using concentric circles, to illustrate the idea that biodiversity is a concept that recognizes a hierarchy of three levels of organization.
5. Explain the factors that lead some observers to label beluga whales as "toxic."
6. Is the use of the term "crisis" to describe biodiversity loss appropriate? Explain your answer.

POPULATION–ENVIRONMENT NEXUS

The links between population factors, biodiversity loss, and degradation of the environment are complex and demand a profound knowledge of geography, demography, economics, and environmental science. There is general agreement among analysts that human pressure on the environment is caused by several major factors, including population growth and distribution, rates of per capita resource consumption, and levels and kinds of technology. Many additional factors, such as the vulnerability or resilience of a particular ecosystem or the adaptability of a species, also have some effect.

All of these interacting factors are linked in a complicated system that makes accurate prediction of outcomes very difficult. Population growth, for example, is affected by fertility rates, which depend on other factors such as the status and education of women. Population growth requires additional food and, consequently, more land. On the other hand, it can also drive the search for new agricultural technologies or result in migration to other places. Per capita resource consumption depends not only on total numbers of people but also on additional factors that change the equation, such as the amount of land needed to produce a unit of food, improvements in technology, changes in diet, and so on. Environmental damage may prompt the development of more environmentally responsible technologies.

Earth as a Lifeboat

Populations of all species, including humans, grow or decline in size over time as a response to environmental processes that affect birth and death rates as well as immigration and emigration rates. As numbers continue to grow within an ecosystem, space and resources become more limited until the **carrying capacity** of the available habitat is reached. Carrying capacity refers to the maximum population size that a habitat can support indefinitely without degrading the resource base.

Because of the complexity of the population–environment **nexus**, no one knows what Earth's actual human population carrying capacity is. Demographers have tried to estimate the total number of people Earth can support, but the estimates range from two billion people living a high quality of life to the Food and Agricultural Organization's (FAO) estimate of 33 billion people living in crowded squalor. The total number of people is not nearly as significant as the total burden of the population's resource use and waste output.

Once the carrying capacity for any species is reached, intense competition can produce stresses that result in a higher death rate and lower birth rate. If the birth rate and death rate are equal, the size of the population will level off as **zero population growth** is reached. In some cases, overpopulation may degrade the environment severely enough to reduce its carrying capacity and a population crash and extinction may occur. Populations that exceed the carrying capacity of the habitat in which they live are not sustainable because the damage they cause to natural systems harms other species as well. It is not only increasing human numbers that are the root cause of the global biodiversity crisis, but the accompanying rapid growth of per capita resource consumption and inadequate use of ecologically sustainable technology.

FACT FILE

A combination of rising incomes, and the spread of western hemisphere diets around the world, have caused meat consumption to increase five times from 1950 to 2000—from 44 to 232 million tonnes. Per capita meat consumption has doubled in the same period to 77 kg per person and the amount is three times higher in developed countries. Feeding one person with a meat-based diet requires 20 times more land and thousands of litres more water than a vegetarian diet.

 See Chapter 10 for more information about population trends.

Tragedy of the Commons

This concept was developed by ecologist Garrett Harding in the 1960s. He described a pastoral village with a common pasture where no one individual owned the land and everyone let their animals graze. If each farmer put more animals on the pasture in order to increase personal wealth, each animal would contribute a small additional amount to the degradation of the pasture. Based on assumed human behaviour, each farmer would increase the number of animals until the common pasture was destroyed.

Some resources, such as the oceans and atmosphere, belong to everyone. These "common resources" are essential for the stability of all ecosystems on Earth and determine the productivity of all the resources on which we depend. A lack of direct ownership of the "commons" tends to encourage overuse and prevent careful conservation. Some ecologists believe that land should be considered part of the commons despite widespread private ownership of terrestrial resources. Many traditional societies of Aboriginal peoples, with a different worldview toward nature, devised rules to deal with depleted resources, or moved on to new lands, leaving the resources to regenerate. In modern societies, particularly in developing countries, those most affected by the loss or degradation of the commons are often unable to take direct action because of inequities in political, legal, and economic systems. The concept of the commons has been useful for

> " The systems approach [to understanding population–environment links ... builds in as many factors as possible; and it does not see human impact on the environment simply as a one-way street. There is feedback. ... The interactions and uncertainties when studying whole ecosystems or the whole Earth are so great that quantitative forecasts are virtually impossible. All that can be offered are 'what if' scenarios that show the possible consequences of a range of trends. "
>
> *Atlas of Population and Environment*

theorizing about humans on the brink of environmental disaster. To avoid the tragedy of the commons, people are required to learn what the limits of the **biosphere** are and to live within them. There is simply no place else for the human species to go.

Endangered Spaces

All ecosystems from the local to global scale are under threat. The biome that is under the greatest siege is believed to be tropical rain forests, which are estimated to contain somewhere between 50% and 90% of the total species living on Earth.

 See Chapter 4 for more information about ecosystem productivity and life support systems at risk.

Temperate rain forests around the world are losing ground almost as fast as tropical forests. **Old-growth forests** are being replaced by second- or even third-growth forests, which support fewer species or by tree plantations of only one species. Fragmentation of habitat creates islands of nature that may be too small to provide the **interior ecosystem** needed by many species. This lowers the size of individual populations, reducing their genetic variability and making them more vulnerable to extinction.

Marine and freshwater ecosystems face serious degradation and species loss. Freshwater ecosystems have been poisoned for years with industrial and municipal pollution and suffer the most frequently from invasive alien species. Over half the world's mangrove forests, rich in unique species, have been destroyed. Coral reef habitats, noted for some of the highest levels of biodiversity on the planet, are seriously threatened by overfishing and destructive fishing techniques such as the use of explosives, water pollution from industry, sewage and fertilizers, tourism, and the phenomenon of **coral bleaching**. Ocean warming of just 1°C can stress corals, causing them to expel the plants living within them and to turn white.

FIGURE 5.5 In 2000, the Global Coral Reef Monitoring Network reported that 27% of the world's coral reefs were severely damaged and that 60% of all reefs were threatened by human activities.

FIGURE 5.4 About 17 million ha of tropical forests are cleared every year—about 4 ha per second.

FIGURE 5.6 Many thousands of people have joined local community groups such as Save the Oak Ridges Moraine (STORM), which are working around the world to protect sensitive habitats.

FIGURE 5.7 Wildlife habitat is becoming increasingly fragmented by land uses like cities, farms, and roads. This aerial photo of the city of Thunder Bay, Ontario (centre), shows the crossing runways of Thunder Bay International airport (southwest), Highways 11 and 17, the Thunder Bay Expressway (north and west), and cultivated fields along the river valley (west).

INTERACT

1. Brainstorm a list of environmental processes that would affect birth and death rates in a population.
2. Use the example of a fish aquarium or an ecosystem of your choice to explain the relationships between carrying capacity, overpopulation, environmental degradation, and extinction.
3. Use the concept of a population–environment nexus to illustrate some of the connections that could result from the trend to higher levels of meat consumption. Include at least five factors in your diagram.
4. **a)** What factors cause a population to reach its carrying capacity?

   b) Explain what happens to a population when the carrying capacity of its habitat is exceeded.
5. Do you believe that Earth has already exceeded its carrying capacity or that it could support billions more people? Defend your viewpoint.
6. Suggest, using specific examples, how technology might increase or decrease the carrying capacity of the biosphere.
7. In your own words, explain the "tragedy of the commons." Give an example of a mismanaged common resource in your local area to support your explanation.
8. Debate the idea of including land as part of the ecological commons. What would be the practical advantages and drawbacks of this idea?

CAUSES OF BIODIVERSITY LOSS

The vast majority of factors threatening the rich diversity of species on Earth are related to people—where we live, how we grow, and what we do; our attitudes, activities, lifestyles, and inequities. The main threat is the destruction and fragmentation of natural habitats, as wilderness lands are converted for human uses. Other direct causes include the introduction of alien or invasive species, overexploitation, pollution, and the use of fossil fuels.

> "Biotic impoverishment is an almost inevitable consequence of the ways in which the human species has used and misused the environment in its rise to dominance. ... The roots of the biodiversity crisis are not 'out there' in the forest or the savannah, but embedded in the way we live."
>
> *World Resources Institute*

Valuing Biodiversity

Generally, humankind values diversity. Biodiversity is important for its own intrinsic value as well as from aesthetic and ethical viewpoints. These values are often reflected in art, literature, and religion, and in people's behaviour toward other species. Species and ecosystems provide all of us with everything we need to survive and prosper: air, water, fertile soil, food, shelter, medicine, and the vast array of products we use. So-called "free" environmental benefits, often referred to as **natural capital**, include nutrient recycling, soil formation, natural foods such as fish and **bushmeat**, waste disposal, pollination, oxygen production, and regulation of climate. Various estimates of the total global value of these goods and "services," in the hundreds of billions of dollars, far surpass total world GNP. Ecotourism and outdoor leisure travel are rapidly growing industries that generate more than $1 trillion a year, and depend on healthy ecosystems. We have begun to reject the idea that Earth's resources are inexhaustible. Why then do societies fail to recognize the essential goods and services provided by natural capital as valuable, and factor that into decision making?

The **ethnobiological knowledge** of indigenous peoples, including genetic materials, food sources, and other plant-based resources, is being sought by transnational corporations who, acting in the interests of shareholders and profits, exploit this knowledge for commercial gain.

Costs and benefits of natural resources and processes are ignored in the economic accounts of countries. The dominant **worldview** is to place a higher value on the small parts of biodiversity that are currently most commercially viable. By undervaluing biodiversity as a whole, the market encourages unsustainable activities that lead to depletion.

 See Chapter 1 for more information about values.

Biodiversity is important to human health because ecosystem disruptions can cause outbreaks of infectious disease or species that humans consider pests. Many of our pharmaceutical drugs are derived from other species. About 80% of the world's population rely on traditional plant-based medicines for their primary health care.

 See Chapters 15 and 16 for more information about ecosystems and human health.

The Human Scale

The impact of the **ecological footprint** of all of humanity is now larger than that of all other species combined. Our impact on ecosystems is

---

FACT FILE

About 120 of the top 150 prescription drugs in North America are synthesized from plants, animals, fungi, and bacteria found by bioprospectors in the wild.

FACT FILE

Of the top 100 prescription drugs in North America, more than 50% are derived from natural plant species. Of the 265 000 known species of flowering plants, less than 0.05% have been studied for their potential medicinal value.

---

occurring faster than we can understand how to respond to and modify the changes.

Population growth, density, and distribution are closely linked to habitat loss. Population growth creates pressure to convert wildlife habitat to space for human activities and to produce wastes that pollute habitats and poison species. As people have spread out and settled over Earth's surface, they have destroyed about 40% of the net primary productivity of the biosphere, leaving the rest for other species and natural processes. The challenge to humankind is to implement policies and technologies that maintain biodiversity, especially in the most heavily populated and developed regions.

> **Only after the last tree has been cut down**
> **Only after the last river has been poisoned**
> **Only after the last fish has been caught**
> **Only then will you find out that money cannot be eaten.**
>
> *Cree prophesy*

Development

As population grows, large-scale landscape changes are inevitable. Settlements ranging in size from small villages to **megacities** spread over Earth's surface. Land is used for farming, transportation, industry, logging, mining, obtaining energy, and for recreation. Rivers are dammed or diverted. Modern industrial agricul-

World Population Density, 1800 and 2000

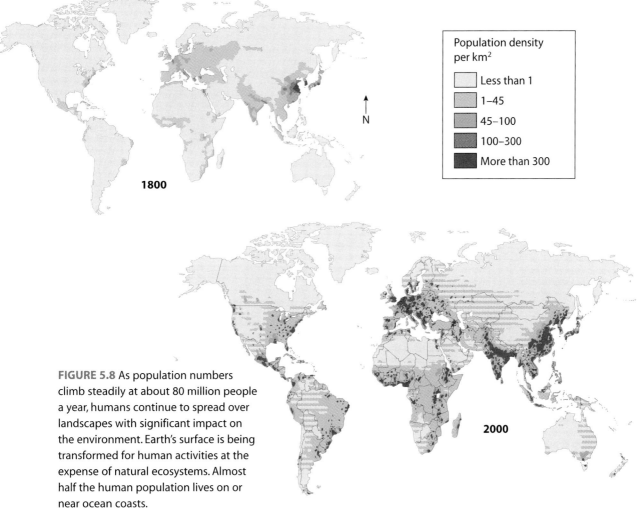

Population density per km²

- Less than 1
- 1–45
- 45–100
- 100–300
- More than 300

1800

2000

FIGURE 5.8 As population numbers climb steadily at about 80 million people a year, humans continue to spread over landscapes with significant impact on the environment. Earth's surface is being transformed for human activities at the expense of natural ecosystems. Almost half the human population lives on or near ocean coasts.

Paul Harrison and Fred Pearce, AAAS Atlas of Population and Environment, University of California Press, 2001, pp. 4–5

ture and forestry, using new technologies and capital-intensive techniques such as irrigation and chemical fertilizers and pesticides, are displacing a huge diversity of plant varieties and sustainable farming methods. As diverse forest ecosystems are cut down, many have been replaced with high-yielding monocultural plantations, which are at much greater risk of disease and pest outbreaks, necessitating additional input of chemical pesticides.

The amount of nitrogen used in fertilizer application has doubled in the last century. People now contribute 50% more to the nitrogen cycle than all other natural sources combined. This contributes to long-term loss of soil fertility in forests and toxic blooms of algae in oceans. Algae blooms, known as red tides, have affected many coastal areas over the past decades, killing large numbers of fish, birds, and marine mammals as well as causing skin and respiratory problems and acute food poisoning in humans who consume the affected sea foods.

Industrial agriculture prefers genetic uniformity. There is no place for some species that are supported in traditional agricultural systems such as bees that pollinate plants or birds that disperse seeds. Large areas of land are planted with single, high-yielding crops. Industrial livestock farming such as beef and hog feedlots produce large amounts of pollution and greenhouse gases and reduce barnyard diversity. While the total number of livestock is growing, many breeds once raised by traditional farmers are now extinct or rare. As the human population grows, so do unnaturally abundant populations of **mutualist species** that use a large amount of the productivity of Earth's ecosystems. In 2001, these species included about 11 billion fowl, 1.7 billion sheep and goats, 1.3 billion cows, 1 billion pigs, and 0.16 billion camels and water buffalo.

Biotechnology

Humans have become a force of evolution as they breed new species. New species can modify habitats and contribute to the extinction of others. While farmers have always developed new breeds of domestic plants and animals by selection of species with favoured characteristics such has thicker wool on sheep, or frost resistance in crops, scientists are now combining genes from across species barriers, creating new life forms with potentially unpredictable results. This form of biotechnology, while largely supported by government and industry, has generated public concern and controversy. Commercial biotechnology promoted by transnational companies and large agricultural research institutes has little to do with feeding hungry people who often cannot afford the new products created. The current gene revolution where new species are created to resist drought, or withstand spraying of company-developed pesticides, is contributing to the spread of monoculture. Since 1900, about 75% of the genetic diversity in agricultural crops has been lost, primarily because of biotechnology and industrial agricultural practices. Farmers in the Philippines used to grow thousands of varieties of rice. Today, just two new varieties developed during the **Green Revolution** are grown virtually everywhere in the country.

 See Chapter 9 for more information about industrial agriculture.

Use of Fossil Fuels

Our world is hooked on fossil fuels. Combustion of oil, natural gas, coal, and byproducts such as propane and gasoline are contributing significantly to air pollution and the increasing amount of greenhouse gases in the atmosphere. The CO_2 content has increased more than 30% and methane 145% since pre-industrial times.

A serious side effect of the air pollution created is global climate change, which is predicted to have enormous effects on biodiversity. Rising sea levels, ocean temperatures, and unpredictable weather extremes are already with us. Many islands and coastal areas in the world will be submerged as sea levels rise, endangering or wiping out many species.

 See Chapter 6 for more information about global climate change.

Biodiversity Loss in Agricultural Species

Global Livestock Populations (millions)

Livestock	Population, 1961	Population, 2000	% Increase
Buffalo	88	167	90
Cattle	941	1,331	41
Geese	36	235	553
Goats	348	714	105
Pigs	406	905	123
Sheep	994	1.060	7
Chickens	3.9 (billion)	14.3 (billion)	267

adapted from *Vital Signs, 2001*, The Worldwatch Institute

Livestock at Risk from Extinction, 1990s

Livestock	Number of Breeds	Breeds at Risk from Extinction
Cattle	787	135
Sheep	920	119
Goats	351	44
Pigs	353	69

adapted from FAO

Diversity Loss in Vegetables (number of varieties held at the U.S. National Seed Storage Laboratory, Colorado State University)

Vegetable	Number of Species, 1903	Number of Species, 1983	% Loss
Asparagus	44	1	97.8
Bean	578	32	94.5
Carrot	288	17	94.1
Lettuce	487	36	92.6
Onion	357	21	94.1
Pea	408	25	93.9
Spinach	109	7	93.6
Squash	341	40	88.3

adapted from World Resources Institute data in *AAAS Atlas of Population and Environment*

FIGURE 5.9

Pollution

Pollutants degrade ecosystems and eliminate sensitive species. Staggering amounts of wastes, gases, and toxic chemicals from industry, energy production, sewage, fertilizers, transportation, and pesticides contaminate air, soil, fresh water, and oceans.

Many of the chemicals persistent in lakes, rivers, oceans, precipitation, and foods consumed by animals and people are placing wildlife populations at risk. Medical and scientific research has linked organochlorine chemical compounds found in pesticides, plastics, polyaromatic hydrocarbons (PAHs), polychlorinated biphenyls (PCBs), and other industrial waste products to thyroid and reproductive dysfunctions, birth deformities, and compromised immune systems in a number of species of birds, fish, and mammals. The research has found that these chemicals either mimic or block the effects of natural estrogen, thereby disrupting the endocrine system. The

FIGURE 5.11 Many species of frogs, considered indicator species, are disappearing and developing genetic disorders. Amphibians are sensitive to environmental contaminants such as low levels of pesticides, acid rain, and increased ultraviolet (UV) light.

World Wildlife Fund (WWF) lists 45 chemicals or classes of chemicals that disrupt reproductive or hormone systems. Alligators studied in one lake in Florida by University of Florida researchers were found to have severe reproductive abnormalities with a mortality rate 10 times higher than expected. The lake contained the pesticide difocol, produced for years at a nearby chemical plant.

 See Chapter 16 for more information about hormone-disrupting chemicals.

Overexploitation

Overexploitation of many species has occurred for commercial and sport activities such as fishing or hunting to extinction. People demand products such as tropical hardwoods that are becoming scarce. Some species have been persecuted as pests or vermin, often based on misconceptions of the danger or nuisance they pose. In the past, attempts were made to eliminate tigers in parts of East Asia. Now, although protected by conservation regulations in many places, tigers continue to be poached for their skins, skulls, or the medicinal use of their bones in traditional Chinese medicine. Some medical practitioners have developed alternatives to

FIGURE 5.10 The Canadian Arctic has lost 18% of its ice cover between 1970 and 2000. Ice shelves, which are a crucial part of the habitat for algae and plankton and support polar bears, are melting as global average temperatures rise.

Amphibian Population Trends in North America and the World

adapted from Nature magazine, vol. 404

Note: Data prior to 1970 are based on very small samples.

FIGURE 5.12

FIGURE 5.13 Rhinos are just one vertebrate that has been hunted to the verge of extinction. In 2001, a rare Sumatran rhinoceros was bred and born in captivity at the Cincinnati zoo.

products from endangered species. Large predators such as wolves, bears, panthers, and cougars have a bleak future in most of North America as they have been shot for sport or killed as predators of livestock. As their natural prey and habitat have been destroyed, they have little choice but to feed on livestock.

Poverty and the Global Economy

A major root cause of biodiversity loss is poverty. Inequities in who manages resources, compared with who receives the benefits, exist between many disparate groups: rich and poor, men and women, and among various ethnic groups.

The world trading system puts pressure on countries to build their economies and compete in the global market. The global economy tends to favour wealthy industrialized countries with the technology and funds to exploit natural resources almost anywhere in the world. They receive a large share of the profits from the development of resources. The economic system discriminates against poor countries, which are still burdened with debt repayments for loans that were obtained in an attempt to start economic growth years ago. In order to pay the interest on the debt, governments in developing countries allow forests to be cleared for cattle ranching or the growing of **cash crops**. Crops such as coffee, cocoa, and tropical fruits are grown on large plantations for export to the developed world. As more and more emphasis is put on fewer and fewer crops, the diversity of species and ecosystems continues to decline. People that depend directly on local natural resources for survival have little opportunity to concern themselves with conservation. They have no other sources of livelihood, little control over managing what natural resources remain, and pay the price of exploiting the resources—environmental degradation.

FIGURE 5.14 Keystone species such as the gray wolf are protected from being shot or poisoned within Algonquin Provincial Park in Ontario. In 2002, they were temporarily protected in regions surrounding the park.

FACT FILE

Profits derived from the development of successful leukemia drugs from the rose periwinkle, native to what is left of Madagascar's tropical forest, are estimated at US$100 million a year. None of that revenue has gone to Madagascar.

FIGURE 5.15 The swift fox was poisoned, shot, and trapped so that it disappeared from the mixed-grass prairie of Canada in the early 1900s. As a result, the Committee on the Status of Endangered Wildlife in Canada (COSEWIC) declared its status as **extirpated**. Two pairs were imported from the U.S. and 800 captive-raised foxes were released in the 1980s. The current population in Canada is estimated to be about 290 animals.

 See Chapter 9 for more information about the global food supply.

 See Chapters 13 and 14 for more information about poverty.

Bioinvasion

An invasive species is one that is not native to an ecosystem. International trade and travel provide an opportunity for some species to "hitchhike" to new marine and terrestrial habitats. A growing number of alien species are posing serious threats to native species through competition for food and space, degradation of water quality, predation of native species, the spread of disease, and interbreeding.

> **" Introductions, like extinctions, are forever. "**
> *J. Ellen Marsden, field biologist*

Some alien species have been deliberately introduced. In the late 1950s, bees were imported from Africa into Brazil in a misguided attempt to improve honey production. The bees display such aggressive behaviour that media

FIGURE 5.16 The cod fishery of Atlantic Canada collapsed in the early 1990s as a result of overfishing, with a serious impact on the local economy and way of life.

reports have called them "killer bees." More than 1000 people and many animals in South and Central America have been killed by swarms of the alien bees. The bees migrated north, crossing into the southern U.S. in the early 1990s where a dozen people were killed. African bees have taken over many bee colonies and have interbred with some native species, making the resulting species stronger and more aggressive.

> **FACT FILE**
>
> There are more than 140 non-native species with significant ecological consequences in the waters of the Great Lakes basin.

Government Policies and Funding

Most government policies are designed to encourage development of industry, energy supplies, agriculture, and forestry. Development policies in developing countries are often

FIGURE 5.17 Ninety percent of wild honeybees in the U.S. have been wiped out by pesticides, competition from invasive African bees, and deadly parasitic mites. Commercial beehives are also at risk with potential losses of billions of dollars.

FIGURE 5.18 The zebra mussel is a mollusc native to the Caspian Sea. It was carried to the Great Lakes in the ballast water of ships. With few predators, it has spread quickly to many other surrounding lakes by attaching itself to boats. While changing fish habitat slightly, its impact has been mainly economic as it clogs pipes at cottages, homes, water treatment plants, and boat engines, and clutters beaches with sharp shells.

adapted from "Pushy Canadian Beaver Invades Russia: Cherished Symbol of Canada is Rolling Through Europe with a Vengeance"

The Globe and Mail
January 24, 2002

"They munched their way through Finland and Sweden. They flooded the remote forests of Tierra del Fuego. Now the Canadian beavers are invading Russia—and the Russians are nervous.

The march of transplanted Canadian beavers across the northern tip of Europe is advancing ever southward, ousting Russia's native beaver population and creating fears of damage to forests and farms.

'It could create a very acute problem. It is an invasion by a species not typical of Europe and their pressure is forcing out the European species and changing the ecosystem,' complained Maxim Sinitsyn, an ecologist at the Institute for Evolution and Ecology, part of the Russian Academy of Sciences.

The Canadian beavers were introduced in the 1950s and 1960s into Finland and Sweden where no native beaver population existed. With no natural predators, they swiftly expanded their area.

The Canadian beavers are more flexible and active and can survive better. They build dams—sometimes huge structures up to hundreds of metres in length—while European beavers don't. As a result they are causing flooding, damage to commercial forestry, and changing the Russian ecology in unpredictable ways.

This isn't the first time the furry Canadian rodent has provoked foreign anxieties. In 1946, Argentina imported 25 pairs from Canada to help the fur industry in Tierra del Fuego. By the 1990s the original pairs had multiplied to 50,000. …

geared toward western-style industrial models required by the structural adjustment policies of the World Bank and International Monetary Fund (IMF), rather than more ecologically appropriate, community-based, sustainable management techniques.

Farmers in some developing countries are given land title or subsidies to clear forests for farming. Some of them have lost the occupancy of their original land through corruption and violence as wealthy landowners and corporations took over. Governments may allow forests to be cleared in order to reduce the pressure for land reform. Lack of property rights and insecure land tenure can result in less interest in looking after the land. The side effect of these policies is loss of biodiversity as people continually spread into undeveloped forest regions.

Because biodiversity is not adequately valued, effective laws are often nonexistent, not enforced, or inadequately funded. A law cannot be enforced if there are no environmental officers hired to do so. In some countries, there are large gaps in responsibility for protection of various biological resources, or opposing and overlapping policies.

FACT FILE

A Sierra Legal Defence Fund report entitled *Ontario: Yours to Pollute* enhances public awareness of the chronic lack of industrial and municipal compliance with environmental regulations and dismal enforcement record of the government. Between 1995 and 1999, the number of violations of water pollution quadrupled. More than 10 000 violations of provincial wastewater laws occurred. Of the 480 industries and facilities cited, only 11 were prosecuted.

INTERACT

1. The quote on page 120 uses the term "biotic impoverishment." What do you suppose it means? Explain how the concept is related to the practice of monocultures.
2. How does the Cree prophesy in the quote on page 121 express a critique of the values of modern society?
3. Create a flow diagram to show how human population growth leads to the loss of biodiversity.
4. Briefly explain how **a)** industrial agriculture, **b)** industrial forestry, and **c)** genetic engineering in biotechnology may reduce biodiversity.
5. Suggest reasons for the two main trends shown by the tables in Figure 5.9, **Biodiversity Loss in Agricultural Species**.
6. For each photograph in Figures 5.13 to 5.16, conduct research to identify measures taken to address each case of threatened species.
7. Investigate any one of the causes of biodiversity loss outlined in this section of the text and write a 500-word case study on a specific example of the cause to explain the situation and evaluate its effects on biodiversity.
8. Use an Internet search engine such as < www.google.com > to find and read a recent Sierra Legal Defence Fund report such as *Ontario's 2000 Dirty Water Secrets* or *Ontario: Yours to Pollute*. Develop a method for classifying the main types of polluters. Write a conclusion about the state of pollution prevention in the province.
9. **a)** Refer to Figure 5.8, **World Population Density**. Analyse the patterns of population distribution in relation to major biomes and ocean coastlines.
   b) On a blank outline map for the world, sketch your prediction for population growth patterns by 2100. On the map, give reasons for the patterns shown and predict the impact on biodiversity.

Biodiversity Hot Spots

Concerned about the prospect of mass extinction of a large number of species, a group of conservation scientists working at Oxford University, UK, and the NGO Conservation International conducted an international biogeographical regional analysis to address the key question of how to protect the most species per dollar invested. Data were collected from professional literature and more than 100 experts in the countries studied. Twenty-five biodiversity "hot spots," each containing at least 1500 of the world's 300 000 plant species, were identified. Ten of the regions contain at least 5000 known species. Species endemism and the degree of threat through habitat loss were two key determinants for hot spot status.

While the hot spots in this analysis cover only 1.4% of Earth's land surface, they form the sole remaining habitat for 44% of plant species and 35% of all species of mammals, birds, reptiles, and amphibians, and face a high degree of risk. Invertebrates, mainly insects, which make up at least 95% of the species within these habitats, were not included in the analysis. Sixteen of the hot spots are in the tropics in developing countries where the threats to biodiversity are the highest and conservation resources are scarce. The greatest threats or "hottest hot spots" appear in Madagascar, the Philippines, Sundaland, Brazil, and the Caribbean.

Two additional hot spots, the Tropical Andes and the Mediterranean basin, are considered "hyper-hot" candidates for conservation support because of their exceptionally high levels of **endemic** plants—20 000 and 13 000, respectively.

Other areas of great biodiversity that are at risk but were not included in the analysis because of insufficient documented data include the Ethiopian Highlands, Angola Escarpment, southeastern China, Taiwan, forests in eastern Democratic Republic of the Congo (formerly Zaire), southwestern Uganda, northern Rwanda, and the tropical forests of Australia's Queensland coast.

There are a few "good news" wilderness areas of 7 million km^2 that have high numbers of endemic species, at least 75% of their primary vegetation, and fewer than 5 people per km^2. These include New Guinea, the Guyana Shield in the northeastern Amazon basin, the lowlands of the western Amazon basin, and the forest of the Congo.

The analysis determined that protection of the 25 habitats could eliminate most of the risk of the expected mass extinction for many of the species.

adapted from "Biodiversity hotspots for conservation priorities" in *Nature magazine*, vol. 403, February 24, 2000

excerpt from
"Biodiversity hotspots for conservation priorities"

by Norman Myers, Russell A. Mittermeier, Cristina G. Mittermeier, Gustavo A. B. Da Fonseca, and Jennifer Kent
Nature magazine
February 24, 2000

"The areas without any protection at all amount to 1.3 million square kilometres or 62% of the total area of the hotspots. This expanse surely represents the greatest biodiversity challenge of the foreseeable future, and should be safeguarded through, for example, a 'hotspots rescue fund'. In some areas outright protection is still the best option. In other areas this is not feasible because of human settlements and other activities long in place. These areas could receive a measure of protection as 'conservation units' that allow some degree of multiple use providing that species safeguards are always paramount. ... The traditional scattergun approach of much conservation activity, seeking to be many things to many threatened species, needs to be complemented by a 'silver bullet' strategy in the form of hotspots with their emphasis on cost-effective measures. We could go far towards safeguarding the hotspots and thus a large proportion of all species at risk for an average of US$20 million per hotspot per year over the next five years,

or US$500 million annually. Although this is 12.5 times the average of the $400 million spent on hotspots over the past decade, it is still only twice the cost of a single Pathfinder mission to Mars, which has been justified largely on biodiversity grounds (the search for extraterrestrial life). The $500 million annually is to be compared moreover, with a recent estimate for a comprehensive conservation programme to protect biodiversity world-wide costing $300 billion annually—a total that should, in turn, be compared with subsidies of various sorts that degrade environments and economies alike, amounting to $1.5 trillion annually world-wide. ... This expanded hotspots strategy offers a large step toward avoiding an impoverishment of the Earth lasting many times longer than *Homo sapiens* has been a species."

Critical Analysis

1. Compare the authors' assessment of the scattergun approach to their silver bullet approach to conservation.
2. What is the main barrier to successful conservation outlined in this commentary?
3. Explain what the authors mean by "subsidies that degrade environments and economies."
4. Evaluate the projected cost of conserving biodiversity in the hot spots.
5. Evaluate the method of "multiple use" of conservation regions.

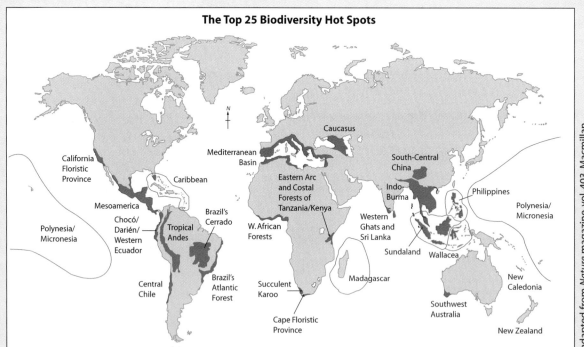

The Top 25 Biodiversity Hot Spots

California Floristic Province · Caribbean · Mesoamerica · Chocó/Darién/Western Ecuador · Polynesia/Micronesia · Tropical Andes · Central Chile · Brazil's Cerrado · Brazil's Atlantic Forest · Mediterranean Basin · Caucasus · Eastern Arc and Costal Forests of Tanzania/Kenya · W. African Forests · Succulent Karoo · Cape Floristic Province · Madagascar · South-Central China · Indo-Burma · Western Ghats and Sri Lanka · Sundaland · Wallacea · Philippines · Polynesia/Micronesia · New Caledonia · Southwest Australia · New Zealand

adapted from *Nature* magazine, vol. 403, Macmillan Magazines Ltd., February 24, 2000

FIGURE 5.19 The regions shown are the highest concentrations of biodiversity in the world that are experiencing the greatest loss of habitat.

MAKE A DIFFERENCE

The World Wildlife Fund vigorously promotes widespread campaigns to:

- enhance public awareness of biodiversity issues;
- stop the poaching, transport, and trade of body parts such as skins, heads, tusks, feathers, and internal organs of endangered species for human decoration or health enhancement;
- provide useful information for people hoping to make a difference in protecting endangered species.

Travellers who fancy a pair of cowboy boots on a trip to Mexico, ivory artifacts from Africa, or black coral jewellery from the Caribbean may not realize they are contributing to harmful practices or illegal trade. You can visit the WWF Web site at <www.wwfcanada.org>. Select "take action" to join in the Conservation Action Network and to communicate with decision makers around the world. This electronic advocacy network has already had success protecting the Galapagos Islands, the Florida Everglades, tigers, rhinos, and sharks.

PROFILE

Birute Galdikas

FIGURE 5.20

Birute Galdikas is a professor of Anthropology at Simon Fraser University. She has devoted most of her life, including more than 20 years spent in the jungles of Borneo, to studying and protecting orangutans. She wanted to know why these apes, whose DNA is 98% identical to humans, did not evolve the way humans did, learning to live in communities. She has won many awards, including the UN Global 500 Award in 1993.

Birute has set up the Orangutan Foundation International as one of her efforts to protect orangutans from the illegal logging that threatens to wipe out their habitat in the forests of Kalimantan, Borneo.

FACT FILE

Of the top 200 ecoregions with outstanding biodiversity in the world, the WWF found that 47% are considered critical or endangered and 29% vulnerable.

PROFILE

Jane Goodall

FIGURE 5.21

Jane Goodall has spent more than 40 years, mainly in Tanzania, working for the welfare of Africa's endangered chimpanzee and gorilla populations. She predicts that chimpanzees in the Congo basin will be gone by 2015. She has written books for adults and children and promoted documentaries in her struggle to raise awareness and money for international conservation efforts.

❝ Look at the very poor law enforcement of animal-protection bills in the developed world. It's pathetic. So it's really not at all surprising that in Africa, unless someone is pushing it, that they will not do something about it. The people just grow up thinking the forests and animals will last forever. The governments... have other things to worry about. War. Political corruption. I'm just trying to change attitudes towards animals. It's very simple, really, I just want to change the world a little. ❞

Jane Goodall, primatologist, conservationist

PROTECTING BIODIVERSITY

The global trends and threats to biodiversity outlined in this and other chapters are indicators of the daunting challenges facing humanity. In order for Earth to continue providing a viable and healthy habitat for humans and other living things, all sectors of society must take action to protect and sustain the ecosystems we all depend on. Biodiversity is not just one issue, but thousands of interrelated issues that cannot be resolved without the work of many different groups and international agreement.

There have been widespread demands, in developed and developing countries alike, for political action to stop the loss of biodiversity. It is clear that population growth, consumption habits, and pollution need to be addressed. Some global progress has been made with population growth.

> **The first rule of intelligent tinkering is to keep all the parts.**
>
> *Aldo Leopold, ecologist*

Fertility rates have been reduced and overall population growth is beginning to slow down, although the impact will not be felt for decades to come.

 See Chapter 14 for more information about poverty solutions.

In order to solve the issues related to biodiversity loss and most other environmental and social justice issues that we face, significant changes must be made in our understanding, attitudes, and lifestyles. Improvements are needed in a wide range of government and corporate policies, including economic incentives that are as strong for protection as they are for habitat destruction, enforcement of stronger legislation, sound land-use planning, efficiency of resource use, allocation of sufficient funds, and development of environmentally sound technology.

> **No politician can hope to get elected on a platform of reducing consumption.**
>
> *Atlas of Population and Environment*

 See Chapter 20 for more information about sustainable solutions.

Conservation Activities

There are some bright spots on the horizon. Populations of several species, including raptors like the bald eagle and peregrine falcon, have begun to recover in North America. Agreements reached at the UN Earth Summit conference in Rio de Janeiro in 1992 form a foundation for international environmental law. One of the agreements was the Convention on Biological Diversity. While the United States did not sign because the agreement interfered with its economic interests, many countries have been working to solve the complex task of conserving endangered spaces and species. Funding for programs is one of the main barriers to success. Without adequate public and private money, it is impossible to transform theoretical policy into practical strategies.

Sources of cleaner energy such as wind, solar, and **biomass** are increasing. The production of ozone depleting chemicals has been reduced by 70% since the late 1980s. Some changes are being made to unsustainable farming and logging practices, making it possible to integrate some wildlife populations within rural landscapes.

Countless initiatives, programs, partnerships, organizations, studies, journals, and international agreements are working around the world to protect biodiversity. **In situ conservation** seeks to maintain viable populations of species in their wild state within their existing range of habitat. **Ex situ conservation** maintains species in seed or gene banks or in captivity, which can result in loss of genetic diversity because of inbreeding. While some of these initiatives are based on utilitarian or economic values, most have made a difference. Many examples of successful **restoration ecology** have improved habitat on lands suffering from deforestation or degradation. Other kinds of local community-based strategies are emerging in many countries. One small example is a diving tax for tourists in Bonaire that is providing revenue for educational materials and conservation rangers to patrol and protect coral reefs. Thousands of non-governmental organizations (NGOs), including the IUCN and Nature Conservancy are having an important influence in setting national and international policies. What follows are just a few of the existing international approaches:

- BioTrade Initiative
- Convention on Biological Diversity
- Intergovernmental Panel on Climate Change
- Kyoto Protocol
- International Whaling Commission
- Convention on International Trade in Endangered Species (CITES)
- Intergovernmental Forum on Forests
- International Coral Reef Initiative
- Biosafety Protocol
- UNESCO World Heritage Sites
- UNEP Assessment of the Status of Closed Forests

CASE STUDY

Protecting Biodiversity in Canada

There is a long way to go before laws and regulations in Canada will ensure adequate management of the biological resources and biodiversity in Canadian ecosystems. Even with overwhelming public support, governments have been slow to protect endangered species and endangered spaces.

A number of overlapping federal and provincial regulations, such as the Fisheries Act and National Parks Act, have provided some protection to some species over the years. A controversial issue in Canada has been the lack of comprehensive endangered species protection, despite public pressure and despite the existence of similar laws in most other developed countries, including the United States and Mexico. The Species at Risk Act (SARA), which passed second reading in Parliament in March 2001, and was submitted for third reading in March 2002, continues to spark controversy. According to 1331 leading scientists who signed a letter to Prime Minister Chrétien in 2001, the main deficiencies of SARA (Bill C-5) are:

66 We just think that Kyoto is not in the interests of the United States or its economy and we don't think it's in the interests of the Canadian economy either. Our two economies are inextricably linked here and we really ought to have a North American strategy. 99

Paul Cellucci, U.S. ambassador to Canada

- the bill does not protect endangered species habitat on provincial land;
- federal lands offered protection make up only 5% of the land needed for habitat protection;
- protection is left to the discretion of the cabinet instead of the previous advisory board of scientists;
- the federal government may not be willing to challenge provincial governments over wildlife responsibility.

While Canada has many national and provincial parks, more than 25% of Canada's natural regions do not contain a single wilderness site with an area of 500 km², the minimum required size for a site to be considered "wilderness," according to WWF Canada.

Parks and reserves are not self-sufficient. As part of the surrounding cultural and economic landscape, they are often associated with mining, logging, hunting, and outdoor recreation and tourism. They commonly contribute to economic diversification in the region and stimulate the local economy, attracting human settlement. Pollution from surrounding activities can affect protected areas. Barriers such as roads and elevated pipelines make it difficult for animals to migrate. If there are already existing roads or other structures, habitat becomes fragmented and travellers on the highways that cut through parks and reserves kill many animals every year. Since there are few remaining habitats suitable for species, buffer zones and natural corridors linking regions of wildlife habitat are important and must be large enough and carefully located to offer adequate protection for the most distinctive species within a region.

Wildlife on the Brink: Endangered Species in Ontario and Canada

Key: Ontario (regular) · **All of Canada** (bold)

	Plants		Butterflies and moths		Molluscs		Fish		Amphibians		Reptiles		Birds		Mammals	
Endangered (regulated under provincial species act)	8		2						1		3		11		1	
Endangered		**30**				**3**		**1**		**1**	5	**2**		**10**		**1**
Threatened	10	**12**					10	**9**	2	**1**	5	**5**	1	**2**		**1**
Vulnerable	6		1				8						8		2	
Special concern		**17**		**1**				**20**		**2**		**5**		**8**		**6**
Extirpated*		**2**		**2**			1	**2**						**1**		
Extinct							1	**3**						**1**	1	
Indeterminate**					1	**1**		**1**					5	**1**	1	**2**
Total by region	24	**61**	3	**3**	1	**4**	20	**36**	3	**4**	13	**12**	25	**23**	5	**10**

FIGURE 5.22

* No longer found in region but living elsewhere in the wild
** Not enough data to determine status

Ministry of Natural Resources in *The Globe and Mail*, Nov. 2, 2000

FIGURE 5.23 A large open-pit coal mine development was to be located in critical wildlife habitat in the land surrounding Canada's Jasper National Park, part of the Rocky Mountain World Heritage site. Environmental lawyers from the Sierra Legal Defence Fund were successful in their bid and subsequent appeal in 2000, to force a new environmental assessment before mining could begin. The project has since been abandoned.

FIGURE 5.24 Some protected areas are used for multiple purposes. For example, Algonquin Provincial Park in Ontario is a protected area that is managed for a variety of uses, including recreational and educational experiences for tourists. Although the park protects and preserves representative ecosystems and species, it allows both logging and hunting within the interior. Some believe that multiple uses of protected areas can work against the motive of conservation.

INTERACT

1. What components of Earth's biodiversity and productivity are not included in the biodiversity hot spots analysis? Explain why.

2. Investigate the efforts of Canadian Birute Galdikas or another conservationist of your choice. Identify several factors that help motivate people to devote so much time and effort to research and species protection.

3. List at least 10 changes that need to be made in order to improve protection of biodiversity.

4. Identify an individual, group, or policy that is working to protect biodiversity in your local community. Identify the issue of concern, explain the initiatives that are being planned or implemented, and evaluate their impact.

5. Evaluate the current policies of Canada's federal government in protecting biodiversity in Canada.

CASE STUDY

Cultural Diversity at Risk

Cultural diversity is the other great realm of living diversity. Language is an important aspect of culture. Just as genetic information in the world's diverse ecosystems is being lost, so is the wealth of cultural knowledge and language of many groups of people. Traditional languages represent an expert, detailed knowledge of traditional livelihoods and local ecosystems. Many cultural geographers and anthropologists believe that complex systems are more resilient—that we may need the vast reservoir of wisdom, ingenuity, and alternative ways of thinking of different cultures when mainstream strategies fail to adequately solve the challenges and problems we face.

Global patterns of biological and cultural diversity tend to coincide. Three **biogeographic** principles explain why places that are high in **endemic** plant and animal species also tend to have the highest number of endemic languages:

- Large countries tend to have higher numbers of species and cultures because of their size, varied ecosystems, and communicative isolation brought on by natural barriers such as mountain ranges
- Island countries are isolated from surrounding land masses and their cultural influences
- The greater species diversity of tropical countries has enabled the survival of many small hunter-gatherer cultures

Many social scientists and international organizations are concerned about cultures facing extinction and that the world's speech is becoming increasingly homogenized. English is quickly becoming the main language of science, commerce, and popular culture. Many languages have fallen to wars, genocide, laws, and assimilation. In South and Central America, hundreds of languages vanished when Spanish explorers conquered the region. Some governments ban minority languages as a way to promote a national identity or cultural conformity. Some children of First Nations peoples in Canada lost the ability to speak their languages in forced residential schools. The government of Kenya promoted Swahili, while the U.S. made it illegal to teach Hawaiian in public schools until 1986. Language is connected to the aspirations of many groups. In the Chiapas region of southern Mexico, the Zapatistas are encouraging the survival of Mayan languages as part of their fight for autonomy.

Vanishing Languages

At least half of the world's 6800 languages, each one spoken by fewer than 2500 people, are expected to vanish. More than half the world's languages are found in eight countries:

Country	Number
Papua New Guinea	832
Indonesia	731
Nigeria	515
India	400
Mexico	300
Cameroon	300
Australia	300
Brazil	234

FIGURE 5.25

FACT FILE

- Four percent of the world's languages originated in Europe, 30% in Africa.

- Four percent of the world's population is considered indigenous, and they speak 60% of the world's languages.

- Sixty-six percent of the worlds' children are bilingual.

COUNTERPOINT These languages are obsolete and have little value in the context of the global economy. Most people in developing countries want to participate in the global economy and will gain the opportunities and advantages it offers if they speak English. Modern technology is much better suited to solving modern problems than is outdated knowledge. Taxpayer money should not be wasted on heritage language programs.

Saving Traditional Languages

Many people of endangered cultures wish to integrate aspects of their traditional cultures with modern education, technology, and political institutions. There are a wide number of initiatives and programs all over the world that work to preserve and revitalize languages, or provide funding for programs.

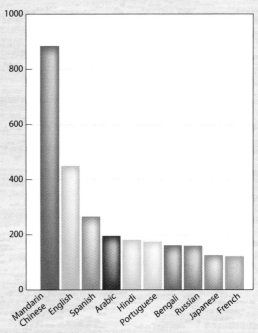

Top 10 Languages in the World
(millions of speakers)

Global Biodiversity Journal, Canadian Museum of Nature, vol. 8, no. 3, Winter 1998

FIGURE 5.26 Half of the world's population speaks one of the "top 10" languages.

Stakeholder Views

"The loss of my people's language has devastating implications. It endangers our ability to think as Sarcee people. When we all become English speaking natives, we sort of belong to the Pan-American group—a generalization of an Indian. It's like lumping all the fishes as a fish, rather than as salmon, trout, or pike. We lose that individuality."

Kevin Littlelight, Tsuu T'ina Nation, Alberta

"Each language has its own way of seeing the world. When you lose a language, you lose that knowledge base and that world view and that impoverishes us."

Arok Wolvengray, professor of Indian languages and linguistics, Saskatchewan Indian Federated College

"Because we include our culture in the education system, our young people understand what effects a major development will have on our traditional way of life. Because our young people now speak English, they understand the major development issues. They now know what land inheritance means."

Gabriel Fireman, Attawapiskat, Nunavut

"Each contracting party shall as far as possible and as appropriate, respect, preserve, and maintain the knowledge, innovations and practices of indigenous and local communities embodying traditional lifestyles relevant for the conservation and sustainable use of biological diversity."

UN Convention on Biological Diversity, Article 8(j)

FIGURE 5.27

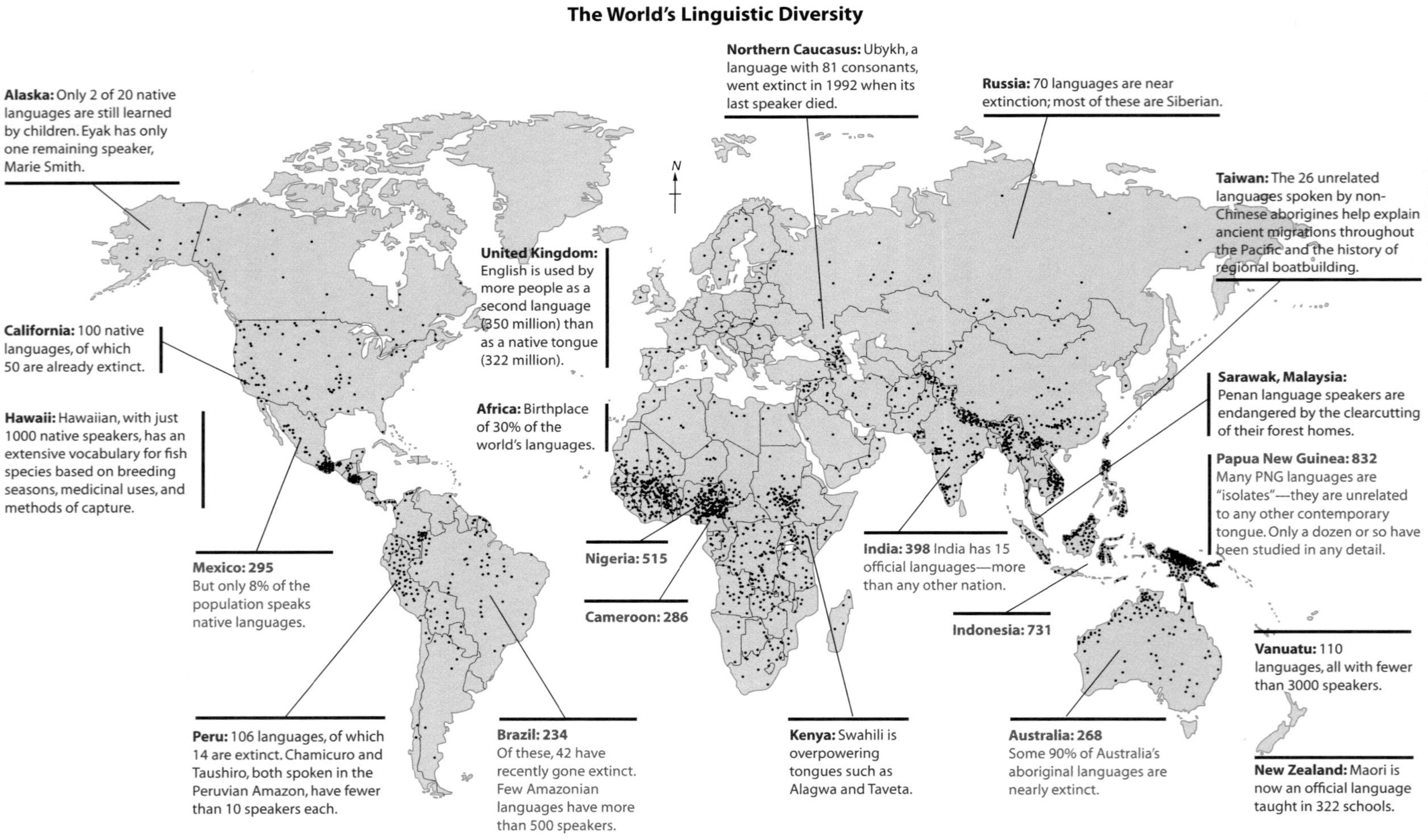

The World's Linguistic Diversity

Northern Caucasus: Ubykh, a language with 81 consonants, went extinct in 1992 when its last speaker died.

Russia: 70 languages are near extinction; most of these are Siberian.

Taiwan: The 26 unrelated languages spoken by non-Chinese aborigines help explain ancient migrations throughout the Pacific and the history of regional boatbuilding.

Sarawak, Malaysia: Penan language speakers are endangered by the clearcutting of their forest homes.

Papua New Guinea: 832 Many PNG languages are "isolates"—they are unrelated to any other contemporary tongue. Only a dozen or so have been studied in any detail.

Vanuatu: 110 languages, all with fewer than 3000 speakers.

New Zealand: Maori is now an official language taught in 322 schools.

India: 398 India has 15 official languages—more than any other nation.

Indonesia: 731

Australia: 268 Some 90% of Australia's aboriginal languages are nearly extinct.

Kenya: Swahili is overpowering tongues such as Alagwa and Taveta.

United Kingdom: English is used by more people as a second language (350 million) than as a native tongue (322 million).

Africa: Birthplace of 30% of the world's languages.

Nigeria: 515

Cameroon: 286

Brazil: 234 Of these, 42 have recently gone extinct. Few Amazonian languages have more than 500 speakers.

Alaska: Only 2 of 20 native languages are still learned by children. Eyak has only one remaining speaker, Marie Smith.

California: 100 native languages, of which 50 are already extinct.

Hawaii: Hawaiian, with just 1000 native speakers, has an extensive vocabulary for fish species based on breeding seasons, medicinal uses, and methods of capture.

Mexico: 295 But only 8% of the population speaks native languages.

Peru: 106 languages, of which 14 are extinct. Chamicuro and Taushiro, both spoken in the Peruvian Amazon, have fewer than 10 speakers each.

N

There are 6 800 dots on this map—one for each of the world's extinct languages. More than half of all languages occur in just eight countries, shown here in green, which give the country language totals.

World Watch magazine, May/June, 2001, pp. 38–39

FIGURE 5.28

They include:

- documenting languages before they disappear;
- language immersion programs for children and adults;
- master–apprentice programs pairing elders with youth;
- control of education programs by Aboriginal peoples;
- rise of new international organizations such as Survival International, which works with more than 80 tribal groups, including Canada's Innu and Terralingua, which works to integrate the understanding and protection of linguistic, cultural, and biological diversity.

FIGURE 5.29 In April 2000, James Wolfensohn, president of the World Bank, participated in the inauguration of the Bank's first Web site in a traditional indigenous language.

INTERACT

1. Compare the map in Figure 5.19, **The Top 25 Biodiversity Hot Spots**, with the map in Figure 5.28, **The World's Linguistic Diversity**. Write a comparative analysis, explaining similarities and any differences between the two maps.

2. Use the Internet to investigate one of the partnerships or initiatives designed to protect linguistic and cultural diversity in Canada. Describe the initiative and evaluate its effects.

3. Using your own values and worldview, write a one-page position paper evaluating the arguments for and against preserving minority cultures and languages.

4. Describe the economic and political aspirations of one traditional culture that is striving to protect its culture and language.

WEB LINKS

- UNESCO (world heritage sites and biosphere reserves): <www.unesco.org>
- International Convention on Biological Diversity: <www.biodiv.org>
- World Wildlife Fund: <www.wwf.org>
- World Conservation Union: www.iucn.org
- Bushmeat Crisis Task Force: www.bushmeat.org
- Jane Goodall Institute, Canada: <www.janegoodall.ca>
- Environmental law: <www.wildlaw.org/Eco-Laws>
- Canadian species at risk legislation: <www.speciesatrisk.gc.ca>
- Ontario's environmental law enforcement: <www.enf.ca/report_2000>
- Statistical data and analysis: <www.fao.org/NEWS/FACTFILE/>
- Survival International: <www.survival-international.org>
- Terralingua: <www.terralingua.org>

RELATED ISSUES

- Impacts of a selected resource development on biodiversity
- World network of heritage and biosphere reserves
- Endangered coral reefs
- Heritage seeds
- Genetically modified salmon

- Frequency and impact of oil spills
- Breeding rare animals in zoos
- Cloning endangered species
- Canada's National Parks in peril
- Protecting local sensitive environments
- Hunting bans or moratoriums such as on grizzly bears in British Columbia

GIS **Species Extinction**

ANALYSE, APPLY, AND INTERACT

1. Apply the frog in the pot and the Tragedy of the Commons analogies to either fish stocks or the atmosphere as a sink for wastes. Write a 300-word scenario of the global future in which the end tragedy for both analogies is reached.

2. Explain why biodiversity is not valued more highly in the market.

3. Explain why it is difficult to make accurate predictions regarding biodiversity and human impact on Earth.

4. Investigate the distribution of land and forest ownership in Canada by the private, federal, and provincial public sectors. Compare this to land ownership in the U.S. What are the implications of land ownership for preserving biodiversity?

5. Choose a hot spot outlined by the biodiversity hot spots analysis on pages 129–130 or an ecoregion that is part of the WWF Global 200 ecoregion study. Produce a detailed case study of your hot spot or region, outlining the location, productivity of the ecosystem, and main threats to biodiversity. Include an annotated sketch map of the region.

6. Identify one threat to global biological sustainability that has an effect on you and your local community. Outline a two-step personal action plan designed to make a difference by being part of a solution to the threat. Carry out your plan.

7. Conduct a cost–benefit analysis of the global trend to monoculture in either agriculture or forestry. Include information on the economic, social, and ecological costs and benefits.

8. Make a list of seven barriers to preserving biodiversity. Conduct a diamond ranking of the barriers. For the top barriers in your ranking, develop a creative solution. Communicate your ideas for the solution to a group or individual that you feel is most able to put it into action effectively.

9. Select one international strategy or agreement designed to protect the global commons. Outline key goals and measures to accomplish the goals, of the strategy or agreement and evaluate its effectiveness in protecting biodiversity.

10. Evaluate the role played by one NGO in protecting biodiversity.

11. Write a 1000-word essay on the impact of aquaculture on the world supply of fish.

12. Investigate the UNEP *Assessment of the Status of Closed Forests* and write a report on the future of the Boreal Forest ecoregion in Canada.

Chapter 6: Global Climate Change

By the end of this chapter, you will

■ analyse geographic issues that arise from the impact of human activities on the environment in different regions of the world;

■ evaluate approaches, policies, and principles relating to the protection and sustainability of the planet's life-support systems;

■ evaluate the effectiveness of methods used by different organizations, governments, and industries to find short- and long-term solutions to geographic problems and issues at the local, national, and global level;

■ demonstrate an understanding of the interdependence of ecology and economics;

■ identify the social, economic, cultural, and political components of selected geographic issues;

■ demonstrate an understanding of how human-induced changes in natural systems can diminish their capacity for supporting human activity;

■ explain how people perceive resources and sustainable development differently at different times and in different places;

■ evaluate some of the ways of promoting sustainable development and assess their effectiveness in selected places and regions of the world;

■ explain the interactive nature of selected natural and human systems;

■ identify current global sustainability issues and environmental threats;

■ evaluate and communicate the perspectives and arguments of various stakeholders involved in a geographic issue;

■ evaluate the effectiveness of an international strategy and agreement that has been designed to protect the global commons or address global issues.

THE GLOBAL CLIMATE CHANGE DEBATE

In 2000, an international panel of 11 climate experts spent nine months carefully considering the evidence on global climate change. The group was sponsored by the National Research Council and included experts on climate modelling, satellite data interpretation, and sea–surface temperature analysis. In the end, the panel could agree on only one narrow aspect of the global climate change debate—that global climate change is, in fact, a real phenomenon. They could not agree on a controversial part of the problem—whether or not human activity is the cause of this climate change. Their efforts to achieve some form of consensus on this controversial debate failed to provide a definitive answer. The debate continues.

The efforts of this panel illustrate the contentious nature of the global climate change issue. While most people can agree that a problem exists, there is little agreement among the experts as to the extent of climate change, its causes, or the implications of the problem. The issue, however, has generated a good deal of confusing rhetoric, strong feelings, and intractable stakeholders. The global climate change debate illustrates the complexity of relationships that develop through human use of the natural environment. In this chapter, we will explore the debate on global climate change to identify the range of viewpoints on the issue and the controversies that arise out of these different perspectives.

> **FACT FILE**
>
> Without greenhouse gases in the atmosphere, Earth's average temperature would be about –17°C. With these gases, the average temperature is about 16°C.

> **FACT FILE**
>
> Although Earth has warmed by only 0.6°C since 1900, that has been enough to disrupt the lives of many plant and animal species.

Points of Agreement

While there are many areas of disagreement, there are some aspects of global climate change on which there is general consensus. To begin, climate change is a product of natural processes. Energy from the sun, in the form of short-wave radiation, heats Earth's surface, radiating the heat back into space as long-wave radiation. Short-wave radiation passes through the atmosphere but some of the long-wave radiation is trapped and retained by the atmosphere. This process acts just like the glass panels of a greenhouse, hence the use of the term "greenhouse effect." The amount of heat retained is a product of the types and amounts of gases in the atmosphere. Greenhouse gases include water vapour, carbon dioxide (CO_2), methane (CH_4), nitrous oxide (N_2O), and more. Without this process, the surface of Earth would be much colder than it is because the heat provided by the sun during daylight hours would be dissipated during the night.

Greenhouse gases are given off naturally through plant and animal respiration and the decomposition of organic material, releases that have normally been in balance with the absorption of gases by terrestrial vegetation and the oceans. These sources collectively release about 10 times more CO_2 than human activity, the other source of greenhouse gases. Here are some generally accepted facts:

- Since the beginning of the Industrial Revolution, atmospheric concentrations of CO_2 have increased by 30%, N_2O concentrations by 15%, and CH_4 concentrations have doubled
- Global mean surface temperatures increased between 0.3°C and 0.6°C over the past century
- The twentieth century's 10 warmest years all occurred in the last 15 years of the century
- Sea levels rose 10–20 cm over the twentieth century

> **FACT FILE**
>
> Ninety-eight percent of U.S. human-induced carbon dioxide emissions are from the burning of fossil fuels to power cars and trucks, heat homes and businesses, and run factories.

The Greenhouse Effect

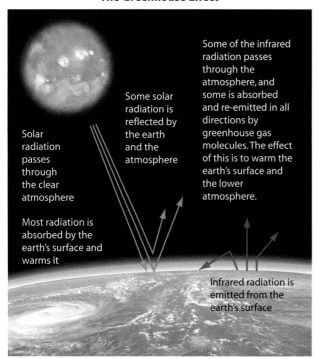

Solar radiation passes through the clear atmosphere

Most radiation is absorbed by the earth's surface and warms it

Some solar radiation is reflected by the earth and the atmosphere

Some of the infrared radiation passes through the atmosphere, and some is absorbed and re-emitted in all directions by greenhouse gas molecules. The effect of this is to warm the earth's surface and the lower atmosphere.

Infrared radiation is emitted from the earth's surface

FIGURE 6.1 Natural and human-generated sources of greenhouse gases work in the same way to warm Earth and the lower atmosphere.

These facts suggest that the world is getting warmer because of increased amounts of greenhouse gases, a trend that the National Research Council panel confirmed. What is causing this? Here is where the debate begins. To many analysts, the cause of the warming of Earth is human activity.

Points of Disagreement

Disagreements about the exact nature and source of climate change occur for a number of reasons, because the data are conflicting or do not provide a clear picture of trends or because of different perspectives and motivations. For example, oil industry representatives will view environmental data from a different

perspective than an environmentalist. Several instances where the data are problematic include:

- human output of greenhouse gases began with the start of the Industrial Revolution (roughly 1750–1800) while global climate change trends were not apparent until the middle of the twentieth century, making it more difficult to identify a cause–effect relationship;

- unlike surface temperatures, there has been no discernible increase in the temperature of the low- to mid-troposphere—the atmospheric layer up to about 8 km—over the past several decades, calling into question the accuracy of computer climate models, which show that the troposphere would heat up;

- variations in climate occur naturally because of long-term trends in such things as solar variations and haze created by volcanic activity, making it difficult to separate naturally occurring warming from human-induced warming and supporting suggestions that correlations between solar activity and climate change are better than between greenhouse gas emissions and global climate change;

- the effect of global climate change is complex and uncertain—extra CO_2 in the atmosphere could stimulate plant growth and the warmer temperatures could lead to the cultivation of colder regions, while the higher temperatures could produce more catastrophic weather

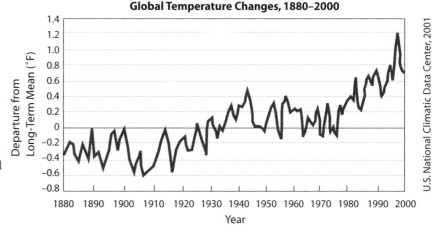

Global Temperature Changes, 1880–2000

U.S. National Climatic Data Center, 2001

FIGURE 6.2

Production of Greenhouse Gases from Human Activities

Greenhouse Gas	Human Activities
Carbon dioxide (CO_2)	Released when fossil fuels (oil, natural gas, and coal), wood, wood products, and solid wastes are burned
Methane (CH_4)	Given off during the production and transport of fossil fuels, the raising of livestock, and through the decomposition of organic wastes in landfills
Nitrous oxide (N_2O)	Emitted during the combustion of fossil fuels and solid wastes and during agricultural and industrial activities
Manufactured gases	Not naturally occurring greenhouse gases include gases that are produced in industrial processes: hydrofluorocarbons (hfcs), perfluorocarbons (pfcs), and sulfur hexafluoride (SF_6)

FIGURE 6.3 Greenhouse gases differ in their ability to retain heat. Nitrous oxide molecules absorb 270 times as much heat as carbon dioxide molecules.

Carbon Dioxide Emissions, Top Ten Countries, 1999

Country	Volume (millions of tonnes)	Percent of Total
United States	1 519.89	25.7
China	668.73	10.9
Russia	400.09	6.5
Japan	306.65	5.0
India	243.28	4.0
Germany	229.93	3.7
United Kingdom	152.39	2.5
Canada	150.90	2.5
France	108.59	1.8
South Korea	107.49	1.7
Other Countries	2 255.68	36.7
Total	6 143.62	100.0

U.S. Energy Information Administration

FIGURE 6.4 Canada generates 2.5% of global CO_2. Canadians make up 0.5% of the world's population.

events including hurricanes, tornadoes, floods, and droughts—which makes modelling the effects of global climate change difficult and requires scenarios to recognize a large range of uncertainty.

The problems with data introduce an element of uncertainty in the debate. This uncertainty allows room for a variety of perspectives on the situation, and gives those who want to oppose the idea of global climate

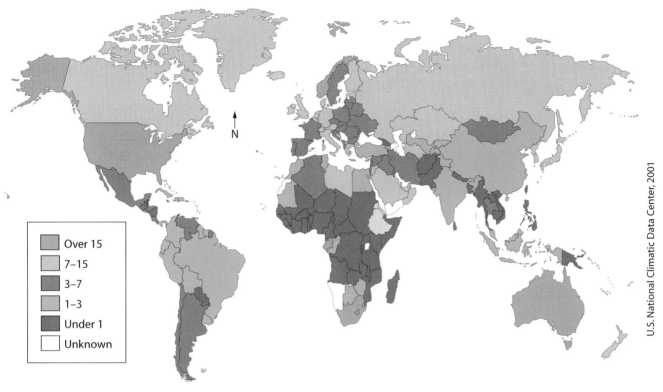

Emission of Carbon Dioxide, 2000 (tonnes per person)

Legend:
- Over 15
- 7–15
- 3–7
- 1–3
- Under 1
- Unknown

U.S. National Climatic Data Center, 2001

FIGURE 6.5 The U.S. produces about 26% of the world's greenhouse gases yet has only 5% of the world's population.

change opportunities to shape arguments. These viewpoints make it difficult to produce a consensus on the problem and how it should be resolved.

Viewpoints on Global Climate Change

Global climate change is seen by many scientists, government officials, and environmentalists as one of the most important environmental problems confronting world decision makers today. Its impacts are viewed as so significant that countries have signed international agreements that obligate them to reduce greenhouse gas emissions, actions that may require substantial financial costs over a long period of time. Critics of the idea of global climate change argue that these drastic changes are not warranted and that the evidence does not support such broad and dramatic responses to the situation. The next section of the chapter will look at the views of those supporting strong action on global climate change and of those opposing actions that will have negative impacts on people and businesses.

" … we have seen no sign of man-induced global climate change at all. The computer models used in U.N. studies say the first area to heat under the 'greenhouse gas effect' should be the lower atmosphere, known as the troposphere. Highly accurate, carefully checked satellite data has shown absolutely no warming. There has been surface warming of about half a degree Celsius, but this is far below the customary natural swings in surface temperatures. **"**

From a briefing paper prepared by the conservative National Center for Public Policy Research

FIGURE 6.6 Consumers in developed countries will face significant impact on their way of life if nations are to reduce their emissions of greenhouse gases.

INTERACT

1. Explain why the lack of certainty in causes and effects of global climate change might lead to differences in viewpoints on the issue.
2. Identify some ways that global climate change has or could have an impact on you personally, on Canadians, and on the global human population.

GLOBAL CLIMATE CHANGE DEMANDS IMMEDIATE ACTION

A host of scientists, environmental organizations, government agencies, and intergovernmental organizations have adopted the view that the world is facing an imminent threat from global climate change. These groups have responded to what some might see as inconclusive data by offering their own explanations. These are some of their positions:

- The lag between the beginning of emissions and rising temperatures can be explained by looking at the effect of the oceans, which acted as a "sink" absorbing carbon dioxide. A carbon sink is a reservoir that absorbs carbon as part of its natural processes. The oceans, along with trees and soils, absorb hundreds of billions of tonnes of carbon each year. It was only in the twentieth century that the output of greenhouse gases exceeded the oceans' ability to absorb it;
- The lack of apparent warming in the higher atmosphere is a product of the short period of data collection, variability or "noise" in the satellite record, and the temperature lowering effects of ozone layer depletion, so the lack of consistent findings in the atmosphere should not invalidate the obvious patterns at ground level;

- The definite rise in sea level and warmer average temperatures are facts that cannot be ignored;
- Inferences from secondary sources of data like ice cores, pollen and fossil data, and tree rings reveal that while global temperatures have been remarkably stable over the past 10 000 years, fluctuating by less than 1 °C between 1000 AD and 1900, they have since risen rapidly, pointing to non-natural impacts on the climate;
- Increasing agreement between computer-generated models of climatic change and observed patterns is a direct result of more sophisticated models that are able to cope with greater complexities and a broader range of evidence coming from a variety of fields of study, leading to predictions of greater and greater certainty.

These explanations lead environmental groups, many scientists, most governments, and the United Nations to the conclusion that global climate change is a real threat. They further conclude that human activity is the cause of global climate change and that immediate action is needed to avoid the worst effects of the problem.

Impacts on Natural Systems

The impacts of global climate change will be felt by natural systems in different ways in different places. Some places may even witness a net drop in surface temperatures due to changes in global circulation patterns. The higher overall temperatures will increase evaporation rates globally, producing drier climates in some regions, but more rainfall in other locations. This regional variability will be very difficult to predict. Globally, average precipitation will increase. Over the twentieth century, for example, global precipitation increased by 1%. Increasing concentrations of greenhouse gases will likely accelerate the warming effect over the next 50 years. It will take at least 100 years for CO_2 levels to return to pre-industrialization levels, largely because the oceans will slowly give off the carbon that they have been accumulating.

The additional heat energy made available by global climate change will power extreme weather events that include tornadoes, hurricanes, and torrential rainstorms. These events will have other associated problems such as ocean surges and flooding.

Plant and animal species will have to respond to changing environments. For example, the algae that give coral reefs their dramatic colours are failing to adapt to warmer waters and the colours are fading, a process known as coral bleaching. Some animals will be able to migrate to more suitable climates as conditions change. However, these migrating animals will likely come into conflict with resident species and human activities. Some adaptable plant species will also be able to expand their range, but the rate of change will far exceed most natural changes that species have confronted. It is expected that some opportunistic plants will find climate change to their liking and will crowd out other plants.

> 66 Apparently small global average changes … led to large climate shifts in the past: Earth's average temperature increased by only about 5°C between the end of the last ice age and today, but much of the Northern Hemisphere went from being buried under [hundreds of metres] of ice to being ice-free. 99
>
> *"Global Warming: Fact vs. Myth,"*
> *Environmental Defense League*

FIGURE 6.7 Commercial air travel produces 15 times as many carbon dioxide emissions per passenger kilometre as travel by bus.

 See Chapter 5 for more information about biodiversity.

Diseases are expanding their ranges as temperatures warm. The migration of the West Nile virus into Canada from the U.S. in 2001 is such an example. This mosquito-borne virus can have fatal consequences for humans. Malaria is another warm-climate disease that has the potential to become a problem in temperate parts of the globe. In the past, cold nighttime temperatures have limited the northward expansion of infectious diseases, but global climate change has produced asymmetric warming with nighttime temperatures reading relatively higher than daytime temperatures. It is thought that the smog and additional water vapour produced by warming help to contain the heat and prevent it from dispersing at normal rates during nighttime hours.

 See Chapter 16 for more information about the environment and human health.

Impacts on Human Systems

Human systems will also be altered by global climate change. Rising sea levels will have a devastating impact on many of the low-lying coastal regions of the world, areas with large populations. Vulnerable cities include Shanghai, Calcutta, Cairo, London, and Miami. A common estimate is that sea levels will rise by 0.6 m over the next century. The additional waters needed for this rise will come from melting glaciers in polar regions.

Global climate change will exacerbate the "heat island" effect in large urban areas. The paving of large surfaces and the use of black roofing materials mean that urban areas trap and hold heat during daylight hours. Temperatures in large cities can be as much as 6°C warmer than the surrounding countryside. This extra heat increases chemical reaction in the atmosphere, producing high levels of smog. For every degree above 20°C, smog increases by 5%. Poor air quality and high temperatures endanger people's health, forcing them to remain indoors and to increase their use of air conditioners, burning fossil fuels in the process. Global climate change means that this problem will become even more chronic.

CASE STUDY

The Collapse of Antarctica's Ice Shelf

In March 2002, a huge part of the Antarctic Larsen B ice shelf crumbled and collapsed into the ocean. This ice had become detached from the Antarctic Peninsula and was 3250 km^2 in area, about half the size of Prince Edward Island. As the ice broke up, thousands of icebergs began drifting out of the area.

The British Antarctic Survey, a research institute with extensive experience on the continent, pointed out that this region has been warming over the past 50 years. Since the middle of the twentieth century, the Antarctic Peninsula has warmed by 2.5°C, a rate of warming about four times faster than the global average. The Antarctic ice is sensitive to climate change because of reflection rates. Ice and snow reflect much of the sun's heat energy back into space while water and bare land absorb the heat. With global warming, more of the surface of the ice shelf is covered by water during summer months, absorbing more heat. The institute predicts that the ice shelves will continue to collapse.

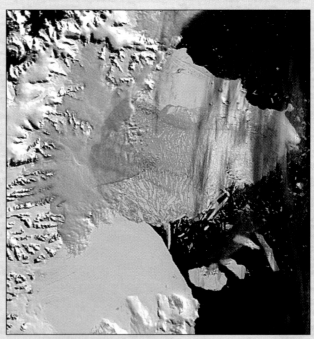

FIGURE 6.8 Collapse of the Antarctic Larsen B ice shelf (March 5, 2002).

This incident did not cause a rise in global sea levels because the ice was already floating. But scientists are concerned that, as the ice shelves melt, the ice caps that cover the continent will also melt or slide into the ocean, raising ocean levels. Antarctica holds 90% of the world's ice.

Forest Fires

Forest fires, often deliberately set for land clearing, contribute as much as 40% of greenhouse gas emissions. Plus, the loss of the forests reduces the global capacity to soak up carbon dioxide. An understanding of the conditions under which fires begin, their behaviour once they get started, and the most effective ways to control them is needed. The World Fire Web brings together scientists and researchers from 16 countries to monitor the extent of fires around the globe. Computer programs are used to search through satellite images to locate hot spots, and global fire maps are generated from the data. Over time, these maps will help national and international agencies better manage fire situations. At the present time, Africa has the most fires, followed by South America, Southeast Asia, and Australia.

FIGURE 6.9 This satellite image shows the smoke plumes from fires burning in eastern Australia.

Climate Change

The Intergovernmental Panel on Climate Change (IPCC), a panel made up of 2000 scientists and other experts, completed a comprehensive review of the body of evidence on climate change in 1999. Using computer models, they extrapolated patterns of carbon dioxide concentrations into the next millennium using three different scenarios. The high scenario is based on the continued intensive use of fossil fuels until they are depleted and/or replaced by less harmful energy technologies. The medium scenario is the IPCC's prediction of CO_2 concentrations if action is not taken to reduce greenhouse gases until 2100. The low scenario requires immediate action to limit emission. This low scenario predicts a temperature peak of about 2°C and a return to pre-industrialization stability in about 500 years. It is the IPCC's view that the medium scenario is the best estimate of what will happen.

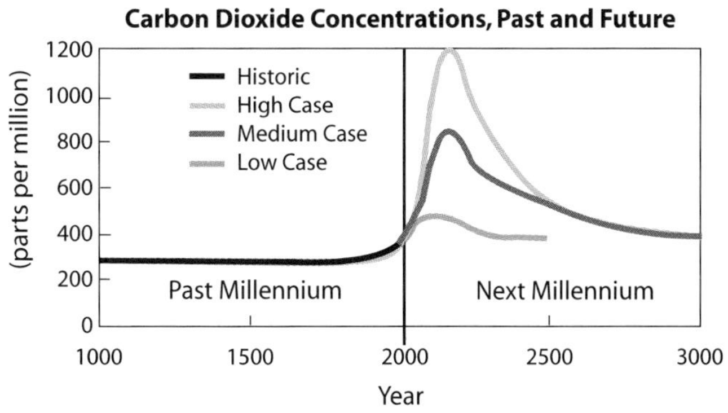

Carbon Dioxide Concentrations, Past and Future

- Historic
- High Case
- Medium Case
- Low Case

Past Millennium Next Millennium

y-axis: (parts per million) — 0, 200, 400, 600, 800, 1000, 1200
x-axis: Year — 1000, 1500, 2000, 2500, 3000

FIGURE 6.10 Even optimistic predictions suggest that temperatures will remain elevated for between 500 and 1000 years.

FACT FILE

In response to the predictions about sea level rise, the South Pacific island nation of Tuvalu (26 km²; 10 800 people) negotiated an agreement with New Zealand that would allow the island's people to become citizens of New Zealand as they are forced from their homes.

Global climate change will produce more deadly heat waves, where temperatures remain elevated for extended periods. In 1995, the city of Chicago endured a heat wave that resulted in over 500 deaths. Temperatures remained above 27°C even during the night.

Higher global temperatures will lead to higher rates of evaporation and the outward expansion of very dry land, reducing croplands in places like North America's interior plains. The moisture could be dropped in unpredictable patterns that could yield greater rates of flooding, ice storms, and blizzards. Temperature could also vary considerably, depending on the altered climate patterns

The direct effect of global climate change, such as extreme temperatures and elevated ocean levels, combined with secondary effects, that will probably include declining food supplies and higher rates of energy use, are predicted by some to have profound impact on living things.

FIGURE 6.12 The impact of global climate change on quality of life could be significant.

Flooding Caused by Rising Sea Level, 2050

FIGURE 6.11 Coastal plains, such as those in the southern U.S. will be particularly vulnerable to rising ocean levels.

INTERACT

1. Identify and explain forces that have some ability to affect or modify natural climatic patterns. For each, identify positive and negative impacts of the forces.
2. Explain why, even if the countries of the world agreed to reduce greenhouse gas emissions to levels equal to the period prior to the Industrial Revolution, the greenhouse effect would still continue for many years.
3. Suppose you accept the argument that global climate change is a real and significant human-induced problem. What level of risk are you prepared to endure? In other words, how much damage do you think is tolerable before drastic action is required to solve the problem? Discuss this idea in a one-page report.

GLOBAL CLIMATE CHANGE DOES NOT WARRANT DRASTIC ACTION

Actions to reduce global climate change usually involve cutting back the amount of greenhouse gases emitted. The 1997 Kyoto Protocol, a key international agreement on global climate change, set targets of reducing emission levels below 1990 levels by 2010. Because of economic growth since 1990, greenhouse gas emissions would have been 30% above 1990 levels by 2010. Therefore, meeting 1990 emission targets will require a dramatic reduction in the consumption of fossil fuels plus substantial retooling of technologies. Adjustments of this magnitude for economies dependent on fossil fuels will not come easily. Some analysts argue that these kinds of changes to solve a "questionable" problem are simply not warranted. In other words, the predicted harm of the cure is probably greater than the harm of the problem.

> " Sceptics say the scenarios of future climate change that are produced by computer models are deeply flawed. They believe the task of simulating the complexities of our climate system is beyond the capabilities of even the fastest supercomputers. "
>
> *Jonathan Amos, environment reporter, BBC News Online*

The oil industry, in particular, has resisted the idea that dramatic cuts in consumption of fossil fuels are necessary. The substantial wealth generated by the use of fossil fuels, and the investment in the infrastructure to support the industry, mean that companies tied to oil production will face substantial reduction in sales if global climate change is to be successfully controlled. To counter this loss of sales, some companies are beginning to diversify into alternative technologies such as hydrogen fuel cells or renewable energy and hybrid vehicles. The worldwide oil industry has developed effective lobby strategies and has friends among some of the world's most powerful governments, especially George W. Bush, president of the U.S.

Harmful Medicine

One approach that governments might use to meet emission targets is a "carbon tax" on fuels to encourage consumers to limit their use. Consumers would see a sharp rise in the costs of heating fuel, electricity, and transportation as additional taxes are attached to fossil fuel energy sources. In the U.S., for example, electricity costs have been predicted to rise between 20% and 86%. The higher costs, in the short term, would encourage consumers to shift their spending patterns, diverting money from consumer spending to taxes. Analysts predict

> " ... the instrument of taxation is often seen as a key tool to be used for environmental objectives. But the track record in many consuming countries is so far poor, with oil products often taxed at levels that have probably already reached a pain threshold. And, while oil is taxed so heavily, other fuels are taxed at far lower levels and are sometimes even subsidized. The time is ripe to reconsider the entire philosophy of energy taxation, by restructuring fiscal systems to address broader concerns than the financial needs of governments ... "
>
> *Dr. Ali Rodriquez Araque, secretary general of the Organization of Petroleum Exporting Countries (OPEC)*

that the tax hikes in the U.S. necessary to achieve below 1990 levels of emission would have the effect of reducing per capita incomes by 10% and would result in 1.3 million job losses. In addition, the burden of the taxes would fall unequally on the poorest 20% of the population, and those on fixed incomes, worsening the poverty gap in the country. The indirect effects of actions to lower emissions would be higher costs for consumer goods and services in all areas, including schools, daycare centres, hospitals, and government agencies. In the longer term, however, tax revenues spent

FACT FILE

A study commissioned by African-American and Hispanic groups in the U.S. concluded that the economic burden of reducing greenhouse emissions would be unequally borne by ethnic minorities, who make up a large share of the working poor, with job losses for these groups more than double the rate for the population as a whole.

wisely would likely result in improved technologies and lifestyle changes that emphasize conservation.

In 2001, the United Kingdom instituted a 7% "climate change tax." This levy, in combination with rising global energy costs, pushed up gas prices charged to industrial customers by 50%. Corporations watched their profits fall. The industrial community complained that the burden of the costs of reducing greenhouse gases was making already difficult times even harder. They wanted action against global climate change put off until times were better and consumers and businesses were better able to pay the costs.

COUNTERPOINT People who support taking action to reduce greenhouse gas emissions argue that the focus on the costs of taxes is simplistic. They point out that not taking action to reduce emissions may well cost many times more than the potential losses due to taxes. These costs would accumulate due to the combination of higher health and social costs because of a warming earth, property losses because of desertification and rising ocean levels, and job losses because of climate-induced poverty. The discussion of taxes, these critics think, is too focused on today's economy, not the future economy.

Another strategy to reduce greenhouse gas emissions has been to establish a system where pollution credits could be bought and sold. Companies able to make reductions in their emissions over government requirements earn credits that could be sold to companies that did not reduce their emissions enough. The earnings from selling credits would stimulate action to reduce emissions. Industries have been very critical of this program, arguing that it has pushed up costs. For example, in southern California it cost just 29¢ to buy credit for 1 kg of nitrogen oxide in 1999, but the price soared as high as $81 during 2000. Not purchasing these credits means that companies face stiff fines.

FACT FILE

One intended outcome of higher taxes on energy sources is that people will switch from using cars to mass transit. Energy prices more than doubled in Britain between 1990 and 2000, yet there were year-on-year increases in traffic. Critics of the taxes argued that the government failed to spend enough to make mass transit more attractive.

FIGURE 6.13 California has established some of the toughest programs to reduce air pollution. Its population growth and high consumption lifestyle, however, negate many of the improvements.

"Viewpoint: Get off warming bandwagon"

by William M. Gray, professor of atmospheric science, Colorado State University
BBC News Online
November 16, 2000

As a boy, I remember seeing articles about the large global climate change that had taken place between 1900 and 1945. No one understood or knew if this warming would continue. Then the warming abated and I heard little about such warming through the late 1940s and into the 1970s.

In fact, surface measurements showed a small global cooling between the mid-1940s and the early 1970s. During the 1970s, there was speculation concerning an increase in this cooling. Some speculated that a new ice age may not be far off.

Then in the 1980s, it all changed again. The current global climate change bandwagon that U.S.–European governments have been alarming us with is still in full swing.

Not our fault

Are we, the fossil-fuel-burning public, partially responsible for this recent warming trend? Almost assuredly not.

These small global temperature increases of the last 25 years and over the last century are likely natural changes that the globe has seen many times in the past.

This small warming is likely a result of the natural alterations in global ocean currents which are driven by ocean salinity variations. Ocean circulation variations are as yet little understood.

Human kind has little to do with the recent temperature changes. We are not that influential.

There is a negative or complementary nature to human-induced greenhouse gas increases in comparison with the dominant natural greenhouse gas of water vapour and its cloud derivatives.

It has been assumed by the human-induced global warming advocates that, as anthropogenic greenhouse gases increase, water vapour and upper-level cloudiness will also rise and lead to accelerated warming—a positive feedback loop.

It is not the human-induced greenhouse gases themselves which cause significant warming, but the assumed extra water vapour and cloudiness that some scientists hypothesise.

Negative feedback

The global general circulation models that stimulate significant amounts of human-induced warming are incorrectly structured to give this positive feedback loop.

Their internal model assumptions are thus not realistic.

As human-induced greenhouse gases rise, global-averaged upper-level atmospheric water vapour and thin cirrus should be expected to decrease not increase.

Water vapour and cirrus cloudiness should be thought of as a negative rather than a positive feedback to human-induced or anthropogenic greenhouse gas increases.

No significant human-induced greenhouse gas warming can occur with such a negative feedback loop.

Climate debate has "life of its own"

Our global climate's temperature has always fluctuated back and forth and it will continue to do so, irrespective of how much or how little greenhouse gases we put into the atmosphere.

Although initially generated by honest scientific questions of how human-produced greenhouse gases might affect global climate, this topic has now taken on a life of its own.

It has been extended and grossly exaggerated and misused by those wishing to make gain from the exploitation of ignorance on this subject.

This includes the governments of developed countries, the media and scientists who are willing to bend their objectivity to obtain government grants for research on this topic.

I have closely followed the carbon dioxide warming arguments. From what I have learned of how the atmosphere ticks over 40 years of study, I have been unable to convince myself that a doubling of human-induced greenhouse gases can lead to anything but quite small and insignificant amounts of global warming.

Critical Analysis

1. Comment on the authority of this writer to offer viewpoints on the topic.
2. What reasons does Gray offer to support his view that global climate change is not a problem?
3. In your own words, summarize Gray's claim that positive and negative feedback loops can be used to show that global climate change is not a significant problem.
4. What does Gray offer as motives for other people's support for global climate change? What is your reaction to this explanation of motives?

INTERACT

1. **a)** Explain how taxes might be used as a tool to reduce greenhouse gas emissions.
   b) Why might governments use this strategy rather than alternative strategies to reduce emissions?
   c) What might be some of the impacts of taxes on consumers, businesses, and governments?

2. The Fact File on page 152 points out that higher energy costs did not produce higher rates of mass transit use. Identify and explain three other factors that could have had an impact on the relationship between energy taxes and mass transit use.

3. Energy taxes have the effect of raising costs for industries, a condition most industries seek to avoid. Complete a costs–benefits analysis for industries for:
   a) a hike in energy taxes, and
   b) the elimination of energy taxes.
   Now, complete the same analysis but from the perspective of society as a whole.

4. Even if you accept that climate change is not a problem, outline some benefits of reducing air pollution anyway.

5. In your opinion, who in a society should bear the greatest burdens for improving a problem situation such as greenhouse gases? Give your opinions in a one-page report.

THE KYOTO PROTOCOL

In spite of the vocal minority view on the issue of global climate change that some suggest is motivated by protection of vested interests, there has been widespread global recognition of a problem. Environmental groups have wholeheartedly endorsed the idea that global climate change is human induced and have mobilized their resources in an effort to bring about sweeping changes. Many governments have also accepted a need for action, in part because of their moral obligation to protect their citizens from harm. Pressure from these two groups, in particular, has led to international efforts to do something constructive about global climate change. In the international arena, taking action involves holding conferences and negotiating international treaties. One of the most influential agreements on human-induced global climate change is the Kyoto Protocol of 1997, negotiated in Kyoto, Japan. This international agreement grew out of a need expressed at the 1992 Rio de Janeiro conference on the environment for action on global climate change. Signatories to this treaty must reduce their levels of carbon dioxide and other greenhouse gases. Eighty-four countries signed the Protocol. This set in motion a process to produce a detailed agreement that the signing nations could take back to their governments for ratification.

The Kyoto Protocol attempted to stimulate action by setting binding targets for reductions of the more important greenhouse gases. As a group, the industrialized countries (representing about 65% of human-induced emissions) have to achieve a reduction of 5.2% below 1990 emission levels between 2008 and 2012. Targets for individual countries were decided based on present emission rates and abilities to achieve reductions. The European Union's (EU) target is 8%, the U.S. has to achieve 7%, and Japan should reach a 6% reduction. Russia is expected to stabilize its emissions. Targets were not set for developing countries on the grounds that per capita emissions are lower than in industrialized countries and the financial burden of reducing greenhouse gases would inhibit economic development.

To ease the pain of cutting emissions in industrialized countries, the Kyoto Protocol included an international emissions trading

The Path to Kyoto and Beyond

1972 ◀	First Earth Summit in Stockholm, Sweden
1982 ◀	Failed Earth Summit in Nairobi, Kenya
1983	
1984	
1985	
1986	
1987	
1988 ◀	The International Panel of Climate Change (IPCC) was created
1989	Toronto Conference on the Changing Atmosphere
1990 ◀	The IPCC's first report
1991	
1992 ◀	Second Earth Summit, Rio de Janeiro, Brazil
1993	
1994	
1995 ◀	Conference of Parties to the Climate Convention (COP I) in Berlin, Germany
	The IPCC's second report
1996 ◀	COP II in Geneva, Switzerland
1997 ◀	COP III in Kyoto, Japan
1998 ◀	COP IV in Buenos Aires, Argentina
1999 ◀	COP V in Bonn, Germany
2000 ◀	COP VI in The Hague, Netherlands
2001 ◀	COP VI-2 in Bonn, Germany
	COP VII in Marrakech, Morocco
2002 ◀	Third Earth Summit in Johannesburg, South Africa

system that would allow industrialized countries to buy and sell emissions credits. A country that was exceeding its target reductions could sell the extra credits to countries not yet achieving their goals. Also, industrialized countries could earn credits by financing projects to reduce emissions in developing countries.

Kyoto's Impact on Developing Countries

The developing countries of the world were eager to see the Kyoto Protocol put into effect. They expected to see an increase in their competitiveness, especially in the production of emission-intensive goods like iron and steel and the processing of metals. These industries use substantial amounts of fossil fuels and the lack of emission targets would mean costs for them would not rise as they would in developed countries. The higher cost in industrialized countries would encourage companies to buy offshore, from producers in developing countries. Predictions suggest that for every 1000 t of greenhouse gases reduced in the industrialized world, there would be an increase of 92 t in the developing world as production shifts.

However, developing countries that are major exporters of fossil fuels will see a decline in revenues as industrialized countries reduce consumption. Mexico's oil industry, for example, sells most of its output to the U.S. where consumption is predicted to drop by 15%. Overall, however, developing countries are expected to benefit economically from the Kyoto Protocol.

Kyoto's Impact on Developed Countries

There is a good deal of debate about the possible impacts of the Kyoto agreement on industrialized countries. An EU report suggests that member countries could achieve 85%–95% of targets without damaging their economic competitiveness. By full implementation in

◀ **FIGURE 6.14** Earth Summits take a broad view of environmental conditions while Conference of Parties (COP) sessions have been meetings to explore, refine, or negotiate specific topics.

FIGURE 6.15 Chief U.S. Negotiator Stuart Eizenstat and Canadian Environmental Minister Christine Stewart at the Kyoto conference in 1997.

is stimulated by governments reforming tax policies so as to encourage research and development of alternative energy sources. Corporations have also been motivated to expand their energy sources: both Shell and British Petroleum have begun funding multimillion dollar investment programs in renewable energies. Car companies have also moved ahead on new fuel initiatives. For example, Ford Motor Company has invested in the Canadian developed Ballard hydrogen fuel-cell technology.

> "To put it simply, the changes we need to make to fight climate change are changes that would make us all better off even if there was no such thing as climate change! That's why a low fossil fuel future is a better future. "
>
> *Greenpeace Canada, "The Kyoto Protocol—a Primer"*

The Bonn Conference

The 2001 Bonn, Germany, conference was one of the follow-up sessions to the Kyoto Protocol. The purpose of the Bonn conference was to fine-tune mechanisms that were agreed to in the Kyoto Protocol. One hundred and seventy-eight countries participated in this meeting, including a good number of nations that had not signed the initial document.

2010, the Kyoto Protocol could cost the EU just 0.06% of its gross domestic product. Japanese economists have established a cost of implementation at about 0.9% of the country's gross national product, or US$47.3 billion. In contrast, American analysts have predicted that the global climate change agreement would have significant negative consequences for the economy, reducing per capita income growth by 5% to 10%. A conservative policy organization estimated that reducing emissions below 1990 levels would cost the average American $862 per year. For Canada, compliance to the Kyoto Protocol has been estimated by different groups to reduce economic growth by 0.66%–2.0% per year. They claim that gas prices would likely have to be raised by 24¢ per litre.

The agreement should encourage the further development of renewable energy technologies that do not emit greenhouse gases. In part, this

FACT FILE

Japanese and European economists have argued that the forced innovation necessary to meet the requirements of the Kyoto Protocol will make these countries more competitive in the world economy.

FIGURE 6.16 This Xantrex Company manufacturing plant is the first factory in North America to operate from 100% renewable energy. Xantrex makes inverters, the electronic controls that regulate power flow from solar panels, fuel cells, and wind turbines.

A key outcome of the Bonn session was the establishment of several new sources of funds to help developing countries limit their emissions and switch to cleaner technologies. Developing countries can use these funds to finance adjustment programs, including training scientists in measuring emissions. One fund provides money to help oil-producing countries diversify their economies so the impacts of the reduced consumption of fossil fuels in developed countries are softened.

> **"** Businesses are starting to use green power in order to market themselves as environmentally sensitive and to position their operations as cutting edge. **"**
>
> *Kevin Hagen, Xantrex Company*

A serious debate surfaced at the conference about the use of carbon sinks as emission credits. Canada, Australia, and several other countries with large forest and farmland areas wanted to claim that these areas of vegetation absorb carbon and, therefore, the countries should earn extra emission credits for them. The countries of the European Union were strongly opposed to such a scheme. In the end, a compromise was reached: countries could take credit for forestry management projects, within strict limits.

The Bonn conference also dealt with penalties for not meeting Kyoto targets. Two penalties were accepted:

- For every tonne of carbon a country emits over its Kyoto limit, it will have to reduce an additional 1.3 t during the second protocol commitment period that will begin in 2012
- Countries that do not meet their targets will be banned from trading for emission credits

All signatory countries are obliged to follow the rules and face international pressure from other countries if they fail to do so.

Critical Analysis of the Kyoto Protocol

The Kyoto Protocol is not binding on signatory countries until it has been ratified or approved by the legislatures of the countries. The agreement will go into force only after it has been ratified by a minimum of 55 countries, representing at least 55% of industrial countries' emissions. By the time of the Bonn conference in 2001, only 34 countries had ratified the Kyoto Protocol, all of them developing countries, with the singular exception of Romania. The U.S.—the largest single producer of greenhouse gases—is unlikely to ratify the Protocol under George W. Bush's administration. Bush has been critical of the agreement—declaring it

FIGURE 6.17 George W. Bush has strong ties to the American oil industry and has not been sympathetic to the goals of the Kyoto Protocol.

fatally flawed—and the obligations it would imply for the U.S. He has come under strong pressure from industry and oil groups not to sign the Protocol. The absence of the U.S. from the treaty would significantly weaken the impact of the Kyoto Protocol.

The need to reach compromises for the agreement to be ratified has weakened its effectiveness. Analysts suggest that the compromises and exceptions negotiated in Bonn have the effect of setting the target at only 2% below 1990 levels, not the –5% that was the goal.

excerpt from

"The Global Warming Debate"

by James Hansen
Goddard Institute for Space Studies

In my view, we are not doing as well as we could in the global warming debate. For one thing, we have failed to use the opportunity to help teach the public about how science research works. On the contrary, we often appear to the public to be advocates of fixed adversarial positions. Of course, we can try to blame this on the media and politicians, with their proclivities to focus on antagonistic extremes. But that doesn't really help.

The fun in science is to explore a topic from all angles and figure out how something works. To do this well, a scientist learns to be open-minded, ignoring prejudices that might be imposed by religious, political or other tendencies (Galileo being a model of excellence). Indeed, science thrives on repeated challenge of any interpretation, and there is even special pleasure in trying to find something wrong with well-accepted theory. Such challenges eventually strengthen our understanding of the subject, but it is a never-ending process as answers raise more questions to be pursued in order to further refine our knowledge.

Scepticism thus plays an essential role in scientific research, and, far from trying to silence sceptics, science invites their contributions. So too, the global warming debate benefits from traditional scientific scepticism.

… [S]ome "greenhouse sceptics" subvert the scientific process, ceasing to act as objective scientists, rather presenting only one side, as if they were lawyers hired to defend a particular viewpoint. But some of the topics focused on by the sceptics are recognized as legitimate research questions, and also it is fair to say that the injection of environmental, political and religious perspectives in midstream of the science research has occurred from both sides in the global warming debate. …

Although scientists have a right to express personal opinions related to policy issues, it seems to me that we can be of more use by focusing on the science and carrying that out with rigorous objectivity. That approach seems to be essential for the success, as well as the "fun" of scientific research. …

As the opinions in the global warming debate do not seem to be converging, it seems to me that one useful thing that can be done is to clearly delineate the fundamental differences. Then, as our scientific understanding advances over the next several years, we can achieve more convincing evaluations of the global warming issue. (Stated less generously, this is a way to pin down those who keep changing their arguments.)…

In summary, all of these issues are ones that the scientific community potentially can make progress on in the near future, if they receive appropriate attention. The real global warming debate, in the sense of traditional science, can be resolved to a large extent in a reasonable time.

Critical Analysis

1. Define these terms: "proclivities," "antagonistic extremes," "scepticism."
2. Explain the role of scepticism in science.
3. The label "junk science" has been used to refer to scientists who use scientific methods to prove their own biases. What might be some reasons that would motivate scientists to practise junk science? Explain why the accusation of "junk science" aimed at legitimate scientific inquiry can be an effective propaganda tool.
4. Summarize Hansen's argument for maintaining "rigorous objectivity" on global climate change.

There are concerns that transnational corporations (TNCs) can benefit from the agreement and avoid taking actions to reduce emissions. By moving their more polluting operations to developing countries that are not required to meet emissions targets, the transnational companies can get away with making only small reductions in emissions.

A number of critics of the Kyoto Protocol have pointed out that the target of reducing below 1990 levels is arbitrary. In spite of all the discussion and negotiation that have gone on around this level, there is no concrete evidence that achieving the target will eliminate or even significantly improve the problem of global climate change. There is growing support for targets to be as much as 50% below 1990 levels.

In general, the Kyoto Protocol has stimulated significant action on a number of fronts to reduce greenhouse gas emissions. Whether the

> " I prefer an imperfect, living agreement to a perfect one that doesn't exist. "
>
> *Olivier Deleuze, Belgian Energy minister*

> " In order to reduce greenhouse gas emissions, you have to innovate and come up with new technologies. If the US does not ratify Kyoto and the EU and Japan do, they will gain a competitive advantage. "
>
> *Professor Kornelis Blok, Utrecht University, co-author of a European Union (EU) report on greenhouse gas emissions, 2001*

cuts are deep enough or fast enough to make a significant reduction in greenhouse emissions are questions that have yet to be answered. The lack of willingness on the part of the U.S.—the world's largest emitter of greenhouse gases—seriously undermines the effectiveness of the agreement, although there remains a high degree of enthusiasm around the world. The success or failure of the Protocol over the next decade will tell the story.

FIGURE 6.18 Environmental groups have tried to pressure government decision makers to push forward on global climate change initiatives.

INTERACT

1. In a chart, identify different viewpoints on the Kyoto Protocol and some of the stakeholders for each viewpoint.
2. Identify the various mechanisms incorporated into the agreement and describe the possible impacts that each could have. Offer reasons to explain why the mechanisms were included.
3. In your opinion, has the Kyoto Protocol been worth the time and effort put into drafting the document? Explain your opinion.
4. Suggest one change that you would make to the Kyoto Protocol. What would be the purpose of your change—to get more countries to sign the agreement or to make it more effective in dealing with climate change? Explain your answer.

CASE STUDY

Canada and Global Climate Change

FACT FILE

Canada signed the Kyoto Protocol on April 29, 1998, and expected to ratify it by late in 2002.

FACT FILE

Converting coal-fired electrical generating stations to much cleaner burning natural gas will reduce their greenhouse gas emissions by 70%.

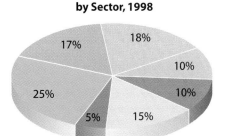

Canada's Greenhouse Gas Emissions by Sector, 1998

18%
17%
10%
10%
25%
5%
15%

☐ Transportation
☐ Electricity production
☐ Oil and gas industry
☐ Buildings
☐ Agriculture and forestry
☐ Indusrty
☐ Other

Government of Canada, Action Plan 2000 on Climate Change

FIGURE 6.19 Transportation is the largest category of emissions, and offers a good deal of opportunity for reductions in greenhouse gases.

Environmentalists Congratulate Federal Government on Climate Change Agreement

Sierra Club of Canada media release
July 23, 2001

The Sierra Club of Canada today congratulated the Canadian delegation and the federal government on the flexibility it demonstrated over the final negotiating session in Bonn, Germany.

After a marathon negotiating session which ran all night, more than 160 countries have come to an agreement on the rules of the Kyoto Protocol. Canada dropped its objections to several parts of the compromise paper prepared... on Saturday night, and was instrumental in helping convince the Japanese delegation to accept a strong compliance system for the agreement.

The successful outcome of this meeting means Canada can now proceed with speedy ratification and begin the hard work of reducing emissions.

Canada got more than it had been asking for on sinks. This means that Canadians will need to be vigilant, and ensure that our use of sinks represents a real increase in carbon storage in forests and soils, and that we commit to reducing our emissions domestically.

Somewhat surprisingly, the Canadian delegation abandoned its demand for the inclusion of foreign sales of nuclear power as a credit under the clean development mechanisms. ...

"It's important to remember that Kyoto is just a first step. If we are going to avert the disastrous effects of runaway climate change, it is vital we start to work on reducing emissions immediately," said Angela Rickman, Deputy Director of the Sierra Club of Canada. "We know what our targets are, and they are attainable. Let's not waste any more time."

FACT FILE

Transnational chemical companies like Dupont, 3-M, and Dow Chemical were already modifying production processes to reduce greenhouse gas emissions well before 2001.

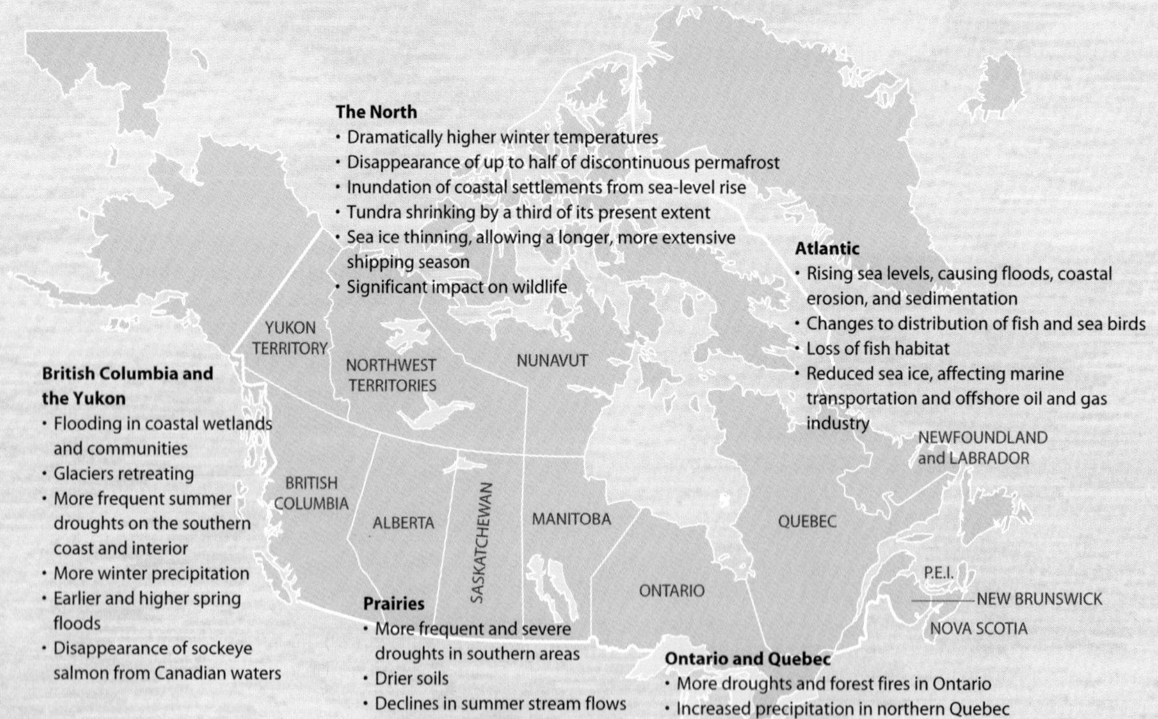

The North
- Dramatically higher winter temperatures
- Disappearance of up to half of discontinuous permafrost
- Inundation of coastal settlements from sea-level rise
- Tundra shrinking by a third of its present extent
- Sea ice thinning, allowing a longer, more extensive shipping season
- Significant impact on wildlife

Atlantic
- Rising sea levels, causing floods, coastal erosion, and sedimentation
- Changes to distribution of fish and sea birds
- Loss of fish habitat
- Reduced sea ice, affecting marine transportation and offshore oil and gas industry

British Columbia and the Yukon
- Flooding in coastal wetlands and communities
- Glaciers retreating
- More frequent summer droughts on the southern coast and interior
- More winter precipitation
- Earlier and higher spring floods
- Disappearance of sockeye salmon from Canadian waters

Prairies
- More frequent and severe droughts in southern areas
- Drier soils
- Declines in summer stream flows
- Longer growing seasons
- Increased crop production in the north where suitable soils exist
- Shrinking seasonal wetlands
- Grasslands migrating northward

Ontario and Quebec
- More droughts and forest fires in Ontario
- Increased precipitation in northern Quebec
- Longer growing seasons
- Increased crop production in the north where suitable soils exist
- Lowered water levels, affecting shipping on the St. Lawrence River and Great Lakes
- More days when heat and air pollution adversely affect public health

FIGURE 6.20 Predicting Canada's climate, 2050

adapted from *Canadian Geographic*, May/June 2002, pp. 40–41

Environmental lobbyists feel Canada's commitment to the Kyoto Protocol is being undermined by industry

Suzuki Foundation news release
November 21, 2001

The Canadian Chemical Producers' Association claims that it will face economic hardship if Canada follows through on its pledge to ratify the Kyoto Protocol. The industry plans to lobby MPs today in order to allow unregulated greenhouse gas pollution to continue.

"This association has been denying and delaying action on global warming for almost a decade," said Gerry Scott, director of the Suzuki Foundation's climate change campaign. "It's time Ottawa stopped listening to the special interests of large industrial polluters and stood up on behalf of all Canadians. It is imperative that this first high-profile assault on the Kyoto agreement be stopped."

> "There is no shortage of solutions to the challenge of climate change, only a shortage of political will."
>
> *The David Suzuki Foundation, Up in the Air, 2002*

> "Cutting greenhouse gas emissions means standing up to powerful vested interests."
>
> *Greenpeace Canada, "The Kyoto Protocol—a Primer"*

Selected Initiatives Announced by the Canadian Government, 2001

Initiative	Value	Activities
Commercial/Institutional Buildings Retrofit Initiative	$30 million	Provides incentives, training, information, and advice to encourage commercial and institutional organizations to carry out energy-efficient retrofit projects
Energy Efficient Housing Initiative	$35 million	Promotes the construction and purchase of energy-efficient houses, and the renovation of existing homes to reduce energy use
Technology Innovation Program	$19 million	Encourages the further development of cost-effective GHG mitigation technologies and skills and encourages research and development partnerships
Clean Development Mechanism	$25 million	Supports Canadian companies' pursuit of GHG credits through project investment in other countries
Canadian Industry Program for Energy Conservation	$2 million	Expansion of activities of this industry organization to reduce emissions among its members
Carbon Dioxide Capture and Storage Initiative	$25 million	Helps demonstrate and commercialize technologies used in the capture, transportation, and storage of CO_2 underground
Future Fuels Program	$3 million	Increases the supply and use of ethanol produced from biomass, such as plant fibre, corn, and other grains

Government of Canada, *Action Plan 2000 on Climate Change*

FIGURE 6.21 The federal government program included 28 initiatives with a total value of $425.15 million.

FACT FILE

A compromise agreement was achieved at the Marrakech conference. Prime Minister Chrétien stated that the agreement opened the door for Canada to consider a decision to ratify the Kyoto Protocol in 2002. Ratification would take place after full consultation with provinces and territories, other stakeholders, and the Canadian public.

FACT FILE

Alberta's premier Ralph Klein declared that ratification of the Kyoto Protocol would cost his province's economy trillions of dollars.

Predicted Reductions from Greenhouse Gas Emissions

Sector	Percent of Total
Industry	15
Agriculture and forestry	20
Buildings	10
Energy (electricity, oil, and gas)	20
Transportation	10
International	25

Government of Canada, *Action Plan 2000 on Climate Change*

FIGURE 6.22 These proposed reductions to help meet the targets under the Kyoto Protocol should total about 65 mt per year for the years 2008–2012.

excerpt from "Is Kyoto a bright move for Canada?"

The Globe and Mail
May 28, 2002

A global problem needs a global cure, says federal Environment Minister, David Anderson....

It is truly important for Canada to be part of the global framework because, while we might only contribute 2 per cent of the emissions that are creating the problem, 98 per cent of the effect of climate change experienced in Canada comes from emissions elsewhere in the world, primarily developed countries.

Canada has a stake in having the rest of the world take action. To expect others to do so, Canada has to do its share.

Canada is the ninth-largest emitter of greenhouse gases in the world and we are in the top three, measured on a per capita basis—about 24 tonnes per Canadian....

On May 15, the government of Canada released a discussion paper that set out four options for how Canada could meet its international climate change commitment...under the Kyoto protocol.

Results so far from federal-provincial modelling work indicate that it is possible to meet our Kyoto target while seeing our economy grow at a robust rate....

These models do not take into account the benefits of accelerated innovation or the increase in quality-of-life for Canadians—such as cleaner air.

Beyond the economic costs associated with taking action we must also consider the significant costs if we don't act. In addition, there are benefits associated with the new technologies in energy efficiency, renewable energy, transportation, and so on....

In some options outlined in the discussion paper, economic growth in parts of the country could be affected more than in others. Alberta has legitimate concerns, and we want to work with the province to address these. The government of Canada's discussion paper does lay out an option that could address these concerns—a way to enable energy intensive industries, such as mines and oil-sands plants, to keep growing....

Under the Kyoto Protocol, Canada is asked to meet the goal of reducing our emissions to 6 per cent less than our 1990 levels over the period 2008 to 2012....

Under Kyoto, we can reshape the future in a way that gives us cleaner air, a more stable climate and a more energy-efficient Canada. We can reshape the future to give ourselves a less wasteful economy.

And we can reshape it to improve the health of Canadians and provide a better environment for future generations.

INTERACT

1. **a)** Evaluate Canada's actions on global climate change, using the information in this section of the chapter.
   b) Investigate current media reports to provide an updated evaluation of Canada's actions.
2. What role do vested interests, including industries, provinces, and NGOs, play in shaping Canada's response to the Kyoto Protocol?
3. In what ways does Canada's position on global climate change illustrate the complexity of negotiating significant international agreements, such as the Kyoto Protocol?
4. Suppose you wanted to try to influence the federal government into taking a new position on global climate change. What are three specific actions that you could take to influence decision makers? Explain your ideas.

WEB LINKS

- Greenpeace Canada:
- Environment Canada's The Green Lane:
- National Consumer Coalition:
- Environmental Defense group (U.S.):
- Scientists for Global Responsibility (UK):
- The David Suzuki Foundation:

RELATED ISSUES

- TNCs and global climate change
- The role of NGOs in bringing about action on climate change
- The value of Earth Summits in focusing attention on environmental issues
- The environmental track records of specific political organizations, such as the American Republican Party or Canada's Liberal party

ANALYSE, APPLY, AND INTERACT

1. Using the debate about global climate change as an example, explain how ecology and economics are interdependent at both the international and national levels.

2. Prepare an ideas web to show the social, economic, cultural, and political components of the global climate change debate. For example, one of your topics might be Transportation. Identify the linkages and connections to this topic and others. You might prepare a poster and include quotations or pictures to show your points.

3. The TV quiz show *Jeopardy* has sets of five increasingly difficult answers (to which the contestants supply questions) arranged under topic headings. Make up five answers for the topic heading of Global Climate Change Debate. Explain why each of your answers would be a good quiz show item.

4. Using global climate change as your specific topic, sketch a cartoon that focuses on ways that human-induced changes in natural systems can reduce their capacity for supporting human activity.

5. Reductionism is the process by which people oversimplify issues. Read the following quotations, both included in the *Instant Expert Guide* published by the U.S.-based Heartland Institute, and explain how reductionism has been used:

   "Immediate action [against global climate change] wouldn't make us any safer, but it would surely make us poorer. And being poorer would make us less safe."

   "A slightly warmer world would probably be greener and a little cloudier than our world today, but otherwise not much different."

6. Working with several partners, role-play a session at the Bonn conference (see pages 156–157 for details) where negotiations focused on mechanisms to implement the Kyoto Protocol. Decide which roles should be played, but at least consider having people represent developing countries, industrial countries, Canada, the U.S., and oil-rich developing countries. Allow time for people to prepare their positions before starting the role-play exercise. Following your session of role playing, conclude by having each person express his/her view about Canada's involvement in negotiations.

7. What strategies do environmental groups use to address the global climate change situation? Examine the actions taken by one environmental organization and comment on its effectiveness.

8. Research to find out the status of the Kyoto Protocol at the present time. How many countries have ratified the agreement? How many countries are likely to meet their target reductions? What important countries have not signed the agreement? What are other interesting developments that have taken place?

9. Make up a personal action plan for reducing greenhouse gas emissions and promoting sustainable development. Set short- and long-term goals for your action plan. Include at least three specific, realistic actions in your plan.

10. Research to determine the current situation of the global climate change debate. Have the viewpoints converged at all? What are some new pieces of evidence in the debate? What new tools are being used to gather evidence?

11. Update the global climate change debate as it applies to Canada. Consider actions taken by governments, initiatives taken by industries, roles of environmental and lobby groups, and changes in living and working conditions for Canadians.

12. China has been an important source of greenhouse gases because of its extensive use of dirty coal as an energy source. Research to determine the role that China has played in the global climate change debate. Evaluate its efforts to reduce greenhouse gases.

Chapter 7: Global Natural Resources

By the end of this chapter, you will

- evaluate the significance of the participation of people in non-violent movements to protect resources and environments;

- demonstrate an understanding of how human-induced changes in natural systems can diminish their capacity for supporting human activity;

- evaluate the economic, social, and ecological impact of current methods for raising or harvesting a selected resource;

- analyse examples of efforts to increase the productivity of a selected natural environment and their short- and long-term economic, social, and environmental impacts;

- produce a case study of a specific situation in which resource development has contributed to the disruption of an ecosystem;

- explain how new technology affects employment and resource management;

- evaluate the sustainability of selected trends related to consumption of the earth's resources;

- evaluate the role played by non-governmental organizations and local community initiatives in different parts of the world in promoting sustainable development and resource management;

- produce an action plan for a local community initiative that contributes to the sustainability of a selected global resource;

- produce scenarios for probable and desirable futures based on current trends in the human use of the earth and its resources, including trends in technology.

PUTTING RESOURCES INTO PERSPECTIVE

In her poignant commentary on change in Australia, the elderly Alice Nannup reflected on the early development of mining in the State of Western Australia:

FIGURE 7.1 The extraction of natural resources often has significant and lasting impacts on natural systems and local communities.

❝ When I was in Fitzgerald Street Aunty Jean was still up in Port Hedland, and she used to come down and stay with me for a couple of weeks at a time. Her hair was that red I'd say to her "Aunty, what's the matter with your hair? You been dyeing it?"

"No," she'd say, "it's the iron-ore, it's all over everything."

… I was up there when that iron-ore first started, when they started loading it on to the boats, and the dust kicked up was terrible. It was really red and it blew from east to west, all over the port. Hedland used to be such a beautiful town but it's ruined now.

Even when they could see how the dust was choking the place they didn't stop, they just kept on going. They even tried putting hoses and sprinklers to stop it from blowing around but it didn't work. When I used to come in from Hillside I couldn't believe it, everything you touched was red. Even the Poinciana trees lost their beauty, and they used to be the pride of Port Hedland when they were flowering.

All that mining and destroying the land is something that worries me a lot. It's not only happening in the Pilbara either, it's everywhere, the world is off its axis, they're destroying everything just to make money…. ❞

excerpt from
When the Pelican Laughed
by Alice Nannup, Lauren Marsh,
and Stephen Kinnane
in New Internationalist
March 1998

FACT FILE

People in the developed countries of the world consume 18 times as much aluminum and 13 times as much iron and steel as people in developing countries.

TAKING MINERALS FROM THE EARTH

The search for mineral wealth was one of the driving forces of European imperialism in the fifteenth to nineteenth centuries. For example, the Spanish conquerors of South and Central America were quick to seize gold and silver and to enslave the indigenous population so that they would have a ready supply of miners. While Africa was conquered somewhat later, by 1870, the British had moved into South Africa to exploit the diamonds and gold of that region. At this point, the British had ambitions to colonize the whole of the continent, from the Cape of Good Hope to Cairo. The political and military domination of the colonized people ensured that resources could be exploited effi-

FIGURE 7.2 While gold and silver were the focus for the early exploitation of minerals in the New World, later mining operations also developed copper, zinc, and iron ore deposits.

To a great extent, this concentration of ownership of the world's minerals has come about through mergers and acquisitions. Transnational mining companies have moved into developing countries seeking new deposits of mineral resources. Local mining companies have not had the resources to compete with the large foreign-owned companies and have had few options but to go into joint ventures or to merge with the larger firms.

❞❞ Large-scale mining is among the most socially disruptive economic activities in the developing world. ❞❞

Keith Slack, Oxfam America

ciently, and the profits from such ventures filled the coffers of European countries.

Imperialism continues to this day, although it now takes the form of economic imperialism. A handful of mining companies from rich countries now control most of the world's mining.

By 1993, the top 10 mining companies controlled almost 29% of the world's mineral production. By 1998, the two biggest companies, Anglo American and Rio Tinto, controlled 18% of the world's metallic output and 90% of the world's rough diamonds. In copper, a key mining sector, the top 10 companies control over 61% of the global output. The example in Figure 7.3, **Leading Uranium Mining Companies, 1999**, shows the domination of mining companies from the developed parts of the world, with 63% of production controlled by four countries.

Leading Uranium Mining Companies, 1999

Company Name	Head Office	Share of World Production (%)
Cameco	Canada	20
COGEMA	France	14
Energy Resources of Australia (ERA)	Australia	11
Western Mining Corporation (WMC)	Australia	9
Rio Tinto (Rossing)	United Kingdom	9
Navoi	Uzbekistan	7
Priargunsky	Russia	6
KazAtomprom	Kazakhstan	4

The Uranium Institute

FIGURE 7.3 The transnational companies listed in this chart have operations in many parts of the world. COGEMA, for example, operates mines in Niger, Canada, and France, and holds reserves in Australia and Kazakhstan.

excerpt from
"Big Mining Companies in Torrid Latin American Affair"
by John Newcomb
Reuters
November 5, 1998

A new breed of conquistador has arrived in Latin America.

This modern-day swashbuckler can be found digging for copper in Chile's Tarapaca region, laying claim to gold in Venezuela's Orinoco Basin and cutting deals from Tijuana to Tierra del Fuego.

Unlike Francisco Pizarro's Spaniards, who plundered their way through the Andes 465 years ago in a largely unsuccessful bid to lay their hands on Inca wealth, mining executives are getting a hearty welcome in the Latin world.

Once a bastion of stringent mining laws and infuriating red tape, Latin American nations, particularly Argentina, Bolivia and Peru, have undertaken dramatic economic reforms and helped trigger a mining renaissance south of the Rio Grande.

This year the world's largest mining companies will earmark about $814 million, or 28.8 percent of their total exploration budgets, toward projects in Latin America, according to Canadian mining consultants Metals Economics Group.

In comparison, the next most popular destination, Australia, will only receive $494 million, or 17.5 percent, of total exploration dollars.

"It (Latin America) has great geology and a welcoming regulatory climate. They are willing to accept mining as an economic activity without putting obstacles in the way. They help a mining company make the business work," said Hugh Leggatt, spokesman for Canada's Placer Dome Inc.

Vancouver-based Placer, one of the world's largest gold producers, has made a strong exploration commitment to Latin America through several option agreements on properties in Chile, Peru and Venezuela.

Placer plans to spend about $46 million this year on exploration in Latin America, one of the largest budgets in the region. The company will allocate about $10 million to Peru alone.

Exploration budgets in Latin America have increased steadily during the past decade as word spread of the region's spectacular mineral potential.

Chile's Candelaria copper mine, 80-percent owned by U.S.-based Phelps Dodge Corp., and Peru's Yanacocha gold mine, operated by U.S. miner Newmont Mining Corp. and by Peru's Buenaventura concern, are two discoveries that have set tongues wagging and investors reaching for their pocketbooks. ...

Analysts say many mining companies have shrugged off sluggish metals markets, preferring to take a long-term view on Latin American exploration.

"If you've already spent $30 million in a country on projects, you wouldn't just leave because of metals prices or your stock price going down," said David Cox, senior research analyst for Metals Economics Group.

"A lot of spending we see from the bigger companies is no longer grassroots but work on their later-stage projects. They've developed projects in Latin America and money is continuing to flow in there," Cox said. ...

Critical Analysis
1. Explain the references in this article to conquistadors, swashbucklers, Francisco Pizarro, and the Rio Grande.
2. According to the article, why are world mining companies interested in Latin America?
3. What might be some benefits of this high level of exploration expenditure for Latin American countries?
4. What might be some of the drawbacks to high levels of foreign ownership in a country's mining industry?

"It is one of the strange economic paradoxes. Why is it that in many cases the economies of countries that have an abundance of natural resources actually perform less well than those of their counterparts that have few resources? What has benefited Korea and Japan for instance, so that their economies have far outstripped those of say, Mexico or Zambia?"

Mining Journal,
April 17, 1998

Environmental Implications of Mining

The search for minerals has led to the decapitation of mountains, the rerouting of rivers, the creation of mountains of waste materials, and the contamination of groundwater. Much of the damage occurs because of the low concentrations of valuable ores; huge amounts of material must be extracted and refined. Refining often requires the use of chemicals and substances that are hazardous to both people and the environment.

Mining operations typically have four stages in their life: exploration, development, processing, and closure. Each stage has its own specific environmental impacts, which are determined by other variables, such as the type of ore being extracted, site characteristics, and the climate of the area.

EXPLORATION STAGE The search for mineral deposits usually requires the building of access roads and the construction of pits and drill pads, activities that may disturb wildlife and drainage patterns. In sensitive environments, such as the Arctic tundra, prospecting activities can lead to erosion and sedimentation in streams. A secondary effect of exploration is that access roads can be used by hunters and campers, exposing sensitive areas to higher levels of human activity. The very nature of prospecting means that only a small percentage of tested sites are ever developed as working mines.

MINE DEVELOPMENT If the ore body is sufficiently rich and transportation costs are low enough, a mine may be built. But first, the infrastructure to support the mine must be constructed, including transportation linkages, power grids, water supplies, and communities for workers, all of which can have detrimental impacts on natural systems. Once this infrastructure is in place, the mine can be built.

Mineral Exploration Expenditures in Canada, 2001

Province/Territory	Expenditures ($ millions)
Ontario	99.0
Quebec	69.6
Northwest Territories	60.1
Nunavut	54.2
British Columbia	45.1
Saskatchewan	41.2
Manitoba	30.5
Newfoundland	24.5
Yukon	10.7
New Brunswick	10.3
Alberta	7.8
Nova Scotia	4.6

Statistics Canada

FIGURE 7.5 Mining companies spend heavily exploring for new mineral deposits.

FIGURE 7.4 Prospecting is the process of gathering information about the subsurface materials. It requires testing at the surface with specialized equipment.

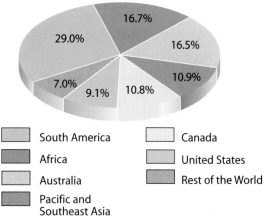

Spending on Exploration for Minerals, 1997

16.7%
16.5%
10.9%
29.0%
7.0%
9.1%
10.8%

South America
Africa
Australia
Pacific and Southeast Asia
Canada
United States
Rest of the World

Minerals Economics Group Survey

FIGURE 7.6 Exploration spending is dependent on several factors, including the geology of regions and demand for minerals.

When the ore is deep beneath the surface, shaft mines are constructed: sloped or horizontal tunnels are dug off main vertical shafts to reach ore deposits that are drilled, blasted loose, and lifted to the surface. The famous nickel mines of Sudbury, Ontario, are of this type. In places where the ore is closer to the surface, open-pit mining is used. In this technique, the overburden of waste rock is removed to expose the ore. The iron ore deposits of Labrador are mined in this way. Open-pit mining allows the use of large-scale extraction methods. The higher volume of material that can be handled with this method means that lower grades of ore can be profitable. The overburden, however, can pose an environmental problem. It has to be put somewhere. The piles of waste can disrupt the natural drainage patterns and often mean that the land cannot be used for other purposes such as forestry or recreation. Open-pit mines produce eight times as much volume of waste as underground mines.

> **FACT FILE**
>
> Over 70% of mineral production in Canada comes from open-pit mining.

> **FACT FILE**
>
> The mammoth excavators used in open-pit mining cost over US$50 million.

MINERAL PROCESSING To extract the useful minerals from the waste materials, ores are crushed and ground and then the materials are treated with chemicals. Cyanide, mercury, sulphuric acid, and organic agents are some of the chemicals used to separate the valuable ore. The waste materials—**tailings**—are filtered and washed and the effluent is discharged to tailing ponds for storage. Treatment of these wastes can lead to 99% recovery of harmful materials from the tailings. Unfortunately, in addition to many instances of leakage from tailing ponds, there have been other incidents. In 1998, a truck carrying sodium cyanide from a Canadian-owned uranium mine in Kyrgyzstan crashed into a river, poisoning an estimated 2500 people, four of whom died.

> **FACT FILE**
>
> Five or six tonnes of ore have to be dug from the ground to produce enough gold to make an 18-carat gold ring.

Estimated Number of Abandoned Mines by Jurisdiction, 2000

Province/Territory	Number of Mines
Ontario	6 015
Alberta	2 100
Quebec	1 000
Saskatchewan	505
Nova Scotia	300
Yukon	120
New Brunswick	60
Newfoundland and Labrador	39
Northwest Territories	37
British Columbia	20
Nunavut	3
Manitoba	n/a
Prince Edward Island	0

adapted from Mackasey, W. O. "Abandoned Mines in Canada" at <www.miningwatch.ca/publications/Mackasey_abandoned_mines.html>

FIGURE 7.8 Poor mining practices in the past have resulted in a large number of abandoned mines. Many of these mine sites pose an environmental hazard.

FIGURE 7.7 Open-pit mines such as this one in Timmins, Ontario, have significant environmental impacts.

In addition to tailings, the smelting of metals in blast furnaces and smelters produces air pollution. Materials injected into the atmosphere include nitrogen oxides, sulphur dioxide, particulate matter, and metals.

MINE CLOSURE Minerals are non-renewable, finite resources, so eventually the deposits are used up and the mines are closed. In the past, and currently in some parts of the world, these sites were just abandoned, with severe environmental consequences. In many cases, the tailings and waste materials have high levels of sulphide that combine with rainwater to form acids. These can leach into the groundwater and contaminate local water bodies. Now in Canada, the sites cannot just be abandoned; they must be returned to some form of useful activity. This **reclamation** requires a carefully thought-out plan and a long-term commitment to monitoring the area. Mining companies are obligated to have an interest in closed mine sites long after they have stopped generating revenues.

Mining and Indigenous Peoples

Many peoples, including indigenous peoples, around the world have long histories of working with minerals, using metals to create the tools and adornments that are part of their cultures. Today, many are employed in the mining industry in all stages of production. In some cases, they share in the revenues that mining generates. However, indigenous peoples have also been victims of the expansion of mining. Some of their complaints against mining are:

- the influx of outsiders into their traditional areas;
- the erosion of traditional livelihoods through the loss of land and resources;
- cultural conflicts with outsiders;
- environmental degradation because of mining activities;
- forced displacement from traditional homelands;
- violence.

The expansion of mining in some places has been seen by indigenous peoples as a threat to culture, the environment, traditional livelihoods, and their own self-determination.

The question of rights to traditional lands usually underlies conflicts that indigenous peoples have with mining. Mining is land-intensive, especially open-pit mining, which requires a great deal of space for the mine, overburden, and tailings. In many countries, mining has been proposed for areas customarily used by indigenous people. In cases where indigenous rights to the land are poorly protected by the laws and constitution of the country, the state has often assumed control of the decision-making. The state usually takes the largest share of the revenue that is generated and is often more concerned about economic interests than the rights of indigenous peoples. A case in point occurred in 1999 in the Philippines. The Subanen indigenous people blockaded a road to a proposed mine site on their ancestral territory on the Zamboanga peninsula. The Canadian mining company, TVI Pacific, had received approval from the federal government for this project on lands the Subanen had claimed ancestral rights to in 1992. The protesters were attacked by an armed group and beaten with rifle butts. Both the Philippines government and TVI Pacific were strongly criticized for this action by religious and civil rights groups, NGOs such as Survival International, and local residents. The Subanen were also supported by local small-scale miners who were displaced by the transnational mining company.

❝ In many, if not most, traditional societies, land is inalienable, communal, and of great spiritual and cultural importance. For most indigenous societies, land is the basis of local economies, providing subsistence produce for consumption and exchange in customary practice. ❞

Frank McShane and Luke Danielson, Mining Minerals and Sustainable Development Project

CASE STUDY

The Los Frailes Tailings Dam Failure

On April 25, 1998, the dam containing the tailings from the Los Frailes lead-zinc mine at Aznalcóllar, Spain, collapsed and released about six million cubic metres of toxic tailings into a nearby river. The mine was owned by Toronto-based Boliden Ltd., a joint Swedish-Canadian operation.

The dam failed when the clay soil that formed its base slid forward under pressure from the accumulated tailings. This caused the dam to collapse. A report prepared for the company two years earlier had pointed to weaknesses in the dam, including the presence of leaks, yet no action was taken to improve the situation. The break in the dam allowed between five and seven million cubic metres of contaminated water to spill into the Río Agrio, raising its surface by three metres. Among the contaminants in the slurry were sulphur, zinc, copper, lead, and other trace elements. There was massive fish kill in the river. The slurry inundated over 5000 ha of farmland,

FIGURE 7.9 The impact of the tailings spill at Los Frailes.

ruining all crops and contaminating the soil. Clean up costs were estimated at US$135 million. The incident resulted in the loss of 5000 jobs in farming, fishing, tourism, and nature conservation.

Within a year of the spill, Boliden decided to reopen the mine. However, an ongoing investigation of the incident heard from experts that the spill was a result of negligence and the company faced significant lawsuits. The company ceased operations at the mine in September 2001 and dismissed its 425 employees. In November 2001, however, Boliden was cleared of criminal responsibility by Spanish courts.

The negative publicity that mining companies receive when they do encroach on indigenous people's land is bringing about some change. Grass-roots movements have learned how to use the attention of the international media to generate interest in their causes. This can result in delays for projects because of community protests and legal action. Indigenous groups have recognized the power in peaceful, organized, public protest.

In response, some mining companies have started to include the different stakeholders in planning projects. Indigenous peoples, local residents, the local business community, and local governments are beginning to have a voice in mining developments.

> 66 Several of the most vicious ongoing wars in the world involve conflicts over minerals. 99
>
> *Chris Baker and Gary Anderson, "Power Hungry People," Insight on the News, June 25, 2001*

FIGURE 7.10 The Ngobe-Bugle Indians protest in front of the Canadian embassy in Panama City against Canadian mining operations on their traditional lands.

Survival International

Survival International is a worldwide NGO that is dedicated to supporting the right of indigenous people to decide their own future. This organization helps Native peoples to protect their lives, lands, and human rights. Survival International was founded in 1969 when people in Britain became incensed about the

❝We believe that public opinion is the most effective force for change. Its power will make it harder and harder, and eventually impossible, for governments and companies to oppress tribal peoples. ❞

Survival International Web site

racist oppression of Brazil's Indians in favour of economic development. The organization now has supporters in over 90 countries and supports tribal peoples in 60 countries around the world. They have offices in London, Milan, Madrid, and Paris. Survival International does not accept money from governments and is financed completely by its supporters, allowing it to have an independent voice on issues.

For Survival International, the most urgent problem for tribal peoples is the

FIGURE 7.11

loss of land. Around the world, indigenous people have lost tribal lands to the invasion of settlers, the appropriation of lands for the extraction of natural resources, or because of government policies, such as road building. Without access to their lands, tribal peoples are less able to feed themselves or acquire the necessities to lead a healthy life. From this organization's perspective, greed and racism underlie this takeover of traditional lands.

Survival International's campaigns are designed to give indigenous people a platform to address the world. They educate people around the world about the situations and issues faced by tribal peoples and encourage their supporters to write letters to the media. Campaigns turn public attention toward governments and companies that are oppressing tribal peoples. Influencing public opinion, this organization believes, is the most effective way to bring about real change for indigenous peoples.

INTERACT

1. Explain the importance of technological change and consumption of consumer goods on the mining industry.
2. Why can it be said that economic imperialism continues to this day in the global mining industry?
3. Which stage in the development of a mine is likely to have the greatest environmental impact? Explain your answer.
4. What strategies would you recommend to limit the conflicts between indigenous peoples and mining activities in Canada? Around the world?
5. Using their Web site, < www.survival-international.org >, research one campaign conducted by Survival International and comment on its success.

ENERGY TO POWER THE WORLD

There are two key observations we can make about the global demand for energy:

- As populations grow, energy demands rise
- As people become more affluent, energy demands rise

Current demographic patterns show that global population growth will continue for most of your lifetime, so global energy demands will escalate over the coming decades simply because there will be more people. And, many people in developing nations, wanting the way of life enjoyed by those in developed countries, struggle to achieve the same energy-rich material wealth. The inescapable conclusion is that energy demands will continue to grow quickly for the foreseeable future, placing a growing demand on the planet's natural resources.

The global consumption of energy increased fourfold over the second part of the twentieth century, a rate far faster than population growth. For part of this period, the world faced a perceived energy crisis. There was concern that supplies of fossil fuels would be used up and the world would face shortages of energy. The concern shifted in the latter part of the century to the environmental effects of our reliance on fossil fuels, largely because we began to understand the relationship between climate change and consumption of energy from carbon-based fuels. The early part of the twenty-first century will see discussions about how to deal with both of these concerns; in other words, how can we meet the growing demand for energy in ways that do not destroy the natural environment?

> As the world's supply of recoverable (inexpensive) fossil fuels dwindles and becomes more important as an agency of international diplomacy, it becomes increasingly clear that the energy dilemma is the most serious economic and environmental threat facing the Western world and its high standard of living.
>
> *John L. Allen, ed., Environment: Annual Editions, 01/02, McGraw-Hill/Duskin*

 See Chapter 6 for more information about global climate change.

Quality of life, including health and well-being, is linked to energy consumption. Those nations that have high levels of energy consumption also have high life expectancies, high literacy levels, low rates for infant mortality, and other such indicators of a high quality of life. Plentiful and inexpensive energy is clearly associated with the conquering of diseases and improvements in living conditions.

Cleaner Energy

The predicted rapid increase in demand for energy over the coming years will bring about catastrophic environmental consequences unless there is

Othmar Preining, "Global Warming Perspective," World Resource Review, Vol. 12, #3, pp. 421–427

Global Energy Future, Modest Scenarios	2000	2050	2100
Global Population (billions)	6	9	10
Gross World Product ($1000 billions)	20	75	200
Energy Demand (giga ton oil equivalent)	10	20	35
Net Carbon Emission (giga tons of carbon)	6	10	6–20

FIGURE 7.12 Global demand for energy will continue to rise over the current century, spurred on by rising standards of living in most countries of the world. The wide range given for carbon emissions reflects the debate about the extent of actions needed now to deal with this form of pollution.

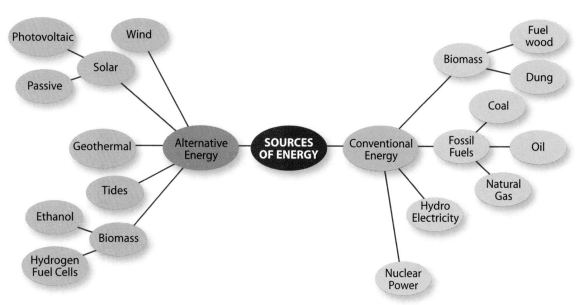

FIGURE 7.13 About two billion people around the world use firewood and animal dung to cook food and heat homes.

International Energy Agency

Global Fuel Sources, 1973 and 1999 (%)

Fuel Source	1973	1999
Coal	13.6	8.2
Oil	47.1	42.7
Gas	14.8	16.0
Combustible Renewables and Waste	13.2	14.2
Electricity	9.7	15.4
Other	1.6	3.5

FIGURE 7.14 These statistics on energy sources show a shift away from high-emission oil and coal toward cleaner energy sources.

Top Energy Consumers, 1998

Country	World Consumption (%)	World Population (%)
United States	25.3	4.6
China	10.0	21.3
Russia	7.0	2.5
Japan	5.9	2.1
Germany	4.0	1.4
India	3.2	16.6
France	2.9	1.0
United Kingdom	2.7	1.0
Canada	2.6	0.5
South Korea	2.0	0.8

United Nations Procurement Division (UNPD)

FIGURE 7.15 According to the data, Canada's ratio of energy consumption to population is 5.2:1. Which country has the highest ratio? Which has the lowest ratio?

a widespread shift to cleaner sources of energy. Fossil fuels—which currently supply about 90% of the energy consumed—produce too much carbon dioxide and other greenhouse gases for their continued use. Fortunately, there has already been some movement toward the use of cleaner fossil fuels. Globally, the consumption of coal has only doubled over the past 50 years, while oil and natural gas use increased seven-fold and tenfold, respectively, reflecting a preference for these relatively cleaner fuels. China,

which has been the largest consumer of coal, has begun to develop other types of energy sources, such as hydroelectric power at its massive Three Gorges project on the Yangtze River, a project that has social and environmental costs as well.

FIGURE 7.16 A plentiful supply of energy is vital to high-consumption lifestyles.

 See Chapter 8 for more information about hydro-electric dams and the Three Gorges project and Chapter 3 for more information about the strategic signifance of the distribution of oil reserves.

Energy Alternatives

Unfortunately, the development of alternatives to fossil fuels has been inconsistent. Construction of hydroelectric projects has slowed as the remaining viable sites have diminished. In addition, environmentalists have campaigned against their construction because of harmful consequences for rivers, surrounding ecosystems, and indigenous peoples. Investment in nuclear power facilities has dropped to one-tenth of what it was in the 1970s over concerns about public safety that were prompted by incidents like the

World Reserves of Fossil Fuels (%)

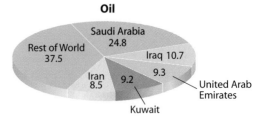

Oil

Saudi Arabia 24.8
Rest of World 37.5
Iraq 10.7
9.3 United Arab Emirates
Iran 8.5
9.2
Kuwait

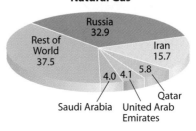

Natural Gas

Russia 32.9
Rest of World 37.5
Iran 15.7
5.8
4.0 4.1 Qatar
Saudi Arabia United Arab Emirates

Coal

United States 25.0
Rest of World 30.0
Russia 16.0
China 12.0
India 8.0 9.0
Australia

British Petroleum

FIGURE 7.17 The distribution of fossil fuels has given some parts of the world strategic importance. The Middle East contains a large part of the world's energy supplies.

Chernobyl accident. There has been rapid development of renewable sources of energy, including solar energy, wind power, and biomass fuels, but these small-scale sources continue to represent a very small portion of the total energy supply and tend to be used mostly where other energy sources are difficult to supply.

One of the problems with the development of alternatives to fossil fuels is that they are viewed as incapable of supplying large populations with cheap and reliable power. Utility companies prefer large-scale projects, citing lower costs and more control over development.

> " In the United States, wind-produced energy is expected to produce 2,500 megawatts of electricity this year [2001], a 60 percent increase from the 1,500 megawatts produced last year. One megawatt provides power for about 1,000 homes. "
>
> *Chris Baker and Gary Anderson, "Power Hungry People,"* Insight on the News, June 25, 2001

Energy Use and Quality of Life Characteristics for Selected Countries, 1999

Country	Commercial Energy Use (kg/capita oil equivalent)	Human Development Index (HDI) Rank	Under the Age of Five Mortality (per 1000 live births)
Algeria	904	107	40
Canada	7 930	1	6
Chile	1 574	38	12
China	907	99	47
Colombia	761	68	30
Costa Rica	769	48	16
Estonia	3 811	46	22
Ethiopia	287	171	173
France	4 224	12	5
Haiti	237	150	130
India	479	128	105
Israel	3 014	23	6
Jamaica	1 552	83	11
Malaysia	2 237	61	10
Mexico	1 501	55	34
Philippines	520	77	44
Poland	2 721	44	11
Saudi Arabia	4 906	75	26
Sudan	414	143	115
Zambia	634	153	202

The World Guide 2001/2002 and Human Development Report, 2000

FIGURE 7.18 The average per capita world consumption of commercial energy is the equivalent of 1684 kg of oil.

The La Grande River hydro-electric project in northern Quebec is a good example of this "bigger is better" thinking. Utility companies have been reluctant to exploit local, renewable alternative sources in spite of the clear social and economic opportunities. Globally, reducing dependency on fossil fuels through expanding alternative-energy technologies would lower oil imports and would encourage entrepreneurs to develop local energy industries. There is a good deal of hope that developing countries will be able to sidestep the "megaproject" approach to energy supplies and develop energy systems based on locally generated power. This "micropower" approach is decentralized and efficient and considered as significant as the move from mainframe computers to personal computers.

There is a huge potential for expanding alternative energy sources if strong support from government policies and tax incentives

FACT FILE

- About 45% of the world's electricity is generated by coal-fired plants.

- About 20% of Canada's electricity is produced by burning coal.

Adding Up the Costs of Coal

adapted from Seth Dunn, "King Coal's Weakening Grip on Power," *World Watch* magazine, September/October 1999, pp.10–19

	Air	Land	Water	Climate
Mining/ Extraction	■ Coal dust causes black lung and other respiratory diseases in miners. ■ Explosions and fires can result from mining. ■ Mining machinery causes fumes and noise.	■ Mining causes soil degradation, erosion, and settling. ■ Farms and forests are destroyed. ■ Communities are displaced by mining.	■ Watersheds are disrupted by mining activities. ■ Drainage from tailings and wastewater pollutes streams and rivers. ■ Drinking water sources are fouled.	■ Mining releases large quantities of methane gas, a greenhouse gas.
Transportation	■ Coal is shipped in open rail cars causing coal dust to be blown into the air.	■ Land is used for building rail lines and roads for transporting coal.		■ The engines and machines used to transport coal release carbon dioxide, a greenhouse gas.
Treatment		■ Smokestack scrubbers used to filter sulphur out of coal emissions produce sludge and other wastes.	■ Coal washing, used to strip sulphur from coal before it is burned, requires large quantities of water.	■ Technologies used to trap sulphur require large amounts of energy, contributing to global warming.
Consumption	■ Particulates, sulphur dioxide, nitrogen oxides, and toxic metals released by burning contribute to cancer risks, impair infant development, cause respiratory illness, and increase death rates.	■ Acid deposition leaches nutrients from soils and damages buildings. ■ Piles of ash from coal burning at power plants take up land.	■ Acid deposition poisons rivers and lakes. ■ Nitrogen oxides cause eutrophication—rapid plant growth cuts off oxygen supplies to other species. ■ Cooling towers heat up large amounts of water.	■ Combustion of coal is the single largest source of carbon dioxide emissions.

FIGURE 7.19 While the market price for coal was about US$40 per tonne for U.S.-produced coal and US$30 for Australian coal in 2002, when environmental and health disruptions are factored into the equation, coal is not as cheap as it may seem. Environmental groups have pressured governments to reduce coal consumption, especially for the generation of electrical power, because of the large number of problems it creates. Globally, the use of coal may already have peaked.

can reduce their initial cost. When all costs of burning fossil fuels are considered, including the costs of the negative impacts on human health and ecosystem destruction, renewable energy sources can be viewed in a more favourable economic light. Some jurisdictions in Canada offer electricity produced from "green" sources to consumers who choose to pay a premium.

FIGURE 7.20 Wind energy produced on wind farms like this one on the Gaspé peninsula in Quebec contribute only a tiny percentage of the total energy supply in Canada. Suggest reasons why a country such as Denmark was able to produce 18% of its power from wind in 2002 and is expected to provide 50% of its energy needs with wind power by 2030.

Percentage Change in Energy Use, 1990–2000

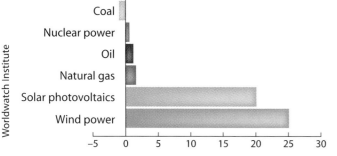

FIGURE 7.21 Renewable energy sources are growing quickly but, in 2000, made up only 2% of the total U.S. energy supply.

Promoting Energy Efficiency

One of the keys to a sustainable energy supply is to improve the efficiency of energy use. Biomass wastes from agriculture, forestry, industries, and cities can produce clean fuels as well as heat and electricity as by-products. There are many opportunities to reduce energy use in homes through better construction techniques, improved insulation, and more efficient lighting and appliances. The R-value of insulation indicates the thermal resistance to heat flow. In Canada, this concept has been adopted for a program called R-2000, where homes are constructed to strict standards for air sealing and ventilation. These homes save about 50% in energy consumption over traditionally constructed homes. Governments have a central role to play in encouraging industries and citizens to change behaviours and to adopt more energy-efficient lifestyles.

About a third of Canada's energy is consumed by industries. These plants and other facilities often use energy-inefficient motors, lights, and machines. There are many opportunities for redesigning industrial processes that allow for energy savings.

Transportation consumes about a quarter of Canada's energy and there are energy savings to be achieved through the use of smaller, lighter vehicles and the development and implementation of hybrid technologies. Honda's *Insight*, for example, combines a gasoline engine with

> **FACT FILE**
>
> The extraction, transportation, and use of coal in Canada creates 73 000 jobs and generates over $5.8 billion in revenue.

" Market forces, greenery, and innovation are shaping the future of our industry and propelling us inexorably towards hydrogen energy. Those who don't pursue it … will rue it. "

Frank Ingriselli, president, Texaco Technology Ventures

> **FACT FILE**
>
> Sport utility vehicles (SUVs) produce 30% more emissions and are 33% less fuel-efficient than average passenger vehicles.

an electric motor to yield the highest energy efficiency of any production vehicle in Canada.

Hydrogen fuel cells are the most efficient, clean, and reliable source of electricity. Hydrogen is already cost-competitive for many uses and its clear-flame gas is safer to use and store than gasoline. Many buildings, cars, and public vehicles such as buses in North America currently run on fuel cells.

Energy efficiency protects the environment, reduces the dangers of climate change, provides jobs, and stabilizes prices. Energy security in a disorderly world can be achieved inexpensively through energy efficient options, reducing the need for large generating plants and transportation by pipelines and transmission lines, all vulnerable to attack.

❝ Energy distributors should be rewarded for reducing customers bills, not for selling more energy; designers should be rewarded for savings achieved not expenditures. ❞

Amory B. Lovins, energy analyst, Rocky Mountain Institute

INTERACT

1. What factors will continue to create larger demands for energy over the coming decades?
2. Identify some of the factors that make a continued reliance on fossil fuels a problem for the world.
3. Identify some recent trends in the world's energy sources and offer reasons to explain these shifts in supply.
4. Use the statistics in Figure 7.18, **Energy Use and Quality of Life Characteristics for Selected Countries, 1999**, to see if there are relationships between energy consumption and quality of life. Create two scattergraphs: the first showing commercial energy use and HDI rank, and the second showing commercial energy use and under the age of five mortality. Describe the patterns.
5. Figure 7.19, **Adding Up the Costs of Coal**, identifies some of the hidden costs of using coal. Make up a similar chart for the hidden costs of relying on oil and natural gas.
6. Identify some of the factors that have limited the development of cleaner alternatives to fossil fuels.
7. Conduct research to produce a case study on the use of an alternative energy source such as wind, solar, or biomass in a location of your choice. Compare your findings with others in your class.
8. What are some strategies that you might recommend to move the developed countries of the world more quickly toward renewable and cleaner sources of energy? Explain your ideas.

SUSTAINING THE WORLD'S FORESTS

Forests cover about 27% of Earth's surface, about 3.4 billion ha in total. Open woodlands (transitional ecosystems in which trees are an important component) and shrubs occupy another 1.7 billion ha. These natural systems are under attack by both human and natural forces. During the 1990s, about 1.5% of the forests of developing countries were destroyed each year, a loss of about 11 million hectares annually. Many people fear for the future of forests in the face of such **deforestation**.

The world's forests are primarily of three types. Tropical forests are located between the tropics of Cancer and Capricorn and are associated with countries like Brazil, Congo, and

Indonesia. They are some of the most productive and diverse ecosystems in the world and are home for at least half of all living species. The temperate forests occur in the mid-latitudes, in places like the U.S., Germany, and New Zealand. These forests thrive in the moderate climates of this temperate zone. Further north, the Boreal forests contain trees capable of enduring colder climates, such as those found throughout Canada, Finland, and Russia. Boreal forests cover about one-third of Canada's land area.

Governments and NGOs began to reach a common understanding of the importance of forests to sustainable development when Agenda 21 and the Statement of Forest Principles was created at the 1992 Earth Summit in Rio de Janeiro. Since then, a number of national and international programs promoting sustainable forest management have begun. The Montreal Process is the largest international initiative, encompassing conservation and sustainable management of the majority of the world's boreal and temperate forests. Its report, Assessing the State of Our Temperate and Boreal Forests, was published in April 2000. Still, we are a long way from fully understanding the nature of truly sustainable forest management.

Why Deforestation?

Forests are being cut down in many places to convert the land to other uses. In tropical areas, forests are removed to create agricultural land—places to plant crops and graze livestock. In **slash–burn agriculture**, farmers chop down a few trees, burn the stumps, and plant their crops in the cleared spaces. These are subsistence farmers and poverty is a compelling force for the clearing of forests. Intensive agriculture is also practised in tropical areas. Large-scale corporate farms remove large areas—many square kilometres—of forests to

> **FACT FILE**
>
> Canada has about 10% of the world's forests. They are made up of approximately 180 tree species.

> **FACT FILE**
>
> Forty percent of the rain forests of Central America have been cleared in the past 40 years, mostly for cattle pasture.

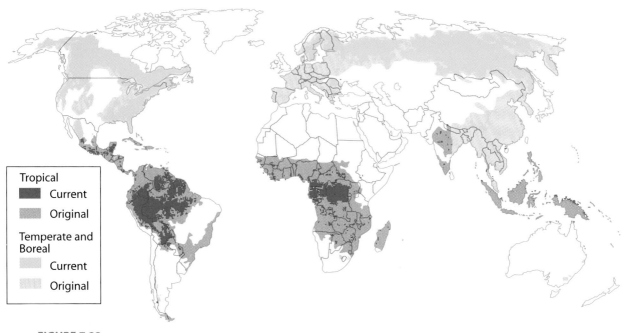

The Current Forest Cover Compared to Original Forests

Tropical
- Current
- Original

Temperate and Boreal
- Current
- Original

FIGURE 7.22

create grazing pastures for cattle that are exported to the world market. These forests are burned to clear the land.

> 66 The economic exploitation of poorer countries by the world's industrialized nations underlies much of the over-exploitation of tropical ecosystems by populations without land or employment. 99
>
> *John Revington, editor,*
> *World Rainforest Report*

Trees are also removed for commercial logging. Valuable species are harvested using heavy machines that damage the unharvested parts of the forest. Other reasons for cutting the forests include building roads, expanding towns, building mines and tailing storage, exploring for oil, and constructing dams and reservoirs.

Farming, logging, and mining are the visible causes of deforestation, but not the underlying reasons. Many analysts have argued that foreign debts, the inequities of the international trading system, and poor government policies are the real factors driving deforestation, particularly in developing countries.

FOREIGN DEBTS The developing nations of the world owe staggering amounts of money to the World Bank and International Monetary Fund (IMF), commercial lenders, and foreign governments. Brazil, for example, a country with huge tropical forests, owed US$232 billion in 1998. These countries exploit their natural resources in desperate attempts to earn foreign currency to pay off loans. They encourage the commercial development of logging, mining, and cash-crop farming as ways of generating export earnings and tax dollars.

FACT FILE

Up to 5 million ha of forests are destroyed annually to grow tobacco.

 See Chapter 10 for more information about foreign debt.

INTERNATIONAL TRADING SYSTEMS International trade encourages large foreign companies to move into developing countries to exploit their resources. They buy up or get rights to forest land, often displacing the local population. And,

FIGURE 7.23 This satellite image of a forest in Rondonia, Brazil, shows the impact of massive deforestation.

FIGURE 7.24 An area where forests were cleared for farmland in Zomba, Malawi. Ironically, the **laterite** soils of tropical rain forests are quite infertile and become virtually useless within a few years.

the pressure to globalize trade discourages countries from using foreign investment regulations to protect their forests.

GOVERNMENT POLICIES Governments in developing countries have often looked to the forests for quick solutions to their problems. For example, Brazil has encouraged the settlement of lands in the Amazon Basin as a way of reducing population pressures in other parts of the country. In Indonesia, Native cultures were forcibly assimilated into the mainstream culture by cutting down the forest that supported and protected them. Throughout Latin America, inequities in land ownership mean that peasant farmers are forced to move onto marginal lands and clear forests if they have any hope of owning their own land. Ill-conceived government policies are impoverishing the people and destroying the forests without solving the problems.

> " Deforestation is the inevitable result of the current social and economic policies being carried out in the name of development. "
>
> *The World Rainforest Movement*

Harvesting the Forest

There are fundamentally different views about how forests should be managed. Should techniques focus on increasing the sustainable yield of timber as well as improving natural conservation values? Should scarce funds be spent on silviculture or should cut areas just be left alone to regenerate naturally? Forest managers and policy makers are continually discovering new information about the economic and ecological impact of different harvesting techniques, fuelling ongoing debate about the most sustainable methods.

Clear-cutting is considered to be the most cost-effective way in the short term, and the safest for loggers. This method removes all the trees from an area that can be many hundreds of hectares in size. Unfortunately, this method fragments wildlife habitat, eliminates biodiversity, opens the soil to the elements, and encourages soil erosion. Current practices are improving based on using the most appropriate technique for each type of forest. For example, partial cutting may be used in birch and balsam forests while clear-cutting is used in fire adapted forests. In order to imitate naturally burned forests, loggers may leave dead trees standing or on the ground and avoid cutting along waterways and roads. While protecting waterways from erosion, these remaining areas are not large enough to provide adequate habitat for wildlife, especially large mammals and birds. Variations on clear-cutting are patch cutting and strip cutting. In both cases, the cut-over areas are left for reseeding from the undisturbed nearby forest. These methods tend to **high-grade** a forest, harvesting the best stands and species of trees and leaving poorer areas untouched. Over time, the forest loses its genetic quality and diversity.

Other methods of harvesting forests leave immature trees to grow to full size. Selective cutting harvests only mature trees of high quality, which are cut individually or in small clusters. This method is used when it is important to maintain a closed forest canopy after cutting. Shelterwood cutting harvests all mature trees, spacing out the cutting over several decades. These methods usually yield less wood, are more labour-intensive, providing more jobs. Labour and transportation costs are higher but the need for more access roads raises environmental concerns. The use of partial cutting methods such as shelterwood is increasing in Canada.

Forest Management and Jobs

The most common development in North America is an increased use of mechanization and labour-saving production techniques, allowing the faster and more efficient removal and

FIGURE 7.25 Harvesting the forest in Dorrington, California, using the latest labour-saving technology.

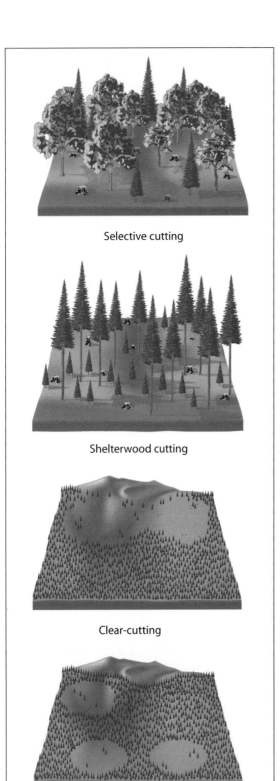

Selective cutting

Shelterwood cutting

Clear-cutting

Patch cutting

adapted from Dianne Draper, *Our Environment: A Canadian Perspective*, Nelson, 2002, p. 309

FIGURE 7.26 Clear-cutting was used to take 85.7% of Canada's forest harvest in 1995.

processing of timber. According to the Sierra Club, during the 1990s there was a 25% loss in jobs for every 1000 m³ of wood harvested on Vancouver Island. Contrary to some publicity campaigns by the industry, jobs are not at stake from environmental protection but from poor forest management techniques, new technologies, and low value-added use of the wood that is cut. Many raw logs are exported that could otherwise be processed here in Canada into products such as furniture, which would increase the number of jobs and enrich the economy.

Silviculture

Where forests that have been clear-cut are allowed to regenerate for future harvests, some sort of **silviculture** may be used. Silviculture is

FIGURE 7.27 Some foresters assert that clear-cutting emulates the ecological conditions left by natural forest fires. Consider the differences in the two photos. Fires (upper) leave many trees standing, enrich soils, kill diseases, and promote growth of some species such as jack pine. Clear-cutting (lower) contributes to erosion, loss of soil fertility, silting of streams, and reduced biodiversity.

the practice of managing forest growth through planting and seeding cut-over areas, encouraging faster tree growth, and protecting the growing forests from damage. In Canada and elsewhere, silviculture involves three steps. Initially, the debris from a cut-over area is slash-burned to encourage faster tree regeneration.

FACT FILE

In 1996, 700 million tree seedlings were planted throughout Canada.

Secondly, seeds or seedlings from one or two desirable species of trees are planted. Finally, the forests are encouraged to grow quickly by removing unwanted species using chemical herbicides. Managed in this way, forests in Canada are cut once they are 60 to 120 years old. At this age, the timber volume added each year begins to slow as the forests reach a mature stage.

Critics of this approach to managing forests argue that silviculture creates more environmental problems than it solves. The slash-burn technique removes natural materials that should be allowed to decay to feed the next generation of trees and destroys the habitat of many animals and birds. In addition, removing this material encourages soil erosion and burning releases greenhouse gases. The planting of a limited number of tree species creates **monocultures** that are less resistant to diseases and are not capable of supporting the diversity of species that natural forests do. The monoculture forests require the use of pesticides in order to protect them from insects and other threats. For critics, techniques that harvest valuable trees but leave the forest largely intact are more desirable. The diversity within a natural forest contributes to a sustainable resource that can support other uses, including recreation and ecotourism.

Sustainable Forest Management in Canada

Until the last two decades of the twentieth century, forest harvesting in Canada did not include effective silvicultural measures. As a result, the industry, which operates mainly in boreal, montane, and coastal forests, continues to rely on wood from natural forests in increas-

Views and Concerns about Sustainable Forest Management in Canada

- Principles of SFM are poorly understood and not always considered in a culture of short-term economic gain.

- Government policy focuses mainly on timber production rather than on incentives for sustainable management and silvicultural programs.

- SFM requirements will reduce the volume of wood cut and raise production costs.

- The interests of First Nations and local communities must be considered.

- Demands for biodiversity protection must be considered.

- The level of understanding of different stakeholders varies widely, making effective public input difficult to obtain.

ingly remote areas to meet demands. It will take decades before harvesting of current reforestation programs can take place. Sustainable forestry practices are gaining momentum across Canada. According to Canadian government departments such as Ontario's Ministry of Natural Resources, which provided country data for a UNEP report, a significant interest in forest certification and sustainable forest management (SFM) has occurred:

- The Canadian Standards Association SFM system was established with the input of many different stakeholders and public participation.
- New forest community partnerships have been established with representatives from government, industry, environmental groups, labour, Aboriginal peoples, private forest owners, academics, and others to achieve a greater balance in the environmental, economic, social, and cultural demands placed on forests.
- Progress towards achieving SFM is continually monitored and improved by government and the industry.

- Private woodlot owners are encouraged to comply with stewardship practices and environmental standards.
- More management activities are based on the principle of landscape ecosystem management, encompassing conservation measures to protect wildlife habitat, social culture, and scenic values.
- Consideration is being given to appropriate training of employees and contractors, integrated management objectives for multiple forest uses, reducing waste, preventing pollution, maintaining connectivity of ecosystems with wildlife corridors, protecting a variety of sensitive habitats, better road construction, and stream crossing techniques.

 See Chapter 2 for more information about Canada's forest resource.

CASE STUDY

Micro-Enterprise Tree Nurseries

The loss of trees from the tropical rain forests of Central America has prompted a number of actions aimed at stopping the cutting and the reforesting of cut-over areas. One program by the NGO Trees, Water and People (TWP) focuses on the underlying cause of deforestation in Guatemala—poverty. This micro-enterprise tree nursery program trains local groups and individuals to run their own tree nurseries. Skills that they learn include seedling production, grafting of stock, managing a nursery, accounting, and marketing. In this region, cashews, lemons, mangos, and other tropical fruit trees grow well. The small nurseries produce and market seedlings throughout the country. Most family farms include a few fruit trees, and the improved varieties sold by the micro-nurseries produce well and are in demand.

A key component of the TWP program is a **micro-credit** fund. Nursery owners borrow US$500 to cover the costs of starting up their operations: seeds, tools, grafting materials, and so on. The money is paid back over two years from the revenues earned by the nursery. Typically, this start-up loan will allow farmers to establish nurs-

FIGURE 7.28 Rafael Ramirez at his micro-enterprise tree nursery. Using their existing land, farmers can expand their operations to include selling nursery stock to other farmers.

eries and earn approximately $500 a year selling about 2500 seedlings. The nurseries can be run part-time on existing farms.

The program benefits the region because it provides additional income to nursery owners, allows other farmers to improve their earnings through the sale of quality fruits, and encourages the planting of trees on lands from which forests have been cut. TWP has also begun a similar program using hardwood tree species such as mahogany.

INTERACT

1. Consult an atlas and other research sources to describe the location and ecosystem characteristics of the world's boreal and temperate forests.
2. Brainstorm ways that forests are important to people other than as sources of wood.
3. This chapter identifies three underlying causes for the destruction of forests: slash-burn agriculture, intensive agriculture, and commercial logging. Do these same causes apply to Canada? Explain your ideas.
4. The Fact File on page 182 points out that large areas of forests are being destroyed in order to grow tobacco to supply the expanding cigarette market in developing countries. Create an ideas web or ideas map to show some of the social, environmental, and political consequences of this trend.
5. a) Compare the environmental consequences of clear-cutting and selective cutting.
   b) Why might forestry companies prefer clear-cutting to selective cutting as a method to harvest forests?
6. The case study of micro-nurseries in Guatemala suggests that replacing forests with fruit trees is a good thing. Do you agree that this is an appropriate way to deal with the loss of forests? Justify your opinion.

WEB LINKS

- Worldwatch Institute:
- Mines and Communities:
- World Rainforest Movement:
- International Energy Agency:
- The David Suzuki Foundation:
- Global Overview of Renewable Energy Sources: <www.agores.org>

RELATED ISSUES

- Foreign aid and protection of natural resources
- Foreign ownership of mining, energy, and forestry companies
- Diamonds mined and sold to finance civil war violence
- Recycling efforts and consumption of natural resources
- Micro-enterprises and resource development
- Softwood lumber trade dispute between Canada and the U.S.

GIS **Energy Use and Quality of Life Indicators**

ANALYSE, APPLY, AND INTERACT

1. Using examples from this chapter, explain how technologies have affected the management of natural resources either positively or negatively.

2. Is the world facing an energy crisis due to increasing population and expanding consumption? Explain your answer.

3. In this chapter, several instances of local responses to the exploitation of natural resources were described. How effective do you feel local organizations and grass roots groups can be in protecting the environment and natural resources? Explain.

4. Explain how cutting the tropical rain forests to create farmland ends up diminishing an area's ability to produce food and wealth.

5. Compare the issues that are part of mining, energy production, and forestry and make some general observations about the use of natural resources that apply to all three sectors.

6. Debate this statement with others in the class: "The need to create wealth to improve our quality of life justifies the exploitation of the planet's natural resources, no matter how harmful it might be to the natural environment or communities."

7. **a)** Using Figure 7.18, **Energy Use and Quality of Life Characteristics for Selected Countries, 1999**, calculate the correlation coefficient between commercial energy use and under the age of five mortality, using the rank correlation statistical analysis technique described in Interact Question 4b on page 313. Explain what the outcome of your analysis shows.

   b) Using the Data Appendix, select one other variable for analysis. Determine the correlation coefficient between this second variable and commercial energy use for the same countries in Figure 7.18, **Energy Use and Quality of Life Characteristics for Selected Countries, 1999**.

8. Suppose that over the next 20 years the amount of fossil fuels used was reduced by 50% because of the development of renewable fuels and conservation. Brainstorm the consequences for this shift in energy supply, considering the economic, social, and political implications.

9. Research a hydro-electric project in North America or somewhere else in the world to find out about the impact of this development on the indigenous people of the area. Specifically, look at the compromises made by the indigenous people and the government in order for the project to go ahead.

10. Complete a case study of one country, examining its development of natural resources, particularly minerals, energy, and forests. Identify areas of strength and weakness in the sustainability of resource development in the country. Make suggestions for how the country might more effectively use its natural resources.

11. Using the Internet and other sources, research and report on a specific situation in which resource development has contributed to the disruption of an ecosystem. You might, for example, discuss a mine or energy megaproject that has been criticized for its destruction of natural systems.

12. What could the people in your community do to help protect forests from destruction? Working with one or two others, prepare a plan that your school or local community could put in place that would help in the protection of forests. As part of your plan, include a way of evaluating the effectiveness of your actions.

Chapter 8: The World's Water Supply

By the end of this chapter, you will

- analyse geographic issues that arise from the impact of human activities on the environment in different regions of the world;

- evaluate approaches, policies, and principles relating to the protection and sustainability of the planet's life support systems;

- demonstrate an understanding of how human-induced changes in natural systems can diminish their capacity for supporting human activity;

- explain how people perceive resources and sustainable development differently at different times and in different places;

- explain the interactive nature of selected natural and human systems;

- produce a case study of a specific situation in which resource development has contributed to the disruption of an ecosystem;

- demonstrate an understanding of how scarcities and inequities in the distribution of resources contribute to uprisings and conflicts;

- evaluate the sustainability of selected trends related to consumption of the earth's resources;

- evaluate the role played by non-governmental organizations and local community initiatives in different parts of the world;

- demonstrate an understanding of the possibility of a number of alternative solutions to any geographic problem or issue;

- analyse cause and effect and sequence relationships in geographic data;

- use maps to analyse change over time in a place.

Water—Views and Myths

"The Great Man-Made River"

excerpt from *Water*
by Marq de Villiers
Houghton Mifflin Co., 2000

Just off the road near Tazirbu is a small well that has been known to travellers for centuries, the Birbu Atla, not much more than a metre deep, the clear water mesmerizing to a thirsty passer-by. It bubbled as you looked into it, little bubbles of air coming up from … where? Traveller's tales often speculated, though no one knew for sure. In the past, camel caravans took eighty days to plod their way from Timbuktu to Marrakech on the western route, or from Cairo to Gao on the eastern, threading through a scanty network of oases, following the veins of water.

Ahmed was only 60 kilometres from the Birbu Atla now. He manoeuvered his huge vehicle—a crane, really a mobile crane capable of lifting up to 200 metric tons—until it was parallel to the gouge in the ochre earth that ran straight-arrow to the north, vanishing up the road to the coast, so many hundreds of kilometres away. On his back—Ahmed thought of the cradle of his immense carrier as his own flesh and blood—was a section of pipe. He lowered it gently into the waiting trench, and another machine, made just for this purpose, nudged it into place with a solid

thud…. what it would transport was more important than anything, more important than oil, although oil was paying for it in the end. This pipeline would be one tributary of what Colonel Gadhafi was calling, with no hyberole at all, the Great Man-Made River. What it would transport was, in this dry country, the most precious thing of all: water.

The pipeline was to take water from the deep desert and carry it to the populated coast. The Sahara was giving up its last secret, something it had kept hidden for ten thousand years. Down there, deep down, was water—lots of it.

Critical Analysis

1. Using a map of northern Africa in an atlas, locate as many of the places named in the commentary as possible. (In some atlases, Timbuktu may be shown as Tombouctou, Cairo as El Qa-hira.)
2. Considering that Ahmed was working in the Libyan part of the Sahara Desert, use a climate map of the world or of Africa to write a description of characteristics of the climate in the region.
3. What is meant by the statement that the pipeline is paid for by oil?
4. Explain the paradox that the Great Man-Made River Project is transporting water from the world's largest desert to coastal cities on the Mediterranean Sea.
5. Evaluate the sustainability of this water transfer project.

Many people in the world are living in regions that have a water shortage. Their perception of water may be very different from your own. All life depends on water, yet views on water vary widely around the world. These differences are based on inequities of supply and access to this precious substance as well as on one's views of nature. Some people see water as far too essential to be called a resource. They consider it a public trust to be protected by all levels of government. Others see water as an economic resource, flowing uselessly and wastefully into the lakes and oceans, a commodity that should be sold for a profit to provide jobs and boost the economy. In countries where water is scarce or shared by others, it can be seen as a strategic resource that generates fierce competition.

There is considerable international debate on whether water should be viewed as a human need or a human right. If water is a human right, governments should be charged with providing adequate supplies for their people. The question of how water should be valued was one of the most controversial challenges identified by the United Nations (UN) World Water Forum held in The Hague,

FACT FILE

Water consumption dropped as much as 25% after the installation of water metres in homes and offices in many Canadian municipalities.

> "It is not enough to draw water from nature for use in agriculture, industry and everyday life without also taking account of nature's needs."
>
> *UN World Water Assessment Programme*

Netherlands, in 2000. The idea of putting a price tag on something as intrinsically valuable as water is unacceptable to some people. Yet most people recognize that water access should be more equitable and that water services must be paid for.

Most people in Canada give little thought to where their water comes from or to who "owns" or controls it. Many assume that water is an endless renewable resource that keeps recycling its way through the **hydrologic cycle**. Why should Canadians be concerned with water when, with 0.5% of the world's population and with estimates of 20% of the world's fresh water and 9% of the world's renewable freshwater supply within our borders, we have so much?

Daily per capita personal domestic water use for the average Canadian is about 330 L. When all uses, including industry and agriculture, are factored in, the daily per capita use is 4500 L.

According to Environment Canada, Canadians are profligate water wasters, using more per capita than any other country in the world except the United States. Millions of people in water scarce regions of the world exist on less than 10 L of water per day.

International agencies suggest 50 L of water for each person per day as an adequate level of consumption for requirements such as drinking, sanitation, bathing, and food preparation. More than a billion people have less water than that while many households in developed countries use up to 15 times that amount.

Water users in most parts of North America are just now beginning to recognize the true cost of having an adequate supply of clean fresh water, not only for people, but for all the other living things on the planet. Sufficient clean water for freshwater ecosystems is essential if we intrinsically value **biodiversity** and **ecosystem** health.

For individuals, a water ethic requires an evaluation of lifestyle and water consumption habits and how to reduce personal impact on Earth's finite supply. It also requires the knowledge and values that will enable effective and responsible action. Whatever our views of water, it contributes meaning to our lives, links us with others on the planet, and is a complex and essential part of the human spirit. This meaning is expressed through a wide range of artistic media including music, art, film, dance, legend, and photography.

> 66 Water which is vital for life, costs nothing, whereas diamonds, useless for life, are valued highly. 99
>
> *Adam Smith, eighteenth-century economist (1723-1790)*

FIGURE 8.1 Less than 3% of municipally treated water in Canada is used for drinking. How does our use of such words as "resource" reflect our view of nature and our place in it?

FIGURE 8.2 Human activities have recently transformed Earth's water supply in unprecedented and unforeseeable ways. Some places transport water from thousands of kilometres away. Irrigating deserts for agriculture can provide food and employment, but has been strongly criticized by some water analysts.

O'BRIEN, Lucius Richard, Cdn. 1832-1899. NIAGARA, 1892. Watercolour over graphite on paper. 71.1 x 55.2 cm ART GALLERY OF ONTARIO, Toronto. Gift of the Government of the Province of Ontario, 1972.

FIGURE 8.3 "Niagara" by Lucius O'Brien. Many artists express their views on the importance of water and document what is happening to it.

FIGURE 8.4 Water makes life possible for all things.

River History

excerpt from *Silenced Rivers: The Ecology and Politics of Large Dams* on the International Rivers Network Web site, <www.irn.org/index.asp?id=/basics/damhistory.html>
by Patrick McCully

The role of rivers as the sustainers of life and fertility is reflected in the myths and beliefs of a multitude of cultures. In many parts of the world, rivers are referred to as 'mothers': Narmadai, 'Mother Narmada'; the Volga is Mat' Rodnaya, 'Mother of the Land'. The Thai word for river, mae nan, translates literally as 'water mother'. Rivers have often been linked with divinities, especially female ones. In Ancient Egypt, the floods of the Nile were considered the tears of the goddess Isis. Ireland's River Boyne, which is overlooked by the island's most impressive prehistoric burial sites, was worshipped as a goddess by Celtic tribes.

The rivers of India are perhaps wrapped in more myths, epic tales and religious significance than those of any other nation. Environmentalist Vijay Paranjpye describes a sacred text, which holds that 'all sins are washed away by bathing thrice in the Saraswati, seven times in the Yamuna, once in the Ganges, but the mere sight of the Narmada is enough to absolve one of all sins!' Another ancient text describes the Narmada River as 'giver of merriment', 'flavourful', 'of graceful attitude', and 'one who radiates happiness'.

Of the life sustained by rivers, salmon have perhaps been imbued with the most mythological significance. The 'Salmon of Knowledge', legend had it, swam in a pool near the source of the Boyne. Anyone who tasted the fish would acquire understanding of everything in the world, past, present and future. Native Americans in the Pacific Northwest believed salmon to be superior beings who ascended rivers for the benefit of people, died, and then returned to life in a great house under the ocean, where they danced and feasted in human form. Some tribes welcomed the first salmon of the season with the ceremony due to a visiting chief.

While rivers provided life, they also brought death. Settlement on the plains, which enabled people to take advantage of the rich alluvial soils, also exposed crops and villages to the risk of catastrophic floods. Gilgamesh, the earliest surviving epic tale, tells of a great flood unleashed by God to scourge the sinful in Mesopotamia. Myths and legends of huge floods are common to many cultures around the world, from Old Testament Jews to the Norse and the indigenous people of the Americas.

WHAT ARE THE ISSUES?

How we make choices as individuals and societies about the use of water resources, and the consequences of our decisions on the quality of all life are at the heart of water issues. Because of the systemic nature of Earth's water supply and how it interacts with human activities, none of the issues can effectively be analysed in isolation.

Human activity transforms and degrades complex ecosystems with a wide variety of impacts on water quantity and quality.

Equitable access to safe water is becoming a global crisis. The UN reported in 2002 that, by 2025, 5 billion people around the world would be living in areas where it would be difficult or impossible to meet freshwater needs. Many parts of the world are already facing shortages of fresh water that result in threats to human and ecosystem health as well as prospects for sustainable development. If development improves economic conditions in developing countries, changes in income distribution and lifestyle, particularly related to improved sanitation and greater use of household appliances, will create a greater demand for water.

Competition over scarce or unequally distributed water can and has led to political tension and conflict.

> 66 Many different interests are at stake and equitable solutions must be found: between cities and rural areas, rich and poor, arid lands and wet lands, public and private, infrastructure and natural environments; mainstream and marginal groups, local stakeholders and centralized authorities. At the regional and international level, many river basin and aquifer authorities are developing integrated approaches that stress cooperation of the shared resource. 99
>
> *Potential Conflict to Cooperation Potential, UNESCO programme*

World economic activity has grown five times since 1950. Continued economic growth is expected to increase the demand for water-related services despite increased efficiency of use and changes in the way goods and services are provided. Rapid urbanization is increasing the demand for water services. If current growth trends continue, particularly in the developing world, the percentage of the world's total population living in cities may reach 60% by 2030 and 70% by 2050.

Water management technologies such as greater use of recycled water, higher water prices, increased efficiency of infrastructure and irrigation projects, and enforcement of improved environmental standards are not widely practised or promoted around the world, leaving significant room for improvement in the search for solutions to water issues. Larger-scale technological solutions such as dams, irrigation schemes, and water diversion projects have not been sufficient to meet the growing need for water and may have created new problems and issues.

FACT FILE

Leaks of water from infrastructure pipes are common. In most Canadian systems, leaks account for 10% to 20% of total water supply. The water lost from Mexico City's supply system is enough to meet the needs of a city of several hundred thousand people. One city that has made tremendous improvements in reducing the amount of water wasted is New York City, where a program of fixing leaky pipes, watching for leaks with computerized sonar equipment, and providing low-flush toilets saves millions of litres of water a day.

INTERACT

1. Make a list of all the things you do on an average day that you could not do without water.
2. Identify 10 current trends that will affect water use in the future.
3. Conduct research to find an example of Canadian art, music, or media with a theme related to an aspect of water. Explain the message portrayed and how closely it follows your own views on water.
4. Consider the photos in Figure 8.2. Suggest why land uses such as golf courses and irrigation located in deserts are considered wasteful by some water analysts.
5. a) Refer to the UNESCO quote on this page. For each of the potential conflicts listed, identify a possible situation of conflict and for each situation, suggest two possible stakeholders that would have opposing views of water.
   b) What is meant by an "integrated approach" to solving water issues?
6. a) How much water would your family save per year by switching to a low-flush 6-L toilet?
   b) List at least eight methods mentioned so far in the chapter that could be used to solve water supply problems.
7. Make a list of 10 water-related issues. Select one of the issues and construct a graphic organizer that shows how the issue is complex and has economic, political, cultural, and environmental causes or implications.

MAKE A DIFFERENCE

Planning is ongoing for the UN-sponsored series of World Water Forums including one in March 2003 in Japan. The forums encourage the participation of all stakeholders in the goals of sharing information, finding workable solutions to the world's water problems, and eliminating life-threatening water shortages, contamination, and floods.

A corresponding Youth World Water Forum is based on the view that the voice of young people must be heard. Water will be a theme for serious consideration on the international agenda for the next few decades for students and young people interested in water issues and water-related careers. At the second World Water Forum in the Netherlands in 2000, about 200 young people from around the world met to discuss the issues. They developed a Youth Action Plan and Vision Statement. A task force was created called the Youth Water Action Team. A number of action projects, organized and managed by young participants around the world, followed. Two projects include:

■ **Children's Book Project** This initiative was organized by a university student from the U.S. and supported by the United Nations Children's Fund (UNICEF). A series of stories, from places such as regions of the Aral Sea, mountains of Pakistan, regions in India, and along the Zambezi River in Africa, were written and produced to raise awareness of water issues for children.

■ **Twinning of River Basins** In March 2001, university students from France, Belgium, and the Netherlands met. Their goal was to bring students and professors in Romania and Hungary together through conducting a systems analysis and sharing of information for two shared river basins in order to promote sustainable river basin management. The project involved a detailed analysis of different aspects of the Tisza and Scheldt Rivers, including economy, navigation, ecology, water quality, pollution sources, safety, culture, resources, infrastructure, and political and economic forces in the field of conflict between upstream and downstream nations. The project started with a three-day excursion to each river basin, and meetings with different stakeholders. The students created a vision for different possible futures for the river basins for 30 years as a "stepping stone," and for 100 years into the future. Their findings were presented to water policy experts in the countries involved and to the World Water Forum.

WATERY PLANET

Water is the most common substance on the planet. Educated estimates suggest that there are 1.4 billion km^3 of water in liquid and frozen form. That number represents a staggering and incomprehensible amount, but do we have enough? It seems incongruous that, with such a watery planet and a continuously recycling hydrologic process, a water deficit is a serious problem in many parts of the world.

The amount of water on Earth is finite. There is not going to be any more of it and there are signs that we are effectively reducing the availability of the existing supply. No one really knows our **water carrying capacity**: the number of people that can be supported by Earth's water supply. Much of it is not available for our use and we are not the only species dependent on it. Chemical pollution and other forms of contamination such as acid rain, sewage, eroded silt, salinity, and algae add significantly to water supply problems.

Where Is the Water?

With one-third of the planet experiencing arid climates, water is unevenly distributed not only over space, but also over time. Some places and seasons have too much while others have too little. Mount Waialeale in Hawaii gets more than

The Watery Planet

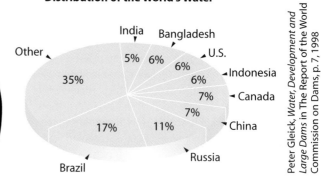

97.3% of Earth's water is in oceans and seas

2.1% of Earth's water is in glaciers and icecaps

FIGURE 8.5 Seventy-one percent of Earth's surface is covered with water but less than 1% of Earth's water is available fresh water.

Distribution of the World's Water

Other — 35%
India 5%
Bangladesh 6%
U.S. 6%
Indonesia 6%
Canada 7%
China 7%
Russia 11%
Brazil 17%

Peter Gleick, *Water, Development and Large Dams* in The Report of the World Commission on Dams, p. 7, 1998

FIGURE 8.7

FIGURE 8.6 If all the water on Earth were represented by 5 L, the amount of fresh water available would take up less than one teaspoon.

> 66 Statistical studies indicate that floods are becoming more frequent. From 66 major floods in 1990, the number rose to 110 in 1999. The number of people who died in floods in 1999 was more than double the number killed by floods in any other year in the 1990s. 99
>
> *Jamie Bartram, coordinator, World Health Organization's (WHO) Water, Sanitation and Health Programme*

11 m of rainfall in some years, while parts of the Atacama Desert in Chile received no precipitation at all for 40 years in a row. In arid regions such as southern Africa, most of the year's rain may fall in just a few days. Rivers in northern Canada are also highly seasonal with minimum flows during winter and flooding during spring or summer melt. In regions experiencing monsoon climates such as Southeast Asia, almost all the rain and run-off occurs over three or four months, and may cause serious flooding.

China and Canada have equal amounts of water but China has 40 times more people. Access to clean water depends not only on global and regional distribution patterns but, on many other factors including population, chang-ing climate, available technology, economic development, political conditions, and conflict. For billions of people living in arid and underdeveloped regions, the daily struggle to find water dominates their lives.

Patterns of Water Use

Over the twentieth century, global water consumption is estimated to have increased nine times, more than double the rate of population growth.

Competition among the major users of water is increasing, as will future demand for food production. Agriculture, which consumes the most water globally, faces increasing competition from domestic, municipal, and industrial demands. Demand is also increasing for more equitable access

FACT FILE

A UN report in November 2000 stated that there are more than one billion people who do not have access to clean drinking water, 2.9 billion lack adequate sanitation services, and as many as 20 000 children die every day from water-borne diseases.

FACT FILE

Forty percent of the global food supply comes from irrigated cropland.

to water for the world's poor and marginalized peoples as well as for freshwater ecosystems.

The UN compared water consumption with availability and found that many countries are water-stressed. A country is considered water-stressed if there is less than 1700 cubic metres per person per

year. Countries with less than 1000 cubic metres per person per year are considered water-scarce. In 2000, 20 countries were water-scarce and 31 were water-stressed. By 2025, the number of water-scarce and water-stressed countries is predicted to be 35 and 48, respectively. Countries with a water supply problem, including India, China, and many developing countries, contain 35% of the world's population. The evidence shows that we are falling behind in our attempts to solve the water crisis.

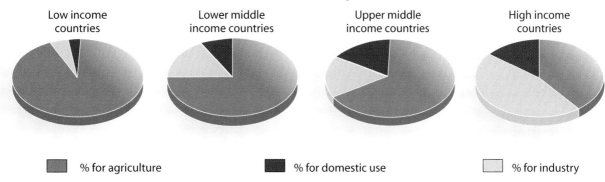

Annual Fresh Water Withdrawals as a Percentage of Total Resources Withdrawn

Low income countries • Lower middle income countries • Upper middle income countries • High income countries

■ % for agriculture ■ % for domestic use ☐ % for industry

World Bank, 1999

FIGURE 8.8 In most parts of the developing world, about 85% of water used is for agriculture, 5% for domestic needs, and 10% for industry. Most developed countries employ about half their total water used for industry, but this can vary widely. For example, more than 90% of water consumed is used for agriculture in parts of some western U.S. states, including Colorado and California.

FACT FILE

■ One kilogram of steak from a beef feedlot operation requires more than 20 000 L of water.

■ Producing one automobile requires 50 times its weight in water.

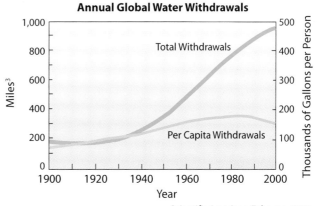

Annual Global Water Withdrawals

Total Withdrawals

Per Capita Withdrawals

Miles³ — Thousands of Gallons per Person

Year: 1900, 1920, 1940, 1960, 1980, 2000

Scientific American, February 2001

FIGURE 8.9 Total water withdrawals continue to rise. If growth trends continue, industrial water consumption is predicted to double by 2025.

Water Availability for Selected Countries, 1995 and Projected 2025

Country	Total Annual Water Available (km³)	1995 Per Capita Water Available (m³)	2025 (median projection) Per Capita Water Available (m³)
Afghanistan	50.00	2 543	1 105
Argentina	994.00	28 590	21 077
Australia	343.00	19 198	14 333
Bangladesh	2 357.00	19 936	13 096
Bolivia	300.00	40 464	22 847
Botswana	14.70	10 138	5 707
Brazil	6 950.00	43 707	32 087
Canada	2 901.00	98 667	79 731
Chile	468.00	32 935	23 941
China	2 800.00	2 295	1 891
Colombia	1 070.00	29 877	20 316
Costa Rica	95.00	27 745	16 940
Cuba	34.50	3 147	2 924
Egypt	58.10	936	607
Eritrea	8.80	2 775	1 350
Germany	171.00	2 096	2 114
India	2 085.00	2 244	1 567
Indonesia	2 530.00	12 813	9 192
Iraq	109.20	5 434	2 625
Israel	2.15	389	270
Jamaica	8.30	3 363	2 463
Japan	547.00	4 374	4 508
Kuwait	0.16	95	55
Madagascar	337.00	22 657	9 775
Mali	67.00	6 207	2 726
Mexico	357.40	3 921	2 745
Myanmar (Burma)	1 082.00	23 988	15 996
Namibia	45.50	29 622	15 172
Netherlands	90.00	5 813	5 576
Nigeria	280.00	2 506	1 175
Norway	392.00	90 489	84 084
Philippines	323.00	4 761	3 071
Portugal	69.60	7 091	7 374
Russian Federation	4 498.00	30 298	34 233
Saudi Arabia	4.55	249	107
Thailand	179.00	3 073	2 591
United Kingdom	71.00	1 222	1 193
United States	2 478.00	9 277	7 453
Zaire (Congo D.R.)	1 019.00	22 419	9 620
Zimbabwe	20.00	1 787	1 034

FIGURE 8.10

Population Action International

FIGURE 8.11 Many irrigation systems are inefficient. In many cases, less than half the water diverted to irrigate crops actually reaches the plants. Water evaporates quickly in semi-arid regions, it seeps or leaks away, or is used for water-hungry crops such as cotton or corn. Irrigation can contribute to degradation of soil due to **salinization** and **waterlogging**.

INTERACT

1. Make a list of factors that are fueling increased demand for water.
2. Refer to Figure 8.7, **Distribution of the World's Water**. Find the total population for the eight countries shown on the graph. Draw a chart to illustrate the following data for the eight countries: population, percent of world population, percent of the world's water. Write a one-paragraph analysis of your results.
3. Contact your local municipal water management office or utility. Write a description of the pattern of water use in your community. Include seasonal patterns, costs, and different categories of use. Construct graphs to illustrate your findings.
4. Refer to Figure 8.8, **Annual Fresh Water Withdrawals as a Percentage of Total Resources Withdrawn**. Brainstorm a list of factors that would affect the percentage of water used in a region for the three categories.

5. a) Using the data in Figure 8.10, **Water Availability for Selected Countries, 1995 and Projected 2025**, decide on four categories of per capita water availability, then select four colours and (on world outline maps) shade in each country according to which category it fits into, to produce two thematic choropleth maps, one using 1995 data and one using projected data for 2025.
   b) The countries that fit into the category with the lowest per capita water availability are water-stressed. Add a water-stressed symbol on top of the shading you have used for each of these countries.
   c) In a written analysis, describe the patterns shown by each map and describe general and regional trends by comparing the two maps.
   d) Compare your maps with a world water surplus and efficiency map in an atlas. Briefly explain any similarities or differences.

THE HYDROLOGIC CYCLE IN ACTION

The hydrologic cycle includes all the water on the planet and is a closed system of water circulation that transfers water from one form and place to another. From 15 km above Earth's surface to about 5 km below it, this includes the process of rainfall and surface run-off, rivers flowing into lakes and oceans, water stored in the soil and underground, cloud formation in the atmosphere, transpiration from plants, and evaporation. A complete trip through the system for a molecule of water can take millions of years. About 35% of all the rain that falls on Earth flows back to the oceans through rivers and groundwater run-off. This is the renewable part of our freshwater supply.

> 66 The interconnectedness of the hydrologic cycle is not something that the editorialists of the *Globe and Mail* or the *National Post* like to contemplate… to them, water is just another commodity that can be owned, sold and disposed of by anyone. But the reality is that water is different. It might rise on your property, but it is not yours—it is just passing through. You can use it and abuse it, but it is not "property." It is a basic part of our life-support system. 99
>
> *Marq de Villiers, water analyst,* Canadian Geographic *magazine, May/June 2000*

Despite the natural ability of the hydrologic cycle to renew and purify water, intensive development and water withdrawal greatly influence the supply of fresh water. Humans interact in complex ways with the world's natural water system. These interactions include withdrawing water from the springs where many people in North America get bottled drinking water, withdrawing large amounts of groundwater for irrigating agricultural crops, clearing forests for lumber, mining, roads, and homes, increasing

FIGURE 8.12 Even the local car wash is an example of human systems interacting with and having an impact on the hydrologic cycle.

run-off and the risk of floods, and many forms of contamination.

Components of the Hydrologic Cycle

Less than 1% of the total water on the planet is found in surface water, yet this makes up most of the water available for use by humans and many other species. The remaining 2% of fresh water is found in glaciers and **aquifers**. Surface water consists of all the water that falls on the land and is contained in lakes, ponds, rivers, streams, and wetlands.

In 2000, 3800 km^3 of water was being withdrawn each year from the world's lakes, rivers, and underground aquifers, twice the amount that was withdrawn in 1950. Heavy water withdrawals have had serious negative impacts on many of the world's river and groundwater systems—many of them irreversible over a reasonable time frame.

WETLANDS Four percent of Earth's surface is covered in wetlands. They can vary in size from small shallow pools to areas larger than the Great Lakes. Until recently, wetlands in most developed countries were considered stagnant, mosquito-infested wastelands. People did not realize the vital natural and human functions they performed, including:

- storing rainfall to regulate watersheds;
- preventing flooding;
- preventing shoreline erosion;

- storing water during dry periods;
- recycling groundwater;
- purifying dirty water;
- filtering sediments and toxic substances;
- storing carbon dioxide, helping to balance increasing greenhouse gas emissions;
- providing resources such as cranberries, blueberries, wild rice, sphagnum moss, and fish;
- supporting rich **biomass** productivity;
- providing food and habitat for many species of plants and animals;
- providing recreational areas for activities such as hunting, fishing, and birdwatching.

Many wetlands have been drained primarily for agriculture and urban development. Since the time of European settlement, 20 million ha or 14% of Canada's wetlands have been drained. In the most densely populated parts of Canada, between 70% and 80% of the wetlands are gone.

There are also extensive wetlands in semi-arid regions such as the inland delta of the Niger River in Mali or the Okavango Delta in the Kalahari Desert. These wetlands form essential water sources for communities. Most have been

FIGURE 8.14 Some lakes become dumping grounds for municipal and industrial wastes. Many of the world's lakes suffer from **eutrophication**, excessive growth of algae that consumes oxygen and produces toxins. This occurs when there is an increase in water temperature or when large quantities of nutrients such as phosphorus and nitrogen from fertilizers, sewage treatment plants, and household products enter the lakes through rivers, rain, or snow melt.

FIGURE 8.13 Namibia has proposed a pipeline to take 20 million m^3 a year from the Okavango Delta (upper left) to supply its growing population with water. Dams and reservoirs in the Botswana area of the wetlands are already affected by a decade of drought. The two countries have taken their dispute over water use in the region to the International Court of Justice in The Hague, Netherlands.

the focus of development projects designed to meet human needs and some have become the focus of international disputes.

RIVERS Rivers are the circulatory systems of the hydrologic cycle. The **riparian zone** along the edges of riverbanks, even in deserts and tundra regions, shelter so much life that, along with wetlands and tropical rain forests, biologists call them nurseries of biodiversity. People tend to treat rivers as effective flushing mechanisms and have only recently begun to realize the great extent of the impact of industrial, agricultural, and engineering activity on the biological productivity of these habitats. Factors that threaten the world's river watersheds include population growth, pollution, deforestation, and withdrawing water for irrigation and municipal supply. The factor that has the greatest physical impact, fragmenting and transforming watersheds, is dam construction.

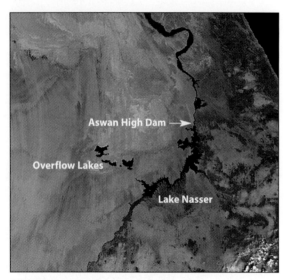

FIGURE 8.15 Artificial lakes that are large and deep, such as Lake Nasser in Egypt, have been constructed as a source of water for agricultural, industrial, recreational, and municipal uses as well as for flood control and power generation.

LAKES There are hundreds of thousands of lakes on Earth's surface, containing mainly fresh water, although some are brackish or salty. Lakes in many parts of the world have been subjected to significant abuse by human activity, resulting in declining water quality, loss of ecosystem integrity, and reduced ability to meet human needs.

Once a lake becomes degraded, restoration is an expensive and difficult task, if it is viable at all. Restoration usually has to coincide with continued use of the lake, which is particularly problematic in developing countries where local people must continue to exploit the water supply to survive. Restoration technologies such as installation of wastewater treatment facilities, dredging polluted silt from lake bottoms, and using chemicals to reduce acidity have created some success stories in developed countries, including Lake Washington in Seattle, many larger lakes in Europe, and Lake Erie.

 See Chapter 16 for more information about the Great Lakes.

GROUNDWATER About two-thirds of the water that falls on the land and percolates down through the soils and into spaces and cracks in bedrock is stored under Earth's surface as **groundwater** or in an aquifer. In arid and semi-arid regions, groundwater is an essential resource. Some aquifers are filled with ancient or glacial water that recharges only over thousands of years. Withdrawing large quantities of fresh water faster than the recharge capability from precipitation and seepage can lead to depletion, and, in some cases near oceans, movement of saltwater into the groundwater supply.

AQUIFER AT RISK The Ogallala underground reservoir is the world's largest supply of groundwater. Found under the Midwestern states of the Great and High Plains region of the United States, this aquifer holds 80% of the water in the region. Most of the area is dry and unsuited to farming, yet agriculture is the main economic activity. More than half the irrigated farmland of the Great Plains depends entirely on water drawn from the Ogallala, where the water table dropped as much as 18 m to 30 m in parts of Kansas, New Mexico, and Texas up until the 1980s.

More than 150 000 drilled wells withdraw water mainly for irrigation but also for domestic use. Some hydrologists predict that the reservoir will be pumped dry by about 2030. This could have a serious impact on food production and the economic base not only of the region but of the entire U.S. In response to this potential crisis, high-efficiency pumping and irrigation and the failure of many farm operations has significantly reduced water consumption and water table decline.

It will take 25 000 years to replenish this natural reservoir if precipitation amounts remain fairly constant. However, climate change predictions suggest that this region may experience more drought in the future. This situation is a clear example of how human-induced changes in natural systems can diminish their capacity to support human activity.

CLOUD FORESTS Cloud forests, tropical and subtropical mountain forests that are permanently covered in clouds or mist, are a part of the hydrologic cycle that are rarely mentioned, yet they provide billions of litres of clean

> 66 The cloud forests will all be gone in the next ten years. We don't know about our resources—80–90% of the cloud forests are a mystery to us all. Scientists have barely begun assessing the wide range of species that cloud forests harbour. In a small area the size of Machu Picchu, we can find the same plant diversity as on the whole continent of Europe. We are working with National Aeronautics and Space Administration (NASA), using satellite images to get some idea of what's there before it is gone. There aren't any field guides available. 99
>
> *Percy Nunez, ethnobiologist*

filtered water. Cooler temperatures on mountain slopes between 1500 m and 4000 m above sea level cause the mist to form. Leaves and branches of the trees collect water from the saturated air that would not otherwise fall as rain and filter the water that goes into local river systems. Water is "harvested" from the cloud forests, using fine polypropylene mesh nets stretched between poles, collecting large drops of water that run down a gutter into a collecting reservoir.

Cloud forests, which form the habitat of millions of species of plants and animals, are seriously endangered as they are constantly being cleared for logging, roads, cattle grazing, and plantation agriculture. The Tropical Montane Cloud Forest Initiative, designed to conserve these valuable water and biodiversity sources, was founded in 1999 by a coalition of non-governmental organizations (NGOs), including the World Conservation Union (IUCN) and the World Wildlife Fund (WWF) along with the UNEP.

> ## FACT FILE
>
> ■ The cloud forest in La Tigra National Park in Honduras supplies 40% of the water used by the 850 000 residents of the city of Tegucigalpa.
>
> ■ In Tanzania, cloud forests of the Udzngwa mountains provide the water used to operate hydro-electric dams that provide power to the city of Dar es Salaam.

GEOGRAPHIC METHODS

Geographic Technologies

Geographic technologies are used to manage water supplies in many ways. In one example, hydrologists measure water levels of wells drilled into the Ogalalla reservoir every January, using global positioning systems (GPS) and digital maps to locate wells and organize and guide their work. Measurements provide an accurate picture of water level trends. The resulting databases are used by landowners and local water officials when making water management and agricultural decisions.

FIGURE 8.16 A GPS device that measures location, elevation, and direction from satellite data is used with a GIS in many fields. These include navigation, aviation, surveying, recreation, mining, fishing, forestry, and emergency rescue. It is even used to track stolen rental cars and measure tectonic movements of Mount Everest.

Municipal and Industrial Groundwater Reservoirs

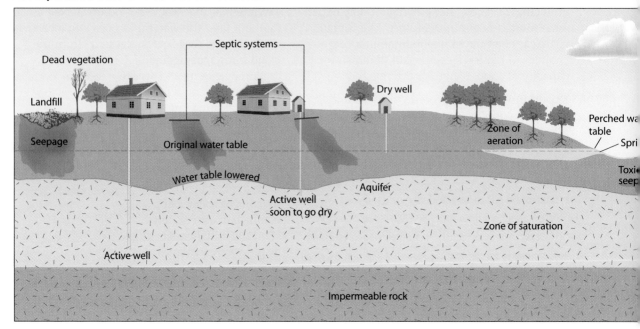

FIGURE 8.17

The World's Cloud Forests

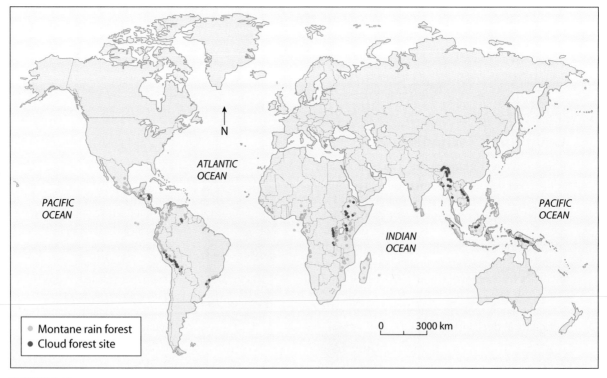

FIGURE 8.18

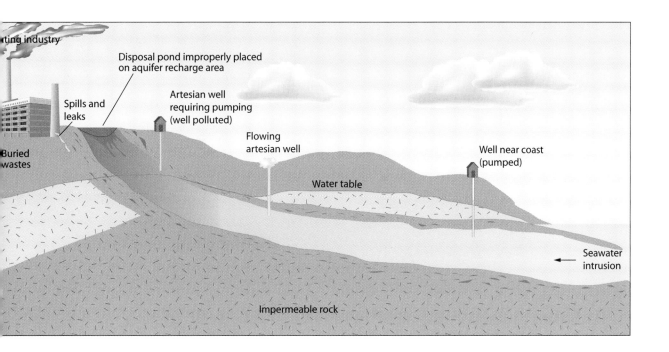

ting industry

Disposal pond improperly placed
on aquifer recharge area

Spills and
leaks

Artesian well
requiring pumping
(well polluted)

Buried
wastes

Flowing
artesian well

Well near coast
(pumped)

Water table

Seawater
intrusion

Impermeable rock

FIGURE 8.19 A cloud forest in Huangshan, China.

CANADA'S WATER ISSUES

The main water issues facing Canadians relate to water quality, drought and flood control, water exports, water conservation, and managing a sustainable water supply for the future.

Canadians have become much more aware of water issues and are beginning to demand protection of the life-sustaining element. While the Canadian Heritage Rivers System protects some rivers from degradation, and national and provincial parks also help keep some lakes and rivers in a more natural state, only a small percentage of the total water is protected. Many municipalities and some of Canada's largest cities, including Victoria and Quebec City, still flush raw or minimally treated sewage into waterways.

A huge increase in the demand for spring or treated water in plastic bottles has occurred in Canada and elsewhere, fuelled by concerns over water quality and increased concern for health and fitness. Sales of bottled water increased six times over the 1990s and are expected to increase 15% a year for the first decade of the twenty-first century. Worldwide sales of bottled water were more than $35 billion in 2001. There is a wide demand for Canadian bottled water from countries as far away as China.

Most current corporate decision making accepts that some pollution is the cost of "doing business" and promoting economic growth. However, government attempts at making corporations and other polluters pay for their share of the real costs of pollution, as in the **polluter pays principle**, may be seen as an unfair tax that could affect global competitiveness.

Changing conditions in Canadian and global economies have resulted in some decisions to reduce government support for programs such as environment ministry inspection and prosecution of pollution complaints and water quality monitoring. In May 2000 in Walkerton, Ontario, a groundwater well contaminated with a lethal

FACT FILE

The International Joint Commission is an organization that studies and looks for solutions to problems in the lakes and rivers along the border shared by Canada and the United States. In 1972, both governments signed the Great Lakes Water Quality Agreement.

Letter to the Editor

by Danny Beaton
The Globe and Mail
February 7, 2002

On Monday [February 4, 2002], the chiefs of nine James Bay Cree communities approved a $3.4 billion deal with Quebec that grants the Crees more control over logging and their economy in return for accepting Hydro-Quebec installations on the Eastmain and Rupert Rivers.

Many native people, however, are deeply concerned over some of the Cree leadership advocating development of the North. If we native people change our attitude about protecting Mother Earth and her rivers and fish, we will no longer be thought of as noble, honest protectors.

Our ancestors taught us that, if we destroy the Earth, then we will destroy ourselves. The thousands of square miles of flooded land at James Bay will be a catastrophe, an ecological disaster on a level with the devastation of the Amazon. It will mean death to the polar bears and seals and it will shatter the culture of traditional Cree Indians.

This is the most destructive energy project in North America. If it is completed, dams and dikes will block rivers, flooding will cover millions of acres, roads will be built through the wilderness, and airports, power lines and power plants will replace natural environments.

One of the Earth's great wild areas, with thousands of pristine lakes and rivers, with the largest caribou herd in North America, with Beluga whales and freshwater seals, with black bears, lynx, beaver, moose, ducks and geese, will be lost forever.

Who is going to benefit from the destruction of Mother Earth? Who is going to buy the power from dead rivers?

Native activist of the Mohawk nation, Danny Beaton has directed and produced four films for Canadian national television: Indigenous Restoration, 1991; Indigenous Restoration, 1992; Mohawk Wisdom Keepers; *and* The Iroquois Speak Out for Mother Earth. *He is currently working on his fifth production,* The Second Thanksgiving.

---

strain of *E. coli* bacteria, likely from agricultural wastes in run-off, caused seven deaths and serious illness in thousands of people.

Many of the large dams constructed in Canada have been in the north, where they have had a significant impact on the environment, health, and way of life of Canadian Aboriginal peoples.

 See Chapter 16 for more information about water pollution and human health.

Exporting Water from Canada

A current issue facing Canadians is whether or not we should allow exports of bulk water to people in other countries, primarily the United States and potentially the Caribbean. This issue highlights the concern for water and the natural environment that spurs citizens to take action. It focuses on a number of questions: who owns the water in our lakes and rivers and who has a right to use, divert, or extract it?

Water is considered a "good" in the General Agreement on Tariffs and Trade (GATT), which rules out restrictions on the quantity of a good that a country can export. The draft text of the agreement under negotiation at the World Trade Organization (WTO) meeting in Doha, Qatar, in November 2001 included a clause that supports the sale of fresh water and does away with export controls, making it illegal to restrict the export of bulk water for commercial purposes. Countries are not allowed to use "non-tariff" barriers such as environmental laws to interfere with trade liberalization. This means that standards to protect Canada's water could be challenged. If any permits are granted for water exports, then a precedent would be set whereby water would be considered an economic good. Some people fear that this would lead to further attempts to export Canada's water under the North American Free Trade Agreement (NAFTA). Others believe that selling some of our water to people who need it makes economic sense.

In 1999, the federal government asked the provinces, who are primarily responsible for resources, to declare a moratorium on large-scale water exports using supertankers, pipelines, or dug trenches until a national water policy can be negotiated. However, in 2002, more than 250 companies had permits to pump and export non-bulk Canadian water.

FACT FILE

Sun Belt Water Inc., a company based in California, sued the Canadian government under the provisions in Chapter 11 of NAFTA for damages of more than CDN$10 billion for profits lost because of the moratorium on water exports in British Columbia.

FACT FILE

A company based in the United Kingdom has constructed huge plastic bags to tow water across the sea from Greece to dry resort islands nearby. A company based in Norway is making similar water deliveries from Turkey to Cyprus using fabric containers. Called "bag and drag," water bags are a cheaper alternative to transporting water by tanker.

CASE STUDY

🍁 The Tay River Watershed

The Tay River runs through the town of Perth, Ontario, about 100 km southwest of Ottawa. The watershed includes a network of 46 lakes heavily populated with recreational cottages, and forms part of the Rideau Canal navigation system. The river supplies drinking water to residents of the region, including the town of Perth. The river is already stressed because it serves as a source of water for maintaining water levels in the Rideau Canal system for summer recreational navigation. In recent summers, lake levels in the system have dropped 1–2 m.

The controversy centres around a permit that was granted in August 2000 to OMYA, a Switzerland-based transnational mining company. The company operates a limestone quarry and calcium carbonate processing plant nearby. Heavy truck traffic through the rural region of small villages carries the material from the quarry to a processing plant 35 km away 24 hours a day, 7 days a week. The permit allows OMYA to take greater amounts of water from the Tay River, as the groundwater supply it is currently using is inadequate for a planned expansion in operations. The permit allows the company to take 1.5 million L a day from the river until 2004 when it will be allowed to take 4.5 million L, provided monitoring shows no adverse effects. This amount is more than the town of Perth takes from the river for domestic use. The water is mixed with ground calcium carbonate from the quarry to form a slurry and exported by tanker truck and rail car for making paper, paint, drywall, toothpaste, and for use at other manufacturing operations across North America. Many manufacturing operations involve a **closed loop system** that treats and returns water to its source. This operation will take the water out of the watershed and not return it.

Stakeholder Views

"I believe that a blanket prohibition on the export of water by tanker is a cruel and inhumane response to the real needs of people throughout the world. Whenever the subject of the export of water arises in Canada, we go a little goofy. I would suggest that a properly managed water-export industry would be a real benefit to Canada and to the thirsty peoples of the world."

John Carten, British Columbia lawyer on behalf of California's Sun Belt Water Inc.

"It is safe to say that a company that invents a cheap and energy-efficient way to desalinate seawater will make a Bill Gatesian-style bundle. And that will be that for Canadian water exports."

Marq de Villiers, water analyst

"It seems strange that you would issue a permit before you had all the information. We normally issue the permit after the information is gathered."

David Ballinger, senior Parks Canada official responsible for the Rideau Canal

"There is nothing in NAFTA that obliges Canada to export bulk water."

Roy MacLaren, Canada's international trade minister

"Water is a renewable resource and is constantly replaced by rainfall. It's part of a complete cycle. Water flowing in the Tay River goes into the St. Lawrence River and leaves the area (anyway)."

Olivier Chatillon, general manager of OMYA (Canada) Inc.

Opponents of the OMYA plan are cottagers and residents, including a former RCMP officer, local MP and MPP, environmentalists, the Council of Canadians, and environmental lawyers. They have tried to convince the Ontario Environmental Review Tribunal, which heard the appeal, to revoke the permit. While a solution is pending, concerns are based on a number of related issues:

- An environmental impact assessment to be conducted by the federal government was not completed before the permit was issued;
- Biologists testified that such a large withdrawal of water must have an impact on the ecosystem, despite studies that predicted no significant impact on water levels or aquatic habitat in the river and connected lakes;
- No consideration was given to the impact on future trade obligations under NAFTA to export water—by permitting water to be exported, future challenges from other companies who are refused permits by Canadian provinces are expected;
- Because water levels in the Rideau Canal system are already low in summer, cottagers and residents fear the water withdrawal will restrict navigation and recreational use of the watershed;
- Changing weather patterns and the threat of global warming have created increased interest in water management issues for local citizens and a belief in the need for caution in managing water resources;
- Because the water that is being exported is mixed with calcium carbonate as a slurry, it is considered a "product" by the company, the provincial Ministry of the Environment, federal water policy analysts, and provincial trade policy analysts, no different from water in beverages like soft drinks or beer, and, therefore, exempt from the moratorium on bulk water exports;
- The Ministry of the Environment maintains that the permit can be revoked for just cause (e.g., if negative ecosystem effects become visible); however, it is not clear how monitoring will take place and the government agrees that there is insufficient technical data to support the company's request.

INTERACT

1. How are Canada's water issues different from and similar to global water issues?
2. Conduct research on current hydroelectric power developments in the James Bay region. Explain the differing views of a variety of stakeholders in the controversy referred to in the letter to the editor on page 207.
3. Provide several reasons for the growth of bottled water from a niche to a mainstream market in Canada. What are the implications of this trend for the future, considering the use of water and plastic?
4. **a)** Identify the major stakeholder groups in the Tay River conflict that are for and those that are against the OMYA water permit.
   b) Construct a For and Against chart that shows the argument that each side would make about the seven related issues listed on page 209.
5. Use an Internet search engine such as < www.google.com > to find the results of the citizen appeal against the OMYA water permit.
6. **a)** Develop an appropriate question or two for a survey that will provide data on people's views about exporting Canada's water.
   b) Conduct a survey of 5 to 10 people, then combine your results with those of others in your class. Analyse the combined results.
   c) What is your view on the issue?
7. Research the role and recent major accomplishments of the International Joint Commission.

DAMMING THE RIVERS

Dams are often at the heart of disagreements or even violent confrontations over how economic and social development in a country should progress. Whether dams are seen as a benefit or a hazard depends on many factors, including how broad one's base of knowledge is, one's **worldview**, and how one will be affected. Most dams provide benefits for a country or region as a whole, while people who are most affected and bear the brunt of the costs usually live in the river valley or close to the river's edge.

The first dams built for generating electric-

> **❝** An estimated 40 to 80 million people have been physically displaced by the construction of dams. They have been flooded out, forced to move. One of the world's most massive engineering projects, the Three Gorges Dam in China, if completed could force the relocation of nearly 2 million people. **❞**
>
> *Curtis Runyan, associate editor, World Watch magazine*

FIGURE 8.20 An ancient dam near Turpan, China. People have been transforming rivers and building dams since ancient times. Anthropologists have studied the ruins of dams, aqueducts, and irrigation canals in the Middle East, Central America, and China that are as much as 8000 years old.

ity were constructed in the 1890s. By 1900, several hundred large dams had been built all over the world for hydropower, irrigation, flood

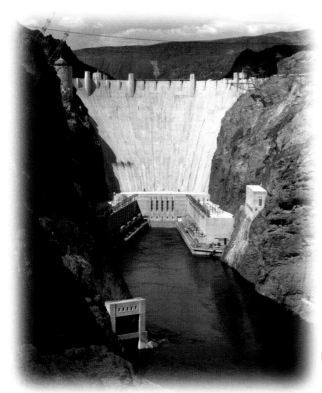

FIGURE 8.21 When the Hoover Dam was built, dams were considered technological wonders, essential for energy, agricultural production, flood control, water supply, economic prosperity, or national security. At the time, people were not as aware of the environmental and social consequences of these megaprojects.

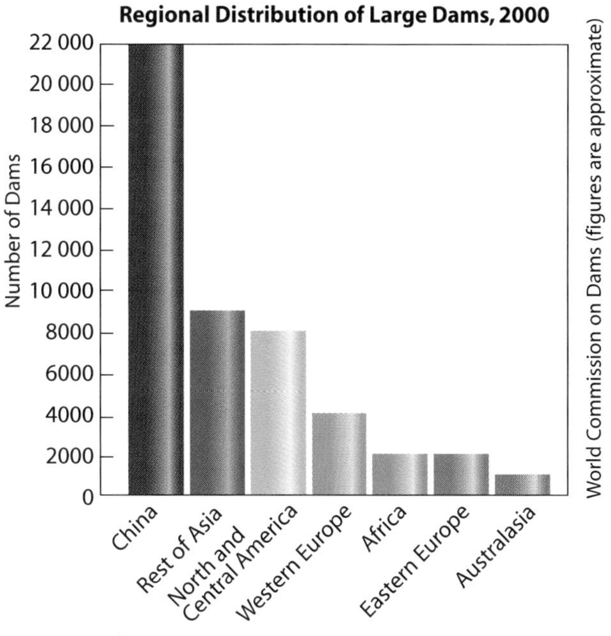

Regional Distribution of Large Dams, 2000
Number of Dams
22 000
20 000
18 000
16 000
14 000
12 000
10 000
8000
6000
4000
2000
0
China
Rest of Asia
North and Central America
Western Europe
Africa
Eastern Europe
Australasia
World Commission on Dams (figures are approximate)

FIGURE 8.22

control, and year-round water supply. By 2000, more than 45 000 large dam projects had been erected on rivers in 140 countries, including 3000 reservoirs that have flooded over 48 million ha of land. Developed countries in Europe and North America now regulate the flow of more than 65% of their rivers.

FACT FILE

Early dam builders had little information on rainfall, river flow, or how to engineer dams safely. Ten percent of all the dams built in the United States before 1930 collapsed. More than two thousand people were killed in Johnstown, Pennsylvania, in 1889 when the earth dam that held back the country's largest reservoir collapsed.

International development agencies, engineers and consultants, governments, and financial-lending institutions all believed dams to be an important route to economic development. Most still do. Dams have provided many thousands of jobs for engineers, consultants, government officials, bankers, and labourers. They have provided more equally distributed access to the water supply, irrigated vast amounts of land to produce food for hungry people, generated almost 20% of the world's electricity, and reduced the dangers of drought and flooding in some places—all benefits believed by some to outweigh the costs.

However, awareness and concern about the economic, social, and ecological costs of dam projects has become widespread, causing significant change in how dams and development in general are viewed. By the 1970s, public reviews and environmental impact assessments were being conducted. By the mid-1990s, NGOs representing some of the people affected began to play an increasingly significant role in the planning process. It became clear that significant improvements in knowledge and practices related to water management were needed.

FACT FILE

The U.S. has recently removed close to 500 large dams.

In 1994, 326 activist groups and coalitions of NGOs from 44 countries signed the Manibali Declaration, calling for a moratorium on World Bank-funded large dams until an independent review of all World Bank-funded projects had been completed. The mainly grass-roots movement has spread to international agencies and major lenders of megaprojects who are beginning to change the way they do business. In 1996, the World Bank conducted a sample review of the performance and impacts of 50 bank-funded large dams. While 90% of the dams met the bank's standards and guidelines for mitigating adverse social and environmental impacts at the time they were built, 75% of the dams failed to meet the bank's updated standards. The World Bank has withdrawn from a number of dam megaprojects, including the Sardar Sarovar project on the Narmada River in India and four dams on the Chico River in Indonesia. The NGO movement is not against dams as much as it is in favour of sustainable, equitable development priorities and policies, more efficient alternatives and technologies, and more democratic decision-making processes.

> " It is only fair to note that popular action has also supported dams. Farmers in Madrid recently marched to demand more water and more dams for irrigation. "
>
> *The Report of the World Commission on Dams, 2001*

FACT FILE

The Three Gorges Dam, at more than 182 m high and 2.4 km wide, with a 640-km-long reservoir will be one of the few man-made structures visible from space.

> " The view that environmental and human rights groups have singled out large dams as their main target is misleading. One assessment found that, of the 36 World Bank-supported projects that NGO activist groups have targeted with some success, only 12 are dam projects, compared to 14 forest and natural resource management projects, 5 mines or industrial management projects and two urban infrastructure projects. "
>
> *"Dams and Development: A New Framework for Decision-Making," The Report of the World Commission on Dams, 2001*

FIGURE 8.23 About 2 million people from 1400 towns and villages will be displaced by the Three Gorges Dam and resettled on land designated by the Chinese government.

A Canadian national registry of large dam projects shows a decline in new projects. The last large dams completed include the Oldman River project in Alberta and the Rafferty–Alameda Dam in Saskatchewan, both subject to a great deal of public protest and expensive litigation. Several provinces have shelved plans for dams in recent years, including the Meridian dam on the Alberta–Saskatchewan border in 2002.

FACT FILE

More than 7000 families living closest to the Narmada River, who will be flooded out by the Sardar Sarovar Dam, received notice of their "resettlement" from the government through a registered letter.

World Commission on Dams

Because of the growing controversy surrounding dam projects, a World Commission on Dams was set up as an independent body by the World Bank in 1998. Working to keep all the different stakeholders with widely divergent views involved in discussion, it released an extensive report in 2001, outlining a decision-making framework and setting out a number of principles and recommendations by which to evaluate dam projects—past, present, and future. Activists and NGOs are more in favour of the report than are governments and stakeholders from the dam building industry. Costs and benefits of any project clearly need to be determined on a case by case basis as the economic, political, cultural, and environmental aspects of each dam project are unique.

World Commission recommendations include:

- dams should not be built without the agreement of affected people through negotiated decision-making processes;
- impact assessment should include all people in the reservoir, upstream, downstream, and in **catchment** areas whose properties and livelihoods are affected and should also include those affected by dam-related infrastructure such as canals, transmission lines, and resettlement developments;
- the efficiency of existing water and energy systems should be improved before building new projects;
- mechanisms should be developed to provide compensation for those suffering the impacts of dams and for restoring damaged ecosystems.

Viewpoints on the Report by the World Commission on Dams

"Had the planning process proposed by the World Commission on Dams been followed in the past, many dams would not have been built."

Patrick McCully, International Rivers Network

"While there may be a few welcome instances of progress towards enhanced human rights and equity, to say there is a global trend towards these goals would indeed be erroneous."

Medha Patkar, anti-dam activist

"... the report notes some positive contributions of large dams. However, the "Global Review" concentrates on the shortcomings in the planning and decision process for dams. There is little mention of the benefits derived from dams and that dams should be included as an option for future water resources and energy development. It would have been appropriate to present a more balanced focus and presentation to include 1) the successful role that dams have played in water resources development; 2) credit for the improvements in the environmental and social aspects in recent years; and 3) the fact that dams provide sufficient quantity and quality of water and energy to meet future needs."

Arthur H. Walz Jr. president, United States Society on Dams

"The new framework for negotiation is vague, its criteria and guidelines a bureaucratic morass. If you mentally transfer yourself to the Narmada Valley, you know that very little of this could happen. There is no capacity for it to happen, even if the will existed."

Maggie Black, editor, New Internationalist magazine, July 2001

Central Issues in the Dams Debate Identified by the World Commission on Dams

Issue	Debate Highlights
Performance costs and benefits	■ The difficult task of evaluating performance over the life cycle of the dam and accurately determining costs and benefits
Environmental impacts and sustainability	■ How to measure environmental impacts and whether they are reversible ■ What value should be placed on biodiversity and ecosystem health, compared to development needs
Social impacts and equity	■ Fundamental human rights of those who are resettled and lose their livelihoods and how to pay reparations to those affected
Governance and participation	■ How and how much all stakeholders, including local people most affected, should be involved in decisions
Wider development impacts	■ The potential of a dam to contribute to export earnings ■ The best use of public funds in an overall development budget
Alternatives to dams	■ Whether other options offer less costly or more sustainable water development or energy objectives, including conservation and alternative renewable energy options
	■ The value of smaller-scale community-based projects such as pumps and wells, or smaller dams and reservoirs, to collect and store local run-off, conservation, renewable energy, etc.
Cross-cutting issues	■ The role and influence of different domestic and international stakeholder groups, including developers, contractors, suppliers, development and commercial banks, and insurers ■ Corrupt practices such as patronage, bribery, and embezzlement that can influence decision making ■ Transboundary conflicts on shared rivers

FIGURE 8.24

Some of the World's Controversial Dam Projects

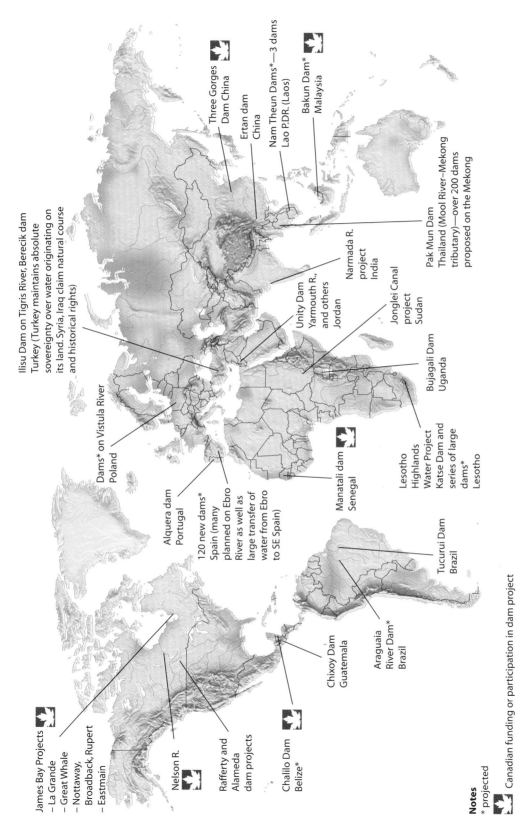

James Bay Projects
- La Grande
- Great Whale
- Nottaway, Broadback, Rupert
- Eastmain

Nelson R.

Rafferty and Alameda dam projects

Challlo Dam Belize*

Chixoy Dam Guatemala

Araguaia River Dam* Brazil

Tucurui Dam Brazil

Alquera dam Portugal

120 new dams* Spain (many planned on Ebro River as well as large transfer of water from Ebro to SE Spain)

Dams* on Vistula River Poland

Ilisu Dam on Tigris River, Berecik dam Turkey (Turkey maintains absolute sovereignty over water originating on its land. Syria, Iraq claim natural course and historical rights)

Three Gorges Dam China

Ertan dam China

Nam Theun Dams*—3 dams Lao P.DR. (Laos)

Bakun Dam* Malaysia

Pak Mun Dam Thailand (Mool River–Mekong tributary)—over 200 dams proposed on the Mekong

Unity Dam Yarmouth R., and others Jordan

Narmada R. project India

Jonglei Canal project Sudan

Bujagali Dam Uganda

Manatali dam Senegal

Lesotho Highlands Water Project Katse Dam and series of large dams* Lesotho

Notes

* projected

Canadian funding or participation in dam project

FIGURE 8.25

CASE STUDY

Narmada River: The Facts

adapted from *New Internationalist* magazine, July 2001

India suffers from widespread water scarcity

Rain comes in one seasonal period of deluge. Dams allow the deluge to be impounded and stored so that it can be used year-round in the same area or transferred to a water-short area by pipeline or canal. India has over 4000 large dams. Three-quarters of India's dams are in the three states of Gujarat, Maharashtra, and Madhya Pradesh and most are for irrigation. The map on page 217 shows the location of the 30 megaproject dams proposed, underway, or completed in the Narmada River Basin. There are an additional 135 medium-sized dams and 3000 smaller dams proposed on the various tributaries.

Opposition to dams

The Narmada Bachao Andolan (NBA), especially, is representative of wider resistance to "development gigantism." The NBA:
- is a people's movement that started in 1985;
- employs tactics that are entirely non-violent: sit-ins, fasts, rallies, and marches;
- is a founder member of the national alliance of people's movements;
- has attracted an international network of support;
- receives no funds from outside India;
- leadership is provided by Medha Patkar and other activists, unsalaried.

The achievements of the NBA include:
- Exit of the World Bank from Sardar Sarovar in 1993
- Halt of Sardar Sarovar construction 1994–95 [reinstated 2000]
- Withdrawal of foreign investors from Maheshwar dam 1999–2001

Pros and cons

- Indian food production rose from 50 to 200 million tonnes in the period 1950–1997; two-thirds of this increase is from irrigation.
- Data does not make clear what proportion of the increase was contributed by large dams; estimated 10%; Government claims 30%.
- Before 1978, all dams were built without an environmental impact assessment (EIA). EIA became statutory only in 1994.
- Estimates of those displaced by large dams in India in the last 50 years vary from 21 to 56 million people.
- Forty percent of those displaced are *adivasis* (tribal people).
- Less than 50% of people displaced by large projects are rehabilitated.
- Construction occurs under the Official Secrets Act; access is denied, information is withheld, and "participation" is non-existent.
- The costs of dams are systematically underestimated and their benefits are inflated.
- The accepted cost–benefit ratio for large dams is not met in 8 out of 10 cases.
- Heavy silting shortens the life of many dams.
- There have been 17 cases of earthquake tremor induced by large reservoirs in India.

Narmada River Valley

Maheshwar Dam
- First privately constructed dam in India
- Anticipated finance: US and Germany
- Height: 36 m
- Purpose: Hydroelectricity
- Construction: 1996–
- Submergence: 5697 ha
- Villages: 61
- People displaced: 35 000

NBA Action:
1998: First capture of dam-site
1998: Task Force review
1999: Sit-in and 26-day fast in Bhopal
1999: US and German companies withdraw
2000: German Government refuses loan guarantee
2000: US company Ogden withdraws

Sardar Sarovar Project
- Final height: 139 m
- Reservoir length: 214 km
- Canal network: 75 000 km
- Submergence: 37 690 ha
- Villages: 245
- People displaced: 200 000
- Irrigated area: 1.8 million ha

NBA Action:
1985: Mobilization begins in tribal belt
1988: Total opposition to dam
1989: Marches, sit-ins, fasts, arrests
1993: World Bank withdraws
1993: "Sacrifice in water" threat
1994: National level review
1994: Petition in Supreme Court
1995: Construction halts
2000: Supreme Court judgement

Bargi Dam
- Construction: 1984–90
- Submergence: 26 797 ha
- Villages: 162 (anticipated: 90)
- People displaced: 114 000 (anticipated: 70 000)
- Proportion tribal: 43%
- Irrigated area: 8000 ha (anticipated: 437 000)

NBA Action:
1992: First mass action for just resettlement
1993: 55-day sit-in as waters rise
1994: Mass action in Bhopal
1997: Sit-in and hunger strike
2001: Many issues still outstanding

Projects under construction:
1 Sardar Sarovar, **24** Indira Sagar, **26** Maheshwar, **27** Upper Veda, **28** Maan, **29** Goi, **30** Jobat

Projects completed:
8 Matiari, **9** Bargi, **17** Barna, **18** Tawa, **19** Kolar, **22** Sukta

FIGURE 8.26

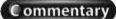

excerpt from

"The Cost of Living"

in *World Watch* magazine
by Arundhati Roy
January/February 2001

"Big Dams started well, but have ended badly. There was a time when everybody loved them—the Communists, Capitalists, Christians, Muslims, Hindus, Buddhists. There was a time when Big Dams moved men to poetry. Not any longer. All over the world there is a movement growing against Big Dams.

In the First World, they're being decommissioned, blown up. The fact that they do more harm than good is no longer just conjecture. Big Dams are obsolete. They're uncool. They're undemocratic. They're a Government's way of accumulating authority (deciding who will get how much water and who will grow what where). They're a guaranteed way of taking a farmer's wisdom away from him. They're a brazen means of taking water, land and irrigation away from the poor and gifting it to the rich. Their reservoirs displace huge populations of people, leaving them homeless and destitute. Ecologically they're in the doghouse. They lay the earth to waste. They cause floods, waterlogging, salinity, they spread disease. There is mounting evidence that links Big Dams to earthquakes.

Big Dams haven't really lived up to their role as the monuments of Modern Civilization, emblems of Man's ascendancy over Nature. Monuments are supposed to be timeless, but dams have an all too finite lifetime. They last only as long as it takes Nature to fill them with silt. It's common knowledge now that Big Dams do the opposite of what their Publicity People say they do—the Local Pain for National Gain myth has been blown wide open. ...

Over the last fifty years, India has spent 870 billion rupees [US$20 billion] on the irrigation sector alone. Yet there are more drought-prone areas and flood-prone areas today than there were in 1947. Despite the disturbing evidence of irrigation disasters, dam-induced floods and rapid disenchantment with the Green Revolution (declining yields, degraded land), the government has not commissioned a post-project evaluation of a *single one* of its 3300 dams to gauge whether or not it has achieved what it set out to achieve, whether or not the (always phenomenal) costs were justified, or even what the costs actually were...

According to a detailed study of 54 Large Dams done by the Indian Institute of Public Administration, the *average* number of people displaced by a Large Dam in India is 44,182. Admittedly, 54 dams out of 3300 is not a big enough sample. But since it's all we have, let's try and do some rough arithmetic. A first draft.

To err on the side of caution, let's halve the number of people. Or, let's err on the side of *abundant* caution and take an average of just 10,000 people per Large Dam. It's an improbably low figure, I know, but... never mind. Whip out your calculators. 3300 × 10,000 = 33 million people. That's what it works out to. Thirty-three *million* people

Displaced by Big Dams *alone* in the last 50 years. What about those that have been displaced by the thousands of other Development projects? In a private lecture, N. C. Saxena, Secretary to the Planning Commission, said he thought the number was in the region of 50 million (of which 40 million were displaced by dams). We daren't say so because it isn't official. It isn't official because we daren't say so. You have to murmur it for fear of being accused of hyperbole. You have to whisper it to yourself, because it really does sound unbelievable. It *can't* be, I've been telling myself. I must have got the zeroes muddled. It *can't be true*. I barely have the courage to say it aloud.

To run the risk of sounding like a sixties hippie dropping acid ("It's the System, Man!"), or a paranoid schizophrenic with a persecution complex. But it *is* the System, man. What else can it be?

Fifty million people. Go on government, quibble. Bargain. Beat it down. Say *something*. I feel like someone who's just stumbled on a mass grave.

Fifty million is more than the population of Gujarat. Almost three times the population of Australia. More than three times the number of refugees that partition created in India. Ten times the number of Palestinian refugees. The western world today is convulsed over the future of one million people who have fled from Kosovo.

A huge percentage of the displaced are tribal people (57.6 per cent in the case of the Sardar Sarovar Dam). Include Dalits ["Untouchables"] and the figure becomes obscene. ... If you consider that tribal people account for only 8 per cent, and Dalits 15 per cent, of India's population, it opens up a whole other dimension to the story. The ethnic "otherness" of their victims takes some of the pressure off the nation builders. It's like having an expense account. Someone else pays the bills. People from another country. Another world. India's poorest people are subsidizing the lifestyles of her richest.

Did I hear someone say something about the world's biggest democracy? What has happened to all these millions of people? Where are they now? How do they earn a living? Nobody really knows. ...

Critical Analysis

1. Who is the author and what is her purpose in writing this account?
2. Describe Roy's bias with respect to the Narmada Dam projects.
3. What persuasive techniques does Roy use to influence public opinion?
4. What evidence is provided to support the argument that democracy in India is questionable?
5. How would Roy likely feel about the recommendations of the World Commission on Dams?

Positive Aspects of Dams
- Help a country meet energy and water needs
- Provide a wide range of water and energy services
- Contribute to export earnings and support economic development
- Increase amount of agricultural land and productivity with water for irrigation
- May develop recreational activities and commercial fisheries in reservoirs
- Just one integral part of resource development strategies
- Improved dam safety and concern for environmental and social issues over the last decade

Negative Aspects of Dams
- Affect critical, life-sustaining resources
- Lack of attention to appropriate alternatives to dams and acceptable solutions to their social and environmental impacts
- Huge inequities in who bears the costs and receives the benefits
- Rich fertile agricultural land rather than marginal land is usually flooded
- Displacement of people as their homes and villages are flooded
- Resettlement programs have been unsuccessful as people may lose their livelihoods, and rural and urban lands may already be densely populated and owned by others
- Require huge investments that are irreversible
- Many have not met their projected targets for productivity
- Corruption and embezzlement of funds by officials
- Block fish passage and migration
- Mercury released from flooded soil and bedrock can poison fish and other species and affect human health
- Water temperature, quantity, and sediment can have negative effects on ecosystems

FIGURE 8.27

PROFILE

Probe International

Many Canadians are not aware of the technical expertise and financial support provided by Canadian businesses and banks to a number of projects in developing countries. On the surface, these international links appear to be beneficial, but mainstream media coverage rarely considers the negative aspects that might exist with development projects.

Probe International is an independent NGO that believes in the rule of law and the democratic process. It works with a number of other NGOs to provide information to Canadians about the environmental, social, and economic effects of Canada's trade and aid that are devastating to some people and environments. It holds Canadian agencies such as the Canadian International Development Agency (CIDA) and the Export Development Corporation (EDC) and Canadian corporations accountable for all aspects of the projects they are involved in. Probe International obtains official documents that may be secret, challenges policies of international agencies and transnational corporations, and lobbies to have people whose environment, heritage, and livelihoods are most affected included in the planning and decision-making process.

FIGURE 8.28

Some of the main campaigns the organization is involved in are large dams, including the Three Gorges Dam in China, and Canadian mining operations in several countries. Funded mostly by small donations from Canadians, the organization is supported by a number of known citizens, including wildlife artist Robert Bateman. A visit to the Web site of this NGO, <www.probeinternational.org>, rounds out the media picture with a great deal of information about Canada's international role that would not be available in official sources. Video clips from a public broadcasting documentary on the Three Gorges Dam can be seen as well as a number of successes Probe International has had.

WATER WARS

Ismail Seralgaldin, vice-president of the World Bank, predicted that the wars of the twenty-first century would be about water. As some ecologists say, we are all downstream from somewhere else. This interconnectedness among places has given rise to complicated political situations, many disputes, and even armed conflicts over control of water supply and water quality. This issue is likely to become more contentious with continued population growth and development. Almost all water at some time in its movement across the landscape crosses regional or national borders. More than 300 river systems in the world cross national boundaries. For example, the water resources of the Jordan River watershed must be shared by Jordan, Lebanon, Syria, and Israel. The 1967 Arab–Israeli war was fought partly over access to the Jordan and Yarmouk Rivers. Turkey has diverted waters of the Tigris and Euphrates Rivers on which Syria and Iraq depend. In Africa, the waters of the Nile must be shared by 10 countries, including Egypt, Ethiopia, Sudan, Uganda, and Eritrea.

The issues that arise centre on questions such as Does a country have the right to use all the water in a river just because it rises on their soil? What about the country that is downstream where the mouth of the river is dry? International law tries to promote an ethic of equity among countries with regard to shared watersheds, but clearer and more enforceable criteria are needed to judge appropriate levels of use and

FIGURE 8.29 A dispute between Canada and the United States has surfaced over the draining of Devils Lake into the Red River to reduce serious flooding in North Dakota. The photo shows flood waters rising in the border town of Emerson, Manitoba. Manitoba is concerned that the Red River flood risk will increase and that alien species will invade the river ecosystem.

ways of sharing the water. A country will usually consent to international laws because the long-term benefits usually outweigh the costs. Most countries strive to work out agreeable terms and treaties. In order to share the waters of the Rio Grande and Colorado Rivers, the U.S. and Mexico have signed treaties that guarantee minimum quantities of water flow and water quality as the rivers cross the international boundary. However, high water salinity because of dissolved salts from irrigation in the U.S. degrades the water flow that does make it to Mexico.

The Aral Sea Disaster

The Aral Sea has been called an environmental disaster and a toxic desert. It is one of the world's worst examples of how human-induced changes can diminish the capacity of natural systems to support human activity and a healthy ecosystem. Five Central Asian countries, formerly republics of the now collapsed Soviet Union, are squeezing as much water out of the Amu Darya and Syr Darya Rivers, which feed the Aral Sea, as possible. Fifty years of diverting water from the two rivers to irrigate millions of hectares of arid land for cotton and rice has caused a loss of 60% of the Aral Sea's water. The lake has shrunk from 65 000 square km to

FIGURE 8.30 Most years, the Colorado River (top centre) does not make it to the ocean via the Gulf of California (lower right). All of the water in the river each year has been allocated to various uses before it crosses the border into Mexico. This not only causes political conflict, there are negative consequences for the river's riparian, delta, and estuary ecosystems.

less than half that size. Salt concentrations have increased from 10% to 23%, devastating the fishing industry. Dust storms have blown 75 000 tons of exposed salts and pesticide residues causing serious health hazards in the area, including very high rates of cancer and respiratory diseases. The water quality continues to drop and water experts predict that by 2010 the region will be a desert.

> " If you're short of water, the choices are conservation, technological invention, or the politics of violence. ...
>
> Water survival strategy 1: If you need more water, get more water. That means you either import water from some place where there is a surplus, or you make more fresh water yourself.
>
> Water survival strategy 2: If you can't get more water... then use less of it. Reduce demand. This can be done in three ways: by conservation; by pricing mechanisms; or by making existing water consumption efficient through a combination of a new water ethic and skillful use of imaginative technologies.
>
> Water survival strategy 3: Water use will go down if there are fewer people. But is this likely to happen? Was Thomas Malthus, the doomsayer who forecast worldwide famines because populations were growing faster than the food supply, right after all?
>
> Water survival strategy 4: Steal water from others. "
>
> *Marq de Villiers, Water, Houghton Miffin Co., 2000*

Statistical Indicators in the Aral Sea Region

Indicator	1960	2000
Population	14 million	50 million
Irrigated land area	5 million ha	8 million ha
Water intake	65 m³/year	110 m³/year

FIGURE 8.31

The Shrinking Water Levels of the Aral Sea

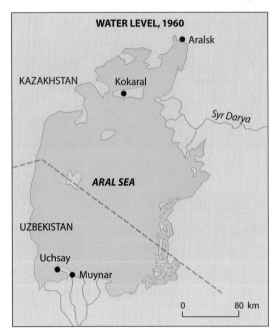

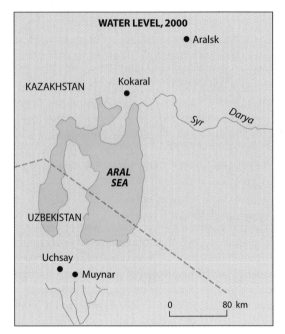

FIGURE 8.32 The Aral Sea disaster is the result of rapid population growth and the damaging agricultural policies of the former Soviet government, including wasteful irrigation methods and monoculture. The Aral Sea shoreline has receded up to 100 km in some places and the lake has lost 75% of its water volume.

INTERACT

1. **a)** Conduct research on the Aral Sea region. Describe the economic, political, cultural, and environmental aspects of the situation in the Aral Sea watershed.

   b) Use your findings to analyse the change over time shown by the two maps in Figure 8.32, **The Shrinking Water Levels of the Aral Sea**.

2. What evidence supports the view that the situation in the region is a disaster?

3. **a)** Conduct research to investigate the International Law Association's Helsinki Rules or the United Nations' Convention on the Law of the Non-navigational Uses of International Watercourse.

   b) Identify five factors that are relevant to equitable sharing of water resources when more than one country shares a water source.

4. What measures have the five Central Asian states in the Aral Sea region taken to share the water?

5. Conduct a case study on one of the water supply issues facing one part of the world such as Egypt or Mexico that is dependent on the flow of water from another country. Communicate the results of your findings, using a fully labelled and annotated sketch map of the river basin within the water sharing countries.

6. Refer to the quote by Marq deVilliers on page 221. Identify the most appropriate water survival strategies for the country in your case study from Question 5.

RELATED ISSUES

- Water pollution and health
- Water quality guidelines in Ontario before and after the Walkerton disaster
- Climate change from greenhouse gas emissions from reservoirs
- Canada's role in dam projects in other countries such as Belize
- Restoration technologies

GIS **Water Availability—The Implication of Growing Demands**

ANALYSE, APPLY, AND INTERACT

1. Provide evidence to either support or refute the argument that there is a world water crisis.

2. Explain why it is important to consider the complete hydrologic cycle when making decisions on how to use water.

3. Identify three significant trends in water use. Predict and analyse how each trend will affect global water requirements in the future.

4. Describe your own personal water ethic and give at least one specific example of how your actions reflect your ethic.

5. Refer to the data in Figure 8.10, **Water Availability for Selected Countries**.
   a) Select one of the countries listed that appears to be water-stressed and conduct a case study on the water sources, water use patterns, and issues facing the country as well as the measures being taken to manage its water crisis. Prepare a written report with analysed graphs and maps that illustrate your findings.

   b) For each of the countries in Figure 8.10, **Water Availability for Selected Countries**, select one statistical indicator of economic development such as per capita GDP (Gross Domestic Product) or GNI PPP (Gross National Income in Purchasing Power Parity) as a variable to create a scattergraph to assess the relationship between economic development and 1995 water availability.

   c) Analyse the correlations that exist between levels of economic development, water availability, and water use.

6. Investigate the current state of acidified lakes in eastern and northern Canada. Prepare a television news report to present to members of your group or class.

7. Choose one large dam project in Canada or another country and conduct research to produce a cost–benefit analysis that evaluates the project with respect to the issues identified by the World Commission on Dams.

8. Refer to the Web site <www.on.ec.gc.ca/coa/2001/intro-e.html> and provide an update on Canada–Ontario agreements to protect water resources in the various components of the hydrologic cycle in the Great Lakes watershed.

9. Make a brief prediction of the probable future of agriculture in the Great Plains of the United States. If you were a water policy analyst in the region, produce a plan of action that outlines the integrated approach and "water survival strategies" that you would take to address the groundwater depletion problem.

10. Brainstorm a list of water-related careers. Select one career that might interest you and investigate the educational requirements and daily responsibilities/activities for the career.

11. Use specific examples to explain how the media can influence public opinion on water-related issues. Include media forms such as Web sites, organization newsletters, art, and cultural myths or legends.

12. Evaluate the role that NGOs have played in promoting sustainable water resources management.

Chapter 9: The World's Food Supply

By the end of this chapter, you will

- analyse selected global trends and evaluate their effects on people and environments at the local, national, and global level;

- evaluate the cultural, economic, and environmental impact of changing technology;

- demonstrate an understanding of how human-induced changes in natural systems can diminish their capacity for supporting human activity;

- analyse the impact of past and current trends in agriculture on natural and human systems;

- analyse examples of efforts to increase the productivity of a selected natural environment and their short- and long-term economic, social, and environmental impacts;

- evaluate factors that may compound problems of hunger and poverty in a selected country;

- explain how new technology affects employment and resource management;

- evaluate the sustainability of selected trends related to consumption of the earth's resources.

THE HUNGER ISSUE

Because everyone must eat in order to survive, food, unlike other commodities and services, is a necessity. In a world where some enjoy huge food surpluses and where overconsumption of food leads to problems of obesity, millions of children go to bed hungry every night. Over the past few decades, the supply of food has grown faster than the human population. This means that, globally, there is more food available per person now than there was in your parents' and grandparents' youth. Yet, programs on television continuously remind us that there are starving people in the world, showing us images of gaunt, emaciated people in destitute countries. Even in wealthy countries, the media report line-ups at food banks and the need for breakfast programs for hungry school children. The evidence indicates that there is a global hunger problem. In this chapter, we will examine the reasons why some parts of the world

> " There is enough food to feed 120% of the world population on a vegetarian diet although not on a western diet. "
>
> *Lester Brown, editor, Worldwatch Institute*

suffer from hunger and consider how these conditions could be changed. We will evaluate our connections to the global food production system as the food choices we make reverberate around the world.

It is a fact that 815 million of the world's people face chronic **endemic** hunger. They are not able to acquire and eat enough food to provide their bodies with the nutrition that they need to live a healthy life. Over 400 million of these hungry people are children.

The World Health Organization (WHO) estimates that one-third of the children of developing countries are malnourished and that half of all deaths of children under the age of five can be attributed to malnutrition. Almost 80% of the malnourished children in the developing world live in countries with food surpluses. In the long term, these food tragedies will get worse as global population growth continues over the next few decades, passing the 8 billion mark.

FIGURE 9.1 Hunger and starvation persist in a world with plenty of food.

a)   b)   c)   d)   e)   f)

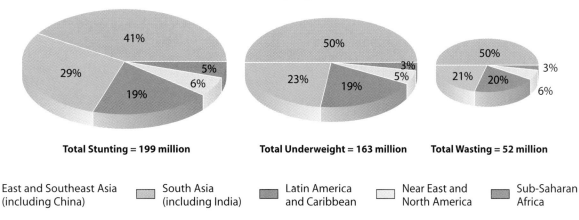

Children Suffering from Undernourishment by Region, 1995–2000

Total Stunting = 199 million

Total Underweight = 163 million

Total Wasting = 52 million

- East and Southeast Asia (including China)
- South Asia (including India)
- Latin America and Caribbean
- Near East and North America
- Sub-Saharan Africa

United Nations Food and Agriculture Organization (FAO)

FIGURE 9.2 At the stunting level of hunger, children will likely not achieve their full physical and intellectual development. For those at the underweight level, hunger will mean a life of poor health and limited intellectual development. Children at the wasting level are in danger of not surviving to adulthood.

The Geography of Hunger

Hunger is a complex geographic issue with economic, cultural, social, political, and environmental causes and effects. The issue centres more on a socio-economic imbalance in the distribution of healthy foods than on a shortage in the total supply available. Statistics reveal that some parts of the world have improved their food supply over the last half of the twentieth century. Asia, Europe, and large parts of the Americas have made improvements to their per capita food production totals. Developing countries, as a group, have seen per capita food supplies grow from less than 2000 calories per day in 1962 to over 2500 calories per day in the 1990s. Improved technologies—in seeds, breeding techniques, pesticides, irrigation, harvesting methods, and storage facilities—have caused global food availability to expand faster than the population. But Africa, parts of Latin America, and the republics that were part of the Soviet Union before 1991 have had different experiences. Africa has witnessed a steady erosion of its per capita food supply as its people struggle to expand their food producing systems to meet the demands of a rapidly growing population. Fully one-third of the population of sub-Saharan Africa—roughly 260 million people—will suffer from hunger by 2010. Countries of the former

FACT FILE

A Canadian federal government study of hunger in 1996 estimated that 1.6% of Canadian families—roughly 75 600 families in total—experienced hunger. Of the families reporting hunger, 62.5% had occasional hunger, 11.2% said they experienced hunger every few months, 19.8% faced hunger regularly, especially at the end of the month when their money ran out, and 6.5% endured hunger even more often.

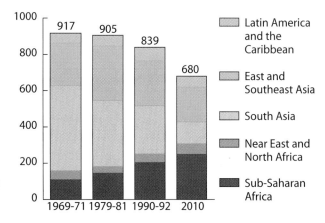

Millions of Persons Suffering from Undernourishment

- Latin America and the Caribbean
- East and Southeast Asia
- South Asia
- Near East and North Africa
- Sub-Saharan Africa

WRI

FIGURE 9.3 The problem of hunger is being improved in some parts of the world, but sub-Saharan Africa will continue to struggle with food supply.

Soviet Union have had to deal with the disruption of shifting from a centrally planned economy to a more open economic system. While food production fell as a result of the economic turmoil, these places may see improvements in the coming years. Hunger in all of these regions indicates inequities in the distribution of the world's food.

"Fighting hunger is a moral obligation. Without biological integrity of the human being which requires his daily bread, there can be no real lasting progress in the struggle for more justice and equity in the world."

Dr. Jacques Diouf, director-general, FAO

Hunger and Natural Disasters

Natural disasters have caused temporary famine but have *not* been a major cause of hunger. Droughts, floods, or insect infestations do contribute to hunger in some places, but these causes represent only about 10% of the overall hunger problem. They often receive a good deal of publicity, which tends to inflate their importance as causes of hunger. Nonetheless, global climate change *is* already beginning to have an impact on food production. In some regions of Africa and the Middle East, climate change is being blamed for many years of drought. Southern Iran and Afghanistan, for example, have experienced extreme drought with devastating effects on traditional livestock agriculture.

FACT FILE

In Toronto, Ontario, an average of 140 000 people used food banks every month during 2001.

Measures of Food Supply for Selected Countries, 1997

Country	Daily per Capita Supply of Calories	Daily per Capita Supply of Protein (grams)	Daily per Capita Supply of Fat (grams)	Food as a Percent of Household Spending
Botswana	2183	70	60	37
Canada	3119	98	126	9
Egypt	3287	89	58	44
Fiji	2865	74	106	30
Granada	2768	67	93	26
Hungary	3313	85	137	14
Japan	2932	96	83	11
Mali	2029	61	42	48
Pakistan	2476	61	65	40
Romania	3253	100	82	24
Spain	3310	107	145	17
Sri Lanka	2302	52	46	38
Thailand	2360	54	47	23
Vietnam	2484	57	36	40
Zambia	1970	52	30	47

Human Development Report 2000

FIGURE 9.4 The figures given here are averages for the populations of the countries and do not reflect what individuals would consume.

FIGURE 9.5 The destruction of food sources in Mozambique after Cyclone Eline in February 2000 prompted a large emergency assistance effort on the part of the international community.

A good example of disaster-related hunger occurred in Mozambique in 2000. Cyclone Eline tore through that country, killing scores and leaving hundreds of thousands of people without homes. The flooding washed away almost all the food crops and survivors faced a severe famine. However, soon after the situation was made known to the rest of the world, a massive humanitarian aid effort was launched. South African and French Air Force planes were used to deliver international aid to the hungry people of Mozambique.

The natural disaster in Mozambique illustrates several characteristics of disaster-related hunger:

- There is a virtual absence of food—a famine
- The hunger is localized, usually occurring only in parts of a country
- The hunger is short-term; the situation usually improves with the next growing season
- Humanitarian aid can help the people survive the crisis

These characteristics set disaster-related hunger apart from the conditions experienced by chronically hungry people. Around the world, close to a billion people are plagued by chronic, persistent hunger, which:

- is a condition of undernourishment, where there is not enough good quality food;
- occurs over the whole country or region;
- has existed for a very long time, and will not likely improve in the immediate future;
- involves so many people that humanitarian aid will have little lasting effect.

Hunger and Population

Like natural disasters, overpopulation *seems* to be an obvious explanation for hunger; too many people eating the available food must mean that there is not enough for everyone. This idea was considered by Thomas Malthus in his 1798 book, *An Essay on the Principle of Population*. Malthus pointed out that populations grow at a geometric rate (i.e., 1, 2, 4, 8, 16, 32, and so on) while food supplies grow at an arithmetic rate (i.e., 1, 2, 3, 4, 5, 6, and so on). Because of this difference, populations must exceed food supplies at some point. Malthus predicted that famine, violence resulting from food shortages, and diseases due to overcrowding would reduce the population to a size that could be accommodated by the food supply. These negative population controls have been referred to as Malthusian checks.

 See Chapter 10 for more information about population trends.

The theory developed by Malthus underestimated the capability of technology to increase food supplies and did not anticipate the reduction in birth rates that has occurred around the world, especially in developed countries, where birth rates are expected to fall to replacement levels by the middle of the twenty-first century.

A high population density does not cause hunger. Some of the most densely populated parts of the world are well-fed. For example, the Netherlands has 385 persons per square kilometre while Japan has a density of 335 persons per square kilometre. The daily per capita supplies of calories for these countries are 3284 and 2932, respectively—well above the world average of 2791 calories per person per day. On the other hand, the African country of Chad has a population density of 6 persons per square kilometre, with 2032 calories per person per day. The Congo (Kinshasa) has one of the world's lowest food supplies at 1755 calories per person per day and a population density of 22 persons per square kilometre. The size of a population is not a determining factor for

FIGURE 9.6 Weather changes such as this drought in Zabul district, Afghanistan, can devastate an entire year's harvest, resulting in famine and reducing a region's food security.

Commentary

"Using Statistics to Look Behind the Questions"
Human Development Report, 2000

Imagine a country in which 87% of children are enrolled in secondary school. What does this reveal about the right of a child to an education? Certainly, the final goal—secondary education for all—has not been reached. But have all the obligations of those involved been met? Answering means looking beyond this one statistic, deeper into the issues.

If we discover that only 77% of girls are enrolled and 97% of boys, then much of the failure is due to discrimination. Do opinion polls reveal that parents discount the importance of girls' education? Then parents are failing to respect the rights of their daughters to a literate future and the government is failing to raise awareness and change that norm. Or do surveys reveal inadequate provision of school facilities, such as a lack of separate classrooms for girls or very few female teachers? Then the government is failing to promote the rights of girls to real access to an education.

Perhaps there is gender equity—but discriminatory legislation enforces apartheid and grossly underprovides for schools for children of the oppressed ethnic group, with only 40% of them in school. That would be a failure of the government to respect the rights of all people without discrimination, calling for an immediate change in legislation, but also for changes in institutions and norms.

Or perhaps there is no discrimination—but all schools lack resources and cannot provide quality education. Is the government giving enough priority to education? It depends on resource availability. In a country spending twice as much on military power and presidential palaces as on secondary education, the answer would be no—and the government would be failing to adequately fulfil rights. But in a country spending 0.5% of revenues on national security and 8% on secondary education, the answer would be quite different: a lack of resources, not a lack of priority, would be the constraint.

And what about progress? If a country had raised enrolments from 50% to 87% in five years, it would be making strong progress in realizing rights—but if the country had let enrolments fall from 95% to 87%, it would be headed backwards.

If resources are lacking, what are donors and the international community doing? How much development assistance are they providing? What percentage is allocated to the education sector?

Clearly, statistics alone cannot give conclusive answers—but they do help open key questions. They need to be embedded in a deeper analysis of the actors involved and their range of obligations. But if statistics can reveal whether or not those obligations are being met, they help to create accountability and, ultimately, to realize rights.

Critical Analysis

1. This article raises serious concerns about the use of statistics. What does it suggest as the real benefit of statistics?
2. What do you suppose the article suggests with the idea that statistics "… need to be embedded in a deeper analysis of the actors involved …"?
3. What might be some key questions to ask about the statistic that, in 1990, there were 150 million fewer hungry people than two decades earlier?

hunger. Something else must be a more important causal factor. Some analysts believe that global efforts should focus on creating a more equitable economic system that enables the poor to be self-sufficient.

> 66 For the poor, it doesn't matter if there's a lot of wheat out there. You can't buy it anyway. 99
>
> *Mark Rosegrant,*
> *International Food Policy Research Institute*

FIGURE 9.7 A floating market in Damnoen Saduak, Thailand. There is a wide range of views on the links between a growing population and persistent hunger. Will limiting population growth put an end to hunger?

Hunger and Poverty

Poverty is a major cause of hunger and malnutrition. Poor people lack the money to buy food, or lack access to the means to produce food. For the 1.3 billion people who live on $1 a day or less, a modest rise in the price of wheat or rice can mean food is not accessible. Developing countries lack the social infrastructures that exist in the rich countries to protect the poorest of the poor—safety nets like food banks and social assistance. In many places around the world, if you cannot buy food, you go hungry.

 See Chapters 13 and 14 for more information about poverty.

> 66 The number of chronically hungry people in the world has increased since the early 1990s, after declining steadily during the previous two decades. This is mainly because there has been little progress in reducing poverty. The widening gap in income distribution in many parts of the world is also a worrying trend for undernourishment. 99
>
> *FAO,*
> *"The State of Food and Agriculture,"*
> *1998*

Agricultural Indicators by Region

	Irrigation (% of arable land)	Fertilizer Use (kg/ha)	Cereal yields (kg/ha)
Africa	7	22	1225
Sub-Saharan Africa	4	9	986
Near East/North Africa	29	69	1963
South Asia	39	109	2308
East and Southeast Asia	32	241	4278
Latin America and Caribbean	12	85	2795
World	20	100	2067

de Haen, Hartwig, "Trends in Reducing Global Hunger and the Challenges to Agricultural Growth," FAO

FIGURE 9.8 This table shows a clear relationship between the use of fertilizers and irrigation and the production of cereal crops. What other factors might affect this relationship?

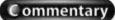

"Poverty and Globalization"
in the BBC Reith Lectures 2000 series
by Vandana Shiva, physicist, ecologist, and activist

Who feeds the world's poor? My answer is very different to that given by most people.

It is women and small farmers working with biodiversity who are the primary food providers in the Third World, and contrary to the dominant assumption, their biodiversity based small farms are more productive than industrial monocultures.

The rich diversity and sustainable systems of food production are being destroyed in the name of increasing food production. However, with the destruction of diversity, rich sources of nutrition disappear. When measured in terms of nutrition per acre, and from the perspective of biodiversity, the so-called "high yields" of industrial agriculture or industrial fisheries do not imply more production of food and nutrition.

Yields usually refers to production per unit acre of a single crop. Output refers to the total production of diverse crops and products. Planting only one crop in the entire field as a monoculture will of course increase its individual yield. Planting multiple crops in a mixture will have a high total output of food. Yields have been defined in such a way as to make food production on small farms by small farmers disappear. This hides the production by millions of women farmers in the Third World—farmers like those in my native Himalaya who fought against logging in the Chipko movement, who in their terraced fields even today grow Jhangora (barnyard millet), Marsha, (Amaranth), Tur, (Pigeon Pea), Urad (Black gram), Gahat (horse gram), Soya Bean (Glycine Max), Bhat (Glycine Soya)—endless diversity in their fields. From the biodiversity perspective, biodiversity based productivity is higher than a monoculture productivity. I call this blindness to the high productivity of diversity a "Monoculture of the Mind", which creates monocultures in our fields and in our world.

The Mayan peasants in the Chiapas are characterized as unproductive because they produce only 2 tons of corn per acre. However, the overall food output is 20 tons per acre when the diversity of their beans and squashes, their vegetables and fruit trees are taken into account.

In Java, small farmers cultivate 607 species in their home gardens. In sub-Saharan Africa, women cultivate 120 different plants. A single garden in Thailand has 230 species, and African home gardens have more than 60 species of trees. Rural families in the Congo eat leaves from more than 50 species of their farm trees.

A study in eastern Nigeria found that home gardens occupying only 2 per cent of a household's farmland accounted for half the farm's total output. In Indonesia, 20 per cent of household income and 40 per cent of domestic food supplies come from the gardens managed by women.

Research done by FAO has shown that small biodiverse farms can produce thousands of times more food than large, industrial monocultures. And diversity in addition to giving more food is the best strategy for preventing drought and desertification.

What the world needs to feed a growing population sustainably is biodiversity intensification, not chemical intensification or the intensification of genetic engineering. While women and small peasants feed the world through biodiversity we are repeatedly told that without genetic engineering and globalisation of agriculture the world will starve. In spite of all empirical evidence showing that genetic engineering does not produce more food and in fact leads to a yield decline, it is constantly promoted as the only alternative for feeding the hungry.

Take the case of the much flouted "golden rice" or genetically engineered Vitamin A rice as a cure for blindness. It is assumed that without genetic engineering we cannot remove Vitamin A deficiency. However nature gives us abundant and diverse sources of Vitamin A. If rice was not polished, rice itself would provide Vitamin A. If herbicides were not sprayed on our wheat fields, we would have bathua, amaranth, mustard leaves, as delicious and nutritious greens that provide Vitamin A. But the myth of creation presents biotechnologists as the creators of Vitamin A, negating nature's diverse gifts and women's knowledge of how to use this diversity to feed their children and families.

That is why I ask, who feeds the world?

Critical Analysis
1. a) Explain the difference between yield and output.
   b) How does the way in which yields are defined hide the reality of food production?
2. Investigate to find the credentials and accomplishments of Vandana Shiva.
3. What is meant by Monocultures of the Mind?
4. Suggest ways in which the dominant mainstream assumptions about who feeds the world's poor are promoted.
5. What evidence is offered by Vandana Shiva to support the view that small diverse farms are more productive and sustainable than modern industrial monocultures?
6. Conduct research to produce a case study that describes and evaluates "golden rice" and its role in solving world hunger.
7. Identify three additional micronutrients (other than Vitamin A) that are essential for good nutrition and identify some foods where they can be found.

There is a constant, steady increase in the price of food. This is because, as the population grows and consumption increases, there is a rising demand. In addition, water supplies are being overconsumed and cities are expanding onto farmland, which contributes to the reduction of food supplies. The poor will be the first victims. Some analysts speculate that poverty and hunger will force people to use violence to change conditions, and that the disruption will ultimately trigger more hunger. Solving the global hunger problem means solving the poverty problem.

> "Hunger is a question of maldistribution and inequality—not lack of food. This is why, despite abundance, hunger hovers; despite progress, poverty persists."
>
> *WHO, "Determinants of Malnutrition," 2001*

INTERACT

1. Write your own definitions for "chronic hunger," "endemic hunger," "famine," and "malnutrition."
2. What evidence suggests that improvements have been made in the global hunger situation? What evidence is there to suggest that we may be facing even greater hunger in the future?
3. Describe the geographic distribution of hunger.
4. Use an atlas and other resources to create a map showing the global distribution of arable land. Compare your map to the patterns shown on other world maps in the text such as population distribution and biodiversity hot spots. Analyse the burden faced by agriculture in competing with other land uses. In your analysis, include suggestions for integrating agriculture with other land uses.
5. In your view, is fighting hunger a moral obligation? Explain your opinion.
6. Use a flow diagram to explain how poverty is an important contributing cause of hunger.
7. Conduct research to find recent examples of dumping of surplus foods in developed countries and explain why this occurs.

THE GLOBAL FOOD SYSTEM—A SOLUTION FOR HUNGER ISSUES?

The global food system is based on large-scale commercialization, domination by large transnational corporations (TNCs) who control trade and pricing in food commodities and vast amounts of farmers, workers, and land, and on an increasing emphasis on growing cash-crops for export. Many developing countries are economically dependent on single commodities. Commodity and food prices have not risen significantly in the past decade while the cost of input has risen dramatically. A huge increase in advertising around the world is one indicator of the rise in the global food trade.

 See Chapter 3 for more information about commodity prices.

The global food system responded to the demands of a rapidly growing population throughout the second half of the twentieth century with some success. But not all the world's peoples enjoyed this expansion of food supplies. With problems such as the depletion of fish stocks and the exhaustion of farmland, it is clear that our present methods of producing, processing, and distributing food will not solve world hunger. The discussion of the Green Revolution that follows underscores this conclusion. The world needs new approaches to the issue of food security to ensure that all people will have access to the food that is produced.

The Failure of the Green Revolution

The **Green Revolution** is the name given to the widespread attempt, beginning in the 1960s, to increase crop yields around the world. At this time, the global population stood at 3.7 billion, about 900 million of whom faced hunger. This period of agricultural expansion focused on planting new, improved varieties of grain crops, irrigating croplands, and using fertilizers extensively. In many places, the results were quite spectacular. In India, for example, the introduction of high-yield,

> 66 While the Green Revolution averted the predicted crises, it was not enough to banish hunger completely. 99
>
> *International Food Policy Research Institute*

drought-resistant varieties of wheat increased production from 11.2 million tonnes in 1965 to 59.1 million tonnes in 1994. For countries like Thailand and Malaysia, expanding agriculture stimulated widespread economic development that reduced poverty levels substantially. But this approach was not universally successful, as close to a billion hungry people will attest. The new crops often required precise control of moisture to maximize production, and needed heavy applications of fertilizers and **pesticides**, both costly commodities unaffordable for many farmers. In the final analysis, the Green Revolution had little impact in Africa where poverty prevented most farmers from adopting the innovations.

There is now a good deal of concern that food production has reached a "yield plateau" or "yield stagnation." For example, wheat yields grew an average of 2.9% per year from 1961 to 1979, but have averaged only 1.8% growth since then. Growth rates for corn (maize) slipped from an average of 2.9% to 1.3% for the same time periods. These slower rates of growth may be explained by several trends:

- Most higher quality land is already in production and only lower quality land is available for further crop development.
- Farmers in lower latitudes have intensified crop production by raising two or three fast-growing harvests per year on their land and cannot plant additional crops.

Methods Used in the Past to Increase Food Supply

Strategies that have been used to increase the global supply of food from crops fit into six categories:

- Increase the amount of land under cultivation
- Increase the yields per hectare of crops
- Increase the number of crops grown on each hectare of cropland
- Replace lower yielding crops with higher yielding crops
- Reduce post-harvest losses
- Reduce the use of feed for animals
- Reduce overconsumption and waste of food

FIGURE 9.9 There are a limited number of ways to improve food supplies and some, such as increasing the amount of land under cultivation, have little potential left. Strategies like reducing wastes still have good potential to increase the amount of food available to hungry people.

FIGURE 9.10 The Green Revolution stimulated a good deal of activity in plant engineering. Important goals were to generate more grain per hectare and to increase resistance to drought, pests, and disease. Biotechnology continues this type of work. This scientist is developing new strains of rice at Plantech in Yokohama, Japan.

- Poor farmers cannot afford the investment in seeds, fertilizers, and pesticides required of new crop varieties and some small farms achieve only one-fifth of the potential of the crops they plant.
- Efforts to squeeze more food from the available resources have resulted in the destruction of large areas of tropical forests, the depletion of groundwater supplies by irrigation, and the degradation of productive soils that become water-logged and contaminated with salts.

This slowing of growth rates points to greater hunger in the future.

The Green Revolution, and the industrial agriculture with which it is linked, has been criticized for other problems. Women farmers, who produce a large part of the food in developing countries, are often shut out of the advances by banking restrictions and lower levels of literacy. Lending systems in general do not make available the capital that farmers need to take advantage of newer technologies. Those farmers who have access to capital expand, while those who do not often lose their farms and face a growing income gap; poverty remains pervasive. In addition, the heavy reliance on fertilizers and pesticides is damaging **ecosystems**. These chemicals are easily washed off fields and end up in streams, and over-spraying affects nearby natural areas. The extensive use of irrigation has lowered water tables and led to the contamination of soils by salts through evaporation. The reliance on only a handful of crop varieties significantly reduces the **biodiversity** of farming areas. By the mid-1980s, just two varieties of rice occupied 98% of the entire rice-growing area of the Philippines. In recent years, the controversy over genetically modified foods has cast further suspicion on the goals and practices of the Green Revolution and modern industrial agriculture.

> **FACT FILE**
>
> Since 1900, an estimated 75% of the genetic diversity of agricultural crops has been lost. Livestock breeds are disappearing at a rate of six breeds per month.

 See Chapter 5 for more information about biodiversity of domestic crops and livestock.

World Grain Production, 1950–2000

Year	Yield (kg/person)
1950	247
1955	273
1960	271
1965	270
1970	291
1975	303
1980	321
1985	339
1990	335
1995	301
2000	303

U.S. Department of Agriculture

FIGURE 9.11 While grain yields have risen in absolute terms, on a per capita basis, there has been a levelling in production.

Post-Harvest Rice Losses in Southeast Asia

Activity	Estimated Range of Loss (%)
Harvesting	1–3
Handling	2–7
Threshing	2–6
Drying	1–5
Storing	2–6
Transporting	2–10
Total	10–37

FAO

FIGURE 9.12 Spoilage and pests produce a high level of accidental waste in some parts of the world. In some wealthier countries, such as Canada, crops are purposely not grown or are destroyed in order to keep supply in line with demand so that prices stay higher.

By the 1990s it became clear that the Green Revolution's focus on producing more food through technological solutions would not solve all hunger-related issues. Sustainable and appropriate technological efforts must be accompanied by change that ensures that the benefits reach all areas of a society. For example, providing $50 000 in aid to buy two tractors might be inappropriate in a region where access to fuel is difficult or costly and where there is a surplus of labour. Spending that money, instead, on 10 000 garden hoes and other tools might be far more appropriate. Poor people need jobs to buy the land and tools, and to get the credit to grow food. Defeating poverty requires community, national, and international policies that address the social, economic, and cultural aspects of food production and consumption and that prioritize food security by providing access to education, health care, and employment opportunities for the poor, keeping food prices low, and solving issues of deprivation for women. Food security is enhanced when food is locally produced, processed, stored, and distributed. In addition, the resource base must be protected from overuse and mismanagement. Food producers must operate within a sustainable system that respects natural systems.

 See Chapter 14 for more information about solving the problems of poverty.

FACT FILE

In the United Kingdom, US$198 million a year is spent removing agricultural pesticides from drinking water.

Integrated Pest Management

For areas of the world facing food shortages, the loss of even a small percentage of the total yield can mean hunger and possibly death for some people. Losses because of pests are seen as unacceptable and preventable. In the past, applications of pesticides have been the first course of action. However, pesticides are expensive and have harmful consequences for the natural environment and for human health, especially for the agricultural workers who apply them. Integrated Pest Management (IPM) is an approach to controlling pests that is economically practical and more environmentally responsible.

The IPM approach uses chemical pesticides only when other techniques do not control the pest problem. Instead, IPM relies on prevention through such strategies as:

- maintaining biologic diversity, so the pests are controlled through natural enemies;
- practising crop rotation to break pest life cycles;
- incorporating host plant resistance, using varieties that have natural resistance to pests;
- removing debris and other materials that promote pest infestations;
- selecting sites that are best suited to the crops being grown;
- monitoring crops for signs of infestation.

The IPM approach also recognizes that crops can tolerate some level of pest attack before there is a loss in production. Farmers use chemical solutions mainly when they believe the benefits of taking action are greater than the losses of not taking action.

The benefits of IPM are well documented. First, pests have less potential to develop resistance to chemical pesticides, a problem that is occurring with a variety of pests. Resistance requires even greater use of pesticides in subsequent applications. Second, costs for pesticides are reduced, a significant advantage in developing countries where chemical pesticides are generally imported. Third, human exposure to chemical pesticides is reduced, both in the short-term and the long-term. Advocates of IPM argue it can reduce the environmental consequences of agriculture without reducing yields.

FACT FILE

In 1997, 20 000 banana plantation workers were successful in a class action suit against nine corporations including Dow, Shell, Chiquita, and Dole for sterilization caused by the nematicide dibromochloropropane (DBCP), which was banned from use in the U.S. in 1977.

 See Chapter 16 for more information on IPM and organic agriculture.

ACHIEVING SUSTAINABLE AGRICULTURE

From a global food perspective, the world is facing a difficult future. The efforts of the past to improve food supply, such as the Green Revolution, have had considerable environmental consequences and do not appear to be sustainable. Because of these problems, most people agree that a different approach is necessary, but there is no consensus on the best course of action. There are generally two perspectives on solving hunger issues that can be labelled "freedom to trade" and "freedom from hunger."

Freedom to Trade

Many people argue that the international free market system can solve global hunger issues. This idea is substantially different than the practices of the past that emphasized national self-sufficiency in food and used tariffs and trade barriers to protect domestic producers. Under a freedom to trade strategy, global free market forces encourage corporations to produce food to export for profits, using techniques such as genetically-engineered seeds, which require more intensive use of fertilizers and pesticides, and an expansion of irrigation. International competition would force companies to develop innovative products and services that would ultimately produce enough food to meet the global demand. It is theorized that global food security would be achieved because it would be in the best interests of transnational companies to be efficient, productive, and cost competitive. Supporters of this view argue that the most productive setting would be created through:

- the deregulation of markets, so that corporations would not have restrictions placed on their activities by governments;

FIGURE 9.13 A Greenpeace protest at a research field of Monsanto, one of the giant agribusinesses operating around the world. Agrochemical and agribusiness TNCs have taken advantage of economic deregulation to become ever larger and more powerful players in the global food system.

- the privatization of food-producing resources, so that all aspects of food production could be developed by corporations;
- strategies to encourage foreign investment, such as dismantling tariffs, so that corporations could have access to global markets.

Within this global trading system, supporters of the strategy argue that transnational food corporations are able to utilize their human and physical resources most effectively to generate profits.

Movement toward a global free market food-producing system has already begun. Some forms of tariff protection and subsidies for agriculture have already been dismantled through trade agreements like the North American Free Trade Agreement (NAFTA). However, developed countries are often criticized by groups in the developing world, such as the Group of 77, for continuing to subsidize aspects of agriculture despite their calls for freer trade. Structural adjustment programs demanded by the International Monetary Fund (IMF) and the World Bank have forced countries to accept more foreign investment. And, TNCs have an ever-larger role to play in producing the world's food. All of these changes are creating a global food system based on trade in food. This has often meant a significant change in thinking about the land and other food-producing resources.

Benefits accrue to everyone, according to the supporters of this globalized food-producing system. People around the world would have far more food choices, there would be a positive transfer of technology and capital from rich to poor countries, and the economic growth stimulated by food companies would

> " The private sector is the great untapped frontier in the world war on hunger. "
>
> Dan Glickman,
> U.S. Secretary of Agriculture

> " The ability of agribusiness to slide around the planet, buying at the lowest possible price and selling at the highest, has tended to tighten the squeeze ... throwing every farmer on the planet into direct competition with every other farmer. "
>
> Brian Halweil,
> "Where Have All the Farmers Gone?," WorldWatch magazine,
> September/October 2000

Global Chocolate Sellers

Company	Subsidiaries
Nestlé	Curtiss Brands (U.S.)
	Rowntree (UK)
	Goplana (Poland)
	D'Onofrio (Peru)
	Maltschika (Bulgaria)
	Cololadovny (Czech Republic)
	Intercsokolade (Holland)
	Buitoni Perugina (Italy)
Philip Morris	Freia Marabou (Holland)
	Lacta (Brazil)
	Kuanas (Lithuania)
	Poliana Zah (Romania)
	Republica (Bulgaria)
	Terry's (UK)
	Olza (Poland)
	Csemege (Hong Kong)
	Figaro (Slovakia)
	Cote d'Or (Belgium)
Cadbury-Schweppes	Piasten (Germany)
	Neilson (Canada)
	Bouquet d'Or (France)
	Productos Santi (Argentina)
	Poulain (France)
	Hueso (Spain)
Hershey	Sperlari (Italy)
	Guber Schokoladen (Germany)

"Chocolate—the facts," *New Internationalist*, August 1998

FIGURE 9.14 The ownership of chocolate companies shows the extent of transnational corporations in the food industry. There has been a general consolidation of the industry as larger companies have taken over smaller ones.

help to raise incomes. The economic benefits, it is felt, would "trickle down" to people at even the lowest income levels; their additional earnings would solve their hunger problems.

> " While the farmers growing grain cereals—wheat, oats, corn— earn negative returns and are pushed close to bankruptcy, the companies that make breakfast cereals reap huge profits. In 1998, cereal companies Kellogg's, Quaker Oats, and General Mills enjoyed return on equity rates of 56%, 165%, and 222% respectively. While a bushel of corn sold for less than $4, a bushel of corn flakes sold for $133. ... maybe farmers are making too little because others are making too much. "
>
> Canadian National Farmers Union

The Changing Face of Canadian Agriculture

Canada's small family farms are rapidly disappearing as large industrial farms spring up. The most recent statistics from the Canada 2001 census reveal that:

- since 1996, the number of farms in Canada has fallen by 10.7%;
- between 1991 and 2001, the number of corporate industrial farms not owned by families increased by 2.9% while family-owned farms decreased by 12%;
- total farm acreage increased by 4.2%;
- the average farm increased in size by 11%;
- the number of livestock including cattle, hogs, and chickens are at record high numbers;
- the 2001 census measured organic farms for the first time, showing 2230 certified organic farms;
- farm operating costs consumed 87% of farmers' revenue, up from 83% in 1996;
- more than 40% of farms use computers, doubling computer use since 1996;
- some family farmers are moving away from traditional farming and diversifying into more profitable crops (e.g., oilseeds, lentils, soybeans, ginseng, maple syrup, greenhouse operations) and livestock (e.g., hogs, sheep, bison, llamas) in response to changing global markets.

Questioning the Benefits of Globalization

COUNTERPOINT There is strong opposition from non-governmental organizations (NGOs), academics, and some governments to the current global food system. A main concern is that globalization has failed to reduce poverty and hunger or to achieve food security. For example, in India in the mid-1990s, trade liberalization produced 70% more food exports. This increase in exports netted food companies an additional $1.3 billion: at the same time, food prices for Indians increased by 63%. Throughout India, poverty rates rose, suggesting that the trickle down of economic benefits was not taking place. In fact, as some analysts claimed, the process of deregulating and privatizing the nation's economy widened the gap between the rich and the poor; in effect, producing a "trickle up" effect. Those who argue that wealthy interests in developed countries are not manipulating the free market system to their own advantage fail to explain why international market structures should work any better than national market structures, which also fail to adequately protect the

> **FACT FILE**
>
> During the 1990s Canadian farmers' net income, adjusted for inflation, fell more than 50%.

"Whether from despair or from anger, farmers seem increasingly ready to rise up, sometimes violently, against government, wealthy landholders, or agribusiness giants."
Brian Halweil, "Where Have All the Farmers Gone?" WorldWatch *magazine, September/October 2000*

"I have 150 chickens eight weeks old, but people would rather buy those foreign chicken parts. If I lower my price, I'll be selling at a loss. Our produce rots in the fields even though people are starving here in Jamaica and around the world because foreign produce floods the market with too much of the same type of stuff. Because of the bad roads no outside buyers come here."

Woman farmer, Millbank, Jamaica

"To understand why people go hungry you must stop thinking about food as something farmers grow for others to eat, and begin thinking about it as something companies produce for other people to buy. Food is a commodity.... Much of the best agricultural land in the world is used to grow commodities such as cotton, sisal, tea, tobacco, sugar cane, and cocoa, items which are non-food products or are marginally nutritious, but for which there is a large market."

Richard H. Robbins, Readings on Poverty, Hunger, and Economic Development

excerpt from "The end of farming?"

by David Roberts
The Globe and Mail
March 16, 2001

There are too many farmers in Canada still clinging to the antiquated notion—the sad historical hangover of postwar federal farm policy—that a nation must protect its domestic food supply, and it should support farming at all costs.

The situation many of our 250,000 farmers and their $30-billion industry face today is that their work is simply no longer sustainable in its present form: The "at all costs" notion is bad for the national treasury, it's worse for farmers.

It may now be time Canadian taxpayers began paying farmers to quit farming. The challenges on the farm today are excruciatingly complex, but this much is clear: Food is more abundant and cheaper than ever, technology has given way to unprecedented efficiencies of scale, and many farmers are still losing their shirts. We need a new plan....

They should be supported not by a short-term fix ... but they should be paid instead as keepers of the land. The bottom line is that it is time for some farmers to be compensated for doing something other than farming.

They might, then, be inclined to take marginal land out of production. On the prairies this is especially cogent since too much land there should never have seen a plow in the first place. Farmers should have an opportunity to turn this land back to nature, to non-food uses, to permanent pasture, to animal habitat: marshes, wildlife preserves, a place where the buffalo might again roam. This way farmers would be paid to become stewards of this great legacy, the land, for the rest of us. In the U.S., the Conservation Reserve Program does just this. It is, in essence, a landscaping subsidy. You city-slickers want a nice-looking countryside? Okay, you help pay for it....

Today's farm woes are precipitated by a sharp cyclical downturn in commodity prices, rising input costs, and, believe it or not, over-production. It is ironic that the current farming "crisis" in Canada is in large measure caused by a vast surplus—not a poor harvest. Historically, a farm crisis has been precipitated by blighted crops, low yields, a shrinking food supply, and higher prices leading to hunger and even starvation in some parts of the world.

It is true that fuel and fertilizer costs have risen 50 per cent or more in the last 12 months, and some farmers, particularly Western Canadian grain farmers, are too cash-poor to plant a crop this spring. But farming is an inherently high-risk enterprise. And Canadian farmers are not alone in feeling the downturn in commodity prices.

But calling for more production aid for Canadian farmers ignores the fact that 80 per cent of Canada's grain product is for export. Who benefits from this? By contrast, in Europe and the U.S. most grain must be grown for domestic consumption. European and American governments are largely subsidizing the production of food for their own taxpayers.

Any further taxpayer-funded, production bail-out for Canadian farmers would be a short-sighted strategic error, motivated by political expediency. The notion of more support for growing export grain is unsustainable....

Critical Analysis

1. Brainstorm a list of activities in a farming operation that require fuel.
2. Investigate to find the characteristics of marginal land in Canada. Why should it never have been farmed?
3. What reasons are offered in the commentary for rejecting agricultural policies that aim for national self-sufficiency in food?
4. Create a definition for "sustainable," as the term is used in this commentary.
5. What are the forces that are having a negative impact on agriculture, according to the commentary? What does this tell us about the food-producing system in Canada?
6. In what ways might the suggestions offered affect the global hunger situation?

interests of the poor. They claim that trade liberalization has undermined the livelihoods and expropriated knowledge from many farmers and indigenous people around the world.

Another concern is that globalization undermines self-sufficiency in the local food producing system. Subsistence farmers in developing countries and family farms in Canada are bought, forced out of business, or contracted out to large corporations. Their small size means that they do not have access to the capital, credit, and technology needed to produce crops for the export market. Rising production costs and rents make their operations unprofitable and imports of food are "dumped" at prices below the cost of production at the local level. **Vertical integration** of agribusiness results in control of a product throughout the whole system as TNCs own profitable seed, pesticide, processing, and farm equipment companies as well as research and development. Faced with these challenges, it is not surprising that many farmers sell out or abandon their farms, increasing poverty rates and destabilizing the social, economic, and cultural fabric of farm communities. This pattern was apparent in India where up to two million farmers a year have stopped producing food.

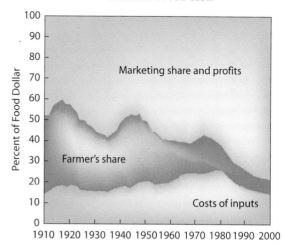

Consumer's Food Costs

FIGURE 9.16 Returns to farmers have declined in recent years. It does not take much of a reduction in revenues to make farming unprofitable in most countries.

Critics of a globalized food system point to the environmental impacts of producing cash crops. The resulting monocultures of non-indigenous plants often result in pest problems that require heavy applications of chemical pesticides. For example, a typical banana plantation in Central America sprays an average of 30 kg of pesticides per hectare each year. The costs for pesticides for melons can average over $2000 per hectare. The tendency for insects to develop

resistance to pesticides means that increasing applications are necessary, a pattern known as the "treadmill effect."

Another criticism of the globalization of the food supply system is that "free trade" is not always "free" but in some cases works to the advantage of developed countries who continue to subsidize their agricultural industries to protect their enormous international political influence, economic strength, and affluent lifestyles. Developed countries do not always give products from developing countries access to their

FIGURE 9.15 Wheat harvesting in India.

markets. For example, in 2002 Canada imposed tariffs on 60% of imports from Least Developed Countries. This rate of tariffs was 10 times higher than on our trade with Japan or Europe, undermining the poverty-reduction advantages touted by supporters of globalization.

Opponents of the way the free market food-producing system is structured argue that the emphasis on profits, corporate independence, and high-tech chemical solutions has exacerbated many of the problems that create hunger and food insecurity. Globalization has the effect of reducing the influence and power of local and national economies.

Freedom from Hunger

People who oppose the globalization of food production believe that the focus should be on national food self-sufficiency. They argue that priorities, policies, and practices should be aimed at ensuring that each country can meet its food needs by producing what it needs. This view is based on the idea that food is a basic human right and, therefore, governments are responsible for creating the conditions that allow everyone to get enough food.

> ❝ Feed the family and trade the leftovers. ❞
>
> *Brewster Kneen,*
> *Canadian trade activitist*

Since these are national problems, new food initiatives will have to bring together governments, food producers, and consumers in order to be effective. Small-scale farming will have to be encouraged and farmers will have to be given access to resources such as land and capital.

Secure land tenure is a critical first step. Farmers must be able to own and maintain land for the long term. This gives them incentive to improve the quality of soils through appropriate soil management methods and to develop sustainable practices that include crop rotation. An important part of stable land tenure is ensuring that farmers earn reasonable incomes through working the land.

FIGURE 9.17 Global food security can be accomplished through efforts at the local and national levels such as these women growing vegetables in the desert of Mauritania.

The Small Farmer (Praising the Simple Life)

by Rolf Jacobsen
translated from the Norwegian by Maisie Steven

It is the small farmer
Who is the loser in this world.
…
It was the small farmer's cows they took,
Along with his field, for yet another motorway.
He it is, now, who sleepless lies night after night,
With worries about repaying all he owes,
So that the banks can build their houses, huge like palaces.
He it is who has been driven to the cities
To fill great blocks of flats ('He adjusts well enough')
He it was who milked his cows
And laboured on his farmland to gather stones
Where now we reap and sow with ease.
It was the small farmer
Who knew how barley should be sown,
And how calves came to birth.
And knows all about the clouds, the wind, and winter,
And how hard it is.
The whinnying of horses he knew well.
Now he knows the tractor, and lending rates,
And when payment is due.
Yet still he leaves the door ajar, the small farmer.
Still he hears when grass is growing, and is aware
When soil gives birth anew.
He who has lost. Until now.
For soon perhaps we shall be asking him the way.
The way back from whence we came.
There, there is growth.

New Internationalist, July 1987

MAKE A DIFFERENCE

Fair Trade

You can make a difference to the world's food supply by supporting fair trade. A Fair Trade label on a product in a store guarantees that a fair proportion of the price is returned to the original producer. This movement started in response to the smaller and smaller share that was making its way back to the farmers or artisans, and the larger and larger share that was filling the coffers of wholesalers and retailers. The increased incomes for producers mean that farmers can build decent homes, send their children to school, pay their workers livable wages, and feed their families nutritious meals. Consumers pay more for fair trade products than for products sold by TNCs, but many consumers feel an obligation to make moral buying choices.

Fair trade has been very successful in Europe. Consumers are demanding that bananas from Costa Rica and Ghana carry the Fair Trade mark, and are prepared to pay up to 10% more for the fruit. This effort was launched in the Netherlands in 1996 and has extended across Western Europe. Over 20% of the bananas sold in the region come from 12 fair-trade organic producers.

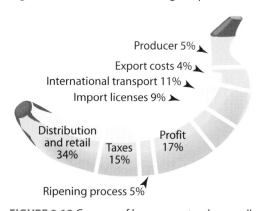

FIGURE 9.18 Growers of bananas get only a small share of the revenue that their crops generate. Fair trade programs try to return a greater share to small producers by reducing costs and profits to non-producers.

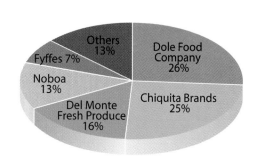

FIGURE 9.19 Banana production is dominated by a handful of large TNCs.

In most situations, small-scale farming has proven to be more sustainable than larger farms. Smaller production units are more likely to produce a variety of food and use approaches such as complementary planting and natural pesticides rather than industrial forms of food production that rely on single crops and tight control of conditions. Smaller-scale farmers are also more responsive to local market conditions and are better able to feed the local population.

Improving food security does not mean returning to traditional food producing practices that did not meet food needs in the past and could not satisfy present and future demands. Food producers have to be able to take advantage of innovations and technological improvements to meet the food needs of a growing population. But these changes will be more successful if implemented within a system that supports local food producers. Achieving food security, according to the freedom from hunger perspective, involves encouraging local self-reliance, empowering workers, promoting participatory decision making, and using environmentally benign farming practices.

> " For the poorest countries, an increase in agricultural productivity is the key to improving food security. In these countries, imports play a small role in the domestic food supply because of limited foreign exchange availability. "
>
> Economic Research Service Report, *August 1999*

Clearly, changes need to be made in the way food is produced and distributed. Greater effort must be put into solving problems of poverty and developing environmentally sustainable practices. Since these are fundamentally national problems, new food initiatives will have to bring together governments, food producers, and consumers in order to be effective.

Grass-Roots Action

Change in food producing systems often starts at the **grass-roots** level. Farmers are increasingly forming growers' co-operatives so that they can market their food and compete more effectively.

In Ecuador, the Union Regional de Organizaciones Campesinas del Littoral is made up of local banana growers. Its activities have helped to raise living standards in the community by reducing the middlemen who skim off parts of the profits, increase incomes, and improve environmental practices, thereby ensuring a brighter, healthier future.

Grass-roots action can also take place among the consumers of agricultural products. A growing number of consumers in Europe and North America have been demanding foods produced under conditions that promote social justice and environmental protection. These organizations have asked for higher wages and working standards, including an end to child and slave labour, stronger protection of the natural environment, collective bargaining, and fair prices for producers. For example, OXFAM is working in British Columbia with a local group to import organically grown bananas from Central America under conditions that give producers fair incomes for their crops. Other "fair trade" co-operatives have been set up by organizations to help consumers change their buying habits by offering alternatives to a globalized food system.

GEOGRAPHIC METHODS

Precision Farming

Global Positioning Systems (GPS) are being used to make farming more productive and less environmentally harmful. As farmers work their land, GPS location data are being picked up from satellites by computers and integrated with existing data. Potassium distribution, soil moisture, slope of the land, weed types, insect distribution, and crop yields are sets of information that can be combined. These data allow farmers to fine-tune the location and amount of fertilizers and pesticides they apply to fields to minimize costs and maximize yields. One additional advantage of precision farming is that the accurate control of pesticides and fertilizers means that fewer chemicals are released into the environment. GPS systems with accuracies of two metres are being custom-fitted to tractors and combines. A further refinement of the precision-farming technique, called Differential GPS, combines GPS locations with ground-based radio signals that produce accuracies within one metre. Promoters of precision farming envision a future in which control of growing conditions will become virtually personalized for each plant.

INTERACT

1. Explain what is meant by food security.
2. In what ways might the globalization of food production improve food security? In what ways might it reduce food security?
3. Conduct research to create a diagram that illustrates all the operations in the global food system, from agricultural inputs, through post-harvest activities such as food processing and transportation, to your table. Write an account of the environmental implications for each step in your diagram.
4. Investigate to find out how much is spent on diet foods and programs in North America. Suggest how this information is linked to the global food system.
5. What are some of the environmental and social consequences of a globalized food system?
6. What might be some advantages of an approach that emphasized national self-sufficiency in food? What might be some drawbacks?
7. Explain how fair trade works to improve conditions in developing countries. Why would consumers support these programs?
8. Develop a rationale that could be used by supporters of globalization of the food supply under a free market system.

WEB LINKS

- WRI: <www.wri.org>
- *AAAS Atlas of Population and Environment*: <www.aaas.org/international/atlas/contents/pages/>
- International Food Policy Research Institute:
- The FAO: <www.fao.org/english/index.html>

RELATED ISSUES

- Organic farming and its future in a hungry world
- Global fisheries as a food source
- Agricultural implications of the war on drugs in Colombia
- Microbanking and farming innovations
- Land ownership and reform in developing countries
- Genetically modified food and food security
- Child agricultural labour and slavery
- Urban agriculture and agriforesty
- Animal rights and industrial farming

ANALYSE, APPLY, AND INTERACT

1. Use the statistics in Figure 9.4, **Measures of Food Supply for Selected Countries, 1997**, to construct a scattergraph showing the relationship between food as a percentage of household consumption and calories per day. What do the data suggest?

2. Survey ten people and record their answers to the question "What is the most important cause of hunger on a global scale?" Organize their answers and analyse the results in view of the causes discussed in this chapter.

3. Use specific examples to explain how our food choices shape the world's food production system.

4. In the final analysis, would you declare the Green Revolution to have been a success in improving food security? Explain your ideas.

5. Modern agriculture has reduced the number of species we use for our food. Explain why this concentration takes place. What are the potential negative outcomes of this trend?

6. In 1966, the United Nations (UN) declared that people have a universal right to adequate food. In your opinion, is an adequate food supply a human *right*? Explain.

7. Identify some of the ways that the globalization of agriculture might have harmful effects on natural systems and the environment.

8. Evaluate activities or initiatives in your own community that improve food supplies both nationally and internationally. What activities do you see as possibly harming food security?

9. Investigate fair trade or organic farming initiatives that can be found in your community or province. Comment on the success of these initiatives.

10. Conduct research to identify the food situation of a developing country or region in Africa. You should attempt to identify the important causes of food shortages, efforts that have been made to improve conditions, and areas that could be improved in the future.

11. Conduct research on hydroponics, aquaculture, or some other recent initiative to identify its impact on food security for the world's population. Identify problems that may prevent these methods from becoming more widely used for food production.

12. Prepare a bulletin board display or Web site, examining the pros and cons of genetically modified foods.

13. Write a 1000-word position paper on significant global interconnections by evaluating how the successful ratification of the Kyoto Protocol and the Stockholm Convention on Persistent Organic Pollutants (POP) might have an influence on global food security.

PART THREE: QUALITY OF LIFE

Chapter 10: Population Trends—An Exploding Population?

By the end of this chapter, you will:

- describe selected world demographic trends and explain the factors influencing them;

- explain how economic and cultural considerations influence a country's population policies;

- predict global demographic changes for the future and assess their economic, environmental, and social implications;

- demonstrate an understanding of the need to consider social differences when analysing global problems and issues;

- use statistical analysis techniques to interpret and analyse data.

HERE WE GROW AGAIN

The world's human population reached one billion about the year 1800. It took all of human history to reach that mark. The population will reach seven billion people in 2013, having gone from six billion to seven billion in just 14 years. At this rate of population growth, 83 million additional people are added to the global population every year. Each one of these new humans requires food, water, a home, education, a job, and material possessions. Each one of these new humans consumes natural resources and produces wastes, contributing to the destruction of the world's natural ecosystems. This rapidly growing demand for resources, combined with a finite supply of natural resources, has caused many people to claim that the world is facing a population crisis. Simply put, they argue that there are too many people and too few resources.

 See Chapter 11 for more information about population policies.

Is this a realistic view of the situation, or are these people simply doomsayers? Certainly the world is facing some serious challenges related to food supply and use of resources. But not all analysts would blame these problems on the size of the population. They might instead point to an unequal sharing of the planet's resources and the overconsumption of resources by the peoples of some regions. And, from another perspective, large and growing populations are a benefit and represent success. More people equals larger markets, a stronger society, a bigger workforce, and a more powerful military. Cultures in some parts of the world mark their worth by their ability to produce children. Clearly people have different perspectives on the consequences of a large and growing world population. A close look at population trends and the implications of those trends reveals patterns of global population growth.

FACT FILE

To put a billion into perspective, you will have lived for a billion seconds when you are 31.7 years old.

Number of Years to Add a Billion People

Billions	Year	Length of time
1	1800	All of human history
2	1930	130 years
3	1960	30 years
4	1974	14 years
5	1987	13 years
6	1999	12 years
7	2013	14 years
8	2028	15 years
9	2054	26 years

Population Reference Bureau

FIGURE 10.1 What are some conditions that affect the rate of population growth?

FIGURE 10.2 A street scene in a Mumbai, India, fish market. Not everyone sees this crowded scene in a negative way.

TRENDS IN GLOBAL POPULATION CHANGE

One of the most outstanding advancements in the twentieth century was our ability to prolong life by delaying death. Mortality rates plummeted throughout the century. For example, in Canada, in 1921, death rates stood at 11.6 deaths for every 1000 people in the population. The death rate had reached 7.4 by 1999. Similar improvements in death rates could be found in all developed countries.

Other demographic rates reflected this improvement, including life expectancies. In 1931, the average life expectancy for a Canadian born in that year was 61 years. By the end of the century, the average life expectancy had risen to over 78 years. Globally, the improvements were even more impressive. In 1950, life expectancies averaged 46.5 years for males and females combined, but stood at 66 years in 2000. This represents an increase of 20 years of life in just a 50-year time span. Some countries—China and Saudi Arabia, in particular—experienced improvements of 30 years.

Infant mortality rates—the number of children under one year old that die per 1000 live births—fell sharply throughout the century. Maternal death rates declined as did deaths from infectious diseases. These improvements in measures of mortality led to the human population explosion that so concerns many people today.

More and More and More

Without question, the world has witnessed a human population explosion. Figure 10.3, **World Population Growth, 1750–2050,** shows this pattern of population growth. The roots of this demographic shift were laid in the several centuries leading up to the last. But the most rapid growth occurred in the twentieth century and continues today.

> 66 The power of population is infinitely greater than the power in the earth to produce subsistence for man. 99
> *Thomas Robert Malthus, economist (1766–1834)*

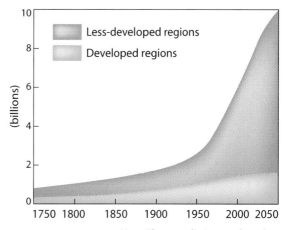

World Population Growth, 1750–2050

(billions)

Less-developed regions
Developed regions

Note: These predictions are based on medium-level population projections.

FIGURE 10.3 Of the 83 million people added to the population each year, 82 million are added to developing countries.

Figure 10.3, **World Population Growth, 1750–2050,** shows another significant trend in the data. Most of the growth in population in the past hundred years or so has occurred in parts of the world that we consider to be developing countries. This includes all of Africa, the Middle East, most of Asia (excluding Japan), and some parts of Oceania and Latin America. This pattern becomes even more obvious by looking at average annual rates of population increase. For example, as a group, developing countries had average annual population growth rates of 2.1% in the years 1975–1980. Compare this with average growth rates of 0.6% for developed countries during the same time. Rates for both developing and developed countries slowed in the decades that followed—to 1.6% for developing countries for 1995–2000 and to 0.3% for developed countries. It is clear, however, that most of the world's population increase in the first half of the twenty-first century will occur in developing countries—countries struggling to improve economically. This rapid population growth will tax these countries' abilities to provide the necessities of life for the people and will result in slower rates of economic growth and social development.

Annual Population Growth, 1995–2000

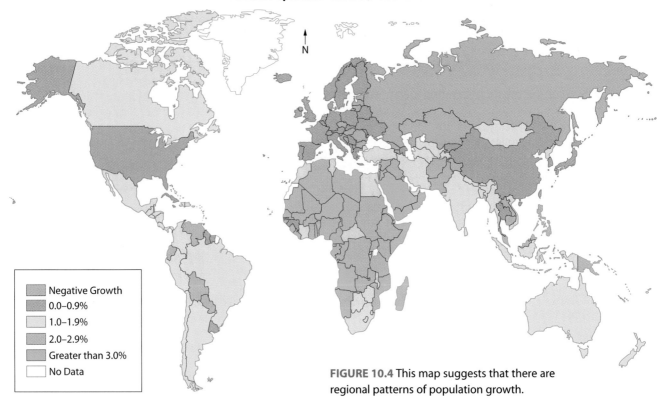

Legend:
- Negative Growth
- 0.0–0.9%
- 1.0–1.9%
- 2.0–2.9%
- Greater than 3.0%
- No Data

FIGURE 10.4 This map suggests that there are regional patterns of population growth.

FACT FILE

Highest Average Annual Population Change, 1995–2000		Lowest Average Annual Population Change, 1995–2000	
Liberia	8.2%	Latvia	–1.5%
Rwanda	7.7%	Georgia	–1.1%
Somalia	4.2%	Bulgaria	–0.7%

FIGURE 10.5 In the developed countries of the world, birth rates are low in large part because couples have chosen to have few, if any, children.

Regional Distribution of Global Population (% of world)

	1750	1800	1850	1900	1950	2000
Developed Countries						
Europe	21	21	22	25	22	12
North America	—	1	2	5	7	5
Japan, Australia, New Zealand	3	3	3	3	4	2
Developing Countries						
Africa	13	11	9	8	9	13
Asia , Oceania (less Japan, Australia, New Zealand)	60	62	61	55	52	59
Latin America and Caribbean	2	2	3	4	7	9

Population Reference Bureau

FIGURE 10.6 Identify the pattern of change for each of the regions given in the table. Which regions have changed most dramatically?

World's Most Populated Countries, 2000 and 2050

Country	2000 Population (millions)	Rank	Country	2050 (est.) Population (millions)
China	1265	1	India	1628
India	1002	2	China	1369
United States	276	3	United States	404
Indonesia	212	4	Indonesia	312
Brazil	170	5	Nigeria	304
Pakistan	151	6	Pakistan	285
Russia	145	7	Brazil	244
Bangladesh	128	8	Bangladesh	211
Japan	127	9	Ethiopia	188
Nigeria	123	10	Dem. Rep. of the Congo	182
Mexico	100	11	Mexico	154
Germany	82	12	Philippines	140
Philippines	80	13	Russia	128
Vietnam	79	14	Vietnam	124
Egypt	68	15	Egypt	117

Population Reference Bureau

FIGURE 10.7 In absolute numbers, India will see the greatest growth, adding 626 million people to its population by 2050. Which country will have the greatest percentage increase?

INTERACT

1. Create a scattergraph to explain the relationships between a rising global population and one of the demographic variables of death rate, life expectancy, or infant mortality rate.
2. Analyse the pattern of population growth identified in the map in Figure 10.4, **Annual Population Change, 1995–2000**. Consider these questions in your analysis:
   a) In which areas is growth the fastest?
   b) Where is growth the slowest?
   c) Which regions seem to have a consistent or uniform pattern of growth?
   d) Which regions have the most diversity?
   e) Create and answer two more such questions.
3. Use Figure 10.7, **World's Most Populated Countries, 2000 and 2050**, to examine rates of population change by region of the world. Use these regional divisions: North America, Latin America, Africa, Europe, South Asia, East Asia, Oceania. Calculate the percentage increase in population for the 15 countries in 2050. (Note that the population of Ethiopia in 2000 was 63 million and that of the Democratic Republic of the Congo was 52 million for the same year.)
   a) Determine an average rate of growth for each region. Suggest why the pattern that is apparent in your analysis is important.
   b) Why are Japan and Germany not in the 2050 estimates?

UNDERSTANDING THE POPULATION EXPLOSION

A simplistic explanation for the population explosion is that people are having more children than they did before. Unfortunately, this explanation is just not true. In fact, in almost every country in the world, birth rates are *lower* now than they were at the middle of the last century. The population explosion is a result of dropping death rates, not rising birth rates.

Growth occurs in a country's population because of two variables:

- **net natural increase** (when births are greater than deaths)
- **net migration** (when in-migration is greater than out-migration)

On a global scale, ignoring migration, growth is a function of the difference between birth rates and death rates. Even though birth rates have fallen around the world, death rates have fallen even faster, producing rapid population growth. Figure 10.8, **Birth and Death Rates for Sri Lanka, 1900–2000**, shows birth and death rates, and net natural increase, for Sri Lanka. We need to understand the forces that cause both birth and death rates to fall in order to understand population growth.

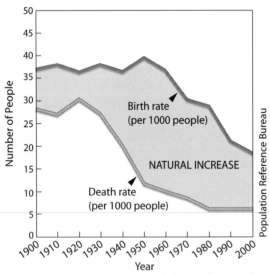

Birth and Death Rates for Sri Lanka, 1900–2000

Population Reference Bureau

FIGURE 10.8 Around what year did Sri Lanka's death rate start to fall? When did birth rates decline? When was this country's rate of natural increase the greatest?

Death Control

Our ability to prolong life came about because humans made progress toward solving some of the threats to life that had forever plagued humankind. Key improvements occurred in disease control, improved food supply, and greater material well-being of the population. To a great extent, these improvements in mortality patterns grew out of the scientific revolution of the seventeenth century and the Industrial Revolution of the eighteenth century, and improvements are still being made today. These developments reduced the wide fluctuations in mortality rates that occurred in previous times due to epidemics, famines, and natural disasters.

> **❝** It may not be the first way we think of ourselves, but all of us alive today are children of the world population explosion. **❞**
>
> *Nicholas Eberstadt,*
> *The Washington Post*

CONTROL OF DISEASE Life expectancies have risen because people are not as likely to fall victim to diseases at a young age. An understanding of the need for personal hygiene to discourage the spread of disease reduced deaths due to cholera and gastrointestinal infections from sewage-contaminated water. Inoculations against epidemic diseases such as smallpox also meant that death rates fell. Drugs have been developed to treat and cure medical conditions. A better understanding of nutrition has lead to an improved overall health of the population. Often these improvements came about because of system-wide actions, including

Life Expectancy at Birth (years)				
	1975–1980		**1995–2000**	
	Female	**Male**	**Female**	**Male**
Developed Countries	76	68	79	71
Developing Countries	58	56	65	62
World	61	58	68	63

United Nations Population Division

FIGURE 10.9 Do the data in the table suggest that the gap in life expectancies between developed and developing countries is improving? Explain.

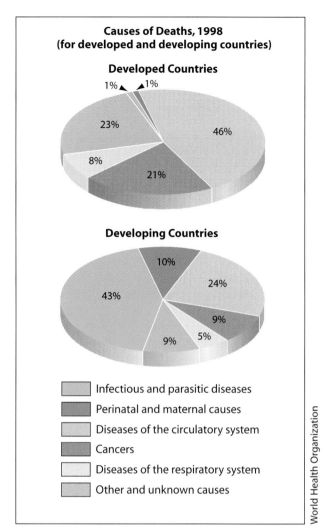

**Causes of Deaths, 1998
(for developed and developing countries)**

Developed Countries

1%   1%
23%
46%
8%
21%

Developing Countries

10%
24%
43%
9%
9%
5%

Infectious and parasitic diseases
Perinatal and maternal causes
Diseases of the circulatory system
Cancers
Diseases of the respiratory system
Other and unknown causes

World Health Organization

FIGURE 10.10 Into which category do you suppose HIV/AIDS would fit? For what reasons do you suppose that infectious and parasitic diseases are such a significant cause of death in developing countries?

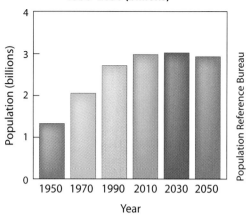

Global Population Under Age 25, 1950–2050 (billions)

Population (billions)

Year

Population Reference Bureau

FIGURE 10.12 One outcome of improved mortality rates is a larger, younger population. This creates a "population momentum" for future growth as the population in their childbearing years continues to expand, leading to more children in the future.

such programs as pasteurization of milk, national health education programs, and municipal water treatment efforts.

 See Chapter 15 for more information about health and disease factors.

IMPROVED FOOD SUPPLY Continuous improvements in animal husbandry and crop production have resulted in more and more food being available per person globally, and in improved quality of food that delivers better nutrition. Equally important was progress in food storage methods that meant that nutrition could be maintained

Infant Mortality Rates (per 1000 live births)					
	1995–2000	**2000–2005 (est.)**	**2010–2015 (est.)**	**2020–2025 (est.)**	**2045–2050 (est.)**
World	59.6	54.5	43.4	34.7	19.4
Afghanistan	164.7	161.3	143.8	127.0	83.9
China	41.4	36.5	28.6	22.2	13.3
Canada	5.5	5.4	5.0	4.8	4.1

United Nations Population Division

FIGURE 10.11 In what way are factors such as improved food supply expected to lead to improvements in such measures as infant mortality?

year round. Losses because of pests and disease were also controlled, yielding more stable food supplies. Well-fed, stronger populations are better able to resist diseases and to thrive, a pattern that is evident by looking at how the youngest members in a population fare.

BETTER MATERIAL WELL-BEING More material wealth helped to lower death rates by improving living conditions and generally making life more comfortable. For example, widespread electrification allowed people to refrigerate food for greater freshness, control temperature for more comfort, and control light for longer productive activity. Generally, improved material well-being allowed people to have more leisure time and to live and work in safer, more comfortable conditions. This progress led to longer lives and lower death rates.

> **The increase in the world's population represents our victory against death...**
>
> *Julian Simon, American writer and academic*

FACT FILE

Water use tripled in the second half of the twentieth century and is predicted to increase by 40% between 2000 and 2020.

INTERACT

1. Explain how rising population totals are *not* the result of higher birth rates.
2. Create flow diagrams to show the relationships or connections that allow each of the following to contribute to a population explosion:
   - Improved understanding of hygiene
   - Better food
   - Improved material well-being
3. Identify ways that you and your classmates have had a demographic advantage over previous generations. In what ways are future generations likely to have demographic advantages over you?
4. Discuss: If rapid population growth because of lowered death rates creates hardships in a population (such as food shortages or poverty), do governments have an obligation to improve the situation? What could they try to do?
5. For Figure 10.11, **Infant Mortality Rates**, suggest factors that might have the opposite effect and cause increasing infant mortality rates in the future.

THE REPRODUCTIVE REVOLUTION

Our abilities to prolong life brought about higher rates of natural increase and a global population explosion. Currently, some countries are struggling with burgeoning populations that are doubling in size in as little as 19 years, for example, the war-torn African country of Eritrea. On average, women in these countries bear more than five children in their lifetimes. Other countries are experiencing remarkably different situations. A number of countries in Eastern Europe have seen their birth rates fall below their death rates, so that these countries are shrinking in population. Latvia, for example, had an average natural increase rate of −1.5% in the period 1995–2000. In this country, the average woman bears 1.3 children in her lifetime, a rate below what is necessary to maintain a stable population. On a broad scale, population stability requires the average woman to bear 2.1 children (to allow for instances of infertility), a figure known as the **replacement level**.

Birth Control

The example of Latvia points to a reproductive revolution that has been going on in most countries of the world, but especially in the developed countries. Simply put, birth rates are falling. For the years 1975–1980, the global **fertility rate** (average number of children per woman) was 3.9 children; this rate stood at 2.7 children for the 1995–2000 period. The dropping birth rate is a product of a number of cultural and economic factors, including changing socio-economic conditions, the status of women, and access to family planning services.

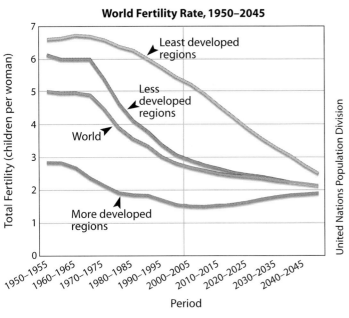

World Fertility Rate, 1950–2045

Y-axis: Total Fertility (children per woman)
X-axis: Period

Least developed regions

Less developed regions

World

More developed regions

United Nations Population Division

FIGURE 10.13 By the middle part of the twenty-first century, globally, births will have fallen to about replacement levels.

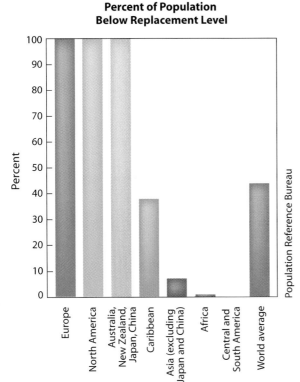

Percent of Population Below Replacement Level

Y-axis: Percent

Categories: Europe, North America, Australia, New Zealand, Japan, China, Caribbean, Asia (excluding Japan and China), Africa, Central and South America, World average

Population Reference Bureau

SOCIO-ECONOMIC CONDITIONS The twentieth century was a time of great change in the social, political, and economic conditions within most countries. These changes were brought on by a number of forces at work around the world, including mass literacy, better transportation and communication, improved health conditions, and a growing concern about issues such as human rights and the environment. This new socio-economic "environment" was more accepting of change and less tied to tradition than previous generations. This openness allowed roles that people play in society and the family to shift.

STATUS OF WOMEN In the 1960s, globally, about one-third of women participated in the labour force, working for a wage in the formal, paid economy. By the end of the twentieth century, this number had climbed to 54%. This statistic points to a change in the roles women play in society, where paid work is considered a normal part of women's lives in most countries of the world. Along with this new economic status are changing attitudes about women's access to education, political and social responsibilities, reproductive roles, control of resources, and the like. These broader expectations—beyond traditional domestic responsibilities that include bearing children—encourage women to develop interests outside of the home and, consequently, to desire fewer children.

 See Chapters 13 and 14 for more information about women and poverty.

FAMILY PLANNING When couples make decisions about the number and timing of the children that they produce, they are planning a family. To make these decisions, they need access to knowledge about human reproduction and the technology that controls births. The development of **family planning** methods has allowed couples to avoid unwanted pregnancies.

FIGURE 10.14 Europe, North America, Australia, and New Zealand have birth rates already below replacement level. In Asia, countries making up only 7% of the total population have growth rates below replacement level. No country in Central and South America has growth rates below replacement levels.

Average Fertility and Female Literacy Rates for Selected Countries

Country	Average Fertility Rate, 1995–2000 (average number of children per woman)	Female Literacy Rate, 1985–1996 (% of women aged 25+)
Algeria	3.8	20
Belgium	1.6	100
Botswana	4.4	60
Brazil	2.3	75
Canada	1.6	100
Central African Rep.	4.9	13
Chile	2.4	93
Ecuador	3.1	81
Egypt	3.4	21
El Salvador	3.2	64
Fiji	2.7	77
Indonesia	2.6	66
Italy	1.2	100
Jamaica	2.5	83
Japan	1.4	100
Kenya	4.5	46
Malawi	6.8	25
Mexico	2.8	80
Nepal	4.5	11
New Zealand	2.0	100
Saudi Arabia	5.8	45
Sweden	1.6	100
Thailand	1.7	89
Turkey	2.5	60
Turkmenistan	3.6	95

UN Statistical Division, UN Population Division

FIGURE 10.15 Does there appear to be a connection between literacy and fertility, based on the data?

Globally, the use of family planning jumped from less than 10% in the 1960s to about 60% in 2001, substantially reducing birth rates in most parts of the world.

 See Chapter 10 for more information about population policies.

BIRTH CONTROL TECHNOLOGY The technology for preventing and terminating pregnancies has advanced over time. Couples can choose to use

UN Population Division

Median Age by Major Area (years)

Area	1950	2000	2050 (est.)
World	23.6	26.5	36.2
Africa	19.0	18.4	27.4
Asia	22.0	26.2	38.3
Europe	29.2	37.7	49.5
North America	29.8	35.6	41.0
Latin America	20.1	24.4	37.8
Oceania	27.9	30.9	38.1

FIGURE 10.16 One of the products of a reduced birth rate is a higher median age in the population. How do you account for the difference of 22.1 years between Africa's and Europe's medians in 2050?

United Nations Development Programme

Birth Control Use, 1998

		Rate (%)
World		58
Developing Countries	Africa	20
	Asia	60
	Latin America and the Caribbean	66
	Oceania (less Japan, Australia, and New Zealand)	29
Developed Countries	Europe	72
	North America	71
	Japan, Australia, New Zealand	76

FIGURE 10.17 "Rate" refers to the use of birth control methods by married women of reproductive age. What might be some factors that would influence birth control use?

"natural" methods such as coitus interruptus or abstinence; mechanical methods, including condoms and cervical caps; or invasive techniques like abortion or vasectomy (see Figure 10.18, **Methods of Birth Control Used in Family Planning**). Unfortunately for couples in developing countries, the more effective methods of birth control are also generally more expensive than less reliable methods. The cost of birth control is an important factor, limiting the use of contraceptives in many parts of the world. In addition, cultural values can also discourage the use of some or all forms of birth control.

The Roman Catholic Church, for example, has opposed the widespread use of contraceptive devices and has condemned the use of abortion as a form of family planning. This stand on abortion and contraceptives has placed this church at odds with organizations that are encouraging family planning and an overall lower birth rate.

Demographic Transition

The fact that all countries have experienced both falling death and birth rates led researchers to develop a general model to help understand this **demographic transition**. Developed countries like Japan, France, and Canada are now at or close to the end of the transition, having achieved stable populations, or even slow decreases. Developing countries are still at the stage of the model where death rates have dropped and birth rates are following. The gap between birth and death rates for these countries produces faster rates of growth. These countries can expect their populations to begin to stabilize in the coming decades, which may allow them to see some positive per capita improvements in quality of life.

Countries started their demographic transitions at different times and will move through the stages at different speeds. Canada, for example, moved out of the pre-industrial stage in the early part of the 1800s. Death rates dropped slowly, with each new innovation in medicine or hygiene producing an incremental improvement in death control. Developing countries did not start the demographic transition until much later, not until the early or middle part of the 1900s. Death rates dropped sharply as these populations enjoyed the accumulated improvements in death control. Most developing countries are currently experiencing rapid growth

> **FACT FILE**
>
> The use of family planning is lowest in sub-Saharan Africa. Nineteen percent of couples use contraception in this region.

Methods of Birth Control Used in Family Planning

Method	Description	Failure Rate
Contraceptives	prevent ovulation, implantation of the ova, or entry of sperm into the cervical canal. Oral contraceptives are common.	Less than 1%
Spermicides	chemicals inserted into the vagina using sponges, foams, jellies, or creams that kill sperm	3–20%
Intrauterine device (IUD)	device inserted into the uterus to prevent implantation of ova by mechanically stimulating an inflammatory response	1–5%
Cervical caps	mechanical blocks to stop sperm from reaching the cervix	3–10%
Diaphragm	device that blocks the entrance to the cervix and is used with spermicidal jelly or foam	3–14%
Condom	mechanical barrier preventing entry of sperm into the vagina	2–10%
Douche	flushing of the vaginal area with water and/or spermicide after intercourse	about 40%
Coitus interruptus	withdrawal of the penis from the woman's vagina prior to ejaculation	9–20%
Rhythm	timing of sexual intercourse to avoid the period when the woman is fertile	13–20%
Vasectomy	cutting and/or tying the tubes that carry the sperm from the testes	0.2%
Tubal ligation	tying the oviduct between the ovary and uterus to prevent the passage of ova	0.1%
Abortion	terminating a pregnancy before the fetus is capable of living unassisted outside the womb	
Abstinence	avoiding sexual intercourse	

FIGURE 10.18 The failure rate is the number of pregnancies per year while using the birth control method compared to no birth control. On average, heterosexual intercourse without birth control will result in pregnancy about 10% of the time.

Health and Welfare Canada

while birth rates decline slowly toward stability. Birth rates are closely linked to social and economic conditions. Unfortunately, those countries that are having difficulty with economic progress will see birth rates decline slowly. This delay results in a longer period of rapid growth, compounding economic difficulties.

Even if developing countries were to now quickly achieve lower birth rates, they would still experience the effects of **population momentum**. In many developing countries, the majority of the population is under 18 years of age. In the Central African Republic, for example, 43% of people are under 15 years old, while in Syria the figure is 41%. As these young people mature and have families of their own, even with lower birth rates, the national populations will continue to grow.

The rapidly growing developing countries of today do not have the benefit of the population "pressure release valve" of migration that was available in the past. While European populations were in their high-growth transition periods, population growth rates were moderated by high levels of emigration. Surplus populations migrated outside of the region, to the Americas and to places like Australia and New Zealand. For example, the population of the United States increased sixfold from 1790 to 1850 largely due to European emigration. This shift in population to other continents served to reduce the harmful impacts of rapid population growth in Europe. Unfortunately, few countries today (save Australia, Canada, and the United States) allow substantial immigration and the number of migrants is tiny compared to the total increase in population in developing countries.

Is the World Overpopulated?

The demographic transition model allows us to see the two "revolutions" that occurred over the past century or so. The mortality revolution caused populations to grow in size, while the reproductive revolution is serving to slow population growth. The predictions are

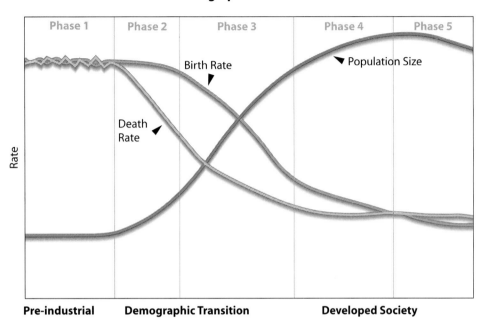

FIGURE 10.19 It takes several generations before populations reduce birth rates after death rates have fallen.

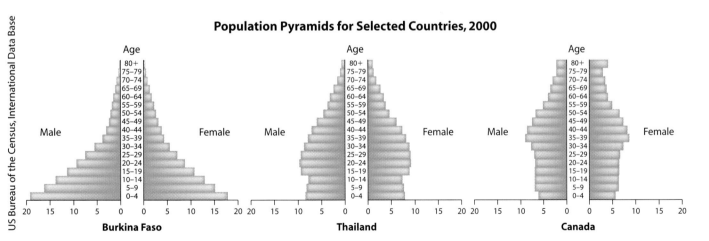

FIGURE 10.20 These population pyramids illustrate the changes in age structure that occur as countries move through their demographic transitions.

Population Changes During the Demographic Transition

	Birth Rates	Death Rates	Life Expectancy	Population Growth
Phase 1	High	High, but fluctuates due to famines, wars, etc.	Low	Very slow
Phase 2	High	Dropping due to improving conditions	Increasing	Increasing
Phase 3	Declining due to changing conditions for women	Low	Increasing	Rapid, but beginning to slow
Phase 4	Low	Low	High	Slow
Phase 5	Low and stable	Rising somewhat due to high median age of the population	High	Decreasing

FIGURE 10.21 At Phase 1, a country has seen little modernization. In order for a country to move through the phases, there must be dramatic changes in conditions.

that it will be around 2050 before all countries have completed their demographic transitions and the global population will be between 8 and 12 billion people. Is this population too large? Is the world overpopulated? Consider the notion of overpopulation and how it connects to ideas about quality of life and sustainability.

Carrying Capacity

Carrying capacity is an estimate of the number of people that an area can support, given its resource base and the population that inhabits the place. Some of the factors that must be considered in determining carrying capacity are:

- physical characteristics, including landforms and climate;
- natural resources, such as vegetation, minerals, and water;
- the size of the population;
- the technological capabilities of the people;
- levels of consumption of the people;
- attitudes of the people toward their environment.

The earliest humans were hunters and gatherers who roamed large territories in search of food and numbered no more than about 1 million. However, over time, people developed new technologies that allowed them to exploit the environment more effectively, including

FIGURE 10.22 International migration rates are not able to moderate the impacts of high rates of population growth in developing countries.

mastering fire, domesticating dogs, and developing stone tools. Their numbers rose to several million. It was the development of agriculture

What Is Overpopulation?

Staff editors
Population Reference Bureau, 2001

… Let's start with…a reasonable working definition of overpopulation…:"…when there are more people than can live on the earth in comfort, happiness and health and still leave the world a fit place for future generations."

For each component of this definition, there are many issues that need to be considered. For example, under the category of "comfort," housing, food, health, and perhaps employment are a few topics that come to mind. But the standard by which these items should be judged is subjective. For example, on the issue of housing, the following questions might be asked. What kind of housing? How much space for each person? Is there heat or air conditioning? What is necessary for comfort? Here is where the problem lies. What some people might consider necessities for basic survival, others might consider luxuries. Is a North American's idea of comfort the same as a Chinese person's or a Nigerian's? …

Is it possible to come up with a definition of "happiness" that would satisfy everyone in the world? One person's definition of happiness might be "to provide adequate shelter, food, and health care for my family," while another's might be "to have two cars, a big house, servants, and a swimming pool." Again, carrying capacity would be affected by the determinants chosen to define happiness.

What about health? Certainly health affects comfort and happiness, but what health standards are appropriate? Do we want to eliminate infant and child mortality completely? Do we want to have a life expectancy at birth of 58 or 75 years? Do we want to save everyone's life at any cost? The standards of health considered to be appropriate in a society would certainly have an impact on its carrying capacity.

And finally, consider "leaving the earth a fit place for future generations." What, for example, is "fit"? Does that mean completely pollution free? Can we assume that future generations will develop technologies to create or tap new energy resources and eliminate pollution? Or do we assume that future generations will basically have the same resource limitations that we do? Is the damage caused by pollution, desertification, and deforestation reversible? These are some of the questions that might be asked about the state of the planet.

Many other issues could be discussed here. For example, should each country be considered separately or should we think of the world as one community when we consider the issue of "overpopulation"? After all, most countries depend upon resources from others for survival. So a seemingly simple interpretation of "overpopulation" leaves a lot of room for differences of opinion. …

Obviously the term "overpopulation" is not as simple to delineate as it may seem at first glance. Each community is different and cannot be judged by a universal standard. When debating the status of a community, consideration must be given to population growth rates, standards of living, lifestyle, culture, technology available, resources, type of economy, as well as a host of other variables. …

FIGURE 10.23 Cultural biases may cause many people to see this setting on the outskirts of Shanghai, China, as an undesirable home. Yet, people live here. They experience love, affection, enjoyment, and excitement—It is a home.

Critical Analysis

1. Why might it be useful or important to engage in a discussion about overpopulation?
2. In what ways is the concept of "overpopulation" subjective and open to interpretation?
3. Part of the working definition offered in the first paragraph includes the idea of leaving the planet fit for future generations. How important do you think this consideration is in defining overpopulation? Explain your answer.
4. Write a definition for "overpopulation" that seems to make the most sense for you.

about 10 000 years ago that remarkably expanded the carrying capacity of the land. A much more secure and abundant supply of food meant that communities could be constructed and large populations supported. The human population expanded from about 5 million people to roughly 250 million people by 2000 years ago. Further innovations in food supply and resource extraction expanded the carrying capacity of Earth and allowed the human population to expand to over 6 billion by the start of the twenty-first century.

In addition to their technological improvements, humans changed their social behaviours, moving from living in small, dispersed family groups to living in metropolitan areas of many millions of people.

Changes in carrying capacity have come about through an evolutionary process over several million years. Some people are concerned that the rapid rate of growth of the human population over the past several centuries—and particularly the last century—has exceeded our technological improvements over the same time. Simply put, we have surpassed the carrying capacity of the planet.

Commentary

excerpt from Populate or perish: Canada needs 100 million people

by Doug Saunders
The Globe and Mail
March 31, 2001

Canada is undergoing a crisis of underpopulation.

Its 31 million people, spread thinly over a vast expanse, have become too few to support the cultural institutions needed in a global culture. Unlike that of any other major trading nation, Canada's market is too small and its infrastructure too expensive to support a cultural voice of its own…

If you have ever worked in the business of creating culture in Canada, you will have experienced that feeling of deep alarm: The realization that your job, given the size and nature of Canada's market, is close to being impossible.

We can do better. The coming hundred years could truly become Canada's century… if we take on the sort of national project that was last entertained in Laurier's day: A deliberate effort to triple the country's population over the next century. One hundred million Canadians drawn from all over the world, attracted by advertising campaigns and screened for education, temperament and ability.

By the end of this century, given the global spread of education and sexual equality, demographers believe that the world's population growth may slow to a halt. When that happens, Canada should make sure it is one of the approximately 20 nations that will be in the 100-million club.

Why 100 million? It would provide an ideal balance of comfort and creativity…

One hundred million is no arbitrary figure. The United States passed that mark shortly before 1920, and it was then that Americans began to create their own important forms of literature, music, cinema and theatre, becoming one of the most influential economic and cultural forces in the world…

A tripling of Canada's population would not entail a huge increase over the current intake of 300,000 people a year—perhaps a third more. As a country of immigrants, we already know the benefits of newcomers…

Critical Analysis

1. Given the efforts to define "overpopulation" in the reading, how do you think that Saunders would define "underpopulation"?
2. Saunders considers the need to maintain strong cultural industries in his article. Should culture be given such importance in planning our demographic future? What other aspects should be considered as well?
3. Brainstorm a list of potential problems and opportunities for a Canada of 100 million people. Given your analysis, would you support such a plan? Explain your answer.

INTERACT

1. a) Use the data in Figure 10.15, **Average Fertility and Female Literacy Rates for Selected Countries**, to create a scattergraph showing fertility rates and female literacy rates for the 25 countries given in the table. Put one variable on the horizontal axis and the other on the vertical axis. Plot a dot for each country at the intersection of the two variables.

   b) What is the general trend in the dots on your scattergraph?

   c) What might be an explanation for the patterns shown in your scattergraph?

2. Write a letter to the editor either advocating that governments in developing countries should support the widespread distribution of free birth control materials, or arguing that they should not. In either case, include in your letter ideas about the changing roles of women in societies and how these roles affect population growth.

3. Explain why the demographic transition will have more profound impacts on the population totals of developing countries than it did on developed countries.

4. Using a two-column chart, summarize the evidence that would suggest that the world has a population problem, and the evidence that indicates that there is not a problem. Refer to the demographic transition model as you fill in your chart.

WEB LINKS

- World Resources Institute:
- United Nations Population Fund:
- Population Reference Bureau:
- Facing the Future: People and the Planet:

RELATED ISSUES

- Impacts of population growth on natural systems
- Religion and population growth
- Impacts of disease and epidemics on population growth
- Impacts of population growth on a selected country
- Population growth rates and poverty

GIS **Average Fertility Rate/Female Literacy**

1. Describe the pattern of growth of the world's population over the past 10 000 years.

2. Identify the factors that are most at work to create or modify population trends on a global scale.

3. Based on the evidence presented in this chapter, what would you consider to be the most significant population trends and patterns for the twenty-first century?

4. Describe and explain the differences in population growth rates between developed and developing countries.

5. Identify ways that social circumstances affect population growth rates. Explain your answer.

6. In spite of improvements, significant gaps remain in life expectancies and other measures of mortality between developing countries and developed countries.
   a) Offer reasons to explain why these gaps exist.
   b) Suggest actions that could be taken on the part of developing countries to reduce or eliminate the gaps.
   c) What are actions that people in developed countries could take to improve conditions in developing countries?

7. Use the statistical information in Figure 10.15, **Average Fertility and Female Literacy Rates for Selected Countries**, to calculate a correlation coefficient for the two variables. See Chapter 13, page 313, Question 4, for help in calculating correlation coefficients.

8. Twenty years from now you will be approaching the statistical midpoint of your life. Based on the evidence, describe global population characteristics that you will experience at that time.

9. Design an advertisement that might be used in a developing country to market condoms as an inexpensive form of birth control.

10. Based on your understanding of population trends, do you think that the world is overpopulated? Give your opinion on this question in a well-organized one-page essay.

11. Write a short stage play or radio drama focusing on the changing role of women in developing countries and the broader acceptance of family planning. In your play, have a young couple in a developing country discuss their future, considering topics like education, careers, family responsibilities, and use of birth control.

Chapter 11: Population Policies

By the end of this chapter, you will:

- evaluate approaches, policies, and principles relating to the protection and sustainability of the planet's life-support systems;

- explain how points of view and paradigms influence an individual's perceptions of a place;

- demonstrate an understanding of the roles and status of men and women in different parts of the world;

- explain how economic and cultural considerations influence a country's population policies;

- predict global demographic changes for the future and assess their economic, environmental, and social implications;

- evaluate the effectiveness of an international strategy and agreement that has been designed to protect the global commons or address global issues;

- demonstrate an understanding of the possibility of a number of alternative solutions to any geographic problem or issue;

- evaluate the effectiveness of techniques used to predict the future.

WHAT ARE GOVERNMENT POLICIES?

People often criticize the government. Their criticisms are tied to what they think are illogical or inconsistent policies or plans of action of those in power. For example, they may see officials claiming that the government is environmentally responsible, yet hear about funding cuts for key environmental protection programs. Most general discussions produce any number of such inconsistencies. The blame for these problems may be tied to the failure of governments to make and implement effective policies, or make their policies known, or to the failure of citizens to find out what the policies are.

The Role of Population Policies: Setting Directions

Government policies are statements that provide direction for the activities of the government. They are developed out of the philosophical beliefs of the people in government, and those that they represent. All the different policies that are in place should be tied into the overall or broad goals of the government. A country like Singapore that values free enterprise should have policies that encourage individual economic action and entrepreneurial spirit. Iran is a country that takes its belief system from the Islamic religion, and its policies will value adherence to the religion and the traditions that grow out of it. In a democratic country like Canada there is a continuous process where citizens of all viewpoints express their opinions and the government of the day listens and develops policies that are consistent with their goals. Policies are expressed in the laws, regulations, and programs that governments put in place.

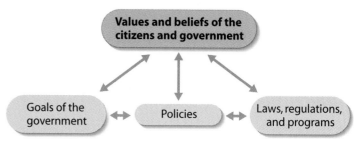

FIGURE 11.2 In theory, all of the actions taken by a government should be linked back to the beliefs of citizens.

Population policies are designed to influence the most intimate and profound decisions in an individual's life. Governments take action to influence the three agents of population change—births, deaths, and migration—as a way to improve the quality of life for the people. In most countries of the world, population policies are intended to promote social and economic development.

Looking Back on Population Policies

Widespread interest in population policies grew out of the interests and concerns of the United Nations (UN). By the 1950s, it was clear that improvements in medicine and hygiene had created a global population explosion. Such rapid growth was viewed as detrimental to development, leading to greater poverty and undermining progress in such areas as literacy and health care. Some countries established population policies that encouraged smaller family size and more family planning in an effort to slow growth rates. India, for example, initiated a national policy in 1952. On a global

FIGURE 11.1 A crowded scene in a market in Guatemala. What do you think a government's policy should be about population growth?

scale, however, these actions were piecemeal and had little overall impact.

The UN held its first meeting on the global population situation in 1954, and followed up with a second conference in 1965. These meetings were important in that they brought together experts and leaders for face-to-face discussions of the issues. Much of the activity at these meetings focused on how countries could reduce birth rates by encouraging the use of family planning services, including contraceptives. These ideas were not willingly accepted by all. Limiting family size goes against the cultural values of many societies, and governments in these places resisted making strong statements supporting family planning. The Roman Catholic Church, in particular, was concerned about the connection between abortion and family planning practices. In the end, the meetings provided a useful guide for those countries that wished to create population policies.

> 66 Without [population] policies, Earth may soon have to hang out the 'no vacancy' sign. 99
>
> *Werner Fornos, president of the Population Institute*

FIGURE 11.3 Population policies in the first few decades of the UN emphasized birth rate reduction. Analysts were becoming increasingly concerned that exploding populations were contributing to poverty and suffering in developing countries.

PROFILE

IPPF

The International Planned Parenthood Federation

FIGURE 11.4

The International Planned Parenthood Federation (IPPF) was founded in 1952. It is the largest non-profit, non-governmental family planning and reproductive health organization in the world. The IPPF links national family planning associations from 180 countries. Promoting the right of women and men to decide freely the number and spacing of their children and the right to the highest possible level of sexual and reproductive health is the IPPF's first priority. They believe that improving the quality of life on the planet requires a balance between the world's population and its natural resources and productivity. The organization mounts campaigns at the local, regional, and international levels, distributing new methods of contraception, providing education on sexuality, and working to prevent unsafe abortions. The organization's goal is to increase support among policy makers, opinion leaders, professionals, and the media for reproductive health and family planning worldwide. Their charter commits the IPPF to promoting for the world's population the right to:

- life;
- liberty and security of the person;
- equality and to be free of all forms of discrimination;
- privacy;
- freedom of thought;
- information and education;
- choose whether or not to marry and to plan a family;
- decide whether or not to have children;
- health care and health protection;
- the benefits of scientific progress;
- freedom of assembly and political participation;
- freedom from torture and ill treatment.

A positive action that came out of the UN population meetings was the commitment of a number of developed countries to support family planning efforts in developing countries. The UN set up the United Nations Population Fund (UNFPA) in 1969 to coordinate this assistance.

UN population conferences were held in 1974 and 1984. By this time, the full force of the population explosion had been felt in developing countries and more and more of these countries had initiated population policies to slow growth. The formal declaration produced by the delegates of the 1984 conference in Mexico City prodded governments "as a matter of urgency" to make family planning services "universally available."

FACT FILE

The declaration in 1984 was weakened by actions taken by the United States at the conference. Anti-abortion activists convinced the U.S.—the largest single donor of population assistance—to withdraw funding from any organization that provided abortion counselling or services. A similar policy was maintained under President George W. Bush.

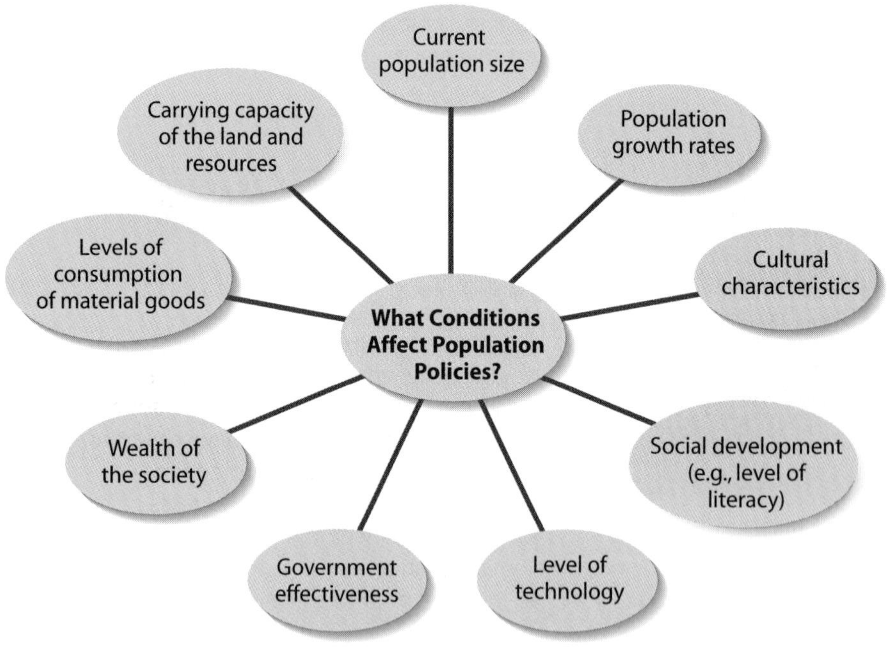

What Conditions Affect Population Policies?
Current population size
Population growth rates
Cultural characteristics
Social development (e.g., level of literacy)
Level of technology
Government effectiveness
Wealth of the society
Levels of consumption of material goods
Carrying capacity of the land and resources

FIGURE 11.5 Some of the variables that help shape a country's population policy. What are two other variables that you might add?

The 1994 Cairo Population Conference

Even as the delegates to Mexico City announced their declaration, criticisms of population policies were growing. Women's rights advocates were especially critical. They argued that population policies generally did little to support women's rights to reproductive freedom—the right to make decisions about families for themselves. To meet national goals, family planning programs were narrowly focused on targets and quotas and delivered in the most cost-efficient manner, not the manner that best suited women's needs or social and cultural settings. For example, women were often told about only one form of contraception—the method that the national planning body considered most appropriate. Women were not given choices. The family planning programs simply did not take into consideration the subtleties of decision-making roles in family planning, childbearing roles, and the use of contraceptives. These issues were front and centre during the 1994 population conference held in Cairo. Here, many delegates pushed to include women's sexual and reproductive health and rights in the final declaration. The Vatican and some Roman Catholic and Muslim countries resisted the inclusion of abortion as a

FACT FILE

More than 11 000 delegates from governments, non-governmental organizations (NGOs), and international agencies attended the Cairo population conference. Over 1200 NGOs participated (compared to 139 who had observer status in 1984).

universal reproductive right. In spite of such sharp ideological differences, by the end of the conference, all but a few nations endorsed a new approach to population policies.

Cairo's Programme of Action provided a more humane and effective way to slow population growth. It made a direct link between slowing population growth and improving conditions for people, and called for action to improve health care, education, and human rights, especially for women. The program suggested that family planning services should be provided as part of a larger package of reproductive health care. This care should include:
- family planning services;
- pregnancy support;
- abortions where legal;
- prevention and treatment of sexually transmitted diseases;
- counselling on sexuality;
- elimination of harmful practices against women, such as forced marriage.

Cairo's Programme of Action reoriented population discussions and called on countries to shift population policies away from slowing population growth to improving the lives of citizens, especially women.

FIGURE 11.6 Prime Minister Hage Geingob of Namibia, president of the special session of the UN at the UN General Assembly's Beijing+5, one of several conferences held since the Cairo conference, to address gender issues such as the advancement of women, poverty, illiteracy, violence against women, and conflict. Links between population and these other development issues have been clearly established and have become increasingly the focus of international attention in the search for effective solutions to global problems.

Doing without Family Planning Services

According to the UNFPA's *State of the World Population 1997* report, the lack of sexual and reproductive rights produces:

- the deaths of 600 000 women—one every minute—from pregnancy-related causes;
- 400 million couples without the means to limit or space their offspring;
- 75 million unwanted pregnancies every year;
- 45 million abortions, 20 million of which are unsafe.

FIGURE 11.7 Do you consider the costs of providing family planning services worldwide a worthwhile investment?

Evaluating the Cairo Agreement

In the years that followed the signing of the Cairo Programme of Action, a number of criticisms have been levelled against it and the manner in which it was drafted.

POPULATION GROWTH The populations of many developing countries are still growing quickly and immediate action is seen by many as necessary. Although improving conditions for women, such as making education more accessible, has a direct link to lower birth rates, it takes time to produce more literate women, who see themselves as having a variety of roles in life in addition to producing children, before a society realizes lowered birth rates.

PERSISTENT POVERTY The huge inequalities in wealth around the world mean that some countries simply do not have the financial resources to put in place the services recommended by the Cairo agreement. The struggle for survival far outweighs other concerns, including sexual and reproductive rights.

FEMINIST AGENDA The high profile given to NGOs allowed women from developed countries to have a good deal of input into the agreement. These representatives were active in committees and their views on gender equity were influential in shaping the final program.

> " The goal is a world where women have control over their own lives and their own bodies; where they have education, employment, and access to good health services; a world where a woman has the ability to chose to have the number of children she wants; not to have unsafe sex; not to be genitally mutilated or married at a very young age; not to be beaten or raped. "
>
> *Nikki van der Gaag, editor, journalist*

ENVIRONMENTAL CONCERNS Environmentalists have argued that the agreement does not give a high enough profile to the relationships between population growth, overconsumption of the world's resources, and environmental degradation. The shift in focus to social development may divert people's attention from the environmental impacts of a growing population.

HIV/AIDS The growing problem of HIV/AIDS, especially in Africa where population growth rates are high, could divert attention and resources from the changes needed to implement the Cairo program. Available resources will be used up in the battle against the disease.

A review of the Cairo agreement took place in June 1999 at a UN General Assembly session. This review suggested some modest changes, but essentially supported the directions contained in the agreement. Given the pattern, the next UN population conference could be expected in 2004 or 2005.

FIGURE 11.8 An NGO school in Afghanistan. The efforts of NGOs at work in developing countries contribute to young girls having more choices for the future than their mothers did.

INTERACT

1. Explain what is meant by sexual and reproductive health and rights. How can population policies reflect these rights?
2. In your mind, in what ways are population conferences and population policies beneficial?
3. In light of the criticisms of the Cairo population conference and the agreement it produced, suggest two ways the agreement could work more effectively in the real world.
4. Script a debate between two delegates at the next international population conference—a delegate who wants women to enjoy a greater range of sexual and reproductive rights and services, and a delegate who opposes the inclusion of abortion in family planning and birth control programs. Support the points made by both delegates with facts and opinions.

CASE STUDY

China's One-Child Policy

The most widely discussed population policy in the past several decades is China's one-child policy. This policy was put into force in 1980 as a way to slow China's rapidly growing population.

By the 1960s, China was experiencing the early stages of demographic transition: death rates had dropped while birth rates remained at traditionally high levels. From 1962 to 1972, the country had average annual birth totals of 26.7 million, so that the population of the country stood at 800 million by 1969. The Chinese government viewed this growth as an economic and social development problem—it was hindering their advancement in areas like education, health care, and material well-being—and

FIGURE 11.10 The high profile given by the government to China's one-child policy indicated its importance. Few couples could ignore the pressure exerted by government officials and community members.

> 66 China always considers population and family planning an important component part of the strategy for the sustained national economic and social development, and they are planned and implemented together with economic and social issues. 99
>
> *Chinese government White Paper on Family Planning, 1996*

encouraged family planning and the use of contraceptives. However, birth rates remained unacceptably high in the eyes of government officials. In 1979, the government made population control and family planning part of its basic state policy, even incorporating it into the constitution of the country. The heart of the policy was a strict limit on the number of children that couples were allowed to produce—one in the cities, two in rural areas. Some small allowances in the policy were made for ethnic minorities and couples facing "difficulties," such as the birth of a disabled child.

FACT FILE

After 20 years of implementing the one-child policy, China passed a family planning law that took effect in September 2002 to reinforce the policy and cap population at 1.6 billion by 2050.

FIGURE 11.9 Rapid population growth, among other factors, has contributed to widespread hunger and poverty in China.

Voluntary Compliance?

In this centrally controlled state, Chinese officials had the means to enforce their policy. First, incentives encouraged couples to give birth to only one child. These incentives included tax breaks and job promotions. An extensive advertising program made sure that couples were reminded of the need for the country to take this course. Disincentives made it painful to break the one-child rule. Couples that had more than one child faced systemic discrimination in the community and on the job. They paid stiff fines, often more than three times their annual income, and higher taxes, and their children were given lower status in schools. A whole system of national, regional, and community monitors were set up to encourage couples to delay marriage and then to delay childbearing. Neighbourhood representatives monitored women's menstrual cycles to detect unauthorized pregnancies. A woman who became pregnant without state approval faced strong community pressure to abort the fetus, even late in the pregnancy. The aggressive enforcement of the policy throughout the 1980s and 1990s prevented an estimated 300 million new Chinese citizens from being born.

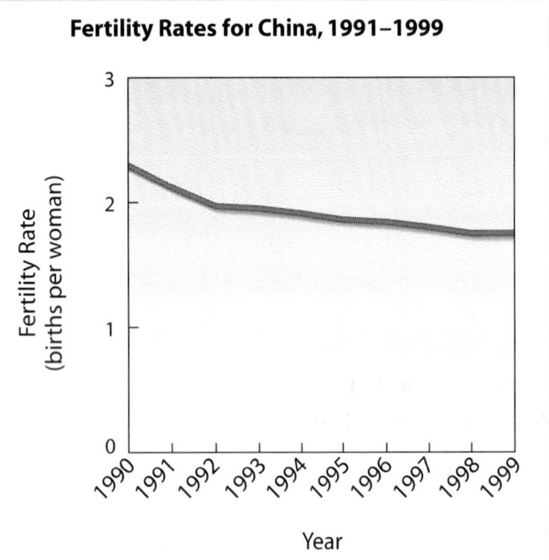

The one-child policy produced some obvious results. The national fertility rate dropped from an average of 3.3 children per mother for the period 1975–1980 to an average of 1.8 children for 1995–2000. Rates in urban areas are lower than in rural areas where enforcement of the policy has not been as effective. Nationally, 40% of women have agreed to sterilization. In Hunan province, almost 90% of women aged 30–34 years have been sterilized. The population of the country will achieve zero population growth around 2040 when it peaks at about 1.6 billion people. The Chinese government recommitted itself to the policy in 2002.

Lin Jintang and Lin Fude, "Zero Growth: Long-Term Effect of China's Family Planning Program" at <www.cpirc.org.cn/e-view1.htm>

Fertility Rates for China, 1991–1999

FIGURE 11.11 After just over a decade of the one-child policy, fertility rates had fallen below replacement levels in China.

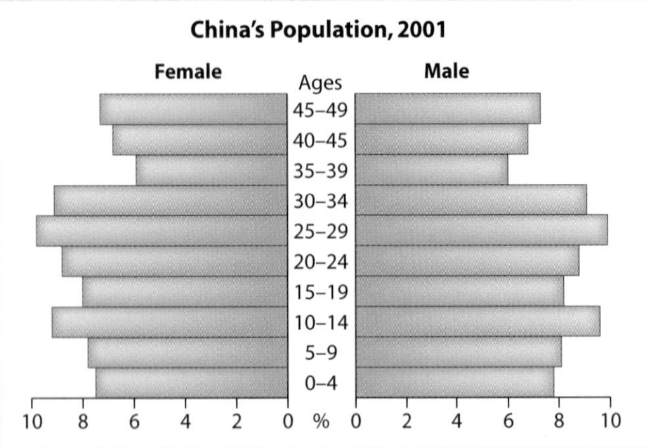

China's Population, 2001

FIGURE 11.12 The narrowing base on China's population pyramid is an indication of the effectiveness of the country's one-child policy.

The Role of Population Predictions

All population policies, including China's one-child policy, rely on population projections to set long-term goals. Projections are developed using a variety of factors and assumptions about how those factors will behave over the life of the projection. Figure 11.13, **Low, Medium, and High Projections for China's Population, 2000–2100**, gives three projections where assumptions about fertility rates are made. In reality, many conditions could affect fertility rates. Actual population totals may not match long-term projections, but those projections are one tool that demographers can use when helping decision makers set population policies.

COUNTERPOINT There is no shortage of critics of China's one-child policy. Opponents to the policy use terms like "barbaric," "forced," and "coercive," and describe people who have disobeyed the rules as "ostracized by the community." Critics are particularly opposed to how the policy ignores the rights of women and couples to make reproductive decisions on their own, free of government pressure.

Another criticism focuses on the desire for Chinese couples to have a male child. In the traditional Chinese society, male children are responsible for elderly members of the family. This tradition has prompted many couples to act to ensure that their one child will be male. Abortion rates were so high that the government had to

FIGURE 11.14 The average family size in China was reduced from 4.54 persons in 1980 to 3.36 persons by 2000.

outlaw the use of the medical procedure amniocentesis as a way of determining the gender of a fetus. Child abandonment, female infanticide, and adoption of female children are also strategies used to get around the one-child policy. In the eight years after the one-child policy came into effect, the number of children who were made available for adoption in China jumped from 200 000 per year to over 500 000, almost all female babies. Critics are concerned about both human rights violations and the long-term effects of an imbalance in the male–female ratio of the population.

A third concern about the policy is its impact on the age structure of the population. This forced, rapid reduction in birth rates means that there are fewer and fewer young people in a population that is quickly aging. In a society where younger generations have traditionally cared for the elderly, this artificially achieved demographic transition may mean that care for seniors will simply not be available in the future.

An International Perspective

The Chinese government claims that the world owes China a word of thanks for the one-child policy. Because it is the most populated country in the world, both the Chinese people and the world's people have a dual responsibility to slow growth rates in China. Without the one-child policy, the world would have pierced the six billion mark much sooner than it did and would be facing even higher estimates for the peak global population.

Low, Medium, and High Projections for China's Population, 2000–2100 (billions)

Year	Low-variant	Medium-variant	High-variant
2000	1.270	1.270	1.270
2010	1.344	1.353	1.369
2020	1.393	1.420	1.466
2030	1.396	1.442	1.518
2040	1.352	1.423	1.547
2050	1.272	1.369	1.544
2060	1.168	1.294	1.528
2070	1.068	1.225	1.527
2080	0.967	1.154	1.522
2090	0.879	1.092	1.529
2100	0.800	1.033	1.533

Lin Jintang and Lin Fude, "Zero Growth: Long-Term Effect of China's Family Planning Program" at <www.cpirc.org.cn/e-view1.htm>

FIGURE 11.13 Computer modelling of population change involves making different sets of assumptions about conditions in the country. The low-variant projection assumes the fertility rate for China will continue to decline following its recent pattern and then stabilize at 1.62 births per woman. The medium-variant projection assumes a stable fertility rate at 1.8 births per woman, the current level. The high-variant projection is based on a rise in the fertility rate to replacement levels of 2.1 births per woman on average. Notice the impact of fertility rate on the size of the population predicted for 2100.

Commentary

excerpt from US Congress clears funds for UN population fund

by Jay Newton-Small
Earth Times News Service
December 27, 2001

In the last day before [U.S.] Congress broke for the winter, funding for the UN Population Fund (UNFPA) was agreed upon…

"I am very grateful for the strong support the Fund has received from the United States administration and Congress—in effect, a vote of confidence in our work to promote reproductive health including family planning, safe motherhood and prevention of HIV/AIDS, along with gender equality and population-related strategies to reduce poverty," said Thoraya A. Obaid, Executive Director of UNFPA.

Congress, after much debate, decided to increase funding. The original request from the White House was for $25 million, the same amount as last year. Before Thanksgiving, lawmakers agreed to up that number to $34 million…

China has been the main sticking point for the Republicans. Conservative Republicans accuse the Fund of helping China force women to have abortions in their "one child," program. While noting the success the program has had in helping China control its population growth, the Fund has repeatedly stated that it only works in areas outside of the "one-child" rule.

In years past the Fund has lost complete funding because of China, and their support of the legalization of abortion globally. The final compromise makes $34 million the ceiling, but allows the President himself to decide the real amount that will go to UNFPA.

The compromise came when the Democratically controlled Senate threatened to overrule what has become known as the "Mexico Rule". While in Mexico City on his first presidential trip outside the US last spring, US President George W. Bush barred all US funding of international family planning non-governmental organizations (NGOs) that supported abortion abroad…

Since then many NGOs have been forced to choose between providing abortions in developing countries, and their US support. The Senate could have the power to overturn the Mexico Rule, as it is the Senate Committee on Foreign Affairs that actually doles out the aid money, but rather than a potentially public and embarrassing fight over the rule, the Democrats allowed the bill to pass with a higher ceiling of funding given to the UNFPA.

What remains to be seen in the new year is whether or not Bush will grant the maximum of $34 million to the UNFPA, thereby alienating his own party's conservatives, or the minimum of $0, daring the Democrats in the Senate to overrule his Mexico Rule.

Critical Analysis

1. Why does the U.S. Congress not want to support the UNFPA in China?

2. Explain the Mexico City Rule in your own words.

3. Research to find the latest U.S. allocation of funds to the UNFPA. Evaluate the U.S. government's policies in reducing population growth.

1. Write a two-page report in which you evaluate China's one-child policy, noting both the positive and negative aspects of this population strategy. Clearly indicate if you personally support this policy or not.
2. Brainstorm a list of conditions that could affect fertility rates.
3. Create a multiple-line graph to show the population projections given in Figure 11.13, **Low, Medium, and High**

Projections for China's Population, **2000–2100**. Record two observations about the trends in your graph.
4. What are some problems that could occur in predicting population size using low-, medium-, and high-variant techniques?
5. Do you agree that China's population growth should be the concern of both the Chinese people and the people of the rest of the world? Explain your answer.

INDIA'S POPULATION POLICY

India's population passed the one billion mark in 2000. Many people around the world did not celebrate this milestone, nor do they rejoice in the knowledge that India will surpass China as the most populous country around 2050. India's growth is an indication of the failure of the country's population policy.

The Population Picture

FACT FILE

India's population grows by 30 people per minute.

Even though India adopted family planning programs in 1952, it has not been able to rein in its high annual population growth rates, which averaged 1.6% between 1995 and 2000. Fertility rates for the same time period averaged 3.1 births per woman, a figure well above replacement levels. There have been some modest successes: growth rates are down from the 1975–1980 period when they averaged 2.1%, and fertility has dropped from the 4.8 births per woman average at that time. A significant factor in keeping growth rates high is the age structure of the population: one-third of its population is under 15 years of age. Even if these young people have fewer children than their parents did, there are so many of them to begin with that the population will continue to

FIGURE 11.15 An electronic billboard in New Delhi shows the population of India in September 1999. The UN estimated that India passed the one billion mark in August 1999, but the Indian census commissioner claimed the actual date was in May 2000.

grow for the next 60 or 70 years. This phenomenon, known as the "youth bulge," leads to the **population momentum** that keeps growth rates high.

Population Densities in India

FIGURE 11.16 India already has very high population densities over much of its land area. Continuing high rates of growth exacerbate the overcrowding.

Increases in Population in India, 1991–2001

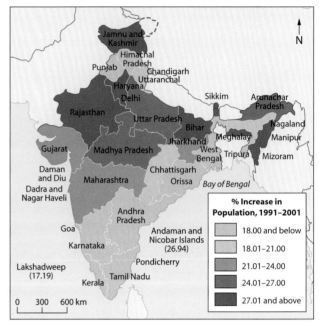

Note: Boundaries are representational, not exact. Uttaranchal, Chhattisgarh, and Jharkhand are states that were created since 1991.

Source of data on population increase: Registrar General & Census Commissioner, India, Census of India 2001—Provincial Population Totals, March 2001.

FIGURE 11.17 Population growth rates vary considerably across India. What might be some factors that would affect rates of growth?

The evidence suggests that India is still undergoing a demographic transition and the population has not naturally curbed its birth rate. Couples are still having large families. In part, this is because children can have an economic value to families, as labour on farms and in factories or as domestic servants, or in the informal sector in large cities, selling small goods, begging, or working in the sex trade. In part, high birth rates occur because couples do not have access to birth control or cannot afford it. And, in part, families remain large because of the value placed on children by the culture—children can be a poor family's wealth. The encouragement offered by family planning programs to lower fertility rates has not met with widespread acceptance given these incentives to have children.

Part of the reluctance of Indian people to embrace family planning stems from a disastrous experiment with forced sterilization in the 1970s. Family planning policies

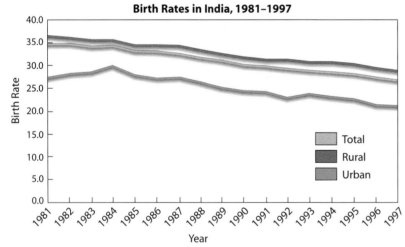

FIGURE 11.18 People who live in urban areas are much more likely to reduce birth rates than are those who live in rural areas. What might be some reasons for this pattern?

excerpt from

"India proposes retooled population policy"

by O. P. Sharma
Population Today
April 1, 2000

Fifty-three years after independence, India is still looking for a viable policy to control population growth. ...

As Indians contemplate becoming a population "billionaire" on May 11 [2000], the Minister of Health has just announced an ambitious new national population policy. The National Population Policy 2000—released on Feb. 15—aims to bring the total fertility rate (TFR) to replacement level by 2010 and to achieve a stable population by 2045, at a level consistent with sustainable economic growth, social development, and environmental protection.

Although these objectives are higher and the time frame to achieve them is shorter than with past programs, the 2000 policy may be more appealing to the public. It envisages achieving replacement level TFR (about two children per woman) through "promotional and motivational measures" that emphasize quality of life, rather than through numerical targets for the use of specific contraceptive methods, which plagued previous programs. The proposed policy talks of better management of public health, education, and sanitation, and focuses on women's employment.

Addressing unmet needs for basic reproductive and child health services [e.g., family planning counselling],

supplies [e.g., contraceptives], and infrastructure [e.g., accessible clinics] is foremost among the policy's goals. Other goals are keeping girls in school longer, raising the age at which girls marry to 18 or 20, reducing infant and maternal mortality, and achieving universal immunization of children against vaccine-preventable diseases. ...

The success of the population policy, if it is implemented, will depend on a judicious mixing of the roles of males and females. It is well known that women in India generally do not decide their reproductive behaviour. Although most contraceptive methods are for women, many women have no say in limiting their family size or in adopting a particular preventive method. The proposed policy would focus information and education campaigns on men to promote small families and to raise awareness of the benefits of birth spacing, better health and nutrition, and better education.

Critical Analysis

1. Summarize the new population policy outlined in this reading.
2. In what ways does this new policy reflect a greater understanding of population planning methods and approaches?
3. Speculate on reasons why "women in India generally do not decide their reproductive behaviour." In what ways might this fact affect the success of population policies?
4. Evaluate, in a one-page report, the chances of success for India's new population policy as described in the reading.

have also failed because they were too target-oriented, with agencies focused on reaching sterilization totals rather than helping couples with family planning.

> " The fact that India is reaching the 1 billion mark is not a cause for anything but concern and shame. India had the first official family planning program of any developing country, but its population control policies have repeatedly failed the people. Even today, family planning services in many areas are atrocious or non-existent. "
>
> *Michael Vlassoff, UNFPA*

Policies without Power

As a democratic country, India has had to convince people to choose smaller families. The government does not have the coercive means available to them that the centrally controlled government of China has to implement its one-child policy. But as the article by O. P. Sharma

(above) indicates, the government is trying a new strategy, one that it hopes will have greater resonance with the Indian population. This new population policy is not bound by numerical targets but offers incentives for two-children families and for delaying marriage. With the new policy, the focus is on the role and responsibility of men.

Hampered by a lack of financial resources and undermined by a general unwillingness to reduce family sizes below replacement levels, India's population policies in the past have not had much success. Growth rates will remain high for decades because of population momentum. This is a problem for this nation struggling to improve its economic and social development. The new approaches to family planning offer some room for optimism, but critics generally remain pessimistic about India's population future. What should they do to effectively implement their population policies?

WHAT SHOULD BE CANADA'S POPULATION POLICY?

While population policies in China and India are focused on controlling growth rates, the developed countries of the world face different circumstances. Given that most developed countries have achieved stable or even declining populations, their population policies may actually encourage growth. The United States, for example, has personal income tax structures that offer greater deductions for larger families. Australia has an ongoing debate that can be summarized as "populate or perish," with many people arguing that the country has to maintain high rates of immigration to keep up with its more rapidly growing neighbours. The fear for many in developed countries is that population decline equates with lowered economic vitality and weaker defence capabilities because of smaller armed forces.

An Absence of Policy

Two key factors contribute to eventual population outcomes: government policies related to immigration and population issues and personal choices made about family size. Population projections are based on assumptions about natural increase and net immigration. Scenarios based on variations in these assumptions have predicted that the population of Canada will

Canada's Population Growth Components

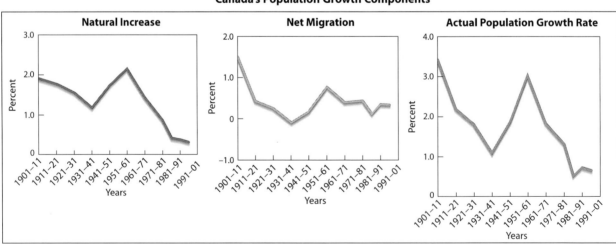

FIGURE 11.19 The first graph shows the growth due to births, the second graph shows the growth due to immigration, and the third graph is the sum of the two growth components. Note that, with the lowered birth rates due to the demographic transition, immigration has greater importance in Canada's population growth.

grow to somewhere between 35 million and 50 million people by 2040. The 2001 census reported that Canada experienced one of the smallest rates of growth ever with a population increase of 4% over 1996 numbers. In Canada, the demographic trend is clear. Most of the population growth is due to immigration because fertility rates are below replacement level. While Canada has separate policies that set guidelines for the number and type of immigrants and refugees allowed to enter the country, as well as policies on human rights, abortion, and child credits, it has not adopted a comprehensive long-term population policy.

The Challenge of Population Planning

There are many questions to consider if Canada is to develop a population policy. Should the country maintain a growing population or aim for a zero growth policy? Should all Canadians be encouraged to have larger families as in Quebec? Is Canada a vast empty land with a strong infrastructure and endless resources that should be shared with the less fortunate from many other countries? How many immigrants should Canada accept? Should we allow natural forces to create a shrinking population? How many people can Canada's land, water, and other natural systems support into the future without endangering other species? Are plans to increase Canada's population through immigration contrary to Kyoto Protocol objectives to reduce greenhouse gas emissions? A population policy for Canada should consider a number of factors:

THE IMPACT OF IMMIGRATION While newcomers may encounter difficulties with language, cultural values, or systemic institutional discrimination in the job market, Canada's legal system and Charter of Rights and Freedoms as well as government and NGO assistance programs work to create a generally tolerant and respectful Canadian society that welcomes and protects people from around the world. Most immigrants settle in Canada's largest cities, most notably Toronto and Vancouver, putting additional pressure on urban infrastructure including transportation, housing, and social services. Immigration has a direct impact on the econ-

omy and employment. The vast majority of immigrants come to Canada to find a better life for themselves and their families. Their skills, talents, and abilities contribute to the well-being of Canada as a whole. Because many of them are young families or people of childbearing age, their personal choices increase the population. Immigrants expand the demand for and provide a larger market for goods and services and are generally less likely to receive welfare than the native-born population.

Canada looks for highly skilled workers and professionals or entrepreneurs and investors who create jobs for Canadians, thereby providing spin-off and multiplier benefits. On the other hand, changing economic conditions that result from globalization have reduced opportunities to those who are unskilled and have replaced many jobs with labour-saving technology. A population policy that incorporates the

FIGURE 11.20 Immigration has always been an important part of the demographic situation in Canada. The decline in births in the second part of the twentieth century made immigration relatively even more important.

Immigration to Canada, 1990–2001

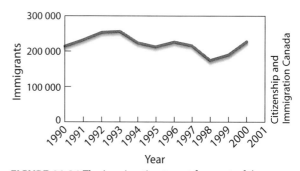

FIGURE 11.21 The immigration target for most of the time period shown in the graph was 300 000 immigrants, or roughly 1% of the population of the country.

impact of immigration would consider the kind of people that would best fit in with current economic realities.

DEMOGRAPHIC TRENDS AND PATTERNS Where, within Canada, are people migrating? For example, between 1996 and 2001, the provinces and territories with the highest growth rates were Alberta (10.3%), Nunavut (8.1%), Ontario (6.1%), and British Columbia (4.9%). Urbanization grew from 78.5% of the population living in urban settlements of greater than 10 000 in 1996 to 79.4% in 2001. Calgary was by far the fastest growing city. Rural areas and small towns declined slightly overall in Canada, although this pattern changed to one of growth in those regions where more than 30% of the population commuted to an urban centre.

What is the impact of an aging population? If the trend to increased longevity continues, as more baby boomers experience longer retirements, collect more social security benefits, and require more health care, a greater burden falls on younger people who have to pay for these benefits. Or an aging population may decide to work longer, affecting labour force trends. Changes in public policy will be required in either case.

CARRYING CAPACITY What would be the environmental impact of higher numbers of people in Canada demanding a high quality of life? Although a great deal of ecological information is available, it lies in hundreds of different databases in different locations and jurisdictions. We do not really know how many people Canada can support, considering that the most habitable

Canada—Population Change, 1996–2000.

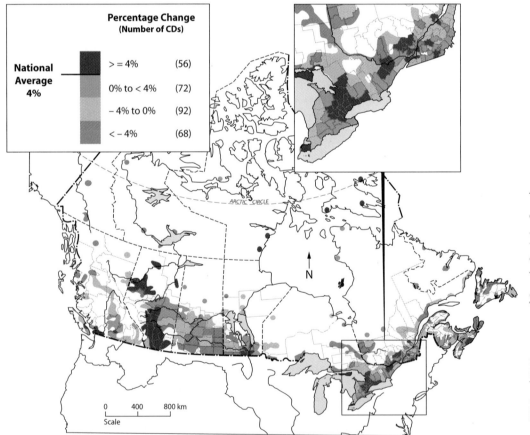

Percentage Change (Number of CDs)		
National Average 4%	>= 4%	(56)
	0% to < 4%	(72)
	– 4% to 0%	(92)
	< – 4%	(68)

1996 and 2001 censuses of Canada, Statistics Canada

FIGURE 11.22 This map from the Geography Division of Statistics Canada in 2002 provides information on population changes that occurred between the 1996 census and the 2001 census.

part of Canada, the narrow band of land that lies within 300 km of the Canada–U.S. border, is already densely populated. Considering that many policy makers are economists rather than ecologists, this gap in mainstream understanding is not surprising. We tend to believe that Canada is a land of vast resources despite contrary evidence such as the collapse of cod and salmon fisheries, inadequate water access and quality, and an increasing number of endangered species and national parks at risk. The more people there are, the more waste and pollution created, the more land is needed to grow food and fibre, the more infrastructure, social services, houses, roads, schools, hospitals, offices, malls, landfills, sewage systems, emergency services, and other things are needed. Considering human numbers in the context of the ecosystems that support them is one way of determining sustainable levels of population and development.

Planners, policy makers, and citizens need reliable information and projections on interacting factors and trends in order to make effective decisions about population policy and to prepare for future changes. Many analysts believe that all countries have a responsibility to control population growth within sustainable limits. Whether this challenge can be met without major changes and initiatives in all areas of society, including government population policy, is debatable.

INTERACT

1. Explain the relationship between population policies and immigration policies.
2. In Canada's situation, immigration policies have become de facto population policies. For what reasons is this a concern to some people?
3. Work with a partner to develop a set of goals and principles that, in your opinion, should form the basis for a Canadian population policy. Does your list deal only with population size or have you included items that relate to other factors? Prioritize your list.
4. Discuss the following statement with several classmates: "Immigration rates should be held to a level that stabilizes Canada's population and holds it at a constant level." Compile evidence that will support your point of view.
5. a) Write a detailed analysis of population patterns and trends across Canada as shown on the map in Figure 11.22, **Canada—Population Change, 1996–2000.**
   b) Suggest several ways that this information could be useful to planners and citizens.

WEB LINKS

- U.S. Population Reference Bureau: <www.prb.org>
- International Planned Parenthood Federation: <www.ippf.org>
- The global reproductive health forum: <www.hsph.harvard.edu/Organizations/healthnet/>
- Canada Census 2001 Population: <www.statcan.ca/english/Pgdb/People/popula.htm>

RELATED ISSUES

- The role and impact of NGOs in shaping the activities of international organizations like the UN
- Cultural roles of women and their influence on shaping social attitudes worldwide
- The causes and effects of female infanticide
- The role of the U.S., the Vatican, and other nations in shaping global population policy

ANALYSE, APPLY, AND INTERACT

1. Explain the purpose and value of national population policies.

2. Economic and cultural considerations influence a country's population policies. Give two examples to show this statement to be true.

3. Explain how people's points of view influence their perceptions about China's population policies.

4. Write a script for an advertisement that the Indian government might use to promote its population policy. For the points you make in your advertisement, explain why you see them as important or effective in convincing people to adopt family planning.

5. Write a conversation that might have taken place between an Indian population expert and a Chinese population expert. In the conversation, have each person offer ways that the other country might try to improve the effectiveness of their population policy.

6. Write a letter to the editor in which you criticize Canada's lack of a population policy and suggest directions that the government should take with a population policy.

7. Draw a cartoon that satirizes Canada's lack of an effective population policy.

8. The three countries profiled in this chapter show a number of alternatives to dealing with the population problem through policies. Compare the effectiveness of these policies by examining their methods and their results. Which policy or policies do you think were effective? Explain.

9. The government of a developing country has asked you to help them draft a population policy. What information about the country would you want to gather before starting to develop a policy? Give reasons for your ideas.

10. Religion plays an important role in shaping population policies. Using the Internet and library resources, research to find the policies of two countries that are strongly influenced by religion. You might, for example, compare the policies of Mexico (a predominantly Roman Catholic nation) and Saudi Arabia (an Islamic nation). Key words that you might use in your research are population policies, values, religion.

11. Conduct a small survey to find out about the attitudes of friends and relatives on the topic of Canada's population. Questions should explore people's attitudes toward maximum population size, immigration levels, desirable characteristics, and the like. Produce your results as a poster or Web site.

12. Working with other students in the class, hold a debate on this statement:
Resolved: Governments of developing countries should be required to undertake population growth control measures before they receive foreign aid from developed countries.

Chapter 12: Are Urban Systems Sustainable?

By the end of this chapter, you will:

- analyse selected global trends and evaluate their effects on people and environments at the local, national, and global level;

- evaluate the cultural, economic, and environmental impact of changing technology;

- analyse the impact of urbanization and urban growth on natural and human systems;

- evaluate some of the ways of promoting sustainable development and assess their effectiveness in selected places and regions of the world;

- identify current global sustainability issues and environmental threats;

- explain how local participation in the development process can build sustainable communities;

- explain, using specific examples, how strategic lawsuits against public participation (SLAPPs) affect the public participation process;

- evaluate the sustainability of selected trends related to consumption of the earth's resources;

- evaluate and communicate the perspectives and arguments of various stakeholders involved in a geographic issue;

- demonstrate an understanding of the value and use of geographic representations and methods;

- collect data, using field study techniques, and analyse the data to identify patterns and relationships.

CITIES AS DYNAMIC URBAN SYSTEMS

Cities have been called the "human nest" as the world's population becomes predominantly urban. These places are dynamic organisms that change and grow in unpredictable ways. Ecosystem concepts can be applied to complex urban systems. These include the *input* of resources that cities need to survive, the *output* of wastes, goods, and services they produce, and the *feedback* or repercussions from these interacting forces. For example, cities cannot survive without using and redistributing energy from a variety of sources. As they do so, they generate pollutants and heat that can alter the local **microclimate** and produce health-threatening smog. How sustainable are these systems?

This chapter examines the process of urbanization and the challenge of providing for the needs and wants of so many people living so closely together. Most cities face similar issues, including scarce affordable housing, inadequate or declining infrastructures, traffic congestion and planning for efficient mass transportation, overburdened services, high unemployment, health risks, and environmental concerns as sprawling cities use up more and more land. The greatest potential for change in urban systems lies in the developing world with its high population growth rate and rapid rural–urban migration. According to the Canadian International Development Agency (CIDA)'s report, *An Urbanizing World*, the viability of the world in the twenty-first century will depend on achieving sustainable development within cities everywhere. Attempts to meet these challenges are already under way in many parts of the world as governments, international institutions, and local citizens examine solutions and consider alternatives.

> ## FACT FILE
>
> Ninety-five percent of the water that goes into a city each day is used to convey wastes from one location to another—from homes to sewers, from factories to rivers, and from lawns and pavement to streams and groundwater.

GLOBAL PATTERNS OF URBANIZATION

The world is currently undergoing the largest population movement that it has ever experienced. It is not the migration of people from one country to another, or even one continent to another, rather, it is the shift of people from the countryside to cities. This rural to urban migration will continue to radically change the living conditions for most of the human population.

The process whereby people leave their homes in rural areas and move to cities—urban areas—is called **urbanization**. This is not a new phenomenon: urbanization has already dramatically affected the developed countries of the world. For example, in 1871, only 19.6% of Canadians lived in urban places. By 1971, just a century later, 76.1% of Canadians were urban dwellers. Clearly

> ## FACT FILE
>
> Overall, urban areas are growing 1.5 times faster than the world population as a whole. Virtually all the population growth in the world expected during the period 2000–2030 will take place in urban areas.

FIGURE 12.1 Every year, millions of people in developing countries such as these people displaced by the Yangtze Three Gorges dam in China leave their homes in the countryside to move to cities, seeking better lives.

Canadian society had undergone a dramatic change. The global figures show a similar trend. In 1900, only 14% of the world's population lived in cities; the figure had reached 29% by mid-century and 50% by 2000.

An estimated 66.7% of the world's population will be urban dwellers in 2050. Cities have become very important economically, socially, and politically. To understand many of the problems and issues of this urban world, we need to understand what triggered this population shift and its effects on people and the environment.

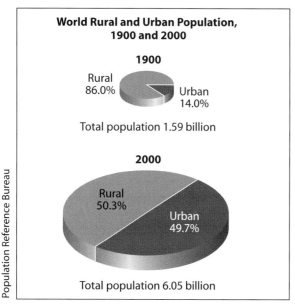

FIGURE 12.2 The sizes of the circles in this graph are in proportion to the total populations of the world. So, while populations have grown, the proportion living in cities has grown as well.

Urbanization and Developed Countries

Urbanization occurred in the developed countries over the past two centuries. It came about largely because of technological change that altered the ways that people earned their livings. Three forces were instrumental in creating these changes:

- Machines were performing more of the jobs that needed to be done, including those industries that were at the heart of the Canadian economy—fishing, farming, logging, and mining. This **mechanization** displaced workers from rural work forces.
- Mechanization triggered the widespread development of manufacturing industries. Factories functioned best in locations where transportation services, raw materials, energy, and labour could be readily combined, which usually meant the fast growing urban areas. So, **industrialization** focused economic activities in urban areas.
- Technological change, particularly in the fuel sources available for industries, helped to spur on industrialization. New, more transportable fuel sources (more heat per unit of weight), including coal, petroleum, and electricity, could be easily transported to cities to service the factories and populations developing there. A second technological change

Population Reference Bureau

UN Population Division

World Urban and Rural Populations, 1900–2000 (millions)

	1900	1920	1940	1960	1980	2000
Urban Population	223	360	570	1012	1807	3008
Rural Population	1367	1500	1725	1973	2567	3046

FIGURE 12.3 Notice from the data that the total population in rural areas has increased, yet the percentage living in rural areas has decreased over this time period. How can this be the case?

FIGURE 12.4 By 1906, Toronto was already a booming metropolis. The potential opportunities there pulled migrants out of rural areas.

that helped cities grow was improvement in the way food was processed and transported. Fresh and perishable food could now be transported long distances to feed growing urban populations.

For Canada and most developed countries, urbanization and industrialization were closely linked. Displaced rural workers found employment in cities and the economies of cities grew to provide more and more goods and services to the urban populations.

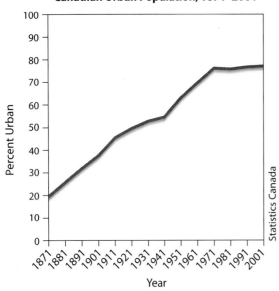

Canadian Urban Population, 1871–2001

Statistics Canada

FIGURE 12.5 By the 1920s, Canada was an urban nation, and the process continues. The 2001 census reports that 79.4% of Canada's population is urban. Identify variations in the trend and explain their significance.

Urbanization and Developing Countries

The developed countries of the world experienced urban transformations similar to Canada's at roughly similar times. Developing countries, though, have had different experiences. Many of these countries are still early in the process of urbanizing and are largely rural in their make-up. Most developing countries did not start to industrialize until well into the twentieth century. To a great extent, this delay was because they were colonies of European imperial powers that did not want industrial activi-

ties in the colonies. The colonies existed to provide raw materials such as minerals, sugar, or wood to the colonizer, and to buy the colonizer's manufactured goods. Without the impetus of industrialization, the developing countries did not start to urbanize until they became independent nations. Some have progressed to the point where urban centres dominate their economies. Bolivia, for example, was 65% urban by 2000 and the Philippines was 59% urban. On the other hand, some countries have barely started the process, including Burundi at 9% and Nepal at 12% urban in 2000. A variety of factors help determine the degree of urbanization, including levels of literacy, available resources, openness to new ideas from outside the country, and colonial experiences.

The technological changes that stimulated urbanization in the developed, industrialized countries were already well established before the developing countries started to urbanize. For these countries, the forces causing people to leave rural areas and move to cities are somewhat different. Three forces are instrumental in creating the present-day movement to cities:

- There are few jobs in rural areas. Better productivity in agriculture has displaced some workers. Large transnational corporations (TNCs) have bought up large areas of land for mechanized cash cropping in a number of countries, and the lower taxes they pay do not encourage the landowners to use the land to its full potential. These factors all work to create both high unemployment and high **underemployment**, and many workers simply do not have access to the land or capital to get into or remain in rural-based businesses. The lack of jobs pushes them out of rural areas.

- Many basic services are not available in rural areas to the same extent that they are available in urban areas. These services include health care, education, potable water, and energy supplies. The greater development of urban areas (at least perceived, if not actual) pulls people toward cities.

- Economic globalization encourages urban growth. As countries struggle to establish and keep competitive industries, they put their development resources into urban areas where productivity levels are higher. Urban

Percent Urban Population, 1950, 1990, and 2030

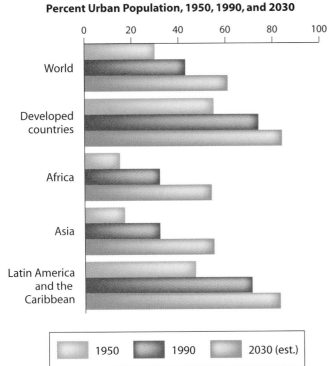

Legend: 1950, 1990, 2030 (est.)

FIGURE 12.6 For some parts of the world, the urbanization trend will continue for decades to come. What are the issues that arise from this trend?

Cities of 10 Million or More People, shows that most of these megacities will be in the developing world.

Problems with Rapid Urban Growth

Unfortunately, developing countries experiencing rapid urbanization have few resources to deal with the crush of people. The hundreds of thousands of people who migrate into some larger cities such as Calcutta, India, and Lagos, Nigeria, need housing, infrastructure services such as electricity and water, jobs, and educational facilities. These cities simply do not have the financial and human resources to provide these services efficiently. So, urban growth is unplanned and uncontrolled, with services woefully overloaded. This can be seen in places like Delhi, India, where electricity is turned off in parts of the city for up to six hours a day and in Bangkok, Thailand, where drivers can spend the equivalent of 44 working days sitting in traffic jams every year.

> **FACT FILE**
>
> In the year 2000, about 262 million people, representing 4.3% of the world's population, lived in cities of more than 10 million people. That percentage is predicted to rise to 5.2% by 2015, and equal 379 million people.

One very visible indicator of the problems that result from rapid urbanization is the prevalence of **squatter settlements** around the edges of large cities. These shantytowns are given different names around the world—"villa miseries" in Argentina, "barriadas" in Peru, "bustees" in India, "favelas" in Brazil. Up to one-third of the population of Manila, Philippines, and over one-third of Lima, Peru's, residents live in squatter settlements. Rio de Janeiro's largest favela is home to roughly 300 000 people. The flood of migrants to the cities means that the housing stock cannot keep up with the demand. For example, 60% of city dwellers in Bangladesh cannot find accommodations in the existing housing. This unmet demand pushes prices for existing homes beyond the reach of most migrants.

Many migrants begin their lives in cities by squeezing into the overcrowded homes of relatives, or just living on the streets, but then

areas will get such things as improved communication systems or new colleges because they are seen as having a greater ability to stimulate real economic growth than rural areas.

Megacities

One of the best ways to see the rapid growth of cities in developing countries is to look at the largest cities in the world—**megacities**. In 1950, only one city in the world had a population greater than 10 million people—New York. By 2015, 23 urban areas are expected to pass that mark and five cities—Tokyo, Bombay, Lagos, Dhaka, and Sao Paulo—are expected to exceed 20 million people. Figure 12.9,

> **FACT FILE**
>
> Globally, cities are growing at an average rate of 2.5% per year. In developing countries, the rate is 3.5% while it is about 1% in developed countries, which account for a smaller part of the world's population.

Distribution of Population, 1975, 2000, and 2015 (%)

	Range of City Size	1975	2000	2015 (est.)
World	5 million and over	4.8	6.9	8.7
	1 to 5 million	8.0	11.6	14.1
	Less than 1 million	25.1	28.5	30.6
	Rural population	62.1	53.0	46.6
Developed Countries	5 million and over	9.3	9.5	9.9
	1 to 5 million	13.9	18.5	20.6
	Less than 1 million	46.8	48.1	49.3
	Rural population	30.0	24.0	20.3
Developing Countries	5 million and over	3.2	6.3	8.5
	1 to 5 million	6.0	10.0	12.7
	Less than 1 million	17.6	23.7	26.8
	Rural population	73.2	60.1	52.0

UN Population Division

FIGURE 12.7 When interpreting data given in a large table such as this, it is useful to isolate statistics and look for trends. For example, what has been the trend for cities of one to five million globally? How does this compare with the trend for cities of one to five million people in developed countries? In developing countries? What might be an explanation for differences in these trends?

move to underused land at the edges of the cities. The people do not own the land, but authorities do not drive them away since there simply is nowhere else that they can go.

FIGURE 12.8 A shanty town in Caracas, Venezuela.

Squatters construct tiny homes out of plastic sheeting, tin sheets, cardboard, planks, or whatever they can find. Settlements are unplanned and have few services like water supply or sewage disposal. Residents do not see these as permanent homes; they hope for a better future. But, it may take many years for some of them to acquire the wealth to move to more substantial housing.

Urban Problems

Overcrowding and lack of services in places dealing with rapid urban growth contribute to serious urban problems. Poverty and unemployment are at the root of the problems. Migrants often arrive without the skills necessary to earn a liveable wage and poverty becomes a barrier to increased affluence. These people cannot afford education for themselves or their children, they have to live at the fringes of the cities far from available jobs and services, and hunger erodes their health. Poverty and lack of opportunities often lead to lives lived with challenges such as pollution, crime, discrimination, family breakdown, homelessness, and sexual and/or substance abuse. While these same problems exist in the large cities of the developed world, their impacts are magnified by the rate of urban growth in the developing world.

Children are the most vulnerable to urban problems. Aside from the harmful effects of growing up in an unhealthy physical environment, children are victims of poverty. Most large cities have large populations of street children—homeless young people who are forced to live their lives at the edges of society. In some cases, they have

Cities of 10 Million or More People

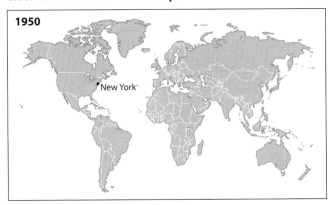

1950

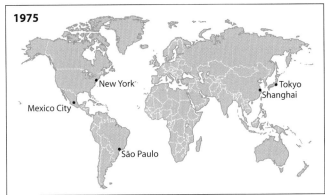

1975

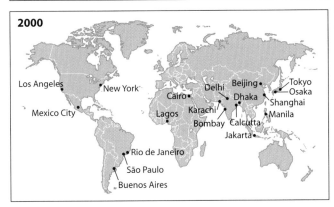

2000

FIGURE 12.9 What trends do the maps show? How can you explain the trends?

FIGURE 12.10 The rapid growth of cities means that the infrastructure is often very inadequate for the demands placed on it. This is a major roadway in Cameroon.

FIGURE 12.11 Open sewers in a residential neighbourhood of Kyoto, Japan.

been abandoned by parents struggling with poverty, and in other cases they have fled a dangerous home. Now on the streets, the children live through begging, scrounging, stealing, or working in the sex trade. These children are often victims of sexual predators and sometimes targeted by police. For example, in Rio de Janiero before the 1992 Earth Summit, dozens of children were kidnapped and relocated and some were killed in an effort to improve the city's image for the conference. High rates of HIV/AIDS are typical of street children populations. There are an estimated 100 million street children in the large cities of the world. In places like Sao Paulo, Brazil, street children can make up 10% of the population.

The Future of Large Cities

It is clear that there are a host of problems associated with urbanization and the rapid growth of large cities. Higher costs of living, overcrowding, crime, pollution, and a deteriorating physical environment are all negative outcomes that are easily identified. On the other hand, cities offer social, cultural, political, and economic opportunities that rural areas cannot match. Migrants do survive and prosper, often by working together to improve their communities. In a number of cities, effective community action has resulted in substantial improvements in the living conditions of shan-

tytowns, including giving ownership of the land to residents. In Recife, Brazil, for example, local neighbourhood associations teamed up and worked with the city government to install sanitary sewers. Neither the residents nor the government had the resources to do the job on their own, but, co-operatively, they accomplished something that improved the lives of

Commentary

excerpt from

"The Urban Demographic Revolution"
by Martin Brockerhoff
Population Today
August/September, 2000

… There is debate about whether some of the world's poorest megacities, such as Dhaka and Lagos, can effectively absorb the millions of additional residents anticipated in the near future (according to the UN, 9 million more for Dhaka and 10 million more for Lagos by 2015). Alarmists point to the plight of poor residents of Chicago, London, Manchester, New York, and other cities of now-industrialized countries during the era of these cities' most rapid growth, 1875 to 1900. Although such cities experienced economic progress, they also tended to have higher mortality than rural areas, because of occupational hazards and infectious diseases associated with high population density and poor water and sanitation infrastructure.

The Dickensian conditions of that earlier time—child labor, dilapidated housing, crime, and class tension—are also observed in megacities of poor countries today but on a much larger scale. And they are often accompanied by high levels of pollution and fatalities from motor vehicles, illicit drug use, and widespread sexually transmitted infections such as HIV/AIDS. The greater magnitude of problems in megacities today is suggested by their rapid growth to enormous sizes.

There are also environmental concerns. Modern urban systems require large amounts of energy, and consequent emissions of carbon dioxide and nitrogen oxides from fossil fuel combustion trap excess heat and lead to climate change, rising sea levels, and changes in vegetation.

On the other side of the debate are those who point to the benefits that megacities in developing regions could enjoy in the future. Many economists argue that cities have always been the engines of national economic growth, and that they achieve megacity size only because they are economically efficient for their countries. As international capital becomes more mobile with globalization, large pools of relatively low-skilled labor can attract foreign investment that leads to job opportunities in manufacturing and indus-

try. The growth of Internet technology enables city governments to inexpensively share information regarding effective approaches to poverty alleviation, waste management, affordable housing, and other critical issues of giant cities.

Anthropologists have shown that the urban poor living in slums, shantytowns, and urban fringe areas of megacities are not marginal residents suffering social malaise, but industrious and resourceful people attempting to better their lives. Community mobilization and grass-roots initiatives organized and led by poor constituents have made hundreds of city neighborhoods more liveable and could increase the productivity of labor in megacities if applied widely.

Regardless of how megacities are perceived, urban scholars, demographers, and decision makers have reached consensus on two issues regarding their treatment in the future. First, effective urban governance is needed to ensure the well-being of all residents. Second, there remains a need to improve the estimation and projection of megacity populations. Expanded data collection through conventional censuses and surveys, as well as through the use of new satellite imagery technology, will be necessary to provide better data for research and policymaking in the world's largest cities.

Critical Analysis

1. Do you agree with the author's argument that the rapidly growing megacities of today represent even worse conditions for people than the rapidly growing large cities of the developed world a century ago? Explain your answer.
2. Use the above reading to create an advantages/disadvantages chart on rapid urban growth.
3. Effective governance is seen as being essential for the well-being of residents in large urban areas. For you, what would be the characteristics of "effective governance"? Give examples to explain your ideas.
4. The author of this reading suggests that satellite images can be used to improve conditions in large cities. What kinds of data about large cities do you suppose could be gathered by satellites and why would these be useful?

people in the favelas. This type of action is essential on a larger scale in the future.

In addition to the problems in urban areas, we need to acknowledge the consequences of urbanization for rural areas. Some migrants are young, ambitious, and talented and leave seeking better lives in cities.

The trend in rural to urban migration is likely to continue until rates in developing countries match those in developed countries.

> 66 The poorer you are, the greater the threat. In human settlements especially in large cities, the poor, without a doubt, are disproportionately threatened by environmental hazards and health risks caused by air and ground pollution, inadequate housing, poor sanitation, polluted water and lack of other basic services. 99
>
> *United Nations Centre for Human Settlements*

FIGURE 12.13 Street children in Brazil. The lost potential of these young people is staggering. Their homelessness means that they have little opportunity to attend school or learn a trade.

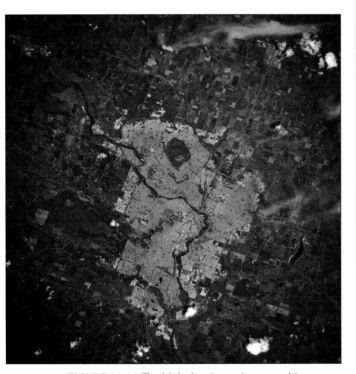

FIGURE 12.12 The high density and geographic extent of Calgary, Alberta, (centre) is clearly shown by this satellite image. What pressures do cities like Calgary, with such a large ecological footprint, place on the surrounding hinterland?

PROFILE

Lester R. Brown

FIGURE 12.14

Often called one of the world's most influential thinkers, Lester R. Brown has been a leading voice on a great number of significant global issues. Brown founded Worldwatch Institution in 1974. This organization is a private, non-profit research institute that analyses global environmental and environment-related issues. Brown's focus has been on identifying and detailing the threats to the biosphere and motivating decision makers to take action. For example, Brown has campaigned to have leaders and decision makers reassess the future of the automobile and to design transportation systems that do not threaten our natural systems and our food supply. His message was heard loudly when a group of eminent scientists presented China—a nation that had announced in 1994 that it was going to make the automobile industry one of its growth sectors—with a paper explaining the virtues of public transit systems. China has since committed to the building of over 2000 km of subway and light rapid transit lines by 2050.

Worldwatch's annual *State of the World* reports are translated into many languages and have become the doctrine of the global environmental movement.

HOW CAN CITIES BE MADE SUSTAINABLE?

From an ecological perspective, large urban areas are disasters! Cities, with their large ecological footprints, gobble huge quantities of resources, produce prodigious amounts of waste, and significantly disrupt natural systems. Imagine the impact on natural systems of cities with more than 20 million people! The environmental impacts of cities will only grow as urbanization continues and people keep moving to cities. But is there anything that can be done? Do we have to give up the benefits of cities in order to have a healthy environment? A growing number of researchers and analysts are arguing that it is possible to have cities *and* a healthy environment if we change the way we organize and build urban areas. We need strategies to create sustainable cities.

Because of their uncontrolled and unplanned rapid growth, few cities in the developing world can begin to explore ideas about sustainability. Most of their resources are consumed meeting day-to-day needs, not planning for the future. Cities in developed countries have far greater resources to address urban issues. Many of the following examples for sustainability have been explored. See if you can identify ways that these ideas could be adapted to urban areas in both developed and developing countries.

What Are Sustainable Cities?

In order for a system to be sustainable, the system must operate without depleting the resources that are available for the future. Natural systems maintain their resources through recycling. In a forest environment, for example, decaying plant and animal materials are reused through processes like nitrogen and carbon cycles: the forest system can function effectively for very long periods of time because resources are not withdrawn from the system. If we apply the same process to cities—urban systems—then they too must operate without depleting the available resources. Figure 12.15, **Characteristics of Sustainable Cities**, identifies some of the characteristics that sustainable cities should have.

Traditional ways of thinking about cities separate the three critical aspects of cities that make them workable. These aspects are:
- the economy;
- the environment;
- the community.

Decisions about each of these aspects are usually made in isolation, so a decision made about the economy may take no notice of environmental or community concerns. For example, the decision to construct an expressway might make economic sense, but the expressway could have important negative consequences for the natural environment and the sense of community in a city. Or, the decision to preserve a sensitive ecological area could discourage economic activity and cause

Characteristics of Sustainable Cities

Sustainable cities should have:	Unsustainable cities have:
efficient transportation systems that encourage use of public transit, minimizing energy consumption for transportation;	inefficient transportation systems, emphasizing automobile use;
well-developed infrastructures that include water supply systems, sewage treatment, waste recycling, health care facilities, education and energy supplies, maintaining high qualities of life;	incomplete or underfunded infrastructures, making access to systems and services difficult or inconsistent;
maximized alternative energy sources, including solar and wind power, reducing dependencies on fossil fuels;	relied on non-renewable sources of energy, especially fossil fuels;
mixes of land uses that put workplaces near homes, minimizing commuting and higher densities;	segregated land uses, requiring transportation to move from residential areas to workplaces;
heterogeneous mixes of housing types, from affordable to luxury, meeting the needs of community members;	housing in homogeneous blocks, emphasizing low-density single-family dwellings;
high qualities of life through the development of civic amenities, such as green spaces and cultural centres.	few opportunities for the people to experience the amenities of the community and to engage in rewarding cultural interactions.

FIGURE 12.15 Building sustainable cities will require changing the way we think about the use of space and the provision of services in cities.

FIGURE 12.16 The first step in building sustainable cities involves changing the ways that decisions are made. The economy, the environment, and the community have to be considered at all stages in decision making.

unemployment rates to rise or a change in the types of jobs available in the community. A sustainable approach to cities would link all three critical aspects, giving equal importance to the quality of community life, the strength of the economy, and the health of the environment. The benefits of this approach are cities that are healthy places to live and work without diminishing the environment—sustainable cities.

Sustainable Cities and the Automobile

One of the biggest barriers to achieving sustainable cities is the automobile. Not only do cars burn incredible amounts of non-renewable fossil fuels and use huge amounts of metals and plastics, but accommodating cars in urban settings forces planners and urban developers to use strategies and techniques that are simply not sustainable. Public policies for transportation have almost universally emphasized private automobiles over public mass transit systems.

FIGURE 12.17 Quality of life is an important measure in an urban environment. What aspects of these scenes from two cities (Bangkok, Thailand [left] and Istanbul, Turkey [right]) indicate something of quality of life?

In the developed world, where car ownership is high, relatively cheap, and comfortable, automobile use has encouraged the construction of suburbs around large cities in an urban form we might refer to as "the automobile city." Suburbs have become popular because, while they have urban qualities, they also offer something reminiscent of the idyllic countryside, a notion that has become romanticized in most highly urbanized cultures. The low population density of suburban living is the main attraction. Single-family homes, each with its own lawns and gardens, are the norm. The suburbs act as bedroom communities for the larger cities to which they are attached. They compare sharply with the high-density apartment blocks and townhouse complexes of urban areas. Cars allow suburban dwellers to leave their residences and to commute to the parts of the city where jobs are located. Often this is in the core of the city, although, increasingly, economic activities are locating in some suburban areas where land costs are lower. This movement of people to and from work gives rise to the phenomenon of rush hours, congestion, gridlock, smog, and "road rage."

> **FACT FILE**
>
> Automobiles are the largest single source of greenhouse gases that cause global climate change.

Urban Sprawl

City planners have labelled the outward growth of cities and their suburbs as **urban sprawl**. The shantytowns of developing countries are clear examples of this process. Criticisms of this uncontrolled outward expansion of cities include:

- Suburbs are built on farmland that is lost forever to food production. The best farmland is typically flat and well drained, exactly the conditions needed to build roads, factories, and homes easily and cheaply. Estimates place the loss of farmland in the United States alone at 400 000 ha per year. In China, urban sprawl in the Pearl River Delta over a 14-year period used up 1500 km^2 of very productive cropland.

- Urban sprawl is not an effective way to deal with population growth in cities. Expanding the edges of cities outward to ease overcrowding and lack of housing encourages people to use larger plots of land for their homes, requiring more land to solve the same problems. Building more expressways to solve the problem of traffic congestion just encourages people to buy more cars and to commute farther. In Los Angeles, California, for example, traffic delays because of over-

> **"Asphalt is the land's last crop."**
> *Rupert Cutler, environmentalist*

Forms of Cities

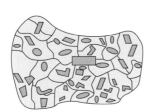

Symbolic City

These are cities that are constructed to represent a perfect form designed along religious, political, or philosophical concepts. Beijing's Forbidden City is a good example of a symbolic city, with the emperor's palace at its centre.

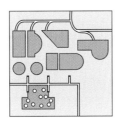

Organic City

All the activities in the city are part of an integrated whole, with residential uses mingling with commercial activities, connecting to religious centres, and the like. Old European cities developed in this manner, including Amsterdam and London. Many cities in Africa and Asia still take this form.

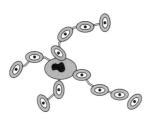

Planned City

Typically laid out using a grid, these cities carefully separate various uses, with commercial activities in one area, industrial uses in another, and residential zones somewhere else. North American cities that developed with industrialization tend to look like this, including Edmonton, Alberta.

Transit City

Transit lines running out from the centre of a large city encourage the growth of subcentres along the lines, each with its own character but intimately connected to the main centre. New York City is a good example of a transit city.

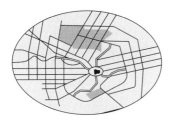

Automobile City

Cities that developed after the widespread ownership of cars usually take this form. The city grows out in all directions with expressways linking the parts of the urban area to the centre. Toronto fits this model nicely.

Cranny, M., *Counterpoints*, Prentice-Hall, 2001, p. 378

FIGURE 12.18 While all of these city forms exist, accommodating automobiles creates a clear preference for the automobile city.

Facts about Cars and Land

- The developed countries are home to 80% of the world's 520 million automobiles.

- In India, there is one vehicle for every 143.2 people. In Canada there is one vehicle for every 1.8 people.

- Mexico City and Bangkok have half of all the vehicles in Mexico and Thailand, respectively.

- In the United States, each car requires 0.07 ha of paved land for parking and roads. Every five cars added to the country's fleet requires that an area the size of a football field be paved.

- One-quarter of all land in North American cities is used for transportation, mostly roads and parking lots.

- More densely populated developed countries need less paved area than the U.S. Japan, Germany, and the United Kingdom pave an average of 0.02 ha per car.

- If China was to achieve the same car ownership rate as Japan, that country would have a fleet of 640 million vehicles and would have to pave 13 million ha of land, mostly cropland.

FIGURE 12.19 The automobile has a significant impact on the shape and function of cities.

FIGURE 12.20 A crowded expressway in Kuala Lumpur, Malaysia. Six hectares of land are lost for every kilometre of expressway built.

crowded expressways during rush hours cost residents $12 billion a year. Expanding cities at the edges sets up leapfrog development.

- Urban sprawl is expensive. The infrastructure of the urban area has to be expanded to service the new suburbs. This cost is estimated in the U.S. to be equivalent to $45 000 per household. A typical North American city like Phoenix, Arizona, estimates their costs of building new fire stations alone in suburban developments at $15 million a year over the next 20–30 years. It costs roughly $10 million per kilometre to build expressways. Expanding the infrastructure consumes huge quantities of taxpayers' dollars.

- Urban sprawl shifts the focus for spending in an urban area, often leaving older areas to decay. Because the new suburbs are consuming resources quickly, the older parts of the urban area can be short-changed. For example, Arizona estimates that it costs $23 000 to service each new home, but that home contributes only $1700 in property taxes each year. The older, established parts of the city make up the financial shortfall. The tax structure of cities can encourage this core/suburb division, for example, giving little support to public transit but offering incentives for highway construction. The results can be a deterioration in housing stock and roadways in the cores of cities.

- The car-based culture of the suburbs does not encourage a sense of community. Land uses are separated, with strip malls and shopping centres isolated in one area, homes in another, and offices somewhere else.

Travelling between these places protected by a steel-and-glass shell does not encourage a sense of community or emotional attachment to a place.

GEOGRAPHIC METHODS

Satellite Imagery and Urban Sprawl

Science News, March 4, 2000

Researcher Marc. L. Imhoff, from the National Aeronautics Space Administration (NASA)'s Goddard Space Flight Center, used satellite images to identify agricultural areas of the United States that are threatened by urban sprawl. He used military satellite images of nighttime illumination to get a detailed picture of population densities. Imhoff then compared these images to daytime satellite images showing surface greenness, which was used as a measure of plant cover. Finally, the patterns were overlaid on a UN-produced map of the soil's potential to support crops. The data clearly showed how urban development is encroaching on valuable farmland. For example, 16% of California's best soils are already covered by cities and fully 55% of the remaining first-class soils are threatened by nearby expanding cities. Imhoff predicts that these soils will be paved in the coming years if action is not taken to stop urban sprawl.

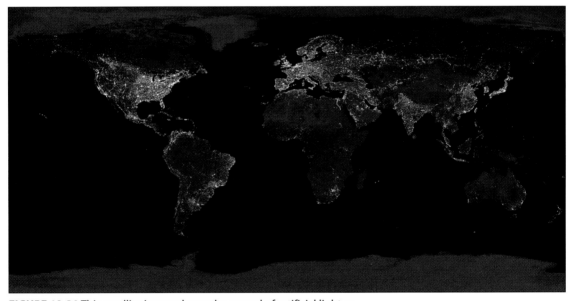

FIGURE 12.21 This satellite image shows the spread of artificial light as urbanization is making real darkness a thing of the past. Light pollution is thought to affect animals and to cause depression and disease in humans.

Smart Growth

One strategy for controlling urban sprawl and creating sustainable cities has been labelled "smart growth." Smart growth aims to limit the outward growth of cities by increasing densities within the existing city. To avoid problems that come with overcrowding in cities, smart growth requires a different view of cities than that of the past. New techniques are designed to create

FIGURE 12.22 Strip malls are a product of suburban living. You need an automobile to do the most basic of activities, like picking up a few groceries or renting a DVD.

Population Change for Detroit, 1990–2000

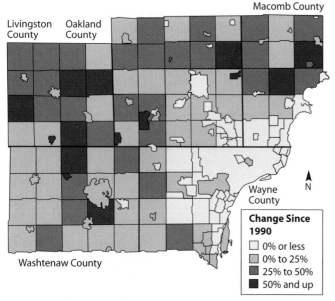

FIGURE 12.23 Since 1950, the population of the city of Detroit has fallen from 1 850 000 to 950 000 people. Yet, by 2030, another 110 000 ha of farmland at the fringes of the city will be urbanized.

more liveable urban places, using things like narrower streets, on-street parking, plenty of trees, open spaces, gathering places, services within walking distance, and clustering of buildings and affordable housing that is spread throughout the community. The results are compact, accessible communities with integrated workplaces, shopping, and community services, where car use is discouraged. Smart growth communities use about one-quarter of the land of typical suburbs, housing the same number of people. Residents of smart growth communities drive only about 50% as many kilometres as suburbanites. Supporters of smart growth argue that this method of designing minimizes ecological damage by limiting the amount of pavement and impervious surface coverage. They also argue that it is much more cost-effective, making resources like fire and police protection and public transit more efficient.

Smart growth requires limiting the outward expansion of cities through some form of development control. A number of cities have designated an urban growth boundary—a line around the city at a distance that will allow growth for a few years but beyond which urban development is prohibited. This gives developers a few years to prepare for the new conditions and the city time to redirect infrastructure development, such as water supplies and energy, to serve higher densities, not greater distances. Portland, Oregon, is one city that has put smart growth into practice. The plan came about because the city involved all citizens in its design in an interactive way. The vast majority of residents had to agree to the important changes in the way the city will grow and how it will impact on their lives. By 2040, the city within the urban growth boundary will house 67% more people than if controls had not been

Smart Growth

FIGURE 12.24 The urban growth boundary requires a strong municipal or regional government to provide efficient services to a population living in relatively high densities.

FIGURE 12.25 An example of "cluster" housing. To allow greater population density in the city of Portland, Oregon, lot sizes were reduced. Before smart growth strategies, there was an average of eight houses per hectare. Now, new developments average 15 houses per hectare.

used. One unforeseen problem that Portland is facing is that the city is such a desirable place to live that population growth has been greater than anticipated!

As you might expect, land and housing developers are not generally in support of urban growth boundaries and other measures to limit the outward growth of cities. Organizations that speak for developers would much rather see free market conditions where consumers can make decisions unhampered by government controls and artificial limits.

The SLAPP Response to Sprawl Control

Developers and some governments opposed to urban growth controls have used SLAPPs—Strategic Lawsuits against Public Participation—as one strategy for undermining those voices calling for controls. The strategy is simple. Multimillion-dollar lawsuits are filed by corporations against individual citizens and groups, claiming that their actions have injured the corporations. Among the actions that have been cited as injurious are writing letters to newspapers, circulating petitions, organizing meetings, picketing or protesting, meeting with politicians, and organizing boycotts. The SLAPP actions are typically without merit and rarely succeed in the courts, but the damage has been done to the opposition. Because they fear being the target of lawsuits that will cost a great deal of money to fend off, others refrain from speaking out on the issues. This strategy was used by a developer in Saanich, British Columbia, in 1999 when local residents opposed a large-scale care facility in their neigbourhood. In ruling on the case, Justice T.M. Singh was of the opinion that the action was "an attempt to stifle the democratic activities of the defendants, the neighbourhood residents" and found the developer's conduct "reprehensible."

Are Cities Sustainable?

As they exist, most cities are not sustainable. Their forms and functions have been shaped by the automobile in developed countries (and will be in developing countries), which produces urban sprawl. Some hope exists, if cities can adopt new ideas like smart growth. Under such plans, the outward growth of cities would be checked, and they would grow in a more compact fashion, with higher population densities. Not everyone agrees with these new directions, including consumers of new homes. Cities will be sustainable only if residents make real efforts to change their attitudes and behaviours, to accept a new form for cities for the future.

excerpt from

"Fact and Fiction on Smart Growth and Urban Sprawl"
Competitive Enterprise Institute (CEI)

…Environmental activists argue that suburban development, pejoratively called "urban sprawl," is destroying the environment. Loss of farmland and open space, they argue, requires a federal "smart growth" program. However, not only is a federal "sprawl" program unwise, but their plans to curb suburban growth will hurt the environment. Consider the claims made by "smart growth advocates," and the facts.

[Environmentalist] claim Smart growth protects the open spaces we enjoy.
[CEI] fact Smart growth provides incentives to destroy the open spaces we actually use—open spaces in urban areas and personal open space (such as yards). In Portland, which proponents of smart growth hail as a model of smart growth, the amount of parkland per 1,000 residents has declined from 21 acres [8.5 ha] to 19 acres [7.7 ha] this decade alone. Smart growth promotes densification, which means that urban open spaces are developed (including parkland), crowding the few parks that remain.

[Environmentalist] claim Suburban development is destroying our beautiful farmland.
[CEI] fact From 1945 to 1992, the amount of cropland remained constant at 24%, according to the U.S. Department of Agriculture. In fact, the federal government spends billions of dollars each year paying farmers to idle their land, suggesting there is a surplus of farmland, not a shortage.

[Environmentalist] claim Increased population density is better for the environment.
[CEI] fact While increased population density may reduce development pressures in rural areas, increased urban density correlates with increased traffic congestion and air pollution. According to the [U.S.] Environmental Protection Agency's own data, smog worsens as densities increase.

[Environmentalist] claim Public transit, especially light rail, is fast, efficient, and will attract enough riders to dramatically reduce traffic congestion.
[CEI] fact Mass transit ridership has been falling for decades and shows no sign of reversing, despite substantial government subsidies. From 1990 to 1995, the number of public transport boardings dropped 5.5 % nationwide. Public transit fails to provide the speed, flexibility, and comfort that today's commuters demand, so they use their cars instead…

Critical Analysis

1. The CEI is a non-profit, industry-supported public policy group dedicated to the principles of free enterprise and limited government. What ideas or evidence in the reading confirms this description?
2. Identify three methods that this reading has employed to counter the claims made by environmentalists.
3. For each of the CEI "fact" statements offered in this reading, suggest how an environmentalist would reply.

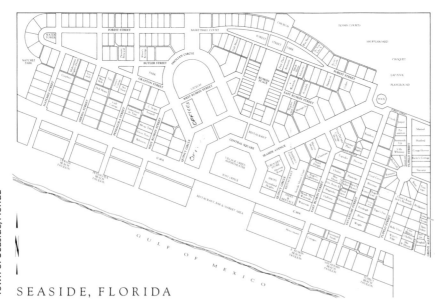

Town of Seaside, Florida

SEASIDE, FLORIDA

FIGURE 12.26 Neo-traditional communities like Seaside, Florida, increase the density of communities without reducing quality of life.

INTERACT

1. Explain why cities are a threat to the environment and global sustainability.
2. Complete an Advantages and Disadvantages chart for the automobile in urban areas.
3. Is smart growth an effective way to make cities sustainable? Evaluate this strategy by producing a PMI (pluses, minuses, and interesting) chart. Use examples in your local area to explain why this is or is not an effective approach.
4. Is your own community a good example of sustainability? Identify three problems or conditions that prevent progress toward becoming a fully sustainable city.
5. Identify bias or logic problems for each environmentalist claim and CEI fact in the reading by the Competitive Enterprise Institute on page 300.
6. Investigate car-free city intiatives. Design a plan to incorporate one or two of the initiatives to reduce car use in your community.
7. Who do you think is responsible for urban sprawl—the developer or the consumer?

WEB LINKS

- Smart Growth British Columbia:
- Worldwatch Institute: <www.worldwatch.org>
- Population Reference Bureau: <www.prb.org>
- Urban Development Institute: <www.udiontario.com>

RELATED ISSUES

- Urban poverty and homelessness
- Rural depopulation
- Pollution control in large urban areas
- Barriers to community participation in urban renewal
- Social or cultural conflicts in large cities

ANALYSE, APPLY, AND INTERACT

1. Compare the process of urbanization in the developed world with urbanization in the developing world. Organize your ideas in a chart.
2. Has urbanization been a positive change for people? Evaluate the changes urbanization has produced by examining its effects on people and environments at the local, national, and global level. Summarize your conclusion in a two-page report entitled "Urbanization: The Challenges" or "Urbanization: The Rewards."
3. What groups of people in a society are likely to support the rapid growth and outward expansion of urban areas? In general, what groups will likely oppose such change?
4. Prepare a collage on one topic that is related to rapid urbanization, such as shantytowns or street children. In your collage, attempt to show how urbanization is connected to the problems associated with that topic and suggest ideas for solutions.
5. Prepare an advertisement that might be used to convince urban dwellers to adopt higher

population densities and less urban sprawl. Explain the images and ideas that you have used in your advertisement.

6. Prepare a case study of one of the world's largest cities. Note particularly its rate of growth, problems that result from growth, and local problem-solving initatives. Include pictures and statistical data in a written report.

7. Explain how local participation in the development process can help to build sustainable communities. Give a local example where this has occurred.

8. Suppose you were asked by your boss, the editor of a local newspaper, to cover a community meeting on the question of urban growth controls. Summarize the arguments that you would expect to hear from people in favour of controls and those opposed to them. Give your own opinions on this topic.

9. Suppose the government of your municipality proposed building a freeway across most of the urban area. Working with four other class-mates, discuss this proposal in a role-play. The roles are:

- a commuter who lives in the city
- a construction worker
- a resident of a quiet neighbourhood near the route of the freeway
- a resident whose land will be expropriated
- a business person
- a resident concerned about human and ecosystem health

Discuss the benefits and costs of such a freeway.

10. Investigate the concept of neo-traditional communities and the work of architects Duany and Playter-Zyberk. What features of their plans conform to smart growth principles?

Chapter 13: Patterns of Poverty

By the end of this chapter, you will:

- analyse the causes and effects of economic disparities around the world;

- analyse selected global trends and evaluate their effects on people and environments at the local, national, and global levels;

- demonstrate an understanding of the interdependence of countries in the global economy;

- select and compare statistical indicators of quality of life for a variety of developed and developing countries in different parts of the world;

- analyse the causes of selected examples of economic disparity in the local or regional community;

- analyse the economic and environmental consequences for selected countries of colonialism in the past and economic colonialism in the present;

- demonstrate an understanding of how quality of life and employment prospects are related to the global economy;

- evaluate factors that may compound problems of hunger and poverty in a selected country.

THE POVERTY EXPERTS

Before making its World Development Report 2000/2001, the World Bank wanted a deeper understanding of the characteristics and causes of poverty and of what can be done to respond to this immense and intractable issue. It conducted a massive global study of 60 000 poor people from remote rural villages to large urban settlements in 60 countries. It listened directly to the voices of the poor—the real experts on poverty. The direct quotes of these people revealed their "resilience, their struggle against hopelessness, their determination to accumulate assets, and their will to live for their families—particularly their children. The stories reveal some of the reasons why poor people remain poor, despite working long hours day after day." The study concluded that effective poverty reduction solutions must involve the real experience, energy, priorities, and recommendations of poor people themselves. It must encourage governments to promote policies that invest in poor people's assets and capabilities, protect their rights in a culture of inequality and exclusion, and address gender inequities and children's vulnerabilities.

Voices of the Poor: From Many Lands

from the World Bank report, 2002

"Someone who is doing well has a house that doesn't leak, bedding, shoes, fishing nets, a plate-drying rack, and drinks tea with milk. Poor people are those who sit on the floor… They go to the garden without eating first; they cook under the sun; they have no pit latrine or bathing area and no plate-drying rack."

Women, Phwetekere, Malawi

"Here there is battering all over the place. Women hit men, men hit women and both hit children."

16-year-old girl, Novo Horizonte, Brazil

"You have to pay the dentist up front, otherwise they just stuff your tooth with sand and it all falls out."

discussion group participant, Russia

"There has never been anyone who represented us in any of the different governments."

woman, Thompson Pen, Jamaica

"Far from defending us, the police mistreat us; they come in and rough up teenagers and don't do anything to the real criminals… The gangs pay them off."

discussion group, Dock Sud, Argentina

"There is enough money to go around the country and make life worth living, but corrupt practices would not allow us to share in the national wealth"

discussion group, Umuoba Road-Aba waterside, Nigeria

"A woman always gets 50 per cent less than a man on the excuse that a woman cannot work as hard as a man."

woman, Nurali Pur, Bangladesh

THE SCOURGE OF POVERTY

Every morning around the world, countless millions of people—women, men, and children—awake to another day of poverty. They emerge from their makeshift homes, often made of plastic bags or cardboard, to spend the day looking for work or scrounging for something to eat. They live on the margins of society, fearing for their personal safety, lacking political influence, living with little access to health care or education. Often they are unable to read or write. In short, they live precarious lives that offer few comforts. They live, perhaps, in the hope that the future for themselves and their children will be brighter than the present.

Even rich countries such as Canada, the United States, and Germany have people who live in poverty. They can be found on the streets of larger cities or in line-ups at food banks. But,

> 66 Poverty anywhere is a threat to prosperity everywhere. 99
> *International Labour Organization*

FIGURE 13.1 Poverty is a condition of life for many people living in Port-au-Prince, Haiti.

while not to minimize their struggles, viewed from a larger perspective, these poor people are the exceptions in their countries. They are minorities in nations where most people have enough money to feed, house, and clothe themselves. This is not the case for large parts of the populations of other countries in the world. Consider these facts about the global patterns of poverty:

- Half of the world's people live on less than US$2 a day
- The number of people living in extreme poverty increased by 200 million between 1995 and 2000

- In 2000, 1.5 billion people lived in extreme poverty
- Poverty is one of the major factors driving 250 million children into the labour force
- The combined wealth of the three richest people in the world is greater than the combined Gross National Product (GNP) of the 48 poorest countries
- The income of the richest 20% of the world's population is 74 times larger than the income of the poorest 20% of the population
- The average family living in Canada is 60 times richer than the average family living in Ethiopia

Poverty in poor countries affects people directly: in the deaths of millions of children due to malnutrition and preventable childhood diseases, through shortened lives because of inadequate medical care, and because of lost opportunities as a result of illiteracy. Many experts view poverty as one of the greatest challenges facing the human population. This chapter will examine the global extent of poverty, the causes of poverty, and the impacts poverty has on societies.

> **FACT FILE**
>
> Nearly a billion people began the twenty-first century unable to read a book or sign their names.

People Living on Less than US$1 a day, 1998 (millions)

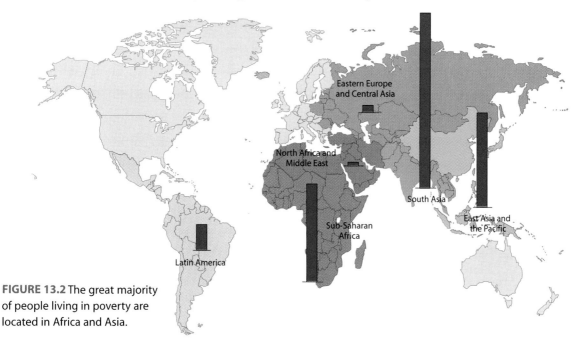

FIGURE 13.2 The great majority of people living in poverty are located in Africa and Asia.

Defining Poverty

Before we can begin to understand the causes and consequences of poverty, we have to agree on a definition of the term. Poverty can be defined in many ways, and the labels that are used are often politically charged. The label "poor" has negative connotations: few people want it applied to themselves. And, identifying people as poor can commit a government to social programs to assist those identified. So governments and agencies use the label with care.

Part of the problem with defining poverty is that there are no internationally accepted definitions. Some definitions are **absolute measures**: you are poor if you lack the money to buy essential goods and services. What goods and services are deemed essential varies by place and over time. For example, is a refrigerator a necessity? In places such as Canada, many people would consider a refrigerator a necessity, but in other countries it would be considered a luxury. Agreeing on what constitutes "necessities" has been a problem. Other definitions of poverty are **relative measures**: you are poor if you have much less than most other people in your society. But, how far below other people is necessary for poverty to exist? Does 50% below the average equal poverty, or should the figure be 40% or 60%? Both approaches require some arbitrary choices, which makes agreeing on a definition of poverty difficult.

In Canada, the federal government uses a relative measure. It sets the poverty line (below which one can be identified as poor) at about half of the income for average families living in the community. Since the amount of money needed to live in large cities is more than in small cities, and larger families need more money to live than smaller families, the poverty line varies by location and family size. Single-parent families headed by women and elderly people make up a high proportion of those living in poverty in Canada. Other countries use different measurements to establish the extent of poverty within their countries.

> " Comparative definitions lead us… into endless difficulties. If poverty means being worse off than somebody else, then all but one of us is poor. "
>
> *Henry Hazlitt,*
> *American economist*

Poverty and Quality of Life

Level of income is an important indicator of poverty for all countries. On a global scale, the World Bank has defined poverty as earning US$1 a day or less, yielding a pattern shown in

"Poverty Lines" in Canada, 1999

Family Size	Population of Community of Residence				
	Fewer than 30 000	30 000– 99 999	100 000– 499 999	More than 500 000	Rural
1	$14 176	$15 235	$15 341	$17 886	$12 361
2	$17 720	$19 044	$19 176	$22 357	$15 450
3	$22 037	$23 683	$23 849	$27 805	$19 216
4	$26 677	$28 669	$28 869	$33 658	$23 260
5	$29 820	$32 047	$32 272	$37 624	$26 002
6	$32 962	$35 425	$35 674	$41 590	$28 743
7+	$36 105	$38 803	$39 076	$45 556	$31 485

The Canadian Council on Social Development

FIGURE 13.3 Campaign 2000, one of Canada's leading coalitions on child poverty, reports that the average poor family in Canada has an annual income of $16 700 compared with an average income of $54 800 for all Canadian families with children.

Populations Below the Poverty Line for Selected Countries, Mid-1990s

Population Below National Poverty Lines (%)			
Country	Rural	Urban	National
Bangladesh	39.8	14.3	35.6
China	4.6	<2.0	4.6
Colombia	31.2	8.0	17.7
Honduras	51.0	57.0	53.0
Morocco	27.2	12.0	19.0
Peru	64.7	40.4	49.0
Philippines	51.2	22.5	40.6
Sri Lanka	38.1	28.4	35.3
Thailand	15.5	10.2	13.1
Tunisia	21.6	8.9	14.1

World Development Report 2000/2001

FIGURE 13.4 Figures given here are for the poverty lines established by the countries themselves. In almost all countries, poverty is greater in rural areas than in cities. This helps to stimulate rural-to-urban migration.

Figure 13.2, **People Living on Less than US$1 a Day, 1998**. But poverty is linked to a host of other variables and these too have been used to determine the extent of poverty in countries. Figure 13.5, **The World Divided by Income Categories**, shows the world pattern, using just incomes, and Figure 13.6, **The World According to the Human Development Index, 2000**, categorizes countries based on their ranking on the UN's Human Development Index (HDI), a broader measure that links income levels, access to education, and life expectancy. On the HDI, some countries with relatively high incomes, such as Saudi Arabia (thirty-ninth in average GNP/capita), score relatively poorly (seventy-eighth on HDI) because the other variables counter high-income figures. Again, these various definitions make international generalizations about poverty difficult.

Consequences of Poverty

In spite of the difficulty of precisely defining poverty levels and rates, we can begin to understand the impacts it has on people's lives.

People who live in poverty suffer on three important dimensions: lack of basic necessities, powerlessness, and vulnerability.

LACK OF BASIC NECESSITIES Basic necessities include food, water, shelter, and clothing, but we can also add minimum levels of health care and education to this list. These are the goods and services that people must have access to in order to live their lives with dignity. People living in poverty cannot satisfy their basic needs because they lack the assets to do so. The assets that they need include:

- human assets (e.g., good health, capacity for labour);
- financial assets (e.g., income, savings);
- social assets (e.g., family connections, business networks);
- physical assets (e.g., access to transportation, building materials);
- natural assets (e.g., ownership of land, safe water).

Access to these assets gives people the tools that they need to acquire the basic necessities, which usually means that they get and hold jobs or that they have land that they can farm. Indigenous people around the world have struggled to regain their most important asset—the land. Having access to the land means that they can generate incomes to acquire assets.

 See Chapter 17 for more information about the indigenous people of Chiapas.

POWERLESSNESS People who live in poverty feel that they do not have power or influence in their society—they do not have a voice. Poor people suffer from harsh treatment and exploitation from the general population because of their condition. They are discriminated against by society and by government agencies within the society. On a day-to-day basis, they must deal with shame, humiliation, and anger. Their condition makes it difficult to support themselves and their families or to acquire things of value, which means that they have difficulty getting

> **❝** So long as every fifth inhabitant of our planet lives in **absolute poverty** [lacking sufficient resources to buy basic necessities], there can be no real stability in the world. **❞**
>
> *Kofi Annan, secretary-general of the United Nations, Nobel Peace Prize Winner, 2001*

The World Divided by Income Categories

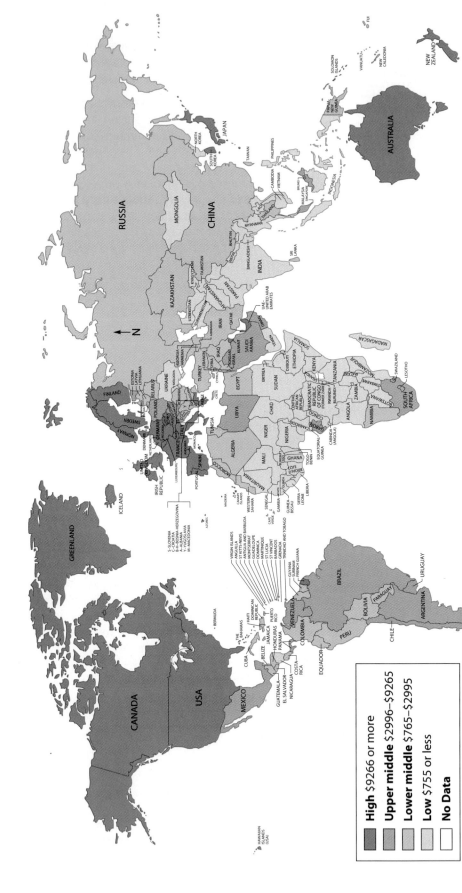

World Development Report 2000/2001

FIGURE 13.5 Organizing the countries of the world into categories of income gives us some insights into patterns of poverty, but does not reveal the desperate conditions of those living in abject poverty.

The World According to the Human Development Index, 2000

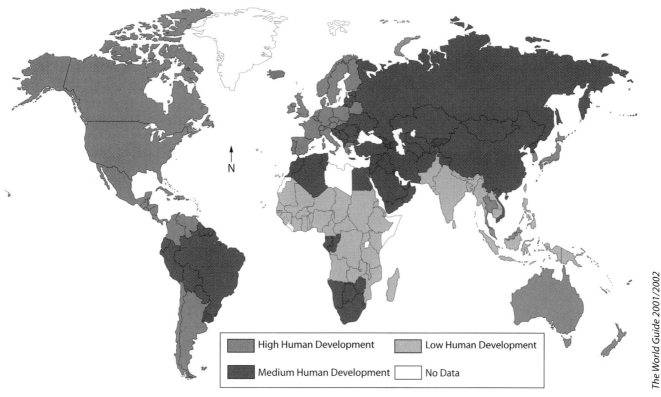

High Human Development
Low Human Development
Medium Human Development
No Data

The World Guide 2001/2002

FIGURE 13.6 For the 2000 ranking, Canada was knocked out of the first place spot it had held throughout the 1990s and was ranked third. This decline was attributed to the effects of funding cuts by various levels of government in the country. Globally, the HDI ranges from a high of 0.939 to a low of 0.258.

Howard White, "Pro-poor growth in a globalized economy," *Journal of International Development, July, 2000* and the UN's *Human Development Report 2001.*

HDI over Time for Selected Countries

Country	1913	1950	2000
Argentina	0.521	0.758	0.842
Chile	0.360	0.620	0.825
France	0.611	0.818	0.924
India	0.055	0.160	0.571
Japan	0.381	0.607	0.928
United Kingdom	0.730	0.844	0.923
United States	0.733	0.866	0.934

FIGURE 13.7 As conditions in countries improve, so does their HDI score.

FIGURE 13.8 The poor everywhere, even in rich cities such as Toronto, Canada, are often ignored, as though they do not exist.

FIGURE 13.9 In conflict situations, the poor suffer disproportionally more than others because they lack the resources to flee the area and often end up as internally displaced people or refugees, such as these people from Afghanistan.

housing and in meeting other basic needs. This pattern perpetuates poverty by ensuring that poor people's children are powerless as well.

VULNERABILITY The poor in a society are vulnerable to shocks and conditions that wealthier people can endure. Because of their situations, poor people:

- have precarious employment and face losing their means of earning incomes;
- are at higher risk of contracting diseases;
- are more likely to be victims of arbitrary arrest and discrimination;
- are more likely to suffer loss from natural disasters such as droughts.

Their poverty means that they lack the resources to reduce the risks of or to deal with the harmful aspects of unforeseen events. Their vulnerability creates a downward spiral of events; for example, the loss of a job means that less food is available so the family's health deteriorates, making holding a job less likely.

Poverty Cycles

As a result of their poverty, conditions of life remain difficult or even deteriorate for the poor because of negative spirals of consequences.

Poverty has demographic consequences. Populations with lower incomes, such as those in sub-Saharan Africa, have higher birth rates. The majority of people in these countries live in rural areas, are largely dependent on agriculture, and have low literacy rates. For them, children are an available labour force and offer hope for security in their senior years. As a consequence, national population growth rates remain high—between 2% and 3% per year—and these countries struggle to make the demographic transition to lower fertility rates. Connected to this rapid population growth are poor rates for other indicators of quality of life, including infant mortality, life expectancy, and literacy. In a real sense, rapid population growth reinforces poverty.

> **"** We can't divorce mass poverty from issues of inequality, social disintegration, the erosion of moral values and environmental decline. These coupled with the more traditionally recognized problems of poor health, hunger, infant mortality, illiteracy, poor housing and the lack of any communal infrastructure are all part of that intricate web which we struggle to untangle. **"**
>
> *Ron Shiffman, director of the Pratt Institute Center for Community and Economic Development*

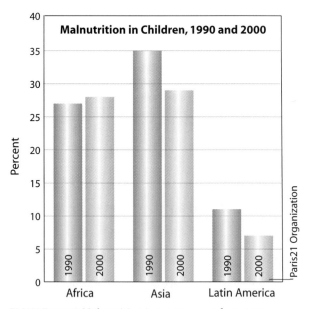

FIGURE 13.10 Malnutrition is a symptom of poverty. While other parts of the world have seen improvements in some aspects of quality of life, poverty and its associated consequences have weighed so heavily on Africa that this continent has actually suffered declines.

Quality of Life Indicators for Selected Countries, Late 1990s

Country	Malnutrition in Children under the Age of 5 (%)	Mortality Rate for Children under the Age of 5 (per 1000 people)	Life Expectancy at Birth (years)	
			Males	Females
Sub-Saharan Africa				
Burkina Faso	33	210	43	45
Kenya	23	124	50	52
South Africa	9	83	61	66
Middle East and North Africa				
Algeria	13	40	69	72
Egypt	12	59	65	68
Syria	13	32	67	72
South Asia				
Myanmar	43	118	58	62
Nepal	57	107	58	58
Sri Lanka	38	18	71	76
East Asia and the Pacific				
China	16	36	68	72
Papua New Guinea	30	76	57	59
Philippines	30	40	67	71
Eastern Europe and Central Asia				
Kazakhstan	8	29	59	70
Mongolia	9	60	65	68
Romania	6	25	66	73
Western Europe				
Germany	<1	6	74	80
Ireland	<1	7	73	79
Portugal	<1	8	72	79
Latin America				
Brazil	6	40	63	71
Guatemala	27	52	61	67
Jamaica	10	24	73	77
North America				
Canada	<1	7	76	82
Mexico	<1	35	69	75
United States	1	—	74	80

World Development Report 2000/2001

FIGURE 13.11 There is a clear connection between poverty and lower quality of life.

See Chapter 10 for more information about population patterns.

" We estimate that tens of thousands more children will die worldwide and some 10 million more people are likely to be living below the poverty line of $1 a day because of the [September 11, 2001] terrorist attacks. This is simply from loss of income. Many, many more people will be thrown into poverty if development strategies are disrupted. "

James D. Wolfensohn, president of the World Bank

 See Chapter 9 for more information about the global food supply.

Widespread poverty has a host of other consequences. The environment is degraded as poor people lack the resources to protect natural systems and are forced to use whatever meager resources they can find. **Desertification** on the fringes of the Sahara Desert, for example, is a direct result of the cutting of trees for fuel wood and the overgrazing of livestock by local people struggling to survive. Social systems remain underdeveloped as governments lack a tax base to finance the building of schools and hospitals. Poverty in India has resulted in high rates of illiteracy where distance and a lack of teachers means many children are unable to attend schools. Governments around the world have

FIGURE 13.12 Poverty is an important factor that leads to the destruction of natural environments. The poor have few other options and destroy the environment to meet basic needs.

not had the resources to combat HIV/AIDS and infection rates are climbing in some of the poorest countries of sub-Saharan Africa. These conditions affect children disproportionately; not only do they suffer the day-to-day conditions of life, but they lose their future as they grow up illiterate and malnourished.

Poverty has serious consequences for both the people who must endure it and the nations where it remains widespread and intractable.

Incomes and Female Literacy and Access to Safe Water Rates for Selected Countries

Country	GDP per Capita, 2000 (US$)	Female Literacy Rate, 1995 (%)	Access to Safe Water, 1990–1997 (average %)
Albania	1 490	76	100
Argentina	10 300	78	63
Bangladesh	1 380	29	95
Bolivia	3 000	78	63
Botswana	3 600	78	90
Cambodia	700	20	30
Canada	22 400	97	100
Chad	1 000	31	24
Costa Rica	6 700	95	96
Egypt	2 850	42	87
Ethiopia	560	31	25
Fiji	6 700	90	77
India	1 720	44	81
Italy	20 800	98	100
Jamaica	3 300	90	86
Myanmar	1 200	80	60
Papua New Guinea	2 400	55	32
South Africa	6 800	84	87
Syria	2 500	58	86
Vietnam	1 770	91	43

FIGURE 13.13 Globally, there are wide inequities in these measures of quality of life.

INTERACT

1. What do you think is a suitable definition for "poverty"? Explain your reasoning.
2. Describe the complex nexus between poverty and other issues. Refer to the quote by Ron Shiffman on page 310 in your answer.
3. How is poverty apparent in your community or region? With a partner, identify several indicators of poverty and develop an explanation for why poverty exists in rich countries such as Canada. Compare your explanations with others in the classroom.
4. Use the information in Figure 13.13, **Incomes and Female Literacy and Access to Safe Water Rates for Selected Countries**, to calculate a rank **correlation coefficient** between incomes and one of the other two variables. Create a table with the headings shown below.
   a) Record the values for the GNP/capita and one of the other two variables in the appropriate columns. Then, rank each of the variables, giving the highest value a "1," the second highest a "2," and so on. Give tied values the same rank, but then skip the next rank. (For example, in access to safe water, three countries show 100%; they would each have a rank of "1," but then the next country in order would receive a rank of "4.") Calculate the difference of ranks by subtracting the rank for variable 2 from the rank for GNP/capita. Record the differences in the second last column. Square the differences of the ranks and record the squared value in the last column.
   b) Add up the differences squared and record this total as "$\Sigma d^2 = .$"
   c) Calculate the Rank Correlation Coefficient using the following formula:
   $$1 - \frac{6(\Sigma d^2)}{n(n^2-1)}$$
   where n = the number of countries in the analysis (n = 20).
   d) This formula yields a correlation coefficient between +1.0 and –1.0. If the sign is positive, this indicates that the variables are rising or falling together; if the sign is negative, one variable is rising while the other is falling. A coefficient around zero suggests that there is no relationship between the two variables. A coefficient close to +1.0 or –1.0 suggests a strong relationship between the two variables. Describe the relationship of the two variables you used in your analysis.

Country	GNP/capita	Rank GNP/capita	Variable 2	Rank Variable 2	Difference of Ranks	Differences Squared

CAUSES OF POVERTY

Trying to identify the causes of poverty is very difficult; whatever conclusion you give may be questioned by others. Explanations for poverty are very much tied to one's understanding of the political and economic relationships among groups and individuals in an economy. Someone from a social democratic or "left-wing" position will likely argue that people are poor because they have been exploited by those with power. From this perspective, poverty is a result of the unequal relationships among groups in a society and an unequal sharing of resources. Someone in a "right-wing" position would likely suggest that people are poor because they lack the skills, knowledge, or motivation to succeed. From this perspective, poverty is a result of the personal failure of people to take advantage of any resources that are available to them. There are many middle positions from these two extremes, and a variety of other perspectives as well.

 See Chapter 3 for more information about the political spectrum.

Nevertheless, because it is important to understand the reasons why poverty exists before we can begin to look for solutions, we will attempt here to offer explanations that have some general acceptance in our society. In general, poverty can be explained as a result of the colonial experience of countries and the crushing burden of national debt.

Imperial Powers and the Colonial Experience

Most of the developing countries of the world were, for a time, colonies of European imperial powers. The process of colonizing the world began in earnest in the final years of the 1400s with the exploration of the New World and the subsequent race by European powers to plant their flags all around the world. For the next several centuries, most of the surface of Earth was controlled by a handful of imperialist countries that sought to control the economic, political, and social affairs of the rest of the world. Following a ludicrous line of reasoning that was justified as "the white man's burden," these countries imposed their values on a great variety of peoples and cultures. From the perspective of the twenty-first century, these forms of cultural imperialism were thinly veiled disguises for the economic imperialism that was taking place. The economies of most of the regions of the world were transformed to provide the European powers with inexpensive natural resources and convenient markets for manufactured products. So, while the European countries expanded their economies by exploiting their colonies, most of the rest of the world was stripped of its resources. Perhaps nothing so vividly demonstrates the relationship between the imperial powers and the rest of the world as the slave trade between Africa and the New World, a trade that provided the European-owned mines, sugar mills, and cotton plantations of the New World with cheap labour at the expense of an entire continent. The effects of the colonial experience are continuing to this day and help to maintain conditions of poverty for most developing countries.

The most important result of imperialism was the unequal distribution of resources. European companies, and those local people closely aligned to European power, took control of land, transportation resources, banks, communication services, education, and

FIGURE 13.14 The imperial powers exerted control over much of the world largely because they had the military strength to impose their rule.

The Impacts of European Imperialism on Former Colonies

Cause →	Effect →	Consequence
European economic self-interest	Focus on resource extraction; no manufacturing established in colonies	Weak, immature economies based on unstable prices
European desire for cultural domination	Loss of native languages, cultural identities, and social hierarchies	Cultural conflict as ethnic and religious groups seek to establish identities and relationships
Political domination to maintain control of the population	Local, traditional power structures destroyed and replaced with subservient leaders; control of affairs by European powers	Loss of traditions and institutions for decision making and conflict management

FIGURE 13.15 The legacy of European colonialism is political instability, cultural conflict, and poverty.

political infrastructures. They consolidated their power and manipulated their systems to keep out others, perpetuating their power arrangements. In Latin America, the Spanish and Portuguese conquerors took over the land and forced the indigenous people into servitude. In 1950, 1.5% of the population—those descended from European conquerors—owned 65% of the farmland. The land was worked by penniless *peons* whose land was taken over. Since the rich elite generally is unwilling to give up their position and power, these disparities are only overcome through revolution. The socialist Sandinista revolution in Nicaragua in the 1980s and the continuing overthrow of European landowners in Zimbabwe in 2002 demonstrate the resentment that local populations have for colonial remnants.

The focus on extracting natural resources from colonies meant that the economies of these places were set up only for this purpose. In many countries in Africa, for example, railway lines ran from mining or forestry centres to ports, bypassing more populated areas that could have benefited from the facilities. There was no attempt to establish manufacturing or other types of economic activity. After independence, these countries had few economic options and were forced to finance their development activities through sales of natural resources, such as minerals, forest products, or agricultural goods such as coffee or sugar. They increased output

only to find that prices dropped as a result of oversupply on world markets as other countries did the same. More recent efforts to diversify economies into manufacturing and services have had limited success because of the lack of investment capital among the poor population and continued exploitation of their resources by foreign companies.

The colonial experience had other impacts. In spite of democratic traditions in the imperial powers, democracy was not offered to the colonies. They were ruled from Europe and had

FIGURE 13.16 The poverty of the population means that there is little money for investment in businesses, perpetuating the poverty.

no real political expression of their own. Independence, when it was taken by force or given by imperial powers looking to discard unwanted obligations, brought with it the need to establish effective political decision making. For many developing countries, the lack of democratic traditions and institutions has resulted in political instability, widespread corruption, and ineffective administrations. Nigeria, for example, since independence, has experienced a series of weak elected governments that have been ousted by tyrannical military dictatorships, resulting in poor economic and social progress. Weak, ineffective governments have allowed other types of organizations to hold and enforce political power over others, including religious groups, large corporations, and non-governmental organizations (NGOs).

COUNTERPOINT Some people suggest that the colonial experience is a convenient scapegoat on which the developing countries blame their misfortunes. These analysts argue that most former colonies have been running their own affairs long enough that colonial conditions can no longer be seen as the source of problems. Most African countries, for example, achieved their independence in the 1960s, and several generations have grown up under home rule. As well, these voices argue that those colonies that were most affected by European influences—Morocco and South

Africa to name two—have been most successful. The European-influenced education systems, political structures, and economies have allowed these now independent countries to more easily connect their economies to global systems.

 See Chapter 3 for more information about democracy in Africa.

Foreign Debt and Structural Adjustments

In the decades following World War II, many poorer countries sought economic progress by borrowing money to finance development projects. In part, this money was available because of new attitudes to foreign aid that had sprung from the success of the Marshall Plan in Europe. Under the Marshall Plan, help was given to war-torn European countries so that they could rebuild and strengthen their economies. The richer countries such as the United States recognized the value of a prosperous Europe that could afford to buy American exports. World leaders supported the practice of extending foreign aid to poorer countries around the world. Often the aid was given in the form of loans or in loan guarantees to lending agencies.

By the mid-1970s, another source of borrowing for developing countries was banks stuffed with money earned from oil exports. From 1973 to 1976, the Organization of Petroleum Exporting Countries (OPEC) raised the price of a barrel of oil from $3 to $30, a move that pushed the world into a severe recession. OPEC members deposited this unexpected wealth in large, international banks. With few corporations wanting to borrow money because of the recession, the banks had to look elsewhere for borrowers. The developing countries were eager to borrow investment capital for projects such as hydro-electric dams, railways, and port facilities. For example, in 1982, Brazil and Paraguay jointly began construction of the Itaipú Dam, the world's largest hydro-electric project. Some of the borrowed money, unfortunately, went into less fiscally sound projects, such as elaborate government buildings, sophisticated military equipment, and unnecessary beautification

FIGURE 13.17 President Yoweri Museveni of Uganda. This regime took power in January 1986 following a military coup.

Top Nations for Foreign Debt, 1998

Country	Total Foreign Debt (US$ millions)	Debt Service as a Percent of Exports	Foreign Debt Per Capita (US$)
Brazil	232 004	74.1	1 399
Russia	183 601	12.1	1 245
Mexico	159 959	20.8	1 669
China	154 599	8.6	815
Indonesia	150 875	33.0	731
Argentina	144 050	58.2	3 988
South Korea	139 097	12.9	5 958
Turkey	102 074	21.2	1 583
India	98 232	20.6	100
Thailand	86 172	19.2	1 429
Philippines	47 817	11.8	656
Poland	47 708	9.7	1 232
Malaysia	44 773	8.7	2 091
Venezuela	37 003	27.4	1 592
Chile	36 302	22.3	2 449
Colombia	33 263	30.7	815
Peru	32 397	28.3	1 306
Pakistan	32 229	23.6	218
Egypt	31 964	9.5	484
Algeria	30 665	42.0	1 019
Nigeria	30 315	11.2	285
Hungary	28 580	27.3	2 825
Czech Republic	25 301	15.2	2 461

The World Guide 2001/2002

FIGURE 13.18 Highlight those countries with over US$25 billion in foreign debt on a map and describe in words the pattern that you find.

works. In a number of cases, borrowed money simply lined the pockets of the countries' elite.

By the end of the 1980s, the developing countries began to realize the extent of their debt situations. High interest rates combined with a weak global economy meant that the countries' economic growth was far short of predictions. They had to borrow simply to make payments on the debts already taken. The situation became a crisis in 1982 when Brazil halted repayments on its $100 billion debt for several months. At this point, the lending agencies recognized their vulnerability: if large and relatively powerful Brazil could not pay its debts, there was little hope that the host of smaller, weaker countries could pay theirs. The threat of loan defaults sent shock waves throughout the financial community. Loans immediately became much harder to get, putting developing countries into financial straitjackets. They were still obligated to pay off their existing loans but could not borrow to pay operating expenses. Efforts to find the money to make payments—such as drastically reducing public expenditures by cutting civil work forces, closing facilities such as hospitals and schools, and not making pension payments—caused turmoil and the dissatisfaction threatened to bring down governments. Faced with a collapse of huge proportions, the lending community rescheduled many of the loans, spreading repayment over longer periods of time. Since then, most developing countries have repaid much more in interest alone than the original value of the loans.

> **FACT FILE**
>
> The developing world spends $13 on debt repayment for every $1 it receives in assistance.

A Helping Hand?

Two agencies that have a role in helping developing countries deal with their financial crises are the World Bank and the International Monetary Fund (IMF). The World Bank gives loans for long-term development projects that will make countries more economically viable. For example, the World Bank has provided over $30 billion in loans and credits for education in 82 countries since 1963 and has committed $1.3 billion per year in lending for health, nutrition, and population projects in developing countries. World Bank interest rates on loans vary according to global lending rates, duration of loans, and the financial conditions of the country.

The IMF provides short-term help for countries that are experiencing balance-of-payments problems. In effect, these countries are spending more money on loan repayments and imports than they are receiving from exports and loans. In the short term, this is not necessarily a problem if the countries' international reserve funds are healthy. Over the long term, however, deficit balance of payments can bring on financial crises where countries cannot meet their obligations and must borrow from the IMF. Money borrowed from the IMF must be paid back within months. The poorest countries pay little interest on IMF loans, but other countries must pay the going rates on borrowing plus a surcharge of 4%, which is designed to discourage excessive use of the IMF.

Both the World Bank and the IMF demand that the borrowers change their operating procedures to make sure that funds are available to pay off the loans. These prescribed **structural adjustments** are designed to cut the governments' social expenditures by eliminating such things as food subsidies, welfare payments, housing programs, and unemployment assistance. Structural adjustment policies also are designed to make business environments more competitive through such actions as removing minimum wage requirements, lowering safety and environmental standards, and encouraging foreign investment. These are changes that are also encouraged by the World Trade Organization (WTO) to strengthen globalization. In many countries, the imposition of structural adjustment policies has produced soaring unemployment and rising prices for basic items such as food and housing. The poor, then, are trapped between the removal of supports by governments and deteriorating living and working conditions. In essence, repayment of debts leads to a downward spiral of poverty and suffering.

Some people claim the demands for structural adjustment by the IMF and World Bank are immoral. Because of the cancellation of social programs, many people, particularly chil-

> **FACT FILE**
>
> Globally, seven million children die each year as a direct result of foreign debt repayment.

> **FACT FILE**
>
> The poorer the country, the more likely it is that debt repayments are being extracted from people who neither took out the loan nor benefited from it.

dren, face deeper, more devastating poverty. Their already limited access to education and health care is eroded and the elimination of food subsidies means that hunger and malnutrition become more widespread. The policies are seen as condemning whole generations of citizens to lives of poor health and missed opportunities. Opposition to the IMF and World Bank policies prompted many critics to protest at key meetings such as the WTO meeting in Seattle, Washington, in 1999 and the Summit of the Americas conference in Quebec City in 2001.

New Internationalist, October 2000, p. 8

FIGURE 13.19 Many people have criticized organizations such as the World Bank, the IMF, and the WTO for putting economic development above the suffering of the poor.

Commentary

"UN report finds improvements in external debt situation of poor countries"
UN News on Africa
September 28, 2000

Developing countries have improved their external debt situation, but more must be done to help them meet payments, according to a report by Secretary-General Kofi Annan. ...

"The year 2000 has seen some improvements in the external debt indicators of developing countries and transition economies," the report states. "With the total stock of debt virtually unchanged in nominal terms, and gross national products (GNP) growth rates exceeding 5 per cent in both developed and transition economies, debt to GNP ratios improved in all regions, and provisional figures for debt to exports ratios even show larger improvements."

At the same time, Mr. Annan cautions that "these improvements should be interpreted with care," pointing out that different countries experienced different levels of growth and export earnings. The cost of servicing debt "continues to represent a heavy burden for many developing countries," while last year, arrears on interest payments rose in Latin America and East Asia.

Drawing policy conclusions in response to these conditions, the Secretary-General calls for improving the initiative for Heavily Indebted Poor Countries (HIPC), which aims to

facilitate relief for those States. "Evidence is increasingly suggesting that the debt sustainability exercises undertaken in the context of HIPC have been overly optimistic regarding the estimation of the level of indebtedness that countries would be able to sustain after receiving debt relief," the Secretary-General observes, stressing the importance of making an independent assessment of debt sustainability.

The report also calls for increased official development assistance (ODA) to help poor States. "This requires ODA to be raised in accordance with the needs of recipient countries," Mr. Annan writes, calling on donors to provide fresh funds to HIPC States without reducing overall levels of multilateral financing.

Critical Analysis
1. What conditions have led to the claim that the debt situation is improving?
2. Do you agree that these changing conditions represent a real improvement in the foreign debt situation?
3. What does the fact that "arrears on interest payments rose" mean for the debt situation?
4. This article quotes UN Secretary-General Kofi Annan. From the comments, would you think that he is optimistic or pessimistic about the debt situation? Explain your answer.

Improving the Debt Crisis

It is clear that foreign debt and the burdens of debt repayment have yielded poverty and human suffering. There is a rising chorus of voices from religious organizations and NGOs calling for debt relief, through lenders forgiving loans or reducing interest rates. On the whole, little debt relief has happened, as banks argue that such a strategy is not fair to their shareholders. Some suggest that rich national governments should buy the loans from private banks, and then forgive them, but, generally, governments have not been quick to take up this suggestion, pointing to concerns about fiscal responsibility. The Government of Canada has provided some debt relief. Most of the CDN$1.2 billion foreign debt owed to the government is held by the Export Development Corporation (EDC). When the government of Canada chooses to offer debt relief, it pays off the loan held by the EDC, so the money remains in Canada.

" Debt relief is often resisted on grounds… that it rewards the reckless and penalizes the prudent. But were not the lenders often just as reckless and irresponsible as the borrowers? Can it really be moral for them to insist on full interest and full repayment if the result is that children, not yet born when the debts were contracted, are denied even a subsistence diet or an elementary education? "

Kofi Annan, secretary-general of the United Nations

An important action on foreign debt came from the United States in 1989. In that year, the U.S. Treasury Department, under Nicholas Brady, developed a new strategy for dealing with foreign debt that became known as the Brady Plan. In situations where both the debtors and commercial lenders agree, loans can be bought out or exchanged by the Treasury Department. The debtor countries have to agree to make substantial economic reforms aimed at improving the vitality of the countries. The lenders lose some of the value of the loans, but get credit "enhancements" through the Treasury Department. By 1999, a total of 16 countries had used this strategy, resulting in over $150 billion in debt reduction. However, in spite of this and other modest efforts at debt relief, foreign debts are likely to remain a significant cause of poverty for years to come.

FACT FILE

Jubilee 2000 is the broad-based initiative promoted by churches, service groups, and NGOs to convince lenders to forgive foreign debts on compassionate grounds.

MAKE A DIFFERENCE

One innovative strategy for helping countries deal with their foreign debt problem involves trading debts for land protected from development. Non-profit organizations in the richer countries of the world raise money that is used to buy the debt of developing countries from the lenders. The organizations then forgive the debt in exchange for the developing countries allocating the equivalent in domestic currency for protecting sensitive environments, mostly rain forests, from disruption. In this way, the countries have less debt and the environmental organizations like the World Wildlife Fund (WWF) have preserved key ecological regions. You can contribute by donating to an NGO. To contact organizations working in this area, go to <www.oneworld.net/> and click on their debt button.

Illegitimate African Debt

The NGO, Africa Action, calls for the outright cancellation of debt deemed to be illegitimate. Debts are considered illegitimate if:

- they were contracted by dictatorships or repressive regimes;
- the funds were stolen by corrupt leaders or senior officials;
- they were contracted and used for improperly designed projects and programs (responsibility rests with the creditors who loaned the money);
- the debts were swelled by high interest rates and other conditions imposed by the lenders;
- repaying the debts would impoverish a country's people; or
- the debts are owed by a poor country to a rich country.

This attempt to identify illegitimate debt recognizes that the lenders are also responsible for the foreign debts of developing countries.

Who Are the Working Poor?

A lack of jobs is one cause of poverty in both the developed and developing worlds, but there is a growing number of people who work at jobs that do not provide a living wage. These people are the working poor. They are victims of changing economic conditions, rapid techno- logical change, deterioration in the quality of jobs, and changes in government policies. In developed countries, including Canada, there is a clear shift in employment patterns away from full-time work with secure tenure to less secure employment in a global, **just-in-time** economy. While there is growth in well-paid, highly skilled jobs in areas such as computer applications and financial services, the majority of jobs created are seasonal or part-time and unstable, paying low wages and providing few benefits.

In Canada, a job no longer provides a living wage for many thousands of fami- lies with children. In 2002, more than 52% of Canadian workers earned less than $15 an hour and more than 37% of working single mothers earned less than $10 an hour. Forty-five percent of adult workers between the ages of 25 and 59 were employed in part-time, contract, or full- time non-tenured work. Social factors such as gender and family structure play a role as women have higher poverty rates than men and families headed by single women are more likely to be poor. In 2000, more than 60% of Canadian families headed by single-parent women were poor compared with about 12% of two-parent families. Child poverty remains a serious problem in Canada, with 21% of chil- dren living in low-income families.

Competition created by globalization has created a downward pressure on wages, encour- aging businesses to downsize the number of workers and replace them with lower cost part- time workers and mechanization and to relo- cate to places where the cost of labour is lower. Many people are unable to climb out of poverty because of disabilities, age, or lack of skills, and because they lack access to affordable housing, child care, work clothing, or transportation. In addition, government income redistribution programs do not provide enough benefits to lift recipients above the poverty line and monetary policies affect levels of employment in the country. Some developed countries have social programs, known as the social safety net, that provide free or subsidized services such as basic health care, day care, and education. However, social programs are not sufficient to eliminate poverty. Many governments have attempted to reduce spending by encouraging or forcing unemployed people to leave social assistance programs and to find work. Many studies have shown that, unless work is reason- ably paid and secure, the welfare-dependent poor may merely become the working poor. There is clearly a strong need for more effective government programs and community-based poverty reduction initiatives.

> ❝ Behind the veil of the official story, which speaks of sustained economic growth and a job creation boom, lies a deeper reality of a crisis within the Canadian labour market. This is a crisis of sustaining employment, a crisis centred around the deterioration in the quality of the job stock both in terms of employment security and income sufficiency. ... Yet governments continue to defend their economic records largely on the basis of job creation figures without taking into account the quality of employment generated. Consequently, there is a need for innovative and alternative ways of approaching the question of sustained employment. ❞
>
> Mike Burke and John Shields, *The Job-Poor Recovery: Social Cohesion and the Canadian Labour Market,* Ryerson Social Reporting Network, Ryerson University, Toronto, 2002

Poverty and Aboriginal Peoples

Aboriginal peoples make up a disproportion- ately large share of the world's poor people. From northern Canada, to the plains of the United States, to the Amazon rain forest, to the tropical forests of central Africa, and to the interior highlands of India, Aboriginal peoples share a common characteris- tic—enduring poverty. The statistics show a clear pattern of suffering and alienation because of poverty:

FACT FILE

In Canada, 43.4% of Aboriginal peoples were poor in 1995, significantly higher than for the Canadian population.

- Indigenous women in the Peruvian Amazon are dying from lack of access to medical facilities, prescription drugs, and health care equipment.

- Nearly one-third of Aboriginal men in Australia are arrested over a five-year period and are significantly over-represented in crime statistics.
- The Bagyeli Pygmies of Cameroon have had their forest invaded by construction workers building a huge oil pipeline and have not been compensated for the loss of their economic and cultural heritage.

FIGURE 13.20 Poverty is widespread among Aboriginal peoples, such as these Innu people sitting in the living room of their house in Davis Inlet, Newfoundland. Many of the homes in the remote Innu community have no running water or toilets.

- The Innu of Davis Inlet in Labrador have lived for decades in a squalid village of two-room shacks and outhouses.
- Violence against the Truká Indians in the state of Pernambuco, Brazil, has been increasing in recent years as settlers have pushed onto traditional lands.
- Overcrowding of reservations for Indians in the state of Mato Grosso do Sul, Brazil, has reached a critical state. The reservations were fixed in size in 1915 while the population has grown rapidly.

Aboriginal peoples have been dispossessed of the land that supported them but have not been accepted in the societies around them. Consequently, they face futures of ongoing poverty and suffering.

FACT FILE

A recent UN report on Canada expressed serious concern that this country has made little or no progress toward the alleviation of social and economic deprivation among Aboriginal peoples. The report specifically referred to shortages of housing, endemic unemployment, high rates of suicide, and the lack of safe and adequate drinking water.

INTERACT

1. Write a paragraph in which you summarize the causal relationship between the colonial experiences of developing countries and poverty.
2. In what ways has foreign debt produced poverty in developing countries?
3. Create a flow diagram to show how foreign debt leads to enduring poverty in countries around the world.
4. Consider the quote on page 320 by Kofi Annan. Do you think that the lending agencies should bear some of the blame for the debt crisis? Explain your point of view.
5. How should the government of a country respond to the problem of the working poor? Explain your ideas, giving examples where appropriate.
6. Identify several demographic factors that are linked to poverty and several barriers to reducing poverty.
7. Explain why traditional statistics such as unemployment rates and GDP do not provide an accurate picture of the well-being of Canadian society.

CASE STUDY

Poverty in Nigeria

Nigeria illustrates the causes and consequences of poverty in a vivid way. The majority of its citizens are poorer today than they were when the country achieved independence from Britain in 1960. This, in spite of the fact that Nigeria is the largest country in West Africa, has a relatively literate population, and is one of the world's largest oil exporters. Nigeria is a country driven to poverty by its colonial roots, its inflated foreign debt, and the structural adjustment policies that repaying that debt has generated.

The Effects of Colonialism

The map of Nigeria is an artificial creation of colonialism. The boundaries of the former colony were drawn by British politicians and government offi-cials with no regard for the ethnic organization of the people in the area. They were mostly interested in exploiting the tin, forest, and agricultural resources of the colony. Nigeria contains 300 different ethnic groups with the Hausa-Fulani, Yoruba, and Igbo making up about 71% of the population. Many of these groups have historic animosities and deeply held suspicions of others. These differences are compounded by more recent religious conversions from traditional African beliefs. The majority of people in the northern parts of the country have adopted Islam, while Christianity is strong in the southeast and southwest. These differences have produced a very fragmented society that has few things to unite groups into a functioning state. There is no common African language: English is the country's official language.

 See Chapter 17 for more information about tribal Africa.

Ethnic differences resulted in a devastating civil war from 1967 to 1970. The southern Igbo-controlled region of Biafra objected to the control of the country by northerners. It seemed to them that the government of Nigeria was determined to isolate them politically and economically from

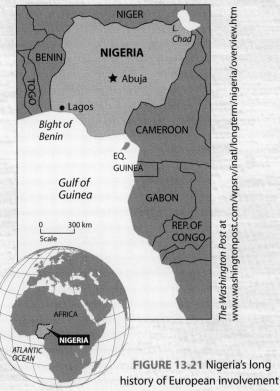

The Washington Post at www.washingtonpost.com/wpsrv/inatl/longterm/nigeria/overview.htm

FIGURE 13.21 Nigeria's long history of European involvement began in the sixteenth century largely because of its accessible location on the Atlantic Ocean.

Facts about Nigeria

Population (1999)	108 945 000
Annual Growth Rate	2.8%
Children Per Woman	5.1
Urban Population	41.3%
Literacy	57%
Access to Safe Water	49%
GNP Per Capita	$300
Development Aid Received (1997)	$202 million
HDI Rank	146

The World Guide 2001/2002

FIGURE 13.22 By 2015, Nigeria's population will total 153 million people.

the rest of the country because of ethnic differences. Biafra unilaterally seceded. A bitter war of attrition followed. In January 1970, the better-equipped federal forces finally overcame the rebels. Over a million lives had been lost.

Colonialism created a very uncertain political situation for Nigeria. In its first 40 years of independence, the country lived through six coups and a presidential assassination. There were only 10 years when democratically elected governments ruled the country. Each democratic government was overthrown by the military to "rescue" the country from corrupt civilian rule. In May 1999, Olusegun Obasanjo, a freely elected president, took over leadership of Nigeria. However, within the first year of his presidency, the country witnessed considerable conflict, with thousands of lives lost over issues such as the imposition of Islamic law, demands for autonomy by ethnic Yoruba militants, and conflicts over control of oil-rich territories. These issues, combined with concerns over the nation's dilapidated infrastructure and widespread corruption, are critical challenges for the elected government. In spite of the problems, Nigerians are optimistic about Obasanjo's government. They see it as an opportunity to throw off the bonds of oppression, this time not the oppression of British colonialism, but the internal colonialism of military dictatorships.

As a result of the political instability in Nigeria, political corruption, and the country's need to generate foreign currency through the sale of oil, the Niger Delta has been plundered by oil companies, principally Shell Oil. Shell took control of the area with the support of corrupt leaders immediately following the Biafran civil war. Much of the revenue has been diverted to foreign bank accounts or spent on luxury goods.

FIGURE 13.23 General Abacha ruled Nigeria from 1993 to 1998. Military dictatorships have controlled Nigeria for much of its period of independence.

The local communities most affected by this development have seen little of the income. When the people of the Niger Delta began to protest this exploitation of their homeland, they were brutally silenced by the Nigerian army and the oil company's own armed forces. In one instance, over 80 villagers were massacred during a peaceful demonstration in the village of Umuechem in 1990. Poverty is now a fact of life in the area. The natural environment of the delta has been destroyed by the exploration, drilling, and pipeline building.

Nigeria's Foreign Debt

Nigeria has a foreign debt of US$30.3 billion—roughly equal to its annual economic output. This debt was built up over the years as the various military dictatorships spent lavishly on maintaining strong forces, in part to stifle public discontent with their heavy-handed rule. Another portion was spent on government megaprojects and imports of consumer goods. Billions of dollars of the loans were stolen during the Abacha dictatorship by corrupt government officials and were deposited in banks in London, UK. Other loans were incurred to develop the oil and gas infrastructure, so that the nation could continue to sell energy, primarily to the United States. By mid-1985, fully 44% of Nigeria's export earnings were needed to pay the interest on the debts. The current Nigerian government must now repay more than $3 billion per year.

The foreign debt means that Nigeria has no state-supported social assistance system. One-third of Nigerians lack access to basic health care, in large part because most treatment centres are located in cities. Facilities are understaffed, under-equipped, and have few medical supplies. Patients often have to buy their own supplies and medications. The result has been an infant mortality rate of 112 per 1000 live births and a life expectancy of 50 years.

Due to government underfunding, rising school fees, the deterioration of buildings, poor instruction, and limited prospects for graduates, only about two-thirds of children attend the compulsory first six years of education. The enrolment rate for secondary schools is 34%.

Nigeria's foreign debt threatens democracy in that country. The democratically elected government needs to create stable political and social

FIGURE 13.24 Poverty in Nigeria remains a fact of life for most people because of the crushing foreign debt.

environments to have any chance of succeeding. Its inability to effectively fund social programs means that large parts of the population will continue to feel resentment and frustration with the government. Experts around the world have argued that alleviation of Nigeria's debt burden is a priority. For any real chance of success, this most populous African country needs to get out from under its mountain of debt and begin to make some real progress on social conditions.

INTERACT

1. Summarize the effects of colonialism and foreign debt in creating poverty in Nigeria.
2. Identify the causes of poverty in Nigeria using an ideas web.
3. If poverty is the key issue in this study, who are the stakeholders and perpetrators? What are the social, economic, and political implications of this situation?
4. What are three actions that the elected government of Nigeria could take to deal with Nigeria's poverty? For each action, explain why you see it as being an appropriate means of improving the situation.
5. Would you personally support some form of debt forgiveness for Nigeria? Explain your answer.
6. Produce a case study of the Ogoni people of Nigeria, analysing the impact of oil development on their well-being.

WEB LINKS

- United Nations:
- Global Issues organization:
- Jubilee 2000:
- *The World Guide*:

RELATED ISSUES

- Poverty and its impact on the environment
- Poverty and war
- Child labour
- The role of transnational corporations (TNCs) in poverty

GIS **Top Nations for Foreign Debt, 1998**

ANALYSE, APPLY, AND INTERACT

1. **a)** Using the World Bank Report, *Voices of the Poor: From Many Lands*, at <www.worldbank.org/poverty/voices/report.htm>, choose one of the 14 Country Case Studies and analyse the causes and effects of poverty in that country. Communicate your findings and compare them with those of others in the class on different countries.

   b) Identify the factors that are creating those problems. Attempt to identify possible solutions for the country. Communicate your findings.

2. Review the different variables that could be used to compare quality of life in different countries using sources like the *CIA World Factbook* or *The World Guide* by New Internationalist. Select five indicators that you think would most effectively allow us to understand the conditions in these countries. Use these statistical indicators of quality of life to compare three countries in different parts of the world. Compare your findings with those of others in the class.

3. Using poverty as your focus, explain how quality of life is related to the global economy.

4. In Canada, the Atlantic region and the North suffer from regional disparities when compared with central Canada and the West. Do the causes of poverty discussed here on a global scale have any application to understanding the poor economic conditions in regions of Canada? Conduct research to answer this question, preparing a 300-word report of your findings.

5. Give three examples to show how economies and environments in some places may be affected by decisions made in other places.

6. Debate this statement with several other members of the class: "People suffer poverty through their own actions or inaction. We are not responsible for solving the poverty of others."

7. Leaders in developing countries have argued that globalization has effectively replaced the imperial colonialism of the past with a new form of economic imperialism, in which the developing countries are still under the control of decision makers in more powerful countries. Do you agree with this line of thinking? Select one developing country and research its economic conditions. For this country, analyse the economic and environmental consequences of colonialism in the past and economic colonialism in the present.

8. Research the Jubilee 2000 actions to reduce foreign indebtedness. Assess their efforts and results.

9. People in poverty have attempted to express their feelings about their conditions. Conduct a search of literature and poetry sources for examples of works that deal with living in poverty. Display your findings, or read them aloud to your classmates.

Chapter 14: Poverty—Closing the Gap?

By the end of this chapter, you will

- analyse selected global trends and evaluate their effects on people and environments at the local, national, and global levels;

- demonstrate an understanding of the interdependence of countries in the global economy;

- describe the structure, membership, and activities of an international economic alliance in Africa or Asia;

- demonstrate an understanding of how economies and environments in some places may be affected by decisions made in other places;

- demonstrate an understanding of how quality of life and employment prospects are related to the global economy;

- evaluate factors that may compound problems of hunger and poverty in a selected country;

- demonstrate an understanding of how the work of the United Nations and other organizations on poverty, disease, and the environment is directly related to your own life;

- demonstrate an understanding of the need to consider social differences when analysing global problems and issues.

POVERTY REDUCTION

In September 2000, the General Assembly reaffirmed the United Nations (UN)'s Millenium Declaration goal for poverty reduction—to cut in half the number of people living on less than $1 a day by 2015. Forecasts indicate just how difficult this goal may be to achieve. One scenario extended each country's performance during the 1990s until 2015. This projection suggested that only 11 countries are on track to meet the target on poverty reduction, while 70 countries will see little improvement, or may even slip further behind. A second, more optimistic forecast that assumes some broad-based improvements in economic growth in the world still predicts that only 29 countries would halve the number of people living in poverty. In this scenario, some 50 countries are not expected to reduce the gap between rich and poor. Both scenarios point to the conclusion that only East Asia as a region is likely to reach poverty reduction goals, and that poverty will get worse in sub-Saharan Africa. These predictions suggest that, without significant changes in strategy, poverty will continue to be a chronic, severe challenge for the world in the foreseeable future.

What can be done to try to improve conditions for people living in poverty? This chapter will address this question and investigate approaches that have some potential to improve the poverty situation in the world.

A great deal of effort has already gone into reducing poverty in the last century, yet many people are still poor in a world of plenty. The World Bank, in its massive 2000 study of 60 countries called *Voices of the Poor*, confirmed that 2.8 billion people live on less than $2 a day. Government policies in most countries have clearly not been effective. Better ways to solve issues of poverty must be found. International institutions and non-governmental organizations (NGOs) are beginning to realize that a paradigm shift is needed. The World Bank report identified some new ways of thinking and concluded that governments should take immediate action to initiate economic and social policies to help poor people make a living in their own communities, whether rural or urban, and to improve their quality of life. The report provided strong evidence that no matter what the issue—forestry, irrigation, roads, credit, sewage, or drinking water— poor people are able partners, make wise decisions, and can protect their assets and investments better than any government agency or externally imposed economic development model.

> 66 Poverty can be reduced only if we build strategies around what we have learned from poor people. ... by urging an empowering approach to development that views poor people as resources, as partners in poverty reduction. 99
>
> *Voices of the Poor,*
> *World Bank Report*

> 66 We believe ... poverty to be intolerable in a world of plenty. And we are all here because we are convinced— indeed we know—that this poverty can be ended in our lifetime, with our own hands, with our own minds. 99
>
> *Kofi Annan,*
> *secretary-general of the UN*

 See Chapter 13 for more information about patterns of poverty.

FIGURE 14.1 New approaches to poverty reduction are being identified by groups such as this NGO village group in Bangledesh. Consultation with civil society in poor communities can provide an opportunity for them to play a role in their social and economic development.

Key Poverty Issues and Ways to Address Them

Issues that Emerged in the *Voices of the Poor* Study	Effects of the Issue	Government Policies Needed to Address the Issue
• The importance of poor people's assets and capabilities needs recognition.	• People often lose property and material goods to natural disasters or war, or sell them to pay debts, feed their families, or provide a marriage dowry. • People need access to credit, information about markets, technology improvements, and their rights. • Economic shocks and policy changes have a strong impact on poor people.	• Collect accurate data to address unique situations of poverty such as people displaced by war in Bosnia, collapsed support for pensioners in Russia, or lower castes in India. • Invest in public assistance programs, education, and skills. • Provide information about people's rights concerning wages, jobs, property, and discrimination. • Develop roads, bridges, and other aspects of infrastructure so people can get their produce or goods to market.
• Government and societal institutions exclude and discriminate against poor people.	• Poor people are often isolated, alienated, and ignored by those who are better off. • Activism of community-based organizations is seen as "making trouble." • Legal and court systems discriminate against the poor. • Police repression, corruption, and lack of accountability in governments and industry are widespread.	• Promote greater micro-business opportunities. • Promote partnerships with the people themselves and with the institutions that they trust in their communities. • Help local groups network, negotiate, and influence policies and events that affect their lives. • Reform police to protect people's safety and rights.
• Women and children are vulnerable to widespread inequities and barriers in households, the workplace, and in public affairs.	• Silence surrounding violence against women is widespread. • Women have a very heavy work burden and earn less than men. • Gender roles are changing in many societies, causing stress and family conflict. • Children cannot afford to stay in school and may be forced into labour in inhumane conditions. • Children and youth are in danger from inadequate supervision, street crime, drugs, and pollution.	• Provide child and youth care and nutrition programs. • Provide scholarships for poor youth and universal access to primary education. • Collect and analyse accurate poverty data by gender, and use this as a base for investment decisions and to tailor strategies to fit the problem. • Encourage micro-credit lending to women. • Provide legal aid. • Remove gender-based barriers. • Enforce laws against discrimination.

FIGURE 14.2

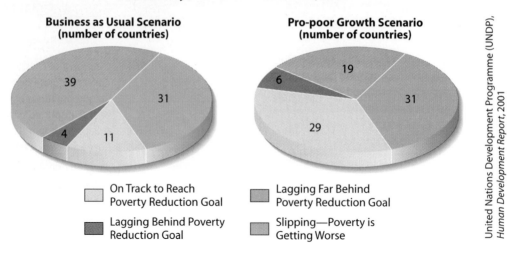

UN Poverty Reduction Predictions, 2001

Business as Usual Scenario (number of countries)

39
31
4
11

Pro-poor Growth Scenario (number of countries)

19
6
31
29

☐ On Track to Reach Poverty Reduction Goal

■ Lagging Behind Poverty Reduction Goal

☐ Lagging Far Behind Poverty Reduction Goal

☐ Slipping—Poverty is Getting Worse

United Nations Development Programme (UNDP), *Human Development Report, 2001*

FIGURE 14.3 Even an optimistic view of poverty reduction suggests that conditions are not likely to improve significantly by 2015 for a large number of countries, most of which are in Africa.

INTERGOVERNMENTAL ORGANIZATIONS AND POVERTY REDUCTION

Intergovernmental organizations are officially recognized bodies within which national governments work together to achieve common goals. The UN is the largest intergovernmental organization dealing with the problem of poverty. The Association for Southeast Asian Nations (ASEAN) is an example of a regional intergovernmental organization that has a role to play.

The UN

The UN has a pivotal role to play in reducing poverty among the nations of the world. The directors see the UN's role as co-ordinating the various players in reducing poverty, and complementing these activities with their own actions and programs. The other parts of the international community that have a role include:

- non-governmental organizations (NGOs) (e.g., the Red Cross);
- regional intergovernmental organizations (e.g., Organization of American States);

- national governments;
- local governments;
- multinational corporations;
- local enterprises and organizations.

Programs such as the UN's Decade for the Eradication of Poverty (1997–2006) are used to raise awareness about the issues and to encourage clear directions among all the stakeholders in the fight against poverty. Where necessary, the UN may take direct action to ensure that improvements are taking place in the poorest countries, such as delivering emergency food aid in times of famine.

The UN views poverty as a multidimensional problem. It is not enough to raise incomes or to ensure that people have enough money to meet their short-term needs. Reducing poverty means treating the problems of inequity that create the poverty in the first place. From the UN's point of view, treating issues of gender equality, improving infant and maternal mortality rates, addressing problems of the urban poor, attacking HIV/AIDS, and promoting sustainable development are actions that must happen before poverty can be eradicated. In fact, the UN has identified three broad strategies to reduce poverty:

- Improve economic development

- Create an equitable distribution of wealth
- Address problems of social development

ECONOMIC DEVELOPMENT One strategy that has been used in an effort to reduce poverty is to accelerate economic growth. But economic growth that is focused on just producing more goods is often harmful to an economy. The growth consumes more natural resources and it usually benefits only the already wealthy because they control resources and capital. Economic development must be widespread and have immediate benefits for the poorest in society. Since most people in the poorest countries are tied to the land, development strategies may work best when they emphasize rural change, such as improving agriculture and encouraging small-scale rural manufacturing and services. National and local governments need to develop and implement policies that provide incentives for farm and non-farm rural businesses, so that incomes are improved for those people who need it most. This would have the added advantage of slowing rural-to-urban migration rates.

Achieving economic development means applying appropriate technologies that do not destroy natural systems. Using the current methods of producing goods and services to meet the needs and wants of all the world's people would require between five and ten times more resources. This is clearly not sustainable.

Many of the UN's strategies include promoting foreign trade. The World Bank estimates that improved international trade could generate an additional $80 billion to $200 billion for developing countries. Achieving this growth, however, requires further integration of the economies of developing countries into the world economy. Many of the promises of freer trade made to developing countries at meetings of the World Trade Organization (WTO) have not been honoured. Tariffs and quotas are lower among wealthy countries than between wealthy and poor countries. For example, textile and clothing industries represent a chance for workers, especially women, to earn independent income and to raise their living standards. Exports of these products contribute to overall economic stability because they add more value to the economy than unprocessed agricultural exports. They also provide managerial jobs.

Canada has imposed very high tariffs on these products from other countries. The average tariff on all goods exported to Canada is 1%, while most of these products are subject to tariffs of more than 15%. Although Canada announced its intent in 2002 to eliminate tariffs and quotas on products from the least-developed countries in Africa, none of the developing countries have so far been exempt from paying the tariffs. Many analysts believe that Canada should follow the lead of countries such as New Zealand, Norway, and The European Union (EU) and get rid of tariffs and quotas completely on products from developing countries. Although exports from poor countries in 2002 represented only 2.5% of total Canadian textile and clothing imports, Canadian industries claim that the poorest countries will not be helped because they lack these industries anyway and Canadian jobs will be threatened.

DISTRIBUTION OF WEALTH Raising the total wealth of a country will do little to reduce poverty if the wealth ends up in the hands of those who are already rich. Governments need to improve the gap between rich and poor as a

FIGURE 14.4 Small-scale technology, including solar energy for village lighting, recharge wells, smokeless biogas cooking units, or this methane gas tank that captures the gas from pig manure and uses it for cooking are more appropriate forms of technology that can help resources such as firewood and water become sustainable and improve the quality of life of poor people in rural areas.

first step in fighting poverty in both developed and developing countries. Policies could redistribute the wealth in a more equitable way, allowing the poor to satisfy their basic needs. This could be accomplished through higher taxes for profitable corporations and wealthy landowners and by ensuring that the poor have access to assets, such as land, education, or capital. Unfortunately, these actions are not likely to be welcomed by those who are already rich. The wealthy often see efforts to improve the income gap as an attack on their position and status; they feel that they are forced to share their wealth for the benefit of others. In addition, current economic thinking has been very critical of strategies such as taxes and public spending, suggesting that it has the effect of reducing economic growth. However, it is clear that the productivity of the poor is improved by giving them greater access to resources, something that can best be accomplished with strong government policies.

SOCIAL DEVELOPMENT Although social conditions tend to improve with economic development, social development must also be targeted for action. Gender inequality is a social condition that limits economic development. Improving literacy and providing access to credit for women has the double advantage of expanding the role of women in the work force and helping to reduce birth rates. When these efforts focus on the urban poor, where population growth rates are staggering, there are real benefits in creating employment, improving quality of life, and protecting the environment.

Addressing the HIV/AIDS epidemic is another important area for social development that can reduce poverty, especially in Africa. The loss of

FIGURE 14.5 An AIDS facility in Mali. The loss of human potential because of HIV/AIDS is a contributing factor to Africa's growing poverty.

adult family members has severe economic consequences for families in developing countries. Children who have lost one or both of their parents to AIDS will likely live in poverty, usually accompanied by malnutrition and illiteracy. Providing preventative education, victim support services, medical facilities, and free access to anti-retroviral drugs will help to reduce infection rates and keep parents with their families, reducing poverty.

 See Chapter 15 for more information about the AIDS pandemic.

The UN at Work

The Economic and Social Council of the UN is largely responsible for action on poverty through its various commissions and organizations. Agencies that have particularly important roles are identified in Figure 14.7, **Key UN Organizations in the Fight against Poverty**.

The UN's primary focus is on encouraging countries to assume responsibility for their own actions against poverty and to mobilize their own resources. In essence, this means encouraging national economic development where wealth is created and distributed throughout the society. However, an interim progress report in 2001 on the success of the Decade for the

> FACT FILE
>
> Seventy percent of the world's poor are women and 80% of the world's refugees are women and children.

66 Generosity has been stagnant for too long, and there are now many parts of the world—especially in sub-Saharan Africa—where the only hope for getting desperately poor people on track to a better future is an infusion of resources. 99

Paul Knox, The Globe and Mail, March 15, 2002

excerpt from

"The Governance Factor"

in *OECD* (Organisation for Economic Co-operation
and Development) *Observer*
by Donald J. Johnston
December 14, 2000

Traditionally, we have always considered poverty to be a lack of means. It is certainly that in part. Without resources, people cannot satisfy even their most basic physiological needs. But a more meaningful definition of poverty is based on deprivation of capability, a concept associated with Nobel prize winner Amartya Sen. ... Capability deprivation means that people are unable to play a full part in society, are economically inactive, marginalized by conflict or discrimination. While they lack income, simply providing more money will not be sufficient to lift them from their deprivation. In any case, being incapacitated inhibits people's abilities to earn a living.

...[T]he poor themselves often allude to the importance of non-material deprivation. They often define their lot in these terms. Not 'lack of money' but lack of empowerment. Resources are important, and a measure of economic dynamism is a prerequisite for making progress against poverty. But while the economic engine may be revving, the transmission may be faulty. And often governance is the missing link.

In today's developing world, the overall lack of resources is commonly not the stumbling block, the use of them is. In countries where progress towards poverty alleviation is slow, public spending intended for basic social services is not put to best use and may not always reach the needy. Sound governance makes the links more solid between resources and needs. If people have a say in the choice of elected decision-makers, can give expression to their views through a free media, and can have fuller access to information about government activities, resources are more likely to be used productively.

Empowering the poor is itself a means of overcoming poverty, because it allows the poor to gain greater control over their lives rather than remaining the hapless recipients of benefits delivered from some far away centre. Take the case of Andhra Pradesh in India. There, village women have organized themselves into self-help groups and with their own resources are increasingly able to respond to the growing needs of the poor for access to credit, information, skills and technology. Similarly, in Cambodia's Seila initiative, local communities are encouraged to formulate their own anti-poverty projects. In Ghana, district authorities are raising their own revenues for poverty reduction projects. In Uganda, the government has made efforts to increase the transparency of its budget procedures, both at the central and at the local government level, and set up a poverty reduction strategy, the Poverty Eradication Plan, with broad participation.

These examples demonstrate that through governance the leaders of the poorest countries have the power to make a direct attack on poverty. By helping to decentralize power and authority, promote **land reform** [change in ownership of the land], encourage community solidarity and the emergence of independent civil society organizations, governments can make a difference.

Critical Analysis

1. Define the following terms or theories: "capability deprivation," "marginalized," "incapacitated," "empowerment," "economic dynamism," "decentralize power." For each, give an example to illustrate the concept.
2. Draw a visual representation to show how capability deprivation leads to poverty.
3. According to the commentary, what are actions that could be taken to deal with capability deprivation?
4. Brainstorm a list of factors that might work against sound governance. Identify the three factors from your list that are likely to be most important. Compare your list with that of a classmate.
5. In your view, are large agencies such as the UN or small, local organizations more likely to result in improvements in poverty? Explain your answer.

Eradication of Poverty pointed to a significant roadblock—few developing countries can attract private investment on a scale large enough to have an impact on poverty.

One UN proposal to deal with the lack of investment leading to poverty reduction calls for the creation of a World Solidarity Fund. This voluntary fund is designed to co-ordinate donations from international organizations, individual countries, institutions and foundations, the private sector, and individuals. The money can then be used to attack the problem of poverty, supplementing those private and public efforts that already exist. Some analysts suggest that the unique nature of this fund may encourage innovative thinking in dealing with the problem. However, reports in 2002 revealed that the UN was having difficulty building the actual resources in the fund verbally committed to by volunteers. The real benefit of the UN's work, in

Principal Organizations of the United Nations

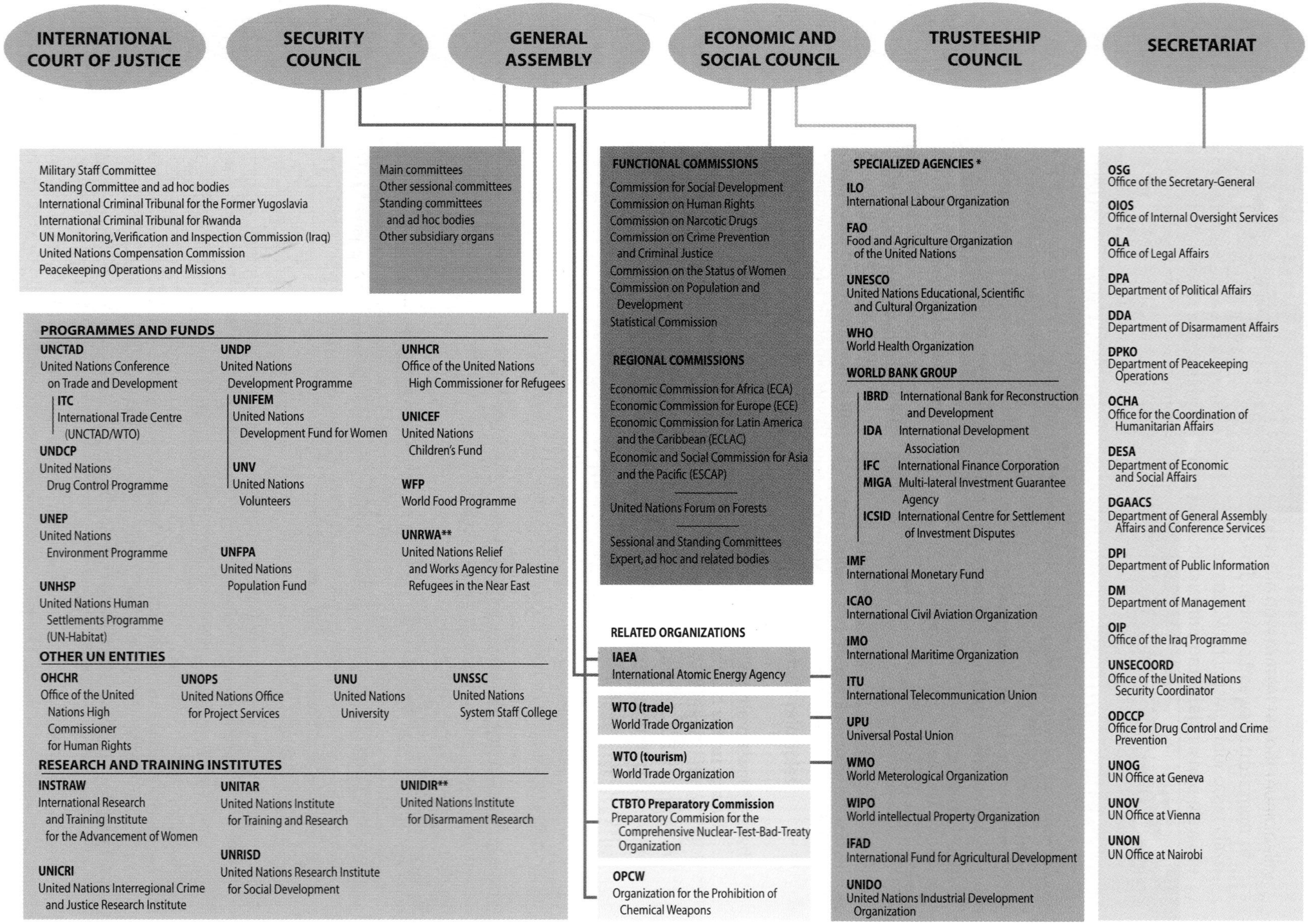

SECRETARIAT

TRUSTEESHIP COUNCIL

ECONOMIC AND SOCIAL COUNCIL

GENERAL ASSEMBLY

SECURITY COUNCIL

INTERNATIONAL COURT OF JUSTICE

SECRETARIAT

OSG Office of the Secretary-General

OIOS Office of Internal Oversight Services

OLA Office of Legal Affairs

DPA Department of Political Affairs

DDA Department of Disarmament Affairs

DPKO Department of Peacekeeping Operations

OCHA Office for the Coordination of Humanitarian Affairs

DESA Department of Economic and Social Affairs

DGAACS Department of General Assembly Affairs and Conference Services

DPI Department of Public Information

DM Department of Management

OIP Office of the Iraq Programme

UNSECOORD Office of the United Nations Security Coordinator

ODCCP Office for Drug Control and Crime Prevention

UNOG UN Office at Geneva

UNOV UN Office at Vienna

UNON UN Office at Nairobi

SPECIALIZED AGENCIES *

ILO International Labour Organization

FAO Food and Agriculture Organization of the United Nations

UNESCO United Nations Educational, Scientific and Cultural Organization

WHO World Health Organization

WORLD BANK GROUP

IBRD International Bank for Reconstruction and Development

IDA International Development Association

IFC International Finance Corporation

MIGA Multi-lateral Investment Guarantee Agency

ICSID International Centre for Settlement of Investment Disputes

IMF International Monetary Fund

ICAO International Civil Aviation Organization

IMO International Maritime Organization

ITU International Telecommunication Union

UPU Universal Postal Union

WMO World Meterological Organization

WIPO World intellectual Property Organization

IFAD International Fund for Agricultural Development

UNIDO United Nations Industrial Development Organization

FUNCTIONAL COMMISSIONS

Commission for Social Development

Commission on Human Rights

Commission on Narcotic Drugs

Commission on Crime Prevention and Criminal Justice

Commission on the Status of Women

Commission on Population and Development

Statistical Commission

REGIONAL COMMISSIONS

Economic Commission for Africa (ECA)

Economic Commission for Europe (ECE)

Economic Commission for Latin America and the Caribbean (ECLAC)

Economic and Social Commission for Asia and the Pacific (ESCAP)

United Nations Forum on Forests

Sessional and Standing Committees Expert, ad hoc and related bodies

RELATED ORGANIZATIONS

IAEA International Atomic Energy Agency

WTO (trade) World Trade Organization

WTO (tourism) World Trade Organization

CTBTO Preparatory Commission Preparatory Commission for the Comprehensive Nuclear-Test-Bad-Treaty Organization

OPCW Organization for the Prohibition of Chemical Weapons

GENERAL ASSEMBLY

Main committees

Other sessional committees

Standing committees and ad hoc bodies

Other subsidiary organs

PROGRAMMES AND FUNDS

UNCTAD United Nations Conference on Trade and Development

ITC International Trade Centre (UNCTAD/WTO)

UNDCP United Nations Drug Control Programme

UNEP United Nations Environment Programme

UNHSP United Nations Human Settlements Programme (UN-Habitat)

UNDP United Nations Development Programme

UNIFEM United Nations Development Fund for Women

UNV United Nations Volunteers

UNFPA United Nations Population Fund

UNHCR Office of the United Nations High Commissioner for Refugees

UNICEF United Nations Children's Fund

WFP World Food Programme

UNRWA** United Nations Relief and Works Agency for Palestine Refugees in the Near East

OTHER UN ENTITIES

OHCHR Office of the United Nations High Commissioner for Human Rights

UNOPS United Nations Office for Project Services

UNU United Nations University

UNSSC United Nations System Staff College

RESEARCH AND TRAINING INSTITUTES

INSTRAW International Research and Training Institute for the Advancement of Women

UNICRI United Nations Interregional Crime and Justice Research Institute

UNITAR United Nations Institute for Training and Research

UNRISD United Nations Research Institute for Social Development

UNIDIR** United Nations Institute for Disarmament Research

Military Staff Committee

Standing Committee and ad hoc bodies

International Criminal Tribunal for the Former Yugoslavia

International Criminal Tribunal for Rwanda

UN Monitoring, Verification and Inspection Commission (Iraq)

United Nations Compensation Commission

Peacekeeping Operations and Missions

FIGURE 14.6 Many of the agencies of the UN have direct or indirect involvement in the struggle to reduce poverty.

Key UN Organizations in the Fight against Poverty

Agency	Focus of Activities
Food and Agriculture Organization (FAO)	The link between food insecurity and poverty Malnutrition
International Labour Organization (ILO)	The condition of the working poor Productive employment and social protection
International Monetary Fund (IMF)	Connections between development policies and progress on poverty Health of financial systems
United Nations Educational, Scientific and Cultural Organization (UNESCO)	Implications of poverty for world peace, security, and stability Impacts on "social capital"
United Nations Children's Fund (UNICEF)	Impacts of poverty on children Achievement of social goals of poverty reduction

FIGURE 14.7 In addition to these agencies, the regional commissions play an active role in those areas where poverty reduction programs are given high status.

any case, is to keep the plight of the poor in the spotlight of global humanitarian action, so that progress, however slight, can take place.

THE PARADIGM SHIFT Some analysts point out that the model of economic development that the World Bank and International Monetary Fund (IMF) have imposed for decades is the wrong kind of development for poor countries and is doomed to fail. The emphasis on investment, rapid trade liberalization, and structural adjustment has wiped out some small- and medium-scale industries and forced governments to reduce spending on social programs in order to service their debts. As poor countries lack internal markets for their products, they must rely on exports, mainly of unprocessed natural resources. The type of economic development that is needed would build up the capacity of civil society in poor countries so that it could force good governance, prioritize social programs, attract invest-

> **❝** There is growing and compelling evidence that the poor can solve their own problems if only they are given fair access to financial and business development services. **❞**
>
> *Kofi Annan,*
> *secretary-general of the UN*

ment on its own terms, and build up the manufacturing and agricultural sectors for the benefit of its own people. In addition, the G8 countries must follow through with their 1999 promise of cancelling many of the debts facing developing countries. For example, between 2002 and

FIGURE 14.8 UN-financed refrigeration plant for use by local fishermen on the island of Rarotonga, Cook Islands.

Domestic and Foreign Investment Flows for Low- and Middle-Income Countries, 1998

Region	Domestic Investment (US$ millions)	Foreign Direct Investment (US$ millions)
East Asia and the Pacific	67 249	64 162
Europe and Central Asia	54 342	24 350
Latin America and the Caribbean	126 854	69 323
Middle East and North Africa	9 223	5 054
South Asia	7 581	3 659
Sub-Saharan Africa	3 452	4 364
All low- and middle-income countries	267 700	170 942

World Development Report 2000/2001

FIGURE 14.9 The high-income countries of the world received over $448 billion in foreign direct investment, almost three times more than all the low- and middle-income countries.

2007, Zambia is scheduled to pay between US$150 million and US$200 million in debt interest alone. This amounts to a large part of the country's total budget and, if paid in full, would amount to significantly more than the original debt.

MICRO-CREDIT Community banks, developed by local NGOs, have become a successful and cost-effective way to reduce poverty and to contribute to self-sufficiency at the local level. Based on the model of the Grameen bank, founded in rural Bangladesh by Professor Muhammad Yunus, the banks collect savings and provide small loans without the need for collateral. While there are many different micro-credit organizations in 30 different countries, the Grameen bank alone has more than 2.4 million members in 40 000 villages in Bangladesh, 95% of whom are women. In some countries, all of the borrowers are women. The repayment rate for loans for these community-based banks is between 97 % and 100%.

> " If poverty eradication is the objective of aid, as it ought to be, then in the current trade set up and way global institutions now run, you can't get there from here. "
>
> *Gerry Barr, president of the Canadian Council for International Cooperation*

FIGURE 14.10 Fair trade products provide higher, fairer prices for small-scale farmers and artisans, cutting out the middlemen who extract the bulk of profits. Products are available at some health food and grocery stores or from trading organizations such as Oxfam Canada's Bridgehead.

FAIR TRADE Fair trade is the label given to trading practices that ensure that producers of products receive a fair share of the revenues generated by the products. Fair trade practices

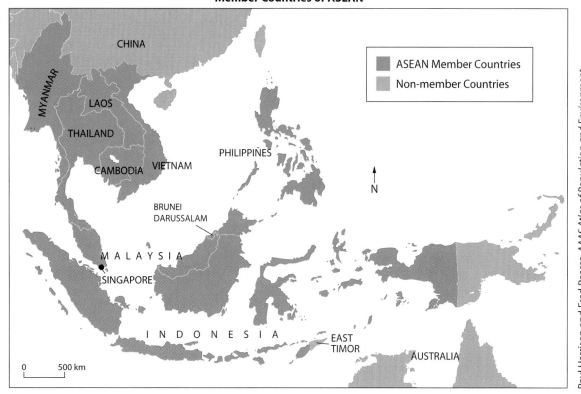

Member Countries of ASEAN

◼	ASEAN Member Countries
◻	Non-member Countries

Paul Harrison and Fred Pearce, *AAAS Atlas of Population and Environment*, University of California Press, 2001, pp. 4–5

FIGURE 14.11 ASEAN includes several member countries that have been identified as "emerging economies." They have been experiencing rapid growth and economic development over the past several decades, with the exception of the late 1990s when the Asian region experienced a severe economic recession.

have been established for agricultural products such as bananas and coffee and for manufactured goods, including carpets. Usually, the products are marketed through farmers co-operatives and alternative trading organizations, such as Oxfam, Equal Exchange, or Fairtrade Labeling Organizations International (FLO), that work to reduce the proportion taken by wholesalers and retailers and put more money in the hands of the small-scale producers. This strategy benefits whole communities through local business and family networks.

 See Chapter 9 for more information about fair trade.

The ASEAN and Poverty Reduction

The ASEAN is an example of a regional intergovernmental organization that is addressing the challenges of poverty as part of its overall agenda. This organization includes all 10 countries of southeastern Asian and represents about 500 million people. Its broad goals are to create a spirit of co-operation within the region to better encourage peace, stability, and prosperity. Poverty reduction is at the heart of the ASEAN Plan of Action on Rural Development and Poverty Reduction. This plan has as its focus:

- socio-economic disparities within member countries and between urban and rural communities;
- needs of vulnerable and disadvantaged people, including women;
- unemployment, underemployment, and low productivity;
- lack of basic infrastructure and social amenities;
- impact of environmental degradation;
- internal migration within and between member countries;

Selected Statistics for ASEAN Member Countries, 2000

Country	Population (1999)	GDP per Capita (US$)	Rate of GDP Growth (%)	Trade Balance (US$ millions)
Brunei	321 000	14 094	3.0	1 869
Cambodia	10 946 000	289	4.5	−245
Indonesia	209 255 000	723	4.8	25 087
Laos	5 297 000	315	5.7	−87
Malaysia	21 830 000	4 016	8.5	20 926
Myanmar	45 059 000	155	6.2	−797
Philippines	74 454 000	990	4.0	6 915
Singapore	3 522 000	25 864	9.9	11 400
Thailand	60 856 000	1 986	4.3	5 519
Viet Nam	78 705 000	396	6.7	628
ASEAN	510 245 000	1 121	5.4	71 215

The World Guide 2001/2002, ASEAN Statistics

FIGURE 14.12 The 10 countries of ASEAN are moving toward greater integration of their economies by establishing an Asian free-trade area.

Indicators of Poverty in ASEAN Member Countries

Country	Population with Access to Safe Water (%)	Female Secondary School Enrollment (%)	TV Sets per 1000 People	Population Aged 0–14 Years (%)
Brunei	—	—	417	33
Cambodia	30	31	9	45
Indonesia	75	53	232	30
Laos	44	53	10	45
Malaysia	78	69	228	35
Myanmar	60	53	7	36
Philippines	84	79	125	37
Singapore	100	75	361	21
Thailand	81	47	167	24
Viet Nam	43	54	180	34

Canadian Global Almanac 2001, World Resources 2000–2001

FIGURE 14.13 There are significant variations in poverty indicators among the countries of the intergovernmental organization.

impacts of globalization and information technologies.

One of the challenges of the program is to measure effectively the degree of poverty and the progress that is being made to combat it. Part of the Plan of Action involves developing a common set of socio-economic indicators of poverty and the statistical agencies to compile the data.

 See Chapter 2 for more information about international organizations and alliances.

Strategic Initiatives in ASEAN's Plan of Action

1. Develop human resources among the poor to allow them to cope with the challenges of modernization and globalization.

2. Develop skills in the different levels of government in formulating policies and implementing appropriate programs.

3. Encourage the sharing of experiences, information, and resources to tackle the problem of poverty.

4. Promote the active participation of the private sector and NGOs.

5. Promote networking among the national and regional research institutes dealing with the problems of poverty and rural development.

6. Encourage collaboration with other relevant national and international organizations.

7. Develop common approaches and positions on the issues among ASEAN member countries.

INTERACT

1. Create a diagram or illustration to show the role of the UN in the struggle to reduce poverty.

2. Suppose you were a UN official seeking funding from richer nations for your programs. Explain why you think that there should be a focus on social development in poverty reduction activities.

3. Explain why countries with high rates of poverty find it difficult to attract investment capital.

4. Assess the focus statements used by the ASEAN in their battle against poverty. Is the organization targeting appropriate types of change? Suggest other useful areas to target.

5. Use Figures 14.12, **Selected Statistics for ASEAN Member Countries, 2000**, and 14.13, **Indicators of Poverty in ASEAN Member Countries**, to calculate an index of poverty for the ASEAN countries. Start by creating a six-column table. In the first column, record the names of the ASEAN member countries. From the information given in the two figures, select four variables that you feel are good indicators of poverty and record the headings in the next four columns of the table. For each variable, rank the countries, giving the value showing the least poverty a "1" and the value showing the most poverty a "10." For example, if you chose GDP per capita from Figure 14.12, Singapore would be ranked 1 while Myanmar, with the lowest value, would be ranked 10. In the final column of your table, sum the ranks for each country. The country with the lowest total has the best "poverty index."

Foreign Aid and Poverty Reduction

For many developing countries, the real barrier to improvements in poverty rates is the lack of investment capital. Private investors and local entrepreneurs are discouraged by the economic uncertainty in developing countries. For these countries, the only significant source of external investment money is **official development assistance (ODA)**—more commonly known as foreign aid. ODA includes both bilateral aid (government to government) and **multilateral aid** (international organization to government). The World Bank is one organization that gives multilateral assistance to countries. ODA is given in the form of loans and grants or goods and services and is provided for a variety of purposes, including support for particular projects, food aid, emergency situations, or peacekeeping. The richer countries of the world have generally agreed to donate ODA at a level equal to 0.7% of their GNP. Unfortunately, most countries have not achieved this target and, in fact, ODA contributions have declined in recent years. For example,

between 1999 and 2000, assistance dropped 6% globally to equal only 0.22% of the GNP of the richest countries. In 2002, during a UN summit on financing for development, held in Monterrey, Mexico, the leaders of a number of developed countries did pledge to increase their foreign aid budgets. However, this additional funding was tied to the recipient countries doing whatever was necessary to attract foreign investment and increase trade. Many critics were not pleased that the generosity came with strings attached.

Canada's Official Development Assistance

Canada's ODA is given through the Canadian International Development Agency (CIDA). Poverty reduction is the focus for CIDA's activities, and its actions fit into seven programs:

- Basic human needs (e.g., providing health care facilities)
- Gender equity (e.g., education for females)
- Infrastructure services (e.g., improving water supplies)
- Human rights (e.g., helping to improve court systems)

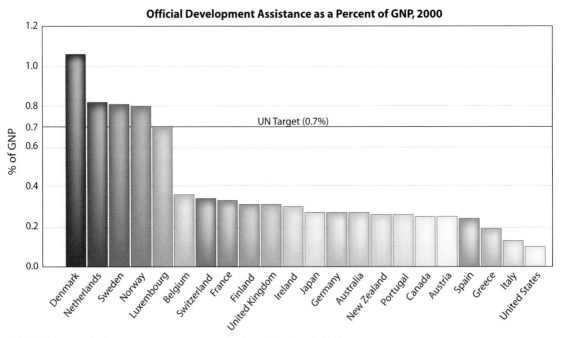

Official Development Assistance as a Percent of GNP, 2000

UN Target (0.7%)

% of GNP

Denmark, Netherlands, Sweden, Norway, Luxembourg, Belgium, Switzerland, France, Finland, United Kingdom, Ireland, Japan, Germany, Australia, New Zealand, Portugal, Canada, Austria, Spain, Greece, Italy, United States

OECD Observer

FIGURE 14.14 Only four countries contribute foreign aid at levels higher than the UN's target. Where are these four countries located?

Distribution of Canadian Bilateral ODA (%)

Region	1994–1995	1995–1996	1996–1997	1997–1998	1998–1999
Asia and Oceania	27.2	30.7	26.4	30.4	30.6
Central Asia and Middle East	2.1	2.7	2.6	2.9	2.2
Europe	1.0	2.3	2.4	1.4	1.7
Africa	52.5	46.0	50.3	45.6	46.6
Latin America and Caribbean	17.2	18.3	18.3	19.7	18.9

CIDA

FIGURE 14.15 Events in different parts of the world, such as natural disasters or civil conflict, cause regional ODA figures to vary. What is important to note is that aid for Africa, the most needy continent, generally declined over the 1990s as aid-giving priorities shifted.

- Democracy and good governance (e.g., providing training of police)
- Private sector development (e.g., helping small businesses)
- Environment (e.g., helping to stop soil erosion)

The environment and gender equity are seen by CIDA as fundamental, overarching concerns. The main sector supported by Canadian bilateral aid is social infrastructure, which accounts for almost half of total aid. More and more, human rights and good governance are also priorities for CIDA. Haiti is an example where Canadian ODA was designed to build the organizations and institutions that allow democracy to function effectively.

FACT FILE

In 1999, Canada assigned more than 10 000 advisors with different areas of expertise to developing countries. Twenty percent were specialists in government and civil society, 18% in population and health, and 17% in education. The majority of experts went to the Americas, followed by Africa and Asia.

Analysts point out that CIDA's agenda is very ambitious. Its programs are wide ranging and require actions to be taken on a number of issues simultaneously. The difficulty is that funding for ODA was reduced throughout the 1990s as part of national austerity programs. CIDA has responded to the funding cuts by shifting operating procedures to focus on results rather than intentions, and by developing cost-sharing partnerships with the private sector and institutions. So, while public support for international aid remains strong, CIDA is faced with the challenge of maintaining its programs in the coming years.

FACT FILE

In June 2002, Prime Minister Jean Chrétien pushed for higher levels of foreign aid, allocating $500 million for Africa and promising to increase Canada's aid budget by 8% a year.

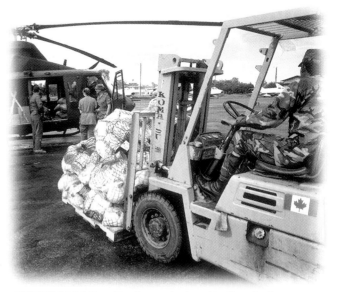

FIGURE 14.16 Canadian humanitarian aid efforts in the Aguan Valley, Honduras.

" Thus, at the end of the 1990s, there is a paradox at the heart of Canada's internationalism. The determination continues to be involved in a very wide range of issues and with as wide a range of partners and multilateral organizations as possible, while the aid budget has been cut by 29 per cent over six years. This paradox raises concerns about Canada's ability to meet expectations about Canada's role in the world, both at home and internationally. "

Development Assistant Committee,
"Development Co-operation Review of Canada"

The Efficacy of Aid

One of the problems with ODA is that it does not always go to the poorest countries. As Figure 14.18, **Canadian Share of ODA for Asian Countries, 1998–1999**, shows, in 1999 the poorest countries received about the same amount of assistance as the middle-income countries. This statistic points to a problem with ODA—it is not always given on the basis of need. For example, Israel had a GNP per capita of US$16 180 and received US$148 per capita in aid in 1999, while Bangladesh had a GNP per capita of US$350 and received US$9 per capita in aid in the same year. Motivating forces behind ODA decisions include furthering the donor country's own economic interests, political persuasion, and military influence. These different reasons give shape to the programs and projects of the donor countries and help to determine which countries get assistance.

ECONOMIC MOTIVES While on the surface it appears that aid giving is an act of generosity, in fact, most of the economic benefits of aid are gained by the donor. Most bilateral assistance is given as **tied aid**, where there are conditions on the use of the assistance, usually that the funds must be spent in the donor country. Recent donor initiatives tie greater access to

" It is true that Africa remains in an exploitative relationship with the rest of the world. And until the developed world relents on such issues as writing off Africa's debt, and opts for a truly free market in people and goods and not the selective patchwork of free markets and protectionism… the claims of neo-liberals for the global economy will always be a bad joke on the weak. "

Ken Wiwa, son of Saro-Wiwa

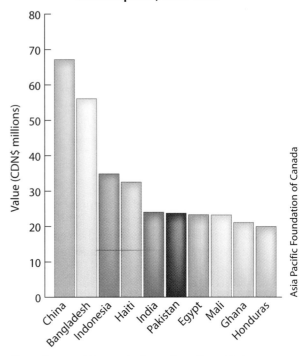

Largest Canadian Bilateral ODA Recipients, 1998–1999

Value (CDN$ millions)

Asia Pacific Foundation of Canada

FIGURE 14.17 This graph shows Canadian aid given directly to the governments of other countries. It is more difficult to report multilateral aid contributions by country since organizations like the World Bank pool donations and distribute the funds according to their programs.

recipient markets as part of aid packages. Donor governments prefer tied aid because recipient countries have to clearly account for its use and the impacts of these public expenditures can be determined. Tied aid is also a way of promoting export and creating employment in the donor country.

FACT FILE

In 2000, Canada earned $9.89 billion from developing countries. Official aid to these countries totalled $2.75 billion, an income of $3.60 for every $1 spent on aid.

POLITICAL MOTIVES ODA is given to improve political ties between donor and recipient countries. This assistance creates a visible and public connection between nations that, to some degree, obligates the recipient nation to support the interests of the donor nation. For example, Canada gives ODA to Francophone countries

Canadian Share of ODA for Asian Countries, 1998–1999

Country	Total ODA (CDN$ millions)	Percent of ODA from Canada	Percent of Canadian ODA that Was Bilateral	Percent of Canadian ODA that Was Partnership	Percent of Canadian ODA that Was Multilateral
Bangladesh	1 855	5.2	58.0	0.6	41.4
Cambodia	500	1.9	52.5	8.7	38.9
China	3 498	3.2	60.2	7.2	32.6
India	2 365	2.7	37.7	6.6	55.7
Indonesia	1 865	2.1	89.5	6.0	4.5
Laos	417	1.8	16.3	6.9	76.8
Malaysia	300	1.8	58.7	28.2	13.1
Nepal	600	2.8	45.3	3.6	51.1
Pakistan	1 557	3.4	44.8	0.2	55.0
Papua New Guinea	536	0.2	38.5	7.3	54.2
Philippines	900	2.7	76.4	12.8	10.8
Sri Lanka	727	2.1	35.0	4.8	60.1
Thailand	1 024	0.9	88.6	6.5	4.9
Vietnam	1 725	3.9	25.9	3.6	70.5

CIDA, UNDP

FIGURE 14.18 This breakdown of Canadian aid to Asia illustrates the patterns of aid giving around the world. Partnerships involve the Canadian government working with Canadian companies, NGOs, and institutions in delivering ODA. Bilateral assistance is usually preferred because it provides clear linkages between Canada and the recipient countries.

❝ An NGO is an efficient tool with which to harvest donor money. ❞

Adam Roberts,
"International NGOs:
New Gods Overseas"
in The Economist

❝ Many Europeans and Americans are painfully aware of the fact that the Euro-American civilization has undermined and destroyed the autonomy and singularity of non-European cultures. They feel it was their fault, and thus feel the need to make amends … by longing to 'help' them in one way or another. To my mind this is a false way of going about it that … contains within itself … the same familiar feeling of superiority, paternalism, and fateful sense of mission to help the 'rest of the world.' It is again that feeling of being the 'elect.' It is in fact, colonialism inside out. ❞

Vaclav Havel, President of the Czech Republic

around the world. This is seen by many as a strategy to undermine the political ambitions of Quebec separatists; the recipient countries have a clear political connection to Canada, rather than to an independent Quebec.

MILITARY MOTIVES Foreign aid can be used to further military interests on regional or international levels. Poverty reduction programs, support for debt repayments (or outright forgiveness), and emergency food aid can have the impact of stabilizing domestic situations of strategically important military allies. For example, in 2001, the U.S. pumped aid dollars into Pakistan in an effort to prop up the government of that country. Pakistan was strategically critical in the U.S.-led war on terrorism that was focused on neighbouring Afghanistan.

Poverty in Canada

COUNTERPOINT Some Canadians argue that this country cannot afford to give foreign aid. As proof, they point to the persistent levels of poverty in Canada, especially among Native peoples and single-parent families headed by women. For example, conditions on a number of Native reserves match conditions found in countries in the lower half of the Human Development Index more closely than conditions in the rest of Canada. Across the whole of Canada, one in five children lives below

> " Africa doesn't want charity; they want assistance, because the colonial powers have exploited the continent, and it is the time now that they put these resources back for the development of the continent. "
>
> *Nelson Mandela*

Aid Dependency for Selected Countries, 1999

Country/Group	Net Official Development Assistance (US$ millions)		Aid Per Capita 1999 (US$)	Aid as a Percentage of Gross National Income
	1994	1999		
Albania	164	480	142	12.8
Benin	256	211	34	9.0
Chile	151	69	5	0.1
Ethiopia	1 071	633	10	9.9
Haiti	601	817	129	15.6
India	2 324	1 484	1	0.3
Israel	1 237	906	148	0.9
Malaysia	66	143	6	0.2
Nepal	448	344	15	6.7
Pakistan	1 605	732	5	1.2
Russia	1 847	1 816	12	0.5
Sierra Leone	275	74	15	11.3
Vietnam	891	1 421	18	5.0
Low-Income Countries	29 422	22 399	9	2.2
Middle-Income Countries	24 531	22 924	9	0.4
High-Income Countries	2 197	1 823	2	0.0

World Development Indicators, 2001

FIGURE 14.19 Global foreign development assistance fell from $67.5 billion in 1994 to $59.1 billion in 1999.

excerpt from "Walk raises $2.6-million to assist world's poor"

by Gay Abbate
The Globe and Mail
May 27, 2002

... tens of thousands of Canadians ... participated yesterday in the World Partnership Walk, organized by the Aga Khan Foundation Canada, to raise money for development projects in the poorest parts of Asia and Africa.

The 18th annual walk brought in an estimated 2.6-million, a 25-percent increase over last year's total. Walks were held simultaneously in Vancouver, Victoria, Edmonton, Calgary, Winnipeg, Kitchener, London, Ont., Toronto, Ottawa and Montreal.

Organizers had not completed an official tally of participants last night, but believed the sunny weather and warmish temperatures ... brought out a record number of people from all walks of life, cultures and religious beliefs. The number is expected to have increased by at least 20 per cent from last year's 20,000 participants. ...

Narmin Hassam, an Edmonton organizer, said one of the most remarkable aspects of the event was about 400 Girl Guides, many of whom completed the walk balancing steel buckets and water-filled urns on their heads or with log bundles strapped to their backs.

"It was part of their sense of awareness to do this and experience what women in developing countries experience," said Ms. Hassam, who estimated they had raised more than $250,000. ...

In Toronto, about 7,000 people walked the course—double last year's number—and raised about $1-million.

Rasika and Nizar Mawani have participated in each of the 18 walks. This year they brought their daughter, Amyn, and seven-year-old nephew, Hussein.

The couple said the walk is an opportunity to support the rest of the world. "We feel it's necessary to help the rest of the global village in

the area of education, hospitals, health care and poverty," Mr. Mawani said. ...

The walk, the largest of its kind in Canada, is "a meaningful way to bring everyone together in partnership with those living in poverty," said Deputy Prime Minister John Manley as he kicked off the walk in Ottawa.

Thousands of volunteers and about 800 corporate sponsors, including *The Globe and Mail* and CTV, supported this year's event. "Canadians are looking for what they can do to make a difference, and we're responding to that," Globe publisher Phillip Crawley said in a statement.

All of the money raised goes to support to fight world poverty, the foundation said. The Aga Khan Foundation is a registered Canadian charitable organization that helps the poor in Africa and central Asia, including Afghanistan.

the poverty line. In most larger Canadian cities, poverty rates exceed 20% of the population. Some critics of Canada's foreign assistance program argue that we should take care of our own poor before we address poverty in the rest of the world.

The Benefits of Foreign Aid

The motives for giving aid and the significant reduction in ODA over the past number of years has undermined the effectiveness of foreign assistance in reducing poverty around the world. However, there seems to be few viable alternatives that can deliver support for developing nations at a level that will make a difference. In the final analysis, ODA still has a key role to play in the struggle to reduce poverty rates in the poorest countries of the world.

NGOs have become increasingly influential in the distribution of ODA. With reduced governmental budgets and fewer civil servants in the field, NGOs have taken over the job of distributing ODA for many programs. The NGOs often have the expertise and connections in developing countries. They are linked through international networks and are tied into political decision making. One chief advantage of NGOs is that they can deliver assistance without the baggage that is attached to official government-to-government disbursement of aid. For example, an NGO such as Médecins Sans Frontières (Doctors Without Borders) can provide services within a war-torn area that Canadian officials would never attempt to enter because of official complications. In addition, NGOs have the ability to attract even more money from the private sector and the general public to complement official sources. Donating to NGOs can have significant positive impacts on conditions in developing countries. Some high-profile NGOs with strong track records are Médecins Sans Frontières, Greenpeace, Amnesty International, Oxfam, Care, Red Cross, and the Aga Khan Foundation.

A problem with donating to NGOs is determining which are legitimate and reputable. Currently there are over 30 000 international NGOs and millions of domestic organizations around the world. In the United States, an estimated 8% of workers are employed in some sort of non-profit group. Inevitably, there will be those who establish NGOs for the express purpose of taking money from public and private donors. Much of the money directed to these groups is used to support their fund-raising activities, and little, if any, finds its way to those for whom it was collected. Donors need to research the NGOs that they might care to support.

Donors must ask questions:

- What portion of donations is delivered to those in need?
- How are the recipients of the programs chosen?
- What opportunities do recipients have to determine the nature of the support?
- What values does this organization seek to promote through its work?
- Are these values consistent with my own values?
- What reporting mechanism is used to keep donors informed of the actions of the organization?

GEOGRAPHIC METHODS

Using Geographic Information Systems (GIS) in Famine Relief

Programs and projects to reduce poverty are frequently undermined by natural or human disasters that produce famine. Poverty reduction programs have little chance of success as long as people are starving and dying. In order to better predict the occurrence of famines in high-risk parts of the world, the United States Agency for International Development (USAID) set up the Famine Early Warning System Network (FEWS NET) as one of its programs. Data is fed into the network from the US Geological Survey/Earth Resources Observation Systems, the National Aeronautics and Space Administration (NASA), the National Oceanic and Atmospheric Administration (NOAA), and Chemonics International, Inc. Among the data used are such variables as rainfall totals and stream flows of rivers. GIS technologies are applied to analyse the data to identify potential famine conditions and predict their occurrences. This information can be relayed to appropriate decision makers who can mobilize relief efforts, so that poverty reduction programs can continue.

1. The richer countries of the world have set 0.7% of their GNP as their target for aid giving. What is your opinion on this target? Is it set too high or too low? Is setting a target for charity an appropriate course of action? Explain your opinions on this topic.
2. Using the information in this section of the chapter, as well as current information that you can access, evaluate Canada's ODA, considering how much is given, the programs that are undertaken, and the recipients of Canadian aid. Use your evaluation to design a new approach for Canada to take in the disbursement of aid.
3. In day-to-day conversations, you will hear the opinion that one of the problems of foreign aid is that developing countries become dependent on handouts from richer countries and lose their motivation to work for their own success. Does the evidence presented in this section of the chapter support this view? Explain your answer.
4. Explain why the various motivations for giving aid can lead to the inefficient use of ODA.
5. Explain what writer Ken Wiwa means by a "truly free market" in the quote on page 342.
6. Conduct research on the New Partnership for African Development (NEPAD). Produce a case study outlining its major initiatives and current arguments for and against it, and evaluate its potential to have a real effect on reducing poverty in Africa.

CASE STUDY

Battling Poverty in India

Since India achieved its independence from Britain in 1947, it has seen a good deal of change. Economically, India has embraced new technologies that have given it both a satellite industry and a computer industry. Socially, there has been significant progress in improving caste discrimination and freedom for women. Politically, India is a working democracy that has increased the participation of women and all groups in society in its decision-making processes. Yet, all of this progress has been overshadowed by India's persistent poverty. At the beginning of the twenty-first century, over one-third of the population still lived in poverty, unable to earn sufficient income to buy food adequate for healthy living. There are striking disparities in India's poverty. Conditions in the state of Kerala are similar to those found in the richer countries of the world, with low infant mortality rates, long life expectancies, and high levels of literacy. However, conditions in states like Uttar Pradesh and Orissa are much worse, with life expectancy fully 20 years less than in other parts of the country and an illiteracy rate approaching 75% for women.

Measuring the extent of poverty has been a controversial problem in India. Differences in assumptions and criteria can lead to quite different estimates. For example, in 1993, the official Planning Commission estimated that 19% of Indians lived below the poverty line. Estimates generated by a survey organization based on actual spending were much higher, at around 36% for the same year. Setting the poverty level is an important step as it has implications for government spending on social programs and poverty reduction efforts. The higher the rate, the greater the pressure on the government to respond.

FIGURE 14.20 Two contrasting views of India. Poverty rates vary from a high of over 50% in Uttar Pradesh to a low of less than 2% in the Punjab.

Facts about India

Statistic	India	Canada
Population (2000)	1 008 940 000	30 857 000
Annual growth to 2015 (%)	1.3	0.9
Children per woman	3.1	1.6
Life expectancy at birth (years)	63	79
Infant mortality (per 1000)	69	6
Doctors per 100 000 people	48	221
Daily calorie supply per capita	2 415	3 056
Pupils per primary school teacher	64	16
TV sets (per 1000 people)	64	709
Per capita GNP ($)	440	19 170
Energy consumption (kg of oil equivalent per capita yearly)	479	7 930
Human development index (HDI) rank, 2001	115	3

FIGURE 14.21 These statistics paint a picture of a country that has been improving on many fronts but still has a long way to go in creating a better quality of life for its citizens.

The poverty line in India is set as the level of spending on food that one needs for good health. Below this standard, families were deemed to be poor. Currently, India's poverty line is the monetary equivalent of a minimum 2400 calories per person in rural areas and 2100 calories per person in urban areas.

A Futile Struggle

India's poverty rate has remained high in spite of a long-standing campaign to attack the problem. Critics of India's poverty reduction efforts have argued that the country has failed to lower rates because programs have only dealt with income levels. Poverty reduction efforts through the 1990s sharply focused on improving incomes throughout the whole country. However, there is no automatic link between higher incomes and fewer people living in poverty. While the economy of India certainly grew over the years, the additional wealth was not distributed to the poor. For example, government policies emphasized heavy industry and public enterprises, yet ignored small businesses and farming; public money was pumped into higher education, while elementary schools were neglected. So, while the majority of the people benefited to some extent from economic policies, the poor remained poor. To a large extent, this was a product of the centralized planning approach favoured by the Indian government, who administered development programs through large bureaucracies. There was little consultation with the poor or decision making at the local or village level.

Critics also argue that the government has been ineffective in managing food supplies, and food prices have risen as a result. The Indian government relies on an open market mechanism to set prices for food. When harvests are poor and

> 66 India has always had the intention to eradicate poverty. It is one of the few issues on which there exists a strong political consensus. The real issue is not the intent, but the nature of public action. Much of it has been guided by displaced concerns and misplaced priorities. 99
>
> A. K. Shiva Kumar, "Poverty and Human Development in India: Getting Priorities Right" UN Occasional Paper 30

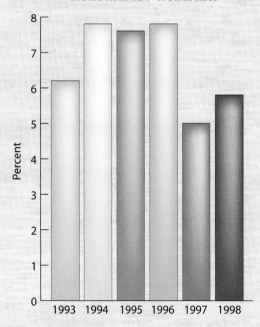

India's Real GDP Growth Rate

FIGURE 14.22 India had sustained economic growth throughout the 1990s, but the poverty rate for the country remained high.

supply is lower than demand, the higher purchasing power of urban residents causes food to flow to the cities. Food prices rise in rural areas. The rural poor are then trapped between higher unemployment rates because of lower agricultural output and rising food prices. The urban poor, as well, cannot afford the more expensive food. The end result is that poverty rates remain high, and more people move to cities.

Fighting Poverty

Poverty reduction efforts must focus on human deprivation, not just raising incomes. Analysts have identified these key areas linked to poverty reduction:

■ Basic services, including sewage and clean water
■ Sustainable livelihoods
■ Child labour
■ Discrimination against women and girls
■ Illiteracy
■ Prostitution
■ Caste discrimination
■ Environmental destruction

Facts about India

Population with Access to Safe Water (%)

	1985	1998
Rural	56.3	86.7
Urban	72.9	90.6

Population with Access to Adequate Sanitation (%)

	1985	1998
Rural	0.7	6.37
Urban	28.4	49.3

FIGURE 14.23

The causes and consequences of these issues are directly interconnected to the poverty experienced by the people of India. Poverty reduction will only be successful if there is a balance between economic growth for the country as a whole and growth in social, economic, and political opportunities for the poor.

The Role of Intergovernmental Organizations and Foreign Aid

Intergovernmental organizations have a role to play in making sure resources over and above what can be supplied within the country are available to Indians as they tackle poverty. Much of these additional resources will come through official development assistance. In a large measure, the important resources are funds, technological support, and expertise. ODA programs in countries such as Japan and the United States are already involved. It is important to note, though, that poverty reduction will be accomplished largely through the efforts and resources of the Indian people. ODA will supplement domestic resources, but will not, on its own, create sweeping change.

Japan is the largest ODA donor to India. It is, however, critical of India's handling of assistance. Japan has challenged India to become more efficient in implementing and delivering assistance, including dealing with corruption so that aid gets to those who could make the best use of it. In addition, Japan would like to see changes in the economy of India so that the economy can function more effectively. They have encouraged the Indian government to make tariff cuts to encourage more foreign investment and to withdraw

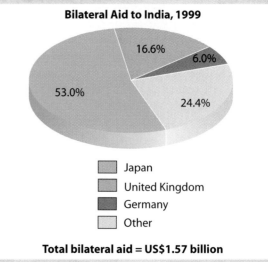

Bilateral Aid to India, 1999

16.6%
6.0%
53.0%
24.4%

- Japan
- United Kingdom
- Germany
- Other

Total bilateral aid = US$1.57 billion

FIGURE 14.24

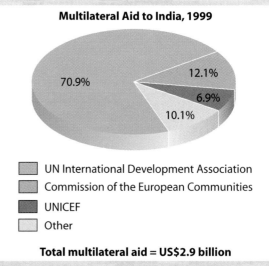

Multilateral Aid to India, 1999

70.9%
12.1%
6.9%
10.1%

- UN International Development Association
- Commission of the European Communities
- UNICEF
- Other

Total multilateral aid = US$2.9 billion

FIGURE 14.25

from sectors of the economy where private industry can work effectively. Japan has also been critical of India's development of nuclear weapons. In 1998, India conducted underground tests, contrary to international treaties. Japan strongly condemned this action and suspended all new ODA, but continued to provide support for projects underway and aid of an emergency or humanitarian nature. In 2001, as a part of the war on terrorism in the Middle East, Japan restored its ODA relationship with India.

India's persistent poverty will remain a troubling problem for the foreseeable future. The international community has a role to play in helping to address the problem.

Priority Areas for Japan's ODA to India

Economic Infrastructure—Japan's focus has been on the energy and transportation sectors, such as the Simhadri Thermal Power Station and the Delhi Mass Rapid Transport System project.

Alleviation of Poverty—Direct assistance in the social sector is important, especially for health and medical services, agricultural and rural development, population and AIDS prevention measures, and small businesses.

Environmental Conservation—Japan's support emphasizes pollution control, improvements in water quality, water supply, reforestation, and improvements in urban environments.

FIGURE 14.26 Japan's ODA programs have supported the theory that poverty is the biggest obstacle to sustainable development.

INTERACT

1. Explain why government actions and international strategies have failed to significantly reduce poverty in India.
2. Canada's aid to India in 1999 totalled $24 million, equal to 2.7% of the ODA received by that country. In your opinion, what are the obligations of India to Canada? What obligations does Canada have to India?
3. Suppose you could make decisions about the amount of ODA given by Japan to India. Identify circumstances that might cause you to offer more assistance. What might cause you to reduce your assistance? Explain your comments.
4. Use an Internet search engine such as <www.google.com> to conduct research and produce a case study on one of the thousands of development alternative strategies (such as Gram Vikas) working to reduce poverty in local Indian communities.

WEB LINKS

- Development Assistant Committee: <www1.oecd.org/dac/htm>
- ASEAN: <www.aseansec.org>
- The Asia Pacific Foundation of Canada: <www.asiapacific.ca>
- CIDA: <www.acdi-cida.gc.ca>
- The UN: <www.undp.org/>
- India's Development Alternatives Group: <www.devalt.org>
- Gram Vikas Development Organization: <www.gramvikas.org>
- TRANSfair Canada: <www.transfair.ca>
- North-South Institute: <www.nsi-isn.ca>

RELATED ISSUES

- Canada's role in NEPAD
- The role of NGOs in delivering assistance
- Funding for the UN
- Consideration of the environment in foreign aid programs

GIS **Poverty in the ASEAN Member Countries**

ANALYSE, APPLY, AND INTERACT

1. Explain why solving the problem of poverty is not just about raising income levels, but involves questions of social justice.

2. Using the struggle for poverty reduction as an example, explain how countries in the global economy are interdependent. Cite three specific cases where the actions of one country had an impact on the economies of others.

3. Identify the root causes of poverty presented throughout the chapter. Compare poverty in Canada and poverty in developing countries to identify connections and similarities in the root causes.

4. Suppose you were the minister of external affairs for a developing country seeking Canadian international development assistance. Outline the points that you would make to convince CIDA officials to look favourably at your application.

5. **a)** Explain how UN and ODA programs have a positive effect on poverty and quality of life for people in developing countries.
   b) What might be some negative effects of these programs?

6. The 1990s and the beginning of the twenty-first century were times of declining ODA budgets. Identify three consequences of this trend for recipient countries.

7. Research an intergovernmental organization other than the UN or ASEAN to identify the actions that it has taken to reduce poverty. You might choose the Organization of American States, the Organization for African Unity, La Francophonie, the Arab League, or another organization. Write your findings as a case study.

8. The UN has had its share of successes and failures. One of its long-standing problems is maintaining its funding. Conduct research to find out where the funds that the UN uses to operate its programs—including poverty reduction—come from, and what some of the issues are that surround UN funds.

9. Using the Internet and other sources, prepare a case study of one developing country that is struggling to overcome poverty. Examine the causes of their poverty, actions that the government has taken to improve conditions, factors that have limited the success of poverty reduction efforts, and the role of the UN, intergovernmental organizations, and ODA in dealing with poverty. Prepare your report as a project proposal for an aid package that the UN would administer.

10. Following the motto "think globally, act locally," prepare a list of five things that young people in Canada could do to have an impact on poverty in other parts of the world. Working in a small group, choose one thing that you can do, and do it!

11. Research the foreign aid situation of one sub-Saharan African country. Determine how much aid the country receives, where the money comes from, what programs are in place in the country, and the overall effectiveness of the aid.

12. Research poverty in Canada. Using statistics, describe the levels of poverty that exist in this country, who is poor, and what is being done to address the problem. Report your findings.

Chapter 15: Global Health Issues

By the end of this chapter, you will:

- select and compare statistical indicators of quality of life for a variety of developed and developing countries in different parts of the world;

- analyse selected global trends and evaluate their effects on people and environments at the local, national, and global level;

- demonstrate an understanding of how human-induced changes in natural systems can diminish their capacity for supporting human activity;

- describe selected world demographic trends and explain the factors influencing them;

- identify individuals who have made significant contributions to addressing global issues and evaluate their impacts;

- demonstrate an understanding of how quality of life and employment prospects are related to the global economy;

- evaluate the performance of a selected transnational corporation with respect to the promotion of environmental sustainability and human rights;

- demonstrate an understanding of how the work of the United Nations and other organizations on poverty, disease, and the environment is directly related to your own life;

- explain how local participation in the development process can build sustainable communities;

- evaluate the role played by non-governmental organizations and local community initiatives in different parts of the world;

- demonstrate an understanding of the need to consider social differences when analysing global problems and issues;

- demonstrate an understanding of the role and status of men and women in different parts of the world.

THE PERIWINKLE STORY

In 1984, a healthy nine-year-old girl spent the summer doing all the things young children love to do during their vacation: swimming, climbing trees, playing with friends. Just before school started, she discovered a painful growth in her groin. Doctors could not find anything to be concerned about and the growth was removed. She did not get better, however, and spent the next month severely ill, under the care of Duke University's highly respected medical team. The pediatric oncologist could find no sign of cancer. In early October, her parents were given the devastating news that their daughter had only a few days to live. At the end of that same week, the medical team finally discovered that the source of her illness was a rare blood cancer—T-cell lymphoma. Only two other cases had ever been reported in the U.S. Cancer research specialists revealed that an experimental drug had been discovered but that it had not yet been approved for use. Were her parents willing to take the chance?

Today that girl is a healthy adult. The drug that put her disease into remission came from the cancer-fighting alkaloids, vincristine and vinblastine, developed from the Madagascar or rose periwinkle (Catharanthus roseus), a small plant native to the island of Madagascar.

At the time of her illness, over 90% of the tropical rain forests of Madagascar that form the world's only natural habitat for the rose periwinkle had already been cut down. Just as that plant is now dependent on wise human action for its survival, we are dependent on it for saving our children's lives. Children with leukemia now have a 94% chance of remission compared to only a 5% chance before the discovery of the rose periwinkle's cancer-fighting compounds. This true story has become a symbol for our recognition of the intrinsic value of all organisms on the planet and the interconnections among natural and human processes and systems. The story illustrates how dependent we are on nature for our well-being, on medical research, and on human activity that affects the environments in which we live.

GLOBAL HEALTH MATTERS

This chapter will give you an opportunity to learn about and analyse just a few of the many health and disease issues that surround us in our communities and around the globe. The issues are complex, since the health of an individual or population depends upon many interacting social, political, economic, cultural, biological, and environmental factors. Many of the issues focus on inequities in global health. These issues are among the most serious ethical challenges facing the world today.

FACT FILE

The World Health Organization (WHO) defines health as "a state of complete physical, mental, and social well-being and not merely the absence of disease or infirmity."

Globally, health conditions have improved more in the past 50 years than in all of human history. The rate of new discoveries in medicine, sanitation, and health care practices has increased enormously. Smallpox has been eradicated worldwide, and polio, leprosy, and other diseases are close to disappearing as well. Average life expectancy has risen steadily. The average global citizen born today can expect to live to be 65 years old. Even in the poorest countries in the world, those in sub-Saharan Africa, life expectancy has risen from 36 years in 1950 to

FACT FILE

Studies of diarrhea show that the simple act of hand washing using soap reduces the incidence of disease by 35%. A three-year project in Burkina Faso that used positive motivation to encourage people to use soap and water for hand washing resulted in a tripling of the use of soap.

52 today. Recent changes to these positive trends have been in the transitional economies of Eastern Europe, where a small decline in life expectancy for men has occurred, and in sub-Saharan Africa as a result of human immunodeficiency (HIV)/acquired immunodeficiency syndrome (AIDS). Death rates overall, especially for children, have decreased dramatically. In 1950, 287 children of every 1000 born died before they reached their fifth birthday. By 1995, the figure was down to 90 of 1000.

The Looming Health Threat

Despite the many improvements, the state of health in many parts of the world is dismal. Averages tell us very little. There are huge gaps between the richest and poorest countries and between rich and poor people within most countries. There are more than a billion people who have not shared in the progress in improved public health. Today, even in our technological world, 20% of all people living in developing countries will not live to be 40 years old, and 20% of the children born in the least developed countries will die before they reach the age of five.

In rich developed countries, less than 1% of children will suffer the same fate. But in this part of the world, hormonal dysfunctions and immune system disorders, along with some forms of cancer and heart disease, are increasing.

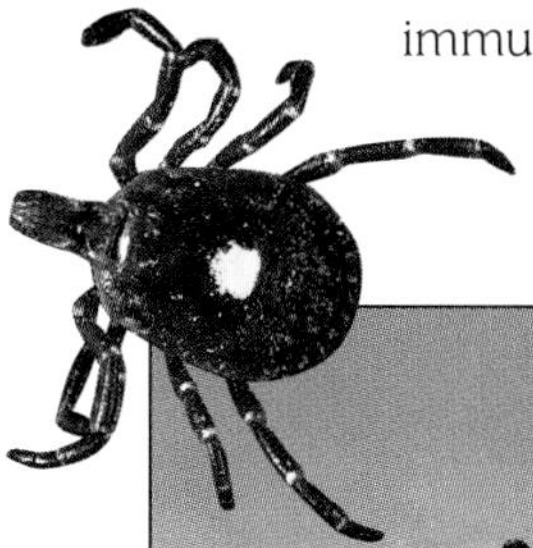

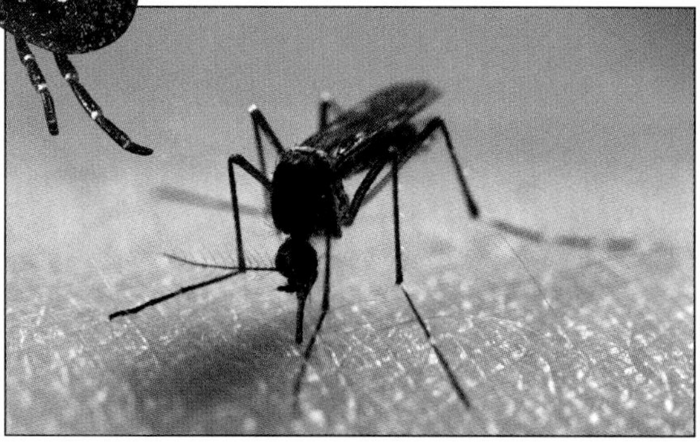

FIGURE 15.1 Many infectious diseases are vector borne. This means that disease-bearing pathogens such as bacteria, viruses, or parasites are transmitted from person to person by an agent such as the tick (the vector for Lyme disease) and the mosquito (the vector for malaria and West Nile virus).

Emerging new infectious threats include AIDS, caused by HIV, which was unknown until 1983, West Nile virus, and new types of hemorrhagic fevers such as the Ebola virus, which is fatal in most cases. The sources of these diseases and the reasons for the new outbreaks are not well understood. The Central Intelligence Agency (CIA) of the U.S. government produced a study in January 2000 called "The Global Infectious Disease Threat and Its Implications for the United States." The report warned that 20 diseases, including malaria, tuberculosis, cholera, and dengue fever, were increasing and spreading to new regions, becoming more deadly than ever. All diseases, particularly avoidable ones, are tragedies and act as constraints to economic and social development.

> **FACT FILE**
>
> Sierra Leone has the lowest life expectancy in the world at 38 years—half that of Japan, which is almost 80 years.

How West Nile Virus Makes its Move

Dead birds found to be infected with the virus are just part of the transmission chain.

Carrier
Birds carry the infectious form of West Nile for one to four days after infection.

Agent
After about two weeks of incubation, the virus resides in the mosquito's salivary glands and is injected into any animal from which it sucks blood.

Human hosts
An infected human may take three to 15 days to exhibit signs of infection, which include fever, body aches, and often rashes.

Other mammals
Horses, deer, and even house pets are susceptible. But like humans, they rarely develop the virus's infectious form and are thus "dead-end" hosts.

The Globe and Mail June 5, 2001, p. R7

FIGURE 15.2

High Alert for West Nile Virus

by Patricia Healy
Spring, 2001

First identified in Uganda in the 1930s, West Nile virus has spread throughout Africa, Asia, southern Europe, and now into North America. It is expected to reach southern Ontario this summer, but there is no plan to deal with the potentially fatal disease. The disease, which killed seven people in New York state last year, has been found in several blue jays and crows in Ontario. A mosquito that bites an infected bird can pass the virus on by biting a human. Most people who are infected show only a skin rash and swollen lymph glands, but severe infections can result in high fever, headaches, convulsions, paralysis, and death. There is no treatment for West Nile, nor is there a vaccine.

To reduce the risk, health officials will ask landowners to empty standing water in containers, old tires, and buckets—anywhere that mosquito larvae may hatch. Spraying with pesticides will only be done as a last resort, as it is expensive and causes health problems, especially for people susceptible to respiratory diseases. New York City used citywide chemical spraying, but it was ineffective and resulted in other health problems.

"Despite health officials' best efforts, Canadians should expect that West Nile will establish itself as an infectious disease threat in Canada," said Dr. Jay Keystone of the Travel and Tropical Medicine Centre at Toronto General Hospital.

Be sure to use insect repellent, especially at night, and take other precautions against being bitten by mosquitoes. Notify health officials immediately if you find dead birds on your property.

Resistance to Antibiotics

The rise and spread of disease pathogens that are resistant to antibiotics is another new health threat, with more than 35 reports of emerging or recurring infectious threats around the world in the past two decades. There are more than 100 different antibiotics but bacteria have evolved to become more lethal than ever. When antibiotics were first developed, they were considered miraculous. Many people felt that disease would soon become a hazard of the past. Unfortunately, the overuse of antibiotics in North America, the widespread use of antibiotics to promote growth in livestock animals that are not sick, and the normal genetic survival mechanism of parasites, bacteria, and viruses are causing some of these to mutate. This can render our most powerful antibiotics ineffective, leaving researchers, doctors, and health care workers with no way of coping. We now need to find new drugs and new international institutions for detecting and tracking these changing diseases.

INTERACT

1. **a)** Explain how changes in the natural environment in Madagascar have diminished its capacity to protect human health everywhere on the planet.
   b) Create a diagram that illustrates how the situation in Madagascar is connected to a number of global issues.

2. **a)** Conduct research to identify examples of other situations and issues related to how human-induced changes in a natural system can diminish its capacity to protect the health of humans and/or other species.
   b) Present your findings to other members of your class and compile a world map, showing the locations and issues of threats to global health caused by

human-induced changes in the natural environment. Add an appropriate title and legend for your map.

3. **a)** Identify several trends in disease threats facing Canadians.

   b) Choose any one of the new or recurring health threats and create a concept web that suggests the social, economic, and environmental implications of the threat. Add arrows to the items on your web or choose some other way to indicate connections among the implications.

4. Conduct research to find:

   a) a specific example of a disease pathogen that has become resistant to antibiotics in Canada; and

   b) a research or medical initiative designed to counter the threat. Share your findings with the class.

5. **a)** What precautions can you take to reduce your risk of contracting a tropical disease such as malaria or West Nile virus that is spread by a mosquito vector?

   b) Draw up a plan consisting of three or four strategies that could be implemented in your community to reduce the risk of contracting West Nile virus. Present your plan in chart form, indicating a predicted effect of each strategy, or write a letter to your Department of Public Health that encourages them to consider your plan.

PATTERNS AND TRENDS

It can be difficult to get accurate information on health and disease issues. Statistics do not give us a complete picture. They are much more accurate for developed countries, where people have better access to health care. The WHO had information about cause of death for only 13 million of the 52 million people in the world estimated to have died in 1996. Statistics do not reveal the reality that the age at which a disease occurs or how long it lasts has an impact on quality of life. For example, if a young child gets river blindness, the impact on the family and the community is severe, due to lost potential.

More Than Just Another Statistic

While statistics are useful for determining patterns and trends and for analysing issues, and while it is hard to grasp the concept of billions of people, every statistic represents real people with real lives. The United Nations (UN), governments, and non-governmental organizations (NGOs) base their estimates on scientific studies, census statistics, and the observations of those who work in the health field. We hear that thousands of children are dying each day from curable diseases. Whichever side of the

equation one is on, whether born into developed or developing countries, whether rich or poor, elderly or young, healthy or sick, each part of one of the "statistics" is a human being with the same basic needs and rights.

The Sanitary Revolution

Imagine working long hours as a child in a dark, damp factory, never being able to shower or bathe in clean water or eat nutritious food. The toll on your health would be dramatic. In the nineteenth century, epidemics and diseases such as typhoid, scarlet fever, diphtheria, cholera, and tuberculosis were common. Industrial cities in Europe and North America were overcrowded dirty places with unsafe living conditions, especially in the slums and tenements of the poor.

> **FACT FILE**
>
> If a jumbo jet carrying a full load of children crashed, it would make headlines around the globe. Yet the number of children who die every day from hunger and disease is equivalent to 50 jumbo jets full.

The amazing improvements in society that occurred over the first half of the twentieth century have been called the sanitary revolution. In Canada, health boards created in the 1880s investigated disease outbreaks, enforced

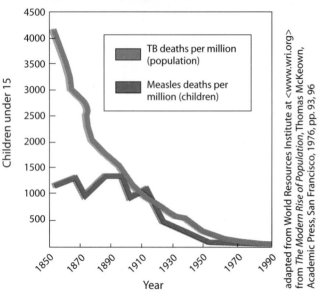

Death Rates for Tuberculosis and Measles in Children under 15, England and Wales, 1850–1990

Legend:
- TB deaths per million (population)
- Measles deaths per million (children)

Y-axis: Children under 15 (500 to 4500)
X-axis: Year (1850 to 1990)

adapted from World Resources Institute at <www.wri.org> from *The Modern Rise of Population*, Thomas McKeown, Academic Press, San Francisco, 1976, pp. 93, 96

FIGURE 15.3 This strong downward trend in infectious diseases resulted from the sanitary revolution in developed countries.

quarantines to reduce the spread of disease, and ran compulsory vaccination programs, resulting in a sharp decline in death rates by the early twentieth century. This gradual change resulted from efforts by governments and organizations to improve working conditions and to eliminate practices such as the dumping of dirty water and raw sewage directly into rivers, although there are many places, even in developed countries, where that practice continues.

Conditions like clean water may seem like basic necessities for most of us, but to many people living today in developing countries, they are unattainable luxuries.

Factors that reduced the incidence of infectious, communicable diseases include:

- awareness that bacteria and viruses cause disease;
- sewage treatment;
- safe drinking water;
- garbage removal;
- improved working conditions, including ventilation;
- better housing;
- laws against child labour;
- food inspection and regulation;

- advances in health care practices such as sterilization of instruments;
- increase in number of health care workers;
- creation of public health departments employing public health specialists;
- discovery and availability of vaccines and antibiotics;
- education about healthy practices and sexually transmitted disease.

The Double Burden

As a result of the sanitary revolution, developed countries in Europe, North America, Asia, and Australia experienced a shift in disease patterns from infectious diseases such as tuberculosis, polio, and measles to chronic diseases like heart disease, stroke, diabetes, and cancer. These chronic diseases are responsible for 86% of all

Main Causes of Death, 1990

Developed Countries
- 86.3%
- 7.6%
- 6.1%

Legend:
- Infectious diseases
- Chronic diseases
- Injury related

Developing Countries
- 47.4%
- 42%
- 10.6%

FIGURE 15.4 Economic development, investment in health care, and social programs can make a big difference within some developing countries. The averages can be misleading. China and India have a similar population size and level of wealth. However, over 50% of deaths in India are from infectious diseases compared with only 16% of deaths in China.

deaths in developed countries. People are living longer and rarely get infectious diseases because of the major overall improvements in health care. This shift from one kind of disease to another is called the **epidemiologic transition**.

The transition is currently occurring in most of the developing world. In middle-income countries in Latin America and Asia, chronic diseases now affect more people than infectious diseases.

People in the poorest countries, however, still suffer from infectious diseases and, without having addressed this burden, also have to cope with the rise of chronic non-communicable diseases. Antibiotic-resistant malaria and tuberculosis are just two of the diseases that are killing millions of people in developing countries and Africa is suffering from an AIDS pandemic that is having a devastating impact on societies.

FACT FILE

The incidence rate of tuberculosis in Canada's Aboriginal population is four times as high as that in the general population.

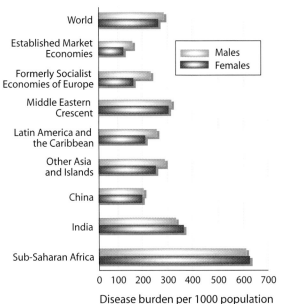

Disease Burden by Gender and Region, 1996

Disease burden per 1000 population

FIGURE 15.5 Africa clearly bears a disproportionate disease burden.

World Resources Institute at <www.wri.org/wr-98-99/dalys2.htm> from *The Global Burden of Disease: Volume 1*, pp. 541–612 (World Health Organization, Harvard School of Public Health, and the World Bank, Geneva, 1996) Christopher J. L. Murray and Alan D. Lopez, eds.

INTERACT

1. Analyse the graphs in Figure 15.4, **Main Causes of Death**, and Figure 15.5, **Disease Burden by Gender and Region**, giving reasons for your observations.

2. Refer to Figure 15.5, **Disease Burden by Gender and Region**, and explain the dichotomy of the disease burden in India and China.

3. Using an atlas, Web site, or the Data Appendix, choose any three statistical indicators of quality of life and include them in a chart comparing each of the 14 countries found in the Fact File on page 370. Other than a low rate of measles immunization for children in all these countries, what differences and similarities in quality of life can be seen?

4. **a)** Write a 250-word comparative analysis of the leading causes of death in developed and developing countries.

   b) Take on the role of an average citizen in a developed and in a developing country of your choice. Write two scenarios describing the daily health risks you face as a member of each society.

5. With other members of your class, discuss the factors that reduce the incidence of infectious disease listed on page 358. Classify the factors according to which of the following three jurisdictions in a developing country that you think should be responsible for implementing them: local municipal government, regional/national government, citizens within the community.

   a) Within each category, reclassify the factors according to low, moderate, or high cost.

   b) Choose any three of the factors that you feel would be most effective in addressing the "double burden" of disease facing the least developed countries.

FACTORS AFFECTING HEALTH AND DISEASE

Despite efforts by the international community, especially over the last half of the twentieth century, our world is still one of poverty, inequity, and inadequate access to food, health care, and other resources.

Poverty and Hunger

Poverty is the key, overriding factor that causes ill health. Most developing countries have not been able to fully develop and finance health care systems and have recently been forced to reduce their budgets. This adds to inequities in health and undermines the potential for economic and social development, creating a vicious circle—poverty causes ill health while ill health contributes to poverty. There are a number of complex underlying factors that must be considered together rather than in isolation before solutions can be implemented.

Nutrition is a key factor because it defines health for everyone. While 22 million children and more than 200 million adults are obese and at significant risk of chronic disease, billions of others suffer from malnutrition or vitamin and mineral deficiencies. A regular intake of the proper mix of high-quality nutrients enables us to grow, develop resistance to infection, work, learn, and enjoy physical and mental well-being. People who are hungry are more vulnerable to disease and malnourished children have poor levels of mental, intellectual, and physical development.

Our food comes from the soil, waters, and forests. The economic structures of a place, its social organization, political stability, how the food is produced, the health of the natural environment, and natural and human-induced hazards all interact to determine the potential for a well-nourished population. Unemployment, lack of income, substandard shelter, lack of education, and sex-based discrimination are all related to poverty and all represent barriers to good nutrition.

In wealthy countries such as Canada, people with low incomes are more likely to be in poor health, suffer diseases, and have a lower life expectancy. Studies have shown that health is linked to level of education and risky behaviour such as poor nutrition, smoking, drinking heavily, and lack of exercise.

> **FACT FILE**
>
> In 1999, the WHO predicted that deaths from tobacco use are expected to increase from 4 million to 8.5 million in 2020, with the largest increases in Asia. This would represent 10% of the whole disease burden worldwide, making tobacco the single largest cause of disability and premature death.

> 66 The gap between what is potentially achievable and what we actually achieve is wider than ever before. Bridging this gap—dealing with the unfinished agenda of the twentieth century—is not only key to improving the health of millions, it is fundamental to a much larger goal—reducing the number of people that live in absolute poverty. 99
>
> *Dr. Gro Harlem Brundtland, director-general, World Health Organization*

Population Growth

Continued population growth combined with rapid urbanization, especially in developing countries, results in overcrowded, unsanitary conditions where infectious diseases spread easily. Over 90% of the population growth in the coming decades will occur in Africa, South Asia, and Latin America. As people with little immunity encroach on tropical forests, they will have contact with diseases such as malaria and yellow fever.

 See Chapters 10 and 11 for more information about population issues.

The Water and Sewage Factor

Providing safe drinking water and proper sewage disposal has the greatest impact on improving the overall health of a population. More than one billion of the world's people do not have access to clean water and 2.5 billion lack sanitary ways to dispose of human waste. Population growth and slowing rates of service provision mean that, in 2000, more people were without access to these basic requirements than in 1990. This sad state in the quality of life exists despite global spending of US$135 billion in the previous decade, with urban areas receiving three-quarters of the total funds. Of the money spent, local governments spent two-thirds while international external organizations spent only one-third. It seems difficult to understand how so many people can exist in the world today without access to these basic necessities of life, when simple and inexpensive measures are readily available.

Water can become contaminated through human, chemical, or industrial wastes, causing many different diseases, most of which Canadians have never heard of. Poor management of irrigation projects has led to a huge spread of schistosomiasis (snail fever) in parts of Africa where it had never existed before. This parasitic disease affects two billion people in the tropical world, an enormous disease burden. Control of the disease requires a single dose of an inexpensive drug, costing only between $0.03 and $0.30 per person, depending on the country. At any one time, half the people in the developing world suffer from one or more of six major diseases associated with water supply: diarrhea, ascaris, dracunculiasis, hookworm, schistosomiasis, and trachoma.

Poor management of farm wastes, lack of skilled personnel at the municipal level, and reduced spending on environmental concerns contributed to the deaths of seven people and illness in hundreds of others in Walkerton, Canada, when the town's water supply became contaminated with E. coli bacteria from hog farm effluent that leaked into groundwater.

Social and Demographic Factors

When analyzing health issues, there is a need to consider social differences and the strong links between human rights and health care.

WOMEN AND CHILDREN Girls and women who are denied access to education, information, real forms of economic, social, and political participation, and freedom from physical and emotional violence are particularly vulnerable to poverty and poor health. Their children suffer consequences along with them.

According to the World Bank, family planning is one of the best ways to have a positive impact on the health of mothers and their children at an annual cost of less than US$2 per person. Yet family planning receives a small fraction of government health budgets and only 2% of all international development assistance.

Some cultural practices rooted in traditional religious and sexual beliefs have had serious effects on the mental and physical health of millions of women and children. These practices include bearing large numbers of children, genital mutilation of young girls, and being forced to stay inside or to completely cover themselves while out, reducing Vitamin D intake. These practices are violations of the United Nations Declaration of Human Rights, the Convention on the Rights of the Child, and the Convention on the Elimination of all Forms of Discrimination Against Women.

The WHO has taken a human rights approach in its efforts to improve the health and nutritional well-being of as many people as possible. The WHO constitution states, "the enjoyment of the highest attainable standard of health is one of the fundamental rights of every human being without distinction of race, religion, political belief, economic, or social condition." In the face of many situations of global conflict—movement of refugees, anti-personnel land mines, suppression of democracy, neglect of human rights, and adverse cultural practices—this goal is a tall order.

MAKE A DIFFERENCE

Nestlé is a huge transnational company that manufactures and sells, among many other products, about half of the world's baby milk formula. In order to sell more formula in developing countries in the 1970s, Nestlé encouraged women to stop breast-feeding their infants and to switch to formula. The company gave away free samples and misinformed mothers and health care workers in promotional literature when it implied that malnourished mothers were better off feeding their babies formula. It went so far as to hire women with no special training and to dress them as nurses to hand out free samples. The breast milk of the mothers dried up, but when the free samples were used up, they were unable to afford the cost of buying the formula. They were often unable to read the mixing directions and the only water available to them was often contaminated.

Because of these unethical corporate tactics, consumers in many different countries began a worldwide boycott against Nestlé products. This boycott campaign raised enough awareness of the issue that the WHO developed an International Code on the Marketing of Breast Milk Substitutes. Most countries signed this agreement in the 1980s, with the United States finally signing on in 1994. For a time, Nestlé and its major competitor, Wyeth, agreed to the code and modified their marketing practices. However, they have been found in violation of the code several times since then, including offering free samples on the Internet. Therefore, the international boycott continues. It is supported by UNICEF, hundreds of health, consumer, and church groups, student and trade unions, political parties, and businesses and celebrities in 20 developed countries, including Canada.

FIGURE 15.6 Some Nestlé and Wyeth products.

An Aging Population A demographic trend that will have a dramatic impact on health issues in the future is the increase in numbers of elderly people living in all countries of the world. In the year 2000, there were about 600 million elderly people aged 60 and over. By the year 2020, more than a billion people will be over the age of 60 with 700 million of them living in developing countries. This aging population is a result of lower death rates and lower birth rates. The decline in death rates, particularly in developing countries, has been remarkable. There are now more than 20 developing countries with life expectancies of over 72 years. Birth rates have fallen in most developing countries outside of sub-Saharan Africa.

 See Chapters 10 and 11 for more information about population trends and policies.

The WHO predicts that by the year 2020, three-quarters of all deaths in developing countries could be age related. Clearly, a rapidly aging global population presents a huge challenge for national and international public health and for economies. More and more people will be at risk of developing chronic and debilitating diseases. There will be a greater need for specialty health care services, less expensive generic drugs, managed home care, and assisted living such as retirement and nursing homes.

> **FACT FILE**
>
> In Canada, in 1999, there were 3.7 million people over the age of 65, or 12% of the population. That is more than double the 5% in 1921 and the percentage is expected to double again by 2040.

> **FACT FILE**
>
> By the year 2020, the "oldest" countries, with around 30% of the total population aged 60 and over, will be Japan, Italy, Greece, and Switzerland, but the countries with the largest total elderly populations will be China, India, Indonesia, Brazil, and Pakistan.

GEOGRAPHIC METHODS

Medical Geography

Medical geography is concerned with the geographic aspects of health and health care such as the factors responsible for the distribution and spread of diseases across geographic regions. Recently, there has been a great deal of research on the geography of AIDS as it has spread from one part of the world to another.

Geographers need to address a number of interrelated factors in analysing health issues from a geographic perspective. Remote sensing and geographic information systems (GIS) are used to address these factors in health studies, including the detection and monitoring of disease outbreaks. GIS is used to facilitate the integration of layers of data obtained from maps, satellite images, and aerial photographs with socio-economic data and information about the quality of health care. There are thousands of wide-ranging applications of these geographic technologies at universities, research institutions, governments, and organizations around the world. These studies include the impact of deforestation on the geographic distribution and intensity of highland malaria; interrelationships between human health and global climate change; and links among ozone layer depletion, ultraviolet radiation, and melanoma (skin cancer). The results of these inquiries are useful in determining strategies for solutions.

Medical geography focuses not only on human health but also on wildlife studies. For example, the Ministry of Natural Resources in Ontario, Canada, has funded geographic studies, using geotechnologies to analyse the spread and control of wildlife rabies.

INTERACT

1. Draw a flow diagram to illustrate the cycle of hunger and poverty and its impact on health.
2. Create a list of 10 specific factors that influence health and disease patterns in developing countries. Compare these with factors that influence patterns in developed countries.
3. Using specific examples of influencing factors, describe the relationship between empowerment of women and the health and life expectancy of their children.
4. How do the health problems of women in developing countries differ from those of women in developed countries?
5. a) What are the social and economic implications of an aging population in Canada?
   b) Predict how your life could be affected by this aging trend by the year 2020.
6. Consider the WHO prediction for tobacco use in the Fact File on page 360. Make your own prediction about how this will affect global demographic trends and identify a social, economic, and environmental implication.

Globalization and Health

Globalization has brought with it a shift to free-market economics with significant implications for health care. The belief that the market system must operate unimpeded has pushed the private sector forward as the best way to create efficiency and growth. Recent government policy in many countries has meant a reduction in overall per capita spending on health care and other social services. Governments have traditionally been the main providers of health services and prevention control programs but are now struggling to keep up. In China, for example, 15 000 villages now have no clinic or health care workers. Allowing privatization of health and hospital services and user fees for these services is a way of bringing the market system into play but private health service providers consider profit as an operating motive. This creates a climate where the type of services that are developed are for those who can pay. Those who cannot afford to pay for medical care usually do without.

Health care workers in developing countries, paid low wages to begin with, are losing their jobs as governments reduce spending on health care. Unemployment in this and other sectors means not only less access to health care, but a declining quality of life, resulting in a vicious circle as rates of alcoholism, mental illness, tuberculosis, and sexually transmitted diseases increase.

Declining international aid and a continued high debt burden have forced many developing countries to follow the structural adjustment policies imposed on them over the past two decades by the World Bank in exchange for loans from the International Monetary Fund (IMF).

The World Bank, in its *World Development Report, 2000/2001*, promises a share for all countries in the benefits of market-led growth and its future policies may encourage more investment in health care and education to improve quality of life for more people.

New international trade regulations, set by the World Trade Organization (WTO), result in liberal policies for large pharmaceutical companies that make drugs at a price out of the reach of the poor. Local manufacturing of generic drugs can be threatened by these trade rules.

Public pressure in the early part of the twenty-first century, particularly relating to the availability of drugs for the AIDS pandemic in Africa, has had some influence, resulting in lower prices or even free essential drugs for some people in some countries. The WHO has developed partnerships with the large pharmaceutical companies in their efforts to cope with rising incidence of disease.

> " Society generally looks at the contribution of development to health. The contribution of health to development has been largely ignored. It is time to reverse this way of looking at things. And it is high time to recognize safe water supply and adequate sanitation to protect health are among the basic human rights. "
>
> *Dr. Gro Harlem Brundtland, director-general, World Health Organization*

FIGURE 15.7 The globalization of infectious diseases means that an outbreak in one country is potentially a concern for the whole world as international trade grows and people and goods are increasingly mobile.

Globalization has brought improved communications technology with better sharing of health information. In the past, doctors in developing countries had little access to current scientific information. Journals of medical schools and research institutions are now available over the Internet to doctors in developing countries at much lower costs than before or are free to the poorest countries, significantly reducing the health information gap.

Health Issues and the Pharmaceutical Industry

It is hard to imagine the state that human health in wealthy countries such as Canada might be in without the wonders of modern medical technology and the many sophisticated drugs that we rely on. Over the past two decades, biotechnology industries have developed drugs for a wide variety of diseases. Without these industries and their pool of financial and human resources, we might all be dying of infectious diseases. Yet there has been a great deal of criticism aimed at the large transnational drug companies, their undue profit from human suffering, and the role they have played in the global health crisis.

Regulatory agencies such as Canada's Drug Safety System and the U.S. Food and Drug Administration have the responsibility of overseeing the drug companies and protecting our health. The formerly adversarial, strictly regulatory role of these agencies appear to have shifted over the years to more of a partnership role. User fees sometimes paid by the companies to the agencies have contributed to the problem. This has led to some recent disasters. Seven well-known and commonly used drugs have been taken off the market since 1993 because of deaths, injuries, and other serious side effects. Potential revenues from sales of the drugs and intense competition among different companies have pushed the partners into "fast-tracking" approvals of some drugs. The industry has been known to mislead the regulatory bodies by excluding essential data and selective interpretation of doctors' reports. The industry claims that their enormous markups in the price of many drugs are necessary because of the high cost of research and development

(R&D). However, a significant portion of the basic research leading to the discovery of drugs has been publicly funded.

Whose Health Revolution?

An important social trend has been the rise of a huge and highly specialized sector of the economy dealing with health care. The health care services industry generates more than US$200 billion a year. We have seen throughout this chapter that the vast majority of services are for a small percentage of the world's people.

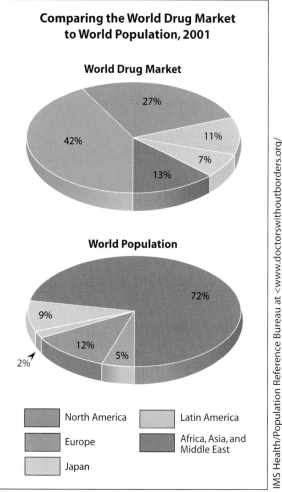

IMS Health/Population Reference Bureau at <www.doctorswithoutborders.org/publication/reports/2001/fatal_imbalance_short.pdf>

FIGURE 15.8 People in developing countries make up about 80% of the world's people but represent only about 20% of world medicine sales. For these people, the imbalance can be fatal. In 2001, an estimated US$70 billion was invested globally in health R&D, with the U.S. private sector alone accounting for US$30.5 billion.

Private sector investment in drugs for infectious diseases in developing countries is minimal. Most of the management attention and financial resources goes to the lucrative market in developed countries rather than focusing on needs across geographic regions. In the spring of 2001, Médecins Sans Frontières (Doctors Without Borders) conducted a survey of the top 20 pharmaceutical companies in the world about the drugs they had developed for neglected diseases in the past five years. Of the 11 companies that completed the survey, none had developed drugs for neglected infectious diseases. However, combined, they had developed eight for erectile dysfunction, seven for obesity, and four for sleep disorders.

Canada joined other developed countries at a G20 summit in Doha, Qatar, in November 2001, in opposing a bid by developing countries to override the patents held by the big pharmaceutical companies, protecting intellectual property rights to the drugs they have developed. This stops developing countries such as South Africa from obtaining cheaper generic drugs even in public health emergencies such as the AIDS pandemic. Some ideas for solutions to the health crisis imbalance have recently been suggested, including a patent exchange. A drug company would be able to extend its patent on a profitable drug beyond the current 20-year period in exchange for investment in a drug to treat a neglected disease.

COUNTERPOINT The European Federation of Pharmaceutical Industries and Associations (EFPIA) represents more than 3350 pharmaceutical companies and associations in Europe. According to their Web site, < www.efpia.org >, "Innovation is the lifeblood of the pharmaceutical industry and the key to any improvement in medical care. Since aspirin™ was invented 100 years ago, the research-based pharmaceutical industry has built up a continuous and steady stream of new medicines targeting ever more complex disease mechanisms. Breakthroughs in pharmaceutical R&D have already produced new or greatly improved treatments for infectious diseases (like diphtheria and tuberculosis), nervous disorders, asthma, hypertension, and stomach ulcers to name but a few.

"Today, over 82 500 pharmaceutical company scientists are researching and discovering in Europe new cures and innovative therapies for cancer, heart disease, HIV/AIDS, Alzheimer's, Parkinson's, arthritis, osteoporosis, cystic fibrosis, and many other diseases. Through its heavy investment in R&D, the pharmaceutical industry's constant search for new life saving and life enhancing medicines provides new hopes and raises expectations that innovation will improve people's health and quality of life—as well as reduce the overall cost of health care.

"Besides contributing to social progress and improving public health, key figures indicate that the pharmaceutical industry's economic strength and ability to deliver innovative medicines also make it a major industrial asset to the European economy."

Some drug companies have recently responded to pressure from international organizations and the public and made some drugs available at lower cost or even as donations. The industry itself can benefit from these measures. Donations of unsold or expired drugs can reduce storage and disposal costs and result in tax breaks as well as good public relations. Some people feel that donating or selling expired or discontinued drugs in developing countries is unethical. Others argue that this is the only way these countries will get some of the badly needed drugs.

> **FACT FILE**
>
> In 1897, a chemist at Germany's Bayer chemical factory prepared the first acetylsalicylic acid, named aspirin™ by Bayer two years later. However, Native people in North America used the bark of the white willow tree to make the substance as a pain-killer in the 1500s, and ancient Greeks prescribed leaves and bark from willow and myrtle for pain and fever as far back as 1500 BCE.

> ❝The G20 action at Qatar will allow massive suffering and death over some ideological issue about patent rights.❞
>
> *Peter Dalgleish, Healthnet International*

excerpt from

Prescription Games: Money, Power and Ego Inside the Global Pharmaceutical Industry

by Jeffrey Robinson
McLelland and Stewart, 2001

North America, Western Europe, and Japan are 80 per cent of the world's drug market. Africa is 1 per cent. The industry claims to invest $27 billion a year in R & D. What it does with the money is what any business does with any investment, it puts it where the consumer power is and caters to the market. The sad thing is that even if it spent its budgets proportionately, and dedicated 1 per cent of its R & D to finding solutions for problems in Africa, that would put only $270 million in the pot, about half the money it takes these days to develop just one new drug.

When you ask about a "floor", they say it doesn't exist. That's because the term they use is "cost-effective" illnesses. Prime Institute's Schondelmaeyer explains, "When it's cost-effective, they find a cure. The opposite, non-cost-effective illnesses, is where there is no economic incentive for anyone to go find a cure. Where you have rare diseases in developed countries with resources, they're likely to get taken care of. But if you have diseases, even with large populations in Africa, but no resources, people die.

Sasich at Public Citizen agrees: "Just look at the drugs that are being developed for malaria."

He points to Glaxo's Malarone, which won approval in Europe in mid-2000. The first anti-malarial developed by a drug company in forty years—the others had all come from institutions—Malarone is preventative, meaning that its main market is the estimated 7 million tourists, business people, and military personnel who travel annually into malaria-affected regions.

"They're marketed to treat travelers from rich western nations going to sub-Saharan Africa," he adds, "not to deal with malaria in Africa. New anti-malarials could probably be used to treat the problem in Africa, but those people don't have any money. So they don't get the drugs."

Glaxo announced it would be donating some quantities of Malarone to Kenya and Uganda. Malaria, nonetheless remains the perfect example of Big Pharma's cost-effective neglect… Sadly, malaria is far from the only disease adversely affected by the cost-effective equation."

When an AIDS conference in South Africa convinced the world's media to spotlight Big Pharma's intransigence, the industries' legions of press and public relations managers went to work. Almost in unison they said, "Of course we're willing to do something. We've always been willing to help, but what's really required is patent protection in the Third World and more respect for intellectual property rights because without

that, if we give our drugs away for free, they'll only wind up being sold on the black market in the West."

The media laid on more heat.

Glaxo Wellcome was first to blink. The company announced that as a gesture of genuine concern, it would reduce the daily price of its AIDS drug, Combivir, from $16.50—which is the retail price in the United States—to a mere $2, which is presumably at, or somewhere above, cost. Could that be an inadvertent admission that drug companies work on an 800 per cent markup?

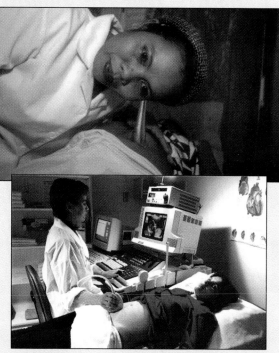

FIGURE 15.9 Pregnancy care in Indonesia (upper) and high-tech maternity care in Canada (lower).

Critical Analysis

1. Explain the bias held by the writer.
2. What role has public opinion played in shifting drug company research and development policies?
3. The incentive in the private sector for finding cures to diseases has always been economic. What other kinds of incentives do you feel different stakeholders could bring into play?
4. What additional information would be useful before making a decision about whether the role of the big pharmaceutical companies is beneficial to or a barrier to addressing global health issues?
5. How will solving the issues surrounding the development and provision of effective drugs at an affordable cost to all people in developing countries affect your future?

MAKE A DIFFERENCE

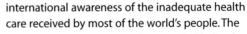

Médecins Sans Frontières

Also known as Doctors Without Borders, this independent medical humanitarian organization won the Nobel Peace prize in 1999. Made up mainly of doctors, the organization operates in the riskiest conflict "hot spots," refugee camps, and poverty-stricken communities in more than 80 countries around the world. Volunteers help people in need regardless of their race, religion, gender, or politics. The organization has been instrumental in raising international awareness of the inadequate health care received by most of the world's people. The pressure they exerted helped persuade some pharmaceutical companies to lower the cost of antiretroviral drugs for treating HIV/AIDS patients and to supply a discounted line of drugs for multi-drug-resistant tuberculosis.

FIGURE 15.10 A doctor with Médecins Sans Frontières, working in a Macedonian refugee camp.

INTERACT

1. Draw a flow diagram to show the "vicious circle" of interconnections among economic and health factors in the society of a typical developing country. In your diagram, include some or all of the following factors: low wages, inadequate government spending, unemployment, alcoholism and mental illness, inadequate access to health care.

2. Explain what is meant by the term "neglected diseases." Suggest two initiatives that could be taken by the WTO and by individual Canadians to address the issues surrounding neglected diseases.

3. Conduct research to find out more about the activities and people involved in Doctors Without Borders, or select another NGO that is involved in similar humanitarian efforts as the focus of your investigation. Create a list of three questions to guide your investigation. Prepare a brief oral report to members of your class in which you answer your questions and evaluate the role played by the NGO in addressing the global health crisis.

4. The World Bank has come under criticism for requiring some governments to adopt structural adjustment policies. Study the quote made by the World Bank director-general on page 374 and the promise made in the bank's *World Development Report, 2000/2001* on page 364. Make a prediction of how likely it is that the World Bank will fulfill its promise to developing countries. Support your view with at least three arguments.

5. Describe recent trends in the pharmaceutical industry. For any one of these trends, analyse the social and economic implications for global health care in the future.

6. Why have recent government policies all around the world had difficulty providing exemplary health care and other social services for their citizens?

7. Use an Internet search engine such as < www.google.com > to discover the focus of at least three GIS applications related to geography of health care, other than those in the text. In a brief point-form note, explain how geographers have used geotechnologies to contribute to problem solving and decision making.

MEETING GLOBAL HEALTH CHALLENGES

Over the past 50 years, there has been a tendency among international health improvement efforts to concentrate on medical intervention to prevent disease and provide drugs, leaving provision of safe water and sanitation as a lower priority. With increased resistance to antibiotics and insecticides, people are now starting to realize the limitations of a strictly medical approach.

" There can be no peace, no security, nothing but ultimate disaster, when a few rich countries with a small minority of the world's people alone have access to the brave, and frightening, new world of technology, science, and of high material living standard, while the majority live in deprivation and want, shut off from opportunities of full economic development; but with the expectations and aspirations beyond the hope of realizing them. "

Lester B. Pearson, prime minister of Canada, 1963–1968

In April 2000, the WHO established a global outbreak alert-and-response communication network that uses electronic communication as a means of improving the tracking and reporting of infectious diseases. Controlling malaria, tuberculosis, and HIV/AIDS, as well as halving the incidence of measles by 2005 and eradicating polio were major strategies of the WHO in 2001. The WHO also stated in its March 2001 report that the health sector must get more fully involved in improving water supply and management.

The need for international co-operative efforts to improve health issues facing all parts of the world is greater than ever before. Strategic partnerships will become an essential tool for addressing health and disease issues and public health failures. Different stakeholders working together as partners can better advocate for the resources needed for research, immunization programs, health education, clean water and nutritional food, healthier natural environments, and improved economic and social development. The solutions put forward must be affordable, needs-based, sustainable,

and actively involve developing countries. Groups that can play a role in these partnerships include:

- UN Agencies such as the World Health Organization (WHO), the Children's Fund (UNICEF), Environment Program (UNEP), and Centre for Human Settlements (UNCHS);
- agencies such as the Pan American Health Organization (PAHO);
- NGOs such as Médecins Sans Frontières (Doctors Without Borders);
- private foundations such as the Bill and Melinda Gates Foundation or Rockefeller Foundation;
- service clubs such as Rotary Clubs International;
- academics and university research teams;
- professional organizations;
- transnational corporations (TNCs), particularly pharmaceutical companies;
- public agencies in national governments;
- media;
- students;
- the general public.

Drugs for Neglected Diseases

In October 1999, a group of concerned scientists, health professionals, representatives from NGOs, pharmaceutical companies, governments of developing countries, and international organizations met in Paris to try to find ways to address the failure of the market to develop drugs to fight the infectious diseases that receive so little attention. The initiative was organized by the WHO, Médecins Sans Frontièries, and the Rockefeller Foundation. The consortium will continue to fund drug development projects in an attempt to reduce the suffering of millions of people.

In March 2001, Canada announced that it would invest $15 million in a tuberculosis drug facility. Canada is the first country in the world to finance this program, fulfilling a promise made by the world's wealthy countries to do more to eradicate this disease. On October 17, 2001, Canada's Minister for International Cooperation announced that the Canadian International Development Agency (CIDA) would provide $10 million over three years to support the Global Alliance on Vaccines and

FIGURE 15.11 Ugandan researchers with the World Health Organization, Tropical Diseases and Research Institute work on African trypanosomiasis (sleeping sickness). Despite chronic lack of funding, scientific research institutes in developing countries conduct research into new medicines and train scientists.

FIGURE 15.12 The Bill and Melinda Gates Foundation has become an important source of funding for developing vaccines and drugs for neglected diseases. The foundation donated US$25 million for developing a malaria vaccine, $25 million to the Global Alliance for Tuberculosis Drug Development, and $15 million for vaccine research for leishmaniasis, a parasitic and often fatal disease transmitted by the sandfly vector.

Immunization (GAVI), a public and private sector partnership aimed at preventing childhood diseases and reducing mortality rates through immunization in the least developed countries. The announcement brings CIDA's commitment to $60 million between 2000 and 2005.

Inadequate policies by the governments of developing countries have compounded the most serious health issues. Governments can make a significant difference and many are beginning to take this responsibility more seriously. For example, the government of Thailand has provided support for the development of the malaria drug Coartem from the ancient Chinese herb artemisinin that cured 90% of the malaria cases in Thailand, and reduced infections in children living in refugee camps on the Thai–Burma border by 90%. Research, development, and production of drugs is increasing in Brazil, India, South Korea, Thailand, Malaysia, and Argentina. The International Vaccine Institute in South Korea is a good model of a non-profit drug development institute for developing countries to follow, while India has a growing pharmaceutical industry with government support.

A Pot of Gold?

In 2001, the UN and its health agencies were negotiating with governments, foundations, and other donors to contribute to a global fund that will be used to combat AIDS, tuberculosis, and malaria. Kofi Annan, the UN secretary-general, hoped to add US$10 billion to the current global spending on these diseases. Donations to the fund have been lower than expected.

FACT FILE

In 1999, 14 countries reported to the WHO that fewer than half their children received the measles vaccine: Afghanistan, Burkina Faso, Burundi, Cameroon, Congo, Democratic Republic of Congo, Djibouti, Guinea-Bissau, Liberia, Madagascar, Niger, Senegal, Somalia, and Togo.

National Immunization Days

An unprecedented alliance, aimed at immunizing 80 million children and thereby eliminating polio, was formed in 16 West African countries. Over a week in October 2001, and with a second round during a week in November, tens of thousands of volunteers and health workers drove, walked, paddled, or cycled to every house in even the most remote villages and densely populated cities, aided by detailed maps. More than 86 000 health care workers provided vaccinations in just one country alone, the Democratic Republic of the Congo. An appeal was made for a halt to violent conflict and safe passage for health care workers in some countries such as Sierra Leone to make the campaign a success. Volunteers also travelled to refugee camps and set up immunization clinics at every border crossing. The cost of this massive campaign was shared by many partners, including the WHO, UNICEF, Rotary International, private foundations, national governments, and political parties. Leaders of the Economic Community of West African States (ECOWAS) signed a document called the Lungi Declaration as part of the global effort to eradicate the wild polio virus by 2005. Similar polio immunization initiatives have occurred in Central Africa, Afghanistan, and Pakistan.

> " Measles is still a major childhood killer, with over 30 million cases and nearly 900 000 annual deaths in recent years. These figures are even more shocking given the fact that effective immunization, which includes vaccine and safe injection equipment, costs just US$0.26 and has been available for more than 30 years. "
>
> *Dr. Bjorn Melgaard, director of vaccines and biologicals, World Health Organization*

> " If we eliminate polio in Sierra Leone but we don't in Nigeria we are not safe. If we eliminate polio in Mali but we don't in Burkina Faso we are not safe. That is why all of West Africa must work together to eradicate this disease. "
>
> *Olusegun Obasanjo, president of Nigeria*

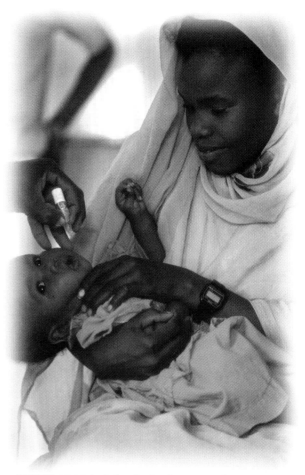

FIGURE 15.13 An infant in Omdurman, Sudan, receives polio immunization.

Solar Energy Initiatives

Health care and energy are closely related factors as health care infrastructure requires energy. Refrigerators are needed to keep vaccines and other medicines cool, especially in tropical climates. There are now over 5000 photovoltaic refrigerators in clinics around the world, primarily in rural areas of Africa, and health care centres often use solar lighting and water heaters. The use of solar cookers for household food preparation has reduced the need for scarce supplies of wood-based fuel and significantly reduced health problems in women caused by long-term exposure to smoke from wood and dung cooking fires.

A highly effective, low cost technique for providing safe water is solar water disinfection

(SODIS), being promoted by the Swiss Federal Institute for Environmental Science and Technology. All that is required is sunlight, which is free, a black surface, and a plastic soft drink bottle. The bottle is filled with water and placed horizontally on a black plastic or corrugated iron surface or, alternatively, the bottom half of the bottle is painted black. Microorganisms in the polluted water are killed by ultraviolet light in the solar radiation and the heat that occurs as the black surface absorbs light. Field studies in Bolivia, Burkina Faso, China, Colombia, Indonesia, Thailand, and Togo have shown the success of this simple process.

Health Care Initiatives

UNICEF's growth monitoring, oral rehydration, breastfeeding, and immunization (GOBI) program is widely accepted as a simple, inexpensive and effective way of providing primary health care for infants and young children in developing countries. GOBI involves a combination of the following medical techniques:

- growth monitoring therapy—continuous monitoring of weight as a sign of well-being;
- oral rehydration therapy (ORT)—a simple but effective sugar, salt, and water solution that reduces dehydration from diarrhea;
- breastfeeding—to provide the best nutritional start for infants;
- immunization—to prevent deaths from six lethal diseases: diphtheria, measles, polio, tetanus, tuberculosis, and whooping cough.

Three additional factors were integrated to form GOBI-FFF in the 1990s. The three Fs stand for Female Education, Family Spacing, and Food Supplements.

Acute gastroenteritis is one of the most common illnesses affecting people all over the world. With diseases and conditions such as food poisoning or microbial infection that result in diarrhea, children are at higher risk because they can become dehydrated much more quickly than adults. In severe cases, there is a mortality rate of over 90%. For centuries, some cultures have had their own effective oral treatments for this debilitating condition, including salted rice water and cereal-based solutions. In India, a thick mixture of soft rice and salt was used for over 3000 years.

The simple, inexpensive solution of sugar and salt called ORT or oral hydration solution (ORS) has saved the lives of millions of children since it was first developed by young medical researchers in the 1960s. The glucose (sugar) enhances the salt and water intake across the mucosal membrane in the intestine, allowing the absorption of essential electrolytes and reducing the dehydrating effects of diarrhea.

ORT has been promoted by the WHO and NGOs as the main treatment in developing countries. Despite its simplicity, ORT has been called the most significant medical advance of the twentieth century.

At the 1990 World Summit for Children, more than 150 countries agreed to work toward achieving ORT coverage of 80% of the child cases and a reduction of 50% of the deaths by 2000. Globally, deaths in children under the age of five have fallen from 5 million in 1980 to 1.5 million in 2000. Case studies in Brazil, Egypt, Mexico, and the Philippines have proven that the use of ORT can cause a significant decline in numbers of child deaths.

ORT must be considered a treatment rather than a solution to the critical global health issues surrounding diarrhea-related illnesses. Solutions require a long-term approach and an integration of many primary health care factors:

- Encourage breast-feeding of infants
- Education
- Improve socio-economic status
- Deliver appropriate technology
- Develop the political will and financial resources to distribute ORT
- Eliminate contaminated water and lack of sanitation that cause diarrhea

Canada Leading the Future

Health care costs continue to rise. In Ontario, Canada, about $0.45 of every tax dollar goes to health care and this cost is increasing. In the future, we may no longer be able to fund many of the treatments for non-life-threatening conditions and diseases such as acne. Our needs may be greater than available resources and decisions will have to be made about where to best allocate our resources. National and international governments and institutions need an ethical and moral framework as a basis for addressing critical public health issues.

What are the ethical and moral principles that should be used to make these decisions? Whether considering stem cells, body parts, gene therapy, or international assistance, new forms of ethics and law will be needed. We need thoughtful discussions and debates on these questions in our society.

New genome-related biotechnologies have great potential for improving prevention, diagnosis, and treatment of common diseases, but they are very costly to develop and very controversial. Canada could take the opportunity to promote the use of these technologies to close the health gap between rich and poor across the country and throughout the world. Many different stakeholders could come together to examine their potential risks and benefits. Public awareness is essential to ensure that citizens of both developed and developing countries have information, understanding, and the opportunity to express their values related to the new technologies.

Canada's health care system is among the top five in the world. Canadian health care professionals should have many ideas to offer developing countries for solving health care issues. If every university medical school in Canada reserved and provided scholarships for just two seats per year for future public health care specialists from developing countries, no one university would be hit too hard and, collectively, such an initiative would be sustainable.

Canada's Programs in Genomics and Global Health and in Applied Ethics and Biotechnology, both based at the University of Toronto, are working with a number of partners, including some in developing countries, to investigate which biotechnologies offer the greatest potential for improving the state of global health.

INTERACT

1. a) Define "primary health care."
   b) Explain how GOBI-FFF can be an effective solution for health problems.
2. a) What initiatives has Canada put forth to address the global health crisis?
   b) Consider the suggestion made on this page about providing scholarships at Canadian universities for medical students from developing countries. In discussion with a group of others in your class, expand this idea to compile a list of additional practical suggestions.
   c) Decide on the most effective way to communicate your ideas to the federal Minister for International Cooperation.
3. Why have strategic partnerships been called essential for solving the global health crisis? Explain why you agree or disagree with this view.
4. a) Study the Canadian Connection on pages 369–370. What is CIDA's per capita financial commitment between 2000 and 2005?
   b) Investigate to find out what percentage of Canada's GDP is spent on foreign aid.
   c) Compare this figure to that of several other developed countries.
5. Canada and the U.S. have been called "fast-food countries." Investigate the links between a diet of frequent fast foods such as hamburgers, fries, and "shakes" and disease. Produce a three-page report on your findings, including statistics that support your conclusions.

CASE STUDY

The Geography of AIDS

The Black Plague of the fourteenth century spread along trade routes across Asia and Europe, killing an estimated 25 million people. Since that time, people have been aware that diseases spread across geographic regions. **Epidemiology**, which studies epidemics, and medical geography are allied fields of study, concerned with analysing the distribution of disease and death at different geographic scales. Medical geographers' inquiries, sometimes called spatio-temporal analyses, attempt to explain how a disease diffuses over space and time. They identify and analyse the cultural, social, behavioural, and political variables that work together to determine distribution patterns, strategies to solve related issues, and why we should care.

> ### FACT FILE
>
> In South Africa, 55% of all new cases of HIV/AIDS infections are women who are vulnerable in a climate of male sexual control.

FIGURE 15.14 Geotechnologies such as GIS are powerful tools that increase the speed and capacity with which geographers can analyse issues.

When studying HIV/AIDS, geographers work with GIS to analyse relationships among data. Information from private and government sources include data sets on factors such as:

- incidence of infection;
- location of health clinics;
- transportation routes;
- migration patterns;
- population density;
- location of urban centres;
- incidence of drug use;
- incidence of prostitution.

A Mosaic of Epidemics

AIDS has been called a **pandemic**, an epidemic that has spread widely to different geographic regions. Patterns of HIV/AIDS diffusion vary dramatically around the globe. Nowhere in the world has been uniformly affected. There has also been a wide range of responses to the pandemic.

AIDS is starting to destabilize entire countries in Africa. Millions of children have lost their parents and teachers. Many industries have lost workers. Economic gains made in countries like Botswana, known for its strong economy and good governance, are seriously threatened. In some countries, the highest risk groups are those who engage in prostitution or unprotected homosexual practices. In others, those who engage in unprotected heterosexual practices are the main groups at risk.

In some South African cities, 45% of women who were tested during pregnancy were HIV positive, a rate that is at least ten times greater than the rate for pregnant women in most countries in Central or West Africa. Along border regions of some countries, such as the borders between Burma, Thailand, and China, and in large urban areas, a higher percentage of people are infected. The disease is increasing in

> " If we had eradicated AIDS in Africa where it was born, it would not be the worldwide disaster it has become today. "
>
> James Wolfensohn, president, World Bank

> ### FACT FILE
>
> In the Brazilian state of Sao Paulo, AIDS has been the leading cause of death in women aged 20 to 34 years since 1992.

Estimated People Living with AIDS and Total Deaths Due to AIDS, 2000

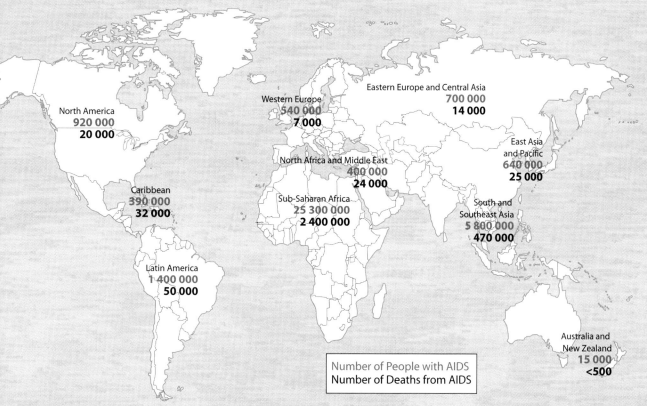

Western Europe
540 000
7 000

Eastern Europe and Central Asia
700 000
14 000

North America
920 000
20 000

East Asia and Pacific
640 000
25 000

North Africa and Middle East
400 000
24 000

Caribbean
390 000
32 000

Sub-Saharan Africa
25 300 000
2 400 000

South and Southeast Asia
5 800 000
470 000

Latin America
1 400 000
50 000

Australia and New Zealand
15 000
<500

Number of People with AIDS
Number of Deaths from AIDS

FIGURE 15.15 The cumulative total of all deaths due to AIDS worldwide is estimated at more than 30 million. There are 14 000 new infections each day, more than 95% of which occur in developing countries.

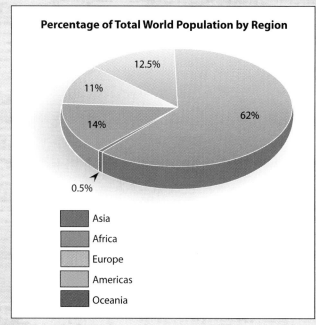

Percentage of Total World Population by Region

12.5%
11%
14%
62%
0.5%

- Asia
- Africa
- Europe
- Americas
- Oceania

FIGURE 15.16

areas that are under great social and economic stress, where migrant workers and traders are mobile, and in regions of political instability. In all countries, HIV/AIDS has spread from high-risk groups and moved into the general population of society.

Coping with the AIDS Pandemic

In November 2001, in Vancouver, two Canadian doctors, Dr. Michael O'Shaugnessy and Dr. Julio Montaner, published an important, widely reported study in the *Journal of the American Medical Association*. The study showed the world that the use of powerful antiretroviral drug cock-

Number of AIDS Diagnoses in Canada

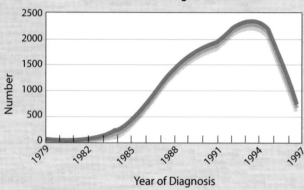

Family Health International "Monitoring the AIDS Pandemic (MAP) Network" Web site, <www.fhi.org/en/aids/impact/mapgva.html>

FIGURE 15.17 In Canada, the proportion of new AIDS cases attributed to men who have sex with men decreased from close to 80% in the 1980s to almost 50% in 1998. The proportion of AIDS cases in women increased from about 5% in the 1980s to 14% in 1997. The downward trend shown on the graph started to go back up in Canada in 2000. The epidemic has moved into new populations, including an increase in infections in the aboriginal population, and in 2000, the declining rate in homosexual males once again began to rise in various cities in Ontario and some other cities, including Vancouver.

tails, used to treat AIDS, which may have powerful negative side effects, can be taken at a much later stage in the disease and still be as effective, possibly revolutionizing future AIDS treatment.

Dr. Kelly MacDonald, the University of Toronto's first chair in HIV/AIDS research, has worked extensively on the disease in Nairobi and is now dedicated to finding a vaccine. Other researchers at the university are working on Canada's largest AIDS study, which began in January 2002, to determine the factors responsible for the rising rate of HIV in Ontario's gay and bisexual men.

A researcher at Laval University in Quebec has developed a heat-activated antimicrobial gel that has prevented transmission of HIV in laboratory conditions. It is under study as an invisible condom.

PROFILE

Stephen Lewis

Stephen Lewis is a Canadian who has been called a humanitarian, diplomat, strategist, investigator, communicator, and grass-roots activist. For decades he has been an outspoken activist in the fight for social justice around the world, particularly for children.

He was the leader of the Ontario NDP party in the 1970s, Canada's ambassador to the UN in the 1980s, and the deputy executive director of UNICEF from 1995 to 1999. He was a member of the Organization of African Unity's investigation of the 1994 genocide in Rwanda. In June 2001, he was appointed by the secretary-general of the UN, Kofi Annan, as the UN's special envoy for HIV/AIDS in Africa.

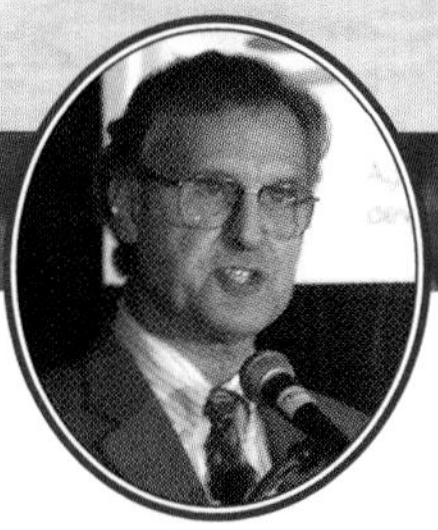

FIGURE 15.18

Stephen Lewis has called the response of the developed world, including that of the World Bank, other multilateral agencies, and the "predatory" transnational pharmaceutical companies, to the AIDS pandemic in Africa "pathetic, and a terribly delinquent moral lapse." He expresses himself in colourful words of frustration and hope in newspapers and television documentaries.

He has helped the rest of the world become aware of the issues connected to AIDS—that millions of people are going to die and that millions of men, women, babies, and orphans are going to suffer. Yet he believes there is not a reason in the world that this has to happen except for the cost of prevention and treatment.

AIDS Timeline

Late 1950s	Origins of HIV, one strain in East-Central Africa, one in West Africa, possibly cross-transmitted to humans from Simian Immunodeficiency Virus (SIV). These events were eventually traced in the 1980s.

Patient Zero, a sexually promiscuous airline steward, vacations in Haiti, the first country in the western hemisphere with a high rate of AIDS. The first reported cases of unusual immune-system failures in North America are concentrated in large cities, including New York, San Francisco, Los Angeles, Miami, Houston, Detroit, Toronto, Montreal, and Vancouver. The disease has spread to all Latin American and Caribbean Nations. — **1980**

1981

HIV is identified as the cause of an epidemic in Africa. — **1983**

1982 — AIDS is named and three ways of transmitting the virus are identified: blood transfusion, mother-to-child, and sexual contact. While the diffusion of the epidemic becomes known around the world, warning signs are largely ignored.

1984

1985 — U.S. Food and Drug Administration (FDA) introduces the first HIV antibody test and begins screening blood donations. The disease spreads to Asia, including Thailand and India, and Europe.

HIV spreads along trade and migration routes throughout Africa in the 1980s. — **1986**

1987 — The WHO establishes the first AIDS program and the first therapy, AZT, is approved.

Health Ministers from a number of countries meet in London to discuss the AIDS issue for the first time. — **1988**

1989

1990

1991

1992 — India establishes the national AIDS Control Organization to carry out prevention and education.

Canada has 1859 AIDS cases. — **1993**

1994

An AIDS outbreak is discovered in drug users in Europe. More effective antiretroviral therapies are developed, which reduce mortality by 80%. — **1995**

1996 — The Joint United Nations Program on HIV/AIDS is created. It predicts that, by 2000, more than 9 million Africans will be infected with AIDS. The actual number turns out to be 25 million.

South Africa passes a law allowing the import of cheaper generic AIDS drugs to protect the health of its citizens in light of the pandemic emergency. The law is never used. — **1997**

1998

1999 — The U.S. and other developed countries spend less than 1% of their international aid budgets on AIDS. The first trials of a potential HIV vaccine in a developing country begins in Thailand.

HIV/AIDS is discussed in the UN Security Council for the first time. — **2000**

Secretary-General Kofi Annan announces a Global Action Plan against AIDS. Three dozen pharmaceutical companies sue South Africa for the 1997 law, which the companies claim violates patents and intellectual property rights. The AIDS toll in Canada reaches almost 20 000 cases.

2001 — The pharmaceutical companies drop their lawsuit against the South African government. Treatment Action Campaign (TAC), an NGO, sues the South African government for not providing sufficient access to neviropene for pregnant women. The South African government is ordered by the courts to provide neviropene to all HIV positive expectant mothers as a result of the TAC lawsuit. Stephen Lewis is appointed as special envoy on AIDS to Africa.

FIGURE 15.19

Local Community Initiatives

While waiting for the mobilization of the international community and the Global Health Fund, there are hundreds of small, local community initiatives in all parts of the world, including counselling, caring for patients and orphans, and prevention programs. Hundreds of small-scale projects provide homes and schooling for orphans throughout Africa, Asia, and Latin America. Although usually underfunded, most of the funds come from religious groups and aid agencies. In Zimbabwe, village leaders have set aside land to be cultivated by villagers to feed orphans and the families of sick people. A number of volunteer women have been recruited to visit households led by orphans to provide basic necessities and emotional support. In Botswana, the president has succeeded in destigmatizing the disease by promoting open discussions on the issues. Huge billboards encourage condom use and community education programs have succeeded in stabilizing and even causing a decline in the high rate of infection in some regions. In South Africa, truckers get free education and condoms at highway rest stops. In Nairobi, Kenya, condom use in prostitutes has risen from negligible in 1985 to 80% in 2000. In Thailand, a concerted effort by government, NGOs, media, and citizens, aimed at encouraging people to stop risky behaviour, along with a national monitoring system, has resulted in a decline in new infections.

FIGURE 15.20 Local community initiatives to fight AIDS in Africa.

"How are we able to do the most monstrous things to each other? What we know can happen in the western world, can improve lives tremendously in Africa. Canada's actual foreign aid and CIDA budget has fallen more than the Prime Minister has told us. Our obsession with deficits and taxes means we rarely think about our contributions to the rest of the world.

These countries are devastated. The infrastructures are shredded. The extended families are destroyed. We're dealing with a kind of contemporary apocalypse.

The entire atmosphere has changed in the most astonishing way in just the last few months. There is a sense of urgency and emergency that is unmistakable. What has happened... is a tremendous consciousness-raising and determination on the part of the African leadership. No one hesitates to talk about [AIDS] any more. The pharmaceutical industry, recognizing tremendous anger around the world and recognizing that they were involved in a public relations disaster.... made a specific policy to change their approach. There began this snowballing effect of one drug company after another, dropping their prices, offering drugs for free, offering sums of money to build clinics in Uganda and Botswana…

The Secretary-General's Global AIDS and Health Fund, which aims to ultimately mobilize $7–10 billion annually in new resources in the fight against AIDS, malaria and tuberculosis in developing countries is a shockwave to the system. A massive commitment of the international community and massive mobilization of health care infrastructure improvement and initiatives in African countries are needed. Will it happen? I don't know. I believe we are on the brink of turning the pandemic around and I'm certainly willing to fight for it.

Finally the world seems to understand that in Africa, this is a gender based pandemic. Unless there is recognition that women are the most vulnerable ... and you do something about the social and cultural equality for women, you're never going to defeat this pandemic. This is the fundamental centrepiece of the whole blessed crisis! Men haven't changed their behaviour, so women somehow have to be strengthened to ward off the men.

It's all terribly late. We've watched for twenty years while millions have died on the sub-Saharan African continent. We've lost 17 million lives and have 25 million people infected, while people with AIDS in industrialized countries have had their lives prolonged for years by antiretroviral drugs. It's only now that we're contemplating treating people in Africa with antiretrovirals. There has been an unacceptable, indefensible double standard... People in Africa who have AIDS have as much right to life as people in the western world."

Stephen Lewis, the UN's special envoy for HIV/AIDS in Africa, Africa Recovery, United Nations

excerpt from **Jwaneng, Botswana**

by Andre Picard
The Globe and Mail
December 10, 2001

The fence, topped with barbed wire and brought into relief by powerful spotlights, stretches as far as the eye can see. The front gate is manned by an impressive private security force. Inside, visitors and employees are under constant surveillance—at any time, a person can be taken aside for X-rays or a full cavity search.

Debswana Diamond Co. Ltd.'s diamond mine in Jwaneng, Botswana, is the richest in the world, producing 11.4 million carats annually, and it prides itself on the security surrounding it's gem-laden crater and processing facilities. Yet a wily thief has been coming back day after day for years, blatantly stealing the company's most precious resource.

HIV-AIDS is stealthily robbing Debswana's workers of their health and their lives, killing at such a prodigious rate that the diamond giant is beginning to worry that it will soon be without an adequate work force. More than 5,500 people work at the sprawling Jwaneng mine, and 1,242 of them are infected.

Although the government has mounted an offensive against HIV-AIDS that has attracted a lot of attention, businesses such as Debswana are coming up with their own solutions to help workers prolong their lives.

Countrywide, it is projected that nearly 40 per cent of Botswana's entire work force will die within a decade, and that the population will fall by at least one-fifth.

Yet this peaceful country in southern Africa has the fastest-growing economy in the world, fuelled by extensive reserves of diamonds and copper and a booming tourist trade.

At Debswana, these two trends are colliding head-on. Sadly, the virus is winning hands down.

HIV-AIDS is not just gobbling up hundreds of lives every week; it is wreaking havoc on the bottom line of corporations and government. By some estimates, the epidemic will soon take a 25 per cent annual bite from the gross domestic product.

"The economic impact of HIV-AIDS is very devastating," Botswana's President Festus Mogae, a former economist, said in an interview. "AIDS is robbing us of our human capital," he said.

Debswana's move will help keep some of those people alive longer. With a budget of $2 million (U.S.), the anti-retroviral program at the single mine site instantly became the largest, most expensive therapy program in Africa, bigger than entire HIV-AIDS programs in many countries.

Tsesele Fanton, who oversees the initiative, said that while the approach is compassionate, it is above all a sound business move…

According to a report by the Washington-based Brookings Institution, the potential impact of AIDS on corporate profits is one of the most overlooked aspects of the epidemic. The report says the disease creates what is in effect an additional payroll tax, in the form of either direct treatment costs or higher health and insurance premiums. Recruitment and training costs also increase.

Mrs. Fanton said Debswana calculated that investing in treatment was the cheapest option. The program was expected to increase payroll costs by up to 10.7 per cent, but a substantial cut in drug prices has cut that estimate to 6.5 per cent…

Spouses are also eligible for the program, but children are not. This has created fears that workers will share their medications, a move that would be dangerous because it would almost certainly result in the virus becoming resistant.

The other controversy associated with the groundbreaking program is the fear that it will lead to mandatory testing and discrimination against people with HIV-AIDS. Mrs. Fanton bristles at the suggestions, saying "our company does not subscribe to the idea of pre-employment testing." Yet Debswana has instituted pre-employment testing for interns, students whose education it subsidizes in return for a promise they will work for the company.

Mrs. Fanton justifies this by saying there is no point investing a lot of money in workers who could be dead by the time they are scheduled to become productive members of the company.

"HIV-AIDS is an emotive issue. But for us, it is a business issue. We are doing this to ensure the future of the mine and the economic security of the workers."

Critical Analysis

1. Suggest factors that could be responsible for the high rate of AIDS incidence in Botswana.
2. How can AIDS be considered a thief to both workers and the company?
3. Explain the economic impact of the AIDS epidemic on governments, workers, and corporations.
4. Evaluate the positive and negative implications of the company's health initiative.

INTERACT

1. Using information from Figure 15.15, **Estimated People Living with AIDS and Total Deaths Due to AIDS, 2000** and Figure 15.16, **Percentage of Total World Population by Region**, comment on the disparity between the AIDS situation in Africa and in the rest of the world.
2. Identify two reasons why Stephen Lewis, the UN's special envoy for HIV/AIDS in Africa, feels frustration and two reasons why he feels hope in the fight against AIDS.
3. Explain how the position of women in a society is a critical factor in shaping the course of the AIDS pandemic.
4. Using an outline map of the world, a map in an atlas showing trade and travel routes, as well as information from this chapter, create a labelled World AIDS Map, using arrows to illustrate the probable diffusion of the pandemic from its origin to the present global spread.
5. Explain the connections among Geography, GIS, and epidemiology.

WEB LINKS

- World Health Organization: <www.who.int>
- Doctors Without Borders: <www.doctorswithoutborders.org>
- Canada's International Development Research Centre: <www.idrc.ca>
- AIDS Educational Global Information System: <www.aegis.com>
- 10 000 links to sources of health information: <www.canadian-health-network.ca>
- Global Health Council: <www.ncih.org>
- Treatment Action Campaign: <www.tac.org/za>

RELATED ISSUES

- Global health in times of crisis: bioterrorism
- Alcohol and tobacco and their impact on health
- Reproductive health issues
- Food safety and health

GIS **Access to Health Care Providers**

ANALYSE, APPLY, AND INTERACT

1. Make a list of the factors discussed throughout the chapter that are barriers to good health for people in developing countries.

2. Produce a case study of global health initiatives designed to address the threat of malaria.

3. Produce a case study of one of the large pharmaceutical transnational companies in which you evaluate its performance with respect to promotion of human rights.

4. Conduct research on the global plan to stop the spread of tuberculosis, launched in October 2001.

5. a) Conduct research to investigate the disease burden facing Canada's Aboriginal people.
   b) Create a chart to compare at least three sets of data on the types and rates of disease and death for the average Canadian population and the Aboriginal population.
   c) Write a one-page conclusion that considers the influence of any two factors on the disease burden patterns shown on your chart.

6. Identify a health issue facing your community within the past year.
   a) What public health services are available within your community?
   b) What role have various public health services played in addressing the issue?

   c) What role has an NGO or a group of citizens played to address the issue?
   d) What steps could you take to address the issue?

7. Write a one-page position paper supporting the argument that human health is related to the global economy.

8. What evidence is there of new ways of thinking with respect to the policies and initiatives designed to address health issues? What impact do you think a paradigm shift will have in addressing the issues?

9. Write a 500-word position paper, using specific examples to put forth arguments that the spread of AIDS is tied to poverty and one additional factor of your choice.

10. In chart form, identify the groups responsible for working to solve the AIDS pandemic. Beside each group, identify their efforts and initiatives to do so. Conclude with a written evaluation of the past and probable future success of the efforts and initiatives of any one of the groups on your chart.

11. Investigate to identify the current status of a) the UN global fund and b) G8 initiatives to combat AIDS, and evaluate their roles in addressing this global health issue.

Chapter 16: The Environment and Human Health

By the end of this chapter, you will

- demonstrate an understanding of how human-induced changes in natural systems can diminish their capacity for supporting human activity;

- explain how people perceive resources and sustainable development differently at different times and in different places;

- explain ways in which trade policies or agreements may affect the environment;

- explain the interactive nature of selected natural and human systems;

- identify current global sustainability issues and environmental threats;

- evaluate the performance of a selected transnational corporation with respect to the promotion of environmental sustainability and human rights;

- demonstrate an understanding of how the work of the United Nations and other organizations on poverty, disease, and the environment is directly related to [your own life];

- evaluate the cultural, economic, and environmental impact of changing technology;

- evaluate the effectiveness of methods used by different organizations, governments, and industries to find short- and long-term solutions to geographic problems at the local, national, and global level;

- explain how local participation in the development process can build sustainable communities;

- assess the environmental and economic impacts of a selected case of environmental deregulation in Canada;

- evaluate the effectiveness of an international strategy and agreement that has been designed to protect the global commons or address global issues;

- describe biases that may inform different viewpoints and perspectives on geographic issues.

A WORLD OF CHEMICALS

Chemicals have become so widespread that they dominate our daily lives. As you get up in the morning to start your day, it is impossible to avoid the reach of a world of chemicals. Plastics, synthetic fibres, synthetic ingredients in detergents, cosmetics, contact lenses, dry cleaning, and the daily newspaper; fire retardants used in electronic equipment and furniture; additives, growth hormones, antibiotics, and genetically modified ingredients in food; chemicals used to treat the water you drink and bathe in, and to treat the sewage you flush away; chemicals in the vehicle or bicycle you use to get to school, and even in the sidewalk and roads on which you travel, are just some of about 70 000 chemicals developed in the twentieth century. The chemical industry develops about 1000 new chemicals each year. Most may not be harmful, but almost 90% of them have never been tested for their short- or long-term effects on human health at either low- or high-exposure levels.

The Chemical Industry

The chemical industry is diverse and complex. Corporations are continually merging to form increasingly bigger conglomerations. For example, the British corporation Zeneca has merged with the Swedish corporation Astra to form AstraZeneca. For some of the world's largest transnational chemical companies, such as ExxonMobil, Shell, General Electric, Novartis, and Monsanto, chemical sales represent a small segment of total sales and products. For others, such as BASF, DuPont, and Dow, chemical sales make up a much higher percentage of total sales.

Monsanto Corporation, which operates in 60 countries around the world, is well-known for the agricultural chemicals it produces, including fertilizers, herbicides and **pesticides**, and aspartame, a synthetic sweetener used in food and beverages. Monsanto is also well-known for its genetically modified seeds and crops. Roundup Ready corn, soybeans, cotton, and canola contain a gene that makes them resistant to glyphosate, the world's most widely used pesticide. Company representatives claim that Roundup poses no risk to human or animal health based on the lethal dose scale or LD_{50}, a test that measures the dose at which approximately 50% of tested subjects—animals such as rats and mice—will die.

Monsanto also claims that the use of Roundup Ready crops will improve the environment, because lower quantities of pesticides will be required. Some studies show, however, that expanded plantings of Roundup Ready soybeans resulted in increases in the use of glyphosate. While glyphosate is known to cause skin and eye irritation and is slightly to moderately toxic to fish, recent studies in Europe show a possible link to cancer in humans.

 See Chapter 9 for more information about the global food supply.

FIGURE 16.1 Children's PVC toys have been found to contain many toxic additives.

excerpt from "Clues to the Early Puberty Mystery, A Puerto Rican Study Links Widely Used Chemicals with Premature Breast Growth"

by Krista Foss
The Globe and Mail
November 14, 2000

It's in glue, perfume and those gummy plastic toys that children love to chew. It's in the sublimely hip—PVC fashions, funky fingernail polish—to the mundane—floor tiles and garden hoses. And it's also an ingredient in medical necessities such as sterile plastic bags and tubes that deliver blood and fluids.

It's a phthalate, a funny-sounding man-made chemical pronounced "tha-late." And according to new research it's in you, skulking around in your bloodstream and ending up in your urine.

Whether or not phthalates, a billion pounds of which are used by manufacturers around the globe each year, pose a danger to our health is hotly contested.

In recent years, animal studies have linked them with altered sexual and reproductive development. European countries have banned their use in toys for tots. And some scientists have dismissed concerns about them

saying the hullabaloo is based on bad science.

All of this has happened before anyone was able to measure human exposure to them in the first place. Just recently, science has begun to catch up to suspicions. And the news on phthalates is both surprising and disturbing.

Dr. John Brock, a senior chemist with the Atlanta based Centers for Disease Control [CDC] and his CDC colleagues looked for clues of seven different kinds of phthalates in the urine of 289 adults between the ages of 20 and 60—and found them. Seventy-five per cent of the adults tested had trace amounts of four different kinds of phthalates in their bodies. Here's the surprising part. Phthalates have been the target of great concern because a couple of varieties of them are in many plastics—put there to create softness and flexibility. This additive never becomes part of the plastic's molecular backbone and as a result slowly gasses off.

In a world practically swathed in plastic, the potential threat appears to loom large.

But of the four types of phthalates floating around in their human subjects, Dr. Brock's team found the three with the biggest presence are those used largely in non-plastic products.

In fact...[they] are found most commonly in detergents, lubricating oils and solvents—the very solvents that help fragrance soaps, and help hair spray, fingernail polish and hand lotions remain stable and colourful.

It's no surprise then that women between the ages of 20 and 40 were found to have significantly higher levels of metabolites of dibutyl phthalates than any other age or gender groups.

And animal studies have shown that dibutyl phthalate has toxic effects—particularly on sexual and reproductive development. Those effects could be just as harmful to men as women: Last year, a study of dibutyl phthalate on animals showed the chemical lowers the ability of the body to make testosterone. Still the evidence is preliminary. ...

In some European countries and parts of Asia, some chemical industry products, including some pesticides and some genetically modified foods and crops, have been banned as potential health risks. In 2001, Canadian beef raised with the use of growth hormones was banned in Europe. The European Union (EU)'s Health and Consumer Protection Directorate found that Canadian government agencies tested only a few carcasses for drug residues, that Canadian officials were unable to provide a summary test report for 1999–2000, and that drug violations were not investigated.

Canada's largest chemical company is NOVA Chemical Corporation. Based in Calgary, the company has petrochemical, plastics, and

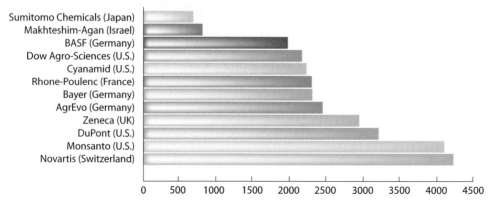

Agrochemical Sales of Leading Companies, 1998 ($US millions)

Sumitomo Chemicals (Japan)
Makhteshim-Agan (Israel)
BASF (Germany)
Dow Agro-Sciences (U.S.)
Cyanamid (U.S.)
Rhone-Poulenc (France)
Bayer (Germany)
AgrEvo (Germany)
Zeneca (UK)
DuPont (U.S.)
Monsanto (U.S.)
Novartis (Switzerland)

0   500   1000   1500   2000   2500   3000   3500   4000   4500

New Internationalist, May 2000, p. 18

FIGURE 16.2 The graph shows only sales of agricultural chemicals, mainly pesticides. Many of the corporations produce a wide range of products, including genetically modified organisms, industrial chemicals, pharmaceuticals, and plastics.

FIGURE 16.3 German Greenpeace activists blaming McDonalds for using genetically manipulated chickenfeed. In 2000, public pressure from consumers and farmers in Europe resulted in the refusal of seven major supermarket chains to carry genetically modified foods. Three large food transnationals, Unilever, Nestlé, and Cadbury-Schweppes, joined the European ban on their use.

research and development operations in North America and Europe. It is North America's largest producer of styrene and polystyrene, and its products end up as carpets, plastic bags, instrument panels of cars, and many other consumer items.

Chemical industry representatives point out that the industry, which is highly regulated, works hard to promote proper handling and safe use of its products. Recent developments in green chemistry, including a program known as Responsible Care, are aimed at reducing emissions and promoting energy efficiency in manufacturing processes and in the products they develop.

Workers in the industry tend to be well-trained. When potential risks to the environment or human health have become known, some products have been withdrawn. For example, in 2000, Dow Chemical withdrew chlorpyrifos (a pesticide commonly used in products such as pet flea collars) in the U.S., after it was found to cause brain damage in rat fetuses.

> **FACT FILE**
>
> The Union of Concerned Scientists ranked chemical pollution above climate change as the greatest risk to human health.

FIGURE 16.4 Recombinant Bovine Growth Hormone (rBGH), a Monsanto Corporation product that increases milk production in cows, has been used in the U.S. since 1993. Despite pressure from the company, the hormone has not been approved for use in Canada.

Different Views on the Chemical Industry

"For the world's food producers, we work to deliver products and solutions to help them reach their goals in ways that meet the world's growing food and fibre needs, conserve natural resources and improve the environment."

Monsanto Corporation, mission statement

"Chemicals are not inherently bad or unsafe if they are properly handled and used."

Susan Walkinshaw, chemist, BASF

"No doubt, the chemical industry has done things it regrets over the last four decades or more. But it probably doesn't regret its crucial role in making us the healthiest, wealthiest people in history."

Michael Fumento, author, journalist

"The principal motives for chemicals are … shaped neither by the needs of the public nor by the limits of nature, but by the exigency of profit and competition."

Murray Bookchin, author

"As a Missouri farm family farmer, I can tell you that the farmers and consumers of the world have been sold a bill of goods because genetically engineered organisms do not perform as advertised. The truth is, genetically engineered crops cost more and yield less. There are four areas of concern—they have to do with health, the environment, and social and economic aspects."

Bill Christison, president, National Family Farm Coalition

Commentary

"Triple Bottom Line Thinking: The Foundation for Green Chemistry at Dow"

from a speech by Dennis Lauzon, CEO and president of Dow Chemical Canada, to a Canadian Society of Chemistry conference at <www.dow.com/dow_news/speeches/spe_lauzon_may.html>
May 30, 2000

Thank you for inviting me here today. Although I'm here to give you examples of Dow's efforts and accomplishments in green chemistry, I'm going to put it in the context of our belief in and commitment to the triple bottom line … also known as sustainable development.

Since about the 1960s, Dow has become more and more focused on making our processes and products as environmentally friendly as possible.

We are committed to reducing emissions by achieving energy efficiency improvements, searching for less energy-intensive manufacturing processes, and producing climate-friendly product solutions for our customers.

Now, you may be wondering why Dow, a global, publicly traded manufacturing company that exists by making a profit, would be focused on this?

Because we believe in the triple bottom line—meeting the social, economic and environmental objectives of our stakeholders. And we know that in order to succeed as a

company, we must meet all three objectives in the decisions we make in order to be credible in their eyes.

Attaining credibility has been a tough goal for chemical companies and the chemical industry to achieve. And because of this, as well as the public outcry for a voice in our decision-making, in the late 1980s the chemical industry in Canada took action. Responsible Care™ is the result.

For those of you who may not know, Responsible Care is a continuous improvement initiative that focuses on the safe handling of our products—from their inception in the research lab, through manufacture and distribution, to their ultimate disposal.

As an industry, we felt that if we didn't do well in those areas, we would not even begin to be trusted or credible in the public's eyes.

And indeed, what started out as a Canadian Chemical Producers' Association initiative in 1985 has expanded to 45 countries. Why? Because at the heart of responsible care is an ethic—an ethic that transcends culture, politics or religion. For us, Responsible Care is about doing the right thing and being seen to do the right thing.

To do business in the 21st century, no one can ignore the needs of our many constituents—our owners, our investors, our governments, our customers, our employees, our communities. Without their support, we risk the ability to grow or even operate. Responsible care is at the heart of business because it aims to integrate elements that historically have been seen at odds with one another: economic needs, environmental needs, and social needs. And by living up to Responsible Care's Codes of Practice, we are able to make better, more sustainable decisions for our world.

So you may be asking yourself how this relates to green chemistry? Our commitment to the responsible care ethic and sustainable development thinking are helping us meet the needs of the 21st century in a way that is more acceptable to the public.

Dow technology and ingenuity play a significant role in these efforts by manufacturing products which, for example, allow the production of lighter vehicles, better insulated buildings and composite materials for improving efficiency. Let me give you [an] example of what I call green chemistry as a result of triple bottom line thinking... STYROFOAM™ insulation, a Dow product for 50 years, is an insulation used in many homes and other types of structures such as office buildings and ice skating rinks. The average North American home, insulated with STYROFOAM insulation, avoids 18,100 pounds of carbon dioxide from being emitted because insulation reduces the use of fossil fuels for heating and cooling. Translated globally, the use of STYROFOAM insulation reduces the annual emissions of carbon dioxide by approximately 6.7 million metric tonnes. This is roughly equivalent to planting 40 million trees per year.

Although there are emissions from the production of STYROFOAM insulation, there is an overall positive balance to the total emissions to the atmosphere because of the energy efficiency that results. ...

Critical Analysis

1. Who is the speaker and what is the likely bias and purpose of his message?
2. How is sustainable development defined by the speech?
3. Who are the stakeholders that are mentioned in the message?
4. Which stakeholders do you feel are the most important to the company and why?
5. What efforts is the company making to protect people and the environment?
6. Conduct research to find one additional example of green chemistry that is currently in use or under development by the chemical industry.
7. Write a two-paragraph evaluation of the term "sustainable development" as outlined in the speech.
8. Use the four-point CARE system outlined on page 37 in Chapter 2 to evaluate the message provided in the speech.

Environmental Risks to Health

Environmental damage occurs when stressors such as hydrocarbons, heavy metals, and **persistent organic pollutants (POPs)** degrade the environment, causing human illness or death. Hazardous wastes are toxic substances that can cause long-term damage to ecosystems and also pose a threat to human health. They are the by-product of industry, including the manufacture of chemicals and petroleum-based products. Hazardous wastes require technologically advanced methods of disposal or treatment to make them less dangerous. Direct discharges of pollutants are known as **point sources**. They are easier to identify and regulate than **non-point sources**, which come from a combination of origins that contribute to agricultural or urban run-off, or contaminated sediments at the bottom of lakes and rivers. Living near gas and oil wells, working near tanker terminals and oil refineries, or inhaling benzene fumes when pumping gas into your car are just a few of a long list of possible occupational and location hazards that put people at greater risk of adverse health effects. Many toxic chemicals can enter the most vital workings of the body and destroy protective enzymes, block oxidation, and initiate genetic changes. Short-term or acute health effects resulting from exposure to hazardous wastes can include lung irritation, dizziness, burns, nausea, headache, muscle cramps, sore throat, internal bleeding, kidney and liver damage, and skin rashes. Long-term or **chronic** health effects can include respiratory damage, neurological damage, birth defects, cancer, arthritis, behavioural abnormalities, reproductive disorders such as miscarriages, and other problems.

The possible risks to human health from these environmental contaminants and hazardous wastes have attracted scientific,

> ### FACT FILE
>
> Hollywood films such as *A Civil Action,* starring John Travolta, and *Erin Brockovitch,* starring Julia Roberts, depict real-life cases of the prosecution of companies responsible for the illness and death of citizens because of the release of industrial toxins.

FIGURE 16.5 The Semipalatinsk nuclear test site in Kazakhstan was used for hundreds of nuclear tests between 1950 and 1990. A 2002 DNA study showed that adults living near the site during testing were found to have an 80% increase in their genetic mutation rates, while rates among their children showed an increase of 50%. Radiation causes atoms in living tissue to take up electrical charges that can change its chemical composition, causing genetic damage and cancer. A desert region in Nevada was used as a similar test site by the U.S. during the Cold War.

government, media, and public attention at local, national, and international levels. Highly publicized environmental disasters such as the explosion that occurred in 1984 at a Union Carbide pesticide plant in Bhopal, India, enhance public awareness of the direct dangers of toxic chemicals. In Bhopal, a cloud of methyl isocyanate, used to manufacture pesticides, was released from storage tanks, resulting in 2000 immediate deaths, more than 14 000 delayed deaths, and hundreds of thousands of injuries, according to recent (2000) Indian government statistics.

 See Chapter 5 for more information about hormone-disrupting chemicals and biodiversity.

FIGURE 16.6 Outdoor air pollution or "smog" in Toronto, Ontario. Smog is believed to be the most significant environmental factor in causing illness and death in Canadians.

Children and Environmental Contaminants

Canadians are worried about the effects that the environment may be having on their own health, but the effect of toxic chemicals on their children's health is particularly worrisome. An

FIGURE 16.7 Workers and their families are exposed to large amounts of toxic emissions from the more than 4000 maquiladora industrial plants, mainly U.S. subsidiaries of plastics, chemical, and electronics industries, that have sprung up on the Mexican side of the U.S. border since the North American Free Trade Agreement (NAFTA) came into effect in 1994. On both sides of the border, there are clusters of birth defects, including high rates of anencephaly, a condition in which babies are born with undeveloped brains.

FIGURE 16.8 Children are at the greatest risk from environmental contaminants.

Eksos poll in September 2000 confirmed that 93% of Canadians were concerned that environmental hazards are having an adverse effect on their children's health.

For their body weight, children receive more exposure than adults, and exposure occurs during a time of critical growth and development. As young children tend to play on floors and outdoors, sometimes putting things in their mouths, they are at greater risk from exposure to environmental contaminants. They tend to eat more foods that are sprayed with pesticides such as apples and grapes. Children living in poverty, in minority communities, or near industrial and toxic dumpsites are often exposed to higher levels of contaminants than others.

INTERACT

1. Identify various stakeholders and compare their views on the chemical industry.
2. What criteria do people base their views on when formulating opinions on the chemical industry?
3. Provide a list of factors that put children at higher risk from adverse health effects due to exposure to toxic chemicals.
4. What is your view about the proliferation of chemicals in our society? Do you have enough information for an informed opinion? What resources would you use to ensure balanced information?
5. Using a specific example, evaluate the role played by NGOs such as Greenpeace, Hollywood films, or song lyrics in alerting people to environmental health hazards.

PESTICIDES

Pesticides are designed to kill specific plants and animals that may harm human health or that reduce our incomes and act as a nuisance. Pesticide manufacturers maintain that their products provide benefits to society, including increasing crop yields. Other groups agree and some studies have shown that there is little risk from proper use of pesticides. Those in favour of widespread use of pesticides may view the environmental costs as acceptable when balanced with the economic benefits that result. However, despite large amounts of pesticides that have been sprayed to eliminate weeds and insects that are considered pests, target species have not been eliminated. Many become resistant or develop immunity to pesticides, which often wipe out their natural predators as well.

Trends show a decreasing use of pesticides in developed countries and the development of newer, safer chemicals. As awareness of the inherent risks increases, most people would prefer to rely on pesticides less, especially if other options are available. An approach called **Integrated Pest Management (IPM)** has become a viable alternative. A successful IPM

FACT FILE

Canada is among the top five world producers of organic grains, with an estimated retail value of CDN$1 billion in 2002.

program can greatly reduce the amount of pesticides required by using a wide range of techniques best suited to the particular situation. These techniques can include crop rotation, planting more than one crop at a time, field treatment, controlling the food sources, predators, and pathogens that affect a pest, developing resistant crop varieties, or use of biological insecticides such as *Bacillus thuringiensis* (Bt). Bt is a bacteria that acts as a pathogen to a number of insects. With IPM, chemical treatments are used only in a crisis and are applied more directly than previous broadcast spraying techniques allowed.

Pesticides are used at many stages of fruit and vegetable growth. Some are used to ensure that the produce has a better appearance for the consumer or to preserve freshness during transportation. While many foods tested do not exceed allowable limits for adult consumption, the cumulative effect of several different residues in our bodies has not been examined. Eating **organically grown food** is one way to avoid pesticides and their residues. Organic foods are those that avoid the use of chemicals, synthetic pesticides, and irradiation, and are not derived from genetic engineering.

Consumer demand for organic food is expanding rapidly in many countries around the world, as both awareness of health issues and resistance to genetically modified foods increase. Mainstream retail grocery chains and transnational food producers have moved into the expanding organic market. The global organic market was US$26 billion in 2002, with an annual growth rate of about 25% per year. The organic sector is expanding rapidly in Canada as well, and retail sales are expected to be more than CDN$3 billion in 2005. Canada is regarded as an ideal location for producing organic food because of its large land base and cold climate that reduces food crop pests and diseases. The growth trend is similar in developing countries, where many farmers are choosing to cultivate their crops organically.

FIGURE 16.9 Canadians and wildlife are exposed to pesticides and their residues regularly, including some that have been banned in some other countries. Canada allows about 500 pesticides, three times the number allowed by countries such as Sweden and Denmark. Because many of the chemicals were reviewed before 1960, Health Canada's Pest Management Regulatory Agency (PMRA) has begun to review a number of organophosphates, some of which are used as weed and insect killers on lawns.

 See Chapter 9 for more information about the global food supply.

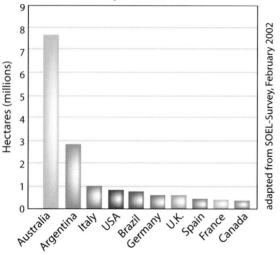

Land Area Under Organic Management, Top 10 Countries

Hectares (millions)

adapted from SOEL-Survey, February 2002

Australia, Argentina, Italy, USA, Brazil, Germany, U.K., Spain, France, Canada

FIGURE 16.10

The World Health Organization (WHO) estimates that at least 3 million people are directly poisoned by pesticides each year, with 200 000 fatalities. More than 25 million agricultural workers experience some health effects. Over half of the fatalities occur in developing countries, even though they use only 20% of the world's pesticides. About 30% of the pesticides that are sold in developing countries every year do not meet internationally accepted quality standards.

FACT FILE

In Ethiopia, there are more than 250 sites that contain 1500 tonnes of leaking, obsolete pesticides. This is a serious issue in many developing countries.

" We used chemicals on our cotton crop and had higher yields than now but we were often sick and had to spend some of the money we earned on medicines. ... This season I grew cotton without any chemical fertilizers or pesticides. We use palm oil cake, ash and cattle manure and we put organic matter back into the soil through cotton leaves, which fall early. We treated the pests with extracts of neem tree. ... "

Kitche Denis, farmer, Mangassa, Benin

" Canada's pesticide regulatory system protects your health. It is one of the most stringent in the world. Before being approved for use in Canada, PMRA [Pest Management Regulatory Agency] requires extensive health studies. For example, PMRA evaluates short-term and long-term repeated exposure studies on animals—over a range of doses—to maximize the potential for identifying toxic effect. The PMRA specifically takes into consideration whether there is a possibility that children are exposed to pesticides. "

PMRA, Health Canada

FIGURE 16.11 Banana plantations in Latin America, where hundreds of agricultural workers become ill or sterile every year because of exposure to pesticides, apply 30 kg of active pesticides per hectare per year—more than 10 times the average for intensive agriculture in Canada.

FIGURE 16.12 About 20% of all pesticides used in North America are sprayed on lawns, gardens, parks, and golf courses.

PROVING THE ENVIRONMENT –HUMAN HEALTH LINK

Scientists around the world are investigating the links between the environment and human health. Thousands of scientific studies have been conducted with a wide range of results. Although it is well-established that the presence of pollution in the environment increases the likelihood of illness, there is a lack of consensus among scientists, NGOs, governments, and businesses on how exposure to environmental hazards is damaging human health. However, the evidence is accumulating and recent studies have found significant and surprising effects, even with exposure to low doses of chemicals. One study, conducted at Cornell University in 1998, analysed population trends, disease rates, and increasing pollution levels. This study estimated that 40% of deaths worldwide are caused by pollution and other environmental factors. Researchers are just beginning to consider that **total pollutant loads**, or low-level exposure to several pollutants, may be affecting large numbers of people.

Despite the abundance of evidence, scientists have been unable to prove beyond all doubt that the proliferation of chemicals in our society is responsible for corresponding trends such as the increases in asthma, learning disabilities, allergies, and some forms of cancer including breast, prostate, and some childhood cancers.

The search for proof of a link between exposure to toxic substances and the impact on human health is complex and controversial. Not everyone who is exposed to a toxin will experience the same effects. Human health implications can vary widely, depending on many factors, including the toxicity of the chemical, how it is ingested, and the frequency or duration of the exposure. Factors such as age, lifestyle, occupation, and general health also play a role. Many toxins are stored in body fat and released gradually over months and even years, causing illness that is difficult to trace.

In an effort to prove a link between the environment and human health, environmental epidemiologists use data from **toxicology** studies that examine the effects of poisons and toxins on living organisms. In addition, they conduct research to find answers to questions that make up the **Components of an Exposure Pathway**. When these questions are answered, researchers may be able to identify a link between an environmental hazard and human health. Recent computer technology, advances in molecular biology studies on DNA, and biological measures of exposure are improving the ability to determine relationships between environmental contaminants and human health.

FIGURE 16.14 An increase in the ultraviolet B (UV-B) rays coming from the sun through a thinner **ozone** layer has been shown to be responsible for damage to people, animals, and plants, including an increase in skin cancer, cataracts, light allergies, and immune system disorders. Human exposure to UV-B rays depends on location, especially latitude, altitude, season, and time of day. Demographic factors such as age and skin colour, as well as lifestyle factors such as the amount of time spent outdoors, and the number and severity of sunburns experienced, can increase the severity of health effects. Children in some parts of Australia are required to wear sunscreen and hats (SLIP, SLAP, SLOP—T-shirt, hat, lotion) before being allowed to participate in outdoor school activities.

adapted from *Detective Work* by Donald Cole, Ross E.G. Upshur, and Brian L. Gibson in *Alternatives Journal* 25:3 Summer 1999, p.27

Components of an Exposure Pathway

1. What is the source and nature of contamination? What is its origin and how is it released into the environment?

2. Where in the environment is the contaminant found (air, water, soil, or other species) and how is it transported to come into contact with human populations?

3. What is the place of exposure—indoors, outdoors, at home or work?

4. What is the route of exposure—are humans exposed by eating, breathing, or touching the hazard?

5. Which groups within the overall population are most likely to be exposed?

6. What are the adverse health effects of the exposure, ranging from subclinical effects, through symptoms of illness, hospitalization, and death?

FIGURE 16.13

> " Waiting for scientific certainty could have dire consequences for the immediate and long-term health of the child and for the adult the child becomes. "
>
> *Sandra Schwartz and Dr. Graham W. Chance, Canadian Institute of Child Health*

> " The social and economic costs of not protecting the environment are much greater than the costs of protecting it. "
>
> *Robert Watson, director of environment, World Bank*

Risk Assessment for Toxic Pollutants

Risk can be defined as the potential danger of injury, loss, or death associated with a particular substance, technology, or activity. Many research programs in countries around the world study the potential for an environmental pollutant to cause human health problems. A risk assessment for a pollutant combines the results of all the available information from studies on the cancer and non-cancer health effects of different levels of human and animal exposure to the substance. The evidence may consist of case reports from physicians or formal studies of groups of people with different levels of exposure. Computer models and mathematical equations are often used to represent variables such as the source, pathway, distance, concentration, biodegradability, and length of time of the exposure.

Factors Considered in Exposure Assessment

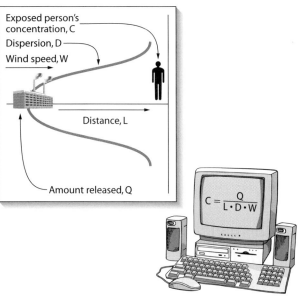

Risk Assessment for Toxic Air Pollutants: A Citizen's Guide, Environmental Protection Agency at <www.epa.gov/oar/oaqps/air_risc/3_90_024.html>

FIGURE 16.15 Exposure Assessment Studies are used to estimate risk.

Understanding the comparative risk of a pollutant can help to identify and rank issues of greatest concern so that action plans and strategies can be developed to reduce environmental threats. It is difficult to develop an accurate ranking of human health hazards because there is a large number of factors that vary by geographic area to be considered. Comparative risk assessments use many different ways to classify environmental risks. Risks are classified by criteria (e.g., number of lives lost or dollars lost), by specific type of pollution or a mixture (i.e., all air pollutants), by source (e.g., industrial wastes or vehicles), by pathway (e.g., surface run-off or air currents), and by receptor (e.g., workers, consumers, or forests). Resources for the Future, a non-partisan **think tank** whose scientists conduct independent research studies, produced a study by David M. Konisky that

Distribution of Individual Risk

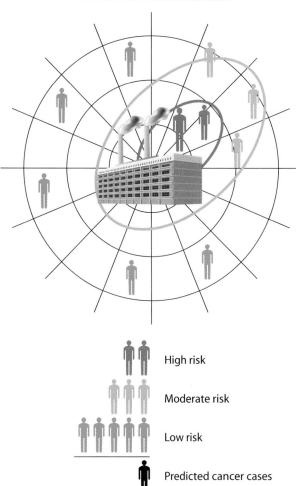

Risk Assessment for Toxic Air Pollutants: A Citizen's Guide, Environmental Protection Agency at <www.epa.gov/oar/oaqps/air_risc/3_90_024.html>

FIGURE 16.16 Distributions of individual risk are used to calculate population risk. The population cancer risk is usually expressed as the expected number of new cases of cancer each year for all people exposed to the pollutant.

addressed this problem by consolidating the results of many studies. It found that the environmental health risks most frequently ranked as the top 10 high risks included indoor and outdoor air pollution, surface water, drinking water and groundwater pollution, lead, pesticides, hazardous waste, toxins, food quality, storage tanks (releases/leaks), stratospheric ozone depletion, accidental releases, and radiation exposure (other than indoor radon).

INTERACT

1. Brainstorm a list of groups in society, other than children, that are at higher risk from adverse health effects due to exposure to toxic chemicals.
2. Draw a diagram that identifies at least five pathways that pollution can take to reach you as a human receptor.
3. Take on the role of an environmental detective: select one environmental pollutant and conduct research on it to answer the questions found in Figure 16.13, **Components of an Exposure Pathway**. Communicate your findings in a way that will inform an audience of your choice of the possible link between the pollutant and health.
4. What are the benefits and drawbacks of risk assessment and comparative risk studies?
5. Brainstorm a list of strategies or actions that could be taken by governments, industries, and consumers to reduce the risk to human health of the highest ranked environmental hazards.

INTERNATIONAL EFFORTS TO ADDRESS ENVIRONMENTAL HEALTH ISSUES

Decisions related to emissions of toxic chemicals made in one country can often affect the environment and health of those living in another country. Many of the contaminants travel across international borders on wind or water currents or in the bodies of migrating animals. Because of widespread recognition that toxic chemicals pose a hazard to the health of people and environments around the world, the international community has reached a consensus on the need for global action. International efforts have resulted in some improvements in co-operation, risk assessment, and more environmentally sound management of toxic chemicals. However, many environmental health practitioners and NGOs are actively advocating for more concrete and comprehensive international steps. Some of the recent agreements and treaties are included in Figure 16.18, **International Efforts to Protect People and the Environment from Contaminants.**

See Chapter 20 for more information about sustainable solutions.

The Canadian and Russian Arctic

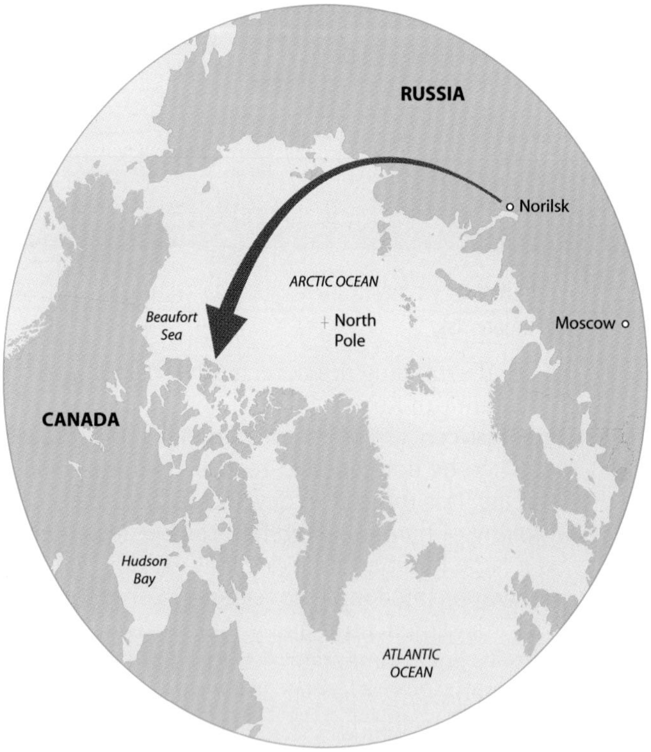

FIGURE 16.17 Pollutants drift into the Canadian Arctic from northern Russia. A nickel refinery in Norilsk produces 10 million tonnes of waste each year, three times the allowable limit, paying about $50 million a year in fines. Aboriginal people in the Arctic were the first to draw attention to contaminants when they noticed significant changes in the animals that form their food sources. High levels of contaminants and toxic residues have been found in the Canadian Arctic environment and its people.

> " The UN report, *Environmental Changes and Human Health*, amasses credible, convincing evidence that environmental deterioration is not a marginal, but a major cause of human death and disease. "
>
> Gus Speth, administrator, United Nations Development Program

> " When carcinogens are deliberately or accidentally introduced into the environment, some number of vulnerable persons are consigned to death. The impossibility of tabulating an exact body count does not alter this fact. The current system of regulating the use, release, and disposal of known and suspected carcinogens—rather than preventing their generation in the first place—is intolerable. "
>
> Sandra Steingraber, *Living Downstream—An Ecologist Looks at Cancer and the Environment.*

Guilty Until Proven Innocent

Large-scale releases of contaminants as in Bhopal, India, or radioactive substances as in the Chernobyl explosion provide irrefutable evidence that toxic substances cause illness and death. However, despite strong evidence from studies on animals, there is a lack of agreement about cause and effect in human health.

New principles for setting protective policies are needed. The **precautionary principle** is a relatively new idea emerging as a principle of international environmental law. If there is good reason to believe that an activity, technology, or substance may be harmful, rather than waiting for absolute proof, action should be taken to prevent the possibility of harm.

Thousands of NGOs have been instrumental in bringing this principle into effect. Initially it was discussed widely by international governments at the UN Earth Summit Conference on Environment and Sustainable Development in Rio de Janeiro in 1992. Principle 15 of the Rio Declaration stated that "In order to protect the environment, the precautionary principle shall be widely applied by states according to their capabilities. ... lack of full scientific certainty shall not be used as a reason for postponing cost-effective measures to prevent environmental degradation." The principle has come into play in the 2001 UN Stockholm Convention on POPs.

Sweden has adopted the precautionary principle in its environmental policies and regulations. Potentially dangerous chemicals are banned until they are proven safe. By 2006, Swedish industries will be required to undertake complete testing for persistence and bioaccumulation of all chemicals that are used in large quantities, and by 2010, all industrial chemicals will be completely tested regardless of quantities used.

International Efforts to Protect People and the Environment from Contaminants

Initiative	Objective
Basel Convention on the Control of Transboundary Movements of Hazardous Wastes and Their Disposal (1992)	This global environmental treaty calls for a reduction in generation and transport of toxic waste as an effective way to protect human health and the environment.
Agenda 21 (1992)	This plan for global action on sustainable development in a number of areas was adopted at the UN Conference on Environment and Development (UNCED) at the Earth Summit in Rio de Janeiro.
Intergovernmental Forum on Chemical Safety (1994)	This non-institutional forum provides guidance to governments, NGOs, and other organizations on developing policies and strategies for promoting risk assessment and management of toxic chemicals.
Declaration of the Environment on Children's Environmental Health (1998)	Leaders of the G8 countries agreed to a guiding framework for developing policies that give priority to children's environmental health issues.
Stockholm Convention on Persistent Organic Pollutants (2001)	This legally binding treaty focuses on the process of minimizing or eliminating the use of 12 priority POPs known as the "dirty dozen." They include pesticides, industrial chemicals, and their unintended by-products.

FIGURE 16.18

CANADA'S ENVIRONMENTAL RECORD

Canada has been a participant in international forums, has ratified treaties on related issues, and has worked actively to reach international agreement on POPs. Several international studies provide composite indicators of the role played by a country in reducing the risk of environmental hazards. Indicators can be used as an effective tool to provide information about complex systems in a meaningful way.

The *Environmental Sustainability Index, 2001* is a study that was conducted by the World Economic Forum based in Geneva, Switzerland, and the Center for International Earth Science Information Network at Columbia University. One hundred and twenty-two countries were ranked according to progress made toward environmental sustainability. The ranking is based on 20 indicators related to human stress on natural systems, the effect of environmental degradation on humans, and the social and institutional capacity for making an effective response to environmental issues. In 2001,

FACT FILE

Volatile organic compounds (VOCs) are a group of hydrocarbons that enter the environment through evaporation from fuel tanks, automobiles, paints, solvents, and consumer products such as perfumes and lighter fluid. They combine with nitrous oxide (N_2O) to form ground level ozone, a component of **smog**.

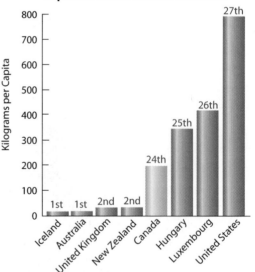

Kilograms of Hazardous Waste per Capita for Selected OECD Countries

OECD environmental data, 1998

FIGURE 16.19 In 1999, the Canadian Institute for Environmental Law and Policy reported that the amount of hazardous waste imported from the U.S. by Ontario grew by 500% to 288 000 tonnes between 1993 and 1998. The increase coincided with a U.S. law requiring all hazardous waste to be incinerated, while Ontario uses mainly less costly landfill burial.

Canada ranked third after Finland and Sweden. By 2002, Canada had moved to fourth place. The U.S. was ranked fifty-first.

A look at other indicators reveals some surprising and disturbing realities. The Organization for Economic Cooperation and Development (OECD) conducts a biannual environmental comparison of its members based on 25 equally weighted environmental indicators in 10 categories related to air, water, energy, biodiversity, waste, climate change, ozone depletion, agriculture, transportation, and population. The study uses data that is published and verified. Canada has one of the worst records of developed, industrialized countries ranking twenty-eighth out of 29 countries. Canada's record was the worst on nine indicators, including per capita greenhouse gas emissions, volatile organic compound emissions, water and energy consumption, energy efficiency, and generation of nuclear waste. Analysts have suggested that some of the reasons for Canada's poor showing include ineffective laws and policies that are not always enforced, inadequate resources for environmental protection and enforcement, gaps in protection because of jurisdictional disputes, and a failure to incorporate environmental limits, values, and costs into the economic system.

While federal and provincial governments have taken some significant steps to manage chemicals and toxic waste, it is clear that there is a great deal more to be done. The regulatory system assumes that there are safe thresholds of exposure to most chemicals but has not evaluated the cumulative effects of low levels of chemicals that we are exposed to in air, water, and food.

The National Round Table on the Environment and the Economy (NRTEE) is an independent advisory body created by the federal government in 1994. It works to find ways to balance economic growth and environ-

FACT FILE

Mercury, once commonly used in dental fillings, thermometers, batteries, and paints, is considered a highly toxic substance. One gram, or less than a teaspoonful, could kill the fish in an 8-ha lake.

Views on Canada's Environmental Record

"The superior progress by other industrialized nations, particularly the northern European countries demonstrates that there are practical, effective solutions to the environmental problems facing Canada."

David R. Boyd, Ecoresearch Chair of Environmental Law and Policy, University of Victoria

"Canadian leaders have done little to live up to their international commitments. As a result, Canada is falling behind other countries, including the U.S., in creating policies to protect children."

Sandra Schwartz and Dr. Graham W. Chance, Canadian Institute of Child Health

"Contrary to public opinion, in most instances objectives for protecting human health and the environment are being met. … Environmental quality in Canada has improved dramatically over the last 30 years, up a full 18% since 1980. Canadians have eight notable reasons to celebrate Earth Day this year [2000]: air quality in Canada has improved dramatically, forest land is plentiful, water quality is improving, scientists are unconvinced there is a global warming crisis due to human activity, economic growth and environmental quality are compatible, the world does not face an overpopulation crisis, Canada does not face an endangered species crisis and there is no garbage crisis in Canada."

Laura Jones, director of Environmental and Regulatory Studies, The Fraser Institute

"The Fraser Institute is about as credible on environmental issues as Don Cherry on figure skating. … The Fraser Institute is correct that emissions of lead, sulphur, carbon monoxide, dioxins and furans have decreased—but it is blinded by ideology when it comes to why. Behind each of these environmental success stories are government regulations—not, as the Fraser institute would like to believe, voluntary corporate behaviour or the market's invisible hand."

David R. Boyd, Ecoresearch Chair of Environmental Law and Policy, University of Victoria

mental protection. NRTEE has identified several environmental health issues not adequately targeted by the federal government:

- Chronic low-level exposure to toxic chemicals
- Chemical **synergies** with multiple exposures
- Air quality and a fourfold increase in asthma in children between 1975 and 2000
- Neurological impairment linked to exposure to environmental contaminants
- Endocrine disruption and immune suppression caused by environmental contaminants
- Increases in rates of some cancers
- Environmental health of children, including a rise in allergies and learning disabilities

NRTEE is concerned about inadequate funding, research, and monitoring of toxic chemicals, and an increasing inability of agencies in Canada to keep up with regulatory action to protect people from existing and new chemical substances. Environmental health protection in Canada falls under the regulatory responsibility of a number of different departments, including health, environment, natural resources, industry, and the food inspection agency. In addition, a number of different provincial government departments is responsible for environmental health care.

FIGURE 16.20 Mercury is still used in some electrical switches, mercury vapour headlights, and anti-lock braking systems in cars. It poses little danger to drivers or passengers, but is released into the air, water, and soil when cars are junked or recycled and represents one of the largest sources of mercury pollution in North America. A general phase out of mercury use in cars has begun. There are few programs for the removal and safe disposal of mercury from the millions of cars on Canada's roads today.

FIGURE 16.21 Electric utilities and Inco Ltd., in Sudbury, are two of the largest sources of air pollution. Coal-fired power plants are the largest unregulated source of mercury pollution in North America.

Positive Steps

In 1996, the Canadian government established the Toxic Substances Research Initiative (TSRI) to promote research of environmental health issues. As the funding for this initiative expired in March 2002, NRTEE made a number of recommendations:

- Continue and increase funding for TSRI
- Establish a Human Health and the Environment Strategic Research initiative as an important tool for addressing environmental health issues
- Develop effective risk assessment tools for measuring toxicity
- Build relationships with other jurisdictions including the U.S.

The Canadian Environmental Protection Act, 1999 has made pollution prevention a key strategy for reducing toxic substances in the environment. One of the requirements of the act is to provide lists of substances considered to be toxic. It also requires that human health be considered as a component of all environmental assessment studies done under federal jurisdiction.

FACT FILE

In December 2001, Canada's federal minister of the environment announced proposed regulations to reduce the sulphur content of diesel fuel by 95% to 15 parts per million. The regulations, designed to protect health by reducing air pollution, are to come into effect in 2006.

The Great Lakes

The agency responsible for watching environmental pollutants under NAFTA, the Commission for Environmental Cooperation, reported in 2001 that about 3.2 million tonnes of waste are generated each year by industries in North America. This does not include the emissions from automobiles or natural resource development such as farming, mining, and forestry. The environmental contaminants are released directly into the air, dumped in water or on land, or into underground wells. The industries recycle about 30% of the total pollutants produced and dispose of the rest either by burning it, or by dumping it down a drain into sewage. Some industries use other more technologically advanced treatments to render toxic substances less harmful before disposal.

FACT FILE

The International Joint Commission has recommended that the U.S. and Canadian governments make Lake Superior a bi-national demonstration site for zero discharge, prohibiting the dumping of any toxic chemicals. Industry groups organized a coalition to oppose this.

"Options to reduce exposure for those substances determined to be 'toxic' were and are being considered, in consultation with stakeholders."

Health Canada Web site, 2002

FIGURE 16.22
As well as legal dumpsites, there are many places, often in rural areas, where illegal dumping of toxic substances and hazardous waste occurs.

> " While there have been many improvements to the environment in this region over the past three decades, these gains are at risk of being lost ... the basin is being subjected to increased environmental pressures, including pollution from industry, municipalities and livestock production. The leadership, innovation, science and diligence that served the basin in the past has diminished. This is a legacy worth protecting and yet there is a sense of complacency, not urgency, and of resignation, not inspiration. "
>
> *Johanne Gelinas, Commissioner of the Environment and Sustainable Development, October 2001*

The Commission's annual report, *Taking Stock*, found that the five worst polluted regions on the continent are Ohio, Texas, Michigan, Indiana, and Ontario. Geographically, the greatest amounts of pollution are concentrated in a band around the shores of the Great Lakes. Forty million people, including 16 million Canadians, live in the Great Lakes Basin, drinking and using the water for many industrial, commercial, and recreational activities. In Canada, the **watershed** supports the highest concentration of industry in the country and its agricultural production is valued at more than CDN$11 billion annually.

Researchers have documented a number of significant health effects, including learning and behavioural problems in children who were prenatally exposed to persistent toxic chemicals when their mothers ate Great Lakes fish. The U.S. Environmental Protection Agency stated that cancer risks from fish consumption in some parts of the lakes are 4500 times higher than the minimum acceptable levels.

MAKE A DIFFERENCE

Monitoring the Environmental Health of Your Community

Canadians can find out how much and what kind of pollution is produced or used in their community. A Canadian government program known as the National Pollutants Release Inventory (NPRI) requires polluters to report on all the discharges, emissions into air, water, land, or underground injection, and shipments transported off-site that they release for about 270 substances, as well as pollution prevention measures taken. The substances identified vary from year to year, depending on annual toxicity lists, but, in 2001, 55 of the substances were known to be toxic or carcinogenic.

The owner or operator of an industry or other facility is legally required to report to Environment Canada if three thresholds are met: there are more than 10 full-time employees; an identified substance is used or manufactured at a concentration of 1% by weight or more; and more than 10 000 kg are used, processed, or manufactured annually. Because of this program, a number of industries have significantly improved the accuracy of their emissions reporting and have reduced emissions of toxic chemicals. Other industries, however, are known to delay action repeatedly, claiming the expense of making improvements and loss of profits as factors.

Three NGOs—the Canadian Environmental Defence Fund, the Canadian Environmental Law Association, and the Canadian Institute for Environmental Law and Policy—have developed a project to help people use and interpret the significance of NPRI data in their communities. Citizens may use the data to approach local polluters or political decision makers and encourage them to make improvements. The Web site, <www.scorecard.org/pollution-watch>, can be used to:

- select facilities from a map of your community;
- conduct a regional or river basin analysis on air and water pollution;
- investigate emissions and transfers of toxic substances and the impact of corporate policies on the environment;
- learn about health and environmental impacts of the emissions;
- learn about related regulations and their impact in reducing toxic emissions;
- understand what information about pollution NRPI does not provide.

First Priority Substances List

Priority Substances List 1 (PSL1)	Priority Substances List 2 (PSL2)
Benzene	Acetaldehyde
Benzidine	Acrolein
Bis(2-ethylhexyl) phthalate	Acrylonitrile
Bis(chloromrthyl) ether	Aluminum chloride, aluminum nitrate, aluminum sulphate
Chlorinated wastewater effluents	Ammonia in the aquatic environment
Chloromethyl methyl ether	1,3 Butadiene
Creosote-contaminated sites	Butylbenzylphthalate
3,3-Dichlorobenzidine	Carbon disulphide
1,2-Dichloroethane	Chloramines
Dichloromethane	N,N-Diemthylformamide
Effluents from pulp mills using bleaching	Ethylene glycol
Hexachlorobenzene	Ethylene oxide
Hexavalent chromium compounds	Formaldehyde
Inorganic arsenic compounds	Hexachlorobutadiene
Inorganic cadmium compounds	2-Methoxylethanol
Inorganic fluorides	N-Nitrosodimethylamine
Oxidic, sulphidic and soluble inorganic nickel compounds	Nonylphenol and its ethoxylates
	Phenol
Polychlorinated dibenzodioxins	Releases from primary and secondary copper smelters and copper refineries
Polychlorinated dibenzofurans	
Polycyclic aromatic hydrocarbons	Releases from primary and secondary zinc smelters and zinc refineries
Refractory ceramic fibres	
Short chain chlorinated paraffins	Releases of radionuclides from nuclear facilities (impacts on non-human species)
Tetrachloroethylene	Respirable particulate matter less than or equal to 10 microns
1,1,1-Trichloroethane	
Trichloroethylene	Road salts
	Textile mill effluents

Health Canada <www.hc-sc.gc.ca/hecs-sesc/exsd/psl1.htm>

FIGURE 16.23 The substances in PSL1 and PSL2 are considered toxic according to Section 11 of the Canadian Environmental Protection Act (CEPA), which requires that they (and others) be assessed to determine the risk posed to human health or the environment.

In 1994, the federal government initiated a plan called Great Lakes 2000 to continue the improvements in the condition of the lakes through better sewage treatment and pollution control that were made by previous agreements with the provinces and the U.S., such as the 1972 and 1987 Great Lakes Water Quality Agreements. Initiatives in Great Lakes 2000 that focus on human health from an environmental perspective include:

- determine the effects of exposure to all forms of contaminants—chemical, microbiological, and radiological;
- implement strategies to reduce or eliminate human health risks caused by pollution;
- provide information to support public education and community action.

The federal and Ontario governments have allowed the Great Lakes 2000 plan to expire and have yet to reach an additional agreement.

Canada's Commissioner of the Environment and Sustainable Development conducts an annual audit of government efforts in addressing environmental issues. The 2001 audit, tabled in the House of Commons in October 2001, revealed the following health related challenges:

- Unlike the U.S., there are no enforceable drinking water standards in Canada
- Current farming practices are unsustainable, as "factory farms" generate manure equal to the sewage of 100 million people, contaminating surface water and groundwater
- Canada has not kept its agreement with the U.S. to clean up the most heavily polluted sites—16 of the original 17 Canadian sites are still highly contaminated
- The federal government has delayed responding to information requests and recommendations from the International Joint Commission

FIGURE 16.24 Pollutants pouring into the Great Lakes ecosystem in Barrow Bay, Georgian Bay.

Great Lakes Areas of Concern for Pollution

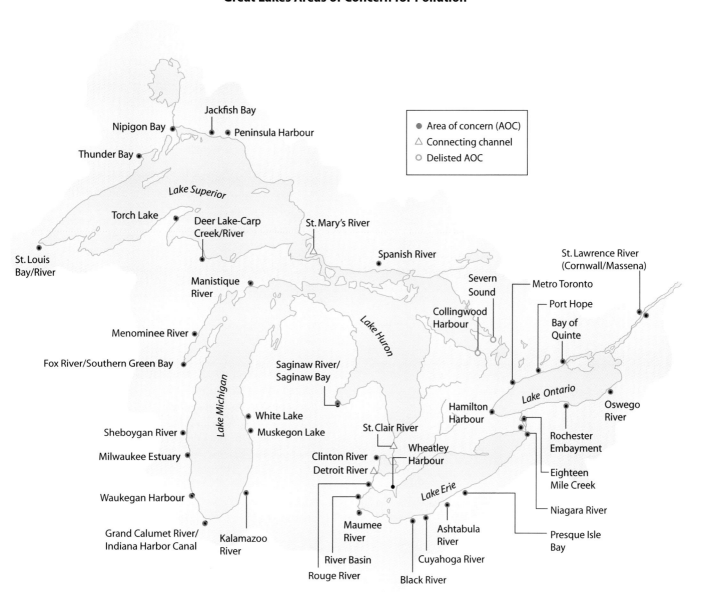

FIGURE 16.25 The 42 areas of concern identified show where remedial action is taking place. Of 17 of the most heavily polluted hot spots identified in 1994, 15 are still in need of remediation. Only Collingwood Harbour and Severn Sound have been improved enough to be dropped from the hot spots list.

CASE STUDY

🍁 Ontario's Environmental Record

According to a number of reports, Ontario is one of the worst jurisdictions in North America for environmental pollution. Throughout the 1990s and early 2000, even the government's own Environmental Commissioner criticized the government for its overall environmental record. A Sierra Legal Defence Fund report showed more than 10 000 violations of Ontario provincial wastewater laws, including more than 3000 in 1999. Fewer than 3% of the violations were prosecuted by the government. Ontario's eight nuclear facilities violated environmental laws 187 times in 1999.

FIGURE 16.26 Environmental pollution from paperplant smoke stacks in Cornwall, Ontario. During the past few summers, in many countries around the globe, smog has become a problem not only in cities but also in rural areas.

Environmental Deregulation

During the 1990s, there was a shift in ideas about the roles that government and the market should take. This resulted in a shift in environmental policy toward deregulation and downloading of environmental responsibility to the private sector or to municipal levels of government. During the second half of the 1990s, the government took a number of actions that had the effect of dismantling safeguards that had previously protected the environment and natural resources. A number of regulations were changed to allow for the voluntary compliance of industry. Just a few of the many steps taken toward environmental deregulation include:

- changes to the limits of allowable discharge for fourteen major polluters;
- repeal of a ban on incinerating municipal waste;
- loss of funding for public transit;
- changes to requirements for farmers using pesticides to be registered, trained, and certified for their use;
- repeal of annual reporting to the public on industrial discharges to waterways.

Funding for government departments such as the Ministry of the Environment and Natural Resources was cut about in half. This reduced the number of environmental inspections, assessments, and monitoring that could take place. A number of agencies that enabled the input of citizens on public environmental policy was cut.

Ontario's much advertised Drive Clean Program, which began in 1999, has tested more than 1.5 million cars for emissions in the most populated parts of Southern Ontario. However, groups such as the Canadian Environmental Law Association and the Ontario Medical Association have said that smog is continuing to get worse.

Provincial policies that support and subsidize highways rather than public transit systems result in more cars on the roads and more pollutants.

FACT FILE

According to Canadian government statistics, air pollution kills 16 000 Canadians prematurely each year. The Ontario government estimates that 1800 people will die prematurely each year due to exposure to air pollutants. Increased exposure to air pollution causes decreased lung function and death, even among healthy people.

While the government is proud of a number of environmental initiatives it has made, such as the Lands for Life program that protects additional land in the province, logging, mining, and hunting will be allowed in many of the protected areas.

Positive Steps

In December 2001, the Ontario government announced a strategy to reduce the dangerous disposal of toxic wastes that are hazardous to human health. If passed into law, under the new strategy:

- 99 000 tonnes of PCBs stored in over 1000 locations will be destroyed by 2004 using advanced technological methods;
- some hazardous wastes will require pretreatment before being dumped into landfills;
- 44 hospital incinerators will be shut down;
- 10 000 tonnes of biomedical waste generated annually by hospitals and medical clinics, including body parts, needles, pharmaceuticals, and human blood, will no longer be dumped in landfill or poured down drains into sewers, but disposed of in hazardous waste facilities;
- 16 000 companies and agencies that generate toxic waste will be charged fees for disposal and monitoring;
- $12 million a year will be used for an electronic monitoring network on the generation, transportation, and disposal of hazardous waste.

FIGURE 16.27 North York General Hospital in Toronto, Ontario. Many hospitals have an ecological footprint that is more than 700 times their actual size. They consume large amounts of energy, produce toxic and biomedical waste, and their incinerators are one of the largest sources of dioxin emissions in Canada.

MAKE A DIFFERENCE

Changing the Way They Do Business
Many companies in Canada can be called environmental success stories. Blount Canada of Guelph, Ontario, is just one example. In 1998, it was the third largest producer of trichlorethylene (TCE), a suspected carcinogen. The TCE was used as a solvent to clean the metal parts it makes for chainsaws. Rather than installing pollution control equipment, and then having to find a way to dispose of the collected toxic materials in landfill or incinerators, as many companies now do, it completely redesigned its processes to eliminate the need for TCE in the first place. Now it heats and spins the metal parts to remove the oil.

FIGURE 16.28 Ninety percent of the dry-cleaning facilities in Canada use a chemical called perchlorethylene, which the Canadian Environmental Protection Act has designated as a persistent, bioaccumulative toxic chemical. Make a difference by looking for a cleaner that uses greener alternatives such as water- or silicon-based processes, or buy clothes that do not need dry cleaning.

MAKE A DIFFERENCE

Detoxify Your Home

Collectively, households in Canada generate large quantities of hazardous waste. A municipality with 100 000 homes will generate more than 2 million L annually. People have disposed of household toxins by putting them in the garbage, or pouring them down the drain or on the lawn or driveway. Disposing of empty containers of household chemicals can leave residues from toxic compounds like benzene or hydrochloric acid in landfill where it can leach into soil and groundwater. Most of the wastes poured down the drain end up in rivers and lakes because sewage treatment plants are designed to treat human waste and do not destroy most toxic chemicals. Adding chlorine as a disinfectant to our water supply can be dangerous since chlorine may combine with organic chemicals to create hazardous trihalomethanes (THM). As consumers, citizens can play a critical role in reducing the amount of hazardous waste that enters the environment.

Replacing hazardous cleaning products and pesticides with some simple alternatives is less expensive and less harmful to our health and the environment. Washing soda, borax, baking soda, vinegar, and cedar chips are just a few green alternatives.

INTERACT

1. Using the Web site < www.environmentalindicators.com >, find and record the overall ranking of OECD nations on 25 environmental indicators. Identify any regional patterns.

2. a) Using the Agency for Toxic Substances and Disease Registry Web site, < www.atsdr.cdc.gov >, find and record the U.S. Top Twenty Hazardous Substances.

b) Which substances appear on the U.S. list of Top Twenty Hazardous Substances that are not included on Canada's list (Figure 16.23, **First Priority Substances List**)?

c) Suggest a reason for the differences between the Canadian and U.S. lists.

3. How have people's views of what constitutes a pest changed?

4. Create a comparison chart on the pros and cons of pesticide use on lawns or for crops.
5. Identify three factors that led to environmental deregulation in Ontario in the 1990s.
6. Make two lists of factors to account for the positive and negative aspects of the record of either Canada or Ontario in environmental protection.
7. Debate the pros and cons of voluntary compliance of industry with environmental guidelines compared with direct enforcement of environmental law based on principles such as the polluter pays principle.
8. Brainstorm a list of products that you use on a regular basis that are made of or include plastics. Write a 250-word scenario of an ordinary day in a future where plastic no longer exists.
9. Evaluate the difference in the difficulty of addressing toxic emissions from point sources and from multiple pathways such as air currents and run-off.

WEB LINKS

- International Safety cards: <http://hazard.com/msds/mf/cards/file>
- Environment Canada warnings and the proper use of pesticides: <www.mb.ec.gc.ca/pollution/pesticides/>
- Green Chemistry: <www.epa.gov/greenchemistry/whatis.html>
- Great Lakes Environmental Atlas: <www.cciw.ca/glimr/data/great-lakes-atlas/intro.html>
- The Agency for Toxic Substances and Disease Registry: <www.atsdr.cdc.gov>
- World Resources Institute, The World Bank and the UN, "Environmental Changes and Human Health": <www.wri.org/wri/wr-98-99>
- Mercury pollution in the automobile industry: <www.cleancarcampaign.org/mercury.html>

- A chronological guide to environmental deregulation in Ontario: <www.cela.ca/Intervenor/24_1/appendix.htm>
- Transnational Corporations: <www.corpwatch.org>
- Resources For the Future: <www.rff.org>
- Canadian Institute for Environmental Law and Policy: <www.cielap.ca>
- Centre for International Environmental Law: <www.ciel.org>
- Global organic food patterns: <www.fao.org/organicag/frame6-e.html>
- Canada's organic food industry: <www.agr.gc.ca/cb/factsheets/2industry_e.phtml>

RELATED ISSUES

- The use of depleted uranium and its impact on health
- Smog as a health hazard
- Costs of cleaning up the environment
- Cross-border transportation of hazardous wastes
- Pesticide use in developing countries
- Light/noise pollution

ANALYSE, APPLY, AND INTERACT

1. Identify the "dirty dozen" POPs, covered by the Stockholm Convention.
   a) Investigate one of the chemicals to find information on its uses and impact on human health.
   b) Use your findings to explain the interactive nature of natural and human systems.
   c) How have people's perceptions of these chemicals varied at different times and in different places?
   d) Explain how agreements such as this could have an effect on you personally.

2. Use an Internet search engine to find the text of the Stockholm Convention on POPs. Evaluate the effectiveness of this international agreement in protecting the health of people and the environment. Consider the following aspects of the agreement: purpose, schedule, public awareness, enforcement, dispute settlement, exceptions, unintentional releases of POPs.

3. Study the quotes found throughout the chapter. Choose one quote that you feel is most significant to the issue of human health and the environment.
   a) Support your choice in a discussion with classmates.
   b) Explain how two quotes that appear to describe opposing viewpoints could both, in some way, be correct.

4. Use the Attorney General of Canada's Web site to find the most recent audit by the Commissioner of the Environment and Sustainable Development.
   a) Assess the progress that has been made in the past year.
   b) Identify the steps outlined by the report that are necessary for the government to take in solving environmental issues.
   c) Make a prediction for the following year based on the government's past performance and the feasibility of implementing the required initiatives.

5. Use the National Pollutants Release Inventory (NPRI) Web site and data to conduct a regional analysis of the pollution in your community.

6. Predict the effect that the Stockholm Convention will have on pollution in the Great Lakes.

7. Conduct a household survey, including the bathroom, kitchen, basement, and garage, to identify products in your home that contain hazardous or toxic ingredients.

8. Explain how public participation in hazardous household waste disposal programs can help to build sustainable communities.

9. Conduct research on household products that can be used as green alternatives to toxic household cleaners, pesticides, and such. Draw up an action plan to detoxify your home. Include in your plan steps to reduce the potential health and environmental risks of using products such as batteries, motor oil, or antifreeze that have no known alternatives.

10. Conduct a case study on a specific example of environmental technology that is being used in your community or another region in Canada. Predict the effect of this technology in reducing the risk of environmental pollution to human health.

11. Investigate the Workplace Hazardous Materials Information System (WHMIS) to find out its impact on the health of people in your school community. How does WHMIS treat pesticides?

12. Conduct research to explain the role of NAFTA's Commission for Environmental Cooperation. Write a 1000-word essay on the impact of this trade agreement on environmental protection in Canada and in Mexico.

13. Using the Web site <www.ciesin.org/indicators.ESI>, find the most recent report on environmental indicators and evaluate the position of Canada compared with previous years.

14. Using the Web site <www.environmentalindicators.com/indicators.htm>, analyse current trends and the impact on human health in Canada for one of the indicators in the OECD environmental indicator study. Evaluate Canada's record in addressing issues related to the indicator.

PART FOUR:
A DISORDERLY WORLD

Chapter 17: Nationalism and the Struggle for Independence

By the end of this chapter, you will:

- demonstrate an understanding of the cultural, economic, and political aspirations of selected groups and the effects of their actions on local, national, and global issues;

- explain why places and regions are important to the identities of selected human groups;

- identify similarities and differences in the economic and political aspirations of selected regional or cultural groups within different countries;

- demonstrate an understanding of the need to respect the cultural and religious traditions of others;

- predict geographic consequences of separation or independence for a region or cultural group that is now part of a larger country;

- demonstrate an understanding of how scarcities and inequalities in the distribution of resources contribute to uprisings and conflicts;

- analyse the economic and environmental consequences for selected countries of colonialism in the past and economic colonialism in the present.

A STRANGE PARADOX

There is a strange paradox in the realm of international relationships. On the one hand, **globalization** has dramatically reformed the way nations and corporations conduct business and think about relationships with other countries. Globalization results in a perspective that sees all parts of the world as interconnected: money, ideas, resources, and labour move easily through porous borders and throughout interconnected economies. National boundaries are in many ways inconsequential, so much so that some argue that boundaries and nations are no longer important. On the other hand, **nationalism** is a force so strong that some countries have been destroyed. Nationalism is a belief that people who share common characteristics, such as culture, religion, or ethnicity, should have their own distinct political identity. Around the world, groups of people are struggling to establish their own nation-states, reasoning that this geographic and political expression is the best way for them to protect their cultural uniqueness and to control their economic and political destinies. These two powerful forces now shape international relationships in the world.

 One man's freedom fighter is another man's terrorist.

anonymous

See Chapter 3 for more information about international relationships.

This chapter will focus on nationalism and its consequences. In particular, we will try to understand the origins of this force and how it can lead to violence.

UNDERSTANDING NATIONALISM

Since 1990, membership in the United Nations (UN) has swelled from 156 countries to over 190 countries. Among the new members were the republics of the former Soviet Union, including Latvia and Uzbekistan, newly independent countries in Eastern Europe such as Croatia and Bosnia and Herzegovina, and tiny countries such as Micronesia, Andorra, and San Marino. These places successfully achieved the status of nation-state and took their places among the other nations of the world. But throughout the world there were stories of peoples whose struggles did not achieve nationhood. They failed in their attempts to become independent and autonomous. Among the list of less successful peoples were the Kurds of Iraq and Turkey, the Catholic Irish of Northern Ireland, the Chechnyans of Russia, the Basques of Spain, and the Quebecois of Canada. Each of these peoples sought independence, sometimes using violence in their quest. These groups illustrate the power of nationalism to drive people to seek autonomy and sovereignty within their own country.

66 From space I saw Earth—indescribably beautiful with the scars of national boundaries gone. 99

Muhammad Ahmad Faris, Syria,
U.S. Space Mission

FIGURE 17.1 Nationalism is a force alive and well in Quebec and can be expressed as separatism.

Imperialism in Africa, 1914

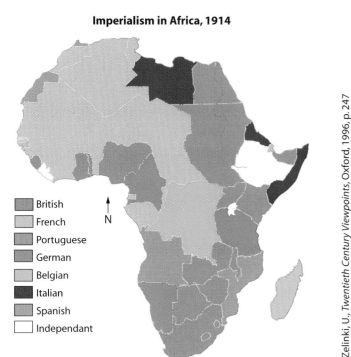

Legend:
- British
- French
- Portuguese
- German
- Belgian
- Italian
- Spanish
- Independant

N

Zelinki, U., *Twentieth Century Viewpoints*, Oxford, 1996, p. 247

FIGURE 17.2 African nationalism stems from the continent's colonial experience under European imperial powers in the nineteenth and first part of the twentieth centuries.

Nationalism is political action taken by peoples who are fighting against the power and control of an external force. It is closely tied to movements for autonomy and self-determination by peoples struggling against European **imperialism**. European imperial powers took control over much of the globe from the fifteenth century to the twentieth century. Spain, Britain, France, Portugal, and to some extent Holland, Belgium, Denmark, Germany, and Italy, imposed their wills over less developed parts of the world, constructing new economies and societies over those that already existed. The frustration and bitterness resulting from these actions have long endured among many groups through their collective memories. The bitterness may not now be directed at the imperial powers themselves, but at the structures that were created by imperialism and that remain to this day, such as national boundaries, political systems, and international economic institutions. In Africa, for example, much conflict has been generated by the European-drawn borders that ignored existing racial and tribal territories and often combined groups

Tribal Divisions in Africa

N

Political Boundaries, 2001

N

adapted from Molyneux J. and M. Mackenzie, *World Prospects*, Prentice-Hall Canada, 1994, p. 263

FIGURE 17.3 Ignoring the traditional tribal structures that had existed before Europeans arrived (left), European imperial powers created political boundaries in Africa in 1885 to suit their own purposes (right). These borders have been called the most dangerous result of colonialism.

with historical animosities. Nationalistic groups are not trying to return to pre-colonial times, but rather to construct new political structures that protect their interests more effectively.

Nationalism is a powerful force and some people are very suspicious of it. In some cases, it is hard to identify the characteristic that is common among a group of people. For example, the many groups who make up the people of East Timor have traditionally been isolated and independent, each with its own languages and customs. Nationalism may appear to be an artificial idea created by some for their own purposes, such as consolidating political power or pushing out a competing ethnic group. These movements use connections such as folk heritage and national symbols. As well, nationalism may be associated with extreme viewpoints, such as fascism, and is closely linked to **xenophobia**, the hatred or fear of other ethnic groups.

Nationalism on the Rise

Why were the 1990s, and the current decade, so troubled by nationalism and ethnic conflict? It is clear that the end of the Cold War and the disintegration of the Soviet Union had much to do with the flowering of nationalism in Europe. By 1990, the authoritarian control of the Soviet Union was gone. For decades, two superpowers—the United States and the Soviet Union—controlled and manipulated less powerful ally nations for their own strategic purposes, maintaining **spheres of influence**. Some nations became pawns in the power struggle between the Soviets and Americans. The nuclear weapon capabilities of both superpowers meant that neither could afford to trigger a conflict or be drawn into one instigated by allies. So, the superpowers kept tight rein on their allies, which meant strong control over internal affairs within these friendly nations, such as separatist movements. The superpowers provided the necessary support for allies to counter demands for autonomy by rebellious groups.

> 66 Once ethnic conflicts begin, I'm afraid you can't solve them. You simply try to manage them. Once fathers are killed, or sisters are raped, you have created an uncontrollable dynamic. 99
>
> *Dr. Rajan Menon, professor of international relations, Lehigh University, U.S.A.*

FIGURE 17.4 The most memorable symbol of the end of the Cold War was the destruction of the Berlin Wall in November 1989. The wall was constructed to keep people inside the communist-controlled part of the city.

For example, the United States propped up the monarchy in Iran by providing weapons and logistical support to keep the more fundamentalist segments of society under control (although this control collapsed with a revolution in 1979). The Soviet Union quieted tension between the Czechs and Slovaks so that Czechoslovakia remained peaceful and united. When these tight strictures were removed with the collapse of the Soviet Union, the nationalistic ambitions of groups were unleashed, often taking the form of ethnic conflict, as was the case in the former Yugoslavia.

 See Chapter 3 for more information about the geopolitical role of superpowers.

But the rise of nationalism after the end of the Cold War does not tell the whole story. Most of the ethnic conflicts that we see today have existed for hundreds of years, yet did not always produce widespread killings and civil wars. For example, the Tutsis and Hutus co-existed in Rwanda in an unequal relationship of the minority ruling the majority for five centuries. There was little violence. In Bosnia and Herzegovina, the Muslim, Croat, and Serb ethnic groups had lived side by side for generations. Something else contributed to the rise of violent nationalism in both cases.

Violence is not a necessary outcome of nationalism. It certainly did occur in places such as Yugoslavia, Azerbaijan, Burundi, and Sudan. The common characteristic in places where widespread violence and civil war was a reality is the lack of effective democratic traditions and institutions. These states simply did not have the democratic structure to allow compromises to resolve conflicts. In the absence of real democracy, the leaders consolidated their power by targeting other groups, using deep-rooted feelings of xenophobia in the population. In Yugoslavia, for example, President Slobodan Milosevic used hatred for ethnic Albanians in the rebellious state of Kosovo to strengthen his popularity among the country's Serb population. Analysts looking at this question have concluded that it is now politically useful for groups to promote nationalism, even if it leads to violent confrontation and revolution. Simply put, these groups now have more to gain by pressing for their own nation-state. Among these groups are the Palestinians, the Chechens, and the Kashmiris. Fortunately, some groups and nations have been able to achieve reasonable, peaceful compromises on issues of nationalism. The native peoples of Belize, a small Central American nation, achieved independence from the United Kingdom in 1981 through diplomacy and negotiation.

Globalization has, ironically, made nationhood useful. In a global economy, only people who have influence and power can begin to control their own destinies. Small groups hidden in a larger population have no power. If a group can break away from the larger population and make itself into a separate nation, it will have at least some measure of strength. As a separate country, the people will:

- have sovereignty, allowing them to choose their own form of government;
- protect their borders, and make decisions about how the country will function;
- be recognized by other countries, by multinational organizations, and by corporations;
- sit in the UN;
- request development assistance;
- compete for international investment dollars;
- negotiate deals and treaties over resources.

In short, they will have a voice. A tiny country such as Tuvalu (with a population of 10 600 people when it achieved independence in 2000) theoretically has the same rights in the international political arena as the United States, China, or Japan.

Challenges to National Sovereignty

In spite of struggles for nationhood, recent trends seem to suggest that nation-states are losing their sovereignty. One of the key advantages of sovereignty is control over transborder movements, whether they are material (e.g., people, goods) or non-material (e.g., cultural influences, information, capital). Technological change has made it very difficult for states to control such movements. Illegal drugs move easily across borders; human smugglers transport migrants from places such as Mexico and China to the United States; the Internet allows information to reach even the most inaccessible locations (in spite of efforts by some fundamentalist societies to block it). Technological change will no doubt continue to erode sovereignty in the future.

Non-governmental organizations (NGOs) are seen by some as undermining the sovereignty of nations. NGOs have been important influences in the past on such issues as abolishing slavery and women's suffrage. In the twentieth century, however, the number of NGOs rose, from about 200 in 1909 to over 20 000

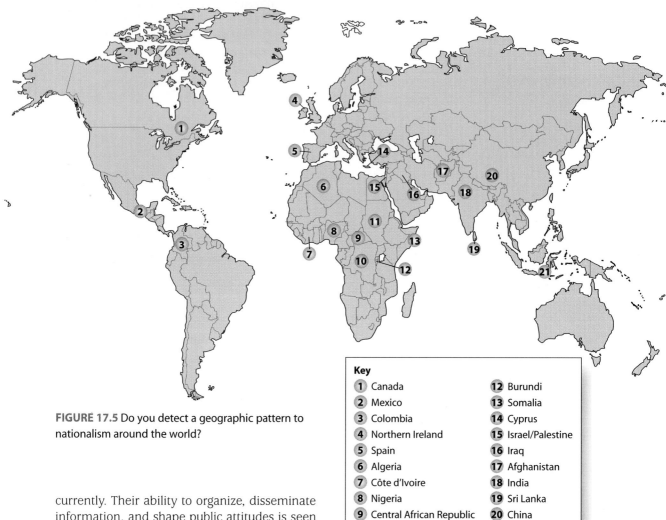

Nationalistic Hot Spots around the World

FIGURE 17.5 Do you detect a geographic pattern to nationalism around the world?

Key

1	Canada	**12**	Burundi
2	Mexico	**13**	Somalia
3	Colombia	**14**	Cyprus
4	Northern Ireland	**15**	Israel/Palestine
5	Spain	**16**	Iraq
6	Algeria	**17**	Afghanistan
7	Côte d'Ivoire	**18**	India
8	Nigeria	**19**	Sri Lanka
9	Central African Republic	**20**	China
10	Congo	**21**	Indonesia
11	Sudan		

currently. Their ability to organize, disseminate information, and shape public attitudes is seen as threatening to domestic decision making. An example of this power is the issue of land mines. Effective action by NGOs in the late 1990s resulted in many countries signing a treaty to ban land mines, changing their official government policies in the process.

But the influence of NGOs is far less significant than the influence transnational corporations (TNCs) have over nations. From setting directions for environmental and trade policies to negotiating contracts, TNCs have substantial clout. Often their actions are attempts to create business conditions that minimize governmental involvement and offer corporations the greatest opportunity to make independent decisions and large profits. Smaller, weaker nations are less able to establish mechanisms to control TNCs.

 See Chapter 3 for more information about the global influence of TNCs.

International organizations are also powerful influences in countries and erode sovereignty. The World Bank and the International Monetary Fund (IMF) have been particularly influential in shaping countries' policies, routinely requiring conditions for financial packages. These conditions are part of **structural adjustment programs** that target government spending,

FIGURE 17.6 Countries give up some aspects of sovereignty when they enter into international agreements such as free trade pacts. Here, protesters at the Summit of the Americas in Quebec City in 2001 voice their disapproval of such loss of control.

forcing cutbacks in areas like education and health care, or improving the climate for international investment, such as reducing protection for workers and unions or for fighting corruption. These policies are designed to ensure that the lending agencies get their investments back, in spite of the costs to the countries.

 See Chapter 13 for more information about structural adjustment programs for developing countries.

In spite of these challenges to sovereignty, nations do have some ability to control conditions within their borders. For example, nations still have the power to manipulate change instruments such as NGOs. Sudan tried to do this by expelling NGOs that supported rebel factions in the country, but the government received sharp criticism from other countries for that action. In addition, nations can still negotiate for the best conditions possible when dealing with TNCs and international organizations. For many groups driven by nationalism, these benefits of nationhood, however slight in practice, are still more attractive than being an invisible minority in a larger country.

INTERACT

1. Create your own definitions for "autonomy," "sovereignty," "nationalism," "xenophobia," "freedom fighter," and "terrorism."

2. In general, would you recommend that a small ethnic minority in a country push for a separate nation-state? Answer this question by comparing the advantages and disadvantages of separation in a specific nationalistic hot spot, recording your ideas in a two-column comparison chart.

3. Based on your knowledge of Quebec in Canada, explain how the Québecois demand for sovereignty:
   a) is an example of nationalism;
   b) has its roots in European imperialism;
   c) is shaped by Canada's strong democratic traditions.

4. Conduct research to identify the cultural, economic, and political aspirations of the people of Nunavut.

5. Design a survey to determine the degree to which your acquaintances would support the struggle for nationalism in Canada and elsewhere in the world. (Or, design your questions about a specific case that is currently in the news and widely discussed.) Try to find out what levels of violence they would accept in a struggle for autonomy and what conditions they would personally be prepared to accept. Report the results of your survey to the rest of the class.

6. Investigate one hot spot from Figure 17.5, **Nationalistic Hot Spots around the World**, Prepare a case study outlining the nature of the conflict and the aspirations of the nationalistic group.

CASE STUDY

East Timor's Struggle for Independence

"We're starting from zero here," explains Luis Ribeiro Carrilho, director of East Timor's new Police Training Academy. It is June 2000, and all around are signs of the destruction and chaos that were part of the struggle for independence in this brand new Asian nation. The new police force is one visible indicator that the people of this war-torn island have finally achieved their independence from Indonesia, a country that brutally occupied their land for 24 years.

The Colonial Legacy

Portugal established the island of Timor as a colony in 1702. In 1913, following 200 years of fighting the Dutch for control, the two countries agreed to share the island. The Dutch occupied the western half and the Portuguese retained control of the eastern half. The Japanese occupied the island during World War II and also faced widespread resistance from the population. From 1940 to 1945, 60 000 Timorese died. Following the war,

the Portuguese resumed control of East Timor, while West Timor was incorporated into the newly created nation of Indonesia. By the 1970s, Portugal had decided to give its colonies independence. East Timor began a three-year decolonization process in 1974, but when Portugal abruptly pulled out of the colony in November 1975, East Timorese leaders quickly declared the independent Democratic Republic of East Timor.

Within ten days, Indonesian forces invaded the abandoned East Timor. One of their motivations for the attack was to prevent the establishment of a communist-inclined government, but they were also after the rich oil and gas reserves found off the coast in the 1960s. A third motivating force was to control ethnic independence; the Indonesian leaders were concerned that an independent East Timor might lead to separatist movements among the diverse groups of people who made up Indonesia. To subdue the country, the Indonesian forces began systematically brutalizing the population, including indiscriminate killings and rapes. Within weeks, by early 1976, they controlled the border and coastal areas. Many East Timorese took refuge in the mountainous interior parts of the country, becoming internally displaced peoples. Over the next few years, Indonesian troops rounded up and relocated the population of occupied regions into resettlement camps far from the border and zones of fighting. Many East Timorese were killed or imprisoned by the military,

FIGURE 17.7 East Timor occupies just half an island in the archipelago dominated by Indonesia.

Quick Facts about East Timor, 2000

Area	14 874 km^2
Population	800 000, composed of 12 ethnic groups, including Timorese, Indonesian, Chinese, and others
Demographic Characteristics	Birth rate—36.5 births per 1000 people Death rate—17.4 deaths per 1000 people Infant mortality rate—135 deaths per 1000 live births Life expectancy for females—48.2 years Life expectancy for males—46.7 years
Economy	GDP/capita US$225 (est.) Agriculture employs over 80% of workforce Rich in oil and natural gas

Canadian Global Almanac 2001

FIGURE 17.8 The government of East Timor is hoping to build its economy on coffee production. The country produces a very high grade of arabica coffee.

disappeared, or died of hunger and disease in the camps. Within a couple of years, 200 000 East Timorese—one-third of the 1975 population—were dead. In spite of these efforts, a resistance campaign continued from isolated parts of the area where Indonesian troops were ineffective.

Initially, Portugal strongly condemned Indonesia's invasion of its former colony, but took no action to stop it. The UN was preoccupied with troubles in the Middle East and a sweeping global recession and did little. The United States had extensive investments in Indonesia, especially in the petroleum sector, and was not willing to risk its close ties to the country over a small island of little consequence to them. Within a short time, this conflict barely made the news pages or the consciousness of most people around the world.

 See Chapter 2 for more information about media coverage of East Timor.

Nationalism in East Timor

Free to do what they wanted in East Timor, Indonesia began a program of systematic repression that was aimed at assimilating the East Timorese people into the Indonesian population. Land was expropriated and given to **transmigrant workers** from West Timor and other parts of Indonesia. Cash-cropping was established, replacing traditional forms of subsistence agriculture. The school system was redesigned to teach children to respect and admire Indonesia's values and practices. The army and secret police were key instruments in this program of repression.

Instead of assimilating the people of East Timor, the repression created a strong nationalist movement. Before 1975, the people did not see themselves as having a separate identity. There are more than 30 indigenous languages on the island, with little communication among the groups because of distance and remoteness. The people did not have the common characteristics that usually inspire nationalism. But, the repression provided exactly the element that was missing. The sense of victimization at the hands of Indonesians stirred outrage in the East Timorese and nationalism was the unintended outcome of the situation. This nationalism pulled together people long accustomed to fighting back against unwelcome occupiers.

Achieving Independence

Internationally, the struggle in East Timor was little known. Two events, however, moved the situation onto the news pages. In 1991, a massacre committed by the Indonesian army was secretly filmed and aired worldwide. It was later determined that up to 270 civilians had been killed. In 1996, the Nobel Peace Prize was awarded to East Timorese Roman Catholic Bishop Felipe Ximenes Belo and resistance activist José Ramos-Horta for their sustained fight for these oppressed people. While bringing international condemnation, these events did not cause the Indonesians to change their tactics. In fact, following the awarding of the Nobel Prize, the Indonesians increased their troop strength from 20 000 to over 30 000 in East Timor and arrested hundreds of people for suspicion of engaging in political activities. The event that finally did bring about positive change occurred within Indonesia. In May of 1998, after months of public protest

FACT FILE

East Timorese voted in their first democratic election in April 2002.

against deteriorating economic and social conditions, Indonesian President Suharto was forced to step down. He had been in power for 32 years, a time during which he and his family had extracted countless billions of dollars from the Indonesian economy. The protest movement compelled the new government to make democratic reforms, including easing repression in East Timor.

> **"** I urge each of you to call on your governments to open a war crimes tribunal on Indonesia. We do not want revenge. We want those who are guilty of war crimes against humanity to be brought to justice. For the sake of those who were murdered. For the sake of those who were burnt to death in their houses. All over the world, we must strive to bring to justice those Indonesian ministers and political leaders who for the past 23 years have executed this crime against a small nation. **"**
>
> *José Ramos-Horta, Nobel Peace Prize winner*

The turmoil in Indonesia inspired separatists in East Timor to push for independence. International attention was now sharply focused on the territory. In May 1999, the Indonesian government was forced to agree to an independence referendum in East Timor, to be held August 30. Then the violence started in earnest. Pro-Indonesia militia groups, supported by the Indonesian army, began herding people across the border into West Timor. Within weeks, fully 200 000 people—about a quarter of the population—had been forcibly removed from East Timor. Many hundreds more were killed. Anything of value that could not be carried away was destroyed, including villages, crops, roads and bridges, farm animals, and fishing boats. At least 80% of all buildings were demolished. In spite of this obvious intimidation, the people of East Timor voted 78.5% in favour of independence. An Australian-led UN peacekeeping force, that included one infantry company from Canada, finally arrived on the island in September 1999 to establish some measure of peace. They found a land in ashes.

Making Independence Work

East Timor declared its independence from Indonesia on October 25, 1999. The task of building a country was daunting, given the level of destruction. The economy was devastated, and few social services remained to help the East

FIGURE 17.9 Some of the destruction that was inflicted on the East Timor population in the lead-up to the independence referendum.

Timorese returning from camps on the other half of the island. Many of the tasks of UN personnel involved supplying basic agricultural necessities, rebuilding roads, and constructing rudimentary schools and health care facilities. Aid began to arrive from other countries and NGOs to help rebuild the economy.

Perhaps more difficult than repairing the economy was putting in place a functional democracy. The UN supported the establishment of a democratic government, but the people of this new nation had no experience in democratic decision making, nor did they have democratic institutions such as courts and political parties. They had to begin building a system from scratch. One of the first problems was choosing official languages for the new country. After many years of occupation, the most commonly understood language, especially among younger citizens, was Indonesian, with Portuguese understood most often by older people—both languages of repressive regimes. No one local language was widespread enough to

FACT FILE

East Timor achieved independence at midnight on May 20, 2002, ending more than 400 years as a Portuguese colony, 25 years of harsh rule by Indonesia, and 31 months under the stewardship of UN peacekeepers.

become an official language. In the end, Tetum, which is understood by about 60% of the population, became the language of commerce and government.

Another important issue to be dealt with by the new government was resolving the animosities created by past violence. Strong resentment remained against East Timorese who had been involved in militia actions and many, fearing reprisals, remained in refugee camps in West Timor, afraid to return to their home villages. These and many other issues have to be resolved before East Timor can be truly independent and peaceful.

FIGURE 17.10 The UN provided equipment and personnel to help rebuild the infrastructure of East Timor following independence.

Commentary

"East Timor: Under Clearing Skies"
by Lisa Clausen
Time International
June 19, 2000

… On foot or in the crowded trays of rusty trucks, they come every second Saturday to family reunion days at Batugade. Here, on the tense border between East and West Timor, thousands of East Timorese queue to enter the field that is neutral ground, where, for six hours, they can try to find family members who have been displaced across the border. More than 250,000 people were forced into camps in Indonesian West Timor during the post-ballot violence and while 162,000 have returned, thousands remain.

… Today's crowd numbers more than 9,000. International peacekeepers are on patrol—there have been disturbances before involving people accusing others of militia acts, and today it happens again, with one man pulled away by soldiers, startling the crowd, some of whom run in panic and weep. Mostly, though, the mood is one of relief and welcome—people shout and hug and eat; surreal picnics in a no-man's-land.

There are glad meetings in the biting sun. A desperate three-month search ends when Diolindo Barros finds his four-year-old daughter Julietta. The child, taken to West Timor during September's madness by an aunt, is feverish and exhausted and Barros holds her close during the two-hour ride home to the town of Maliana. There, the sight of Julietta brings the family running. "We're just happy to be together again," says Barros, as Julietta is kissed and wept over. At this moment, their poor rice harvest and ruined home are forgotten.

Critical Analysis
1. Explain why the border between East Timor and West Timor could be described as "tense."
2. Why would some East Timorese be so frightened of returning to their homes that they would live as refugees in West Timor?
3. What role should international agencies such as the UN play in a situation such as the one described here? Explain your answer.

INTERACT

1. Why did the Indonesian government not support a nation-state for East Timor?
2. Explain how the creation of the nation of East Timor was a product of forces both within and outside of the country.
3. Suppose that you were part of the Indonesian government in the 1990s when the East Timorese were pressing for independence. What strategies would you have suggested to replace the repression and violence that was used? What would you set as your goal in this situation? Explain your ideas.
4. Suppose that you were an East Timorese leader during the struggle for independence. Suggest five strategies that you might have used to try to get international attention for your cause. For each strategy, explain how it might have made a positive difference.
5. Was the creation of an independent East Timor worth the struggle? Give your answer in a carefully thought-out one-page opinion statement.
6. Critically analyse the quotes throughout the chapter and identify opposing views on nationalism.

CASE STUDY

Repression of Indigenous People in Chiapas, Mexico

There is a five-hundred-year history of recurring resistance and rebellion among the indigenous peoples of Mexico. At first, their anger was directed at the Spanish imperialists, and, since independence in 1810, toward the **economic colonialism** of the dominant classes who rule the country. Over the years, the Mexican government has sought to assimilate the indigenous people into the broader society and has had little respect for their cultural and linguistic heritage. The lands of the indigenous peoples have been taken and the people themselves have been exploited as a source of cheap labour. The struggle for the preservation of the unique culture and way of life of indigenous people has been an ongoing theme in Mexico. The rebellion in the southern state of Chiapas that began in 1994 was just a recent flashpoint in this struggle.

One aspect of this situation sets it apart from other nationalistic struggles considered in this chapter—the people of Chiapas are not seeking to create a new nation, but rather to redefine their place *within* the country of Mexico. In a sense, their nationalistic desires can be satisfied by creating conditions that will protect their culture and ensure democracy for themselves within the country, rather than outside of it.

The Situation in Chiapas

Poverty is the dominant aspect of the situation for indigenous people in Chiapas. Most of the people are subsistence farmers, producing enough for their own needs and selling a small surplus to pay for purchased goods such as energy, fertilizers, and medicine. They grow beans, maize, and coffee. Because most of the good land was taken by large landowners and corporations many years ago, the people eke out meagre livings on marginal land that is subject to drought or is hilly and stony. Controls on prices for maize—for the benefit of the poor throughout the country—restrict their incomes while prices for purchased

FACT FILE

The state of Chiapas produces enough electrical energy to meet the needs of all of Mexico, although much is sold to Central American countries. Many communities within Chiapas are not even connected to the electrical grid.

goods continue to rise. The people are trapped in poverty by a system that sees indigenous people on the bottom rung of the social ladder.

Poverty and social alienation were largely responsible for the 1994 rebellion. Demands for reform were obvious well before 1994. Local committees in Chiapas had organized demonstrations and marches, and had produced many petitions asking for land reform, actions that were well within the legally recognized vehicles for protest. The organizers wanted the good quality land that had been confiscated returned to the

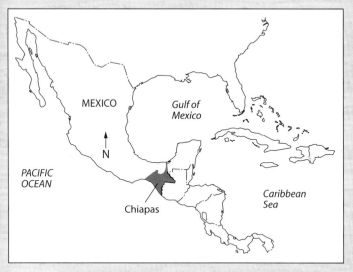

FIGURE 17.11 The location of Chiapas in Mexico.

FIGURE 17.12 The indigenous people of Chiapas want to protect their culture in the face of the transformation of the state into a more modern economy.

Social and Economic Conditions in Mexico and Chiapas, 2000

		Mexico	Chiapas
Population	Total population	97 483 000	3 921 000
	Urban residents (% of population)	74.6	45.7
	Population density (persons per km^2)	50	53
	Ages 0–14 years (% of population)	33.4	38.0
Language	Indigenous language speakers over 5 years old (% of population)	6.8	25.1
	Households where householder or spouse speaks an indigenous language (%)	9.9	29.0
Economy	Employment by sector (% of workers)		
	Primary (agriculture, etc.)	20.7	56.3
	Secondary (manufacturing)	25.0	10.8
	Tertiary (services)	53.9	32.8
	Paid workers earning less than minimum wage (% of work force)	12.3	33.1
Illiteracy	Percent of population who are illiterate	9.5	22.9

Instituto Nacional de Estadística (Mexico)

FIGURE 17.13 The statistics show that the state of Chiapas suffers from **regional disparities** within Mexico.

Indigenous Language Speaking Population, Mid-1990s (% of population)

Less than 3.4%

3.4%–6.8%

National Average = 6.8%

6.8%–13.4%

Greater than 13.4%

N

FIGURE 17.14 The indigenous population has a strong geographic identity in Mexico.

Mexico, which took effect January 1, 1994, triggered open, armed rebellion. To encourage foreign investment in Mexico under NAFTA, Mexican president Carlos Salinas changed the country's constitution to allow the **privatization** of communal land, land that the indigenous peoples depended on for survival and saw as part of their heritage. The move would have, in effect, led to the annihilation of indigenous peoples by taking away the land resource that supported them. The Zapatista guerrilla army moved into action against the Mexican army in the state. Military clashes between the unequal forces lasted for only a few days, but served the purposes of the Zapatistas by bringing international attention to the situation. The conflict then settled into a standoff with a long period of political negotiation. During this time, the presidency

indigenous people, so that they could achieve economic self-determination. The government of Mexico responded in limited ways that were seen by the local people as bureaucratic stalling techniques. Some people became so frustrated with the process that they joined the Zapatista National Liberation Army, a revolutionary group that operated in the mountains and villages of Chiapas. Young people, especially young women, were drawn by an ideology that encouraged people to take control of their lives and resist the traditional Mexican repressive social structures. The Zapatistas also argued that globalization had no benefits for indigenous people and entry into world markets threatened traditional ways of life. Over a period of years, a guerrilla army was created.

    The North American Free Trade Agreement (NAFTA) among Canada, United States, and

> 66 Violence is a form of resourcelessness; in other words, we use violence when we lack the creativity to come up with a non-violent solution. 99
>
> *Ursula Franklin, Canadian academic*

FIGURE 17.15 The leaders of the Chiapas rebellion were able to avoid capture by hiding in the jungles of the state. After the initial skirmishes in 1994, there were few outright battles.

and ruling party of Mexico came under attack for human rights violations, media manipulation, and corruption (a long-standing practice for the party), much of it linked to the situation in Chiapas.

Working Toward a Solution

Resolution of the situation in Chiapas was made difficult by the presence of Mexican troops sent in to quiet the revolution. Eventually, up to 70 000 troops were in the state, in effect, turning it into a police state. There were many reports of human rights violations, including the displacement of indigenous people and rape. The government also armed and trained paramilitary groups. In one incident, paramilitaries killed 45 civilians, including 15 children, in the village of Acteal. In spite of the military presence, the rebellion went on.

> 66 Since the end of 1994, outright attempts have been made to divide the indigenous communities. … In the eyes of the Mexican government, a unified indigenous community would pose a formidable challenge. One of the goals of the military has therefore been to dismantle these communities. Not only have paramilitary groups been created, but they have been given specific military training for this purpose. 99
>
> *Bishop Samuel Ruiz, former president of a peace commission formed in 1998 to examine the conflict in Chiapas, in Alina Rocha Menocal, "The politics of marginalization: Poverty and the rights of indigenous people in Mexico," Journal of International Affairs, October 1, 1998*

FIGURE 17.16 The media attention given to the march to Mexico City by the Zapatista leaders was instrumental in protecting them from prosecution.

There was some hope of a breakthrough in the conflict in 2001. The new Mexican president, Vicente Fox, campaigned on a platform that sought peace with the Zapatistas in Chiapas, a position quite contrary to the long-standing policies of the previous government. For their part, the Zapatistas set three conditions for renewed negotiations—the demilitarization of Chiapas, the release of 100 Zapatista political prisoners, and a new federal law protecting indigenous rights and culture. To support their demands, in March 2001, 23 Zapatista leaders, led by Subcomandante Marcos, left their refuge in the jungles of Chiapas and, with the wide support of the Mexican people, marched unarmed to Mexico City. This display drew the attention of the world's media and put tremendous pressure on the Mexican government to meet the peace conditions. By the end of April, Mexican troops had been withdrawn from the state and some of the political prisoners had been released. New protective laws, however, proved to be harder to implement. An indigenous rights bill that included a series of constitutional reforms was passed by the Mexican Congress in April 2001. It then had to be passed by a majority of the country's 31 states, not an assured thing when only 10% of Mexicans speak indigenous languages. Many non-indigenous Mexicans were reluctant to give up some of their rights or pay an economic price for the protection of indigenous culture and rights. In more northern, wealthier parts of the country, some of the residents felt that the indigenous people were complainers and needed to face the economic realities of a global economy. By May 2001, indigenous leaders had largely rejected the Indian rights bill, claiming that so many compromises had been made to the draft to mollify other groups in society, including business leaders and the military, that the bill no longer protected indigenous interests.

The progress that had been made in the situation was not completely lost and negotiations continued throughout 2001, although with a distinctly less optimistic tone. This conflict showed that nationalism, whether directed at the creation of a wholly new country or at a new relationship within a country, is a compelling force. This conflict has lessons for Canada and its relationships with its indigenous peoples.

Networking on the World Wide Web

The Internet played a key role in the Chiapas conflict. The Mexican government tried to limit damage to their credibility by controlling the media. They painted the Zapatistas as a threat to the political stability of the country. The Internet allowed different points of view about the issue to reach national and international audiences, using already existing networks. News of the situation went out over two informal networks, those established to oppose NAFTA and those built up to promote support for indigenous peoples. Using these networks, official media reports could be challenged and counter-information supplied within minutes or hours. Dozens of Web sites were set up by supporters of the Zapatistas. The rebels began to co-operate with other organizations facing similar situations, which lead to international meetings in 1996 and 1997 attended by thousands of supporters from over 40 countries. The Internet linked the struggle of indigenous people in Chiapas to other issues all around the world and took away from the Mexican government the power that comes from control of information.

Commentary

excerpt from

Racism strangling Mexico Indians' way of life

by Lorraine Orlandi
Reuters
September 28, 2001

… The word racism is rarely heard in Mexico, where the majority of the 100 million citizens are of mixed Indian and Spanish blood, known as "mestizos," and indigenous culture is proudly counted as part of the national patrimony.

But if Mexico's brand of racism seems more subtle than that faced by African Americans in the United States and aboriginal peoples in Australia, it is no less rampant or devastating.

Most of Mexico's 10 million Indians live in extreme poverty in rural villages lacking roads, running water, schools and telephones, in what their leaders call de facto apartheid.

Those who leave that world to seek opportunity in the teeming capital or elsewhere do so against great odds and face unrelenting pressure to leave behind their customs and values.

Many mestizos would willingly call themselves poor but not indigenous. In the popular lexicon, indio is pejorative.

"In Mexico no one recognizes discrimination on the basis of being indigenous. But just look at the insults—'don't act like an Indian'—they all have very colonial, racist origins," said Paloma Bonfil, a senior government official who will attend the UN conference on racism this week in South Africa. …

"Everyone's a Happy Mestizo"

… Mexico's halls of power are occupied mainly by European descendants with surnames like Creel, Zinser and Fox, while members of at least 56 indigenous groups make up the poorest of the poor, with high rates of illiteracy and infant mortality, working long hours and earning far less than the minimum wage of around $4 a day.

Even in their own villages, children may be berated by their teachers for speaking Indian languages. In most places courts and other public institutions provide translators in foreign languages, but not in Indian languages.

Such conditions gave rise to a rebellion in dirt-poor Chiapas state, where about a quarter of 4 million residents are Indians. The 1994 Zapatista uprising over Indian rights came as a shattering blow to a society in which, as political scientist Federico Estevez ironically put it, "everyone's a happy mestizo."

President Vicente Fox took office in December [2000] and pledged to answer indigenous demands with a package of constitutional reforms to guarantee Indian rights.

But the vision of a new pact between Mexico and its indigenous peoples gave way to disappointment.

"The policies of the new government are the same, it's a kind of negation of the indigenous," said Francisco Lopez, a Mixteco lawyer who headed the justice arm of the National Institute for the Indigenous until resigning last week to protest the new Indian rights law. …

The compromise measure that took effect this month falls short of granting Indian citizens full equality, leaders say.

"They tell us we are the sons of the indigenous ancestors, but then they don't give us the opportunity to grow alongside Mexicans," said Benancio Ruiz, a Triqui lawyer who heads a Mexico City organization of indigenous artisans. ...

Critical Analysis

1. What evidence is presented to support the contention that racism is widely practised in Mexico?

2. Francisco Lopez claims that the government policies are a "negation of the indigenous." What does this mean? How would such an attitude affect government policies and actions?

3. Compare the nature and extent of racism in Mexico to that found in Canada. In what ways is the racism the same? different?

NATIVE LAND CLAIMS IN CANADA

As in Chiapas and other parts of the world, the indigenous peoples in Canada are struggling to regain control of their land, arguing that this is necessary to protect both their heritage and their future. The history of this country has shaped the current land claims context. In Canada, aboriginal land claims are based on three types of treaties:

- Pre-Confederation treaties that were signed before Canada became an independent country
- Numbered treaties (11 in total) that were negotiated between 1871 and 1877 with the federal government of Canada
- Modern treaties negotiated under Canada's Land Claims Policy of 1973

The Land Claims Policy is important to the process because it recognizes that Aboriginal peoples have land rights. This policy lays out two types of land claims. Specific claims apply to native bands that have signed treaties but feel that the government has failed to live up to its obligations. In some cases, the claims concern assets such as timber and mineral rights that were improperly administered by the government, or land that was sold from reserves without the consent of the bands. These claims seek redress for specific problems covered by signed treaties. Comprehensive claims are made by native bands that have never signed treaties yet have lost access to resources enjoyed by their ancestors before Europeans arrived. These claims usually include demands for full ownership of some lands, wildlife harvesting rights, guaranteed participation in resource and environmental management, revenue-sharing on natural resources, financial compensation, and efforts to stimulate economic development. Negotiations in comprehensive claims are aimed at ensuring the native bands will become economically self-sufficient.

While the process to settle indigenous land claims seems straightforward, there has been a great deal of criticism of it. For example, Canada's Auditor General, Sheila Fraser, in her 2001 report to the House of Commons, found "fundamental issues" with the negotiation process. She particularly cited the length of time it takes to reach agreements as a problem. This idea is echoed by native groups who have become frustrated with the bureaucratic quagmire that surrounds the process. On the other hand, non-native groups have spoken out against the idea that a small minority of Canadians has rights to large areas of the country simply as a result of ancestry.

> " ...there are differences, if not an outright philosophical schism, between native and non-native Canada. "
>
> *John Stackhouse,*
> *"First step: End the Segregation"*
> The Globe and Mail,
> *December 15, 2001*

FACT FILE

In 2000, the Canadian government settled 16 specific claims. A total of 120 specific claims were in negotiation.

FACT FILE

Since 1973, a total of 12 comprehensive claims have been finalized. In 2000, there were 70 comprehensive land claims in negotiation.

Comprehensive Native Land Claims Agreements as of 2000

Name of Agreement	Area Covered	Year
The James Bay and Northern Quebec Agreement	From the shores of James Bay and Hudson Bay to Labrador	1975
The Northeastern Quebec Agreement	A large part of northeastern Quebec	1978
The Inuvialuit Final Agreement	The islands and part of the mainland along the Beaufort Sea	1984
The Gwich'in Agreement	Parts of northeastern Yukon and northwestern portion of the Northwest Territories	1992
The Nunavut Land Claims Agreement	Eastern part of Northwest Territories, including Baffin Island	1993
The Sahtu Dene and Metis Agreement	Northwestern part of the District of Mackenzie	1993
The Vuntut Wwich'in First Nation Agreement	Part of Yukon Territory	1993
The Teslin Tlingit Council Agreement	Part of Yukon Territory	1993
The Champagne and Aishihik First Nation Agreement	Part of Yukon Territory	1993
Nacho Nyak Dun Agreement	Part of Yukon Territory	1993
The Little Salmon/Carmacks First Nation Agreement	Part of Yukon Territory	1997
The Selkirk First Nation	Part of Yukon Territory	1997

adapted from Elaine L. Simpson, University of Alberta

FIGURE 17.17 The comprehensive land claims settled to date have focused on the northern parts of Canada.

Public opinion in British Columbia against an agreement reached between provincial and federal governments and the Nisga'a people has prompted a subsequent provincial government to consider re-opening the agreement by holding a referendum on the decision. According to many Aboriginal people, the relationship between Aboriginal people and non-Aboriginals in Canada is not substantially different from most other countries of the world, including Mexico.

INTERACT

1. Identify "repressive social structures" in society. Compare the impact of those in Chiapas with those of Canada's Native people.
2. The indigenous peoples in Chiapas are not trying to create a new nation-state. In what ways can their struggle still be considered nationalism?
3. Clearly identify the stakeholders in this situation in Chiapas and explain their points of view on the issues.
4. Write a script for a meeting between Mexican government officials and Zapatista leaders during which both groups attempt to clearly state their posi-

tions on the issues that have caused conflict in Chiapas.
5. Conduct research about indigenous rights and issues in Canada. Compare the issues in Canada to those in Chiapas. Identify some lessons that Canadians should learn from this conflict in Mexico. Investigate the current status of the indigenous people of Chiapas and their nationalistic struggle.

CASE STUDY

The Kurds' Struggle to Protect their Culture

The cause of the Kurds' situation can be clearly tied to imperialism and the impact of imperial powers in other parts of the world. Solutions to the situation are not so apparent.

Background on the Kurds

The Ottoman Empire came to an end with the conclusion of World War I in 1918. This empire had existed from the fourteenth century and incorporated large parts of Eastern Europe, the Middle East, and Northern Africa. Many different groups of people had been subjugated by the Ottoman Empire, including the Kurds, a people who can trace their settlement in the region back to about 2400 BCE. With the defeat of the Ottoman Empire, the Kurds pushed to have a nation-state of their own, to be called Kurdistan. This desire was written into the Treaty of Sèvres that was signed in August 1920 between Turkey and the Allied Powers (Britain, France, Italy, and the United States). Unfortunately, many Turks were not satisfied with this treaty and rallied behind a

FIGURE 17.18 A Kurdish family in Suleymaniyah, Iraq.

FACT FILE

The Kurds are the fourth largest ethnic group in the Middle East, after the Arabs, Turks, and Persians. They make up about 15% of the population of the region.

rebellious nationalistic leader, Mustafa Kemal, who overthrew the existing government and established the Republic of Turkey. Turkish resistance to Allied forces prompted the drafting of a new treaty in 1923, the Treaty of Lausanne. This new treaty did not recognize the demands of the Kurds for their own nation. The area occupied by the Kurds was divided among Turkey and areas controlled by the British and French, which subsequently became the countries of Syria and Iraq. Kurds were also a minority group in Iran.

The Struggle to Survive

In spite of many decades of repression and hostility since the Treaty of Lausanne, the Kurds have refused to give up on their dream of an independent and autonomous Kurdistan.

The Distribution of the Kurdish People

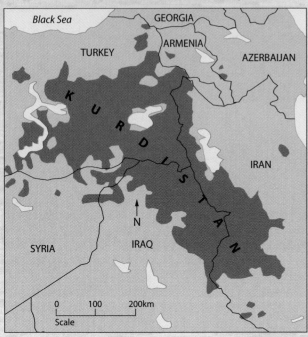

FIGURE 17.19 While a majority in the area they have designated as Kurdistan, the Kurds are minorities in all the countries that currently exist in the area.

Kurdistan and Present-day Countries

Country	Proportion of Area of Kurdistan (%)
Turkey	43
Iran	31
Iraq	18
Syria	6
Other countries	2

FIGURE 17.20 Kurdistan would include a territory of about 500 000 km².

Kurds in Turkey At the time of the signing of the Treaty of Lausanne in 1923, the new government of Turkey claimed that Kurdish interests would be protected. Within a short period of time, however, it was clear that they wanted a different future for the Kurds. The government denied their existence and began a process of assimilation that included

Kurdish Population, 2000 and 2020 (millions)

Country	Population, 2000	Population, 2020 (est.)
Turkey	18.7	32.3
Iran	9.0	16.2
Iraq	6.4	10.9
Syria	1.6	2.7
Other Middle East	0.5	0.9
Total	36.2	63.0

FIGURE 17.21 The Kurds have maintained high birth rates, so that their populations are growing faster than other groups within the various countries. In Turkey, Kurds are predicted to outnumber Turks by 2050.

forbidding the use of the Kurdish language. The Kurds revolted in the face of this discrimination, first in 1925 and then again in 1930 and 1938. Each time, the rebellions were brutally put down and thousands of Kurds were killed. Over the following decades, the Kurds were victims of systemic oppression and were driven into poverty and ignorance. Open, armed rebellion began again in 1979 and has continued to this day. The government of Turkey has responded by declaring a state of emergency and imposing military law in the area. Since 1991, over 1500 Kurdish villages have been evacuated and destroyed. Thousands of Kurds have fled to Iran and Iraq to seek asylum as refugees.

FACT FILE

About one-third of the total area of Turkey would be contained within Kurdistan. In some provinces, 80–90% of the population is Kurdish.

 See Chapters 18 and 19 for more information about civil conflicts and refugees.

Kurds in Iraq The Kurds in Iraq also faced oppression in the years following World War I. Their resistance to oppression resulted in a number of compromises with the Iraqi government. The Kurds were granted some rights to protect their culture, could run their own schools, and operated their own media. In 1970, after a decade of prolonged conflict, the Iraqi government, as part of a peace pact, even agreed to a Kurdish autonomous region within Iraq. Unfortunately, delays in implementing the agreement, and subsequent repressive laws, resulted in renewed violence in 1974. Hoping to pressure the Iraqi government into honouring the agreement, the Kurds sought the support of neighbouring Iran, an action that brought greater hostility from the Iraqis. Subsequently, Iran and Iraq fought a devastating eight-year war over land throughout the 1980s, during which time the Kurds actively sided with Iran. Iraq responded by attacking the Kurds, including using chemical weapons against them.

The Gulf War of 1991 gave the Kurds some glimpse of hope. Iraq, led by Saddam Hussein, invaded Kuwait in 1990. Many countries, including Canada, joined in a coalition of forces to push Iraqi forces out of Kuwait. This coalition also established a protected enclave in the northern, Kurdish occupied parts of the country and enforced a "no-fly zone" to keep Iraqi aircraft out of the area. However, the coalition stopped short of supporting the creation of an independent Kurdish nation. In the years that followed the Gulf War, the drive for an independent Kurdish nation lost its momentum. Competing Kurd groups fought for control of the area—essentially engaging in a civil war—and little progress was made in their struggle for an independent homeland.

Kurds in Iran The Kurds in Iran faced repression similar to conditions in Iraq and Turkey. In the aftermath of World War II, the Kurds in Iran sought to take advantage of unstable political conditions in the region and declared the Kurdish state of Mahabad. This rebellion was quickly put down by the government of Iran, supported politically by

> ## FACT FILE
>
> About one million Kurds live in European countries, seeking work as migrant labourers, or avoiding oppression in their places of birth.

> 66 We have flown the air like birds and swum the sea like fishes, but have yet to learn the simple act of walking the earth as brothers. 99
>
> *Martin Luther King,*
> *American civil rights activist*

FIGURE 17.22 The use of chemical weapons by Iraq against Kurds (this young boy's burns are the result of a phosphorous bomb) outraged the world. For many observers, the Iraqi treatment of the Kurds has been a genocide.

both Great Britain and the United States. Kurdish resistance has continued to this day, first against the U.S.-supported Shah, whose reign ended in 1978, and then against the regime of the fundamentalist **mullahs**.

Kurds in Syria Political opposition is not tolerated in Syria. Kurds have been suppressed, with many ending up in Syrian jails. The media is strictly controlled and the small community of Kurds have little chance to voice their demands for an independent Kurdistan.

The Failure of Kurdish Nationalism

Resistance to oppression and assimilation has cost the Kurdish people dearly. The desire for a nation of their own runs deep within the people. Many thousands have been killed and hundreds of thousands displaced through mass expulsions. Observers consider their experience to be a case of genocide. But after more than three-quarters of a century, the people have little to show for their struggles. Why has Kurdish nationalism failed? Three reasons seem to be important:

- The social structure of the Kurdish people remains traditional, reminiscent of medieval times, with power passed through family and tribal lineage. Political organization is based on sheikdoms and tribes, and land is held in large blocks by hereditary title. Power is fragmented, which has led to strongly contested rifts between Kurdish groups and prevented a united movement for nationalism.

■ The Kurds must simultaneously demand independence from four nations, none of which would benefit greatly from the creation of an independent Kurdistan. The four nations have become allies in opposition to Kurdish nationalism.

■ The Kurds have failed to win international support for their cause. In the past, countries such as the United Kingdom and France have taken actions directly contrary to Kurdish independence, such as financing opposing forces, and, more recently, countries including the United States and Canada have stopped well short of supporting the Kurds in their struggle. This lack of support is because the international community is reluctant to oppose the four countries that are home to most of the Kurds.

Moving to Resolve the Kurdish Situation

It is clear that Kurdish nationalism will not be extinguished by oppression. Continuing to wage civil war against the Kurds has drained the financial resources of Turkey, Iran, and Iraq, as well as destroyed the economy of those parts of the country inhabited by Kurds. Turkey's military bill for direct expenditures in trying to subdue the Kurds is estimated at US$8–10 billion per year. A peaceful resolution through diplomacy and recognition of Kurdish rights would benefit the three countries and the Kurdish people.

Pressure is being applied to Turkey to take a different tact in dealing with the Kurds. Turkey is attempting to join the European Union (EU), to better ensure its economic future. Within such an organization, the country would have to meet European standards for protecting human rights and honouring treaties and agreements. For example, Turkey has signed the UN Declaration on Human Rights, yet has repeatedly and willingly broken the spirit of the declaration in its treatment of the Kurds. In short, Turkey will have to improve its handling of the Kurdish question before it will be respected in Western Europe.

The key to improving the situation for Kurds in Turkey, Iraq, and Iran is international pressure to improve rights. All countries around the world need to put political pressure on the three countries to improve conditions for ethnic minorities within their borders, especially the Kurds. Trade and aid agreements could even be tied to such improvements. Unfortunately, countries such as Canada have avoided strong actions and opted for less overt diplomatic steps. Even the most optimistic of observers have to conclude that an independent homeland for the Kurds is a long way off.

FIGURE 17.23 A demonstration of support for Kurdish independence in Toronto, 1999.

excerpt from
Hansard
April 6, 1995

Mr. Svend J. Robinson (Burnaby-Kingsway, NDP)
Mr. Speaker, last month I had the honour of leading a delegation to Turkey to look into the very serious situation of human rights violations in that country. In particular, I was looking at the appalling human rights violations affecting the Kurdish community in Turkey.

Some 12 million Kurds live in Turkey. They have been denied any democratic rights whatsoever to express their fundamental cultural and linguistic heritage.

Following my return from that delegation, I raised a question in the House last week. I asked the Prime Minister to explain why the Canadian government is seriously contemplating sending a delegation led by a minister of the government to celebrate 75 years of Turkish parliamentary democracy.

It is absolutely appalling that the government would seriously consider sending a delegation of that nature when six members of the Turkish Parliament are locked up in the Ankara prison solely for having spoken out for human rights, democracy and justice....

Second, I raised the issue of the possible sale of 39 CF-5 fighter aircraft to Turkey. We know of the human rights abuses. We know of the burning and destruction of villages. We know of over two million Kurds who have been made homeless in southeastern Turkey. We know of the attacks on journalists. We know of the very profound attacks on many other minorities in Turkey.

This arms deal is fundamentally immoral. I call on the Government of Canada to join with Norway and Germany, two of our strong NATO [North Atlantic Treaty Organization] allies, in imposing an arms embargo on Turkey.

Canada's policy is supposedly not to sell weapons to areas of conflict and not to sell weapons to countries with questionable human rights records. The government says: "No problem, we will get a promise from Turkey that they will not use this against civilians". The Turkish government made a similar promise with respect to tanks sold to them by Germany. That promise was broken as well.

I call on the government to say now, categorically, that it will not participate in this charade of the celebration of Turkish democracy, that it will cancel the Canadian delegation, that it will not sell CF-5 fighter aircraft, that it will impose an arms embargo and call on the Turkish government to arrive at a peaceful solution through political dialogue and peaceful means instead of attacking the Kurdish community....

Mr. Jesse Flis (Parliamentary Secretary to Minister of Foreign Affairs, Lib.) Mr. Speaker, I wish to set the record straight....

I would like to begin by addressing the first two issues. The hon. member received an excellent answer from the Prime Minister when he asked the question on March 28. The Prime Minister in his reply said: "It might be a good occasion for the ministerial delegation to raise the issue of human rights with the government when it is there". He also said: "Perhaps one way is to cancel the delegation or the other way is to send the delegation with a mandate to talk about it"....

I am sure these kind of direct interventions, face to face interventions, go a long way. Boycotting that country and not talking to them is not going to give them the message. We have to get there and approach them eyeball to eyeball on this situation. That addresses the first two issues.

As far as the sale of the CF-5s is concerned, again I do not know why the member is making such a fuss over the issue. Just after question period today I asked the Minister of Foreign Affairs about this. There is no sale of CF-5s to Turkey. That is as recent as today. I hope the hon. member will pass that on to his constituents and to other Canadians. Yes, we have surplus planes. Yes, countries are interested in purchasing them. The price is a little lower because they are surplus and used. As of today, there is no sale of CF-5s to Turkey.

I thank the hon. member for his intervention, but I hope he will not be hypocritical—

The Deputy Speaker Your time has expired.

Critical Analysis
1. Summarize the arguments made by both Svend Robinson and Jesse Flis as they spoke to the House of Commons.
2. Based on the reading, what do you consider to be Canada's policy on the Kurdish situation?
3. What might be some of the implications of Canada's official relationship with Turkey, given that country's treatment of the Kurds?

Amnesty International (AI) is a NGO that has played an important role in protecting people who have been imprisoned solely for their beliefs and who have not used nor advocated violence. They label these people "prisoners of conscience." AI's campaigns seek to free all prisoners of conscience, to ensure fair and speedy trials for political prisoners, to abolish torture and the death penalty, and to end human rights abuses around the world.

AI's strategy is to make public the abuses of human rights. When they identify problem situations, they hold public demonstrations, engage in letter-writing campaigns, put on fundraising concerts, and launch personal appeals. Using their million members in over 160 countries, they can create a significant pressure on offending governments or groups. During 2000, AI worked on behalf of 3685 named individuals, of which 481 were new cases located in 85 countries or territories.

AI is independent of any government, religion, or political point of view. The organization is funded by donations and subscriptions.

> 66 In international practice there is no recognition of a unilateral right to secede based on a majority vote of the population of a sub-division or territory, whether or not that population constitutes one or more "peoples" in the ordinary sense of the word. In international law, self-determination for peoples or groups within an independent state is achieved by participation in the political system of the state, on the basis of respect for its territorial integrity. 99
>
> *James Crawford, University of Cambridge,*
> *in a briefing paper to the Department of Justice,*
> *Canada, 1997*

INTERACT

1. Explain how the situation of the Kurds is a case of nationalism.
2. Write a newspaper editorial expressing your views about the plight of the Kurdish people. In your editorial, suggest actions that could be taken to improve their chances for establishing a homeland.
3. What should be the policy of countries such as Canada when there are strong demands for sovereignty and independence in other parts of the world? Explain your views.

CANADA'S SOVEREIGNTY

Canada faces many issues of national sovereignty, given the changes in Canadian identity brought on by globalization and living within the close sphere of influence of the United States.

Canada has a long history of mutual co-operation with the U.S. Canada is dependent on trade with the world's largest consumer and plays an important role in providing energy and resources to the U.S. Greater continental integration has been the recent trend, beginning with trade and moving to a more strategic defence and security partnership with the U.S. The integration of North and South American markets appears to be having a positive effect on Canada's economy, but there is concern that integration will lead to loss of control over our social and environmental policies.

In Europe, the close alliance of countries is generally balanced in size and power. The relationship between Canada and the U.S. is not balanced and there are important differences between the two countries. Canada and the U.S. do not always agree in foreign policy matters. As a country, Canada has worked hard to eradicate land mines, promote nuclear arms control and disarmament treaties, strengthen the UN, and create an international criminal court. Canadian values centre on an open society and open and free markets, and on helping others to help themselves, including a focus on African development.

Controversial, Defining Geopolitical Issues of Concern to Canadians

Foreign overfishing The European Union (EU) is one of the main culprits in Canada's territorial waters and, by 2002, had not signed a treaty, despite five years of efforts by the Canadian government. Critics say the government has not been forceful enough in attempts to protect the fishery.

Foreign ownership of Canadian resources and industries Half of Canada's oil and gas sector is owned by foreign companies. In 2001, $35 billion worth of Canadian energy companies were taken over by U.S. energy companies.

Preservation of local cultural traditions, skills, artists, and values Global monoculture, with its consumerist corporate paradigm, and American films, music, and television dominate Canadian markets.

The "brain drain" from other countries Canada loses university graduates to the U.S., particularly in health care, engineering, and computer sciences. Yet, for every Canadian graduate who moves south, four university graduates immigrate into Canada.

Continental integration with the U.S. and Mexico Intended for defence and security, is there potential for lost sovereignty?

Defence expansion What will be Canada's position on the greatly expanded missile defence system and militarization of space planned by the U.S.?

Security Who are Canada's real enemies—terrorists and foreign armies or homelessness, poverty, and global climate change?

The Canadian military Should we build an all-purpose military and fight with the U.S. or stick to peacekeeping?

Association with U.S. military operations Does this put us in breach of our international obligations, given the Treaty we signed to ban land mines?

Protection of sovereignty Do we want to protect cultural sovereignty, immigration, refugee policies?

Democracy and human rights What is the best way for Canada to promote democracy and human rights around the world?

Foreign aid Canada, one of the wealthiest countries in the world, has allowed its foreign aid to shrink from 0.45% of GNP to 0.25% in 2002.

Canadians are among the best educated in the world and have a highly technological society. Canadians have more personal computers and Internet connections per capita than any other country in the world and the most advanced fibre-optic network infrastructure. Canada has the lowest cost of living of the G7 countries and, according to the UN's Human Development Index (HDI), ranked first or second during the 1990s and into the twenty-first century. Despite these advantages, with a small population of under 33 million people over the second largest territory, Canada has found it necessary to join coalitions of allies to help defend her sovereignty.

A current issue centres on how closely Canada should integrate with the U.S. on defence policy. As we are asked to form closer ties with U.S. decision making and its move to a more co-ordinated continental defence command, we may be risking our freedom of choice on controversial initiatives such as militarization of space, and the independence to pursue initiatives and policies that reflect our distinctly Canadian worldview.

The changes in Canadian law and policy since the terrorist attacks against the U.S. in September 2001 occurred quickly, with little public input or government debate. Many

FIGURE 17.25 The world's longest undefended border with the U.S. is now under increased security with integrated border enforcement teams and National Guard troops. Canada–U.S. trade is the largest in the world. More of this trade passes across the Windsor–Detroit Ambassador Bridge than any other crossing.

Canadians have called for more serious and widespread public dialogue and debate, with the government leading the way in informing public opinion before making policy decisions on important issues.

While we are already integrated with the U.S. in a number of initiatives for North American defence, as partners in the Alaska–Canada–United States Agreement known as ALCANUS and the North American Aerospace Defence Command (NORAD), the U.S. has a much greater share of command. The Commander-in-Chief of NORAD is American. Although the deputy commander is Canadian, he has no power to act in the commander's absence.

What Is Happening in Canada's Backyard?

Canada is an Arctic nation. Global climate change and environmental protection of the fragile Arctic ecosystems will require effective responses. According to the International Law of the Sea, coastal countries have jurisdiction over the area that fits within a 300-km limit of their coastlines. In 1985, Canada formally asserted control over its Arctic waters and islands after the U.S. ice-breaker ship, Polar Sea, sailed through the North West Passage without Canadian permission.

Analysis of satellite images and Environment Canada field research shows that the ice coverage in Hudson Bay has been shrinking at the rate of 10% over each decade since the 1970s. The total frozen surface of the Arctic Ocean has been reduced by 8% between 1992 and 2002. The Inuit have noticed many indicators of global climate change, including the changing habits of polar bears as they spend more time hunting on land and less on floating ice. As the Arctic ice thins and melts, the brief shipping season gets longer each year.

The North West Passage connects two international bodies of water. As the passage opens up, it will attract commercial ships. In the 1990s, there was an increase in ecotourism cruises and other commercial ships from countries such as Germany, Russia, Japan, and China, as well as U.S. ships and submarines. As the passage melts further, interest in using it will grow. Environmental pollution and the introduction of alien species from the ballast of ships in a fragile ecosystem, as well as increased smuggling and illegal resource exploitation in the area, are concerns for the future. Organized crime could infiltrate the diamond mining of the North and Canada's freshwater supply could be at risk if northern

FACT FILE

In 1990, there were no ecotourist cruises, but by 1998, there were 15 ecotourist cruises through the North West Passage.

66 Canada needs to take some ownership, but it would be really nice if the Canadian government would talk to the people who live here before deciding what should be done about Arctic sovereignty. 99

Inuit elder, Tuktoyaktuk

rivers can be pumped into a foreign ship without detection.

While the U.S. often asks Canada's permission to enter the waters, neither the U.S. nor the EU recognize Canada's claim to sovereignty. According to international law, a country must have monitoring and enforcement capability for a strategic water route, and be able to react to a threat. Canada lacks adequate Coast Guard protection, long-range maritime control aircraft to monitor activities in the Arctic, and search and rescue capabilities. Canadian pollution officers often find themselves working on U.S. Coast Guard or research ships to conduct their research. The central focus of the issue is whether Canada wants to adapt to the effects of climate change on the Arctic on its own terms or according to the interests of international shipping.

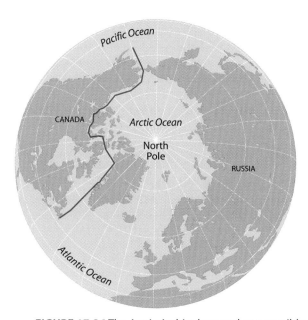

FIGURE 17.26 The Arctic Archipelago and one possible North West Passage route.

INTERACT

1. Define the term "sovereignty" as it applies to Canada–U.S. relations.
2. Communicate creatively in a poster or poem your vision of what should be Canada's role in the global community in the twenty-first century.
3. Identify global trends and events that are having an influence on Canada's Arctic sovereignty.
4. a) Choose one of the controversial, defining geopolitical issues of concern to Canadians outlined on page 435 and conduct research to obtain the most current information on the issue.
   b) Write two 250-word position papers outlining two opposing viewpoints on the issue, evaluating its impact on Canada's sovereignty.

WEB LINKS

- American Kurdish Information Network: <www.kurdistan.org>
- Global Policy Forum: <www.globalpolicy.org>
- Centre for Security Studies and Conflict Research: <www.isn.ethz.ch/cwa>
- East Timor International Support Center: <www.easttimor.com>

RELATED ISSUES

- Refugees and internally displaced people
- Nationalism and racism
- Independence and development
- Role of NGOs in encouraging nationalism

ANALYSE, APPLY, AND INTERACT

1. Develop a comparison chart to record information about the nationalistic experience of the three groups profiled in case studies in this chapter.

2. Imagine that you are a reporter for a major Canadian television network. You have just witnessed acts of violence in one of the three cases explored in this chapter. Script a report, including details and reasons for the violence.

3. Choose a group of people that is seeking to establish a nation-state and write a poem, short play, or story that expresses something of their nationalistic aspirations.

4. Using one of the groups considered in this chapter, write a two-page report in which you discuss how the cultural, economic, and political aspirations of the group affect local, national, and global issues. Local issues include poverty, basic human needs, and the environment; national issues include security, human rights, and political leadership; global issues include the plight of refugees and displaced people, international peace and security, and access to natural resources.

5. Places and regions are important to the identities of the human groups who live there. Compile a collage or poster of images of a place that is important to another group of people, such as the indigenous tribes of the Amazon rain forest or the Aborigines of the deserts of Australia.

6. Conduct research and use your own knowledge to identify similarities and differences in the economic and political aspirations of two regional or cultural groups within Canada. For example, you might compare aspirations of the Quebecois to those of the Inuit of Nunavut, or the aspirations of the people of Western Canada to those of the people of the Atlantic Provinces. Use a chart to record your ideas.

7. A common theme in this chapter is the attempt to assimilate a group of people into a larger population. Using this observation, explain why the need to respect the cultural and religious traditions of others is necessary for ongoing peace on the local, national, and international levels.

8. Using ideas from the case studies in this chapter, predict geographic consequences of separation or independence for the Kurds in the Middle East, or predict the consequences of the separation of Quebec from Canada.

9. Many analysts, including Thomas Homer-Dixon, have theorized that scarcities and inequalities in the distribution of resources will become increasingly important causes of uprising and conflicts. Prove or disprove this theory by looking at nationalism around the world. Choose one particular group and identify the forces that are motivating their actions to see if they are related to scarcities in resources.

10. Choose one civil conflict that is ongoing. Analyse this conflict to determine the extent to which colonialism in the past and economic colonialism in the present contributed to the violence. You might consider the situations in Algeria, India (Kashmir), Sierra Leone, Palestine, Sri Lanka, and Tibet. Write a three-page case study, including your analysis.

Chapter 18: Refugees

By the end of this chapter, you will:

- identify similarities and differences in the economic and political aspirations of selected regional or cultural groups within different countries;

- analyse the causes and consequences of recent events involving refugees in Canada or in another part of the world and evaluate the effectiveness of the relevant policies for dealing with refugees;

- analyse the impact of selected human migrations on natural and human systems;

- analyse geopolitical relationships between selected countries and regions;

- analyse cause and effect and sequence relationships in geographic data;

- analyse how the media influence public opinion on geographic issues.

A STRUGGLE FOR SAFETY

During the 1990s and into the present decade, a large number of intranational conflicts emerged. These were largely confined within one country and were usually based on race, ethnicity, nationality, religion, clan, language, or region. The massacre of about one million people that took place in Rwanda in 1994 was just one instance of civil conflict. As a whole, these civil conflicts have generated more **refugees** and **internally displaced people** than the international wars of the previous era.

Civil Conflicts and Refugees

Civil conflicts are usually fought by deliberately targeting civilians. The objectives of the leaders are to intimidate, overpower, or drive out some part of the population in the country—those considered the enemy. The spirit of the people is more easily broken if non-combatants are hurt or killed than if soldiers are attacked. The goal is not military victory, but psychological defeat. This strategy works best if the violence is based on gender. Young women are systematically raped and humiliated; young men are victims of mass murders or are made to fight for the more powerful side. Children are kidnapped and forced to be soldiers. These atrocities create terror in the civilian population and many people flee, becoming refugees in a neighbouring country.

The war in Bosnia and Herzegovina (1992–1995) is a good example of the targeting of civilians in a civil conflict. During this country's war of independence from the former Republic of Yugoslavia, the three main ethnic groups—Serbs, Croats, and Muslims—fought among themselves for land and power. Atrocities were committed on all sides. Stories eventually surfaced about the confinement and sexual exploitation of young women, the rounding up and massacre of men, and ethnic cleansing. **Ethnic cleansing** is the **forced migration** of other ethnic groups from an area in order to leave only one group. Homes and businesses were destroyed. Thousands of people who had the means sought **asylum** in other countries. Some of these refugees have only returned to Bosnia now that a relative peace has been achieved by using United Nations (UN) peacekeepers from other countries, including Canada.

> ### FACT FILE
>
> The ratio of civilian to military casualties in civil conflicts is as high as nine to one.

FIGURE 18.1 Most current wars are civil wars, fought within a country. These are "Kamajor" civil defence militia fighters fighting in Sierra Leone.

FIGURE 18.2 A Kosavar family flees civil conflict during the civil war in Yugoslavia.

FIGURE 18.3 Rebel soldiers in the African country of Sierra Leone would systematically cut off the hands or feet of civilians as a way of creating terror. Many thousands of people in that country now need prosthetic limbs.

Who Are Refugees?

In 2001, an estimated 150 million people lived outside of their country of birth. This equalled about 2.5% of the world's population. Most of these people voluntarily left their native country and live elsewhere legally, including over five million people who immigrated to Canada. Only about 14 million of the people who live outside of their country of birth are considered refugees. Refugees are defined by the United Nations High Commission for Refugees (UNHCR) as "persons who are outside of their country and cannot return owing to a well-founded fear of persecution because of their race, religion, nationality, political opinion, or membership in a particular social group." In other words, refugees are people who will suffer discrimination, torture, jail, or death if they return to their country of birth. Fearing for your life is a strong **push factor**. Figure 18.5, **Principal Sources of Refugees, 2000**, shows the top 20 countries from which refugees originate that existed as of December 31, 2000, when the world total stood at 14.4 million refugees.

FIGURE 18.4 Civilians such as these in Bosnia and Herzegovina are targeted in civil conflict not for their military value, but because such attacks create fear and undermine the people's resolve.

The definition used for refugees is limited in its scope. The term does not include people who leave a country because they are seeking jobs or more opportunities. It also does not include people who might travel to a neighbouring country because of a drought or famine in their own country. The term "refugee" is only legitimately used for people who fear for their lives or safety through actions on the part of people in power in their native country. These people seek asylum in other countries where their safety is not so threatened.

Places that border countries involved in civil conflict face the greatest numbers of refugees. These are **countries of first asylum**, the nearest safe place for refugees. Safety is a strong **pull factor**. In 2000, for example, 172 000 Afghan citizens fled the brutal, hard-line Taliban regime in that country and crossed the border into Pakistan. Many thousands more scrambled across the same border late in 2001 as the United States retaliated against their government, the Taliban, for hiding members of Al Qaeda, accused of terrorist attacks against the U.S. There they waited until the violence ended and they could be **repatriated** to Afghanistan. Under the 1951 UN Refugee Convention, Pakistan could not have forced the refugees back into Afghanistan even if they had wanted to. This policy of

Principal Sources of Refugees, 2000

Country/Conflict	Number of Refugees	Country/Conflict	Number of Refugees
Palestine/Israel	4 000 000	Eritrea	350 000
Afghanistan	3 600 000	Croatia	315 000
Sudan	460 000	Vietnam	300 000
Iraq	450 000	Bosnia and Herzegovina	250 000
Burundi	420 000	El Salvador	230 000
Angola	400 000	Liberia	200 000
Sierra Leone	400 000	Yugoslavia	190 000
Burma	380 000	China	145 000
Somalia	370 000	Bhutan	144 000
Congo-Kinshasa	350 000	East Timor	120 000

U.S. Committee for Refugees

FIGURE 18.5 This table shows the estimates for numbers of refugees. Estimates often vary substantially from one agency to another. This is because refugees are often on the move and getting precise counts is very difficult.

nonrefoulement is necessary so that refugee applicants are not put in grave danger. Pakistan had to cope with the flood of refugees but asked for help in doing so from the UN. In some cases, other countries will accept some of the refugees for permanent resettlement. Canada accepted thousands of "boat people" from Vietnam in the 1970s, helping to reduce the overcrowded refugee camps in the countries of first asylum around Vietnam, including Hong Kong, the Philippines, and Japan.

Problems of Definition

The world community has agreed on a definition for refugees; the challenge is in identifying just who fits this category. Many people who claim to be refugees had to flee their countries with few or no documents. It is often difficult, therefore, for the asylum country to get the facts and fairly separate those who are real refugees from those who are using the label to their own advantage. The following cases are just a few examples to consider:

- The editor of an independent newspaper writes editorials criticizing the authoritarian

World Refugee Totals, 1992–2000 (millions)

Year	Number of Refugees
1992	17.6
1993	16.3
1994	16.3
1995	15.3
1996	14.5
1997	13.6
1998	13.5
1999	14.1
2000	14.4

U.S. Committee for Refugees

FIGURE 18.6 Statistics are for the end of the year. Totals vary according to events during the year that affect refugee movements. Many refugees, such as the Palestinians, have been outside of their homeland for years or decades.

FIGURE 18.7 Afghan refugees being processed in a UN-sponsored refugee camp in Roghani, Pakistan.

FIGURE 18.9 Most developed countries have tightened entry requirements for immigration. This has prompted more people to use the asylum route, even if they are not genuine refugees.

Refugees and Asylum Seekers Worldwide, 2000

Region	Number
Africa	3 346 000
Europe	1 153 000
The Americas and the Caribbean	562 000
East Asia and the Pacific	792 000
Middle East	6 035 000
South and Central Asia	2 656 000

U.S. Committee for Refugees

FIGURE 18.8 This table includes people who have been accepted as refugees and those who are seeking refugee status in asylum countries. Data are for the end of the year.

government and then receives death threats. She tries to join her sister who emigrated to Australia.

- A subsistence farmer crosses the border into a neighbouring country to find work after his crops and village are burned and destroyed by a rebel paramilitary group.
- A computer programmer joins a group considered heretical in his country. He then applies for jobs outside of the country, claiming that his life is in danger.

Which of these examples deal with legitimate refugees? You cannot rely on information about refugee claimants from their home countries because of the motives or bias on the part of governments. In the example of the newspaper editor above, the government will likely deny any form of coercion because it would not be seen as acceptable in the international community. If countries of asylum take a hard line and insist on full documentation, they risk sending real refugees back to their native countries to face hardship or death. The asylum countries are forced to make decisions about refugee applications every day with incomplete or confusing evidence.

The problem is compounded by the numbers of claimants who are falsely trying to use refugee status to enter another country. By applying as a refugee, they hope to "jump the queue" and avoid the normal process of applying to immigrate to a new country. In many cases, queue jumpers know that they do not have the qualifications that will get them admitted and try to enter the country using the humanitarian route that exists to protect legitimate refugees. During 1999, about 600 people of Chinese origin tried to enter Canada by applying as refugees. Only 24 were accepted, including nine children, while the rest were deported after it

FACT FILE

Worldwide, 131 countries are affected by refugees and displaced persons.

was determined that their lives were not in danger if they returned to China. These people were economic migrants and did not fit the definition of "refugee." Nevertheless, Canada had to systematically work through the process of collecting evidence and judging each applicant in order that no one's life was endangered by deportation.

Who Are Internally Displaced People?

During civil conflicts, most of the attention of the international community is focused on refugees as they cross national borders. These are the people who receive help from the UN and various non-governmental organizations (NGOs) such as the Red Cross. Little attention is given to the people who remain within the country—those who are unable or unwilling to leave. Their lives may be in jeopardy and they may have been dislocated from their homes and communities looking for shelter and safety. These internally displaced people are vulnerable but may not get support from their own coun-

try or international agencies. The UN and other agencies estimated that there were between 17 and 21 million internally displaced people worldwide in 2000. A good example of internally displaced people occurred in Indonesia in 2000. Religious and ethnic violence resulted in 800 000 people being uprooted from their homes and forced to flee for their lives. They received little help from international agencies.

Little support is given to internally displaced people because countries are unwilling to interfere in the domestic affairs of other countries. A nation is sovereign over its lands. Even though they may not like what is taking place within another nation, most countries will not get involved in the situation. Internally displaced

> " ... sovereign states have a responsibility to protect their own citizens from avoidable catastrophe—from mass murder and rape, from starvation—but ... when they are unwilling or unable to do so, that responsibility must be borne by the broader community of states. "
>
> *International Commission on Intervention and State Sovereignty (ICISS)/UN report, "A Responsibility to Protect," 2001*

Ratio of Refugees to Host Country Population for Selected Countries, 2000

Host Country	Ratio of Refugees to Total Population	Host Country	Ratio of Refugees to Total Population
Gaza Strip	1:2	Sudan	1:76
Jordan	1:3	Uganda	1:101
West Bank	1:3	Kenya	1:123
Lebanon	1:11	Dem. Rep. of the Congo	1:188
Guinea	1:19	Thailand	1:285
Yugoslavia	1:22	Germany	1:456
Iran	1:36	Canada	1:566
Zambia	1:38	United States	1:572
Syria	1:44	Bangladesh	1:1042
Tanzania	1:65	India	1:3451
Pakistan	1:75	China	1:3562

U.S. Committee for Refugees

FIGURE 18.10 The Middle East and Africa clearly suffer the greatest burdens in dealing with refugees.

people, if they cannot make their way to a border, are viewed as a domestic or civil matter. Only if displaced people can cross a border can other countries and UN agencies respond to their plight.

The Humanitarian Response

The fact that refugees and internally displaced people are now central to the tactics and goals used in war has made the humanitarian response to their plight more complex. Response now typically involves UN agencies such as the World Food Organization, NGOs including the Red Cross, religious organizations such as World Vision, professional associations such as Doctors Without Borders, national armies, and private contractors. Each has a different role to play in protecting and supporting refugees.

In most refugee situations, the actions of the various "partners" are co-ordinated by the UNHCR. This UN agency ensures that there is little duplication of activities and that supplies and personnel are moving as quickly as possible. Their success in helping refugees resulted in this agency being awarded the Nobel Peace Prize in 1954. In spite of their success, the UNHCR has been criticized for some of its work with refugees. Some argue that continuing to provide relief to refugees may in fact prolong the situation and make it harder to solve. Relief efforts mean refugees are being looked after, taking away some of the urgency to solve issues. Relief efforts may inadvertently stop local efforts to reach compromises. In some cases, such as the war in Bosnia, the actions on the part of UNHCR to protect refugees by gathering them together in safe camps helped some groups' ethnic cleansing efforts.

> " Meeting the needs of the world's displaced people—both refugees and the internally displaced—is much more complicated than simply providing short-term security and assistance. It is about addressing the persecution, violence, and conflict which bring about displacement in the first place. "
>
> *United Nations High Commission for Refugees (UNHCR)*

Principal Sources of Internally Displaced Persons, 2000

Country	Number of Persons
Sudan	4 000 000
Angola	1 100 000–3 800 000
Colombia	2 100 000
Dem. Rep. of the Congo	1 800 000
Burma	600 000–1 000 000
Sierra Leone	500 000–1 000 000
Turkey	400 000–1 000 000
Indonesia	750 000–850 000
Iraq	700 000
Burundi	600 000
Sri Lanka	600 000
Azerbaijan	575 000
Bosnia and Herzegovina	518 000
India	507 000
Syria	500 000
Uganda	500 000
Russia	491 000
Yugoslavia	480 000
Afghanistan	375 000
Lebanon	300 000–350 000
Eritrea	310 000
Somalia	300 000
Ethiopia	280 000
Georgia	272 000
Cyprus	265 000
Israel	200 000–250 000
Algeria	100 000–200 000
Philippines	150 000
Rwanda	150 000
North Korea	150 000

U.S. Committee for Refugees

FIGURE 18.11 Estimates of internally displaced people are usually based on fragmentary evidence and are frequently unreliable.

Major Refugee Populations, 2000

CANADA
There were 54 400 refugees or asylum seekers in Canada at the end of December 2000. They came from a wide variety of countries, including Sri Lanka, China, Pakistan, and Hungary.

UNITED STATES
Refugees from conflicts in Central America and the Caribbean made up the majority of the 481 500 refugees to the U.S. El Salvador was the largest single source, contributing 231 500 refugees.

GERMANY
Most of the 180 000 refugees in Germany arrived during the 1990s, fleeing wars of independence in the former Yugoslavia (123 000). Other refugee sources were Turkey, Iran, and Iraq.

YUGOSLAVIA
The Federal Republic of Yugoslavia (Serbia and Montenegro) was home to 484 200 refugees. About 290 000 fled Croatia during that country's war of independence and 190 000 were made stateless by the conflict in Bosnia and Herzegovina.

JORDAN
Almost all of Jordan's 1 580 000 refugees are Palestinians who fled when Israel was formed. Most have been in the country for over 50 years.

LEBANON
Palestinians made up 376 500 of Lebanon's 383 200 refugees.

SYRIA
Palestinians made up 383 200 of Syria's 389 000 refugees in 2000.

THE GAZA STRIP AND WEST BANK
Over 1 407 000 Palestinian refugees lived in these areas. They lost or fled their homeland with the creation of the state of Israel.

GUINEA
In spite of its own poverty, Guinea accepted 390 000 refugees. These people fled the destructive civil wars in Sierra Leone (300 000) and Liberia (90 000).

UGANDA
This country's proximity to Sudan made it a destination for Sudanese fleeing civil war. About 200 000 of Uganda's 230 000 refugees were from Sudan.

DEMOCRATIC REPUBLIC OF THE CONGO
The Congo hosted 276 000 refugees, largely from Angola (170 000) and Sudan (70 000). The Congo's own civil war produced 250 000 refugees who found asylum in neighbouring countries, including the Republic of the Congo (Brazzaville), Rwanda, and Tanzania.

N

FIGURE 18.12 The countries highlighted on the map show the major locations of the world's refugees, but smaller numbers of refugees are found in many other countries.

IRAN

An enduring civil war in Afghanistan produced 1 482 000 refugees in Iran. Iraqis (387 000) and others made up the 1 895 000 refugees in this country.

PAKISTAN

As a neighbouring country to Afghanistan, Pakistan offered asylum during the long civil war. Two million of Pakistan's 2 019 000 refugees were from Afghanistan, including 172 000 new refugees during 2000.

BANGLADESH

A very poor country, Bangladesh hosted 121 500 refugees from the civil turmoil in Burma.

CHINA

China's 350 000 refugees were largely ethnic Chinese escaping wars in Vietnam (293 000) and North Korea (50 000).

SUDAN

Eritrea's struggle for independence from Ethiopia produced 350 000 refugees, most of whom had been in Sudan since the mid-1990s. Smaller numbers of refugees arrived because of violence in Ethiopia, Chad, and Uganda, bringing the total for the country to 385 000. The ongoing civil war within Sudan has created about 475 000 refugees.

THAILAND

Most of Thailand's 217 300 refugees escaped from violence in Burma (216 700).

INDIA

India was host to refugees from a variety of civil conflicts, including China–Tibet (110 000), Sri Lanka (110 000), Burma (42 000), and Afghanistan (12 700). India had a total of 290 000 refugees.

KENYA

A relatively stable country in a war-torn region, Kenya was host to 233 000 refugees. They included 160 000 from Somalia, 55 000 from Sudan, and smaller numbers from Ethiopia and Uganda.

INDONESIA

All of Indonesia's 120 800 refugees fled during East Timor's struggle for independence from Indonesia in 1999. About 40 000 refugees were repatriated to East Timor during 2000.

TANZANIA

Tanzania hosted the continent's largest number of refugees, 543 000 in total. About 400 000 refugees escaped brutal ethnic violence in neighbouring Burundi. Smaller numbers of refugees were from the Democratic Republic of the Congo (110 000), Rwanda (30 000), and Somalia.

ZAMBIA

The bulk of Zambia's 255 000 refugees escaped from Angola (190 000) while 60 000 were from the Democratic Republic of the Congo.

SYRIA
LEBANON
Gaza West Bank
JORDAN

Faced with the criticisms, the changing nature of refugee crises, and shrinking international assistance budgets, the UNHCR has been changing its tactics. Rather than simply helping refugees once they are outside a war-torn country, the agency is encouraging peace within the countries. An example of this occurred in 2001 with the attempts to find peaceful resolutions between ethnic Albanians and the local population in Macedonia. This strategy helps to avoid the costs and problems of housing and feeding refugees for what could be a long time, and the difficulties of repatriating them following peaceful resolutions. This tactic also encourages resettlement of internally displaced people in their own communities through compromise and peace negotiations. It can have the additional benefit of not involving large numbers of relief workers and support agencies that use up international assistance dollars that could be put to work elsewhere.

FIGURE 18.13 A UNHCR team at work in East Timor. A total of 139 countries have signed the 1951 Geneva Refugee Convention and/or its 1967 Protocol, agreeing to specific definitions for refugees and their treatment.

PROFILE

Dr. Sima Samar

Sima Samar fled Afghanistan in 1984 following the Soviet Union's invasion of that country. Her husband "disappeared" after he was arrested, and Samar feared for her own life. She joined a stream of Afghans seeking safety in Pakistan. Her training as a medical doctor made her invaluable in the crowded refugee camps and she worked in clinics for refugees in Pakistan before opening a hospital for women in 1987. Over the next few years, she set up 10 clinics and four hospitals for women and children inside Afghanistan with funding from international NGOs. She also established schools for girls in rural Afghanistan that eventually provided basic education to more than 17 000 students. In Pakistan, she maintained her hospital and a school for refugee girls.

Dr. Samar is director of *Shuhada*, an organization based in Quetta, Pakistan, that provides health care and literacy services to refugees and Afghan women and children.

Samar has received countless death threats because of her actions in opposition to the Afghanistan ruling regime. She has always spoken out against the wearing of the *burqa*, the head-to-toe wrap that the Taliban regime required of women in public. Her schools and hospitals for women and girls also angered the Taliban. Every time she crossed into Afghanistan, her life was in real jeopardy. Samar remained unafraid, however, stating, "I've always been in danger, but I don't mind. I believe we will die one day so I said let's take the risk and help somebody else."

FIGURE 18.14

In 2001, Dr. Samar was awarded the John Humphrey Freedom Award by the International Centre for Human Rights and Democratic Development. John Humphrey was the Canadian who wrote the first draft of the Universal Declaration of Human Rights. While she was in Canada receiving the award, Samar was informed that she was the only woman named to the interim government of Afghanistan, following the defeat of the Taliban government.

INTERACT

1. Choose one of the countries that is a source of refugees and conduct research to find out the circumstances that led to the refugees fleeing the country. Write a one-page summary and share it with the class.

2. Other terms that are at least superficially related to refugees are "economic migrant," "illegal immigrant," and "environmental refugee." With a partner, write definitions for these labels to clearly distinguish them from a refugee.

3. Using the data in Figure 18.8, **Refugees and Asylum Seekers Worldwide, 2000**, complete a circle graph, showing the distribution of the world's refugees. What conclusion can you draw from the graph?

4. Use the data in Figure 18.11, **Principal Sources of Internally Displaced Persons, 2000**, to complete a map of the world, showing the locations for internally displaced people. Use proportional circles to show the numbers of people in each country. Establish a scale that is appropriate for your outline map. Identify patterns shown by your map.

5. Identify one NGO or international refugee agency and research its activities. Prepare a display to show the extent of its involvement with refugees, the actions that it has taken to support refugees and internally displaced people, and some indication of its success in assisting refugees.

CASE STUDY

The Refugee Crisis in Sudan

In 2001, Sudan's civil war was the world's longest running uninterrupted civil war. More than two million Sudanese had died from war-related causes, and the death toll continued at a rate of 300 per day. Over four million civilians had been left homeless, most of them internally displaced. An estimated 465 000 Sudanese in 2001 were refugees or asylum seekers in other countries.

Ethnic and Racial Conflict in Sudan

Sudan's government came to power in 1989 when a military coup ousted the elected government. This regime is controlled by the National Islamic Front (NIF). The NIF gets its strength from the largely Arab Muslim population in the northern part of the country, who make up a majority of the Sudanese population. Between five and seven million people

Distribution of Sudan's Refugees

Country	Number of Refugees
Uganda	200 000
Ethiopia	70 000
Dem. Rep. of the Congo	70 000
Kenya	55 000
Central African Republic	35 000
Chad	20 000
Egypt	12 000
Various European countries	2 000

U.S. Committee for Refugees

FIGURE 18.15 The numbers in this table are conservative estimates. Real numbers may be much higher than those given.

in the southern part of the country are black Christians or followers of local traditional religions. Because of long-standing racial, cultural, religious, and political animosities between the northern

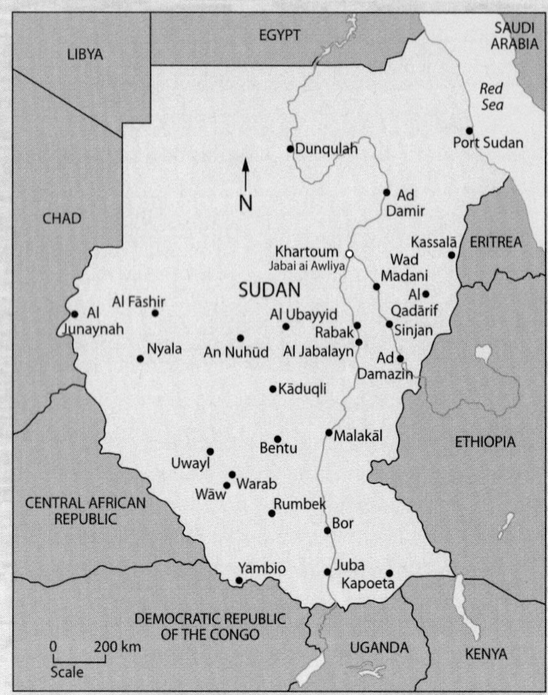

FIGURE 18.16 Sudan became an independent country in 1956. Like other countries in this region, it has been involved in civil and cross-border conflicts for most of its existence as an independent nation.

Muslims and southern Christians, many people in the south have pushed for independence from Sudan and the establishment of a separate nation. The Sudan People's Liberation Army (SPLA) is the chief rebel group that has led this struggle for independence, although many internal divisions in both the south and the north complicate the conflict. The SPLA has fought a guerrilla war against the Sudan government for two decades.

Civilian populations have been repeatedly targeted and exploited by both sides in this conflict. In recent years, government forces have been using a **scorched earth policy**, invading and destroying villages that support southern independence. The government has also launched air strikes against civilian targets and has routinely bombed humanitarian relief centres, at least 152 times in 2000 alone. They have tried to bar international aid from large parts of southern Sudan. There have even been

> 66 If the North wins, they will not have won an ordinary war. They will have won a genocidal war, a war defined by the bombing of clearly marked civilian hospitals ... by the use of famine as a weapon. 99
>
> *Dr. Eric Reeves, Smith College, U.S.*

Quality of Life Indicators for Sudan, 1999

Population	34.5 million people
Population growth rate	2.71%
Fertility rate	5.58 children per woman
Infant mortality rate	70.94 deaths per 1000 live births
Life expectancy at birth	Females—57.44 years Males—55.41 years
Literacy	53.3%
GDP per capita	CDN$930
Defence expenditures	53.8% of government revenue
Employment in agriculture	63.4% of work force
Telephones	6 per 1000 people
Major environmental problems	Dust storms, desertification, unsafe drinking water, overhunting
Major economic problems	Civil war, chronic political instability, poor government policies, high foreign debt, dependence on subsistence agriculture

Canadian Global Almanac 2001

FIGURE 18.17 Conditions in Sudan are some of the worst in Africa, the continent with the lowest overall quality of life.

accusations that the government of Sudan has supported, or at the very least ignored, the taking of slaves from rebel-held areas. Rebel groups, for their part, have reportedly controlled humanitarian aid programs so that their forces receive food that should go to displaced people and refugees. Aid agencies that refuse to co-operate with the SPLA are forced to end their operations in the south. Rebel forces have also conscripted soldiers through force from the refugee camps. During 2000 alone, over 100 000 Sudanese were displaced by the continuing violence.

The disrupted aid programs, destroyed crops and livestock, and collapsing agricultural system triggered a devastating famine in 1998 that killed tens of thousands of people. Serious malnutrition exists throughout the country.

To finance their war efforts, the Sudanese government developed an oil reserve of about 75 000 km^2 in the southern part of the country, with a pipeline running to the north. Production began in 1999 and the government has set targets of 185 000 barrels per day. They have used even greater than normal force to protect this lucrative resource from rebels, including forced depopulation of the region. A Canadian petroleum company, Talisman Energy, was involved in development of the oil fields. The company drilled 40 wells in 2001. Talisman Energy is traded on the Toronto Stock Exchange (TSE) and is included in the TSE 300 index. The Canada Pension Plan has invested in Talisman Energy.

The Plight of Other Refugees

An ironic twist in the Sudanese conflict is the presence of large numbers of refugees from other countries who have sought asylum in Sudan. The border war between Eritrea and Ethiopia in 2000 prompted a wave of 95 000 Eritrean asylum seekers to cross into Sudan, joining many refugees who had been there since Eritrea battled for its independence in the 1990s. As of January 2001, there were 178 745 Eritrean refugees in the country. There were also smaller numbers of refugees from conflicts in Chad, Somalia, Uganda, and Ethiopia. The UNHCR stepped in to provide basic humanitarian assistance to the new refugees until repatriation could take place. Assistance took the form of water, food rations, education, vocational training, and health care. One of the goals for their activities was to shift away from providing long-term humanitarian aid to actively supporting real solutions based on voluntary repatriation of refugees. The UNHCR's budget for 2001 was just short of US$10 million, a value that is not likely to go down in the near future if this region remains as troubled as it has been.

FIGURE 18.18 The majority of the population of Sudan are Arab Muslims. Actions such as the ban on women in the workplace in 2000 have alienated the non-Muslim minority in the country.

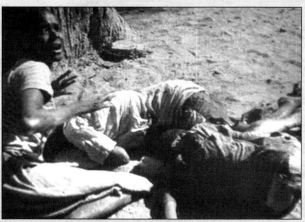

FIGURE 18.19 Victims of fighting in the Sudan civil war.

excerpt from Refugees Target Talisman over Sudan Oil Project

by Nova Pierson
Calgary Sun
December 14, 1999

Sudanese refugees and a group that rescues them from slavery pointed an accusing finger at Calgary-based Talisman Energy yesterday.

Members of Christian Solidarity International [CSI] said despite what Talisman claims, slavery exists in Sudan.

Talisman has been the target of harsh criticism—from such people as U.S. Secretary of State Madeleine Albright—for its role in a Sudanese oil pipeline.

"As long as I see these photos in Sudan, it reminds me of the pain which happened ... how hopeless I was before I knew I was going to be saved," said Natalie Yoll, a 24-year-old who survived three slave raids.

Yoll said she doubts Talisman will learn the truth from ... Sudan's northern-based government, an Islamic dictatorship threatening the predominantly Christian south.

"The Khartoum government is an oppressive one," said Yoll, whose father and two brothers were killed during raids.

About 20 members of Calgary's Sudanese community rallied outside the Palliser Hotel, while officials with CSI inside questioned Talisman's involvement in Sudan.

"It's my belief Talisman is an ethical company who doesn't have a clue what they're into," said Glen Pearson, a London, Ontario-based representative of CSI.

"We believe [Talisman CEO] Jim Buckee hasn't let information get through to shareholders ... not only is there slavery in

Sudan on a grand scale, but the slavery has been aided and abetted by the government of northern Sudan."

Talisman has maintained its partnership in the government pipeline project and has helped the people of Sudan, with a hospital, water wells and inoculations.

"A lot of these human-rights groups have good intentions," said David Mann, Talisman's investor relations manager.

"But if Talisman withdraws, what happens?"

And Mann said Buckee—and all of Talisman—is co-operating with Canadian government efforts to get to the truth.

"The concept of slavery is abhorrent to us," he said.

CSI says it has rescued 15 000 slaves from the control of the northern Sudanese government.

Critical Analysis

1. Summarize the evidence offered in the article that is critical of Talisman Energy.
2. To what extent has the article recognized the viewpoints and reasoning of Talisman Energy?
3. If you were a Talisman Energy official, how would you respond to these accusations? Explain your reasoning.
4. If you were a Canadian government official, how might you react to this report?

Fact Sheet on Talisman Energy's Involvement in Sudan

- Talisman Energy acquired a 25% stake in the Greater Nile Petroleum Operating Company in 1998. State-owned oil companies in China own 40%, in Malaysia 30%, and in Sudan 5% of the company.

- Talisman Energy has invested more than $800 million in the oil fields and in the 1600-km pipeline connecting the fields to Port Sudan on the Red Sea.

- The pipeline supplies the El Obeid oil refinery, which produces aviation fuel that is used in government bombers to attack civilian targets, including refugee centres and hospitals.

- Government officials have stated publicly that earnings from the oil will be used to manufacture tanks and missiles to be used against Christians and Animists in the south.

- Talisman Energy sold its stake in Sudan to India's Oil and Natural Gas Corporation in November 2002.

FIGURE 18.20 Talisman Energy officials responded to the criticisms by putting in place programs that dealt with human rights concerns, including training employees, monitoring human rights in Sudan, and encouraging its partners in the project to adopt a code of ethics on the protection of human rights. Human rights and church groups claim that regardless of who owns the company, oil revenues continue to fuel the civil war.

" There are a lot of people in the Middle East and further east than that who need oil and are less concerned about the political impact. "

Jim Buckee,
Talisman Energy CEO

FACT FILE

In November 1999, the U.S. Senate passed a bill that delisted from the New York Stock Exchange (NYSE) companies that conduct business with the government of Sudan. In June 2002, the U.S. House of Representatives passed a bill that strips oil companies operating in Sudan of access to U.S. capital markets.

INTERACT

1. In a few sentences, summarize the conflict in Sudan.
2. Using an atlas and other map sources, draw a sketch map of Sudan and the area around it. On your map, show the significant flows of refugees in and out of the country. Include significant physical features and cities on your map.
3. In what ways has this conflict created a significant refugee problem?
4. The quotation on page 450 contains the words "the use of famine as a weapon." Explain what that means.
5. Explain to a classmate how the concept of "country of first asylum" has helped to complicate the Sudanese refugee situation.
6. In one or two pages, write an editorial about the involvement of companies such as Talisman Energy in the Sudan situation. Be sure to include current facts to support your opinions.

CANADA'S REFUGEE POLICIES AND PROCEDURES

Recent incidents of people seeking refugee status in Canada have focused a spotlight on this country's refugee policies and procedures. The following are some of the more high profile incidents:

■ Over a six-week period in 1999, a total of 599 Chinese citizens from Fujian Province were dumped by four boats onto British Columbia's coast. They had paid human smugglers to take them to the United States. Most applied for asylum in Canada.

■ In 1999, an Algerian who was allowed to enter Canada seeking asylum was arrested trying to enter the United States in a car loaded with explosives.

■ In January 2000, officials in Vancouver discovered 25 Chinese people in a cargo container on a Liberian registered ship.
Each of these incidents created a groundswell of resentment and hostility toward refugees, with some attitudes bordering on **xenophobia**. Many citizens were highly critical of the Canadian government for even letting large numbers of foreigners land on our shores. These incidents prompted some Canadians to argue that our refugee policies are too soft and that too many false refugees are getting into the country. Critics were especially vocal after the September 11, 2001, terrorist attacks in the United States when it was erroneously reported that the terrorists had strong links to Canada. These Canadians wanted the refugee door into this country slammed shut! Is this an appropriate response? What should be Canada's refugee policy? Before we can answer such an important question, we need to understand how Canada deals with refugees.

Applying as a Refugee

In 2000, the number of asylum seekers applying to Canada was the highest in almost a decade—a total of 36 534 cases.

The first step takes place when the asylum seeker contacts Canada's immigration department. A senior immigration officer makes a decision as to whether or not a claimant has legitimate grounds for application. Sometimes just the homeland of the applicant is enough; if you are from war-torn Sudan, your claim will likely be passed on, but if you are from a country such as the United Kingdom where civil rights are protected, you will not likely be able to claim that the government is threatening your life. Other conditions that will cause a claim to fail will be past criminal behaviour, if the applicant is a threat to national security, or if the person has already been accepted as a refugee in another

FIGURE 18.21 Canada's refugee policy in the mid- to late 1980s was to give a fair hearing to anyone who applied for asylum.

> **FACT FILE**
>
> The countries with the highest approval rates for refugee applications in Canada for 2000 were Afghanistan (89%), Somalia (78%), Sri Lanka (77%), and the Democratic Republic of the Congo (74%).

Refugees to Canada, 1990–2000	
Year	**Number of Refugees**
1990	36 093
1991	35 891
1992	36 943
1993	24 835
1994	19 739
1995	27 753
1996	28 352
1997	24 221
1998	22 787
1999	24 378
2000	36 534

Refugees Branch, Citizenship and Immigration Canada

FIGURE 18.22 The large number of refugees and asylum seekers in 2000 was well above the number for each of the previous seven years.

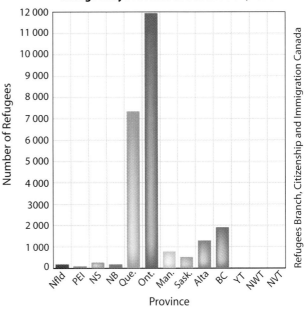

Refugees by Province of Destination, 1999

Refugees Branch, Citizenship and Immigration Canada

FIGURE 18.23 The greatest impact of refugees is felt in only two provinces. How do you think this affects people's attitudes toward refugees?

country. In 2000, 34 253 claims were passed on to the Immigration and Refugee Board (IRB).

Most asylum seekers who are waiting for their cases to be heard are not held in detention, although those that are considered a flight risk might be. Asylum seekers are eligible for social assistance and health services and are authorized to work while their cases are being considered.

The IRB conducts hearings to determine the merit of asylum seekers' claims. Applicants can be represented by legal counsel. They have an opportunity to present their evidence and argue that their lives are in jeopardy should they return to their home country. This can be a relatively speedy process if there are no questions of credibility and their stories are consistent with conditions that are known about the countries. In some cases, such as those of refugees from Somalia and Afghanistan, the IRB requires little documentation since conditions are so bad in those places that few official documents are ever issued. As long as one of the two officials at the hearing rules in the favour of the appli-

cant, that person is granted refugee status in Canada and is allowed to stay in the country. In 2000, the IRB made decisions in 24 124 cases and granted refugee status to 13 990 asylum seekers, a 57% approval rate. Another 4685 cases were abandoned by the applicant or otherwise concluded.

If both official members of the board reject an applicant, that person is ordered to leave Canada. However, there are some appeal steps. The claimant can ask for a judicial review by a federal court; the judge either confirms the decision of the IRB officials or sends the case back to them with a written opinion. This acts as a safeguard to protect legitimate refugees who may lack documentation. The failed claimant can also reapply for refugee status once outside the country.

> **FACT FILE**
>
> During the 1990s, Canada logged an average of 28 000 asylum requests each year, with more than 50% accepted.

Problems in the Refugee Process

One long-standing problem in the refugee system is the length of time that it takes to make decisions on a case. Scheduling hearings, collecting evidence, and making appeals can sometimes take years and the system seems unable to handle the task. This has led to a significant backlog in the process. As we can see from the figures for 2000, even though a total of 28 809 cases were concluded, 34 253 cases were referred to the IRB, leaving a backlog of 5444 unresolved cases. During this time, a claimant's future is uncertain. As well, many Canadians object to the social, health, and education costs that society must bear during this time of uncertainty.

MAKE A DIFFERENCE

"It Takes A Neighbourhood to Welcome a Refugee" is a successful project co-ordinated by Sister Mary Jo Leddy, a Catholic nun who runs Romero House in a middle-class Toronto neighbourhood. Not your average shelter, Romero House provides a place to live and friendly support to the neediest political refugee claimants. Although uncomfortable at first with refugees in their community, neighbours soon came to recognize the courage and dignity of people forced to leave their homelands and of the strengths they bring to Canada. Neighbours and volunteers, many of them young people, have become increasingly involved in providing a home within a welcoming community. Many provide jobs, outings, or just a chance to practise English with a friend. Annual gatherings in the community now include a huge street party for Canada Day. The skilled efforts of Sister Leddy, the goodwill of the neighbours, and the refugees themselves have all enriched the community. Romero House has been very effective in helping refugees; everyone who has lived there has moved into independent housing and started a life in their new country.

Tinkering with the Refugee System

In 2000, the government of Canada responded to the criticisms of its refugee policy and acted on initiatives of its own. The government tabled in the House of Commons the Immigration and Refugee Protection Act, legislation designed to improve the refugee process. The minister responsible for the bill, Elinor Caplan, described the new act as designed to "close the back door to those who would abuse the system but ensure that the front door will remain open both to genuine refugees and to the immigrants our country will need to grow and prosper in the years ahead." "Closing the back door" was to be accomplished with severe penalties for people smuggling, detention for those asylum seekers who enter the country illegally, barring serious criminals from claiming refugee status, and more intense security screening at the time of initial application. Not everyone was happy with these proposals. Refugee supporters claimed that these measures may very well keep out real refugees who do not have the chance or the means to take the legal route. For example, a woman suffering discrimination in

FIGURE 18.24 "When you come to Canada as a refugee ... you need help adjusting to the culture and the language. Romero House was a home—it provided a warm environment for us. Refugees need personal support, people to talk to, a community."

Jaffet, refugee from Eritrea

Sudan can hardly abide by Canada's application procedures and may have to resort to illegal means to escape the country. From the supporters' perspective, closing the back door hurts many of the very people that the refugee policy should protect.

Keeping the front door open in the proposed law involved new rights to appeal decisions and incorporated into law Canada's nonrefoulement obligations. As it turned out, an election was called before the bill was passed into law, but the proposed bill established the response by the federal government to the demands for action following the 2001 attacks on New York and Washington. Canada's refugee procedures were tightened up in the uncertain months that followed the terrorist attacks and the conflict in Afghanistan.

For many, the discretionary power of the government is the most worrisome part of Canada's refugee policy. When the public mood toward refugees is negative, the federal government could respond by tightening rules and regulations—closing the front door. This would have the effect of keeping out legitimate refugees who need humanitarian support. Far better to have in place long-term goals and a strong commitment that would override the uninformed opinions of a public influenced by stories in the media.

INTERACT

1. Work with a partner to brainstorm the conditions that you think are important in establishing the number of refugees and asylum seekers that should be allowed into Canada. Consider conditions both within and outside of the country in your brainstorming.
2. Create a flow diagram or organizational chart to show the steps in the current Canadian refugee determination process. Suggest ways that the process could be improved.
3. What might be some of the implications of a tighter refugee policy? What might be some implications of a more open refugee policy?
4. Is Canada's refugee policy too lenient? Answer this question in a carefully constructed opinion statement.

WEB LINKS

- U.S. Committee for Refugees:
- UNHCR:
- African Newswire Network:
- Talisman Energy:

RELATED ISSUES

- Refugees and the role of UN agencies, such as the World Health Organization (WHO)
- Palestinian refugees
- Refugees and human rights in Canada
- Environmental refugees
- Economic migrants

GIS **Principle Sources of Internally Displaced Persons, 2000**

ANALYSE, APPLY, AND INTERACT

1. Update Figure 18.6, **World Refugee Totals, 1992–2000**, using Internet sources such as the U.S. Committee for Refugees or the UNHCR.

2. Debate the theme of the quote from the Canadian government sponsored ICISS/UN report, "A Responsibility to Protect," on page 444.

3. Looking at refugee flows on a global basis, identify three impacts of these human migrations on natural and human systems within countries of first asylum.

4. Design a diagram or illustration to show how refugee flows have an impact on the geopolitical relationships between countries. Use specific examples of refugee situations in your diagram.

5. **a)** Using the case study of Sudan, identify how aspirations of different cultural groups within the country have contributed to the civil conflicts and human suffering.
   b) What are three actions that you might take to help resolve the issues?

6. Develop a survey or questionnaire to identify Canadian attitudes toward refugees.
   a) Explain how the media influences public opinion on refugee issues. Do you think that influence is positive or negative? How accurately informed do you think Canadians are on refugee issues?
   b) Organize your findings in a report. Include in your analysis a discussion of the implications for Canadian society of the trends or patterns identified.

7. Debate the following statement with other members of the class, using ideas from this chapter. Resolved: Because the current approach to dealing with refugees has not stemmed their flow, every effort should be taken to prevent possible refugees from leaving their country of origin.

8. Identify the strengths and weaknesses of Canada's approach to dealing with refugees. Suggest ways that the policies and procedures might be improved.

9. Interview a current refugee claimant or a recent successful refugee to Canada. Try to find out their thoughts and emotions about the process. Be sure, when you prepare your report, to conceal the actual identity of the person to protect her/his privacy.

10. Using almanacs and Internet sources, identify three organizations in Canada that provide support for refugee claimants and newly accepted refugees. Briefly summarize the work that they do.

11. Based on your understanding of the conditions that create flows of refugees, speculate on where three new sources of refugees will occur over the next few years. Provide the reasons for your choices.

Chapter 19: Conflict and Co-operation

By the end of this chapter, you will:

- analyse instances of international cooperation and conflict and identify factors that contribute to each;

- identify ways in which countries and regions of the world are becoming increasingly interdependent;

- select and compare statistical indicators of quality of life for a variety of developed and developing countries in different parts of the world;

- demonstrate an understanding of how scarcities and inequities in the distribution of resources contribute to uprisings and conflicts;

- identify individuals who have made significant contributions to addressing global issues and evaluate their impacts;

- analyse geopolitical relationships between selected countries and regions;

- analyse the evolving global geopolitical role of a selected region or country and evaluate how its actions contribute to cooperation or conflict;

- research and report on the human and ecological cost of global military spending;

- use different types of maps and images to analyse the consequences of human activities.

Conflict in the Post-Cold War Era

Writing in 1991, Peter Cipkowski, in *Revolution in Eastern Europe*, analysed the changing political conditions in Eastern European countries immediately after the disintegration of the Soviet Union:

> " The collapse of Eastern European Communism shocked that world. Certainly, few supporters or friends of Soviet Communism predicted it. In their view, the countries of Eastern Europe had real governments.... But most conservatives always saw these regimes as nothing more than a bunch of thugs who ruled only by the threat of Soviet guns. If ever the threat were lifted, they claimed, the regimes would be swept away in a matter of days. And that is exactly what happened. "

Peter Cipkowski, Revolution in Eastern Europe,
New York: John Wiley and Sons, 1991, p. 162

The Cold War ended in 1991 with the collapse of Soviet Communism. This led many people to believe that the world had entered an era of peace since international conflicts based on political ideology seemed a thing of the past. The peacefulness of this "new world order" would produce real improvements in the quality of life for all peoples. People referred to the

FIGURE 19.1 American soldiers in Afghanistan in 2001.

Estimated War-Related Deaths

Century	Deaths in Millions	Deaths per Thousand People
First to fifteenth	3.7	—
Sixteenth	1.6	3.2
Seventeenth	6.1	11.2
Eighteenth	7.0	9.7
Nineteenth	19.4	16.2
Twentieth (to 1995)	109.7	44.4

Michael Renner, "How to Abolish War," in *The Humanist*, July/August, 1999

FIGURE 19.2 The twentieth century had the most destructive wars in history, the First and Second World Wars. What will the twenty-first century be like?

expected shift in public spending from the military to social programs as the "peace dividend." Unfortunately, these were naïve expectations. Conflicts have continued, although changed in character and motivation. In Chapter 17, we looked at how nationalism and the desire for autonomy *within* countries is a driving force for conflict and violence. In this chapter, we will explore the forces that are motivating global security concerns that bring about conflict *among* countries. We will also consider approaches that have the potential to help diffuse these conflicts through co-operation.

In this first decade of the twenty-first century, international peace and security concerns have centred on four factors—the struggle for control of resources, the widening gap between the rich and the poor, the worldwide **militarization** of nations, and the strength of religious **extremism**.

Fight for Resources

Over the past several centuries, humans—especially those in developed countries—have come to expect that their material wealth will grow over time. This expectation, combined with an exploding global population, has led to the rapid consumption of resources and the deterioration of natural systems. Many people now

FIGURE 19.3 An oil tanker at Turkey's Yumurtalik oil terminal loaded with 153 000 tonnes of Iraqi oil. The reserves of oil in Middle Eastern countries give this region a huge geopolitical lever.

believe that the finite resource base of this planet has been exceeded and cannot sustain the human populations at current rates of consumption. There simply are not enough resources to go around, resulting in conflicts over control of strategic resources. Energy is an obvious resource to stimulate violence, as the Gulf War of 1991 revealed. But other resources also have the potential to compel countries to fight countries, including water and food.

Energy in the form of oil has great potential to spark conflicts because of its unequal distribution. The Middle East controls over two-thirds of the world's oil. The developed countries of North America and Europe, as well as Japan, Australia, and New Zealand, consume 58% of the world's energy. These countries' own supplies, in places such as the North Sea or the Beaufort Sea, are being consumed at a rapid rate and cannot supply enough energy to meet day-to-day needs. The economies of the developed countries simply cannot function without a stable and reliable supply of oil from the

FACT FILE

The World Health Organization (WHO) estimates that the basic requirement for water is 150 L per household per day. Households in richer countries of the world consume more than 2000 L per day.

Middle East. The United States and other developed countries see the supply of oil as a legitimate security concern and have shown a willingness to use force to maintain its flow.

 See Chapter 3 for more information about oil as a strategic resource.

Water is another commodity that has the potential to spark conflict. The consumption of water tripled in the second half of the twentieth century and is expected to double again by 2020. This increased consumption has significantly reduced available water sources, perhaps no more dramatically than in the Aral Sea, which lost 60% of its volume in the past three decades. About 90% of world consumption is for industrial purposes and irrigating crops, so water is important in both maintaining material quality of life and in feeding populations. Nations will protect their water futures with force, if necessary. Unfortunately, sources of water often cross international boundaries or link several nations. Actions by one user of the resource may jeopardize the supply for other

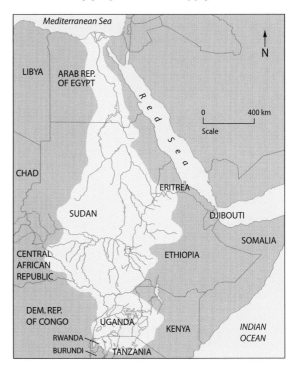

FIGURE 19.4 The Nile River is an international water body. Actions along its length can affect the water supplies of those downstream.

users. The Jordan River, for example, is both a boundary line and a vital water source for both Israel and Jordan, nations that have a history of mutual distrust and conflict.

See Chapter 8 for more information about the Aral Sea and conflicts over water.

Other resources that have the potential to stimulate conflicts are strategically important industrial minerals such as cobalt, tungsten, and phosphate, an essential component of chemical fertilizers. The scarcity of food in significant parts of the world also could trigger violence.

The Widening Gap Between Rich and Poor

Regions of the world are being more sharply defined as either rich or poor. The gap in wealth between those who are rich and those who are poor has been widening. In part, this is because the rich countries of the world have already passed through the demographic transition and have little or no population growth, while developing countries are experiencing rapid growth, hindering economic development. But the rich have also helped to create conditions that hinder progress among developing countries through control of the global economy and resources. The net result is that one-fifth of

FIGURE 19.5 The inequities in wealth in the world are growing larger. This "poverty gap" could lead to violence and conflict.

Distribution of Incomes for Selected Countries, Mid-1990s (% share of income or consumption)

Country	Lowest 20%	Second 20%	Third 20%	Fourth 20%	Fifth 20%	Gini Index
Bangladesh	8.7	12.0	15.7	20.8	42.8	33.6
Brazil	2.5	5.5	10.0	18.3	63.8	60.0
Canada	7.5	12.9	17.2	23.0	39.3	31.5
India	8.1	11.6	15.0	19.3	46.1	37.8
Japan	10.6	14.2	17.6	22.0	35.7	24.9
Mexico	3.6	7.2	11.8	19.2	58.2	53.7
Netherlands	7.3	12.7	17.2	22.8	40.1	32.6
Nigeria	4.4	8.2	12.5	19.3	55.7	50.6
Russia	4.4	8.6	13.3	20.1	53.7	48.7
United States	5.2	10.5	15.6	22.4	46.4	40.8

The World Guide 2001/2002

Note: The Gini Index is a measure of inequality. Zero represents perfect equality, where each quintile would have 20% of the wealth. An index of 100 represents perfect inequality, with one quintile controlling all the wealth.

FIGURE 19.6 Disparities exist within nations as well as on a global scale. The greatest inequities in wealth within nations tend to occur in Latin America and Africa. Richer countries tend to have smaller inequities, although there are exceptions to this pattern.

humanity uses three-quarters of the world's resources. So, while a billion or so people live in relative luxury, billions more struggle to keep body and soul together, including the roughly 800 million people who do not have enough food to meet basic bodily needs. Furthermore, this division is growing because of the higher rates of growth in the poorer countries: by 2030, just one-seventh of the human population will control three-quarters of the wealth.

 See Chapter 13 for more information about the consequences of poverty.

 See Chapter 10 for more information about demographic transition.

There have been some improvements for some countries in the developing world. South Korea, Singapore, and Costa Rica are three countries where qualities of life have improved substantially in the past few decades, but they are the exceptions. For most poorer countries, development has been frustratingly slow. Progress has been hampered by having to repay huge debts owed to large banks or other countries, political instability that leads to violence or turmoil, and economic exploitation by large companies seeking cheap labour or resources. More of the world's people now live in absolute poverty and suffer malnutrition than two decades ago. The wealthier countries of the world show little inclination to help change the circumstances for developing countries. Throughout the 1990s and into the current decade, foreign assistance budgets were cut and, in spite of pressure from non-governmental organizations (NGOs) and religious organizations, most lenders were unwilling to

FIGURE 19.7 People live in poverty in every country of the world. In some cases, such as India, a large proportion of the population have insufficient funds to meet their daily needs.

forgive loans to struggling countries. There is little evidence to suggest that the massive economic disparities will be reduced in the foreseeable future.

 See Chapter 13 for more information about the causes of poverty.

This deep polarization of the world into "have" and "have-not" classes is a source of potential instability. The media allow everyone else in the world to see how the rich live. The people of developing regions think that they too should be able to share in the bounty of this planet. Instead, they see a world in which resources are being consumed at an astonishing rate by a small minority of the population. And, from their perspective, they are being told by policy makers that they have to curtail their activities in order to clean up the messes that the overconsumption of the rich have created, including reducing greenhouse gases and banning ozone-depleting chemicals. Frustration runs deep and affects the relationships that countries have with each other.

Worldwide Militarization

To many, the Cold War and the global arms race are synonymous. During the Cold War, both the United States and the Soviet Union tried to gain advantage over one another by building up their arsenals of conventional and nuclear weapons. Their allies also invested heavily in weapons. While the United States worked with the former Soviet republics in post-Cold War years to reduce nuclear weapons, the stocks of **conventional weapons** remain. Also remaining are the extensive industrial and military infrastructures that produced and used them—a group of economically and politically powerful industries and organizations referred to as the **military–industrial complex**. The people skilled in the design of weapons, the factories used to manufacture them, and the people who know how to use them still exist. Many analysts suggest that the availability of these weapons and systems make military responses to situations much more likely, that countries and groups will use their weapons rather than solving problems through other means. The large arsenal of arms held by Iraq at the end of the Iraq–Iran war in 1988 was seen by Western observers as significant in Iraq's invasion of Kuwait in 1990.

It is in the interests of the weapons industry to maintain the myth that countries are under threat and need to continue to develop their military power. Indeed, some would suggest that potential conflicts have been exaggerated through biased media and **propaganda** to suggest that "the enemy" is stronger or more aggressive than it actually is. In the recent past, for the developed countries of the world, North Korea, Iraq, Libya, and Afghanistan have achieved "rogue state" status. The weapons industry and its supporters then argue that a stronger military is necessary for effective defence. This defence requires continued large-scale spending on upgrading weapons and improving systems. As a consequence, defence expenditures grow steadily and weapons become more expensive and more destructive. Few people stand to oppose such actions: the armed forces get better equipment, politicians gain prestige through increased national strength, arms companies make money, and many jobs are maintained. Those voices that suggest alternative viewpoints are quickly shouted down by the powerful groups in the military–industrial complex.

Unfortunately, this additional spending creates a competitive upward spiral—an arms race—with each nation trying to ensure their own safety by having more military might than others. Countries divert scarce financial resources to build up their military strength while other aspects are ignored, including health care and economic development. Hostility from the population living in abject poverty can produce unstable political systems that may degenerate into violence and war.

The widespread militarization of countries can lead to conflict on two fronts—the tendency to see a military response as the solution to a problem, and the destabilization that occurs through growing resentment of spending on the military.

Top Military Budgets, 2000

Country	Military Budget (US$ billions)
United States	324.8
Russia	56.0
Japan	45.6
China	39.5
United Kingdom	34.5
France	27.0
Germany	23.3
Saudi Arabia	18.7
Italy	16.0
Brazil	16.0
India	15.9
South Korea	12.8
Taiwan	12.8
Turkey	7.7
Canada	7.6
Iran	7.5
Australia	7.1
Israel	7.0
Spain	7.0

Center for Defense Information

FIGURE 19.8 The United States spends significantly more than any other country on its military, and its budget continues to grow.

Military Expenditures as a Percent of Gross Domestic Product, 1996

Greater than 4% of GDP Country	Expenditures	Less than 1% of GDP Country	Expenditures
Croatia	14.5	Japan	0.1
Oman	13.2	Malta	0.1
Saudi Arabia	13.2	Mauritius	0.3
Kuwait	11.9	Mexico	0.4
Jordan	8.8	Lithuania	0.5
Israel	8.7	Ghana	0.6
Syria	6.7	Nigeria	0.7
Lebanon	6.3	Luxembourg	0.7
Sri Lanka	6.0	Guatemala	0.8
Pakistan	5.6	Guyana	0.8
Bahrain	5.4	Latvia	0.8
Burundi	4.9	Madagascar	0.8
Cambodia	4.7	Malawi	0.8
Greece	4.5	Moldova	0.8
Ukraine	4.5	Nepal	0.8
United Arab Emirates	4.5	Austria	0.9
Singapore	4.3	El Salvador	0.9
Turkey	4.3		

The World Guide 2001/2002

FIGURE 19.9 Canada spends 1.4% of its gross domestic product (GDP) on its military.

FIGURE 19.10 Most countries figure the best defence is a strong offence and develop the equipment to fight protracted wars against perceived aggressor nations.

Religious Extremism

In a number of instances, people with extreme religious views have sought to undermine or destabilize political systems and geopolitical relationships of perceived enemies. Their actions are motivated by their interpretations of religious teachings. An example of this is the September 11, 2001 attacks on the World Trade Center in New York City and the Pentagon in Washington, DC, that killed over 2600 civilians. Terrorists linked to Islamic extremism targeted symbols of the United States' economic and military strength. The attacks led to significant economic disruption in the United States and around the world.

Religious extremists seek to impose their religious ideas on others. It is not enough that they personally meet the expectations of their faith, they demand that everyone else does as well. These religious extremists so strongly believe that they are right that they feel justified in imposing their points of view on others, using force, if necessary. Their beliefs justify the intolerance and prejudice that accompanies extreme **fundamentalism**. Adherents of extreme fundamentalist religious groups frequently attempt to intervene in political processes to make sure that the society conforms to their view of the world. Over the centuries, religious extremism has restricted freedoms of groups in society, such as making women and children possessions of males, and has resulted in a great number of human rights abuses, including the imprisonment or death of non-believers.

Religious extremists exist in many faiths in many parts of the world. In North America, Christian fundamentalists such as the Aryan Nations are seen as a potential threat to the political stability of the United States. In the Middle East, Zionist groups such as the Jewish Defence League have been blamed for acts of religious terrorism. Currently, many argue that a serious threat to political and economic stability is from Islamic extremism. In part this is because the Islamic religion has developed a global reach, with significant populations of adherents in many countries around the world. Extremists often are individuals with little allegiance to any particular group, making their identification difficult. Islamic extremists are often committed to holy war against what they view as corrupt or evil influences.

The 2001 attack on the United States demonstrated the threat of religous extremism. The terrorists were able to obtain false documents and to design an elaborate scheme without being tracked by security networks. They blended into local emigrant communities, easily moving across international borders and into position within the United States. The terrorists methodically carried out their suicide missions. After the attack, U.S. officials quickly pointed to Osama bin Laden as the instigator of the terrorist activities. Born in Saudi Arabia, bin Laden possessed enormous wealth and personal charisma, and developed an intense hatred for Western influences in the Middle East. He

FIGURE 19.11 A hijacked American commuter jet was crashed into the World Trade Center in an act of terrorism on September 11, 2001. The religious extremists who caused this terror crashed four aircraft on that day.

created the training centres that prepared terrorists for their missions. The terrorists' knowledge and skills in using modern tools such as cell phones, the Internet, and jet aircraft, combined with traditional zealous dedication, made them dangerous and deadly threats to a country that they viewed as evil and corrupt.

International terrorists motivated by religious extremism have the potential to destabilize countries around the world, producing international conflict and violence.

FIGURE 19.12 Osama bin Laden led a terrorist organization called Al Qaeda from bases in Afghanistan, a country led by the Taliban— Islamic extremists whose beliefs were rejected by most moderate Islamic adherents.

CASE STUDY

Geopolitics and the Middle East

The Middle East has been the central focus of global geopolitics since World War II. Because the links between geography, politics, and economics here are the most dramatic in the world, this region gets more media coverage than any other. The conflicts directly affect many Canadians.

The West, whose influence in the region dates back to World War I and intensified during the Cold War, has been criticized for disregarding Arab history and culture, leading to strong anti-western hostility in some places.

In the past, Northeast Africa and Southwest Asia was a powerful region of trade and culture. Today, known as the Middle East, it has been called a **shatterbelt** of instability, caught between opposing economic, political, and cultural forces. While the region is home to many different ethnic groups, most are Muslims divided into a number of different sects, including Sunni, Shiite, Wahhab, and Druze. The Jews of Israel and Christians in several countries, including Egypt, Lebanon, and Syria, are minority groups.

A large part of the region is inhospitable mountains and desert, so most people live where water supply is more reliable, by oases and along coastlines and river valleys, including the Nile River and the "fertile crescent" of the Tigris-Euphrates Rivers. All the countries in the region have access to a coastline, but most of them are using their water resources to the limit and face critical water shortages in the future as industrialization grows slowly and the population grows rapidly, at 2.9% per year. Without adequate supplies of water, it is difficult to grow enough food in the region, requiring expensive imports. It is expected that 80% of the food supply will be imported by 2005. Most rivers are shared by more than one country and this is a source of ongoing and potential conflict as water consumption increases.

 See Chapter 8 for more information about the world's water supply.

The geographic location of the Middle East makes it one of the most strategically located regions on Earth. It is considered to be one of the world's main "cradles of civilization," where agriculture and the first cities emerged. Three of the world's major religions—Judaism, Christianity, and Islam—began there. It is located at the nexus of three continents—Asia, Europe, and Africa—and has been the hub of world trade routes for centuries. Access to and control of five main strategic water routes has had an impact on trade patterns and influenced geopolitical events. These routes, including the Suez Canal and Strait of Hormuz, are shown in Figure 19.15.

By far the largest resources of the region are the vast wealth of oil and natural gas on which countries around the world are dependent.

Conflict in the Middle East

There have been many wars and disputes over land and borders in the region. These include the ongoing Arab–Israeli Conflict, the Lebanon civil war, the Iran–Iraq War, and the Persian Gulf War of the early 1990s.

> ### FACT FILE
>
> Saudi Arabia contains 25% of the world's known oil reserves while Iran, Iraq, and Kuwait have another 25%.

FIGURE 19.13 The Rub-al-Khali or empty quarter in southern Saudi Arabia is the world's largest sand dune region, receiving less than 8 cm of precipitation annually.

Arab–Israeli Conflict

The most intractable dispute is the Arab–Israeli conflict. The issue has its roots in ancient times as the land was conquered by a succession of many different groups, including Jews, Egyptians, Assyrians, Babylonians, Persians, Jews again, Romans, Crusaders from Europe, and Turks. The conflict currently centres on the right to a state and to security for both Israel and Palestine.

In 1920, when Palestine came under British control, Jewish settlers began moving to the region and buying land. With the rise of the Nazis in Germany in the 1930s and continued persecution of Jews, more Jews began to move to Palestine. By 1940, there were about 450 000 Jews in the region, 30% of the total population. When the horrors of the Holocaust were revealed, **Zionism** grew and many more Jews migrated. The British found it impossible to keep peace between the Palestinian inhabitants and the new settlers, who were demanding a Jewish state, and called on the UN for help. In 1947, the UN voted to partition land that was known as Palestine into a Jewish and an Arab state, which came into effect in 1948.

Drawing superimposed and arbitrary boundaries on a map created the state of Israel and guaranteed decades of conflict. More than 700 000 Palestinian inhabitants were forced to leave their homes and lands. Arab leaders rejected the new plan and neighbouring states surrounding the tiny country invaded the territory when it was only a few hours old. Just over a year later, when Israel had beaten the invaders off, it joined the UN and was recognized by more than 50 countries. During the Six-Day War in 1967, Israel captured what are now called the Occupied Territories: the West Bank and east Jerusalem from Jordan, the Gaza Strip and the Sinai Peninsula from Egypt, and the Golan Heights from Syria. After both the 1967 and 1973 wars, the UN passed resolutions 242 and 338 calling for Israel to withdraw from all territory illegally gained in the wars, including the West Bank and Gaza.

In 1993, the Palestinian Liberation Organization (PLO) agreed that Israel had a right to exist as a state and Israel recognized the PLO, as the official negotiating body for Palestinians. This was part of the Oslo Peace Accord, which unfortunately left the more serious issues for future negotiation. Both Yasser Arafat, the leader of the PLO, and Shimon Peres, the Israeli prime minister, shared a Nobel Peace Prize in 1993 for their efforts to bring peace to the region with the Oslo Accord.

A number of peace agreements, including the Oslo Accord, have failed to resolve the conflict and the violence has continued to escalate, with increased frustration and militancy, particularly among young people on both sides. Both sides have committed acts of terror. Israelis claim they are acting in self-defense. Palestinians claim they are fighting against oppression. There is little security for either Palestinians or Israeli citizens and

Middle Eastern Countries, Resources, and Territorial and Boundary Disputes

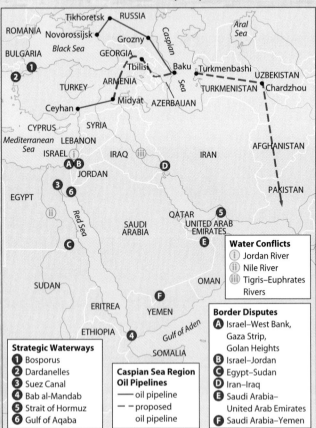

Water Conflicts
- ⓘ Jordan River
- ⓘⓘ Nile River
- ⓘⓘⓘ Tigris–Euphrates Rivers

Border Disputes
- Ⓐ Israel–West Bank, Gaza Strip, Golan Heights
- Ⓑ Israel–Jordan
- Ⓒ Egypt–Sudan
- Ⓓ Iran–Iraq
- Ⓔ Saudi Arabia–United Arab Emirates
- Ⓕ Saudi Arabia–Yemen

Strategic Waterways
- ❶ Bosporus
- ❷ Dardanelles
- ❸ Suez Canal
- ❹ Bab al-Mandab
- ❺ Strait of Hormuz
- ❻ Gulf of Aqaba

Caspian Sea Region Oil Pipelines
- —— oil pipeline
- – – proposed oil pipeline

▶ **FIGURE 19.14** The British government first used the term "Middle East" in the 1930s when its military forces in the area extended from the central Mediterranean into India. Other names that are used to describe the region include the Arab World and the Oil World. None of these names accurately apply to the whole region.

Partition Lands, 1947–1948

Lebanon

Damascus

Lebanon border

Syria

Haifa

Israel

Mediterranean Sea

Sea of Galelee

Jordan River

Tel Aviv

Amman

Jerusalem

Dead Sea

Egypt

Transjordan

Jewish State
Arab State
International Zone

FIGURE 19.15

Israeli Settlements in Palestinian Territories

adapted from *The Globe and Mail*, May 9, 2002, p. A17

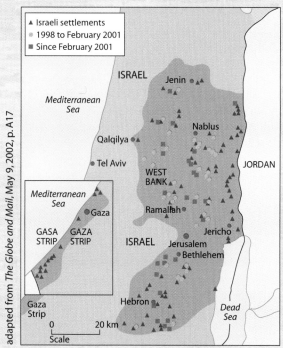

▲ Israeli settlements
● 1998 to February 2001
■ Since February 2001

ISRAEL

Mediterranean Sea

Jenin

Nablus

Qalqilya

Tel Aviv

WEST BANK

JORDAN

Ramallah

Jericho

ISRAEL

Jerusalem

Bethlehem

Mediterranean Sea

Gaza

GASA STRIP   GAZA STRIP

Gaza Strip

Hebron

Dead Sea

0   20 km
Scale

FIGURE 19.16 The number of Israeli settlers in Palestinian territories has grown to more than 200 000 since 1967, when the first settlements were created.

neither side appears to have found a way to end the violence. As in any society, there are people with moderate views and extremists. The most extreme elements on both sides are opposed to peace and want the other group out of the region. Some who have lost friends and family members, or are exhausted from the constant fear and violence, have become angry and militant. Other citizens on both sides genuinely want to live together in peace. Some believe that the only hope for peace will come from the grass roots and not from the government.

Some analysts believe that the only hope for peace is for Israel to give back the land that was taken in violation of international law. Large and growing Jewish settlements have been built on the disputed lands and Israel is opposed to their return. Millions of Palestinians now live in other countries around the region, but many people and their descendants have lived in refugee camps for decades.

Issues in Dispute

- Borders of the proposed independent Palestinian state, which claims the West Bank and Gaza Strip
- If that land is returned to Palestine, what will happen to the Israelis living in illegal settlements?
- Both sides claim Jerusalem, designated as international territory in the original partition, as their capital and a sacred religious centre for Muslims, Christians, and Jews
- The plight and repatriation of Palestinian refugees
- Restrictions on the movement of Palestinians within West Bank and Gaza territory
- Jewish settlements on occupied land, including in east Jerusalem, which the Palestinians want removed or transferred to their control and the Israelis want protected with a permanent buffer zone along the Jordan River in the West Bank
- The water supply in the West Bank
- Security measures to ensure the safety of civilians on both sides

As well as a wide diversity of opinion within the Middle East, geopolitical experts are divided about where the solution lies. There have been many attempts by the international community and by the two sides themselves to bring about peaceful resolution. Polls have shown that a majority of people in Israel support the idea of Israeli withdrawal and a demilitarized national state for the Palestinians within the occupied territories.

The European countries have proposed the recognition of Palestine as a state by the UN and then renewed negotiations with Israel. Crown Prince Abdullah of Saudi Arabia has proposed that the 22 Arab League countries would offer a full and normal relationship with Israel if Israel withdrew from all occupied territories to its legal pre-1967 borders. This plan did not address the problem of the return to Israel of Palestinian refugees and their descendants from the 1948 and 1967 wars, but both of these proposals could be a platform on which to build a peace settlement. Other proposals include the creation of a regional federation of Israel, Palestine, and Jordan, similar to the three **Benelux** countries of Europe, with full diplomatic relations and international aid to help make it work.

Views on the Arab–Israeli Conflict

"The roadblocks in the West Bank won't stop a terrorist from going around or through in another spot. They just make daily life a nuisance or keep people from getting to the hospital."

Palestinian citizen, West Bank, CBC radio interview, March 2002

"The trouble with the Arab–Israeli arena is that the major strategic developments that affect our lives and generate war or peace are usually unpredictable and catch us completely by surprise."

Yossi Alpher, former director of the Jaffe Centre for Strategic Studies, Tel Aviv University

"…Israel, a far smaller entity, has absorbed millions of refugees over the past five decades and integrated them into its society. The Arab countries, meanwhile, have permitted the squalor of the refugee camps to persist for cynical propaganda purposes."

Ed Greenspon, journalist

"We saw both populations, Palestinians and Jews, living in fear. Every Palestinian in the Occupied Territories is affected in a cycle of repression, which is bringing people to despair. Israelis are living in constant fear of suicide bombs and armed attacks, which have deliberately targeted civilians, killing and wounding people in streets, shops and bars. Trampling on people's human rights cannot be justified under any circumstances, not in the name of security and not in the name of freedom. Israeli military aggression has made Palestinians in towns constantly watch the sky in fear. Houses and infrastructure have been shelled and demolished without regard for the rules of the Fourth Geneva Convention… It is unacceptable that without warning or legality tanks and bulldozers demolish the homes of hundreds of families, including thousands of children."

Report of Amnesty International Delegation, February 7, 2002

"We condemn attacks against Israeli civilians, indeed against any civilians, on three distinct grounds: moral, legal and political. The Palestinian people, in spite of the suicidal mood of some of its most desperate youth, will survive. But the chaos into which the Israeli "military option" threatens to drag the whole area, and in which many more innocent lives will be sacrificed on both sides, also threatens world peace and stability as a whole. It undermines any serious effort to isolate terrorists and eliminate terrorism, and it dooms whole new generations to endless wars, destruction and suffering. Will the world stand idle, indifferent or accomplice? Will the international community continue to claim helplessness?"

Editorial, Palestinian National Authority Website, January 19, 2002

Waging War in Cyberspace

One of the Palestinian groups fighting for a Palestinian homeland is Hezbollah. It has used the Internet to inform people of its views and to communicate among its members. In 2000, its two Web sites were "bombed" by a huge volume of e-mails, some of which contained viruses. The sites crashed, but Hezbollah quickly opened seven new ones. Within a few weeks, Israeli government Web sites were likewise assaulted with intense electronic traffic, jeopardizing the functioning of these sites. The widespread use of the Internet for communication has turned Web sites into military targets.

INTERACT

1. Explain how the end of the Cold War and the disintegration of the Soviet Union changed peace and security conditions around the world.
2. For each of the four peace and security concerns discussed in this section of the chapter, complete a flow diagram to show how it could lead to international violence and war.
3. Use the statistics in Figure 19.8, **Top Military Budgets, 2000**, to calculate per capita military budgets. Use an almanac or on-line sources such as the *CIA World Factbook* to find population totals for the countries listed. Analyse the per capita results and report on trends in the data.
4. On an outline map of the world, locate the countries listed in Figure 19.9, **Military Expenditures as a Percent of Gross Domestic Product, 1996**. Shade in one colour those countries whose military expenditures are greater than 4% of GDP, and use a second colour for those whose expenditures are less than 1%. What observation can you make about the pattern on your map?
5. Conduct research on the conflicts between Israel and its Arab neighbours over Palestine. Write a two-page report showing how the four factors discussed in this part of the chapter (i.e., the fight for resources, the widening gap between rich and poor, worldwide militarization, and religious extremism) play roles in the conflict.

THE GLOBAL ARMS TRADE

It costs the nations of the world roughly US$800 billion to maintain their militaries. This is the largest single form of public spending, greater than spending on social programs, economic development, or protecting the environment. Between $160 billion and $240 billion of this total expenditure on the military is used to buy, maintain, or operate weapons. In recent years, about $35 billion a year has been spent globally on the manufacturing and purchase of new conventional weapons (a category that does not include nuclear weapons or other weapons of mass destruction). Here are some statistics about arms sales:

- U.S. sales of weapons make up half of total worldwide sales
- Developing countries spend about $25 billion a year on new weapons

World Military Expenditures, 1992–2000 (US$ billions)										
	1992	1993	1994	1995	1996	1997	1998	1999	2000	% Change 1992–2000
Africa	10	10	11	10	10	11	10	14	14	+40.0
Americas	383	367	348	333	314	315	308	308	318	-17.0
Asia and Oceania	105	108	109	112	115	117	118	120	123	+17.1
Europe	296	278	275	239	235	238	227	235	240	-18.9
Middle East	52	51	51	28	49	53	57	56	61	+17.3
World	847	814	794	742	723	734	720	733	756	-10.7

Stockholm International Peace Research Institute

FIGURE 19.17 Note the different patterns of spending between developed and developing regions of the world.

- Developing countries account for 68 % of U.S. arms sales
- In the period 1997–2000, the United Arab Emirates—a tiny Middle Eastern country—was the world's largest purchaser of arms

The rich, developed countries are the nations with the largest arms industries. They have the technological skill and research and development (R&D) facilities to produce better weapons. The sale of weapons to developing countries represents a massive movement of money from the poorer regions of the world to the richer regions. In recent years, this transfer of wealth has accelerated as civil conflicts have flared in Africa, Asia, and Eastern Europe.

The sale of arms to other countries is important for countries with strong weapons industries. These sales help to offset the high cost of developing their own weaponry and to improve the balance of trade figures. The United States, for example, spends roughly $40 billion a year on military R&D, part of which can be recouped through sales of weapons. The arms-producing countries keep the more recent, most sophisticated technology for themselves, to ensure that they keep a competitive edge, and allow the arms manufacturers to sell obsolete and less sophisticated weapons to willing

buyers. Ironically, arms sellers such as the United States can end up fighting forces equipped with weapons made in their own countries. This happened in the 1991 Gulf War against Iraq: the United States had built up Iraqi weaponry during that country's war against Iran in the 1980s, arms that were still serviceable in 1991. And it happened again in 2001–2002, when the U.S. battled Taliban forces who were using American weapons supplied to them when Soviet forces occupied the country in the 1980s.

> ❝A nation that continues year after year to spend more money on military defense than on programs of social uplift is approaching spiritual doom.❞
>
> *Martin Luther King, Jr., American civil rights activist*

FACT FILE

Canada spent US$97 million on imports of conventional weapons in 1997.

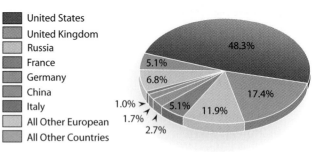

Suppliers of Arms to the World, 2000 (% of total sales)

- United States
- United Kingdom
- Russia
- France
- Germany
- China
- Italy
- All Other European
- All Other Countries

48.3%
17.4%
11.9%
5.1%
6.8%
5.1%
1.0%
1.7%
2.7%

Arms Trade Oversight Project

FIGURE 19.18 The United States and European countries sell most of the arms that are used around the world.

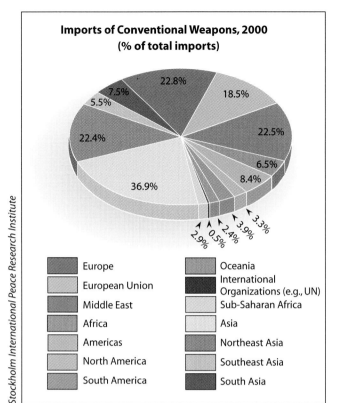

Imports of Conventional Weapons, 2000 (% of total imports)

22.8%

18.5%

7.5%

5.5%

22.5%

22.4%

6.5%

8.4%

36.9%

2.9%
0.5%
2.4%
3.9%
3.3%

Legend:
- Europe
- European Union
- Middle East
- Africa
- Americas
- North America
- South America
- Oceania
- International Organizations (e.g., UN)
- Sub-Saharan Africa
- Asia
- Northeast Asia
- Southeast Asia
- South Asia

Stockholm International Peace Research Institute

FIGURE 19.19 Purchases of arms by rebel groups and other NGOs are included in the regional totals, along with official government purchases.

Consequences of the Arms Trade

Weapons sales are frequently made to countries or regimes run by dictatorships or corrupt governments, where the arms are used to impede democratic movements. Two examples

> 66 This rush to globalize arms production and sales ignores the grave humanitarian and strategic consequences of global weapons proliferation. Already, profit motives in the military industry have resulted in arms export decisions that contravene such U.S. foreign policy goals as preserving stability and promoting human rights and democracy. 99
>
> *"Globalized Weaponry,"* Foreign Policy in Focus, Vol. 5, #16, *June 2000*

illustrate this trend: Western countries, including Canada, have repeatedly sold weapons and military supplies to Indonesia and Turkey for strategic purposes, two countries that have dismal records in their treatment of ethnic

> 66 Every gun that is made, every warship launched, every rocket fired, signifies, in the final sense, a theft from those who hunger and are not fed, those who are cold and are not clothed. This world in arms is not spending money alone; it is spending the sweat of its laborers, the genius of its scientists and the hopes of its children. 99
>
> *U.S. President Dwight D. Eisenhower*

groups, specifically the East Timorese and the Kurds. In the Middle East, the United States has used arms sales to prop up monarchies, with anti-democratic policies and suspicious human rights records, in order to maintain supplies of oil. In Panama, the United States had supported through weapons sales a "friendly" military regime that later turned out to be an important conduit of drugs into the United States. Large arms sales increase the risk of oppression of local people and increase the likelihood that uprisings will be put down with violent means, as was the case in Chiapas, Mexico.

Weapons of Choice

The greatest share of weapons purchases is of light weapons—rifles, machine guns, mortars, grenades, and land mines—that can be easily carried by soldiers. Roughly $5–$10 billion per year are spent on arms of this type. An estimated 80–90% of casualties in recent conflicts have been caused by light weapons. The advantages of this type of weapon are their low cost, accessibility, limited maintenance requirements,

FIGURE 19.20 Mikhail Kalashnikov and his famous AK-47 assault rifle. Other light weapons that are popular in the U.S. are the M-16 rifle, the German G-3, and the Israeli Uzi machine pistol.

Canadian Military Exports, 1990–1999

Country	War Began	War End	War-Related Deaths	Exports ($ millions)
Algeria	1991	—	60 000	8.1
Bangladesh	1975	1992	25 000	2.8
India	1952	—	80 000	4.4
Indonesia	1963	2000	237 000	24.9
Israel	1965	—	15 000	3.1
Mexico	1994	2001	1 000	3.2
Peru	1982	1997	30 000	4.7
Philippines	1972	—	90 000	4.7
Sri Lanka	1983	—	70 000	0.4
Turkey	1984	—	40 000	45.9
United Kingdom	1969	—	1 500	415.3

Coalition to Oppose the Arms Trade

FIGURE 19.21 Part of Canada's arms trade is with countries with poor track records on protecting human rights. There is great concern that Canadian-made equipment is being used to oppress ethnic minorities and to deny democratic rights to citizens.

portability, and killing power. Even children can be quickly taught how to use light weapons. The Soviet-designed Kalashnikov AK-47 is the weapon of choice for most forces. First manufactured in 1947, this automatic assault rifle has been proven to be durable and reliable. Roughly 60–70 million have been manufactured over the years in many countries, including China, Egypt, Iraq, and North Korea.

Light weapons are also widely available from corrupt militaries, black market sources,

FACT FILE

Globally, there are about 125 million light automatic weapons in the hands of soldiers, terrorists, and militia fighters.

Types of Military Equipment Exported by Canada

- Firearms and automatic weapons, and ammunition
- Bombs, torpedoes, grenades, rockets, etc.
- Fire control equipment, range-finding sensors, ballistic computers
- Ground vehicles specially designed or modified for military use (e.g., armoured vehicles)
- Equipment and components for detection of and defence against radioactive materials and biological and chemical agents
- Explosives and fuels specially designed for military purposes
- Naval vessels
- Aircraft, helicopters, unmanned airborne vehicles, and related equipment
- Electronic equipment for military use
- Armoured or protective equipment such as military helmets
- Specialized equipment for military training or for simulating military scenarios
- Imaging or imaging countermeasures equipment
- Software designed for military use

Department of Foreign Affairs and International Trade, 1999

FIGURE 19.22 Military equipment is often manufactured by companies that also produce consumer goods. In many cases, products manufactured for consumers are modified for use by the military, or vice versa.

Top U.S. Military Contractors, 2000

Rank	Company	Value of Contracts Awarded (US$ billions)	Product or Weapons
1	Lockheed Martin Corporation	15.1	F-11, Apache, Trident, and Hellfire missiles
2	The Boeing Company	12.0	F/A-18, F-15, V-22 Osprey
3	Raytheon Corporation	6.3	Patriot, AMRAAM Hawk missiles
4	General Dynamics Corporation	4.2	nuclear submarines, DDG-51 destroyers
5	Northrop Grumman Corporation	3.1	B-2 bomber, F-15, F/A-18
6	Litton Industries, Incorporated	2.7	aircraft and helicopter engines
7	United Technologies Corporation	2.1	DDG-51 destroyers, amphibious assault ships
8	TRW Incorporated	2.0	electronic systems and support
9	General Electric Company, Incorporated	1.6	aircraft and helicopter engines
10	Science Applications International Corporation	1.5	V-22 Osprey, tank engines, helicopters

Center for Defense Information

FIGURE 19.23 Many Canadian corporations have links to the large transnational corporations (TNCs) on this list of top military suppliers.

FACT FILE

The Internet was first developed as a tool for the military. In the late 1960s, the Advanced Research Projects Agency (ARPA) of the U.S. Department of Defense linked mainframe computers in an effort to form a communications network that could survive a nuclear attack or natural disaster, and provide links to its users in remote locations. This early Internet was called ARPANet.

friendly governments, and through theft from government arsenals. Jets and tanks, on the other hand, are only available from a select group of producers, and their manufacture and sale are tracked and reported. The availability of light weapons has made them popular; their effectiveness has made them deadly.

"Kalashnikov Kids"

There is a growing trend to use children as soldiers. Termed "Kalashnikov Kids," children as young as eight years old are forced into brutal and fearful lives. The children are used by military forces because they are easily manipulated through fear, they eat less, and they can be trained to be heartless killers. Children are often sent into the most dangerous places because they are seen as expendable. Girl soldiers are used as sex slaves and boys as labourers and slaves. Often abducted by roving militia forces, the children are brutalized, forced to endure pain and suffering, and to inflict it on others. In many cases they are ordered to kill their own families, so that there is no place for them to return should they try to escape. There are an estimated 300 000 child soldiers in the world, in places such as Sierra Leone, Burma, and Somalia. Those child soldiers who do manage to escape are ostracized by their society and live with the fear that they will be hunted down by their former comrades.

People around the world are trying to end the use of children as soldiers. In fact, this effort is just part of a growing movement to improve the rights of children everywhere. Some other efforts focus on improving the health and education of children, ending the practice of child labour, protecting children in civil conflicts and from the destruction of land mines, and supporting children who have become separated from their families through violence or natural disasters. One agency that has set up a directory to provide information and give access to specific organizations for the whole spectrum of children's rights is the BBC World Service. Their Web site is at <www.bbc.co.uk/worldservice/people/features/childrensrights/help.shtml>. By accessing this site, you can learn about some of the more prominent NGOs and other agencies working in this field, including Save the Children Fund, the Rugmark Foundation, the Disasters Emergency Committee, and Oxfam International.

INTERACT

1. In chart form, identify the benefits and the costs of the arms trade. Include in your chart social, political, environmental, and economic costs and benefits.
2. Tax dollars are used to underwrite at least part of the costs of developing new military technologies. Should Canadians then have the right to demand that weapons not be sold to countries that abuse their citizens and deny them their human rights? Explain your answer to this question of ethics.
3. a) In your opinion, globally, should there be controls placed on the purchase of arms? Explain your answer.
   b) If you replied "yes" to part a), explain how controls would be put in place and who would be responsible for overseeing their implementation. If you replied "no" to part a), explain how the harmful impacts of weapons can be minimized for civilians and peaceful countries.
4. Investigate to find the focus of a public boycott of a TNC such as General Electric.

CO-OPERATING FOR A PEACEFUL FUTURE

In a 1999 issue of *The Humanist*, Michael Renner remarked, "governments still devote far less energy and enthusiasm to the task of conflict prevention and peace building than to war preparation and war-making." Many national governments determine that their goals can more easily be accomplished with violence and force than through peace. These goals include gaining prestige, acquiring resources, eliminating competitors, and strengthening their economy. These governments set achieving their goals above establishing and maintaining peace. Still, some people and governments are prepared to work toward the peaceful resolution of conflicts, and the United Nations (UN) has as one of its mandates

FIGURE 19.24 Canadian peacekeepers in Kigali, Rwanda. Part of the UN strategy for dealing with conflicts is to deploy peacekeepers to attempt to curtail violence and the use of armed force in conflict areas. While this strategy has proven successful in some locations, it has not removed the incentives and inclinations for countries to wage war.

GEOGRAPHIC METHODS

Geographic Information Systems (GIS) as a Peacekeeping Tool

GIS is becoming increasingly important as a tool for peacekeeping responses to conflict situations. Peacekeepers are finding that GIS gives them greater ability to integrate data and analyse information quickly. GIS is particularly effective in recognition of patterns of events, such as vehicle traffic, movements of weapons, and distribution of camps. This tool gives peacekeepers more strength in tracking problems in the mission area and in assessing the impacts of their actions, leading to more effective responses on their part to stop violence.

the prevention of war. The ongoing ethnic and regional conflicts, however, are a clear sign that peace is an elusive goal.

Achieving peace will mean changing some of the normal methods of operating that have been used in the past and replacing them with new strategies and tactics. For the past half century, the world has associated peace with UN peacekeeping activities. But, in reality, peacekeeping efforts are often last-ditch affairs that belatedly dispatch too few ill-equipped troops to attempt to make peace among combatants who do not desire it, even if the civilians do. The limited success of these efforts is a testament to the soldiers, police, and others who have dedicated themselves to the task. A more realistic view suggests that making peace likely will require two important new directions: strengthening the infrastructure that encourages peace and reducing the causes of conflicts.

Promoting Peace

Achieving peace takes planning, dedication, creative thinking, conflict management skills, and effort.

Disarming the militaries of the world is a key step toward peace. In the past, arms controls have attempted to limit the amount and types of weapons that could be stockpiled and used. These initiatives have resulted in UN conventions banning some weapons, specifically chemical weapons in 1993 and land mines in 1997 (although the United States and other key producers of land mines have not signed this convention). However, few weapons have been outlawed and stockpiles of arms have grown significantly over the years. As long as these weapons are available, there will be the temptation to use them. Disarmament would lead to the elimination of militaries and the destruction of weapons of war. It would mean substantial reductions in all types of weapons, including light assault rifles. Done as **multilateral agreements** on a global scale, this would remove the tendency to use war to solve problems and encourage negotiation as a way to resolve conflicts. Costa Rica and Panama are two countries that have taken the step of disbanding their standing armies (save for small forces intended for police action).

> **FACT FILE**
>
> Between 3600 BC and today, there has been an estimated 14 500 major wars, with about four billion casualties. During this whole time, there has been only 292 years of world peace.

FIGURE 19.25 At a student protest in Ottawa demanding an end to land mines, Canada's then minister of foreign affairs, Lloyd Axworthy, adds a shoe to the pile, of which each one is symbolic of a life destroyed by land mines.

An important component of a disarmament strategy would be a binding code of conduct on all countries to prevent the export of weapons to countries in turmoil. This ban would apply to nations that are engaging in armed aggression, are denying human rights to some part of their population, or fail to hold free elections. Over time, this strategy would mean that arms sales would be rare and unusual events, rather than a normal part of international economic activity. It is likely, however, that arms sales would continue as a black market activity.

Because of their destructiveness, one of the most urgent parts of a disarmament program is the elimination of nuclear weapons. At the present time, the world is divided into nuclear "have" and "have not" nations. The Non-Proliferation Treaty was designed to keep the "have not" countries from obtaining nuclear weapons. This treaty does not put an obligation on the "have" countries to destroy their stockpiles, so it gives a small group of countries a monopoly on these powerful weapons. Furthermore, those who have these weapons continue to improve their effectiveness and deliverability. This creates an inequity in national securities, a situation that has and will push some countries into developing or buying their own nuclear capabilities. For example, both India and Pakistan tested nuclear weapons in the 1990s, clearly violating the Non-Proliferation Treaty, each citing perceived threats from the other as reason for their actions. Also of great concern is the chance that nuclear weapons will be bought or stolen by aggressive governments or terrorist groups.

PROFILE

Jody Williams and the International Campaign to Ban Land Mines

In 1997, Canadian Jody Williams was awarded the Nobel Peace Prize for her work to ban land mines. Land mines are indiscriminate weapons and cannot distinguish a soldier from a child, a mother, or a family's livestock. They kill or maim thousands of civilians every year, at a rate of one person every 20 minutes. There are over 110 million land mines in use in the world today, scattered over 64 countries. In 1991, Williams began mobilizing NGOs with the goal of banning land mines. In the following six years, over 1000 NGOs became involved in the task, including churches, service organizations such as the Red Cross, and peace groups. The strong support by NGOs put considerable pressure on governments to respond. A text for the international treaty to ban land mines was negotiated in Oslo, Norway, in 1997 and signed later that same year in Ottawa, Canada. The Nobel Peace Prize acknowledged the important role Williams played in achieving this goal.

FIGURE 19.26

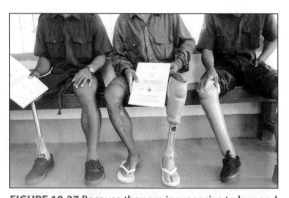

FIGURE 19.27 Because they are inexpensive to buy and use, land mines have been buried in many countries around the world. Unfortunately, they injure more civilians than combatants.

FACT FILE

Cost to buy a land mine: $3–$10

Cost to remove a land mine: $300–$1000

Preventing Conflict

Removing the sources of conflict is seen as the most effective way to solve international peace and security conflicts. Conflict prevention can be accomplished through a fair distribution of wealth. For many, the shift to a global economy in recent decades has made wealth inequalities greater. Globalization has encouraged a "race to the bottom," whereby TNCs prefer those locations that offer the lowest wages, the weakest environmental protection, and the least concern for worker protections. These choices encourage lower wages and weaker standards. This exploitation of the poor leads to a widening poverty gap and, ultimately, frustration, resentment, and conflict. Analysts have argued for policies that encourage full employment, eradicate poverty, and end social inequalities and racism. All people should have access to the resources to generate enough wealth to have a comfortable way of life, free from exploitation. Policies that would accomplish this would strengthen the social fabric of the global society, reducing the underlying pressures that bring about war and violence.

Countries with Nuclear Weapons Capability

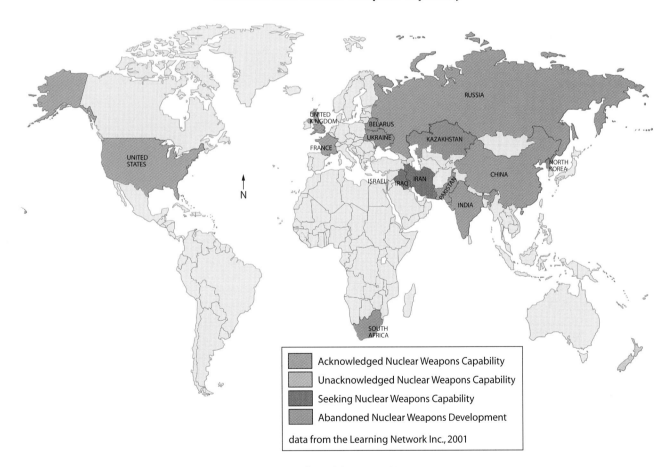

FIGURE 19.28 The number of countries in the "nuclear club" jumped in 1991 with the collapse of the Soviet Union. Some of the former Soviet republics abandoned these nuclear installations and nuclear weapons.

FIGURE 19.29 This weaver in Ecuador is supported by the Canadian International Development Agency (CIDA).

 See Chapter 13 for more information about the causes of poverty.

As they shift their policies, countries will have to answer difficult questions:

- What segments of society should be protected?
- What segments of society should be promoted and encouraged?
- What role will the military play in society?
- What rights will individuals have?
- What rights will be held by the state?
- How much power should international organizations have in our future?

Responding to these questions in ways that reduce the incentive to react in violent and forceful ways is a step in the right direction toward eliminating conflict on a global scale.

Reducing and eliminating global security concerns can be accomplished by removing both the tools to wage war and the motivation to do so.

INTERACT

1. What evidence leads some people to believe that the strategies we have used in the past to work toward peace have been ineffective? What has been suggested as an alternative?

2. Two conditions are given for the reduction of violence among nations in this section of the chapter—reduced militarization and elimination of poverty. In your own words, explain how these changes would reduce wars and violence.

3. Complete a cost–benefit analysis chart for eliminating militaries. In one column, record the benefits for a demilitarized world. In another column, record the costs. For both columns, consider social, political, environmental, and economic factors.

4. What is the likelihood that the ideas for creating peace described here will be used in the future? Write a one-page opinion paper in which you discuss the prospects for improved strategies for peace for the future.

- Peace Pledge Union in the United Kingdom:
- Global Issues organization:
- Military Analysis Network:
- Canada's security agency:
- Middle East Peace Dialogue Network:
- Palestinian Autority: <www.pna.net>

- Environmental impacts of war and conflict
- Child soldiers
- Impacts of the arms trade on developing countries
- Economic impacts of terrorism
- TNCs and the manufacture of weapons

 Quality of Life Versus Military Expenditures

1. Summarize the causes of conflict in the world, ranking them in order of importance.

2. Rivers that are shared between countries are sometimes a source of conflict, especially in arid regions of the world. Using an atlas and an outline map of the world, map the rivers that form boundaries between countries. Use a legend to identify those that have potential to be sources of conflict.

3. Do countries with more neighbours have more conflicts than countries with fewer neighbours? Randomly choose 20 countries from around the world and count the number of countries with which they share borders (for example, Canada shares one border, but the United States shares two borders). Conduct research to determine which of the 20 countries on your list are currently involved or were recently involved in a conflict. Determine if there is a correlation between number of neighbours and potential for conflicts. Compare you results with those of others.

4. Use the data from Figure 19.6, **Distribution of Incomes for Selected Countries, Mid-1990s**, to construct a stacked bar graph, showing distribution of incomes for the selected countries. Draw each country bar 100 mm in height (representing 100%) and divide it into the five quintiles given in the table. What observation can you make from your graph?

5. Using examples from this chapter, identify ways in which countries and regions of the world are becoming increasingly interdependent. Make a sketch or some form of visual to show your ideas.

6. What is the impact of the arms trade on the quality of life in developing countries? Using the Internet and other resources, compare statistical indicators of quality of life for a total of 20 countries in different parts of the world. Record information about spending on the military along with three indicators of quality of life, such as infant mortality rate, life expectancy, and energy consumption. What pattern does your data reveal? How do you explain the pattern?

7. Research and report on the human cost of global military spending. Look for connections between military spending and poverty, the lack of democratic rights, and oppression of groups in society such as women or indigenous people. Write your findings as an article for a news magazine, incorporating factual evidence.

8. Scarcities and inequities in the distribution of resources contribute to uprisings and conflicts. Resources include materials from the

physical environment, but can also include other things that are needed for improving qualities of life, such as technology, skills, entrepreneurial opportunity, and capital. With a partner, brainstorm the broad types of resources that are most likely to lead to uprisings and conflicts. For the three most important items on the list, explain why you think they have the potential to threaten peace and security.

9. Research and report on one organization that is working toward global peace, such as Peace Pledge Union in the United Kingdom. Identify and evaluate its tactics.

10. What is the current situation for the Canadian military? Conduct research to find out about spending trends, size of forces, training efforts, foreign policy, and so on. Display your information in some creative form such as a bulletin board display, poster, or Web site.

11. Using the Internet and other resources, analyse one current instance of international conflict. You might consider border disputes in places like Kashmir or Congo (Zaire), international peacemaking efforts in Eastern Europe, or international terrorism. For each instance, identify factors that contribute to the conflict and examine possible ways of co-operating to resolve the situation.

12. a) Analyse the evolving global geopolitical role of a region, or a country within a region, that could be considered a risk to international peace and security.
    b) Evaluate how its actions contribute to global conflict and co-operation.

PART FIVE:
BUILDING A BETTER FUTURE

Chapter 20: Sustainability—Finding Solutions

By the end of this chapter, you will

- evaluate the significance of the participation of people in non-violent movements to protect resources and environments;

- evaluate some of the ways of promoting sustainable development and assess their effectiveness in selected places and regions of the world;

- demonstrate an understanding of how the work of the United Nations and other organizations on poverty, disease, and the environment is directly related to your own life;

- evaluate the effectiveness of methods used by different organizations, governments, and industries to find short- and long-term solutions to geographic problems and issues at the local, national, and global level;

- explain how local participation in the development process can build sustainable communities;

- predict global demographic changes for the future and assess their economic, environmental, and social implications;

- evaluate the sustainability of selected trends related to consumption of the earth's resources;

- evaluate the role played by non-governmen-

tal organizations and local community initiatives in different parts of the world in promoting sustainable development and resource management;

- produce an action plan for a local community initiative that contributes to the sustainability of a selected global resource;

- produce scenarios for probable and desirable futures based on current trends in the human use of the earth and its resources including trends in technology;

- demonstrate an understanding of the possibility of a number of alternative solutions to any geographic problem or issue;

- explain why it is difficult to make accurate predictions relating to human use of the earth and its resources, and why some predictions are more (or less) accurate than others;

- evaluate the effectiveness of techniques used to predict the future;

- use different types of maps and images to analyse the consequences of human activities or environmental phenomena;

- identify practical applications in the local community of conclusions reached in the independent inquiry.

BUILDING A BETTER FUTURE

Throughout your study of *Geonexus: Canadian and World Issues*, you have examined a number of geographic issues that affect the planet and its inhabitants at all levels—from the personal to the global. The text has provided information about the ways that systems interact. This is essential for helping us manage an increasingly complex, rapidly changing world and for addressing the issues facing us. In analysing these issues, we realize that they are so diverse and interwoven that solutions become elusive. What role, as an individual, can you play in searching for solutions to these issues? What is your role in the future as you move through your education into the working world and new relationships? Is it possible to make a difference?

The extent to which one person can make a difference can be seen in the classic case of Mahatma Ghandi. When faced with the might of the British Empire in nineteenth-century India, Ghandi's solution was radical, non-violent, and brilliant. Britain saw her Indian colony as a huge source of raw cotton fibre for British textile and clothing mills and as a massive market for the products of those mills. Britain imposed import and export laws that supported British industries but practically destroyed the traditional **cottage industries** of hand-spinning and weaving cloth that supported millions of Indians, yet did little to create new employment for those who lost their livelihoods. How to affect change? How to bring down an economic empire? Ghandi devoted daily time to hand-spinning and weaving his own clothes, boycotted the British products, and encouraged his friends, acquaintances, and followers to do the same. It became a matter of pride and unity to wear homespun clothes known as *svadeshi*. Ultimately, the revitalization of this home-based industry led to both economic and political independence for India. One man made a difference.

Martin Luther King once said, "Injustice anywhere is a threat to justice everywhere." This captures the views of many people on the issues that challenge us. Underlying some of the more distressing issues are the great injustices that exist among Earth's inhabitants. These injustices include chronic hunger versus those who consume too much, astounding poverty versus great material wealth, dominance and brutality destroying lives and livelihoods, and a trend toward a single global civilization, with increasing conflicts between nations, ethnic groups, and cultures. The root causes of these injustices are complex and a thoughtful analysis and search for ways to address them must recognize the role that we as individuals play within the global village.

> 6 6 Leadership is the ability to inspire others while making a contribution and personally making a difference. Everything we say or do sends a message, sets a tone, or teaches people what to do or not to do. 9 9
>
> *Sheila Murray Bethel, author,*
> Making a Difference: 12 Qualities
> *that Make You a Leader*

> 6 6 Imagine no possessions. I wonder if you can. No need for greed or hunger. A brotherhood of man. Imagine all the people sharing all the world. You may say I'm a dreamer. But I'm not the only one. I hope someday you'll join us and the world will live as one. 9 9
>
> *John Lennon, musician,*
> *songwriter, "Imagine"*

The Turn of the Tide

As residents of a country with an enviable living standard, Canadians have contributed to the inequities and suffering in the world, as well as to the degradation of **ecosystems** on which we all depend for life. The systems and structures that support the affluence of the majority of Canadians can work to create bleak conditions for others. Solving these injustices requires change to global patterns and power structures. It requires positive, purposeful action. It cannot be done all at once, but must be done one small step at a time. Social and environmental change is not just about marching in protest. It is about everything we do: holding discussions, working on committees, sending letters and e-mail messages, refusing to remain a silent witness in the face of injustice, and changing our behaviours and shopping habits. It takes energy to transform our lives and the lives of others. Imagine a world where everyone's energy went into compassion and acceptance instead of greed and indifference; into co-operation instead of competition; finding common ground instead of using our differences to justify violence. Many people hope that this future is possible. They take courage at the tremendous and bold efforts made by people every day to achieve a better world.

> " There is no need at all for different peoples, religions, and cultures to adapt to one another. It is enough if they accept each other as legitimate and equal partners. They need not even understand one another. It is enough if they respect and honour each other's differences … The salvation of the world cannot begin through the technology of world order. The only way to begin is by seeking a new spirit and a new ethos of co-existence. "
>
> *Vaclav Havel, president,*
> *Czech Republic*

Significant Trends Facing Humankind

- The global population has doubled from about three billion in 1950 to more than six billion. While population growth rates are slowing, the population is expected to grow into the twenty-second century.

- Half of the world's people now live in cities; small- and medium-sized cities are growing the fastest while **megacities** are growing more slowly. These trends are expected to continue.

- Most of the population and urban growth is occurring in developing countries.

- The global economy has grown seven times since 1950 and continues to grow, providing improvements in quality of life for many but increasing the size of humanity's ecological footprint.

- Globalization in all areas has resulted in increased interdependence among countries and regions.

- Technological change has been revolutionary.

- The gap between rich and poor is growing as many people do not share in the benefits of economic growth.

- Some form of democratic government has spread to many countries.

- The world's peoples are becoming increasingly mobile through improvements in transportation technology, the search for better economic opportunities, and as a result of conflict, resource scarcity, and environmental degradation.

- The global supply of food has increased dramatically, yet patterns of food distribution leave a billion people hungry and a billion others overnourished.

- Environmental pollution of water, air, and soil from the massive production of wastes and the use of fertilizers and **pesticides** in agriculture is having a negative impact on **biodiversity** and human health.

- Some diseases have been eradicated while others are growing and new health threats are emerging.

- Emissions of greenhouse gases have increased, resulting in warmer global temperatures and unpredictable and dramatic changes in weather and climate patterns.

- Citizens in communities of all sizes and locations have become increasingly concerned with quality of life issues.

FIGURE 20.1

The State of the Planet and its People

The world in the first decade of the twenty-first century is economically and technologically more developed and ecologically more damaged than anyone could have predicted halfway through the last century.

> **❝** One thing is virtually certain: the next half-century will not see a repeat of the trends of the one just past. Earth simply will not support it. The question is whether humanity will forge a healthier, sustainable future or risk the downward spiral that would be the result of failing to understand the ecological and economic threshold on which we now stand. **❞**
>
> *Christopher Flavin, president, Worldwatch Institute and Klaus Topfer.
> executive director, United Nations Environment Programme (UNEP)*

INTERACT

1. Create a chart that includes an economic, social, political, and environmental impact of Ghandi's actions to protect cottage textile and clothing industries in nineteenth-century India.
2. Create your own definition of leadership. Evaluate the leadership of Mahatma Ghandi based on your definition.
3. Explain how workers in cottage and traditional craft industries could be seen as participants in building sustainable communities.
4. Study Figure 20.1, **Significant Trends Facing Humankind**. Identify one global issue related to each trend. Rank these issues in order of the significance of the challenges they present to the community in which you live.
5. Develop a trend file. Collect articles from a variety of sources that discuss emerging trends that will have an impact on your future.
6. In the quote on this page, explain what is meant by "the ecological and economic threshold on which we now stand."

SUSTAINABILITY

Sustainability was defined in Chapter 4 as the ability of an ecosystem to maintain vital ecological processes and functions, biodiversity, and productivity indefinitely into the future. Simply put, it means making things last into the future without wearing them out or using them up. It means that people must live within the limits of Earth's **carrying capacity**—that excessive consumption by some may prevent others from the opportunity to improve their lives. Thinking, planning, and acting within the context of the ecosystems in which we live, as well as considering social and economic well-being, are essential if we are to build sustainable communities and effectively solve global issues.

Sustainable development is an ambiguous, controversial, and perhaps overworked concept. In theory, it means using Earth's resources and improving quality of life for all without degrading and using up those resources so as to compromise their availability to future generations. However, practical interpretations of the term vary widely. Some people, including some with traditional ecological knowledge, say it is incongruous and impossible to have the two words together; that continued growth and

FACT FILE

Fifty-five experts at the Organization for Economic Cooperation and Development (OECD) spent 12 meetings trying to develop a global standard definition of a sustainable rural community, without success.

development (improving quality of life) cannot be sustained in a finite world.

Some people focus on the sustainable part of the concept and believe that we must consider the health of Earth's life-support systems and its biodiversity as long-term priorities in our decision making and behaviours. Others focus more on the development side of the term and are in favour of continued growth and an increase in demands on the planet's resources. They believe that technology and substitution of one resource for another will enable us to stay within acceptable limits of growth. Despite these differing points of view, a transition to more sustainable ways of improving the quality of life for billions of people has begun in many places.

FIGURE 20.2 Development alternatives make good use of local skills and resources to provide sustainable livelihoods for women in rural communities such as these women in Caliling, Philippines.

Definitions of Sustainable Development

"That 'buzz-word' sustainable development is not a destination but a direction. In reality, we surpassed our own needs a long time ago. Now it's all about achieving balance. We will never know what it looks like, so we need to break it down into bite-size pieces. In a 100 000 piece puzzle of a sustainable future, sustainable development is perhaps only 100 pieces."

David McGuinty, executive director, National Roundtable on the Environment and Economy

"Sustainable development is development that meets the needs of the present without compromising the ability of future generations to meet their own needs."

World Commission on Environment and Development, "Our Common Future," The Brundtland Report

"Sustainable development involves the simultaneous pursuit of economic prosperity, environmental quality and social equity. Companies aiming for sustainability need to perform against the triple bottom line.

World Business Council on Sustainable Development

"To be sustainable, development must be economically viable, ecologically supportable and socially acceptable. If any one of these is not delivered, the others collapse. To be sustainable, development must provide fulfilling jobs and enrich lives and rehabilitate ecosystems. It must redistribute wealth and power, reduce material and energy use, foster civility, build cooperative social involvement and prepare for surprises. It must do all these things more or less at once, because they are all mutually interdependent. … It is not surprising, then, that some of the best development work is done by small, flexible groups with modest projects and the active involvement of local residents."

Robert Gibson, editor, Alternatives Journal, Faculty of Environmental Studies, University of Waterloo

"Sustainable development is a process of changing the character of a society. It is a set of attitudes and values we need to incorporate into our way of life. It involves fundamental changes in the way business is done, what is taught to our children, how we as individuals live and conduct our lives and how government and societies' public institutions address the essential problems affecting our life."

International Institute for Sustainable Development

FIGURE 20.3

Earth's Three Socio-ecological Classes

Overconsumers (1 billion)	Sustainers (3.5 billion)	Marginals (1.5 billion)
■ Huge individual ecological footprint	■ Travel by bicycle and public transport	■ Travel by foot or animals
■ Travel by car and air	■ Eat grains, vegetables, and some meat, much of it grown locally	■ Eat nutritionally inadequate diets
■ Eat high-fat, high-calorie, highly processed diet based on meats, much imported	■ Drink water and some tea and coffee	■ Drink contaminated water
■ Drink bottled water and soft drinks	■ Use few prepackaged goods	■ Use no packaged products
■ Have many material possessions, mostly disposables	■ Live in small, naturally ventilated residences often with extended families	■ Live in simple shelters
■ Planned obsolescence	■ Reuse and recycle	■ Reuse and recycle
■ Live in spacious, climate-controlled, single-family residences	■ Produce little waste	■ Produce negligible waste
■ Discard substantial amounts of waste	■ Have a few items of functional clothing	■ Have few items, secondhand clothing
■ Use large amounts of energy and water		
■ Maintain several image-conscious sets of clothing in wardrobe		

FIGURE 20.4 In which socio-ecological class do you fit?

adapted from The People-Centred development Forum, David C.

Seeking Solutions

Why Is It So Difficult to Solve Issues?
- There are so many issues. Which ones should be the top priorities?
- Complex issues encompass many variables and do not always have predictable outcomes.
- It is difficult to set objectives, work collaboratively, and determine best approaches with others who hold diverse **worldviews** and perspectives.
- Do we need more knowledge or do we already know plenty about why and how to take action?
- At all levels, not enough effective use is made of the knowledge that we do have.
- Many people and organizations act in their own immediate interest.
- Our institutions are not well set up to accommodate divergent views.
- Inertia exists, fostered by a belief that the world's political and economic institutions are beyond question or change.
- Government policies may subsidize negative things such as pollution or suppress energy efficiency by distorting prices.
- Human nature encompasses the paradox of both positive and negative qualities such as generosity and greed.
- The important democratic processes are not always followed even in democratic countries and elected governments often take a short-term approach rather than one that considers future generations.

Steps to Sustainability—New Ways of Thinking

- Shift values away from excessive material consumption.

- Bring agriculture into the city by transforming unused space and even rooftops into areas for plant-or food-producing gardens.

- Encourage government policy support for organic farming.

- Integrate conservation and biodiversity protection with agricultural production policies.

- Use technology to change industrial processes to reduce pollution.

- Increase public participation and citizen involvement in decision making.

- Use education to increase our ecological awareness, our understanding of how our actions are connected, and our ability to challenge our assumptions and to discard obsolete information.

- Raise public understanding of issues through the communications media.

- Establish a balance between carbon emissions and carbon fixation, groundwater withdrawal and recharge, trees cut and forests regenerated, human births and deaths.

- Change linear industrial systems to cyclical or closed loop systems that reuse and transform wastes.

- Increase taxes on advertising, consumption of luxury items, high resource use, and environmental degradation while reducing income tax.

- Provide tax incentives for conservation and ecologically friendly technology.

- Reform international economic institutions originally chartered by the United Nations (UN) such as the World Bank and International Monetary Fund (IMF).

- Corporations are now chartered by the public. Develop laws that would enable the revocation of corporate charters for corporations practicing illegal and harmful acts.

- Encourage 50% of the world's top leadership positions to be held by women.

- Create a world parliament where each country would be represented based on population (China would have 40 times more people in it than Canada).

- Improve efficiency and accessibility of public transport.

- Adjust the price of natural services performed by ecosystems and resources such as water and forests to reflect their true costs in the market.

FIGURE 20.5 "The thinking that brought us to these conditions is inadequate to remedy them." *Albert Einstein*

"Old answers are no longer viable for the new questions we are confronting; just as old paradigms and old solutions are insufficient to respond to the new and unanticipated problems. …"

John L. Brown and Cerylle A. Moffett,
The Hero's Journey: How Educators
Can Transform Schools and Improve Learning

"If women comprised half our leaders, human-centred, sustainable development and an improved global quality of life with an underpinning of ethical considerations would be realistic goals."

Rosina Wiltshire, Sustainable Development Program officer,
International Development Research Center

Despite the difficulty inherent in finding solutions to issues, there are some commonly accepted conclusions about planetary conditions:

- Changes in society, technology, and the environment are inevitable, rapid, and getting faster
- People are part of and dependent on nature
- Nature is much more complex than our current knowledge allows us to understand
- Earth has limits in a finite system
- There is no such place as "away" for getting rid of wastes
- There are a number of unique, legitimate, and complementary alternatives that can be used to address the issues
- All sectors need to be involved in searching for solutions, from local initiatives to international agreements

- Some new ways of thinking and better approaches to planning for the future and solving issues are needed
- Diverse and creative initiatives are already thriving and helping to solve issues at every level
- The cost of doing nothing is greater than the cost of addressing the issues

> " Contemplate being a politician or government bureaucrat charged with the responsibility of ensuring livelihoods and an acceptable quality of life for so many citizens while protecting the ecological heritage and environmental quality of the country—the challenges are extraordinarily daunting.
>
> *Bill Freedman, professor of biology, Dalhousie University*

> " "80% of the technology we will use in our daily lives in ten years hasn't been invented yet. "
>
> *Jim Harris, business consultant, author,*
> *The 100 Best Companies to Work for in Canada*

> " The world is in a race between education and catastrophe. "
>
> *H.G. Wells, author*

FIGURE 20.6 Urban regions, which contain about 40% of the population of China, provide a significant portion of urban residents' food needs. Farmers cultivate vegetables, orchards, and fisheries within cities; this is known as the China Model of mixed and intensive land use.

INTERACT

1. Brainstorm a list of completely unexpected but plausible events that could significantly change your life and the lives of members of your community.
2. Create a list of criteria that could be used to complete one of the following statements: Development is sustainable if it… A sustainable future environment implies that… A sustainable community is one that… .
3. Create a graphic organizer such as a Venn diagram that illustrates the interconnections among ecological, social, and economic sustainability.
4. Design a 10-point checklist of indicators that could be used to test the sustainability of the community in which you live. Submit your list to a community decision maker of your choice.
5. Refer to Figure 20.3, **Definitions of Sustainable Development**. Make a list of all of the criteria that must be met before development can be considered sustainable.

6. Identify five characteristics and qualities of human nature that tend to contribute to local and global problems. Which attributes of human nature do you believe may contribute to solutions for these problems?

7. Add one of your own ideas to the list of barriers that make solving issues difficult on page 488. Select any one of the ideas listed and develop a plan to reduce the effect of the barrier in solving an issue of your choice.

8. Refer to Figure 20.5, **Steps to Sustainability—New Ways of Thinking**. Develop an action plan to encourage the application of one of the new ways of thinking to improve the sustainability of the community in which you live.

VISIONS OF THE FUTURE

Expectations of the future are affected by current beliefs and knowledge and help to shape our actions. There is a growing awareness that human choices and actions taken today can shape what happens in the future, and that developing alternatives for the future can influence what might happen today. In short, proactively anticipating change is preferable to reacting to what has already happened. A number of questions need to be answered before taking action:

■ Where are we now?
■ Where do we want to be in the future?
■ How are we going to get there?
■ What decision made today will help create the best possible future?
■ What unexpected events might stand in the way?
■ What can we do?

Futures Analysis

Futures research and analysis is a multidisciplinary focus on the future and the wide range of powerful forces that play a role in determining it: natural systems and forces, social, political, and economic factors, scientific discovery, technological development and application, rates of consumption, and the capacity of our natural resource base. A number of methods and analytical techniques are used to:

> " The future is sufficiently interesting and complex, that by definition it is unknowable. "
>
> *Alan Turing, mathematician*

■ enhance the capability of people to anticipate, adapt, and deal effectively with change;
■ imagine what the future might be like;
■ explore, create, and test scenarios of possible futures;
■ study the implications of current and potential policies and actions;
■ prepare and plan for possible alternative futures.

FIGURE 20.7

The Right to Rave

by Eduardo Galeano

Let's set our sights beyond the abominations of today to divine another possible world:

the air shall be cleansed of all poisons except those born of human fears and human passions;

in the streets, cars shall be run over by dogs;

people shall not be driven by cars, or programmed by computers, or bought by supermarkets, or watched by televisions;

the TV set shall no longer be the most important member of the family and shall be treated like an iron or washing machine;

people shall work for a living instead of living for work;

written into law shall be the crime of stupidity, committed by those who live to have or to win, instead of living just to live like the bird sings without knowing it and the child who plays unaware that he or she is playing;

in no country shall young men who refuse to go to war go to jail, rather only those who make war;

economists shall not measure living standards by consumption levels or the quality of life by the quantity of things;

cooks shall not believe that lobsters love to be boiled alive;

historians shall not believe that countries love to be invaded;

politicians shall not believe that the poor love to eat promises;

earnestness shall no longer be a virtue, and no one shall be taken seriously who can't make fun of himself;

death and money shall lose their magical powers, and neither demise nor fortune shall make a virtuous gentleman of a rat;

no one shall be considered a hero or a fool for doing what he believes is right instead of what serves him best;

the world shall wage war not on the poor but rather on poverty, and the arms industry shall have no alternative but to declare bankruptcy;

food shall not be a commodity nor shall communications be a business, because food and communications are human rights;

no one shall die of hunger, because no one shall die of overeating;

street children shall not be treated like garbage, because there shall be no street children;

rich kids shall not be treated like gold, because there shall be no rich kids;

education shall not be the privilege of those who can pay;

the police shall not be the curse of those who cannot pay;

justice and liberty, Siamese twins condemned to live apart, shall meet again and be reunited, back to back;

a woman, a black woman, shall be president of Brazil, and another black woman shall be president of the United States; an Indian woman shall govern Guatemala and another Peru; in Argentina, the crazy women of the Plaza de Mayo shall be held up as examples of mental health because they refused to forget in a time of obligatory amnesia;

the Church, the holy mother, shall correct the typos on the tablets of Moses and the Sixth Commandment shall dictate the celebration of the body;

the Church shall also proclaim another commandment, the one God forgot: though shall love nature, to which you belong;

clothed with forests shall be the deserts of the world and of the soul;

the despairing shall be paired and the lost shall be found, for they are the ones who despaired and lost their way from so much lonely seeking;

we shall be compatriots and contemporaries of all who have a yearning for justice and beauty, no matter where they were born or when they lived, because the borders of geography and time will cease to exist;

perfection shall remain the boring privilege of the gods, while in our bungling, messy world every night shall be lived as if it were the last and every day as if it were the first.

Upside Down: A Primer for the Looking Glass World, Metropolitan Books (translation), Henry Holt and Company, New York, 2000, pp. 334–336

FIGURE 20.8 What is your vision of a preferable future?

Many exploratory methods involve data gathering techniques. For example, mathematical and computer models can simulate different conditions and many different assumptions can be made trying to determine which factors may cause which effects in the future. Other data gathering techniques include:

- remote sensing;
- computer mapping;
- geographic analysis (using Geographic Information Systems [GIS]);
- public opinion polling;
- contextual mapping (using diagrams such as future wheels);
- mathematical and computer models;
- simulation games;
- environmental scanning (for early warning signs of probable changes);
- statistical modelling (that focuses on measurable factors such as population density and mobility, crime or traffic congestion);
- creative and lateral thinking (to develop new ways of looking at current ideas and concepts).

Making Predictions

While no one can accurately predict important future events or their impact, geographers, scientists, and planners from many fields of study have used trends and statistical analysis as a basis for making predictions. Trends can be extrapolated into the future, based on current and anticipated events and changes.

Unanticipated events such as developments of new technology, natural hazards, or war and conflict can make this and other methods less reliable. Some predictions made in the past century have come true but many have been way off the mark. For example, predictions about the price of oil rising to more than $100 a barrel by 2000, made during the Organization of Petroleum Exporting Countries (OPEC) oil embargo of the early 1970s, did not come true. Nor did predictions made in the 1970s that, by 2000, Canadians would have a three- or four-day workweek and considerably more leisure time.

One way to spot emerging trends at the local or national level is to analyse stories in a variety of media sources and compare the number of

column inches or amount of broadcast time devoted to particular ideas or events. If we know statistics related to total population numbers, population growth rates, and the demographic structure of a place, we can fairly accurately extrapolate projected changes into the future. To avoid the uncertainties involved in forecasting and making predictions, some planners and analysts use **backcasting**. Backcasting is a method of determining what a preferable future would be like and what steps need to be taken or what policies are required to reach that desired future.

The **Delphi technique**, first used in the 1950s by the Rand Corporation, is still being used today. A group of experts from a wide range of backgrounds meet to answer questions on a particular problem or issue and consider alternative strategies for solutions. The goal for the experts, who possess a wide range of worldviews, data, and understanding, is to reach a consensus on an issue or its solution, by learning from each other.

Focus groups are similar to but less formal than Delphi groups. A panel of fewer than ten but more than six people, chosen from a variety of experiences and expertise, focuses on a key question related to an issue for about two hours. There is general discussion rather than a structured agenda. Throughout the discussion, people attempt to learn from what others say and new ideas often develop. The group usually meets again to keep driving at the issue until alternative solutions are accepted. Focus groups may conduct what is called a **force field analysis**, whereby participants focus on or rank the key driving or restraining factors that directly affect the central focus of the issue. They may plot factors along an axis according to their level of certainty.

Geographers, planners, and futurists use **scenarios** as a useful tool for imagining possible

> " It is vital that a community, comprised of individuals, have the skills collectively to identify its needs and the ability and willingness to collaborate effectively among its various actors/sectors to bring about the desired changes. "
>
> *"APEC Megacities Project: Issues in Developing Healthy Cities"*

Some Areas of Expertise for a Delphi Panel on Transportation Solutions

- regional economics
- population demographics
- land use location analysis and planning
- consumer behaviour analysis regarding shopping and residential preference
- leisure and recreation
- public opinion analysis
- real estate development
- public transit planning

- highway planning
- urban planning
- urban geography
- architecture
- municipal government regulation
- environmental assessment
- environmental quality
- cost–benefit analysis

FIGURE 20.9

futures. Scenarios are an attempt to understand combinations of events that could possibly occur. They can help to answer the key question: what are the critical factors we need to know about the future in order to be able to develop and take effective actions now?

Peter Schwartz, in *Using Scenarios to Navigate the Future*, describes the process of creating scenarios: "Despite its story-like qualities, scenario planning follows systematic and recognizable phases. The process is highly interactive, intense and imaginative. It begins by isolating the decision to be made, rigorously challenging the mental maps that shape one's perceptions and hunting and gathering information, often from unorthodox sources. The next steps are more analytical: identifying the driving forces (social, economic, political, and technological); pre-determined elements that are inevitable (like many demographic factors); and the critical uncertainties (i.e., what is unpredictable or a matter of choice such as public opinion). Scenarios are not about predicting the future; rather they are about perceiving the future in the present. ...The end result of scenario planning is not a more accurate picture of tomorrow but better decisions about the future."

Ten Elements of Good Urban Governance

1. Accountability (serves whole community; free of vested interests and corruption)
2. Transparency (provides reliable and understandable information, in a form people can make use of)
3. Participation (all men and women included in decision making)
4. Rule of law (fair, impartially enforced)
5. Predictability (of the processes of making and changing laws)
6. Responsiveness (serves all stakeholders and reacts to their concerns)
7. Consensus orientation (mediates different interests fairly)
8. Equity (all residents have equal opportunities to improve and maintain their well-being)
9. Effectiveness and efficiency
10. Strategic vision, a long-term perspective and a sense of what is needed to achieve it, that is shared by government and citizens

FIGURE 20.10 Good governance would go a long way toward achieving a sustainable future.

excerpts from "APEC Megacities Project: Issues in Developing Healthy Cities"

at <www.nstda.or.th/apec/docs/>

The "APEC Megacities Project: Issues in Developing Healthy Cities" developed alternative scenarios of megacities for 2020, using combinations of the important factors influencing change, including good governance and economic and political stability, as one creative approach to solving urban issues:

Scenario 3: Fat City

Fat City 2020 is bulging at the seams. Rich in people, in cultures and languages, it overflows its political and physical boundaries, defying definition or limitation. And still people come. While rural to urban migration has slowed to a trickle (and at weekends it goes the other way!), transnational migration to this world class city is still a feature, and one that provides a youthful balance to the aging of the 'indigenous' citizens.

Migrants are welcomed to Fat City for more than 'cheap labor.' Cultural diversity is seen as a major attraction for tourists; in Fat City, you can find better tortillas than in Tijuana, better 'pad thai' than in Thailand. More importantly, their variety of experiences and ways of doing things provide an influx of new ideas to those who are willing to listen.

Another key element is the way Fat City is run. The old central administration had no hope of keeping up with the dramatic doubling of the population. By 2010, the official figures went from under 8 million to 16 million

people, in only 20 years, but most people reckoned there were a few more million on top of that.

By luck, or by necessity, a new system of substantially autonomous community 'nodes' grew up, each committed, through local action, to making life better for their community, but recognizing the need for cooperation with other nodes. They raise their own revenue and receive central government funding for their achievement against national targets of employment and environmental management. Fat City isn't a mega-city at all; it's a concentrated network of connected cities, with only a minimal (but important) overall planning system.

There is still a ceremonial mayor of Fat City, who enjoys opening the big infrastructure projects and travelling the world to market the city to potential investors…. He explains that the city supports a healthy and educated population, and provides partnering funding for many basic infrastructure projects. He also describes the rebate scheme for investors that promote social and environmental good…. Under these conditions, both the knowledge and the cultural industries boomed. Fat City quickly became known as the home of the 5th generation Internet companies….

Entrepreneurs remember the disastrous consequences of the extreme flood/drought cycles of '06–'07. Who could concentrate on their work or even get to it, when the subway was flooded, and schools

and offices had to close whenever there wasn't even water to flush the toilets. Only the bottled water manufacturers did well out of that situation. With drug resistant cholera decimating the poorest and most marginal communities, even the most committed advocates of 'laissez-faire' economics felt that such instability and extremes required coordinated intervention… that didn't come easy. But as the city showed… a crisis can be the spur to turn things around. It went from a plague ridden rubbish dump to the cleanest city in India in only 2 years….

The response to crisis showed in practise that planning and regulatory systems could be simplified immensely, and in just 4 years, Fat City transformed itself from a corrupt and convoluted bureaucracy, to a rational and open administration…. [as] out of desperation communities mobilized to solve their own problems. Residents associations, trade unions, religious and social centers, local institutions like schools, hospitals and firms, sent representatives to regular neighbourhood meetings to decide what to do, and how to organize the means of survival…. Local democracy and participation are key features of the city. Communities remember with pride and confidence, their ability to take control of the direst situation and expect and demand a political system that responds to their needs. This is reflected in local elections, where turnout exceeds 75%…. For Fat City, the good times are here.

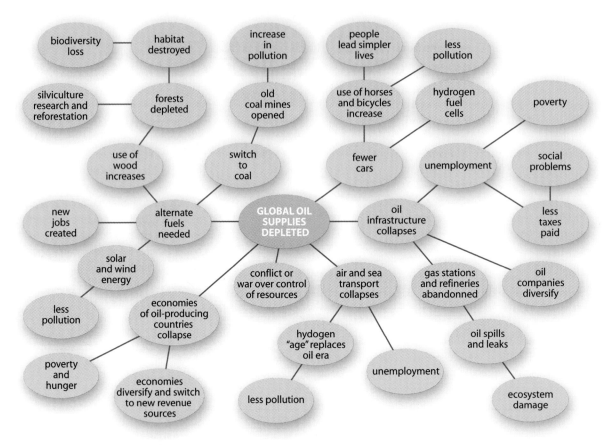

FIGURE 20.11 The future wheel technique follows the possible impacts on various aspects of life and the implications for the future of "what if?" events over time. What if there was a severe shortage of oil as reserves run out?

INTERACT

1. Identify the forces that collectively work to determine our future.
2. Critically analyse the cartoon in Figure 20.7.
3. Identify some of the methods used to conduct a) futures research and b) futures analysis. Conduct further research on one analytical method and evaluate its potential for planning for the future.
4. Refer to the news clip on page 495 and answer the following questions:
   a) Describe the new structure of Fat City.
   b) Outline the events that triggered major changes in the city and identify those changes.
   c) Using Figure 20.10, **Ten Elements of Good Urban Governance**, identify the characteristics of governance that enabled Fat City to improve quality of life for inhabitants.
5. Make a list of 10 general categories of factors that are important to consider when developing scenarios of the future.
6. Consider a "what if" hypothetical situation such as: What if cars were banned from the city centre? Or, what if remote sensing reveals vast oil reserves in Antarctica? Draw a future wheel diagram to connect the situation to predicted effects. On your diagram, circle positive effects in green and negative effects in red.
7. Explain why it is difficult to make accurate predictions relating to human use of Earth and its resources, and why some predictions are more accurate than others.

SHAPING THE FUTURE

As the rate of change accelerates and interactions among human and natural systems become more complex, planning for a sustainable future has become a formidable challenge. However, the trend toward looking for opportunities to create a sustainable future is catching on at individual, local, regional, national, and global levels. Progress is limited in some places and flourishing in others, where people and organizations are making a difference by finding solutions to some of the incredible issues of concern. Individuals as well as governments and institutions are responsible for finding solutions. Individual actions can and do make a difference. Collectively, they must be combined with policies and actions at the community and government level.

> " Never doubt that a small group of citizens can make a difference. Indeed, it is the only thing that ever has. "
>
> *Margaret Mead, anthropologist*

The Individual

While it is not reasonable to expect one person to resolve complex issues such as conflict in the Middle East, the spread of arms and land mines, or global climate change, you can be a force for constructive change. Some people believe that activism is confrontational and extreme, but activism can take a wide range of forms and methods—from the media stunts and civil disobedience of radical activism to promoting public education and wise consumer and lifestyle choices. The link between all forms of activism is the promotion of values, attitudes, and actions that encourage a **paradigm shift** in mainstream society. Public pressure and initiative can and does work to encourage decision makers to address the issues.

No individual lives in a vacuum. We are all connected to the natural world, our community, country, and planet. Individual actions taken and personal choices made can have a ripple effect on people and environments in other places around the world. Silence in the face of injustice or environmental degradation may make one complicit in their continuation. Each small step that an individual takes to reduce his or her ecological footprint and negative impact on others is accepting responsibility for and promoting a healthier, more sustainable planet for all. Individuals can become well-informed and inform others, lead by example, support or work with a non-governmental organization (NGO), connect with the natural environment of your own **bioregion** as well as other places, and reduce unnecessary consumption.

> " The 5 Rs are respect, rethink, reduce, reuse, recycle. Begin by respecting that all of life thrives or dies by our choices. When we truly respect life, rethinking our choices becomes automatic. We discover that we don't need to fill the void with stuff because the greatest things in life aren't things at all and so reducing consumption is easy. Then you look at what you already have and find ways to give objects a life that continues. The very last thing to do is recycle. "
>
> *Julia Butterfly Hill*

FIGURE 20.12 Celebrities often use their influence for social and environmental causes. U2 singer Bono presented a petition to world leaders at the UN Millennium Summit in 2000, calling for the cancellation of the poorest countries' debts. The petition was signed by more than 21.2 million people from 155 countries. The petition broke the world record for the most signatures ever collected on any issue. In 2002, Bono met with the world's financial leaders at the World Economic Forum in New York to urge governments and corporations to fund global health initiatives.

excerpts from "Butterfly Triumphs"

by Nicholas Wilson
The Monitor
<www.monitor.net/monitor/9912a/
butterflydown.html>
December 22, 1999

After living nearly two years and eight days on a small tarp-covered platform nestled in the upper boughs of an ancient redwood named Luna, Julia "Butterfly" Hill's bare feet touched the ground December 18 as she triumphantly ended her world record protest. Her tree sit ended only after reaching an agreement with Pacific Lumber/Maxxam Corporation, the landowner, to permanently protect the tree and a

FIGURE 20.13

200-ft. radius buffer zone from logging. Hill said that the agreement fulfilled her vow not to touch the ground until she had done all she could to preserve the ancient tree whose life had already spanned a millennium….

Julia and her ground crew linked arms in a circle around the 15-ft diameter trunk of the old tree. Gazing up at Luna from the ground for the first time in daylight, Julia exclaimed, "She's even more beautiful than I thought" But her voice choked with emotion as she went on, "I understand all of us are governed by different values. I understand that to some people I'm just a dirty tree-hugging hippie. But I can't imagine being able to take a chainsaw to something like this…. I think before anyone could be allowed to cut down something like this they should be mandated to live in it for two years."

Asked what was her goal, she answered: "When I first climbed up there I wanted to do something for the forest. When I came out here in the summer of '97 I entered the ancient redwoods for the first time, and I had a life-altering experience. There's no way to be in the presence of these ancient beings and not have a new understanding of who we are as people walking on this Earth. And a few weeks later I found out that they were being destroyed."…

"My hope today is that Pacific Lumber/Maxxam Corporation recognizes that we have to do things differently; that we can't keep clearcutting, we can't keep dumping herbicide and diesel fuel. We can't keep cutting on steep hillsides that slide away and destroy people's homes; that there's something greater than a profit, and that's life. We have to begin recognizing the intrinsic and vital value of life that no amount of money can ever replace. And to me that's what this tree-sit is all about.

My hope is that Pacific Lumber, in agreeing to this protection, has seen that no matter what our differences we can find our common ground, and that we as people can learn to work together to find solutions. There's a lot of conflict, and there's a lot of problems; there's a lot of anger, and frustration and sadness in our world. And all of those energies try every day to make us give up and lose hope. But I've learned the lesson of not letting go of hope. I've had to let go of everything else in my life, but hope and love are the two things I've refused to let go of."

Julia Butterfly Hill and her supporters agreed to pay Pacific Lumber $50,000. The company refused her request that the money go to benefit its employees but did donate it to a forestry research program at a nearby university. They dropped their condition that restricted her free speech to advocate for protest and criticize the company.

Proceeds from her books, *The Legacy of Luna*, published in 2000, and *One Makes the Difference: Inspiring Actions That Change Our World*, published in 2002, go to her non-profit Circle of Life Foundation."

COUNTERPOINT " Julia Hill broke the law. She should have been taken down two years ago and arrested. Trees are a crop. Get over it, Butterfly. "

letter to the editor of the Press Democrat,
The Monitor, *December 22, 1999*

" Every day, from the moment we roll out of bed, each of us is faced with thousands of choices about how to live. What do we spend money on? What do we choose to eat? How do we get from place to place? What is the quality of our connections with others? How do we use the earth's resources? What do we do with our time? … Be conscious of those choices and take action… you, yes you, make the difference in the world. One does make the difference. You are the one. "

Circle of Life Foundation

SUSTAINABLE COMMUNITIES

Each individual is a member of some community. The term "community" can mean more than just the place in which one lives. Groups such as NGOs, which were created to fill the gaps left in society by governments and business, make up communities that, collectively, are sometimes referred to as civil society. One of the strongest arguments held by groups in the anti-globalization movement is against the power that is held over local communities from somewhere else in the world.

What would a safe, healthy, and sustainable community look like? Sustainable communities can be developed when the links between the economy, the environment, and society are taken into account. Communities working on projects to improve sustainability should consider many indicators other than the traditional ones of per capita income and housing starts. New indicators include health conditions, traffic patterns and congestion, employment, voter turnout, energy use, air and water quality, biodiversity, housing, green open space, and management of wastes. Communities in all parts of the world are beginning to identify

FIGURE 20.14 Widespread urbanization in Latin America has led to unplanned growth, pollution, slums, and poor delivery of basic services. In an effort to create an alternative transportation system, instead of spending money on new highways, the city of Bogota, Colombia, restricted car use, closing major roads once a week, and invested in wide sidewalks, trees, bicycle paths, and libraries. The benefits have spilled over into many other areas, making Bogota a much safer city. The UN, impressed with the results, organized a conference for mayors of other cities to learn from Bogota's success.

innovative ways to improve conditions for people and ecosystems and to put pressure on their governments and industry to adopt policies that favour sustainability.

It is at the community level where some of the most effective initiatives are working to solve local manifestations of global issues. Large issues can often be best addressed in small ways and the people of a community usually know best about what their future depends on. A simple project designed to empower women at the village level in a developing country may make more of a positive difference than a large-scale foreign aid initiative.

Communities often use different regional planning approaches to guide growth and change and to help shape land use policies and laws related to air and water quality, traffic issues, housing, and livelihoods in the context of ecosystem health. New processes are being developed and used to reconcile competing interests when planning for community projects. Successful projects bring together representatives from all the stakeholder groups, acknowledge that they all have a stake in developing and sustaining the health and wealth of the community, and identify what the stakeholders want the community to be like in the future.

> " To save things everywhere, you have to start by saving them somewhere.
>
> Susan George, author, "
> Life After Debt

FIGURE 20.15 Young people from community and school groups, working with the Environmental Youth Alliance in Vancouver, have successfully harvested food from their beautiful garden planted on abandoned industrial lands. The garden favours native food plants and organic methods such as companion planting, composting, and natural fertilizers. Food donations are made to organizations in the community.

Restoration Ecology

It is not possible to completely restore damaged ecosystems to their original condition, particularly if plant and animal species have been lost, because natural ecosystems take decades or even centuries to develop. Nevertheless, scientists such as geographers, planners, and ecologists and many citizens are actively involved in efforts to reclaim and remediate land damaged by human activities. The goal is often to develop stable, self-maintaining regional vegetation as a habitat for endangered species.

FACT FILE

There are about 25 000 **brownfields** in core urban areas in Canada and 500 000 in the U.S.

FIGURE 20.16 Remediation efforts include adding lime to lakes to reduce acidity caused by acid rain or planting tolerant grass species on old **tailings** ponds as shown in this nickel mining region of Sudbury, Ontario.

FIGURE 20.17 Brownfields are former industrial sites that contain a high degree of environmental contamination. Some communities are beginning to reclaim them for other land uses. In 2001, the Ontario government amended its Brownfields legislation, setting environmental standards and upholding the **polluter pays principle**.

FIGURE 20.18 A Leaside school garden project in Toronto, Ontario.

CASE STUDY

West Muddy Creek—A Green Community for the Future

The Willamette River basin drains an area of 31 460 km² in the western part of the state of Oregon and is home to about 70% of the state's population. A small part of the **watershed** known as the West Muddy Creek bioregion, with a population of over 3000, was at risk of environmental degradation in the 1980s and early 1990s. Public concerns focused on widespread water shortages for irrigation, logging practices, declining salmon fisheries, and water quality. A community project, funded by the U.S. Environmental Protection Agency's Green Communities Program, involved members of the community in a high degree of meaningful citizen participation and decision making for the future.

Measurable criteria using the best available data for several main indicators were chosen as a focus for the project: population projections, biodiversity, water quality, and the management of land use practices. The main goals of the project were to:

- improve understanding of the relationship between human use of the land and its effects on ecological resources;
- use this improved understanding to enhance the ability to predict the effects of people's activities on water quality and biodiversity;
- envision a plausible range of future landscape conditions;
- incorporate divergent views of different stakeholders in the community;
- test options for appropriate policies and development plans that would shape the future.

GEOGRAPHIC METHODS

Geographic Information Systems (GIS) analysis used overlapping layers of altitude, slope, hydrology, soil classes, transportation, land cover, and land ownership to provide detailed and accurate maps. Collection of data and creation of the maps in the GIS process helped to build common understandings among residents about the place in which they lived and the impact of human activities on ecosystems and natural resources.

Possible future scenarios for 2025 were developed related to residential, agricultural, forestry, and preservation components of the watershed's landscapes. The four scenarios represented were high development, moderate development, moderate conservation, and high conservation.

FIGURE 20.19

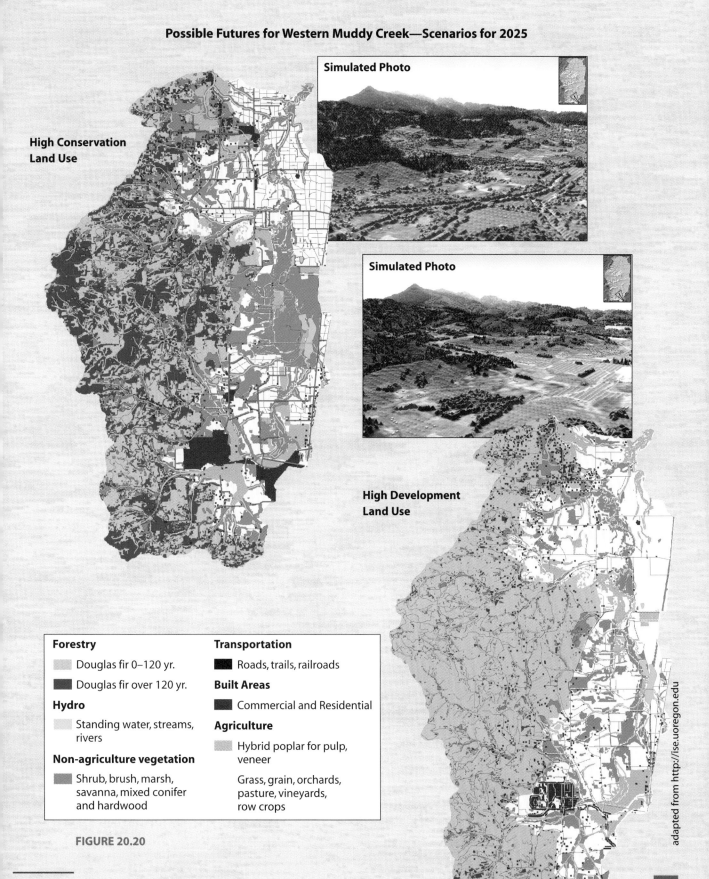

Possible Futures for Western Muddy Creek—Scenarios for 2025

High Conservation
Land Use

Simulated Photo

Simulated Photo

High Development
Land Use

Forestry
- Douglas fir 0–120 yr.
- Douglas fir over 120 yr.

Hydro
- Standing water, streams, rivers

Non-agriculture vegetation
- Shrub, brush, marsh, savanna, mixed conifer and hardwood

Transportation
- Roads, trails, railroads

Built Areas
- Commercial and Residential

Agriculture
- Hybrid poplar for pulp, veneer
- Grass, grain, orchards, pasture, vineyards, row crops

FIGURE 20.20

adapted from http://ise.uoregon.edu

1. Using the maps and simulated photos in Figure 20.20, **Possible Futures for Western Muddy Creek—Scenarios for 2025**, identify the predicted effects of community conservation efforts in creating a more sustainable community for Western Muddy Creek.

2. Explain the benefits of using GIS in the Western Muddy Creek Community Futures Project.

3. Explain how public participation in the development process can help to build a sustainable community in the Western Muddy creek bioregion.

4. Identify a practical way in which a component of the Western Muddy Creek study could be applied in your own community.

THE GREENING OF INDUSTRY

> Canadian citizens are now forbidden by provisions in the Criminal Code from certain kinds of behaviour that would be illegal at home. Surely it's time we had laws for companies in their operations abroad, should they be involved in the denial of fundamental rights of citizens in developing nations.
>
> *Ed Broadbent and Avie Bennett, co-chairs of Canadian Democracy and Corporate Accountability Commission*

Corporations are among the largest and most powerful global institutions. There is a growing demand from consumers, employees, communities, suppliers, investors, and activist organizations to demand they be more socially and environmentally responsible. Developing social and environmental corporate responsibility means doing the right thing for all stakeholders, including respect for human rights, labour standards, and protection for the environment.

Corporate responsibility includes supporting new ways of thinking and planning and new questions: How much profit do we really need? How can we return some of that profit by doing beneficial things for people, the community, and the natural environment? Is it possible to change to a different type of product or process that is less toxic, less energy intensive, has a **closed loop system**, considers the contributions of workers, and so on? How much will it cost society if we do not act?

FACT FILE

The 1999 Millennium poll by Environics surveyed 25 000 citizens in 23 countries on corporate social responsibility. One finding was that 90% of the people surveyed want business and industry to focus on concerns other than just profitability.

Many leaders in the business and industrial sectors have begun to respond with new solutions as they recognize the need to respect people, communities, and the environment. Some leaders meet or even exceed ethical standards, laws, and public expectations. New businesses and processes have developed related to recycling, environmentally benign building materials, renewable energy, organic products, green or ethical investment funds, and certified forest products from methods more sustainable than clear-cutting. A growing number of **empirical studies** have shown that responsible corporate action, including reducing waste and preventing pollution, improves economic performance and does not reduce shareholder returns.

> Bluewash: allowing some of the largest, wealthiest corporations to wrap themselves in the UN's blue flag without requiring them to do anything new.
>
> *New York Times at <www.corpwatch.org>*

In 2000, The Global Compact, which set out a new relationship between the UN and corporations, was officially started by Kofi Annan, UN secretary-general. Some NGOs, fearing that the influence of corporations within the UN may lead to privatization and widespread **greenwash**, have called for a corporate-free UN.

More than 110 companies from around the world have joined the Global Reporting Initiative (GRI), launched in collaboration with the UNEP at UN headquarters in April 2002. GRI goals include corporate transparency and disclosure so that the public is aware of a corporation's policies and actions, as well as providing standards for making sustainability reporting as common as financial reporting.

> " The most important contribution of the socially responsible business movement has little to do with recycling, nuts from the rainforest, or employing the homeless. Their gift to us is that they are leading by trying to do something, to risk, take a chance, make a change—any change. They are not waiting for 'the solution', but are acting without guarantees of success… This is what all of us must do. "
>
> *Paul Hawken, economist, author*

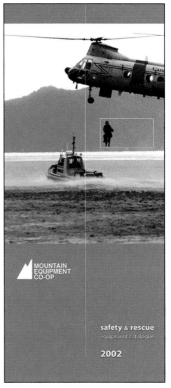

FIGURE 20.21
Many consumers are attracted to carefully cultivated brands that claim socially and environmentally responsible behaviour.

CASE STUDY

Interface Incorporated

Interface Incorporated is the world's largest carpet manufacturing company and is on *Fortune* magazine's list of the "100 Best Places to Work." The industry was known as petroleum-intensive with its use of fossil fuel byproducts as a raw material, a high user of energy, and as a producer of large amounts of unhealthy toxic waste. As consumers want new carpets, the old ones end up in landfill sites, continuing to 'offgas' polluting substances. In 1994, the CEO, Ray Anderson, experienced an emotional response to a book by Paul Hawken, *The Ecology of Commerce*, which argues that industrial leaders are the only leaders powerful enough to change the industrial system and its processes that are destroying the planet. Anderson challenged his 7500 employees with a seven-point plan to initiate ideas for changing company practices so that the company would not only sustain but also restore the environment.

By 2001, Interface had made more than 400 changes to its policies and actions. Carpets are now completely recyclable and the company has

> " If we get it right, our company and our supply chain will never have to take another drop of oil… our goal is not to lose a single molecule of carpeting material. "
>
> *Ray Anderson, CEO Interface Inc.*

introduced a program to rent carpets to customers, and to pick up old carpets for recycling. To offset transportation pollution, many trees have been planted. The CEO is working with chemical and agribusiness transnationals, such as Dow Chemical and Cargill, to find ways to develop carpets from renewable materials such as corn. Renewable energy, including solar energy, powers manufacturing plants.

Interface Incorporated's Seven-Point Plan

1. Eliminate waste with zero waste as a goal

2. Benign emissions, eliminating toxic impact on ecosystems

3. Renewable and efficient energy

4. A closed loop waste system of cyclical material flows

5. Resource efficient transportation

6. Sensitivity Hookup—with all suppliers, employers, and other links moving together in the same direction

7. Redesign commerce to focus on service and value instead of delivery of material and design market incentives that encourage sustainability

adapted from Interface, Inc. at <www.ifsia.com/getting_there/seven.html>

FIGURE 20.22

The National Sphere

Governments face the challenge of finding ways for so many voices and organizations to participate in planning for the future. Countries are required to develop their own policies and strategies to integrate the goals of UN conventions into their decision making. However, countries are not forced to sign or ratify conventions and legal enforcement is not always feasible. Legislation within a country is expensive and difficult to enforce, especially if the community fails to place a value on social justice and the environment. Public opinion and international pressure can encourage governments to design and implement more policies that give people and the environment a much higher priority as well as fewer policies and subsidies that encourage unsustainable industrial and agricultural development, increased energy and water use, and depletion of forests and biodiversity.

66 The challenge now is for each country to put all the pieces of an eco-economy together. 99

Lester Brown, author,
Eco-Economy: Building an
Economy for the Earth

66 A transformation is taking place in one of the most basic aspects of our daily lives—the way we use energy. From Japanese 'hybrid' automobiles to the explosive growth of the Danish wind-turbine industry, nations with vision are shifting to cleaner, more efficient energy systems… as they do, they reduce atmospheric pollution and the risks of climate change, while increasing employment and enhancing their competitive edge in the global economy. 99

David Suzuki, scientist, environmentalist

Governments can create and enforce laws and regulations that protect people and ecosystems from the negative effects of the actions of corporations and results of new technology. The difficulty lies in satisfying the interests and views of many stakeholders. For example, Canada's federal government has made several attempts to pass a law to protect endangered species.

Canada is in an enviable position. It is a wealthy country with vast resources and very few people. Canada has 25% of the world's wetlands, 25% of the world's original forests, the only remaining semi-pristine tundra ecosystem,

"Rebranding Canada in the Global Economy"

by Dr. David Wheeler, Erivan K. Haub Professor of Business and Sustainability, Schulich School of Business, York University, Toronto
for *"Commentary"* on CBC radio

"… Faced with a U.S. dominated continental economy that seems so random in its effects on Canadian industry how should we respond? Are we as ordinary citizens left with just two choices: to acquiesce or protest? Or is there another way?

Like citizens around much of the developed and developing world, Canadians are ambivalent about globalization. But that hasn't stopped the echoes of conflict being felt here. The anti-globalization bandwagon that started in Seattle and found its first martyr in Genoa… rolled through Quebec City earlier in the year, precipitating a serious reappraisal of Canadian values. To many Canadians, the apparent suppression of dissent through physical means and the images of paramilitary policing was more than a little inconsistent with Canada's self-image as peacemaker and protector of democratic values. …

I believe there is another way. … What I see, as a teacher and commentator is an enormous capacity here in Canada to leverage traditional Canadian values of fair play, social justice and environmental concern and to turn those to positive effect for the Canadian economy and *the global commons*.

Many leading Canadian companies are already showing the way—re-inventing their way into new, more sustainable product lines and markets—preparing themselves to be real winners in the second half of the 21st century, not just the next five or ten years. These companies come from all sectors: oil and gas, chemicals, steel, mining, engineering, automotive, forestry and even banking.

In my view, Canada and its most visionary businesses have a huge opportunity to turn Canada's traditional leadership on social and environmental issues into a global 'win–win'.

Imagine if you will, that whenever anyone around the world saw the red maple leaf, or 'made in Canada' on a product or service, they knew that it stood for social justice and environmental responsibility. Imagine if 'Brand Canada', was a bit like 'Intel Inside' in the world of computers: hardwired for sustainability. Imagine if Canadian firms were rewarded in local and international markets based on their reputation for quality and service.

I believe that the world is waiting for such a lead. In a survey conducted by Toronto-based market researchers

Environics in 23 countries around the world, 56 per cent of respondents said their impressions of companies were formed primarily by such factors as labour practices, business ethics and environmental impact. This compared with only 34 per cent citing 'business fundamentals' such as financial performance and company size.

Just imagine the impact on firms in the U.S. and elsewhere as Canadian companies started to gain larger market shares in environmentally and socially sensitive countries and through government purchasing programs. For example, in the European Union [EU]. Imagine the impact on politicians as economic success in global markets began to depend more and more on environmental and social reputation. The signs are there: we are already seeing the growth of anti-U.S. sentiment in Europe because of the Bush Administration stance on climate change.

In a matter of four or five years, if Canada adopted an active strategy of green branding, I believe that Canada could gain economically and the world would gain environmentally and socially. At present the world does not appreciate the leadership already being shown by Canadian firms in these areas. And of course, traditional Canadian modesty and self-deprecation often get in the way. But in my view, Canada has an opportunity *and an obligation* to show what is possible and to commit to a compelling model of environmentally and socially responsible business that will really impact how global markets work in the long term. … Canadian firms are perfectly placed to lead—and benefit from—the sustainability revolution of the next 20 years."

Critical Analysis

1. Define the terms "visionary," "green branding," "global commons," "self-deprecating," and "global win–win," as used in the article.
2. What are the credentials of Dr. Wheeler? What is his bias? Briefly describe his worldview.
3. Draw a sketch or graphic organizer that explains how Canada is connected to the global economy.
4. What does the author consider to be traditional Canadian values?
5. Identify specific steps that would need to be taken at all levels: individual, community, business and industry, and national and global for Canada to successfully "rebrand" itself in the global economy.
6. How could the ideas for solutions be considered creative thinking or "thinking outside the box"?
7. Write a 300-word scenario for Canada in 2010 if Dr. Wheeler's ideas are realized by 2005.
8. Evaluate the contribution that Dr. Wheeler has made by speaking out in public with ideas for solutions.

and the largest populations of large mammals such as caribou and grizzly bear. We are, therefore, in a position to act as responsible global stewards for the rest of the planet—a challenge for the future. Another major challenge facing Canadians is to find a way to foster economic growth while protecting the natural environment and enhancing the quality of Canadian life.

Appropriate Technology

Many people believe that technology can solve the world's problems. The negative feedback of technology is often unknown or not adequately considered when inventions are first developed. For example, when chlorofluorocarbons (CFCs)

> **We must stop being so economically defensive and start being more politically courageous.**
>
> *Kofi Annan,*
> *UN secretary-general, 2001*

were first developed in the 1930s, their inventor presented them as completely friendly and non-toxic by inhaling a sample, then exhaling them to extinguish a candle flame. He and Du Pont, the company that manufactured them, had no idea that they would subsequently become persistent and widespread in the atmosphere or of the impact they would have on depleting the ozone layer. Technology can be a powerful force for making a better future, but it should be developed with consideration for its environmental, social, and cultural implications.

The Global Sphere

In its search for solutions, the UN has made a large contribution to enhancing awareness of the need for action at all levels and promoting fairer and more equitable access to the world's resources. Some people believe that some amazing progress has been made since the 1992 Earth Summit in Rio,

> **FACT FILE**
>
> As of 2002, there were 411 biosphere reserves in 94 countries.

while others feel that not only are we not keeping up, the problems are getting worse. It all

depends on one's perspective. For example, the International Convention on Biological Diversity, the Convention on International Trade in Endangered Species, and the International Whaling Commission have helped to sustain wild species, although success is difficult to assess.

Programs such as United Nations Educational, Scientific, and Cultural Organization (UNESCO)'s Managing Our Biosphere focus on new approaches for the sustainable protection of biological diversity by promoting scientific research and linking it with traditional knowledge about resources to improve the relationship between people and their environment. Globally, the successes of the program are evident in the network of Biosphere Reserves. These terrestrial and coastal ecosystems are regions where solutions to issues combine sustainable use and protection of biodiversity.

> **Parks are not enough for the future in Canada—they are becoming islands of extinction.**
>
> *David McGuinty, executive director,*
> *national Roundtable of the*
> *Environment and the Economy*

Through the United Nations University, the Millennium Project is a massive undertaking. More than 1000 futurists, planners, scientists, scholars, and decision makers from international agencies, governments, NGOs, universities, and corporations from more than 50 countries met in a

> **FACT FILE**
>
> The World Summit on Sustainable Development (WSSD) held in Johannesburg, South Africa, in September 2002 was the twenty-fifth major UN conference in the last three decades to deal with sustainable development issues.

think tank setting to contribute expertise and study a number of important challenges and issues, including:
- measuring and promoting sustainable development;
- globalization;
- peace and conflict;
- rich–poor gap;
- human health, UN reform;
- environmental security;
- environmental issues;
- science and technology issues.

A variety of futures research and analysis techniques were used, including the development of scenarios for 2050 and very long-range scenarios to 3000 on various themes such as technology and human development.

" Four powerful sets of ideas have engaged the UN system over the 50+ years of its existence: peace, independence, development and human rights... and environmental perspectives were brought to bear on development debates over 30 years ago. "

George Francis, professor, Environmental and Resource Studies, University of Waterloo, Canada

FIGURE 20.23 The Niagara Escarpment Biosphere Reserve.

UN University Millennium Project

"Thousands of 100-mile long robotically managed closed-environment agricultural tubes interspersed with photovoltaic strips across the Sahel, produced sufficient food for Africa and exports to Asia. Surplus energy from the strips is currently exported by microwave to earth orbit and relayed worldwide via the satellite energy grid. ...

"Ecological and energy taxes were initiated to create disincentives for inappropriate energy use and tax incentives for less polluting alternative energy sources. ...

"Corporate-NGO partnerships developed model sustainable communities in different settings around the world that were designed around reduced consumerism, sustainability, community values, traffic free, sylvan spaces. ..."

Global Normative Scenario for 2050

WEB LINKS

- Millennium Project: <www.geocities.com/~acunu/>
- The David Suzuki Foundation: <www.davidsuzuki.org>
- Man and the Biosphere: <www.unesco.org/mab/wnbr.htm>
- Global Reporting Initiative on corporate social responsibility: <www.globalreporting.org/AboutGRI.hrm>
- Sustainable Measures: <www.sustainablemeasures.com/Sustainability/index.html>
- Sustainable Communities Network: <www.sustainable.org>
- Planetizen, Urban planning solutions: <www.planetizen.com>
- Commuter Connections: <www.carpool.com>
- Business for Social Responsibility: <www.bsr.org>
- Urban farming: <www.cityfarmer.org>
- Grist Magazine, Earth Day Network: <www.gristmagazine.com>
- Gram Vikas Rural Development Alternatives, India: <www.gramvikas.org/>
- Learning for a Sustainable Future skills activities: <www.schoolnet.ca/learning>

RELATED ISSUES

- Ecotourism
- Alternative eco-communities
- Solving transportation issues
- Corporate responsibility
- Investment in green or ethical funds
- The role of technology in a sustainable future

ANALYSE, APPLY, AND INTERACT

1. Gather current information about an issue of interest to you. Identify one of the trends that is related to the issue and in a 500-word essay, extrapolate two alternative futures related to the trend.

2. Brainstorm a list of values and attitudes that today's youth will need to have in order to become responsible citizens in the twenty-first century.

3. Suggest three important national priorities for Canada for the next 10 years. For any one of the priorities, outline a role that could be played by individuals, institutions, organizations, and different levels of government.

4. Create a labelled map, locating Canada's biosphere reserves.
   a) Conduct research on one of the biosphere reserves and explain the reasons for its selection.
   b) Evaluate the biosphere reserve project as a solution to global biodiversity loss.
   c) In what way could the biosphere reserve concept be applied to a biodiversity issue in your own community?

5. Use a futures method of your choice to predict global demographic changes for the future and assess their economic, environmental, and social implications.

6. Conduct research to produce a case study of a specific community in a developing country that explains how local participation in the development process has helped to build a sustainable community.

7. For any one of the trends related to consumption of Earth's resources, evaluate its sustainability if the trend continues unchanged. Outline steps that need to be taken at all levels to stabilize or reverse the trend.

8. For one significant issue facing either Canada or your community, identify several barriers to solving the issue and several opportunities that could be tapped for finding a solution.

9. Evaluate the sustainability of the trend of increasing consumption in western society.

10. Evaluate the role played by an NGO of your choice in promoting sustainable development.

Data Appendix—Demographic Variables

Country	Population (millions)	Area (km²)	Births per 1000	Deaths per 1000	Projected Pop. 2050 (millions)	Pop. Change 2001-2050 (%)	Fertility Rate (births per woman)	Pop. Under Age 15 (%)	Pop. Over Age 65 (%)	Infant Mortality (per 1000 births)	Life Expectancy at Birth (years)	Urban Pop. (%)
Afghanistan	26.8	652 090	43	19	67.2	151	6.0	43	3	154	45	22
Albania	3.4	28 750	17	5	5.2	51	2.2	15	6	12	72	46
Algeria	31	2 381 740	25	6	51.2	66	3.1	39	4	55	69	49
Angola	12.3	1 246 700	50	25	29.6	141	6.9	48	3	198	38	32
Argentina	37.5	2 766 889	19	8	54.5	45	2.6	28	10	19	73	90
Armenia	3.8	29 800	9	6	3.8	0	1.1	24	9	16	73	67
Australia	19.4	7 741 220	13	7	25.0	29	1.7	20	12	6	79	85
Austria	8.1	83 859	10	9	8.2	1	1.3	17	15	5	78	65
Azerbaijan	8.1	86 600	15	6	11.5	42	2.0	32	6	13	72	51
Bahamas	0.3	13 880	21	5	0.5	46	2.4	31	6	18	72	84
Bangladesh	133.5	144 000	28	8	208.6	56	3.3	40	3	66	59	21
Barbados	0.3	430	14	9	0.3	3	1.6	23	9	14	73	38
Belarus	10.0	207 600	9	14	8.5	-15	1.3	19	13	9	68	70
Belgium	10.3	30 519	11	10	10.0	-3	1.6	18	17	5	78	97
Belize	0.3	22 696	25	6	0.6	132	3.2	41	5	22	72	49
Benin	6.6	112 620	45	15	18.1	174	6.3	48	2	94	50	39
Bhutan	0.9	47 000	40	9	2.0	127	5.6	42	4	71	66	15
Bolivia	8.5	1 098 580	32	9	17.1	100	4.2	40	4	63	62	63
Bosnia-Herzegovina	3.4	51 130	12	8	3.4	-1	1.6	20	8	11	68	40
Botswana	1.6	581 730	31	20	1.2	-26	3.9	41	4	60	41	49
Brazil	171.8	8 511 969	22	7	247.2	44	2.4	30	5	35	68	81
Bulgaria	8.1	110 910	9	14	5.3	-35	1.2	16	16	15	72	68
Burkina Faso	12.3	274 000	47	17	34.3	180	6.8	48	3	105	47	15
Burundi	6.2	27 830	42	17	16.1	158	6.5	48	3	75	47	8
Cambodia	13.1	181 040	28	11	18.1	38	4.0	43	3	95	56	16
Cameroon	15.8	475 440	39	12	34.7	119	5.2	43	3	77	55	48
Canada	31.0	9 970 609	11	8	36.6	18	1.4	19	13	5.5	79	78
Cape Verde	0.4	4 030	37	7	0.4	-6	4.0	43	7	31	68	53
Central African Republic	3.6	622 980	38	18	6.4	78	5.1	44	4	98	45	39
Chad	8.7	1 284 000	49	16	33.3	282	6.6	48	3	103	50	21
Chile	15.4	756 950	18	5	19.3	26	2.3	28	7	10	75	86
China	1273.3	9 559 867	15	6	1369.0	8	1.8	23	7	31	71	36
China, Hong Kong	6.9	1 092	8	5	7.4	8	1.0	17	11	3	80	100
Colombia	43.1	1 138 910	24	6	71.5	66	2.6	32	5	21	71	71
Comoros	0.6	2 230	47	12	1.8	208	6.8	46	3	91	56	29
Congo Dem. Republic	53.6	2 344 860	47	16	181.9	239	7.0	48	3	106	48	29
Congo Republic	3.1	342 000	46	16	10.7	245	6.3	43	3	105	50	41
Costa Rica	3.7	51 100	22	4	5.6	51	2.6	32	5	12	77	45
Cote d'Ivoire	16.4	322 460	36	16	35.7	118	5.2	42	2	112	46	46
Croatia	4.7	56 540	10	11	3.9	-16	1.4	20	12	8	74	54
Cuba	11.3	110 860	14	7	11.0	-3	1.6	22	10	7	75	75
Cyprus	0.9	9 250	13	8	1.0	10	1.8	23	10	7	77	66
Czech Republic	10.3	78 860	9	11	9.4	-9	1.1	17	14	4	75	77
Denmark	5.4	43 090	13	11	6.2	16	1.7	18	15	4	76	72
Dominica	0.1	750	16	8	0.1	14	1.8	33	9	16	73	71
Dominican Republic	8.6	48 730	26	5	14.9	74	3.1	35	5	47	69	61
East Timor	0.8	14 870	33	16	1.4	48	4.4	43	5	135	48	8
Ecuador	12.9	283 560	28	6	24.7	92	3.3	34	4	30	71	62
Egypt	69.8	1 001 450	28	7	114.7	64	3.5	36	4	44	66	43
El Salvador	6.4	21 040	30	7	12.4	93	3.5	36	5	30	70	58
Equatorial Guinea	0.5	28 050	45	14	1.4	193	5.9	44	4	108	50	37
Eritrea	4.3	117 600	43	13	13.3	209	6.0	43	3	80	55	16
Estonia	1.4	45 100	9	13	0.9	-36	1.3	18	14	10	71	69
Ethiopia	65.4	1 104 300	44	15	172.7	164	5.9	44	3	97	52	15
Fiji	0.8	18 270	25	6	0.9	9	3.3	33	4	20	67	46
Finland	5.2	338 130	11	10	4.8	-8	1.7	18	15	4	77	60
France	59.2	551 500	13	9	65.1	10	1.9	19	16	4	79	74
Gabon	1.2	267 670	32	16	1.8	49	4.3	40	6	57	52	73
Gambia	1.4	11 300	43	14	4.2	195	5.9	46	3	82	52	37
Georgia	5.5	69 700	9	9	4.2	-23	1.2	23	13	18	73	56
Germany	82.2	356 733	9	10	70.3	-14	1.3	16	16	4	78	86

Country	Population (millions)	Area (km²)	Births per 1000	Deaths per 1000	Projected Pop. 2050 (millions)	Pop. Change 2001-2050 (%)	Fertility Rate (births per woman)	Pop. Under Age 15 (%)	Pop. Over Age 65 (%)	Infant Mortality (per 1000 births)	Life Expectancy at Birth (years)	Urban Pop. (%)
Ghana	19.9	238 540	32	10	32.0	61	4.3	43	3	56	58	37
Greece	10.9	131 990	10	10	9.7	-11	1.3	15	17	6	78	59
Grenada	0.1	340	21	8	0.1	-2	2.4	38	4	14	65	34
Guatemala	13.0	108 890	36	7	31.5	143	4.8	44	3	50	66	39
Guinea	7.6	245 860	41	19	18.1	138	5.5	44	3	98	45	26
Guinea-Bissau	1.2	36 125	42	20	3.3	167	5.8	44	3	131	45	22
Guyana	0.7	214 970	21	8	0.5	-34	2.5	31	5	40	65	36
Haiti	7.0	27 750	33	15	11.9	70	4.7	43	4	80	49	35
Honduras	6.7	112 090	33	6	12.2	81	4.4	43	4	42	66	46
Hungary	10.0	93 030	10	14	8.0	-19	1.3	17	15	9	71	64
Iceland	0.3	103 000	15	7	0.3	18	2.0	23	12	2	79	93
India	1033.0	3 287 588	26	9	1628.0	58	3.2	36	4	70	61	28
Indonesia	206.1	1 889 700	23	6	304.8	48	2.7	31	4	46	67	39
Iran	66.1	1 648 000	18	6	100.2	52	2.6	36	5	30	70	64
Iraq	23.6	438 320	37	10	53.6	127	5.3	42	3	92	59	68
Ireland	3.8	70 280	14	9	4.5	18	1.9	22	11	5	77	58
Israel	6.4	21 060	22	6	10.6	64	3.0	29	10	5	78	91
Italy	57.8	301 270	9	10	46.0	-20	1.3	14	18	5	79	90
Jamaica	2.6	10 990	20	5	3.9	48	2.4	31	7	24	71	50
Japan	127.1	377 800	9	8	100.5	-21	1.3	15	17	3	81	78
Jordan	5.2	97 740	27	5	11.8	128	3.6	40	5	31	70	79
Kazakhstan	14.8	2 717 299	15	10	10.0	-5	1.8	28	7	20	66	56
Kenya	29.8	580 370	34	14	37.4	26	4.4	44	3	74	48	20
Korea, North	22.0	120 540	21	7	26.4	20	2.3	26	6	88	70	59
Korea, South	48.8	99 020	14	5	51.1	5	1.5	22	7	8	74	79
Kuwait	2.3	17 820	20	2	6.4	181	4.2	26	1	9	73	100
Kyrgyzstan	5.0	198 500	20	7	7.5	52	2.4	35	5	23	69	35
Laos	5.4	236 800	39	14	9.2	72	5.4	44	4	104	52	17
Latvia	2.4	64 500	8	14	1.8	-25	1.2	18	15	11	71	69
Lebanon	4.3	10 400	23	7	5.8	35	2.5	29	7	33	71	88
Lesotho	2.2	30 355	33	13	2.8	31	4.3	40	5	84	53	16
Liberia	3.2	111 369	49	17	10.0	210	6.6	43	3	139	50	45
Libya	5.2	1 759 540	28	4	10.8	106	3.9	37	4	33	75	86
Lithuania	3.7	65 200	9	11	3.1	-16	1.3	20	13	9	73	68
Luxembourg	0.4	2 586	13	9	0.6	33	1.7	19	14	5	78	88
Macedonia	2.0	25 710	14	8	2.1	11	1.9	23	10	15	73	60
Madagascar	16.4	587 040	43	13	47.0	186	5.8	45	3	96	54	22
Malawi	10.5	118 480	46	23	22.2	110	6.4	47	3	104	39	20
Malaysia	22.7	329 750	25	4	43.9	94	3.2	33	4	8	73	57
Mali	11.0	1 240 190	50	20	36.4	230	7.0	47	3	123	46	26
Mauritania	2.7	1 025 520	43	15	8.5	208	6.0	44	2	106	51	54
Mauritius	1.2	2 040	17	7	1.5	24	2.0	26	6	16	71	43
Mexico	99.6	1 958 200	24	5	149.7	50	2.8	34	5	25	75	74
Micronesia	0.1	702	31	6	0.2	108	4.6	44	4	34	66	27
Moldova	4.3	33 700	11	11	4.2	0	1.4	24	9	18	68	46
Monaco	0.03	1	20	17	0.04	15	—	15	23	4	—	100
Mongolia	2.4	1 566 500	20	7	3.9	61	2.2	34	4	37	63	57
Morocco	29.2	446 550	26	6	48.4	66	3.4	33	5	53	69	55
Mozambique	19.4	801 590	43	22	22.9	18	5.6	44	3	135	72	28
Myanmar/Burma	47.8	676 580	28	12	68.5	43	3.3	33	5	92	56	27
Namibia	1.8	824 290	36	17	2.5	37	5.0	43	4	68	46	27
Nepal	23.5	140 800	35	11	49.5	111	4.8	41	3	79	57	11
Netherlands	16.0	40 844	13	9	18.0	12	1.7	19	14	5	78	62
Netherlands Antilles	0.2	800	17	6	0.3	13	2.1	26	7	13	74	70
New Zealand	3.9	268 680	15	7	5.0	29	2.0	23	12	6	77	77
Nicaragua	5.2	130 000	35	6	11.6	122	4.3	43	3	40	68	57
Niger	10.4	1 267 000	53	24	28.5	175	7.5	50	2	123	41	17
Nigeria	126.6	923 770	41	14	303.6	140	5.8	44	3	75	52	36
Norway	4.5	323 900	13	10	5.2	15	1.8	20	15	4	78	74
Oman	2.4	212 460	39	4	7.6	218	6.1	41	2	18	71	72
Pakistan	145.0	796 100	39	11	345.4	138	5.6	42	4	91	60	33

Country	Population (millions)	Area (km²)	Births per 1000	Deaths per 1000	Projected Pop. 2050 (millions)	Pop. Change 2001-2050 (%)	Fertility Rate (births per woman)	Pop. Under Age 15 (%)	Pop. Over Age 65 (%)	Infant Mortality (per 1000 births)	Life Expectancy at Birth (years)	Urban Pop. (%)
Palestine	3.3	6 220	42	5	11.2	239	5.9	47	4	26	72	—
Panama	2.9	75 520	25	5	4.3	48	2.6	31	6	17	74	56
Papua New Guinea	5.0	462 840	34	11	11.3	124	4.8	39	4	69	56	15
Paraguay	5.7	406 750	32	5	14.4	155	4.3	40	5	33	73	52
Peru	26.1	1 285 220	24	6	42.3	62	2.9	34	5	41	69	72
Philippines	77.2	300 000	29	6	129.2	67	3.5	37	4	31	67	47
Poland	38.6	323 250	10	10	33.9	-12	1.4	20	12	9	73	62
Portugal	10.0	92 390	12	11	8.2	-18	1.5	17	15	6	76	48
Puerto Rico	3.9	8 900	15	7	4.2	8	1.9	25	10	10	75	71
Qatar	0.6	11 000	31	4	0.9	45	3.9	27	2	10	72	91
Romania	22.4	238 390	10	12	19.3	-14	1.3	18	13	19	71	55
Russia	144.4	17 075 400	9	15	127.7	-12	1.2	18	13	16	66	73
Rwanda	7.3	26 340	39	21	8.9	22	5.8	44	3	107	39	5
Sahara (Western)	0.3	266 000	46	17	0.6	128	6.8	—	—	140	—	95
Saint Lucia	0.2	620	19	6	0.2	50	2.1	33	6	14	71	30
Samoa	0.2	2 840	30	6	0.2	0	4.5	32	6	25	68	33
Sao Tome and Principe	0.2	960	43	8	0.5	204	6.2	48	4	54	65	44
Saudi Arabia	21.1	2 149 690	35	6	60.3	185	5.7	43	2	21	67	83
Senegal	9.7	196 720	41	13	22.7	135	5.7	44	3	68	52	43
Seychelles	0.1	450	18	7	0.1	15	2.0	29	8	10	70	63
Sierra Leone	5.4	71 740	47	20	15.7	189	6.3	45	3	153	45	37
Singapore	4.1	620	14	5	10.4	151	1.6	17	6	2	78	100
Slovakia	5.4	49 010	10	10	4.7	-13	1.3	20	11	9	73	57
Slovenia	2.0	20 250	9	10	1.7	-15	1.2	16	14	4	76	50
Solomon Island	0.5	28 900	41	7	1.5	217	5.7	43	3	25	67	13
Somalia	7.5	637 660	48	19	25.5	240	7.3	44	3	126	46	28
South Africa	43.6	1 221 037	25	14	32.5	-25	2.9	34	5	57	53	54
Spain	39.8	504 780	10	9	30.8	-23	1.2	15	17	5	76	64
Sri Lanka	19.5	65 610	18	6	23.2	19	2.1	28	6	17	72	22
St. Kitts-Nevis	0.04	360	20	11	0.1	33	2.5	31	9	24	69	43
St. Vincent & Grenadines	0.1	390	19	7	0.1	-19	2.2	32	6	20	72	44
Sudan	31.8	2 505 810	34	11	63.5	100	4.9	43	3	74	56	27
Suriname	0.4	163 270	26	7	0.4	-11	3.0	33	5	27	71	69
Swaziland	1.1	17 360	41	20	2.0	84	5.9	46	3	109	40	25
Sweden	8.9	449 960	10	11	9.5	7	1.5	19	17	3	80	84
Switzerland	7.2	41 284	11	9	7.4	2	1.5	18	15	5	80	68
Syria	17.1	185 180	31	6	35.2	106	4.1	41	3	24	70	50
Taiwan	22.5	36 000	14	6	25.2	12	1.7	21	9	6	75	77
Tajikistan	6.2	143 100	19	4	8.7	40	2.4	42	4	23	68	27
Tanzania	36.2	883 749	41	13	88.3	144	5.6	45	3	99	53	22
Thailand	62.4	513 120	14	6	71.9	15	1.8	24	6	22	72	30
Togo	5.2	56 790	40	11	9.7	89	5.8	47	2	80	55	31
Tonga	0.1	750	27	6	0.2	86	4.2	41	4	19	71	32
Trinidad and Tobago	1.3	5 130	14	8	1.4	6	1.7	26	7	17	71	72
Tunisia	9.7	163 610	19	6	14.2	46	2.3	31	6	28	72	62
Turkey	66.3	774 815	22	7	97.2	47	2.5	30	6	35	69	66
Turkmenistan	5.5	488 100	19	5	7.0	29	2.2	38	4	25	67	44
Tuvalu	0.01	30	30	9	0.02	82	3.1	34	3	56	67	18
Uganda	24.0	241 038	48	19	84.1	251	6.9	51	2	97	42	15
Ukraine	49.1	603 700	8	15	38.4	-22	1.1	18	14	15	68	68
United Arab Emirates	3.3	83 600	18	4	5.1	54	3.5	26	1	19	74	84
United Kingdom	60.0	244 100	12	11	64.2	7	1.7	19	16	6	77	90
United States	284.5	9 363 520	15	9	413.5	45	2.1	21	13	7	77	75
Uruguay	3.4	177 410	16	10	4.5	34	2.3	24	13	17	74	92
Uzbekistan	25.1	447 400	22	5	40.4	61	2.7	38	4	20	70	38
Vanuatu	0.2	12 190	36	6	0.3	51	4.6	42	3	45	65	21
Venezuela	24.6	912 050	25	5	40.2	63	2.9	34	5	20	73	87
Vietnam	78.7	331 690	20	6	117.2	49	2.3	33	6	37	66	24
Yemen	18.0	527 970	44	11	71.1	295	7.2	48	3	75	59	26
Yugoslavia Fed. Rep.	10.7	102 170	12	11	10.2	-4	1.6	21	13	13	72	52
Zambia	9.8	752 618	45	22	20.3	108	6.1	45	2	95	37	38
Zimbabwe	11.4	390 760	29	20	9.3	-18	4.0	44	3	65	40	32

Data Appendix—Economic Variables

Country	GNI PPP per Capita (US$)	Av. Annual Growth in GDP 1990-2000 (%)	Av. Annual Growth in Manufacturing 1990-2000 (%)	Av. Annual Growth in Services 1990-2000 (%)	CO_2 Emissions per Capita (tonnes)	Arable Land (% of land area)	Military Expenditures 1999 (US$ millions)	Aid per Capita (US$)
Afghanistan	—	—	—	—	0.01	21.1	—	142
Albania	3 240	3.3	-6.6	3.8	0.14	21.1	30	3
Algeria	4 840	1.9	-2.1	1.9	0.97	3.2	1 680	31
Angola	1 100	1.3	-0.4	-2.0	0.13	2.4	720	2
Argentina	11 940	4.3	2.8	4.5	1.03	9.1	3 080	55
Armenia	2 360	-1.9	-4.3	6.7	0.26	17.6	100	—
Australia	23 850	4.1	2.4	4.5	2.14	6.2	8 240	20
Austria	24 600	2.1	2.3	1.8	1.38	16.9	1 790	—
Azerbaijan	2 450	-6.3	-21.1	2.3	1.65	19.9	270	9
Bahamas	15 500	—	—	—	0.05	1.0	20	—
Bangladesh	1 530	4.8	7.2	4.5	1.60	62.2	500	2
Barbados	14 010	—	—	—	0.05	37.0	10	—
Belarus	6 880	-1.6	-0.8	-0.5	1.60	29.8	300	34
Belgium	25 710	2.0	—	1.8	2.73	24.8	3 710	—
Belize	4 750	4.7	—	—	0.47	2.0	10	70
Benin	920	—	5.8	4.1	0.03	15.4	30	274
Bhutan	1 260	—	—	—	0.05	2.0	—	38
Bolivia	2 300	4.0	—	4.3	0.41	1.8	120	1
Bosnia-Herzegovina	—	—	—	—	0.35	9.8	210	32
Botswana	6 540	4.7	4.1	6.5	0.66	0.6	200	36
Brazil	6 840	2.9	2.1	3.0	0.49	6.3	13 620	11
Bulgaria	5 070	-2.1	—	-1.3	1.55	38.9	300	24
Burkina Faso	960	4.9	7.0	4.6	0.02	12.4	50	30
Burundi	570	-2.6	-8.0	-2.0	0.01	30.0	60	—
Cambodia	1 350	4.8	8.2	6.9	0.02	21.0	90	33
Cameroon	1 490	1.7	1.4	0.2	0.03	12.8	190	25
Canada	25 440	2.9	3.8	2.6	4.17	4.9	7 620	5
Cape Verde	4 450	—	—	—	0.08	11.0	—	2
Central African Republic	1 150	2.0	—	-0.5	0.02	3.1	40	1
Chad	840	2.2	—	1.2	0	2.8	40	7
Chile	8 410	6.8	—	5.6	1.11	2.6	1 510	—
China	3 550	10.3	4.6	9.0	0.68	13.3	33 450	3
China, Hong Kong	22 570	4.0	13.4	—	1.47	5.1	—	49
Colombia	5 580	3.0	-2.3	4.3	0.45	2.0	1 790	3
Comoros	1 430	—	—	—	0.03	35.0	—	29
Congo Dem. Republic	—	-5.1	-13.4	-15.2	0.01	3.0	—	11
Congo Republic	540	-0.4	-2.8	-3.9	0.18	0.5	80	—
Costa Rica	7 880	5.3	6.7	4.7	0.36	4.4	—	—
Cote d'Ivoire	1 540	3.5	3.8	2.6	0.25	9.3	—	31
Croatia	7 260	0.6	-3.3	0.9	1.21	26.1	850	11
Cuba	4.2	6.3	2.5	0.62	33.10	300.0	5	—
Cyprus	19 080	—	—	—	2.10	12.0	280	—
Czech Republic	12 840	0.9	—	—	3.14	40.1	1 110	31
Denmark	25 600	2.5	—	—	2.76	54.1	2 830	—
Dominica	5 040	—	—	—	0.32	9.0	—	—
Dominican Republic	5 210	6.0	—	5.9	0.67	22.1	120	23
East Timor	—	—	—	—	—	4.9	—	—
Ecuador	2 820	1.8	2.1	1.3	0.59	5.7	350	12
Egypt	3 460	4.6	6.3	4.5	0.44	2.8	2 160	25
El Salvador	4 260	4.7	5.3	5.4	0.27	27.0	80	30
Equatorial Guinea	3 910	—	—	—	0.16	5.0	—	—
Eritrea	1 040	3.9	—	—	—	4.9	250	37
Estonia	8 190	-0.5	2.5	1.8	3.25	26.5	50	57
Ethiopia	620	4.7	6.6	7.1	0.01	10.0	700	10
Fiji	4 780	2.8	—	—	0.25	10.0	30	—
Finland	22 600	2.8	5.8	2.3	2.82	7.1	1 810	—
France	23 020	1.7	2.1	1.9	1.72	33.4	40 380	—
Gabon	5 280	2.8	0.6	3.9	0.66	1.3	120	39
Gambia	1 550	3.1	1.0	4.3	0.05	19.5	10	26
Georgia	2 540	-13.0	3.2	15.6	0.08	11.4	90	44
Germany	23 520	1.5	-0.4	2.4	2.75	33.1	34 490	—
Ghana	1 850	4.3	-3.3	5.7	0.06	15.8	60	32

Country	GNI PPP per Capita (US$)	Av. Annual Growth in GDP 1990-2000 (%)	Av. Annual Growth in Manufacturing 1990-2000 (%)	Av. Annual Growth in Services 1990-2000 (%)	CO$_2$ Emissions per Capita (tonnes)	Arable Land (% of land area)	Military Expenditures 1999 (US$ millions)	Aid per Capita (US$)
Greece	15 800	2.1	—	2.4	2.19	21.4	5 290	—
Grenada	6 330	—	—	—	0.54	15.0	—	—
Guatemala	3 630	4.1	2.8	4.7	0.24	12.5	10	26
Guinea	1 870	4.3	4.1	3.6	0.05	3.6	50	33
Guinea-Bissau	630	1.2	-2.0	-0.6	0.05	10.7	10	44
Guyana	3 330	—	—	—	0.53	2.0	10	—
Haiti	—	-0.6	-10.8	0.2	—	—	34	129
Honduras	2 270	3.2	3.9	3.8	0.23	13.1	40	25
Hungary	11 050	1.5	7.9	1.4	1.58	52.1	580	—
Iceland	27 210	—	—	—	2.06	0	—	—
India	2 230	6.0	7.0	8.0	0.29	54.4	9 520	1
Indonesia	2 660	4.2	6.7	4.0	0.31	9.9	2 060	11
Iran	5 520	3.5	4.7	9.2	1.20	10.7	3 500	3
Iraq	—	—	—	1.0	11.90	1300.0	—	—
Ireland	22 460	7.3	—	—	2.84	15.6	850	—
Israel	18 070	5.1	—	—	2.75	17.0	7 940	148
Italy	22 000	1.6	1.5	1.7	1.97	29.1	18 290	—
Jamaica	3 390	0.5	-1.9	1.1	1.18	16.1	30	9
Japan	25 170	1.3	0.5	2.5	2.45	12.4	42 480	—
Jordan	3 880	5.0	5.4	5.0	0.60	2.7	500	91
Kazakhstan	4 790	-4.1	—	2.8	2.06	11.1	300	11
Kenya	—	2.1	3.3	0.1	7.00	260.0	10	9
Korea, North	—	—	—	—	2.64	14.1	4 000	—
Korea, South	15 530	5.7	7.5	5.7	2.15	17.2	13 290	1
Kuwait	—	3.2	—	7.4	0.30	2230.0	4	—
Kyrgyzstan	2 420	-4.1	-14.3	-6.4	0.38	7.1	60	55
Laos	1 430	6.5	11.7	6.5	0.02	3.8	60	59
Latvia	6 220	-3.4	-7.8	2.5	0.88	29.8	40	40
Lebanon	—	6.0	-4.3	4.1	1.40	17.6	400	45
Lesotho	2 350	4.1	6.6	4.4	—	10.7	30	15
Liberia	—	—	—	0	2.00	—	—	—
Libya	—	—	—	1.9	1.00	1200.0	1	—
Lithuania	6 490	-3.1	-8.5	-0.3	1.15	45.3	110	35
Luxembourg	41 230	—	—	—	4.97	24.0	140	—
Macedonia	4 590	-0.8	-4.4	0.7	1.69	23.1	100	135
Madagascar	790	2.0	0.6	2.5	0.02	4.4	40	24
Malawi	570	3.8	-2.1	3.4	0.02	19.9	30	41
Malaysia	7 640	7.0	9.8	7.2	1.54	5.5	2 100	6
Mali	740	3.8	3.0	2.9	0.01	3.8	50	33
Mauritania	1 550	4.2	-0.5	4.9	0.31	0.5	30	84
Mauritius	8 950	5.3	5.6	6.4	0.41	49.3	20	35
Mexico	8 070	3.1	4.4	2.9	1.07	13.0	1 570	0
Micronesia	—	—	—	—	—	—	—	—
Moldova	2 100	-9.7	—	1.9	0.60	55.0	20	24
Monaco	—	—	—	—	—	—	—	—
Mongolia	1 610	1.0	—	—	0.82	0.8	10	92
Morocco	3 320	2.3	2.7	2.8	0.32	19.0	1 300	24
Mozambique	810	6.4	17.6	1.7	0.02	4.0	70	7
Myanmar/Burma	—	6.6	7.0	6.8	0.05	14.5	1 450	2
Namibia	5 580	4.1	2.7	4.6	0	1.0	120	104
Nepal	1 280	4.9	9.2	6.2	0.04	20.3	50	15
Netherlands	24 410	2.8	—	3.1	2.85	27.0	6 480	—
Netherlands Antilles	1 470	—	—	—	9.93	10.0	—	—
New Zealand	17 630	3.0	—	3.7	2.16	5.8	660	0
Nicaragua	2 060	3.5	1.8	1.8	0.19	20.2	30	137
Niger	740	2.4	2.6	2.6	0.03	3.9	30	18
Nigeria	770	2.4	1.2	1.9	0.20	31.0	1 000	1
Norway	28 140	3.6	2.3	2.9	2.07	2.9	3 080	—
Oman	—	5.9	—	3.4	0.10	1330.0	17	—
Pakistan	1 860	3.7	3.5	4.4	0.18	27.5	2 820	5
Palistine	—	2.8	3.6	2.8	—	27.0	—	180

Country	GNI PPP per Capita (US$)	Av. Annual Growth in GDP 1990-2000 (%)	Av. Annual Growth in Manufacturing 1990-2000 (%)	Av. Annual Growth in Services 1990-2000 (%)	CO$_2$ Emissions per Capita (tonnes)	Arable Land (% of land area)	Military Expenditures 1999 (US$ millions)	Aid per Capita (US$)
Panama	5 450	4.1	2.8	4.0	0.57	6.7	—	5
Papua New Guinea	2 260	4.0	5.6	3.0	0.14	0.1	40	46
Paraguay	4 380	2.2	0.7	1.6	0.24	5.5	90	14
Peru	4 480	4.7	3.8	4.0	0.31	2.9	700	18
Philippines	3 990	3.3	3.0	4.1	0.28	18.6	800	9
Poland	8 390	4.6	—	4.1	2.27	46.2	3 060	25
Portugal	15 860	2.7	—	2.3	1.51	21.5	2 210	—
Puerto Rico	—	3.1	—	—	1.26	3.9	—	—
Qatar	—	—	—	22.1	1.00	1100.0	—	—
Romania	5 970	-0.7	-2.8	-0.5	1.12	40.5	550	17
Russia	6 990	-4.8	—	-1.0	2.66	7.4	18 010	12
Rwanda	880	-0.2	6.6	-0.1	0.02	35.1	110	45
Sahara (Western)	—	—	—	—	0.21	0	—	—
Saint Lucia	5 200	—	—	—	0.36	8.0	—	—
Samoa	4 070	—	—	—	0.21	19.0	—	—
Sao Tome and Principe	—	—	—	—	0.15	2.0	—	1
Saudi Arabia	11 050	1.5	2.7	2.0	3.83	1.7	13 530	58
Senegal	1 400	3.6	4.0	3.8	0.10	11.6	70	—
Seychelles	—	—	—	—	0.71	2.0	10	15
Sierra Leone	440	-4.3	5.0	-10.3	0.03	6.8	—	0
Singapore	22 640	7.8	7.1	7.8	6.46	1.6	3 960	59
Slovakia	10 430	2.1	4.1	6.5	1.93	30.4	290	16
Slovenia	16 050	2.7	4.0	3.9	2.00	8.5	190	—
Solomon Island	2 050	—	—	—	0.10	1.0	—	—
Somalia	—	—	—	—	1.70	—	—	13
South Africa	8 710	2.0	1.2	2.6	2.38	12.1	1 780	13
Spain	17 850	2.5	—	2.7	1.70	27.4	7 530	—
Sri Lanka	3 230	5.3	8.1	6.0	0.12	13.6	570	13
St. Kitts-Nevis	10 400	—	—	—	0.71	22.0	—	—
St. Vincent & Grenadines	4 990	—	—	—	0.40	10.0	—	15
Sudan	—	4.0	6.3	0	7.00	9440.0	8	—
Suriname	3 780	—	—	3.5	1.41	0	20	20
Swaziland	4 380	3.3	3.0	1.7	0.11	9.8	20	30
Sweden	22 150	1.9	6.4	—	1.50	6.7	6 590	—
Switzerland	28 760	0.8	—	—	1.56	10.5	3 730	—
Syria	3 450	4.0	—	2.6	0.90	25.6	3 500	15
Taiwan	—	—	—	-0.4	24.00	0	—	—
Tajikistan	500	-10.4	-12.6	2.7	0.23	5.2	60	20
Tanzania	500	2.9	2.7	3.7	0.02	4.2	80	26
Thailand	5 950	4.2	6.4	0.4	0.87	28.8	2 800	0
Togo	1 380	2.3	2.9	0.3	0.05	40.4	30	4
Tonga	—	—	—	2.7	24.00	0	—	—
Trinidad and Tobago	7 690	3.0	5.9	5.3	4.76	14.6	80	27
Tunisia	5 700	4.7	5.5	3.7	0.65	18.3	350	1
Turkey	6 440	3.7	4.8	-5.8	0.86	31.4	8 410	—
Turkmenistan	3 340	-4.8	—	—	1.76	3.5	170	—
Tuvalu	—	—	—	—	—	—	—	—
Uganda	1 160	7.0	13.6	7.9	0.02	25.7	160	27
Ukraine	3 360	-9.3	-11.2	-1.1	1.90	56.4	1 260	1
United Arab Emirates	—	2.9	—	—	10.23	1.0	1 790	—
United Kingdom	22 220	2.5	—	3.2	2.51	24.6	28 420	—
United States	31 910	3.5	—	—	5.43	19.3	254 630	—
Uruguay	8 750	3.4	-0.1	4.6	0.49	7.2	250	7
Uzbekistan	2 230	-0.5	—	0.3	1.26	10.8	450	5
Vanuatu	2 880	1.6	0.9	0.4	0.09	2.0	—	—
Venezuela	5 420	1.6	—	—	1.82	3.0	870	2
Vietnam	1 860	7.9	4.4	7.7	0.15	17.7	480	18
Yemen	730	5.8	—	5.1	0.23	2.9	820	27
Yugoslavia Fed. Rep.	—	0.6	—	—	1.30	30.0	2 000	60
Zambia	720	0.5	1.2	2.6	0.05	7.1	40	63
Zimbabwe	2 690	2.5	0.4	3.1	0.34	8.3	300	21

Data Appendix—Quality of Life Variables

Country	Physicians per 100 000 people	Health Expenditures per Capita (US$)	Women as Percent of Parliament	Primary Pupil to Teacher Ratio	Newspapers per 1000 people	Pop. with Improved Drinking Water Sources, Urban (%)	Pop. with Improved Drinking Water Sources, Rural (%)	Consumption of Electric Power (kilowatt-hours per capita)	Paved Roads (% of total)
Afghanistan	—	—	—	—	5	19	11	—	—
Albania	129	116	—	18	36	—	—	851	30.0
Algeria	85	—	4	27	38	88	94	566	68.9
Angola	8	—	15	—	11	34	40	64	25.0
Argentina	268	1291	21	17	123	85	30	1 634	29.5
Armenia	316	—	3	19	23	—	—	1 141	100.0
Australia	240	1980	25	18	293	100	100	8 307	38.7
Austria	302	1978	25	12	296	100	100	6 051	100.0
Azerbaijan	360	—	10	20	27	—	—	1 631	92.3
Bahamas	152	658	20	22	99	98	86	—	—
Bangladesh	20	51	—	—	9	99	97	76	9.5
Barbados	125	938	—	—	200	100	100	—	—
Belarus	443	387	18	20	174	100	100	2 607	95.6
Belgium	395	2172	25	—	160	100	100	7 055	80.7
Belize	55	132	14	26	2	83	69	—	—
Benin	6	29	6	52	—	74	55	43	20.0
Bhutan	16	87	9	—	—	86	60	—	—
Bolivia	130	150	10	—	55	93	55	391	5.5
Bosnia-Herzegovina	—	—	5	—	152	—	—	—	—
Botswana	24	267	17	25	27	100	89	—	23.5
Brazil	127	453	6	23	40	95	54	1 743	9.3
Bulgaria	345	230	26	17	257	100	100	3 203	92.0
Burkina Faso	3	36	11	50	1	84	—	—	16.0
Burundi	—	21	14	50	3	96	—	—	—
Cambodia	30	90	9	46	2	53	25	—	7.5
Cameroon	7	—	6	—	7	82	42	181	12.5
Canada	229	2391	24	16	159	100	99	15 829	35.3
Cape Verde	17	119	11	—	—	64	89	—	—
Central African Republic	4	33	—	67	2	80	46	—	2.7
Chad	3	25	2	—	—	31	26	—	0.8
Chile	110	511	9	30	98	99	66	2 011	13.8
China	162	—	22	24	—	94	66	714	—
China, Hong Kong	—	—	—	—	—	—	—	4 959	100.0
Colombia	116	553	12	25	46	98	73	885	12.0
Comoros	7	—	—	52	—	98	95	—	—
Congo Dem. Republic	7	—	—	45	3	89	26	120	—
Congo Republic	25	46	12	70	8	71	17	197	9.7
Costa Rica	141	509	19	29	94	98	98	1 353	21.0
Cote d'Ivoire	9	62	9	—	—	90	65	181	9.7
Croatia	229	—	16	19	115	—	—	2 429	—
Cuba	255	—	28	12	118	99	82	—	—
Cyprus	303	928	11	15	114	100	100	4 817	100.0
Czech Republic	303	—	14	19	254	100	100	6 027	100.0
Denmark	290	2141	37	—	309	100	100	—	100.0
Dominica	—	—	15	—	—	100	90	—	—
Dominican Republic	216	246	15	—	52	83	70	620	49.4
East Timor	—	—	—	—	—	—	—	—	—
Ecuador	170	115	15	25	70	81	51	611	16.8
Egypt	202	—	2	23	40	96	94	803	78.1
El Salvador	107	298	10	33	48	88	61	537	19.8
Equatorial Guinea	25	—	5	44	5	45	42	—	—
Eritrea	3	—	15	17	—	63	42	—	21.8
Estonia	297	—	18	—	174	—	—	3 466	22.1
Ethiopia	—	25	8	43	1	77	13	21	15.0
Fiji	48	196	—	—	52	43	51	—	—
Finland	299	1502	37	18	455	100	100	13 689	64.0
France	303	2102	11	—	218	100	100	6 060	100.0
Gabon	—	198	11	51	29	73	55	—	—
Gambia	4	56	2	30	2	80	53	—	—

Country	Physicians per 100 000 people	Health Expenditures per Capita (US$)	Women as Percent of Parliament	Primary Pupil to Teacher Ratio	Newspapers per 1000 people	Pop. with Improved Drinking Water Sources, Urban (%)	Pop. with Improved Drinking Water Sources, Rural (%)	Consumption of Electric Power (kilowatt-hours per capita)	Paved Roads (% of total)
Georgia	436	73	7	18	—	100	100	1 142	93.5
Germany	350	2488	30	17	311	100	100	5 626	99.1
Ghana	6	85	9	—	14	87	49	276	24.1
Greece	392	1207	9	14	153	100	—	3 493	91.8
Grenada	—	—	9	—	—	97	93	—	—
Guatemala	93	155	9	35	33	97	88	404	27.6
Guinea	13	68	9	49	—	72	36	—	16.5
Guinea-Bissau	17	—	8	—	5	29	55	—	—
Guyana	18	186	18	29	50	98	91	—	—
Haiti	8	61	9	35	3	46	45	42	24.3
Honduras	83	210	9	35	55	97	82	411	20.3
Hungary	357	—	8	11	186	100	98	2 840	43.4
Iceland	326	2358	—	—	537	100	100	—	—
India	48	—	9	64	24	92	86	363	45.7
Indonesia	16	44	8	22	28	91	65	329	46.3
Iran	85	229	3	31	19	99	89	1 163	50.0
Iraq	—	—	8	20	20	96	48	—	—
Ireland	219	1505	14	22	150	100	100	4 559	94.1
Israel	385	1730	13	—	290	100	100	5 069	100.0
Italy	554	1830	9	11	104	100	100	4 315	100.0
Jamaica	140	202	16	—	62	81	59	2 170	70.7
Japan	193	1844	—	19	578	100	100	7 241	74.9
Jordan	166	—	3	21	58	100	84	7 796	100.0
Kazakhstan	353	273	11	—	9	98	82	2 595	86.5
Kenya	13	79	4	30	—	87	31	127	13.9
Korea, North	—	—	20	—	199	100	100	—	—
Korea, South	136	720	6	31	393	97	71	4 847	74.5
Kuwait	189	—	0	14	374	100	100	12 886	80.6
Kyrgyzstan	301	109	7	20	15	98	66	1 372	91.1
Laos	24	35	21	30	4	59	100	—	13.8
Latvia	282	410	17	—	247	100	100	1 758	38.6
Lebanon	210	—	2	13	107	100	100	1 930	95.0
Lesotho	5	—	11	47	8	98	88	—	17.9
Liberia	—	—	11	—	12	—	—	—	—
Libya	128	—	—	—	14	72	68	—	—
Lithuania	395	429	11	16	93	100	100	1 818	91.0
Luxembourg	272	2327	17	—	325	100	100	—	—
Macedonia	204	288	7	19	21	—	—	—	63.8
Madagascar	11	16	8	37	5	85	31	—	11.6
Malawi	—	36	9	59	3	95	44	—	19.0
Malaysia	66	189	15	20	158	94	94	2 352	75.1
Mali	5	30	12	80	1	74	61	—	12.1
Mauritania	14	74	3	50	—	34	40	—	11.3
Mauritius	85	302	6	24	75	100	100	—	—
Mexico	186	—	16	28	97	94	63	1 459	29.7
Micronesia	—	—	—	—	—	—	—	—	—
Moldova	350	177	13	23	60	100	100	1 217	87.3
Monaco	—	—	—	19	—	100	100	—	—
Mongolia	243	—	11	31	27	77	30	—	3.4
Morocco	46	—	1	28	26	100	58	423	52.3
Mozambique	—	28	30	58	3	86	43	47	18.7
Myanmar/Burma	30	—	—	—	10	88	60	57	12.2
Namibia	30	417	20	—	19	100	67	—	9.3
Nepal	4	66	6	—	11	85	80	39	41.5
Netherlands	251	1974	33	—	306	100	100	5 736	90.0
Netherlands Antilles	—	—	—	—	337	—	—	—	—
New Zealand	218	1454	31	—	—	100	—	8 380	58.1
Nicaragua	86	266	10	38	30	95	59	286	10.1
Niger	4	20	1	41	—	70	56	—	7.9
Nigeria	19	23	3	37	24	81	39	84	30.9
Norway	413	2467	36	—	588	100	100	23 499	74.5

Country	Physicians per 100 000 people	Health Expenditures per Capita (US$)	Women as Percent of Parliament	Primary Pupil to Teacher Ratio	Newspapers per 1000 people	Pop. with Improved Drinking Water Sources, Urban (%)	Pop. with Improved Drinking Water Sources, Rural (%)	Consumption of Electric Power (kilowatt-hours per capita)	Paved Roads (% of total)
Oman	133	—	—	26	29	41	30	—	57.0
Pakistan	57	71	—	—	23	96	84	333	—
Palistine	—	—	—	—	—	—	—	—	—
Panama	167	410	10	38	62	88	86	1 152	28.1
Papua New Guinea	7	75	2	21	15	88	32	759	3.5
Paraguay	110	233	8	28	43	95	58	607	9.5
Peru	93	278	18	35	—	87	51	432	12.9
Philippines	123	136	—	35	79	92	80	2 451	19.8
Poland	236	510	13	15	113	100	100	3 206	65.6
Portugal	312	—	19	—	75	100	100	—	—
Puerto Rico	—	—	—	—	126	—	—	—	—
Qatar	126	—	—	—	130	—	—	—	67.6
Romania	184	—	10	20	300	91	16	1 704	—
Russia	421	—	6	—	105	100	96	3 981	—
Rwanda	—	34	26	—	—	60	40	—	9.1
Sahara (Western)	—	—	—	—	—	—	—	—	—
Saint Lucia	—	—	—	—	—	—	—	—	—
Samoa	34	—	—	26	—	95	100	—	—
Sao Tome and Principe	—	—	—	24	—	—	—	—	—
Saudi Arabia	166	—	—	13	57	100	64	4 085	30.1
Senegal	8	61	17	56	5	92	65	107	29.3
Seychelles	—	—	9	17	39	—	—	—	—
Sierra Leone	7	27	—	—	—	23	31	—	8.0
Singapore	163	777	6	22	360	100	100	7 944	97.3
Slovakia	353	728	14	19	185	100	100	4 243	99.0
Slovenia	228	1126	12	14	199	100	—	4 955	90.6
Solomon Islands	—	—	—	24	1	94	65	—	—
Somalia	—	—	—	—	—	—	—	—	—
South Africa	56	623	30	36	32	92	80	3 800	11.8
Spain	424	1202	27	17	100	100	100	3 899	99.0
Sri Lanka	37	95	4	28	29	91	80	227	95.0
St. Kitts-Nevis	—	—	—	—	—	—	—	—	—
St. Vincent & Grenadines	—	—	10	—	—	—	—	—	—
Sudan	9	—	—	29	27	86	69	—	—
Suriname	25	—	18	—	122	94	96	—	—
Swaziland	15	148	6	34	26	100	—	—	—
Sweden	311	1707	43	—	445	100	100	14 042	77.5
Switzerland	323	2739	22	—	337	100	100	6 885	—
Syria	144	90	10	23	20	94	64	776	23.1
Taiwan	—	—	—	—	—	—	—	—	—
Tajikistan	201	63	12	24	20	80	42	2 177	82.7
Tanzania	4	15	22	37	4	89	77	54	4.2
Thailand	24	349	10	—	63	85	38	1 360	97.5
Togo	8	36	5	51	4	100	100	—	31.6
Tonga	—	—	—	—	—	—	—	—	—
Trinidad and Tobago	79	323	21	25	123	—	84	—	78.9
Tunisia	70	287	12	24	31	82	100	709	28.0
Turkey	121	—	4	28	111	100	—	1 275	81.2
Turkmenistan	300	146	26	—	—	—	—	934	—
Tuvalu	—	—	—	—	—	—	—	—	—
Uganda	—	65	—	35	2	72	46	—	—
Ukraine	299	169	8	—	54	100	100	2 449	96.5
United Arab Emirates	181	1495	0	—	156	100	100	—	100.0
United Kingdom	164	1532	17	16	329	100	—	5 241	—
United States	279	4180	14	16	215	98	93	11 822	58.8
Uruguay	370	823	12	20	293	96	78	1 710	90.0
Uzbekistan	309	87	7	21	3	63	94	1 645	87.3
Vanuatu	—	—	—	—	—	—	—	—	—
Venezuela	236	248	10	21	206	88	58	2 488	33.6
Vietnam	48	81	26	—	4	81	50	203	25.1
Yemen	23	—	1	—	15	85	64	93	8.1
Yugoslavia Fed. Rep.	—	—	6	—	107	—	—	—	—
Zambia	7	52	10	39	12	88	48	563	—
Zimbabwe	14	—	10	39	19	100	77	919	47.4

Adapted from Population Reference Bureau, *World Development Report 2000/2001*, United Nations Statistical Division, World Bank, *Human Development Report 2001*, Bonn International Center for Conversion Report 2001. Population figures are for mid-2001 unless otherwise specified. Other data are for late 1990s, 2000, or 2001, the latest data available at the time of publication. The symbol "—" indicates that information was not available for that country.

GLOSSARY

abiotic: components of an ecosystem that are not living such as water, air, or soil but that support life

absolute measures: calculations based on real counts or totals

absolute poverty: the condition of lacking sufficient resources to buy basic necessities

advertorials: stories that appear to be news stories but are actually subtly disguised advertisements (also known as infomercials)

alternative media: forms of mass communication such as newspapers, journals, or television that are outside the norm

analysis: examination of the parts of a whole to discover their nature and their relationship with each other, to interpret patterns and recognize their meaning

anthropocentric: from the point of view of human beings; placing human beings and their values at the centre of the universe

anthropogenic ecosystem: a human-made environment or habitat (e.g., urban, industrial, or agricultural) that disturbs the natural ecosystem

aquifers: water-bearing, underground layers of porous rock, sand, etc. that can be used as sources of water for wells

bacillus thuringiensis (Bt): a bacteria that acts as a pathogen to a number of insects that causes little non-target damage

backcasting: a method of determining what a preferable future would be like and what steps need to be taken or what policies are required to reach that desired future

bilateral aid: government-to-government foreign aid

bioaccumulate: the increasing concentration up the food chain of substances in the fatty tissues of living organisms

biodiversity: the variety of life found within any given area

biogeochemical cycle: the means by which nutrient elements and their compounds cycle continually through Earth's atmosphere, hydrosphere, lithosphere, and biosphere

biogeoclimatic: a classification system of geographic regions, used for forest land management, based on how vegetation, soil, and climate relate to one another; there can be many biogeoclimatic zones within an ecozone

biogeography: the study of the geographic distribution of organisms

biomass: the total amount or mass of living organisms in a given area

biome: an extensive ecological community, especially one having one dominant type of vegetation

bioregion: a region defined by its natural and human characteristics

biotic: the living things within an ecosystem

blocs: a group of persons, companies, or nations, etc. united for a purpose

brownfields: former industrial sites that contain a high degree of environmental contamination

bushmeat: food from the meat of wild forest animals, usually gorillas, chimpanzees, and elephants in Africa

carrying capacity: an estimate of the number of people that an area can support, given its resource base and the population that inhabits the place

cash crops: a crop grown for export rather than for consumption within the region or country

caste: one of the four main social classes of India, no longer officially supported by the state and still part of the Hindu religion; traditionally hereditary (i.e., one could never change one's caste or marry somebody from another caste)

catchment: a reservoir for catching drainage

civil society: the collective capacity of organizations that advocate economic, social, cultural, and environmental goals and aspirations

closed loop system: a water treatment system whereby manufacturing operations treat and return water used in the manufacturing process to its source

collateral damage: a wartime euphemism for civilian deaths and damage to property near a military target under attack

commercial pollution: the presence of excessive advertising media and messages that shape and promote a rampant consumerism by creating an image of necessity

compromise projections: methods of transferring the surface of the globe onto paper that compromises between distortions in the true shape and size of continents

conformal projections: methods of transferring the surface of the globe onto paper that shows the true shape of continents but distorts their size

conventional weapons: a category of weapons that does not include nuclear weapons or other weapons of mass destruction

coral bleaching: the process by which corals expel the algae living symbiotically within them and turn white due to environmental stresses such as ocean warming or changes in salinity

correlation coefficient: a measure of the strength and direction of the relationship between two variables

cottage industries: systems of production in which workers make products at home with their own equipment

countries of first asylum: for refugees, the nearest safe place

cultural diffusion: the spread of elements of culture from their point of origin over a wider area

deforestation: to clear of forest or trees, usually for commercial or agricultural use of land

Delphi technique: a method of future forecasting whereby a group of experts from a wide range of backgrounds meet to answer questions on a particular problem or issue and consider alternative strategies for solutions with the goal of reaching a consensus on an issue or its solution

demographic transition: a change or passing from one population condition, form, stage, etc. to another

dislocated: forced to flee from their normal home

doublespeak: talk that is purposely made confusing or deceptive

ecocentric: from the point of view of the natural environment or habitat; putting the environment at the centre of the universe

ecological footprint: the land area of an ecosystem required to support a level of resource consumption and waste assimilation of an individual or population

economic colonialism: the practice or policy of a nation that rules or seeks to rule over the material welfare of other countries

ecosystem: the system formed by the interaction of all the living things of a particular environment with one another and with their habitat

empirical studies: studies such as the case study that are based on experiment or experience and that use qualitative as well as quantitative data that takes into account the complex interactive effects that take place in the world

endemic: regularly found in a particular people or locality

epidemiological: of or having to do with the branch of medicine dealing with the occurrence, location, spread, and control of infectious and epidemic diseases

epidemiologic transition: the shift from one kind of disease to another

epistemology: the part of philosophy that deals with the origin, nature, and limits of knowledge

equal-area projections: methods of transferring the surface of the globe onto paper that distorts the true shape of continents but not their size

ethnic cleansing: the forced removal of other ethnic groups from an area in order to leave only one group

ethnobiological knowledge: traditional knowledge, held by indigenous Aboriginal peoples, of plants and animals within an ecosystem particularly for food and medicinal purposes

ethnocentrism: the quality or condition of being preoccupied with one's own cultural or national group, believing in the superiority of one's lifestyle, values, and behaviours

eutrophication: excessive growth of algae forms that consume oxygen and produce toxins

ex situ conservation: conservation that seeks to maintain species in seed or gene banks or in captivity

extirpated: removed or destroyed completely; abolished or exterminated

extremism: a tendency to go to political or ideological extremes

family planning: when couples make decisions about the number and timing of the children that they produce

fertility rate: the average number of children born per woman

focus groups: panels of fewer than ten but more than six people, chosen from a variety of experiences and expertise, focus on a key question related to an issue

forced migration: movement of people brought about by the conditions in their home regions, such as war or persecution

force field analysis: a process whereby focus group participants rank the key driving or restraining factors that directly affect the central focus of an issue

fundamentalism: a movement or attitude stressing strict and literal adherence to a set of basic principles, often militant, in any faith

global governance: international government or control

globalization: making global; making worldwide in scope or application

Green Revolution: widespread activities in the 1960–1980 period intended to improve the volume of food output (e.g., plant engineering and broader use of chemical fertilizers and pesticides)

greenwash: a term used to describe practices such as political lobbying, financial contributions to political parties, and the use of public relations campaigns by companies or groups attempting to promote a positive environmental or social image to undermine and minimize the damage done to their brand or reputation by public criticism

Gross National Product (GNP): the value of total incomes earned by domestically based production

groundwater: water that flows or seeps through the ground into springs and wells

hegemony: political domination; especially, leadership or domination by one state over others in a group

high-grade: take only the best timber from a stand

holistic: emphasizing the importance of the relationship between the parts or elements that make up the whole; considering the well-being of the whole person or ecosystem

hydrologic cycle: the circular process in which water evaporates from the ocean, falling to Earth as rain or snow, to return to the ocean from rivers fed by rain or melting snow

ideology: a set of values and beliefs about how people and components of society should relate to one another and how power should be exercised

imperialism: the policy of extending the rule or authority of one country over other countries and territories; the dominating of another nation's economic, political, and even military structure without actually taking government control

indicator species: those species that provide early warnings of environmental damage to ecosystems

indigenous species: species belonging naturally to a region

infant mortality rates: the number of children under one year old that die per 1000 live births

in situ conservation: conservation that seeks to maintain viable populations of species in their wild state within their existing range of habitat

Integrated Pest Management (IPM): pest program that greatly reduces the amount of pesticides required by using a wide range of techniques best suited to the particular pest situation

intergovernmental organizations: officially recognized bodies within which national governments work together to achieve common goals

interior ecosystem: that part of an ecosystem that is large enough to support species that require that size of habitat and that is not degraded by contact with the surrounding built environment

internally displaced people: during civil conflicts, people who remain within the country, who are unable or unwilling to leave; their lives may be in jeopardy and they may have left their homes and communities looking for shelter and safety

Interventionist: one who supports interference in the affairs of another country

invertebrates: animals without backbones, such as jellyfish, worms, insects, and spiders

isolationist: one who objects to his or her country's participation in international affairs

jargon: language that fails to communicate because it is full of long or fancy words, uses more words than necessary, and contains lengthy, awkward sentences

jet stream: a current of air travelling around the planet at very high speed from west to east at high altitudes

junk science: the use of seemingly scientific methods to prove a biased point of view

just-in-time: a method for the delivery of materials just in time for them to be used in the next stage of manufacturing

keystone species: a species on which other associated species depend

land reform: change in ownership of the land

laterite: a soil formed by the decomposition of rocks, red in colour because of its content of ferric hydroxide

LD50: a scale that indicates the dose at which approximately 50% of tested subjects will die from exposure to toxins

mainstream media: forms of mass communication such as newspapers or television with wide public consumption

maximum sustained yields: amounts of a renewable resource such as forests or fish that can be harvested without seriously depleting the supply for future generations

media literacy: the ability to decode or deconstruct the information that is received in order to find out the truth and become better informed

megacities: cities of 10 million or more people

micro-credit: small loans given by non-governmental organizations to family, often women, or small businesses that do not require collateral

militarization: the making of the military organization of (a country) very powerful; the equiping of (a country) with military forces and defences

military–industrial complex: economically and politically powerful military and industrial organizations and infrastructures that produce and use weapons

militias: parts of an army made up of citizens who are not regular soldiers but who undergo training for emergency duty or national defence; the reserve armies

monocultures: the uses of land for the cultivation of a single product

mullahs: a title of respect for Muslims who are learned in Islamic theology and the sacred law

multilateral: involving two or more nations, parties, etc.

multilateral agreements: agreements among a group of countries that bind each country to a set of conditions

multilateral aid: organization-to-government foreign aid

mutualist species: groups of organisms that share a symbiotic relationship or that benefit from interaction with one another

nation: a group of people with a collective sense of belonging based on a common language and cultural background

nationalism: the desire and plans for national independence; the desire of a people to preserve its own language, religion, traditions, etc.

natural capital: the so-called "free" natural processes that provide services on which humans depend such as pollination of crops by insects

neo-liberal economic model: the free flow of money, goods, and services around the world

net migration: the difference between immigration and emigration

net natural increase: in population, when births are greater than deaths

neurotoxic: effects that are harmful to the nervous system

nexus: a connection; link

non-point sources: discharges of pollutants from a combination of origins

nonrefoulement: a policy whereby a host country cannot force legitimate refugees back into their country of origin, intended to protect refugee applicants from grave danger

official development assistance (ODA): foreign aid

old-growth forests: a forest of ancient trees that has never been harvested

organically grown food: food free of the use of chemicals, synthetic pesticides, irradiation, and not derived from genetic engineering

organochlorine chemicals: chemicals used as synthetic pesticides, formed when a chlorine atom replaces one or more hydrogen atoms in a carbon hydrogen compound

ozone: a gas (O_3) consisting of molecules composed of three atoms instead of the usual two, produced by electricity and present in the air, especially after a thunderstorm; an air pollutant in the lower atmosphere

ozone layer: the presence of ozone in the stratosphere that filters out harmful ultraviolet radiation from the sun

paradigm: a general way of seeing the world that dictates which kind of theory and ideas will be acceptable; a set of beliefs and values determining one's outlook or approach to things that may undergo radical change in a paradigm shift

paradigm shifter: a person or organization who works to change mainstream assumptions, values, and approaches

particulates: matter in the form of minute separate particles

persistent organic pollutants (POPs): toxic organochlorine chemicals that take long periods of time to be degraded in the environment by microorganisms or physical agents such as heat and sunlight

pesticide: any chemical agent or other substance used to destroy plants, animals, or microorganisms

photosynthesis: the process by which plant cells make sugar from carbon dioxide and water in the presence of chlorophyl and light

point sources: direct discharges of pollutants from an easily identifiable single source

polluter pays principle: the idea that corporations and other polluters should pay for their share of the real costs of pollution

pop culture: arts, beliefs, habits, institutions, and other human endeavours intended to appeal to the current tastes of the general public and considered together as being characteristic of a particular community, people, or nation

population momentum: when a population achieves replacement fertility, that population continues to grow for several generations before stabilizing because of the young people who are included in the population

precautionary principle: an approach to environmental management where scientific uncertainty is not a sufficient reason to postpone control measures when there is a threat to the natural environment or human health

primary productivity: productivity by organisms such as plants or algae, measured as the amount of biomass that accumulates over time or the amount of carbon stored in vegetation and organic matter

private sector: the portion of an economy in which goods and services are produced by non-governmental units such as firms and households

privatization: the transfer (of public property, services, etc.) from public or government control to private control

propaganda: systematic efforts to spread opinions or beliefs, especially by distortion and deception; ideas, facts, or allegations spread deliberately to further one's cause or to damage an opposing cause

public sector: the portion of an economy in which goods and services are produced by the government or by government-owned agencies and firms

pull factor: a condition that attracts people to a place, especially a country

push factor: a factor, such as the lack of freedom of speech or unemployment, that makes a person want to leave her/his country to go to another one

pyrethroids: pesticides originally derived from chrysanthemums

reclamation: the rehabilitation of a site in order to make it a viable and, if possible, self-sustaining ecosystem that is compatible with a healthy environment

reductionism: attempts to explain any complex problem or phenomenon by reducing it to the simplest factors or a single factor to the point of minimization or distortion

reductive fallacy: mistakenly forming a conclusion that is too simplistic or exclusive by choosing to eliminate any complexities that do not fit with a convenient viewpoint or philosophy

refugees: people who flee for refuge or safety, especially to a foreign country, in time of persecution, war, etc.

regional disparities: the large inequities in quality of life that exist between regions of a country or regions of the world

relative measures: measurements based on some known, given, or normal value

repatriated: sent back or restored to one's own country

replacement level: the number of births needed to maintain a population at a stable number (i.e., about 2.1 births per woman)

rhetoric: language used to persuade or influence others

riparian zone: area on the bank of a river, lake, etc.

salinization: the accumulation of salts in soil

scenarios: the process of describing possible future conditions based on assumptions, projections of trends, the implications of these assumptions and trends, and the analysis of long-term options in an attempt to understand what could possibly occur

scorched earth policy: a government or military policy whereby forces invade and destroy villages and civilian targets that oppose them

silviculture: the branch of forestry dealing with the cultivation and care of forests

slash–burn agriculture: a traditional agricultural system that relies on the periodic burning of small patches of rain forests to create spaces for producing crops, requiring the regular movement of the population throughout a territory

smog: a combination in the air of smoke or other chemical fumes and fog; polluted air from any source hanging low in the atmosphere and perceptible to the eye or nose

spheres of influence: the areas of the planet controlled by a superpower, militarily, economically, and politically

squatter settlements: an area of a city where people live in small, dilapidated houses or shacks

Strategic Lawsuits against Public Participation (SLAPPs): a legal tactic by which corporations attempt to render critics powerless to disrupt their industrial or resource development pursuits; while a SLAPP lawsuit has little or no merit or hope of success, it can deter activists who are usually unable to afford the time and legal cost to defend themselves

structural adjustments: actions required by developing countries in order to make their economies more suitable for foreign investment and usually require the cutting of social programs and the encouragement of globalization

sustainability: the ability to be maintained or renewed indefinitely into the future

sustainable development: development that meets the needs of the present generation without compromising the ability of future generations to meet their needs

synergy: the combined or co-operative action of two or more agents, groups, or parts, etc. that together increase each other's effectiveness

synthesis: a cognitive skill practised widely by geographers; study that combines, integrates, and rearranges information from a variety of sources and perspectives in order to make generalizations, draw conclusions, and create new ideas

system: anything that is made up of different kinds of parts that join together to form an interconnected whole

tailings: waste matter left over after the mining or milling of ore

think–tank: a centre for research and discussion of theories and ideas, or the people working there

third sector: the sector of society made up of non-profit, non-governmental organizations, sometimes equated with civil society

threshold: the point at which conditions reach the tolerance limit of a species in a given ecosystem

tied aid: foreign aid where there are conditions on the use of the assistance, usually that the funds must be spent in the donor country

Tobin tax: a tax on speculative foreign exchange activity as a way of collecting funds for basic environmental and human needs

total pollutant loads: a combination of exposures to more than one pollutant

toxicology: study of the effects of poisons and toxins on living organisms

trade sanctions: an official trade boycott against a country because it defies international law or the policies of other countries

transboundary pollution: pollution that crosses geographic boundaries

transmigrant workers: workers who travel from one area or country to another in search of work

underemployment: the condition whereby people in the work force are not adequately or fully employed or are employed in a way that does not permit the use of their true or full abilities and training

urbanization: the process by which an area becomes urban

urban sprawl: the uncontrolled outward growth of cities and their suburbs

vertebrates: animals with backbones, including fish, amphibians, reptiles, birds, and mammals

vertical integration: where a corporation owns or controls all aspects of the production system from origin to consumer such as a transnational food corporation that owns the animals, hatcheries, feed mills, processing plants, packaging, and transportation companies

water carrying capacity: the number of people that can be supported by Earth's water supply

water-logging: the process of becoming completely soaked with water

watersheds: the regions drained by one river system

worldview: a comprehensive concept or philosophy of life as it relates to the world or the universe and the role of humanity within it

xenophobia: a hatred or fear of foreigners or foreign things

zero population growth: the levelling off of population size when the birth and death rates are equal

Index

A

Abiotic factors, 97, 115
Abiotic/non-living things, 93
Acid rain, 3
Advertising, 38–39
  advertorials, 39
  infomercials, 39
Afghanistan, 3, 33, 341, 441, 443, 448
Africa, 61, 63
  sub-Saharan, 227, 362
Africa Action, 320
African Union (Organization of African
     Unity), 87, 89
Aga Khan Foundation Canada, 345
Agricultural productivity, by region, 231
AIDS. *See* HIV/AIDS
Alaska-Canada-United States Agreement
     (ALCANUS), 436
ALCANUS. *See* Alaska-Canada-United
     States Agreement
Algonquin Provincial Park, Ontario, 125,
     135
Alternative media. *See* Media, alternative
Amnesty International, 434
Amphibian population trends, graph, 125
Annan, Kofi, 72, 307, 319, 320, 328,
     335, 370, 508
Antarctica, 98
  collapse of ice shelf, 148
  garbage dumps at research stations,
     105
Anthropocentric view, 15–16
Anti-Ballistic Missile Treaty, 78
Anti-globalization movement, 5, 6, 68
APEC. *See* Asia Pacific Economic
     Cooperation
Arms trade, 471–475
ASEAN. *See* Association of South East
     Asian Nations
Asia Pacific Economic Cooperation
     (APEC), 78, 89
Association of South East Asian Nations
     (ASEAN), 62, 75. *See also*
     Poverty, reduction
  selected statistics of member countries,
     338
Atmosphere, 2, 94
Australia, 149, 166, 322, 394

B

Bangledesh, 328, 336
Biafra, 323–324
Biodiversity, 92, 106, 113–140, 191
  defined, 115
  food supply, 232
  hot spots, map, 130
  loss of, 115, 116, 120–135
    agricultural species, 123
  protecting, 132–135
Biogeochemical cycle, 99
Biogeoclimatic zones, 95
Biogeography, 95
  principles, 136
Biomass, 93–94
Biomes, 95–99, 104, 118
Bioregion, 97
Biosphere, 92, 94, 118
Biotechnology, 122
  new species, 122
Biotic impoverishment, 120, 128
Biotic/living things, 93
Birth control, 254–257
Borneo, 131
Bosnia, 329, 440, 445
Brady Plan, 320
Brazil, 182, 317, 318, 322
British Antarctic Survey, 148
Broadcast Act, 35
Brownfields, 501
Brown, Lester R., 291
Burma. *See* Myanmar

C

Cairo, 147
Cairo Population Conference 1984,
     268–270
Calcutta, 147
California, 152
Cameroon, 322
Campaign 2000, 306
Canada, 17, 18, 20, 21, 36, 60, 66, 73,
     125, 126, 127, 196
  AIDS diagnoses 1979–1997, 376
  Applied Ethics and Biotechnology
     Program, 373
  CBC. *See* Canadian Broadcasting
     Corporation
  Charter of Rights and Freedom, 279

climate change initiatives, 161
climate prediction 2050, map, 160
Commissioner of the Environment and
     Sustainable Development, 404
dam projects in Alberta and
     Saskatchewan, 212
debt relief for developing countries, 320
Department of Foreign Affairs and
     International Trade, 74
employment patterns, 321
endangered species, 134
energy, 174, 175, 177, 179
environmental record. *See* Human health
     and the environment, Canada's
     environmental record
farming statistics, 239, 240
Fisheries Act, 133
foreign aid. *See* Canadian International
     Development Agency
Genomics and Global Health Program,
     373
global climate change, 159–163
greenhouse gas emissions by sector,
     159
Kyoto Protocol, 160–162
Labrador, Innu, 322
land and forest ownership, 140
land claims of Aboriginal peoples,
     427–428
  comprehensive claims settled by
     2000, 428
military exports
  by country, 474
  type, 474
mineral exploration expenditures, 169
mining operations in Panama, 172
National Parks Act, 133
North West Passage, 436–437
  threat to sovereignty, 437
organic food production, 391
population change 1996–2000, map,
     280
population growth, graphs of compo-
     nents, 278
population planning challenges
  carrying capacity, 280–281
  demographic trends and patterns, 280
  impact of immigration, 279–280
population policy, 278–281
poverty, 306
  Toronto, 309

E

CREDITS

Photo Credits

PART ONE: INTRODUCTION
Chapter 1: Ways of Seeing—World Issues, Worldviews
pp. 2 and 17 HARRIS, Lawren S. Canadian 1885-1970. BEAVER SWAMP, Algoma 1920. Oil on Canvas, 120.7 x 141.0 cm. ART GALLERY OF ONTARIO, Toronto. Gift of Ruth Massey Tovell, in memory of Harold Murchison Tovell, 1953. ; p. 5 ©Dick Hemingway; p. 7a. CP Photo, b. CIDA Photo, c. CIDA Photo: Roger LeMoyne, d. CP Photo/Kingston-Whig Standard/Michael Lea, e. CP Photo/Tom Hanson, f. CP Picture Archive/AP Photo/Pier Paolo Cito, g. CP Photo/Ryan Remiorz, h. CIDA Photo: Roger LeMoyne; p. 13l Toronto Public Library Picture Collection; p. 13tr CIDA Photo; p. 13c CP Photo/Andrew Vaughan; p. 14l CUSO; p. 14r ©Dick Hemingway; p. 16a. Victor Last/Geographical Visual Aids, b. ©Dick Hemingway, c. Elaine Freedman, d. CP Picture Archive/AP Photo/Robert F. Bukaty, e. CP Picture Archive/AP Photo Anders Krusberg, f. CP Photo/Andrew Vaughan, g. Elaine Freedman; p. 18 Copyright © 2001 World Eagle/IBA, Inc. Reprinted with permission from WORLD EAGLE, 111 King Street, Littleton, MA 01460 U.S.A. 1-800-854-8273. All Rights Reserved. www.worldeagle.com/info@worldeagle.com.

Chapter 2: The Media and Global Issues
pp. 25 and 46 ©Dick Hemingway; pp. 28 and 29 ©Dick Hemingway; p. 32 Tom Kruse; p. 33 CP Photo/Lyle Stafford; p. 40t Teresa Smythe; p. 40b Victor Last/Geographical Visual Aids; p. 41t Marcel Crozet/WHO; p. 41b ©Dick Hemingway; p. 43 CP Photo/The Belleville Intelligencer/Frank O'Connor; p. 47 Adbusters Media Foundation; p. 48 ©Universal Press Syndicate; p. 50l Greenpeace/Hunter; p. 50r Sierra Club of British Columbia.

Chapter 3: Geopolitics—Patterns of Global Power
pp. 55 and 68 CP Picture Archive/AP Photo/Scott Nelson; p. 56r Victor Last/Geographical Visual Aids; p. 56l Ruth Lor Malloy; p. 57l CP Picture Archive/AP Photo/David Longstreath; p. 57r Ruth Lor Malloy; p. 61 National Geographic-James Blair; p. 62 Ruth Lor Malloy; p. 64 Victor Last/Geographical Visual Aids; p. 65 CP Picture Archive/AP Photo/Stuart Isett; p. 67 CP Photo/Kelowna Courier; p. 72 CP Picture Archive/AP Photo/Shawn Baldwin; p. 73t UN/DPI Photo/E. Debebe; p. 73b United Nations; p. 80 ©Dick Hemingway; p. 84 Victor Last/Geographical Visual Aids; p. 85 CP Picture Archive/AP Photo/Ajit Kumar; p. 87 Victor Last/Geographical Visual Aids.

Chapter 4: Planetary Systems—Global Connections
pp. 91 and 99b Ruth Lor Malloy; p. 93 NASA; p. 94 ©Dick Hemingway; p. 98 Peter and Barbara Barham; p. 99tl Ruth Lor Malloy; p. 99tr Victor Last/Geographical Visual Aids; p. 100 CP Picture Archive/AP Photo/Saurabh Das; p. 101 NASA; p. 102bl and br Victor Last/Geographical Visual Aids; p. 102t Patricia Healy; p. 105t Elaine Freedman; p. 105br Victor Last/Geographical Visual Aids; p. 105bl Alpine Ascents Collection; p. 106 The Haliburton Forest; p. 107 Susan Roxborough; p. 110 NASA.

PART TWO: SUSTAINING PLANETARY SYSTEMS
Chapter 5: Biodiversity—Endangered Spaces, Endangered Species
pp. 113 and 118l Linda Jo Malloy; p. 114 courtesy University of Montreal, Faculty of Veterinary Medicine; p. 115 Ruth Lor Malloy; p. 118r NASA; p. 119l ©Dick Hemingway; p. 119r Coral Magazine; p. 124b Don Williams; p. 124t Minnesota Pollution Control Agency; p. 125l David Jenike/Cincinnati Zoo & Botanical Garden; p. 125r Jim Rang; p. 126l Canadian Wildlife Service, Environment Canada. Reproduced with permission of the Minister of Public Works and Government Services Canada, 2002; p. 126r Michel Therien; p. 127l Elaine Freedman; p. 127r CP Photo/Belleville Intelligencer/Frank O'Connor; p. 131l Orangutan Foundation International/www.orangutan.org; p. 131r CP Picture Archive/AP Photo/Jean-Marc Bouju; p. 134 ©Third Eye Images/CORBIS; p. 135 Ruth Lor Malloy; p. 139 ©AFP/CORBIS/MAGMA.

Chapter 6: Global Climate Change
pp. 141 and 150 Ruth Lor Malloy; pp.146 and 147 ©Dick Hemingway; pp. 148 and 149 NASA; p. 152 CP Picture Archive/AP Photo/Reed Saxon; p. 156t CP Picture Archive/AP Photo/Katsumi Kasahara; p. 156b Xantrex Technologies Inc.; p. 157 CP Picture Archive/AP Photo/Doug Mills; p. 159 Greenpeace/Geier.

Chapter 7: Global Natural Resources
pp. 165 and 179 CP Photo/Jacques Boissinot; p. 166 Victor Last/Geographical Visual Aids; p. 167 Toronto Public Library Picture Collection; p. 169 Fugro Airborne Surveys; p. 170 Patricia Healy; p. 172t CP Picture Archives/AP Photo/Emlio Morenatti; p. 172b CP Picture Archive/AP Photo/Scott Dalton; p. 173 Survival International; p. 176 Ruth Lor Malloy; p. 182t NASA; p. 182b Victor Last/Geographical Visual Aids; p. 183 CP Picture Archive/AP Photo/Rich Pedroncelli; p. 184t Wildlands League/Evan Ferrari; p. 184b Greenpeace/Varford; p. 186 J. Moses Ceaser/Enlight Storyworks.

Chapter 8: The World's Water Supply
pp. 189 and 205 Ruth Lor Malloy; p. 191 ©Dick Hemingway; p. 192tr, tl Dr. Cherie Northon, University of Alaska Anchorage; p. 192bl O'BRIEN, Lucius Richard, Cdn. 1832-1899. NIAGARA, 1892. Watercolour over graphite on paper. 71.1 x 55.2 cm ART GALLERY OF ONTARIO, Toronto. Gift of the Government of the Province of Ontario, 1972.; p. 192br Canadian Fishing Company; p. 199 Brigham Young University/Sheldon D. Nelson; p. 200 ©Dick Hemingway; p. 201bl Jacques Descloitres, MODIS Land Rapid Response/NASA; p. 201tr Greenpeace/Greig; p. 202 NASA; p. 203 Garmin International Inc.; p. 210 Ruth Lor Malloy; p. 211 Bureau of Reclamation, U.S. Department of the Interior; p. 212 Ruth Lor Malloy; p. 219 Probe International; p. 220 CP Photo/1997/Winnipeg Free Press-Ken Gigliotti; p. 221 NASA.

Chapter 9: The World's Food Supply
pp. 225 and 241 Dinodia Photo Library; p. 226a. and b. Ruth Lor Malloy, c. Victor Last/Geographical Visual Aids, d. UN/DPI Photo by Eskinder Debebe, e. ©Dick Hemingway, f. Ruth Lor Malloy; p. 229 CP Picture Archive/AP Photo/

Enric Marti; p. 230 CP Picture Archive/AP Photo/Khalid Mansoor, W.F.P.; p. 231 Victor Last/Geographical Visual Aids; p. 234 ©Tom Wagner/CORBIS SABA/MAGMA; p. 237 CP Picture Archive/AP Photo/Rodney White; p. 242 FAO/J.Van Acker.

PART THREE: QUALITY OF LIFE
Chapter 10: Population Trends—An Exploding Population?
pp. 247 and 248 Ruth Lor Malloy; p. 250 ©Dick Hemingway; p. 260 CP Photo/Chuck Stoody; p. 261 Elaine Freedman.

Chapter 11: Population Policies
pp. 265 and 266 Ruth Lor Malloy; p. 267t United Nations; p. 267r International Planned Parenthood Federation; p. 269 CP Archive/Richard Drew; p. 270 AFP/CORBIS/MAGMA; p. 271 Ruth Lor Malloy; p. 273 Ruth Lor Malloy; p. 275 CP Picture Archive/AP Photo/John McConnico; p. 279 ©Dick Hemingway.

Chapter 12: Are Urban Systems Sustainable?
pp. 283 and 289t CIDA Photo: Roger LeMoyne; p. 284 Ruth Lor Malloy; p. 285 Toronto Public Library/Baldwin Room, PC1566; p. 288 Patricia Healy; p. 289b Patricia Healy; p. 291l NASA; p. 291t CIDA Photo: Pierre St-Jacques; p. 291b Earth Policy Institute; p. 294l Victor Last/Geographical Visual Aids; p. 294r Ruth Lor Malloy; p. 296 CP Photo; p. 297 NASA; p. 298 ©Dick Hemingway; p. 299 courtesy of Leland Consulting Group, Portland, Oregon.

Chapter 13: Patterns of Poverty
pp. 303 and 312 UN/DPI Photo by Ian Steele ©United Nations; p. 305 UN/DPI photo by Eskinder Debebe; p. 309 ©Dick Hemingway; p. 310 CP/AP Photo/Darko Bandic; p. 314 Toronto Public Library Picture Collection; p. 316 ©Crispin Hughes/Panos Pictures; p. 319 Pail Fitzgerald/POLYP; p. 322 CP Photo/Ryan Remiorz; p. 324 CP Picture Archive/AP Photo/Jerome Delay; p. 325 CP Picture Archives/AP Photo/Saurabh Das.

Chapter 14: Poverty—Closing the Gap?
pp. 327 and 331 Victor Last/Geographical Visual Aids; p. 328 R. Peer/Geographical Visual Aids; p. 332 ©Jim Whitmer; p. 335 Victor Last/Geographical Visual Aids; p. 336 ©Dick Hemingway; p. 341 CIDA Photo: David Trattles; p. 348l Linda Jo Malloy; p. 348r Dinodia Photo Library.

Chapter 15: Global Health Issues
pp. 353 and 368 Médecins sans frontieres/Tommi Laulajainen; p. 355t ©Anthony Bannister/Gallo Images/CORBIS/MAGMA; p. 355b ©Richard T. Nowitz/CORBIS/MAGMA; p. 362 ©Dick Hemingway; p. 364t ©Dick Hemingway; p. 364b Victor Last/Geographical Visual Aids; p. 367t CIDA Photo: Nancy Durrell McKenna; p. 367b CP Photo Archive/Maclean's/Peter Bregg; p. 370l WHO/TDR/Crump; p. 370r CP Picture Archive/AP Photo/Elaine Thomson; p. 371 CIDA Photo: Roger LeMoyne; p. 374 Image courtesy of ESRI Canada; p. 376 CIDA Photo; p. 378t UNAIDS/Louise Gubb; p. 378l, c UNAIDS/G.Pirozzi.

Chapter 16: The Environment and Human Health
pp. 383 and 394 Elaine Freedman; p. 384 Greenpeace Canada; p. 386l CP Picture Archive/AP Photo/Diether Endlicher; p. 386r ©Dick Hemingway; p. 389tl ©Robert Knoth/Panos Pictures; p. 389tr ©Dick Hemingway; p. 389br ©Liba Taylor/Panos Pictures; p. 390 ©Dick Hemingway; p. 391 University of Nebraska, Lincoln Institute of Agriculture and Natural Resources; p. 392 Ruth Lor Malloy; p. 393 ©Dick Hemingway; p. 400t, bl ©Dick Hemingway; p. 400br Patricia Healy; p. 401 CP Photo/The Hamilton Spectator/John Rennison; p. 404 Victor Last/Geographical Visual Aids; p. 406 Victor Last/Geographical Visual Aids; p. 407 ©Dick Hemingway; p. 408 ©Dick Hemingway.

PART FOUR: A DISORDERLY WORLD
Chapter 17: Nationalism and the Struggle for Independence
pp. 411 and 425 CP Picture Archive/AP Photo/Eduardo Verdugo; p. 412 CP Photo; p. 414 CP Picture Archive/AP Photo/Lutz Schmidt; p. 417 CP Picture Archive/AP Photo/John Moore; pp. 420 and 421 International Committee of the Red Cross/Boris Heger; p. 423 CP Picture Archive/AP Photo/Eduardo Verdugo; p. 424 CP Picture Archive/AP Photo/Scott Sady; p. 429 CP Picture Archive/AP Photo/Burhan Ozbilici; p. 431 ©Ed Kashi/IPN/AURORA; p. 432 CP Photo/Rene Johnston; p. 434 Amnesty International; p. 436 CP Photo/Windsor Star/Don McArthur.

Chapter 18: Refugees
pp. 439 and 440r CIDA Photo: Roger LeMoyne; p. 440l CP Picture Archive/AP Photo/Brennan Linsley; p. 441l CIDA Photo: Clive Shirley; p. 441r UN photo by J. Issac; p. 443l UN/DPI photo by Luke Powell; p. 443r CP Photo/Chuck Stoody; p. 448t UN/UNHCR photo by M. Kobayashi; p. 448b CP Photo/Andre Forget; p. 451l CP Picture Archive/AP Photo/Jean-Marc Bouju; p. 451r CP Picture Archive/AP Photo/Stephen Amin; p. 454 ©Dick Hemingway; p. 456 ©Dick Hemingway.

Chapter 19: Conflict and Co-operation
pp. 459 and 476 CP Photo/Ryan Remiorz; p. 460 CP Picture Archive/AP Photo/John Moore; p. 461 CP Picture Archive/AP Photo/Burhan Ozbilici; p. 463 Ruth Lor Malloy; p. 465 CP Picture Archive/AP Photo/Eddie Shih; p. 466t CP Picture Archive/AP Photo/Todd Hollis; p. 466b AP Photo; p. 467 ©1996 CORBIS; Original image courtesy of NASA/CORBIS/MAGMA; p. 473 CP Picture Archive/AP Photo/Vladimir Vyatkin; p. 477 CP Photo/Tom Hanson; p. 478r CP Picture Archive/AP Photo/Alex Brandon; p. 478l Adrian Brown; p. 480 CIDA Photo: Patricio Baeza.

PART FIVE: BUILDING A BETTER FUTURE
Chapter 20: Sustainability—Finding Solutions
pp. 483 and 490 Robb Kendrick/AURORA; p. 487 CUSO; p. 491 Reprinted with special permission of King Features Syndicate; p. 497 CP Photo/Jonathan Hayward; p. 498 ©Shaun Walker; p. 499 ©Jeremy Horner/Panos Pictures; p. 500t ©Environmental Youth Alliance; p. 500b Patricia Healy; p. 501l ©Dick Hemingway; p. 501r Rob Christie; p. 503 David Diethelm, Institute for a Sustainable Environment, University of Oregon; p. 505 Mountain Equipment Co-op; p. 509 Victor Last/Geographical Visual Aids.

Text Credits

PART ONE: INTRODUCTION

Chapter 1: Ways of Seeing—World Issues, Worldviews
p. 6 courtesy Jon Rye Kinghorn; p. 17 Rick Boychuk, *Canadian Geographic*, May/June 2000.

Chapter 2: The Media and Global Issues
p. 35 Haroon Siddiqui, *The Toronto Star*, March 10/2002; p. 43 ©Eric McIntyre; p. 44 From JIHAD VS. MCWORLD by Benjamin R. Barber, copyright © 1995 by Benjamin R. Barber. Used by permission of Times Books, a division of Random House, Inc.

Chapter 3: Geopolitics—Patterns of Global Power
p. 88 Used by permission of *New Internationalist*, August 2000, pp. 20-21.

Chapter 4: Planetary Systems—Global Connections
p. 107 From "The Ingenuity Gap" by Thomas Homer-Dixon, Random House of Canada Ltd.; pp. 110-111 courtesy NASA.

PART TWO: SUSTAINING PLANETARY SYSTEMS

Chapter 5: Biodiversity—Endangered Spaces, Endangered Species
p. 127 Reprinted with permission from *The Globe and Mail*; p. 130 Excerpt from "Biodiversity hotspots for conservation priorities" by Norman Myers, Russell A. Mittermeier, Cristina G. Mittermeier, Gustavo A.B. da Fonseca and Jennifer Kent in NATURE magazine, Vol. 403:853-8, (map) ©Conservation International-Center for Applied Biodiversity Science.

Chapter 6: Global Climate Change
p. 153 ©Professor William M. Gray, Dept. of Atmospheric Science, Colorado State University; p. 158 James Hansen/Goddard Institute for Space Studies; p. 160 courtesy Sierra Club of Canada; p. 161 courtesy the Suzuki Foundation; p. 162 David Anderson, Federal Environmental Minister.

Chapter 7: Global Natural Resources
p. 166 Used by permission of *New Internationalist*, March 1998, p. 14; p. 168 Copyright ©Reuters Limited 1998.

Chapter 8: The World's Water Supply
p. 190 Excerpt from "Shrinking Aquifers", from WATER by Marq de Villiers. Copyright © 2002 by Jacobus Communications Corporation. Reprinted by permission of Houghton Mifflin Company. All rights reserved.; p. 193 From "River History" in *Silenced Rivers:The Ecology and Politics of Large Dams* by Patrick McCully, Zed Books Ltd, UK.; p. 207 courtesy Danny Beaton; p. 218 From THE COST OF LIVING by Arundhti Roy, copyright © 1999 by Arundhti Roy. Used by permission of Modern Library, a division of Random House, Inc.

Chapter 9: The World's Food Supply
p. 230 From HUMAN DEVELOPMENT REPORT 2000 by United Nations Development Programme, copyright ©2000 by the United Nations Development Programme. Used by permission of Oxford University Press, Inc.; p. 232 courtesy Vandana Shiva; p. 240 Reprinted with permission from *The Globe and Mail*; p. 242 Used by permission of *New Internationalist*, July 1987.

PART THREE: QUALITY OF LIFE

Chapter 10: Population Trends—An Exploding Population?
p. 261 courtesy Population Reference Bureau; p. 262 Reprinted with permission from *The Globe and Mail*.

Chapter 11: Population Policies
p. 274 *The Earth Times News Service*, www.earthtimes.org; p. 277 courtesy Population Reference Bureau.

Chapter 12: Are Urban Systems Sustainable?
p. 290 courtesy Population Reference Bureau; p. 295 adapted from Cranny, M., *Counterpoints*, Prentice Hall, 2001, p. 378; p. 300 ©Competitive Enterprise Institute, www.cei.org.

Chapter 13: Patterns of Poverty
p. 319 UN News on Africa.

Chapter 14: Poverty—Closing the Gap?
p. 333 courtesy OECD; p. 345 Gay Abbate/*The Globe and Mail*.

Chapter 15: Global Health Issues
p. 367 *Prescription Games* by Jeffrey Robinson. Used by permission, McClelland & Stewart Ltd. *The Canadian Publishers*.; p. 380 Reprinted with permission from *The Globe and Mail*.

Chapter 16: The Environment and Human Health
p. 385 Reprinted with permission from *The Globe and Mail*; pp. 387-388 ©Dow Chemical Company/CANADA.

PART FOUR: A DISORDERLY WORLD

Chapter 17: Nationalism and the Struggle for Independence
p. 421 ©2000 Time, Inc. reprinted by permission; pp. 426-427 ©Copyright Reuters Limited 1995.

Chapter 18: Refugees
p. 452 By permission of the *Calgary Sun*.

PART FIVE: BUILDING A BETTER FUTURE

Chapter 20: Sustainability—Finding Solutions
p. 492 From UPSIDE DOWN:A PRIMER FOR THE LOOKING GLASS WORLD. Copyright©1998 by Eduardo Galeano; translation, copyright © by Mark Fried. Published by Metropolitan Books, Henry Holt & Co, LLC. All Rights Reserved. Reprinted by permission of Susan Bergholz Literary Services, New York. All Rights Reserved.; p. 495 ©NSTDA; p. 498 ©Nicholas Wilson; p. 507 ©Dr. David Wheeler, Schulich School of Business.